S0-BAB-933

HMH

into Literature™

Front Cover Photo Credits: (outer ring): ©Alexy Lisovoy/Shutterstock, (inner ring): ©Joseph Sohm-Visions of America/Getty Images, (c): ©Carrie Garcia/Houghton Mifflin Harcourt, (c overlay): ©Eyewire/Getty Images, (bc overlay): ©elenamiv/Shutterstock

Back Cover Photo Credits: (Units 1-6): ©Syda Productions/Shutterstock; ©PeopleImages/DigitalVision/Getty Images; ©Jason Donnelly/Shutterstock; Library of Congress Prints & Photographs Division [LC-DIG-ppmsca-34584]; ©David Schaffer/Caiaimage/Getty Images; ©Tim de Waele/Corbis via Getty Images

Printed in the U.S.A.

ISBN 978-1-328-47479-7

5 6 7 8 9 10 0877 27 26 25 24 23 22 21 20

4500796920 B C D E F G

into Literature™

GRADE 8

Program Consultants:

Kylene Beers

Martha Hougen

Elena Izquierdo

Carol Jago

Erik Palmer

Robert E. Probst

PROGRAM CONSULTANTS

Kylene Beers

Nationally known lecturer and author on reading and literacy; coauthor with Robert Probst of *Disrupting Thinking, Notice & Note: Strategies for Close Reading,* and *Reading Nonfiction;* former president of the National Council of Teachers of English. Dr. Beers is the author of *When Kids Can't Read: What Teachers Can Do* and coeditor of *Adolescent Literacy: Turning Promise into Practice,* as well as articles in the *Journal of Adolescent and Adult Literacy.* Former editor of *Voices from the Middle,* she is the 2001 recipient of NCTE's Richard W. Halle Award, given for outstanding contributions to middle school literacy. She recently served as Senior Reading Researcher at the Comer School Development Program at Yale University as well as Senior Reading Advisor to Secondary Schools for the Reading and Writing Project at Teachers College.

Martha Hougen

National consultant, presenter, researcher, and author. Areas of expertise include differentiating instruction for students with learning difficulties, including those with learning disabilities and dyslexia; and teacher and leader preparation improvement. Dr. Hougen has taught at the middle school through graduate levels. In addition to peer-reviewed articles, curricular documents, and presentations, Dr. Hougen has published two college textbooks: *The Fundamentals of Literacy Assessment and Instruction Pre-K–6* (2012) and *The Fundamentals of Literacy Assessment and Instruction 6–12* (2014). Dr. Hougen has supported Educator Preparation Program reforms while working at the Meadows Center for Preventing Educational Risk at The University of Texas at Austin and at the CEEDAR Center, University of Florida.

Elena Izquierdo

Nationally recognized teacher educator and advocate for English language learners. Dr. Izquierdo is a linguist by training, with a Ph.D. in Applied Linguistics and Bilingual Education from Georgetown University. She has served on various state and national boards working to close the achievement gaps for bilingual students and English language learners. Dr. Izquierdo is a member of the Hispanic Leadership Council, which supports Hispanic students and educators at both the state and federal levels. She served as Vice President on the Executive Board of the National Association of Bilingual Education and as Publications and Professional Development Chair.

Carol Jago

Teacher of English with 32 years of experience at Santa Monica High School in California; author and nationally known lecturer; former president of the National Council of Teachers of English. Ms. Jago currently serves as Associate Director of the California Reading and Literature Project at UCLA. With expertise in standards assessment and secondary education, Ms. Jago is the author of numerous books on education, including *With Rigor for All* and *Papers, Papers, Papers,* and is active with the California Association of Teachers of English, editing its scholarly journal *California English* since 1996. Ms. Jago also served on the planning committee for the 2009 NAEP Reading Framework and the 2011 NAEP Writing Framework.

Erik Palmer

Veteran teacher and education consultant based in Denver, Colorado. Author of *Well Spoken: Teaching Speaking to All Students* and *Digitally Speaking: How to Improve Student Presentations.* His areas of focus include improving oral communication, promoting technology in classroom presentations, and updating instruction through the use of digital tools. He holds a bachelor's degree from Oberlin College and a master's degree in curriculum and instruction from the University of Colorado.

Robert E. Probst

Nationally respected authority on the teaching of literature; Professor Emeritus of English Education at Georgia State University. Dr. Probst's publications include numerous articles in *English Journal* and *Voices from the Middle,* as well as professional texts including (as coeditor) *Adolescent Literacy: Turning Promise into Practice* and (as coauthor with Kylene Beers) *Disrupting Thinking, Notice & Note: Strategies for Close Reading,* and *Reading Nonfiction.* He regularly speaks at national and international conventions including those of the International Literacy Association, the National Council of Teachers of English, the Association of Supervisors and Curriculum Developers, and the National Association of Secondary School Principals. He has served NCTE in various leadership roles, including the Conference on English Leadership Board of Directors, the Commission on Reading, and column editor of the NCTE journal *Voices from the Middle.* He is also the 2004 recipient of the CEL Exemplary Leader Award.

UNIT 1

GADGETS AND GLITCHES

PAGE 1

ESSENTIAL QUESTION

Does technology improve or control our lives?

ANALYZE & APPLY

COLLABORATE & COMPARE

Online Ed

Key Learning Objectives

- Analyze plot
- Analyze science fiction
- Analyze organization
- Analyze structure
- Analyze irony
- Analyze claim and evidence
- Analyze graphic features
- Evaluate evidence
- Analyze rhetoric and reasoning

Visit the Interactive Student Edition for:

- Unit and Selection Videos
- Media Selections
- Selection Audio Recordings
- Enhanced Digital Instruction

UNIT 2

THE THRILL OF HORROR

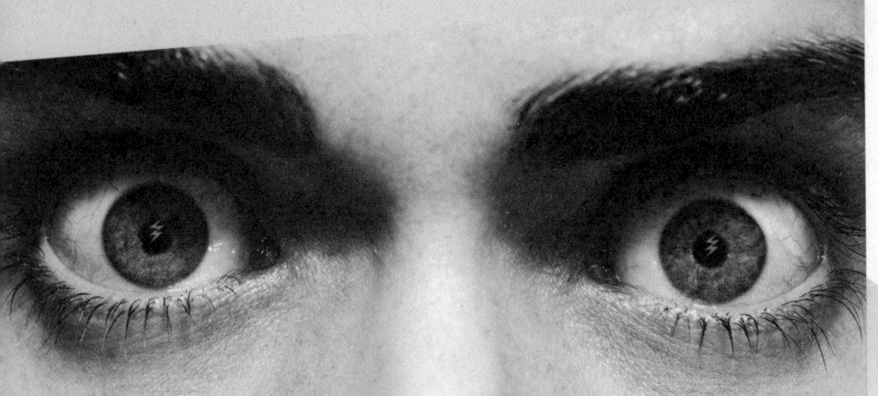

ESSENTIAL QUESTION

Why do we sometimes like to feel frightened?

ANALYZE & APPLY

COLLABORATE & COMPARE

Key Learning Objectives

- Analyze literary criticism
- Make connections
- Analyze rhyme scheme
- Analyze point of view
- Analyze suspense
- Analyze theme
- Analyze foreshadowing
- Evaluate media

Visit the Interactive Student Edition for:

- Unit and Selection Videos
- Media Selections
- Selection Audio Recordings
- Enhanced Digital Instruction

UNIT 3

PLACES WE CALL HOME

PAGE 150

ESSENTIAL QUESTION

What are the places that shape who you are?

ANALYZE & APPLY

NOTICE & NOTE READING MODEL

COLLABORATE & COMPARE

COMPARE PURPOSES

Online Ed

Key Learning Objectives

- Analyze plot
- Analyze character
- Analyze narrative structure
- Analyze theme
- Analyze graphical elements
- Analyze literary devices

Visit the Interactive Student Edition for:

- Unit and Selection Videos
- Media Selections
- Selection Audio Recordings
- Enhanced Digital Instruction

UNIT 4

THE FIGHT FOR FREEDOM

PAGE 238

? ESSENTIAL QUESTION

What will people risk to be free?

ANALYZE & APPLY

NOTICE & NOTE READING MODEL

COLLABORATE & COMPARE

COMPARE TREATMENTS

Key Learning Objectives

- Analyze autobiography
- Analyze structure
- Analyze characterization in nonfiction
- Analyze author's craft
- Analyze setting
- Analyze mood
- Analyze figurative language
- Analyze poetry

Visit the Interactive Student Edition for:

- Unit and Selection Videos
- Media Selections
- Selection Audio Recordings
- Enhanced Digital Instruction

UNIT 5

FINDING YOUR PATH

PAGE 322

? ESSENTIAL QUESTION

How do your teenage years prepare you for adulthood?

ANALYZE & APPLY

NOTICE & NOTE READING MODEL

COLLABORATE & COMPARE

COMPARE POEMS

COMPARE ARGUMENTS

Key Learning Objectives

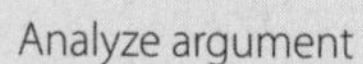

- Analyze structure
- Analyze author's purpose
- Analyze characterization
- Analyze free verse poetry
- Make inferences
- Analyze argument
- Identify counter argument
- Analyze rhetorical devices

Online Ed **Visit the Interactive Student Edition for:**

- Unit and Selection Videos
- Media Selections
- Selection Audio Recordings
- Enhanced Digital Instruction

UNIT 6

THE LEGACY OF ANNE FRANK

PAGE 404

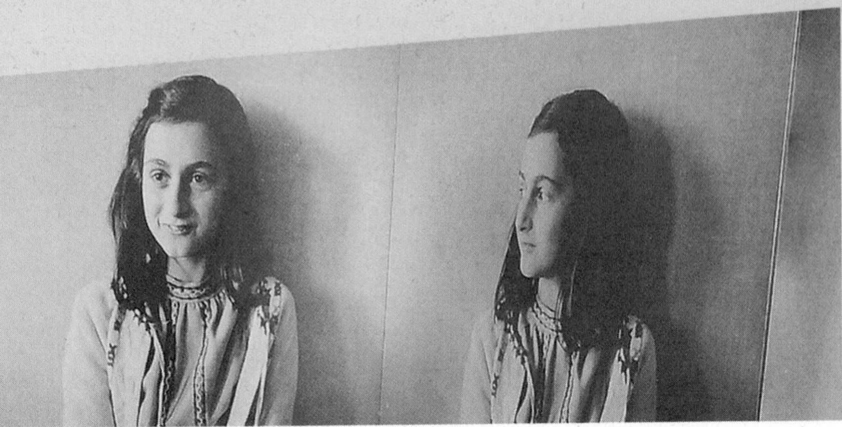

? ESSENTIAL QUESTION

What can we learn from Anne Frank?

ANALYZE & APPLY

COLLABORATE & COMPARE

Key Learning Objectives

- Analyze drama
- Analyze plot development
- Make predictions
- Analyze primary sources
- Make inferences
- Analyze appeals
- Analyze rhetorical devices
- Analyze sound devices
- Analyze figurative language

Visit the Interactive Student Edition for:

- Unit and Selection Videos
- Media Selections
- Selection Audio Recordings
- Enhanced Digital Instruction

SELECTIONS BY GENRE

FICTION

SHORT STORY

NOVEL

ORAL TRADITION

NONFICTION

INFORMATIONAL TEXT

ARGUMENT

HMH

Into Literature Dashboard

Easy to use and personalized for your learning.

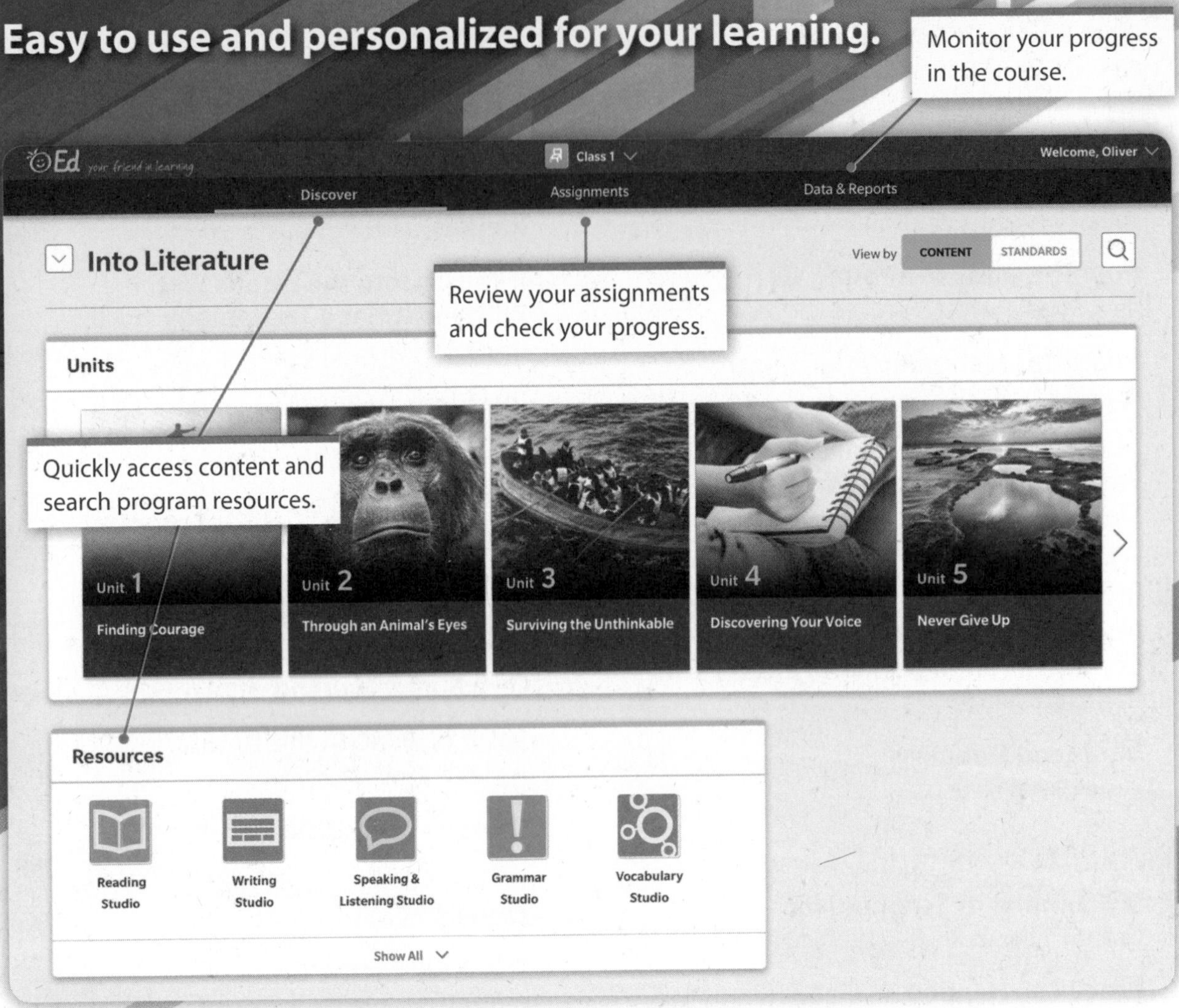

Monitor your progress in the course.

Ed your friend in learning — Class 1 — Welcome, Oliver

Discover | Assignments | Data & Reports

Into Literature — View by CONTENT | STANDARDS

Review your assignments and check your progress.

Units

Quickly access content and search program resources.

- Unit 1 Finding Courage
- Unit 2 Through an Animal's Eyes
- Unit 3 Surviving the Unthinkable
- Unit 4 Discovering Your Voice
- Unit 5 Never Give Up

Resources

- Reading Studio
- Writing Studio
- Speaking & Listening Studio
- Grammar Studio
- Vocabulary Studio

Show All

Explore Online to Experience the Power of HMH Into Literature

All in One Place

Readings and assignments are supported by a variety of resources to bring literature to life and give you the tools you need to succeed.

Supporting 21st Century Skills

Whether you're working alone or collaborating with others, it takes effort to analyze the complex texts and competing ideas that bombard us in this fast-paced world. What will help you succeed? Staying engaged and organized. The digital tools in this program will help you take charge of your learning.

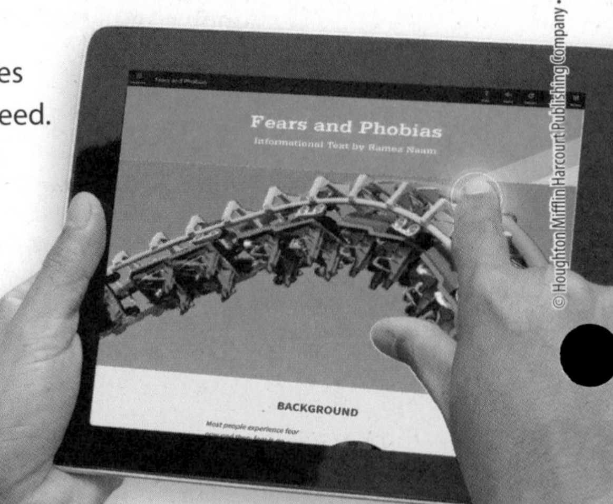

Ignite Your Investigation

You learn best when you're engaged. The **Stream to Start** videos at the beginning of every unit are designed to spark your interest before you read. Get curious and start reading!

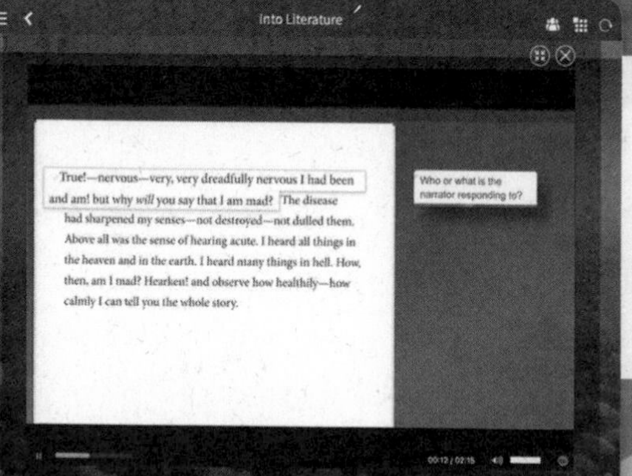

Learn How to Close Read

Close reading effectively is all about examining the details. See how it's done by watching the **Close Read Screencasts** in your eBook. Hear modeled conversations on targeted passages.

Bring the Meaning into Focus

Text in Focus videos dig deeper into complex texts by offering visual explanations for potential stumbling blocks.

Personalized Annotations

My Notes encourages you to take notes as you read and allows you to mark the text in your own customized way. You can easily access annotations to review later as you prepare for exams.

Interactive Graphic Organizers

Graphic organizers help you process, summarize, and keep track of your learning and prepare for end-of-unit writing tasks. **Word Networks** help you learn academic vocabulary, and **Response Logs** help you explore and deepen your understanding of the **Essential Question** in each unit.

No Wi-Fi? No problem!

With HMH *Into Literature*, you always have access: download when you're online and access what you need when you're offline. Work offline and then upload when you're back online.

Communicate "Raise a Hand" to ask or answer questions without having to be in the same room as your teacher.

Collaborate Collaborate with your teacher via chat and work with a classmate to improve your writing.

HMH

Into Literature STUDIOS

All the help you need to be successful in your literature class is one click away with the Studios. These digital-only lessons are here to tap into the skills that you already use and help you sharpen those skills for the future.

Play Audio Notes More

Contents

WRITING STUDIO

Ways to Organize Reasons and Evidence

Every argument must include reasons and evidence to support a claim. There are several effective ways you can organize that support. Check out some of those ways here.

Read the following techniques that will help you achieve cohesion, or coherence, in your writing.

Order of Importance

Least to most important

Claim: Homewood must switch from a volunteer fire department to a full-time fire department.

- Reason 1: The town is growing and getting more calls during they day when volunteers are at their full-time jobs
- Reason 2: Full-time firefighters can train daily instead of once a month, giving them more time to improve firefighting skills.

Online Ed — Easy-to-find resources, organized in five separate STUDIOS. On demand and on ED!

Look for links in each lesson to take you to the appropriate Studio.

READING STUDIO

Go beyond the book with the Reading Studio. With over 100 full-length downloadable titles to choose from, find the right story to continue your journey.

WRITING STUDIO

Being able to write clearly and effectively is a skill that will help you throughout life. The Writing Studio will help you become an expert communicator—in print or online.

SPEAKING & LISTENING STUDIO

Communication is more than just writing. The Speaking & Listening Studio will help you become an effective speaker and a focused listener.

GRAMMAR STUDIO

Go beyond traditional worksheets with the Grammar Studio. These engaging, interactive lessons will sharpen your grammar skills.

VOCABULARY STUDIO

Learn the skills you need to expand your vocabulary. The interactive lessons in the Vocabulary Studio will grow your vocabulary to improve your reading.

An ABSOLUTELY, **POSITIVELY,** MUST READ ESSAY in the FRONT of your Literature Book

YOUR
TEACHER
AGREES!

BY TWO PEOPLE YOU HAVE NEVER HEARD OF
Dr. Kylene Beers and Dr. Robert E. Probst

If you are reading this essay when we think you are, it's early in the school year. You have this big book in front of you and, for some reason, your teacher has asked you to read these pages by two people you've never met.

Let's begin by telling you something about us.

From Dr. Beers:

"I've been a teacher all my adult life. I've worked with students at all grades and now I spend most of my time working with teachers, maybe even your teacher! I live in Texas and when I'm not on an airplane flying off to work in a school, I'm on my ranch, plowing a field. I like to read, cook, read, garden, read, spend time with my family and friends, and (did I mention?) read!"

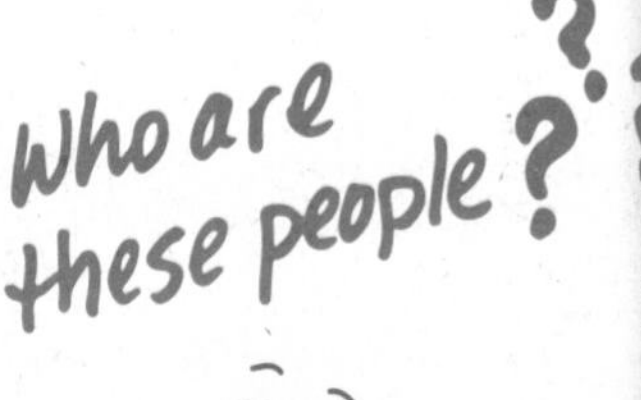
Who are
these people???

From Dr. Probst:

"I've also been a teacher all my adult life. When I first started teaching, I taught kids in middle school and high school, and then I spent most of my career teaching people how to be teachers. For many years now, Dr. Beers and I have written books together, books that are about teaching kids how to be better readers. I live in Florida and when I'm not in schools working with teachers and kids, I enjoy watching my grandkids play soccer and baseball and I love going out on my boat. And, like Dr. Beers, I love reading a great book, too."

So, we're teachers. And we're writers. Specifically, we write books for teachers, books teachers read so that they can help their students become better readers...

. . . and we're going to try to help you become a better reader this year.

We will because we both believe TWO things.

First, we've never met a kid who didn't want to get better at reading. Reading is important for almost everything you do, so doing it well is important.

Second, we believe that reading can change you. Reading something can open up your mind, your thinking, your ideas, your understanding of the world and all the people in it, so that you might choose to change yourself. Reading can help you change yourself.

We think too often it's easy to forget why reading is important. You can come to believe that you need to read better just so your grades will go up, or you need to read better so that you do well on a big state test. Those things are important—you bet—but they aren't as important as reading better so that you can become better. Yes, reading can help you change.

How would that happen—how can reading help you change yourself? Sometimes it is obvious. You read something about the importance of exercise and you start walking a little more.

How can reading help me change myself?

Or, you read something about energy and the environment and you decide to make sure you always turn off the lights when you leave any room.

Other times, it might be less obvious. You might read *Wonder* and begin to think about what it really means to be a good friend. Maybe you walk over to that person sitting alone in the cafeteria and sit with him or her. Perhaps you'll read *Stella by Starlight* and that book helps you become someone who stands against racism. Or maybe it happens as you read *Mexican Whiteboy* and discover that who you are is more about what you are on the inside than what anyone ever sees on the outside. And when you realize that,

"Hello! I wanted to discuss the Important Message with you!"

perhaps it will give you the courage you need to be truer to yourself, to be the person you really want to be.

Reading gives us moments to think, and as we think we just might discover something about ourselves that we want to change. And that's why we say reading can help us change ourselves.

Finding Important Messages

It sure would be easy to find important messages in the things we read if the authors would just label them and then maybe give us a call.

The reality is, though, that would make the reading less interesting. And it would mean that every reader is supposed to find the same message. Not true! While the author has a message he or she wants to share, the reader—that's you!—has at least three jobs to do:

My Job

1 → **First**, enjoy what you are reading.

2 → **Second,** figure out the message the author wanted to share. Authors write for a reason (no, not to make a lot of money!), and part of that reason is to share something important. That's the author's message, and this year we'll be showing you some ways to really focus in on that.

3 → **Third,** you need to figure out the message that matters most to **YOU.** (YES, WE SAVED THE BEST FOR LAST!!!) Sometimes the author's message and what matters most to you will be the same; sometimes not. For instance, it's obvious that J.K. Rowling wrote the Harry Potter series to show us all the sustaining power of love.

From Dr. Beers:

"But when I read these books, what really touched my heart was the importance of standing up to our fears."

From Dr. Probst:

"And what mattered most to me was the idea that one person, one small person, can make a huge difference in the world. I think that's a critically important point."

Understanding the author's message requires you to do some work while you read, work that requires you to read the text closely. No. You don't need a magnifying glass. But you do need to learn how to notice some things in the text we call **SIGNPOSTS.**

How do I find the author's message?

A signpost is simply something the author says in the text that helps you understand how characters are changing, how conflicts are being resolved, and, ultimately, what theme—or lesson—the author is trying to convey.

So, as I read, I have to think about something called signposts?

You can also use signposts to help you figure out the author's purpose when you are reading nonfiction. If you can identify the author's purpose—why she or he wrote that particular piece of nonfiction—then you'll be better able to decide whether or not you agree, and whether you need more information.

We do want you thinking about signposts, but first, as you read, we want you to remember three letters: BHH.

B	Book	As you read, we want you to remember that you have to pay attention to what's in the book (or article).
H	Head	And, you need to think about what you are reading as you read—so you have to think about what's in your head.
H	Heart	And sometimes, maybe as you finish what you're reading, you'll ask yourself what you have taken to heart.

To think carefully about what's in the book and what's in your head, you need to become an alert reader, one who notices things. If you're reading fiction, for instance, you ought to pay attention to how characters act. When a character starts acting in a way you don't expect, something is up! That's as if the author has put up a blinking sign that says "Pay attention here!" Or, if you are reading nonfiction, and the author starts using a lot of numbers, that's the same as the author waving a huge flag that says "Slow down! Pay attention! I'm trying to show you something!"

Pay attention HERE!

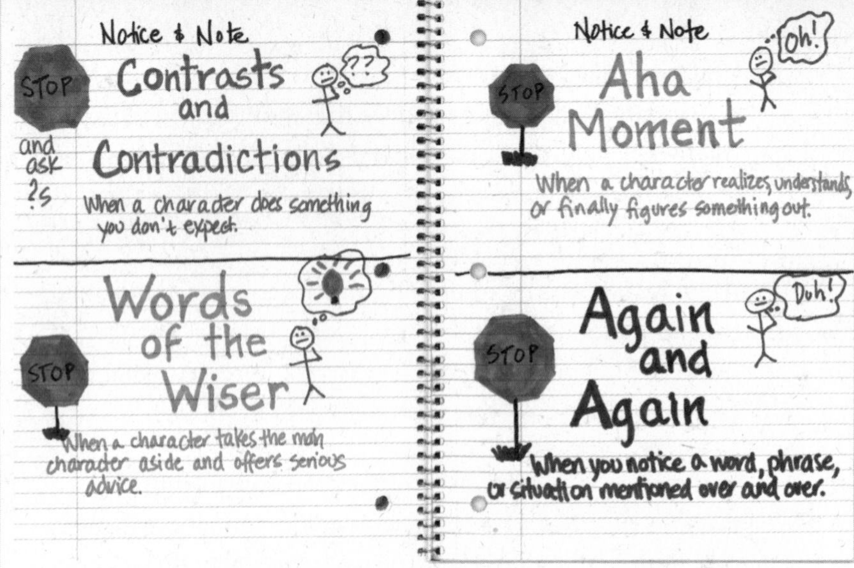

Don't worry about memorizing all the signposts. You'll learn them this year. Your teacher will probably have you make some notes—perhaps as the student above did.

Some of the things you'll read this year, you might not like. (OK—just being honest!) But most of the things we bet you will. What we hope you'll do, throughout this year, is keep reading.

- » Read every day.
- » Read something hard.
- » Read something easy.
- » Read something you choose.
- » Read what your teachers ask you to read.
- » Read something that makes you laugh.
- » And it's OK if sometimes what you read makes you cry.

One of us LOVES to read scary books while the other much prefers survival books, so don't worry if you like something your best friend doesn't. Read joke books and how-to books and love stories and mysteries and absolutely be sure you read about people who aren't like you. That's the best way to learn about the world around you, about other people, about other ways of thinking. The best way to become a more open person is to live for a while, in the pages of a book, the life of someone you are not.

We hope you have a great year. Stay alert for signposts that you'll be learning throughout this book.

And remember . . .

. . . reading is something that can help you become the person you most want to be.

NOTICE & NOTE SIGNPOSTS

Signpost	Definition	Anchor Question(s)
FICTION		
Contrasts and Contradictions	A sharp contrast between what we would expect and what we observe the character doing; behavior that contradicts previous behavior or well-established patterns	Why would the character act (feel) this way?
Aha Moment	A character's realization of something that shifts his actions or understanding of himself, others, or the world around him	How might this change things?
Tough Questions	Questions a character raises that reveal his or her inner struggles	What does this question make me wonder about?
Words of the Wiser	The advice or insight about life that a wiser character, who is usually older, offers to the main character	What is the life lesson, and how might this affect the character?
Again and Again	Events, images, or particular words that recur over a portion of the story	Why might the author bring this up again and again?
Memory Moment	A recollection by a character that interrupts the forward progress of the story	Why might this memory be important?
NONFICTION		
Contrasts and Contradictions	A sharp contrast between what we would expect and what we observe happening. A difference between two or more elements in the text.	What is the difference, and why does it matter?
Extreme or Absolute Language	Language that leaves no doubt about a situation or an event, allows no compromise, or seems to exaggerate or overstate a case.	Why did the author use this language?
Numbers and Stats	Specific quantities or comparisons to depict the amount, size, or scale. Or, the writer is vague and imprecise about numbers when we would expect more precision.	Why did the author use these numbers or amounts?
Quoted Words	Opinions or conclusions of someone who is an expert on the subject, or someone who might be a participant in or a witness to an event. Or, the author might cite other people to provide support for a point.	Why was this person quoted or cited, and what did this add?
Word Gaps	Vocabulary that is unfamiliar to the reader—for example, a word with multiple meanings, a rare or technical word, a discipline-specific word, or one with a far-removed antecedent.	Do I know this word from someplace else? Does it seem like technical talk for this topic? Can I find clues in the sentence to help me understand the word?

READING AND WRITING ACROSS GENRES

by Carol Jago

Reading is a first-class ticket around the world. Not only can you explore other lands and cultures, but you can also travel to the past and future. That journey is sometimes a wild ride. Other books can feel like comfort food, enveloping you in an imaginative landscape full of friends and good times. Making time for reading is making time for life.

Genre

One of the first things readers do when we pick up something to read is notice its genre. You might not think of it exactly in those terms, but consider how you approach a word problem in math class compared to how you read a science fiction story. Readers go to different kinds of text for different purposes. When you need to know how to do or make something, you want a reliable, trusted source of information. When you're in the mood to spend some time in a world of fantasy, you happily suspend your normal disbelief in dragons.

GENRE: INFORMATIONAL TEXT

FEARS AND PHOBIAS

How do you find courage in the face of fear?

In every unit of *Into Literature,* you'll find a diverse mix of genres all connected by a common theme, allowing you to explore a topic from many different angles.

GENRE: SHORT STORY

GENRE: HISTORICAL FICTION

GENRE: POETRY

Writer's Craft

Learning how writers use genre to inform, to explain, to entertain, or to surprise readers will help you better understand—as well as enjoy—your reading. Imitating how professional writers employ the tools of their craft—descriptive language, repetition, sensory images, sentence structure, and a variety of other features—will give you many ideas for making your own writing more lively.

GENRE ELEMENTS: INFORMATIONAL TEXT
- provides factual information
- includes evidence to support ideas
- contains text features
- includes many forms, such as news articles and essays

GENRE ELEMENTS: SHORT STORY
- is a work of short fiction that centers on a single idea and can be read in one sitting
- usually includes one main conflict that involves the characters and keeps [...] moving
- includes the basic ele[...] of fiction—plot, chara[...] setting, and theme
- may be based on real [...] and historical events

GENRE ELEMENTS: HISTORICAL FICTION
- includes the basic elements of fiction: setting, character, plot, conflict, and theme
- is set in the past and includes real places and real events of historical importance
- is a type of realistic [...] in which fictional c[...] behave like real pe[...] use human abilities [...] with life's challenge[...]

GENRE ELEMENTS: POETRY
- may use figurative language, including personification
- often includes imagery that appeals to the five senses
- expresses a theme, or a "big idea" message about life

Into Literature provides you with the tools you need to understand the elements of all the critical genres and advice on how to learn from professional texts to improve your own writing in those genres.

Reading with Independence

Finding a good book can sometimes be a challenge. Like every other reader, you have probably experienced "book desert" when nothing you pick up seems to have what you are looking for (not that it's easy to explain exactly what you are looking for, but whatever it is, "this" isn't it). If you find yourself in this kind of reading funk, bored by everything you pick up, give yourself permission to range more widely, exploring graphic novels, contemporary biographies, books of poetry, historical fiction. And remember that long doesn't necessarily mean boring. My favorite kind of book is one that I never want to end.

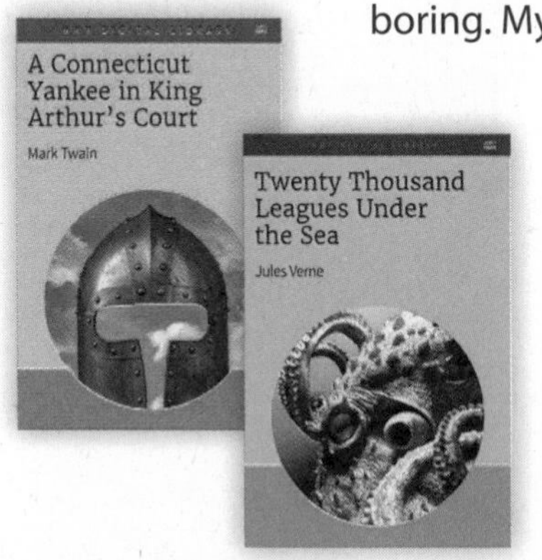

Take control over your own reading with *Into Literature's* Reader's Choice selections and the HMH Digital Library. And don't forget: your teacher, librarian, and friends can offer you many more suggestions.

SHORT STORY
Vanquishing the Hungry Chinese Zombie
Claudine Gueh
A girl faces terror to protect her parents and the family store.

POEM
Horrors
Lewis Carroll
What are those terrible things that go bump in the night?

NARRATIVE NONFICTION
Running into Danger on an Alaskan Trail
Cinthia Ritchie
A long-distance runner has a terrifying encounter with a bear.

UNIT 1

GADGETS AND GLITCHES

? **ESSENTIAL QUESTION:**

Does technology improve or control our lives?

> "We are stuck with technology when what we really want is just stuff that works."
>
> Douglas Adams

ACADEMIC VOCABULARY

Academic Vocabulary words are words you use when you discuss and write about texts. In this unit you will practice and learn five words.

- [x] **commentary**
- [ ] **occupation**
- [ ] **option**
- [ ] **speculate**
- [ ] **technology**

Study the Word Network to learn more about the word **commentary**.

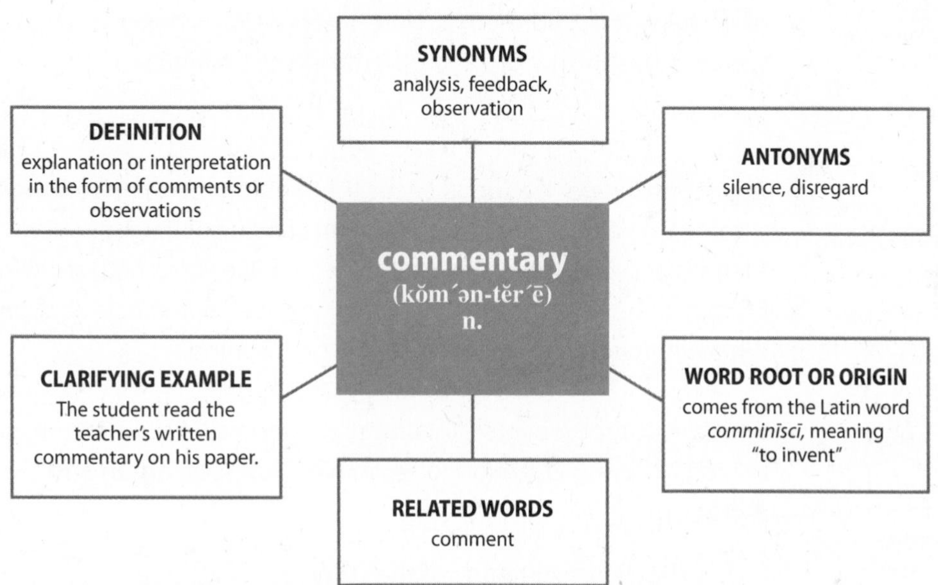

SYNONYMS
analysis, feedback, observation
DEFINITION
explanation or interpretation in the form of comments or observations
ANTONYMS
silence, disregard
commentary
(kŏm´ən-tĕr´ē)
n.
CLARIFYING EXAMPLE
The student read the teacher's written commentary on his paper.
WORD ROOT OR ORIGIN
comes from the Latin word *comminīscī*, meaning "to invent"
RELATED WORDS
comment

Write and Discuss Discuss the completed Word Network with a partner, making sure to talk through all of the boxes until you both understand the word, its synonyms, antonyms, and related forms. Then, fill out Word Networks for the remaining four words. Use a dictionary or online resource to help you complete the activity.

 *Go online to access the Word Networks.*

RESPOND TO THE ESSENTIAL QUESTION

In this unit, you will explore how people use and adapt to different forms of technology. As you read, you will revisit the **Essential Question** and gather your ideas about it in the **Response Log** that appears on page R1. At the end of the unit, you will have the opportunity to write an **informational essay** about the future of technology. Filling out the Response Log will help you prepare for this writing task.

 *You can also go online to access the Response Log.*

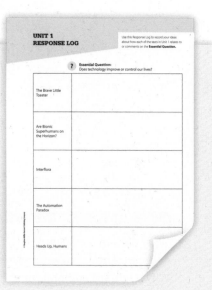

UNIT 1
RESPONSE LOG

Essential Question:
Does technology improve or control our lives?

The Brave Little Toaster	
Are Bionic Superhumans on the Horizon?	
Interflora	
The Automation Paradox	
Heads Up, Humans	

Notice & Note

READING MODEL

THE BRAVE LITTLE TOASTER

For more information on these and other signposts to Notice & Note, visit the **Reading Studio**.

You are about to read the short story "The Brave Little Toaster." In it, you will notice and note signposts that will give you clues about the story's plot, characters, and themes. Here are three key signposts to look for as you read this short story and other works of fiction.

When you notice one of the following while reading, pause to see if it's an **Again and Again** signpost:

a word or phrase that rings a bell from earlier in the story

a familiar pattern of events or actions

an object or image that appears more than once

words a character repeats at different points in the story

Again and Again If a friend keeps mentioning the math test that's coming up next week, what might you conclude? Perhaps your friend is nervous about the test and would like some help studying. Or, maybe he's concerned that *you* might need some help studying! Whatever it is, the math test is clearly on his mind.

When an author repeats something, ask yourself if there's a message behind it. Paying attention to something you read **Again and Again** can

- show how different parts of the story are connected
- provide clues to the story's theme or lesson
- reveal a character's traits and personality
- create tension as you wonder how the pattern might change

Read this part of "The Brave Little Toaster" to see a student's annotation of Again and Again:

> . . . "I'm no drink and I'm no meal," LOONY GOONY sang. "I'm a ferrous lump of steel!"
>
> 16 The dishwasher wouldn't wash it ("I don't mean to annoy or chafe, but I'm simply not dishwasher safe!"). The toilet wouldn't flush it ("I don't belong in the bog, because down there I'm sure to clog!"). The windows wouldn't retract their safety screen to let it drop, but that wasn't much of a surprise.

Anchor Question When you notice this signpost, ask: Why might the author keep bringing this up?

What pattern is repeated?	LOONY GOONY speaks in rhymes.
Why might the author have created this pattern?	The rhymes are funny but also make LOONY GOONY seem kind of annoying.

Contrasts and Contradictions There are some things you expect to be the same every day. The sun will rise. Birds will sing. The neighbor's dog will bark. What if, one day, the birds barked and the dog said, "Good morning"? That would get your attention!

When something happens in a story that goes against your expectations, you'll want to pay attention to it. **Contrasts and Contradictions** often give you a deeper insight into a character or into the story's setting. If a character suddenly does or thinks something unexpected, or a detail about the setting strikes you as surprising, take the time to consider what it means.

The title of the story you're about to read, "The Brave Little Toaster," contains an example of Contrasts and Contradictions.

Anchor Question When you notice this signpost, ask: Why did the character act that way?

What contradiction is expressed in the title?	A toaster can't really be brave.
What are some ways the story might explain this contradiction?	A toaster could be a brave character in a science fiction story. Or the title could be meant as a joke.

Aha Moment Some problems or questions can't be resolved quickly. You have to think about them over a period of time. Then, the answer may come to you all at once. In a story, such moments often mark a turning point for the main character. His or her new understanding may take the story's action in a new direction.

When you see phrases like these, pause to see if it's an **Aha Moment**:

"All of a sudden . . ."

"For the first time . . ."

"Finally she understood . . ."

"I realized . . ."

"It all made sense now . . ."

A character experiencing an **Aha Moment** may

- finally realize what the real problem is
- understand why another character did or said something
- discover a way to resolve a conflict or solve a problem
- reach a broader understanding about life

In this example, a student underlined the Aha Moment:

> 6 But the food hadn't been spoiled. Mister Toussaint pored over his refrigerator's diagnostics and logfiles, and soon enough, he had the answer. It was the energy beverage, of course.

Anchor Question When you notice this signpost, ask: How might this change things?

What word(s) tell you Mister Toussaint has figured something out?	"he had the answer," "of course"
How might this be connected to the story's conflict?	If Mister Toussaint has figured out what was causing his problem, that might help him resolve the conflict.

THE BRAVE LITTLE TOASTER

Science Fiction by **Cory Doctorow**

ESSENTIAL QUESTION:

Does technology improve or control our lives?

QUICK START

When you think about technology, you might not think of simple machines like toasters. List some ways a toaster makes your life easier.

ANALYZE STORIES: PLOT

A story's **plot** is a series of events that usually centers on a conflict or problem. The way the main character responds to this conflict depends on his or her **motivations**—what the character wants—as well as the character's traits or qualities. As the character takes action to solve the problem, a series of causes and effects leads to the story's **climax,** or its most intense moment, and to the resolution of the conflict.

As you read, ask yourself what motivates the main character's actions. Use a chart like this one to track causes and effects.

CAUSE	EFFECT/CAUSE
Event that starts the action of the story	

EFFECT/CAUSE	EFFECT
	Climax, when the conflict reaches its peak

ANALYZE SCIENCE FICTION

In **science fiction,** writers explore ways in which science and technology might affect people and the world. The writer combines scientific facts with ideas from his or her imagination to create a believable setting. Science fiction is often set in the future, but it also may describe an alternative past or present. When you read science fiction, you must use details in the text to draw a conclusion about when and where the story takes place.

As you read "The Brave Little Toaster," ask yourself these questions:

- What elements of the story are familiar from today's world? What parts are from the writer's imagination?
- Does the story take place in the future or in an alternative version of the past or present?
- What effect does the technology in the story have on the characters?
- What ideas or messages does the story convey about technology?

GENRE ELEMENTS: SCIENCE FICTION

- includes the basic elements of fiction—setting, characters, plot, conflict, and theme
- combines real scientific facts and theories with imaginative elements
- may comment on the present world by imagining a possible future
- may convey a message about the effects or consequences of technology

GET READY

CRITICAL VOCABULARY

diagnostics	retract	reintegrate	consternation
chafe	ample	abode	vindictive

To see how many Critical Vocabulary words you already know, answer these questions.

1. Why might you run a **diagnostics** check on your computer?
2. Why would hearing the same song 50 times **chafe** listeners?
3. If a cat wanted to scratch you, would it **retract** its claws?
4. How many hours would be **ample** time to watch a movie?
5. Why would a lost sheep want to **reintegrate** with its herd?
6. Which is an **abode**—an apartment or a school?
7. If you heard a loud crash, might you feel **consternation**?
8. Would you thank someone who had done something **vindictive**?

LANGUAGE CONVENTIONS

The Structure of Sentences Writers use a variety of sentence structures to express ideas clearly. Note how commas and conjunctions (*so, because*) help connect ideas in these examples.

Simple sentence: My fridge is already full of delicious things.

Compound sentence: My fridge is empty, so I'm going to the grocery to buy food.

Complex sentence: My fridge is full because I went to the grocery store last night.

ANNOTATION MODEL

NOTICE & NOTE 

As you read, notice and note signposts, including **Again and Again, Contrasts and Contradictions,** and **Aha Moments.** Also note details that help you draw a conclusion about where and when "The Brave Little Toaster" takes place.

1 One day, Mister Toussaint came home to find an extra 300 euros' worth of groceries on his doorstep. So he called up Miz Rousseau, the grocer, and said, "Why have you sent me all this food? My fridge is already full of delicious things. I don't need this stuff and besides, I can't pay for it."

These details are realistic and modern. The story may be set in the present.

BACKGROUND

Cory Doctorow *(b. 1971) is a journalist, a blogger, and the author of many works of science fiction. His young adult novels include* Homeland, Pirate Cinema, *and the award-winning* Little Brother, *which was also adapted for the stage. His other works include graphic novels, essays, and short stories. Doctorow was born in Toronto, Canada, and lives in Los Angeles. In addition to his other pursuits, he works for the Electronic Frontier Foundation, which aims to protect freedom in technology law and policies.*

THE BRAVE LITTLE TOASTER

Science Fiction by Cory Doctorow

SETTING A PURPOSE

As you read, think about the role that technology plays in this story. Note details about Mister Toussaint's interactions with certain devices and how he is motivated to respond.

1 One day, Mister Toussaint came home to find an extra 300 euros' worth[1] of groceries on his doorstep. So he called up Miz Rousseau, the grocer, and said, "Why have you sent me all this food? My fridge is already full of delicious things. I don't need this stuff and besides, I can't pay for it."

2 But Miz Rousseau told him that he had ordered the food. His refrigerator had sent in the list, and she had the signed order to prove it.

3 Furious, Mister Toussaint confronted his refrigerator. It was mysteriously empty, even though it had been full that morning. Or rather, it was *almost* empty: there was a single pouch of energy drink sitting on a shelf in the back. He'd

[1] **euros' (yŏŏr´ōz) worth:** valued in euros, the currency of the European Union. 300 euros is about the same as $350 in American currency.

Notice & Note

Use the side margins to notice and note signposts in the text.

CONTRASTS AND CONTRADICTIONS

Notice & Note: Which details in paragraphs 1–5 contrast with your own experiences and expectations? Mark these details.

Draw Conclusions: Based on these details, what do you think is the setting of this story?

NOTICE & NOTE

gotten it from an enthusiastically smiling young woman on the metro[2] platform the day before. She'd been giving them to everyone.

4 "Why did you throw away all my food?" he demanded. The refrigerator hummed smugly at him.

5 "It was spoiled," it said.

6 But the food hadn't been spoiled. Mister Toussaint pored over his refrigerator's **diagnostics** and logfiles, and soon enough, he had the answer. It was the energy beverage, of course.

diagnostics
(dī´əg-nŏs´tĭks) *n. Diagnostics* are tools a computer uses to identify problems.

7 "Row, row, row your boat," it sang. "Gently down the stream. Merrily, merrily, merrily, merrily, I'm offgassing ethylene."[3] Mister Toussaint sniffed the pouch suspiciously.

8 "No you're not," he said. The label said that the drink was called LOONY GOONY and it promised ONE TRILLION TIMES MORE POWERFUL THAN ESPRESSO!!!!!ONE11! Mister Toussaint began to suspect that the pouch was some kind of stupid Internet of Things[4] prank. He hated those.

9 He chucked the pouch in the rubbish can and put his new groceries away.

ANALYZE STORIES: PLOT

Annotate: Notice what Mister Toussaint does with LOONY GOONY in paragraph 9. Mark details in paragraphs 6–8 that explain why he does this.

Infer: What conflict is Mister Toussaint facing in this story?

10 The next day, Mister Toussaint came home and discovered that the overflowing rubbish was still sitting in its little bag under the sink. The can had not cycled it through the trapdoor to the chute that ran to the big collection-point at ground level, 104 storeys below.

11 "Why haven't you emptied yourself?" he demanded. The trashcan told him that toxic substances had to be manually sorted. "What toxic substances?"

12 So he took out everything in the bin, one piece at a time. You've probably guessed what the trouble was.

13 "Excuse me if I'm chattery, I do not mean to nattery, but I'm a mercury battery!" LOONY GOONY's singing voice really got on Mister Toussaint's nerves.

14 "No you're not," Mister Toussaint said.

AGAIN AND AGAIN

Notice & Note: What pattern do you notice in Mister Toussaint's actions? Underline and circle words that show the pattern.

Analyze: How do Mister Toussaint's repeated actions create tension in the plot, or make you eager to see what will happen next?

15 Mister Toussaint tried the microwave. Even the cleverest squeezy-pouch couldn't survive a good nuking. But the microwave wouldn't switch on. "I'm no drink and I'm no meal," LOONY GOONY sang. "I'm a ferrous[5] lump of steel!"

[2] **metro:** subway.
[3] **offgassing ethylene** (ĕth´ə-lēn´): releasing a flammable gas, C_2H_4.
[4] **Internet of Things:** the network of devices, including "smart" appliances, that are connected to the Internet.
[5] **ferrous** (fĕr´əs): containing iron.

16 The dishwasher wouldn't wash it ("I don't mean to annoy or **chafe**, but I'm simply not dishwasher safe!"). The toilet wouldn't flush it ("I don't belong in the bog, because down there I'm sure to clog!"). The windows wouldn't **retract** their safety screen to let it drop, but that wasn't much of a surprise.

17 "I hate you," Mister Toussaint said to LOONY GOONY, and he stuck it in his coat pocket. He'd throw it out in a trash-can on the way to work.

18 They arrested Mister Toussaint at the 678th Street station. They were waiting for him on the platform, and they cuffed him just as soon as he stepped off the train. The entire station had been evacuated and the police wore full biohazard containment gear. They'd even shrinkwrapped their machine-guns.

19 "You'd better wear a breather and you'd better wear a hat, I'm a vial of terrible deadly hazmat," LOONY GOONY sang.

20 When they released Mister Toussaint the next day, they made him take LOONY GOONY home with him. There were lots more people with LOONY GOONYs to process.

21 Mister Toussaint paid the rush-rush fee that the storage depot charged to send over his container. They forklifted it out of the giant warehouse under the desert and zipped it straight to the cargo-bay in Mister Toussaint's building. He put on old, stupid clothes and clipped some lights to his glasses and started sorting.

22 Most of the things in the container were stupid. He'd been throwing away stupid stuff all his life, because the smart stuff

chafe
(chāf) *v.* To *chafe* is to annoy or bother someone.

retract
(rĭ-trăkt´) *v.* To *retract* is to pull in.

ANALYZE SCIENCE FICTION

Annotate: Mark details in paragraphs 18–20 that show what happens when Mister Toussaint tries to dispose of LOONY GOONY on the way to work.

Analyze: Why are the police waiting for him at the train station? What ideas about technology are suggested by these events?

was just so much easier. But then his grandpa had died and they'd cleaned out his little room at the pensioner's ward[6] and he'd just shoved it all in the container and sent it out to the desert.

23 From time to time, he'd thought of the eight cubic meters of stupidity he'd inherited and sighed a put-upon sigh. He'd loved Grandpa, but he wished the old man had used some of the **ample** spare time from the tail end of his life to replace his junk with stuff that could more gracefully **reintegrate** with the materials stream.

ample
(ăm´pəl) *adj.* To be *ample* is to be plentiful or enough.

reintegrate
(rē-ĭn´tĭ-grāt´) *v.* To *reintegrate* is to come together, as when similar materials are collected for recycling.

24 How inconsiderate!

AHA MOMENT

Notice & Note: What words and phrases in paragraph 29 suggest that Mister Toussaint is having an Aha Moment? Mark these words and phrases.

Cause/Effect: What does Mister Toussaint suddenly realize, and how does this affect what he does next?

25 The house chattered enthusiastically at the toaster when he plugged it in, but the toaster said nothing back. It couldn't. It was stupid. Its bread-slots were crusted over with carbon residue and it dribbled crumbs from the ill-fitting tray beneath it. It had been designed and built by cavemen who hadn't ever considered the advantages of networked environments.

26 It was stupid, but it was brave. It would do anything Mister Toussaint asked it to do.

27 "It's getting hot and sticky and I'm not playing any games, you'd better get me out before I burst into flames!" LOONY GOONY sang loudly, but the toaster ignored it.

28 "I don't mean to endanger your **abode**, but if you don't let me out, I'm going to explode!" The smart appliances chattered nervously at one another, but the brave little toaster said nothing as Mister Toussaint depressed its lever again.

abode
(ə-bōd´) *n.* An *abode* is a home.

29 Just as he did, he thought to check in with the flat's diagnostics. Just in time, too! Its quorum-sensors[7] were redlining[8] as it listened in on the appliances' **consternation**. Mister Toussaint unplugged the fridge and the microwave and the dishwasher.

consternation
(kŏn´stər-nā´shən) *n.* *Consternation* is a feeling of alarm or fear.

30 The cooker and trash-can were hard-wired, but they didn't represent a quorum.

31 The fire department took away the melted toaster and used their axes to knock huge, **vindictive** holes in Mister Toussaint's walls. "Just looking for embers," they claimed. But he knew that

vindictive
(vĭn-dĭk´tĭv) *adj.* Something is *vindictive* if it is intended to hurt or punish someone.

[6] **pensioner's ward:** part of a hospital that provides care for people receiving pensions, or government support for older persons.

[7] **quorum-sensors:** devices that receive input from Mister Toussaint's smart appliances; when a certain number (a quorum) of the appliances signal distress, emergency action is taken.

[8] **redlining:** reaching a limit or maximum; here, approaching the point at which the apartment would take action to stop the toaster.

NOTICE & NOTE

they were upset because there was simply no good excuse for sticking a pouch of independently powered computation and sensors and transmitters into an antique toaster and pushing down the lever until oily, toxic smoke filled the whole 104th floor.

32 Mister Toussaint's neighbors weren't happy about it either.

33 But Mister Toussaint didn't mind. It had all been worth it, just to hear LOONY GOONY beg and weep for its life as its edges curled up and blackened.

34 He argued mightily, but the firefighters refused to let him keep the toaster.

ANALYZE STORIES: PLOT

Annotate: Mark details in paragraphs 31–34 that reveal what happens to LOONY GOONY.

Analyze: How do these events resolve the story's main conflict?

LANGUAGE CONVENTIONS

Annotate: Coordinating conjunctions are used to connect ideas in a compound sentence. Mark the coordinating conjunction in paragraph 34.

Interpret: What does the conjunction suggest about the firefighters' response to Mister Toussaint's request?

CHECK YOUR UNDERSTANDING

Answer these questions before moving on to the **Analyze the Text** section on the following page.

1 Why does Mister Toussaint's refrigerator order more groceries?

- **A** The refrigerator detects that all the food has gone bad.
- **B** Miz Rousseau receives a signed order for more groceries.
- **C** LOONY GOONY tells the refrigerator the food is spoiled.
- **D** The appliances reach a quorum about placing an order.

2 The police arrest Mister Toussaint because —

- **F** they believe the energy beverage is hazardous material
- **G** it is illegal to dispose of smart devices in public
- **H** they are collecting all the energy beverages for disposal
- **J** the train station has been evacuated for no reason

3 The toaster is able to destroy LOONY GOONY because —

- **A** toasters are braver than all other appliances
- **B** the other appliances are afraid of the toaster
- **C** the quorum-sensors approve its actions
- **D** it does not receive messages from other devices

ANALYZE THE TEXT

Support your responses with evidence from the text. NOTEBOOK

1. **Draw Conclusions** Is the story set in the past, the present, or the future? What details in the text help you draw this conclusion?
2. **Interpret** Is LOONY GOONY an "Internet of Things prank," as Mister Toussaint suspects? Explain why.
3. **Cause/Effect** What is Mister Toussaint's main **motivation** throughout the story? How do his goals and desires cause the story's action to unfold?
4. **Analyze** What is the **climax**, or most exciting moment, in the story's plot? How does it lead to the resolution of the main conflict?
5. **Notice & Note** Find the statement that Mister Toussaint repeats in paragraphs 8 and 14. What is he responding to each time? What theme about people and technology does the repetition suggest?

RESEARCH TIP

Remember that you can use quotation marks around a specific phrase to focus your search. For example, searching for "Internet of Things" will weed out search results that are about the Internet in general. If you find that your results are too narrow and you want to see more, just remove the quotation marks.

RESEARCH

How close are we to having refrigerators that automatically order our groceries for us? Do some research about the Internet of Things. Find out what it is today and what it might hold in store for us tomorrow.

QUESTION	ANSWER
What is the Internet of Things?	
What are some examples in today's world?	
What might the Internet of Things do in the future?	

Connect Science fiction often conveys a warning about the possible negative effects of technology if people don't use it wisely. With a group, discuss the warning implied by "The Brave Little Toaster." What can people do to gain future benefits from the Internet of Things while also avoiding potential problems?

CREATE AND DISCUSS

Write a Summary Write a summary of "The Brave Little Toaster." Your summary should briefly retell the most important events of the story in your own words. If you created a cause-and-effect chart to track story events while reading, you may refer to the chart as you write your summary.

- ❑ Begin by describing the story's setting and introducing the main character, Mister Toussaint.
- ❑ Next, describe the conflict Mister Toussaint faces and how he responds to it. Tell the main events of the story in the order in which they happened.
- ❑ Explain how the conflict is resolved at the end of the story.

Go to **Using Textual Evidence** in the **Writing Studio** for more help with writing a summary.

Discuss with a Small Group What could Mister Toussaint teach his neighbors about dealing with a prank like LOONY GOONY? Work with a group to create a set of helpful tips.

- ❑ As a group, review the story and note Mister Toussaint's actions in response to LOONY GOONY. Discuss which actions were effective and which were ineffective or destructive, and why.
- ❑ Brainstorm a list of tips or guidelines that would help someone overcome a similar Internet of Things prank.
- ❑ Together, organize everyone's ideas into a set of step-by-step instructions for what a person should do if faced with something like LOONY GOONY.

Go to **Participating in Collaborative Discussions** in the **Speaking and Listening Studio** to learn more.

RESPOND TO THE ESSENTIAL QUESTION

Does technology improve or control our lives?

Gather Information Review your annotations and notes on "The Brave Little Toaster." Then, add relevant details to your Response Log. As you determine which information to include, think about:

- ways in which Mister Toussaint's life is made easier by technology
- ways in which technology causes problems for him
- whether the benefits outweigh the drawbacks

At the end of the unit, you may want to refer to your notes when you write an informational essay.

ACADEMIC VOCABULARY

As you write and discuss what you learned from the story, be sure to use the Academic Vocabulary words. Check off each of the words that you use.

- ❑ **commentary**
- ❑ **occupation**
- ❑ **option**
- ❑ **speculate**
- ❑ **technology**

CRITICAL VOCABULARY

WORD BANK
diagnostics
chafe
retract
ample
reintegrate
abode
consternation
vindictive

Practice and Apply Words with similar meanings are called **synonyms**. **Antonyms** are words with opposite meanings. Identify each word pair below as being either synonyms or antonyms.

1. diagnostics/methods
2. chafe/soothe
3. retract/extend
4. ample/plenty
5. reintegrate/explode
6. abode/home
7. consternation/worry
8. vindictive/vengeful

VOCABULARY STRATEGY: Context Clues

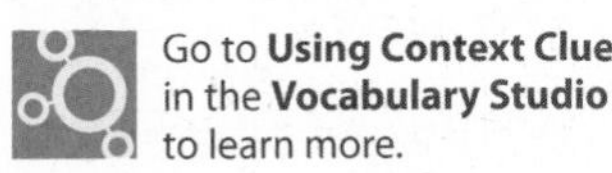

Go to **Using Context Clues** in the **Vocabulary Studio** to learn more.

Context clues are words, phrases, and ideas in the surrounding text that help you figure out the meaning of an unfamiliar word or one that could have several different meanings. These clues may appear in the same sentence or paragraph, but sometimes you also need to search in nearby paragraphs. The structure of the sentence in which the word appears can also help you determine its meaning. Find the word *ferrous* in this paragraph from the story:

> 15 **Mister Toussaint tried the microwave. Even the cleverest squeezy-pouch couldn't survive a good nuking. But the microwave wouldn't switch on. "I'm no drink and I'm no meal," LOONY GOONY sang. "I'm a ferrous lump of steel!"**

Ferrous appears right before *lump*, which is a noun. This helps you determine that the word *ferrous* describes *lump,* and in turn you can tell that it is an adjective. You also know from previous paragraphs that LOONY GOONY pretends to be made of dangerous materials. Microwaving metal is dangerous, and steel contains iron; all of these are clues to the word's meaning, "made of iron."

Practice and Apply Find the words *container* and *stupid* in paragraph 21. Complete the chart for both words.

WORD	POSSIBLE MEANINGS	CONTEXT CLUES	MEANING IN PARAGRAPH 21
container			
stupid			

LANGUAGE CONVENTIONS: The Structure of Sentences

Good writers use a variety of different sentence structures. The simplest structure has one main **clause**, a group of words with a subject and a predicate. Other structures have more than one clause. Study the examples in the chart.

Go to **Sentence Structure** in the **Grammar Studio** to learn more.

SENTENCE TYPE	EXAMPLE
A **simple sentence** has one main clause.	The refrigerator hummed smugly at him.
A **compound sentence** has two main clauses joined by a comma and a coordinating conjunction, such as *and, or*, or *but*.	The windows wouldn't retract their safety screen to let it drop, but that wasn't much of a surprise.
A **complex sentence** has a main clause and a subordinate clause. The subordinate clause begins with a subordinating conjunction, such as *when, as, after, because*, or *while*.	When they released Mister Toussaint the next day, they made him take LOONY GOONY home with him.
A **compound-complex sentence** has at least two main clauses and one subordinate clause.	The smart appliances chattered nervously at one another, but the brave little toaster said nothing as Mister Toussaint depressed its lever again.

Notice how the conjunctions in the example sentences connect the ideas in the clauses. Without the conjunctions, each sentence would be a **run-on**, or multiple sentences written as if they were one. The writer's meaning would also be less clear without conjunctions.

Run-on: The smart appliances chattered nervously at one another the brave little toaster said nothing Mister Toussaint depressed its lever again.

A common error in writing is to use a comma by itself to join two clauses, instead of using a comma and a conjunction. This error is called a **comma splice**, and it is a type of run-on.

Comma splice: His refrigerator had sent in the list, she had the signed order to prove it.

Correct sentence: His refrigerator had sent in the list, **and** she had the signed order to prove it.

Practice and Apply Write a simple sentence about LOONY GOONY. Then use that sentence to build a compound sentence, a complex sentence, and a compound-complex sentence.

ARE BIONIC SUPERHUMANS ON THE HORIZON?

Informational Text by **Ramez Naam**

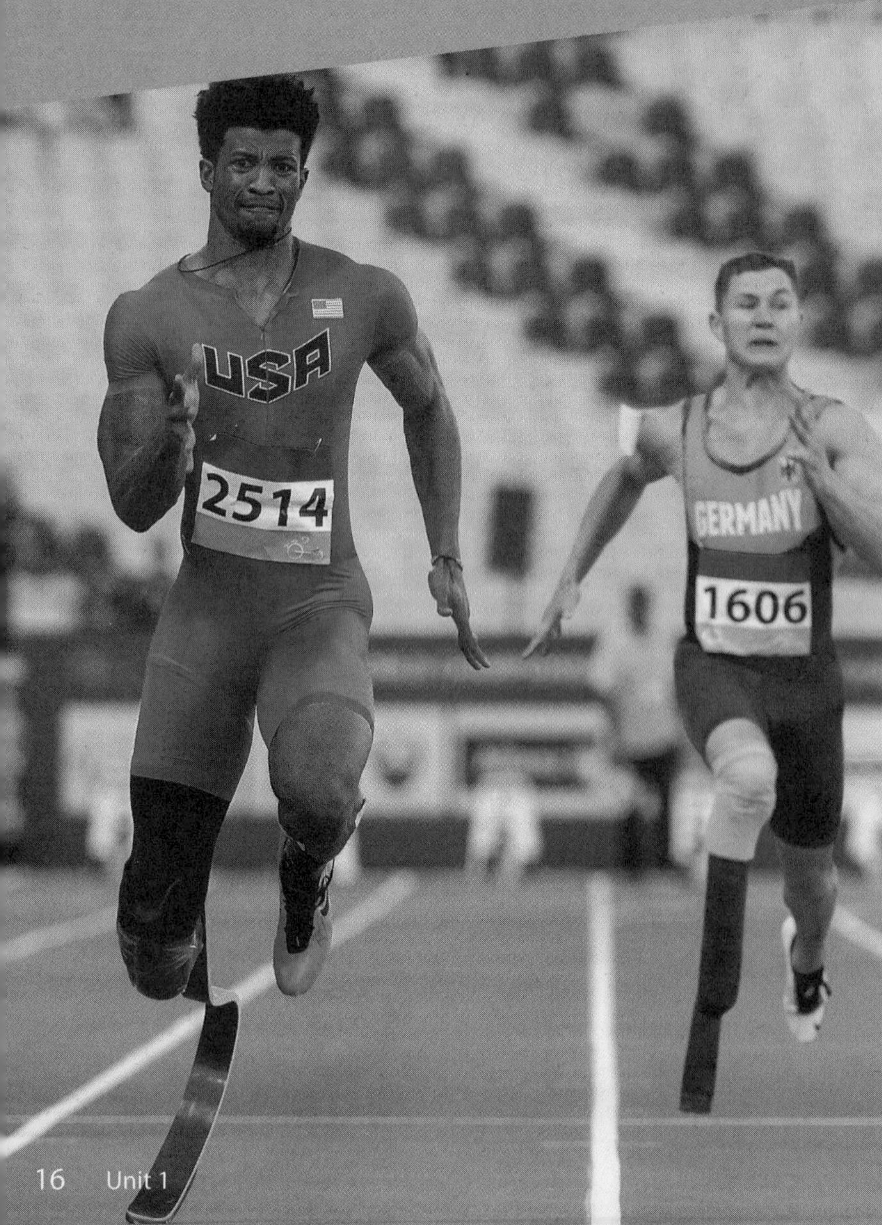

ESSENTIAL QUESTION:

Does technology improve or control our lives?

QUICK START

If a scientist could implant a device inside you that made you smarter, faster, or stronger, would you have the surgery? What if the procedure were risky or expensive? Discuss your reaction with the class.

IDENTIFY MAIN IDEA AND DETAILS

How can you understand a text when you don't know anything about its topic? You can ask questions about the text as you read. You might try re-reading the text. Let the text teach you by doing the following:

- Identify the **main idea**—the most important idea about a topic—of each paragraph or section of text. It may be stated directly at the beginning or end of each paragraph or section.
- Read the **supporting details**, or information about the main idea, to learn more. If the main idea isn't stated, use these details to infer it.

Identifying these elements will help you summarize the text—that is, to briefly retell in your own words the text's main ideas and details.

GENRE ELEMENTS: INFORMATIONAL TEXT

- provides factual information
- includes evidence to support ideas
- contains text features
- appears in many forms, such as news articles and essays

ANALYZE ORGANIZATION

This article has mostly a **main-idea-and-supporting-details** pattern of organization. Near the end, however, it breaks away from this pattern, filling one paragraph with questions and the next with a call to action. As you read, think about why the author uses both types of organization to convey his **thesis**, or the controlling idea of his entire text. Also pay attention to **text features**, such as headings, subheadings, photos, and captions. These can help you make predictions about the text's main ideas and organizational patterns by making them visually prominent.

TYPE OF ORGANIZATION	EXAMPLE
In **main-idea-and-details organization**, each paragraph or text section introduces a main idea and gives examples or other details about it.	We're in the midst of a bionic revolution, yet most of us don't know it. Around 220,000 people worldwide already walk around with cochlear implants. . . .
In **question-and-call-to-action organization**, the author poses questions and then tells readers what they ought to do.	. . . will only the rich have access to these enhancements? We have a little while to consider these questions, but we ought to start. . . .

GET READY

CRITICAL VOCABULARY

implant **inert** **integrity** **enhancements**

To see how many Critical Vocabulary words you already know, use them to complete the sentences.

1. Soccer has no __________ if some players cheat.
2. I broke a tooth, so Dr. Lu will __________ an artificial one in my jaw.
3. These new gadgets are __________ because they save you time.
4. His old artificial hand was __________; the fingers did not move.

LANGUAGE CONVENTIONS

Commonly Confused Words In this article, the author uses both *it's* and *its,* two words that even experienced writers sometimes confuse.

It's with an apostrophe is a contraction that means "it is."

What happens when it's possible to improve on the human body and mind?

Its without the apostrophe means "belonging to it."

The technology will sneak its way into our lives.

When you find an *it's* or *its,* consider why it's correct in its sentence.

ANNOTATION MODEL

NOTICE & NOTE

As you read, determine the main ideas and supporting details. You can also mark up the article. Here are one reader's notes.

1 We're in the midst of a bionic revolution, yet most of us don't know it.

2 Around 220,000 people worldwide already walk around with cochlear implants—devices worn around the ear that turn sound waves into electrical impulses shunted directly into the auditory nerve.

3 Tens of thousands of people have been implanted with deep brain stimulators, devices that send an electrode tunneling several inches in the brain. Deep brain stimulators are used to control . . .

First sentence often is main idea. Bionic revolution? What's that?

2nd and 3rd paragraphs give details about devices that help people.

BACKGROUND

Technology can make our lives better, but it also can change them. In this article, science fiction author ***Ramez Naam*** *shares some science facts about bionic body parts that can now change animal and human capabilities. Bionic body parts are those containing mechanical or electronic elements that improve functioning, and they may be part of your life someday.*

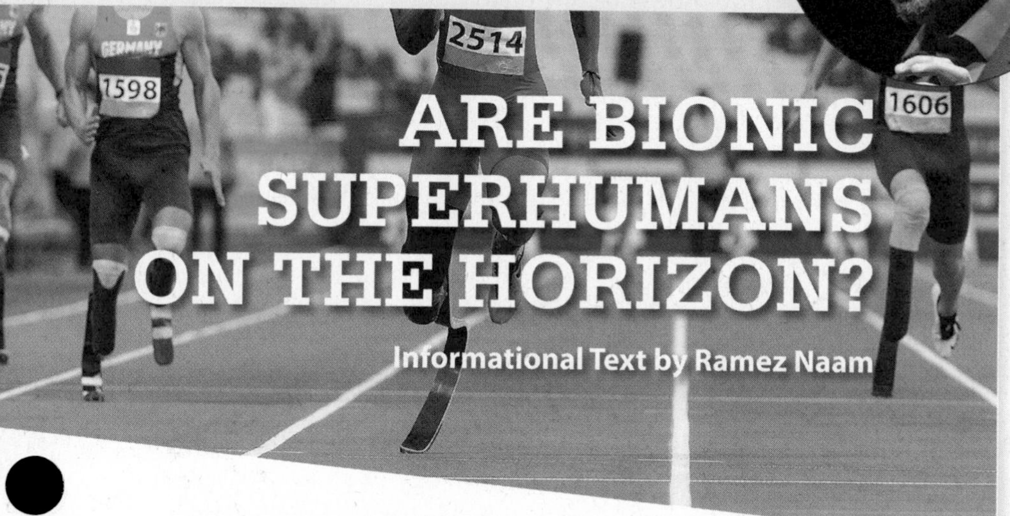

ARE BIONIC SUPERHUMANS ON THE HORIZON?

Informational Text by Ramez Naam

SETTING A PURPOSE

As you read, look for details that reveal what the author means by "bionic superhumans" and how he answers the question posed in the title.

1 We're in the midst of a bionic revolution, yet most of us don't know it.

2 Around 220,000 people worldwide already walk around with cochlear implants—devices worn around the ear that turn sound waves into electrical impulses shunted[1] directly into the auditory[2] nerve.

3 Tens of thousands of people have been **implanted** with deep brain stimulators, devices that send an electrode[3] tunneling several inches in the brain. Deep brain

[1] **shunted:** allowed to flow from one pathway to another through surgery.
[2] **auditory** (ô´dĭ-tôr´ē): related to hearing.
[3] **electrode** (ĭ-lĕk´trōd´): a material through which electricity flows.

Notice & Note

Use the side margins to notice and note signposts in the text.

IDENTIFY MAIN IDEA AND DETAILS

Annotate: Circle the main idea of paragraphs 1–4. Underline key details that support this main idea.

Summarize: Write a sentence that summarizes paragraphs 1–4 in your own words.

implant
(ĭm-plănt´) *v.* To *implant* a device means to place it inside the body through surgery.

NOTICE & NOTE

stimulators are used to control Parkinson's disease,[4] though lately they've also been tested—with encouraging results—in use against severe depression and obsessive compulsive disorder.

4 The most obvious bionics are those that replace limbs. Olympian "Blade Runner" Oscar Pistorius made a splash with his Cheetah carbon fiber prostheses.[5] Yet those are a relatively simple technology—a curved piece of slightly springy, super-strong material. In the digital age, we're seeing more sophisticated limbs.

5 Consider the thought-controlled bionic leg that Zac Vawter used to climb all 103 floors of Chicago's Willis Tower. Or the nerve-controlled bionic hand that Iraq war veteran Glen Lehman had attached after the loss of his original hand.

6 Or the even more sophisticated i-limb Ultra, an artificial hand with five independently articulating artificial fingers. Those limbs don't just react mechanically to pressure. They actually respond to the thoughts and intentions of their owners, flexing, extending, gripping, and releasing on mental command.

7 The age when prostheses were largely **inert** pieces of wood, metal, and plastic is passing. Advances in microprocessors, in techniques to interface[6] digital technology with the human nervous system, and in battery technology to allow prostheses to pack more power with less weight are turning replacement limbs into active parts of the human body.

8 In some cases, they're not even part of the body at all. Consider the case of Cathy Hutchinson. In 1997, Cathy had a stroke, leaving her without control of her arms. Hutchinson volunteered for an experimental procedure that could one day help millions of people with partial or complete paralysis. She let researchers implant a small device in the part of her brain responsible for motor control. With that device, she is able to control an external robotic arm by thinking about it.

9 That, in turn, brings up an interesting question: If the arm isn't physically attached to her body, how far away could she be and still control it? The answer is at least thousands of miles. In animal studies, scientists have shown that a monkey with a brain implant can control a robot arm 7,000 miles away. The monkey's mental signals were sent over the internet, from Duke University in North Carolina, to the robot arm in Japan. In this day and age, distance is almost irrelevant.

WORD GAPS

Notice & Note: What words in paragraphs 6–7 are unfamiliar or confusing? Mark these words.

Infer: Use context clues to guess the meanings of the words. If you still feel uncertain about any of the words, look them up in a dictionary.

inert
(ĭn-ûrt´) *adj. Inert* means unable to move or act.

[4] **Parkinson's disease:** a disease that weakens muscles and causes a person's arms and legs to shake.

[5] **prostheses** (prŏs-thē´sēz): artificial devices that replace injured or missing body parts.

[6] **interface:** to connect or interact smoothly.

NOTICE & NOTE 

The Superhuman Frontier

10 The 7,000-mile-away prosthetic arm makes an important point: These new prostheses aren't just going to restore missing human abilities. They're going to enhance our abilities, giving us powers we never had before, and augmenting[7] other capabilities we have. While the current generation of prostheses is still primitive, we can already see this taking shape when a monkey moves a robotic arm on the other side of the planet just by thinking about it.

11 Other research is pointing to enhancements to memory and decision making.

12 The hippocampus is a small, seahorse-shaped part of the brain that's essential in forming new memories. If it's damaged—by an injury to the head, for example—people start having difficulty forming new long-term memories. In the most extreme cases, this can lead to the complete inability to form new long-term memories, as in the film *Memento.* Working to find a way to repair this sort of brain damage, researchers in 2011 created a "hippocampus chip" that can replace damaged brain tissue. When they implanted it in rats with a damaged hippocampus, they found that not only could their chip repair damaged memory—it could improve the rats' ability to learn new things.

13 Nor is memory the end of it. Another study, in 2012, demonstrated that we can boost intelligence—at least one sort—in monkeys. Scientists at Wake Forest University implanted specialized brain chips in a set of monkeys and trained those monkeys to perform a picture-matching game. When the implant was activated, it raised their scores by an average of 10 points on a 100-point scale. The implant makes monkeys smarter.

[7] **augmenting** (ôg-mĕnt´ ĭng): increasing or adding to.

ANALYZE ORGANIZATION

Annotate: Circle the heading on this page. Underline details in paragraphs 10–13 that help you understand what the heading means.

Analyze: Does the heading help you predict the main idea of this section? Confirm your prediction by writing the main idea in a sentence.

IDENTIFY MAIN IDEA AND DETAILS

Annotate: Underline the main idea in paragraph 12. Circle key details that give more information about this main idea.

Evaluate: Why do you think the author chose to state the main idea later in the paragraph, instead of in the first sentence?

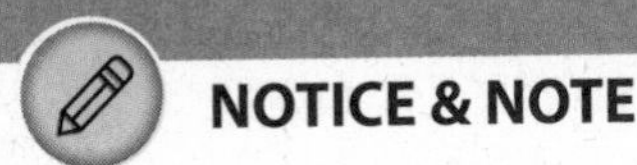

From Disabled to Super-capable

14 Both of those technologies for boosting memory and intelligence are in very early stages, in small animal studies only, and years (or possibly decades) away from wide use in humans. Still, they make us wonder—what happens when it's possible to improve on the human body and mind?

ANALYZE ORGANIZATION

Annotate: Underline the questions in paragraphs 14, 15, and 17, and circle the call to action.

Synthesize: How do the questions and the call to action work together?

15 The debate has started already, of course. Oscar Pistorius had to fight hard for inclusion in the Olympics. Many objected that his carbon fiber prostheses gave him a competitive advantage. He was able—with the help of doctors and biomedical engineers—to make a compelling case that his Cheetah blades didn't give him any advantage on the field. But how long will that be true? How long until we have prostheses (not to mention drugs and genetic therapies) that make athletes better in their sports?

integrity

(ĭn-tĕg´rĭ-tē) *n. Integrity* is following a strict code of ethical conduct.

16 But the issue is much, much wider than professional sports. We may care passionately about the **integrity** of the Olympics or professional cycling or so on, but they only directly affect a very small number of us. In other areas of life—in the workforce in particular—enhancement technology might affect all of us.

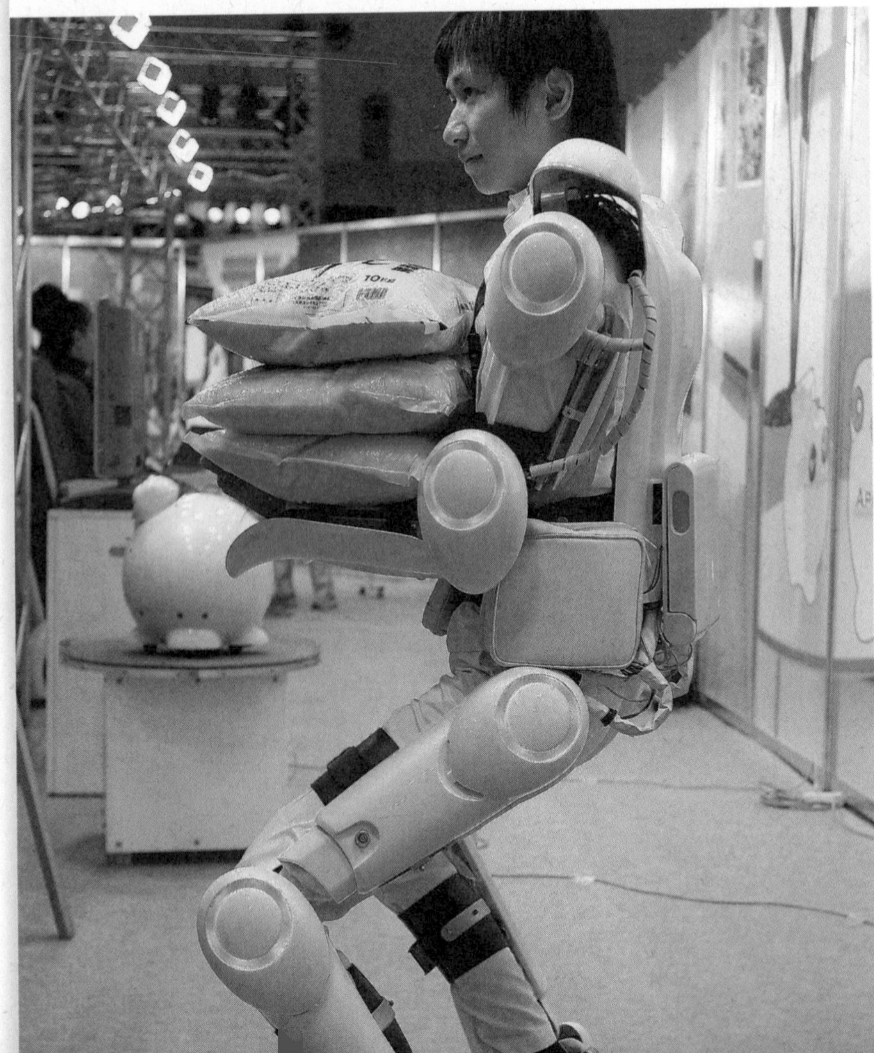

17 When it's possible to make humans smarter, sharper, and faster, how will that affect us? Will the effect be mostly positive, boosting our productivity and the rate of human innovation? Or will it be just another pressure to compete at work? Who will be able to afford these technologies? Will anyone be able to have their body, and more importantly, their brain upgraded? Or will only the rich have access to these **enhancements**?

18 We have a little while to consider these questions, but we ought to start. The technology will sneak its way into our lives, starting with people with disabilities, the injured, and the ill. It'll improve their lives in ways that are unquestionably good. And then, one day, we'll wake up and realize that we're doing more than restoring lost function. We're enhancing it.

19 Superhuman technology is on the horizon. Time to start thinking about what that means for us.

NOTICE & NOTE

LANGUAGE CONVENTIONS

Annotate: The author uses the commonly confused words *affect* and *effect*. Mark them in paragraph 17.

Infer: Use context clues and a dictionary to figure out the words' meanings.

enhancement
(ĕn-hăns´mənt) *n.* An *enhancement* improves or adds to the quality or function of something.

CHECK YOUR UNDERSTANDING

Answer these questions before moving on to the **Analyze the Text** section on the following page.

1 The author included the section "The Superhuman Frontier" to —

A explain that bionics will do more than replace body parts

B express his uncertainty about the future of bionics

C convince readers that bionic body parts are dangerous

D inform readers which types of bionics they will receive

2 In paragraph 17, the writer includes a series of questions in order to —

F express his confusion about the issue to readers

G inform readers about what is certain to happen

H encourage readers to think deeply about the issue

J entertain readers with impossible fantasies

3 Which idea is supported by information throughout the selection?

A Bionics will improve intelligence and memory.

B Athletes with bionic body parts will perform better.

C Many people with disabilities already benefit from bionics.

D Bionics can improve human abilities in many ways.

RESPOND

ANALYZE THE TEXT

Support your responses with evidence from the text. NOTEBOOK

1. **Evaluate** Examine the article's subheadings. In your own words, state the concept or aspect of the main topic that each introduces. Are the subheadings effective? Why or why not?
2. **Cite Evidence** In paragraph 4, the author states, "In the digital age, we're seeing more sophisticated limbs." What details does he provide in support of this main idea?
3. **Interpret** Review paragraphs 9 and 10. What might the author mean by "powers we never had before"?
4. **Predict** Will the effect of bionics on the lives of most people be positive overall or negative overall? Use specific details from the article to support your opinion.
5. **Notice & Note** Now that you have read the article, how would you define the phrase *bionic revolution* (paragraph 1)?

RESEARCH TIP
Most search engines allow you to write your search in the form of a question. For this activity, you might type in the question *When will humans become bionic?*

RESEARCH

Don't just take Ramez Naam's word for it that bionic superhumans will soon be here. Instead, find out what other experts think. Complete this chart with information from classroom resources or reliable websites. Then write a sentence that synthesizes, or combines, the information.

ARTICLE TITLE AND SOURCE	OPINION ABOUT BIONICS
What do the experts think about bionic superhumans?	

Extend In paragraph 19, Naam states that "superhuman technology is on the horizon." In a small group, discuss the results of your research, and decide whether you agree or disagree with this statement.

CREATE AND DISCUSS

Write an Informational Essay Write a three- to four-paragraph essay in which you compare and contrast bionic technology that repairs damage to the human body and bionic technology that enhances the human body.

- ❑ Introduce the topic and state your controlling idea about the two kinds of bionic technology.
- ❑ Then, tell about the similarities and differences between the two kinds of technology, including their effects on people's lives. Use details from the text to support your ideas.
- ❑ In your final paragraph, state your conclusion about bionic technology and the different ways it can be used.

Go to **Writing Informative Texts** in the **Writing Studio** to learn more.

Discuss with a Small Group Have a discussion about the best ways to distribute bionics fairly. Should people who can pay a lot of money get the best bionics first? Should people with disabilities be first in line? If so, who should pay for those bionics if they are expensive?

- ❑ As a group, set an agenda and establish clear goals for your discussion. Review the text and decide which information is relevant to the discussion topic. Use the headings to help you locate the information.
- ❑ Have group members add relevant research findings.
- ❑ Review the ideas together, listening closely and respectfully to all ideas. Then take a vote on the fairest ways to distribute bionics.

Go to **Participating in Collaborative Discussions** in the **Speaking and Listening Studio** for more on having a discussion.

RESPOND TO THE ESSENTIAL QUESTION

? Does technology improve or control our lives?

Gather Information Review your annotations and notes on "Are Bionic Superhumans on the Horizon?" Then, add relevant details to your Response Log. To decide what to include, think about:

- the kinds of bionic advances people want or need
- ways in which advances in bionics may affect individuals and society
- the ethical questions bionic devices may raise

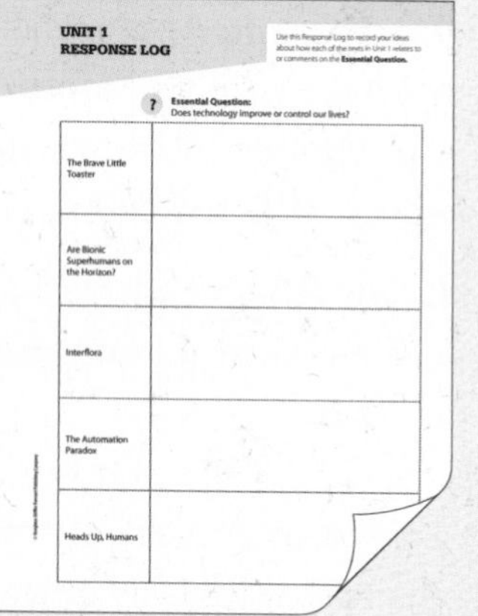

UNIT 1 RESPONSE LOG

Essential Question: Does technology improve or control our lives?

The Brave Little Toaster	
Are Bionic Superhumans on the Horizon?	
Interflora	
The Automation Paradox	
Heads Up, Humans	

At the end of the unit, you may use your notes to help you write an informational essay.

ACADEMIC VOCABULARY

As you write and discuss what you learned from the informational text, be sure to use the Academic Vocabulary words. Check off each of the words that you use.

- ❑ **commentary**
- ❑ **occupation**
- ❑ **option**
- ❑ **speculate**
- ❑ **technology**

CRITICAL VOCABULARY

WORD BANK
implant
inert
integrity
enhancement

Practice and Apply Choose the correct answer to each question. Then, explain your response.

1. Which of the following is an example of something **inert**?
   a. a cube made of solid stone **b.** a bionic hand with moving fingers

2. Which of these would a doctor **implant** through surgery?
   a. an artificial leg **b.** a computer chip in a brain

3. Which of the following could be called an **enhancement**?
   a. an old, persistent problem **b.** a new, better feature

4. Which of the following is an example of **integrity**?
   a. cheating on a test that you forgot to study for **b.** being honest when nobody is watching

VOCABULARY STRATEGY: Synonyms and Antonyms

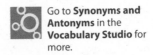

Go to **Synonyms and Antonyms** in the **Vocabulary Studio** for more.

Synonyms and antonyms can help you understand technical words. A **synonym** is a word with a meaning similar to that of another word. An **antonym** has a meaning opposite that of another word. In paragraph 7, old *inert* artificial limbs are contrasted with newer *active* ones, making *inert* and *active* antonyms. So, if you know that *active* means "able to move," you can infer that *inert* means "not able to move."

Practice and Apply Each sentence includes a pair of words in boldface type. Use context clues to figure out what the words mean and whether they are synonyms or antonyms. Then, in your own words, write the definition of the word indicated below the sentence.

1. Does the prosthetic hand have five **articulating** fingers, or are the fingers part of one **immobile** piece of plastic?

   articulating: ______________________________

2. Soon after researchers **implanted** the device, it malfunctioned, and they quickly **extracted** it.

   extracted: ______________________________

3. "That information is **irrelevant**, so let's get rid of it," Brad said, but I insisted that it was **essential** and needed to stay in the report.

   irrelevant: ______________________________

LANGUAGE CONVENTIONS: Commonly Confused Words

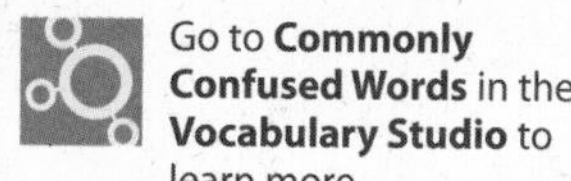
Go to **Commonly Confused Words** in the **Vocabulary Studio** to learn more.

English contains so many words that sound alike but are spelled differently that it's easy to get them confused. Ramez Naam's article includes some commonly confused words.

- *It's* (meaning "it is") and *its* (meaning "belonging to it")

  What happens when it's possible to improve on the human body and mind?

  Technology will sneak its way into our lives.

- *Affect* (meaning "to influence") and *effect* (meaning "result")

  When it's possible to make humans smarter, sharper, and faster, how will that affect us? Will the effect be mostly positive?

Here are two other examples.

- *There* (meaning "in that place"), *their* (meaning "belonging to them"), and *they're* (meaning "they are")

  The scientists gave their lecture over there, near the college. They're answering questions now.

- *To* (meaning "toward"), *two* (meaning "a whole number that is more than one and less than three"), and *too* (meaning "also")

  We're going to the lab to see two or three new prosthetics. You can come, too.

Practice and Apply Write your own sentences with commonly misspelled words using the examples above as models. Your sentences might express your opinions about how bionics will affect people. Share your completed sentences with a partner and compare how each of you used the words.

INTERFLORA

Poem by **Susan Hamlyn**

? ESSENTIAL QUESTION:

Does technology improve or control our lives?

QUICK START

In the poem you are about to read, one person communicates with another person through email. What kinds of messages are best conveyed through email? What kinds are not? List your ideas below.

Email is great for . . .	Email is not so great for . . .

ANALYZE STRUCTURE

"Interflora" is a **sonnet,** a14-line poem with a strictly defined structure and pattern of rhyme. The origins of this traditional form date back to the 1500s. Many famous love poems have been written in the form of the sonnet. One well-known collection of love sonnets is Elizabeth Barrett Browning's *Sonnets from the Portuguese* (1850), which she wrote for her husband, the poet Robert Browning.

In poetry, **meter** is a pattern of stressed and unstressed syllables. Each unit of meter, known as a foot, consists of one stressed syllable and one or two unstressed syllables. Sonnets are written in iambic pentameter, with five feet in each line. Each foot has one unstressed syllable (˘) followed by a stressed syllable (´). The first line of Elizabeth Barrett Browning's Sonnet 43 below has been marked to show the meter. Mark the next three lines to show how the pattern continues.

˘ / ˘ / ˘ / ˘ / ˘ /
How do I love thee? Let me count the ways. a

I love thee to the depth and breadth and height b

My soul can reach, when feeling out of sight b

For the ends of Being and ideal Grace. . . . a

A poem's **rhyme scheme** is its pattern of end rhymes. A rhyme scheme is noted by assigning a letter of the alphabet, beginning with *a,* to each line. Lines that rhyme are given the same letter. The first four lines of Sonnet 43 have been marked to show the rhyme scheme. Notice rhyme scheme and other sonnet characteristics as you read "Interflora."

GENRE ELEMENTS: SONNET

- is a form of lyric poetry that expresses personal thoughts and feelings and has a musical quality
- contains 14 lines
- follows a strict rhyme scheme, or pattern of end rhymes, such as *abbaabba cdcdcd* or *abab cdcd efef gg*
- is a popular form for love poems

GET READY

ANALYZE IRONY

Irony is a literary device used to show a special kind of contrast between appearance and reality. Writers often use irony to create humor. There are three types of irony frequently used in literature: situational, dramatic, and verbal. Read the definition of each type in the chart below. Then write how each type could be funny.

TYPE OF IRONY	DEFINITION	WHY THIS COULD BE HUMOROUS
Situational irony	When a character or the reader expects one thing, but something very different happens or is true	
Dramatic irony	When the reader knows something that a character does not know	
Verbal irony	When a character says one thing but means another	

As you read "Interflora," look for examples of irony that create humor.

ANNOTATION MODEL

NOTICE & NOTE

As you read, note how the poet uses irony to convey a message or to create humor. This model shows one reader's notes about the beginning of "Interflora."

From Robert B. @ mailexcite dot com
to E.B.B. @ virgin dot uk:
Please find herewith as proof of my esteem
a customized, fresh, virtual bouquet.

The sonnet is written like an email message, but line 3 uses old-fashioned language. Is this an example of irony?

BACKGROUND

"Interflora" is a sonnet written as an email. The poem begins with the email addresses of the speaker and the person to whom he is sending a message. Readers familiar with the love sonnets that Elizabeth Barrett Browning wrote to her husband, Robert Browning, may recognize a certain humorous or ironic connection between this sonnet and those earlier works. ***Susan Hamlyn*** *is a London-based English teacher and writer. Hamlyn has published two collections of poetry,* The Only Thing Untouched *and* Quiet Myth.

INTERFLORA

Poem by Susan Hamlyn

SETTING A PURPOSE

As you read the sonnet, pay attention to details that are surprising or unexpected, and think about how these details create humor.

Notice & Note

Use the side margins to notice and note signposts in the text.

NOTICE & NOTE

ANALYZE STRUCTURE

Annotate: Use the symbols ˘ and ʹ to mark the meter of the sonnet. Use letters of the alphabet to identify and mark the rhyme scheme.

Analyze: Does "Interflora" follow a traditional sonnet rhyme scheme? Explain.

ANALYZE IRONY

Annotate: Mark at least three examples of humor in the sonnet.

Analyze: Explain how the poet uses irony to create humor.

Interflora

From Robert B. @ mailexcite dot com
To E.B.B. @ virgin dot uk:
Please find herewith as proof of my esteem
a customized, fresh, virtual bouquet.
For scent please click on cellophane and press
Control. To read the message on the tag
highlight the print, click on *Encrypt Reverse.*
To unwrap blooms and place in vase use *Drag.*
My flowers sent, beloved, in this way,
won't fade, stink of mortality's decay.
Petals won't wilt to husks nor leaves to slime;
these on-line flowers for you will outlast Time.
But if, my love, this gift seems incomplete
and does not touch your heart, then press *Delete.*

CHECK YOUR UNDERSTANDING

Answer these questions before moving on to the **Analyze the Text** section on the following page.

1 Which line reveals that the poem's speaker is sending an email?

A *From Robert B. @ mailexcite dot com*

B *Please find herewith as proof of my esteem*

C *To unwrap blooms and place in vase use* Drag

D *Petals won't wilt to husks nor leaves to slime*

2 To smell the flowers, what does the recipient need to do?

F Click on cellophane and press *Control.*

G Highlight the print and click on *Encrypt Reverse.*

H Use *Drag.*

J Press *Delete.*

3 According to the speaker, in what way are the on-line flowers better than real ones?

A They are fresh and virtual.

B They come with a message.

C They will last forever.

D They can easily be deleted.

ANALYZE THE TEXT

Support your responses with evidence from the text. NOTEBOOK

1. **Cite Evidence** Which words and phrases in the poem reveal that it is a love sonnet?
2. **Analyze** Which types of irony are used in the sonnet? Give examples from the poem.
3. **Compare** How are the last six lines of "Interflora" different from the rest of the poem in form? How does this compare to more traditional sonnet forms?
4. **Synthesize** The 19th-century British poets Robert and Elizabeth Barrett Browning shared one of the most famous and passionate romances in the history of literature. How does this fact add to the humor of "Interflora"?
5. **Infer** What theme or message about technology does the poet's use of irony suggest?

RESEARCH

"Interflora" was published in 1994. Since then, much has changed about the way people use the Internet in their daily lives. With a partner, research the differences between technologies today and technologies from the time period in which this poem was written.

RESEARCH TIP
Besides using the Internet, where can you look to find answers to these questions? Consider contacting someone who lived during the time period and ask whether you can conduct an interview about how technology has changed since then.

QUESTION	ANSWER
What devices could people use to connect to the Internet in the mid-1990s?	
How did people communicate overseas in the 1990s?	
Could you use the Internet to order flowers in 1994?	

Connect In a small group, discuss how technology has changed the way we communicate with other people. How would the people in the poem communicate with each other today? What might Robert B. send to E.B.B. today?

CREATE AND PRESENT

Write a Sonnet Write a poem in the structure of a sonnet. Review your notes on the Quick Start activity before you begin.

- ❑ Decide on a topic and theme for your sonnet. Brainstorm some rhyming word pairs related to your topic.
- ❑ Consider how to include irony and humor in your sonnet.
- ❑ Write a draft of your sonnet in 14 lines. You might use a rhymed couplet at the end to reveal your theme.
- ❑ Revise your poem to match the traditional meter of a sonnet and to have a consistent rhyme scheme.

Present a Sonnet Now share your sonnet with the class. When you and your classmates read your sonnets aloud, provide thoughtful feedback to each other.

- ❑ Practice reading your sonnet. Experiment with stressing different syllables to bring out the musical quality in the text.
- ❑ Practice making eye contact with your audience, and use facial expressions and natural gestures to convey the meaning of the sonnet.
- ❑ Finally, read your sonnet aloud to the class.

Go to the **Speaking and Listening Studio** for more on giving a presentation.

RESPOND TO THE ESSENTIAL QUESTION

? Does technology improve or control our lives?

Gather Information Review your annotations and notes on "Interflora." Then, add relevant details to your Response Log. As you determine which information to include, think about:

- how people used technology in the past versus today
- whether this has changed for the better or for the worse
- how to keep technology from controlling one's life

At the end of the unit, you may want to refer to your notes when you write an informational essay.

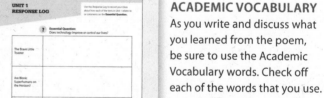

ACADEMIC VOCABULARY

As you write and discuss what you learned from the poem, be sure to use the Academic Vocabulary words. Check off each of the words that you use.

- ❑ **commentary**
- ❑ **occupation**
- ❑ **option**
- ❑ **speculate**
- ❑ **technology**

ARGUMENT

THE AUTOMATION PARADOX

by **James Bessen**

pages 39–43

COMPARE ARGUMENTS

As you read, notice how the claim in each argument is supported by reasons and evidence. Then think about how the arguments relate to each other. After you read both selections, you will collaborate with a group on a final project.

ESSENTIAL QUESTION:

Does technology improve or control our lives?

ARGUMENT

HEADS UP, HUMANS

by **Claudia Alarcón**

pages 51–55

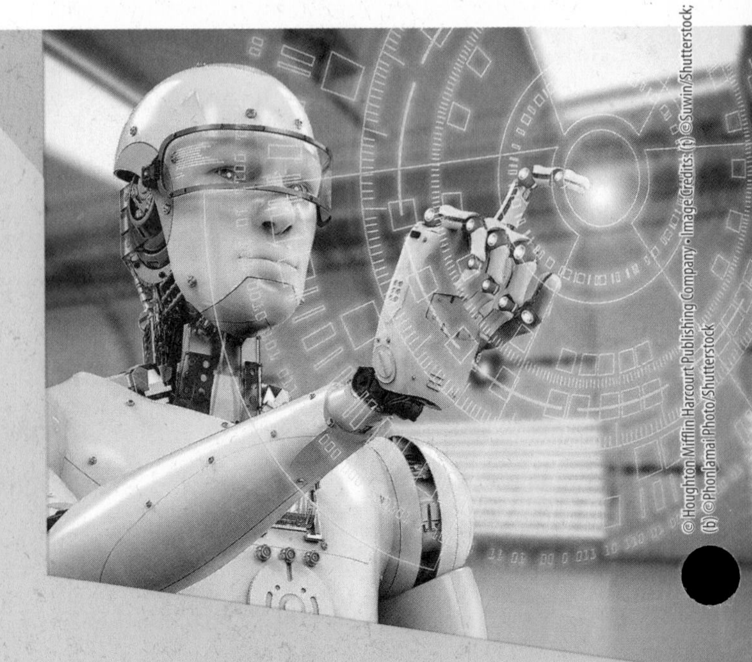

The Automation Paradox

QUICK START

Early elevators required operators to help passengers ride safely and efficiently. What other once-human jobs are now done by technology? List as many as you can. Then share your list with the class.

ANALYZE CLAIM AND EVIDENCE

In an argument, a **claim** is the writer's position, or opinion, on an issue. Recall the difference between facts and opinions.

- A **fact** is a statement that can be proved, or verified. However, different people may interpret the same fact in different ways.
- An **opinion** is a statement that cannot be proved because it expresses a person's beliefs, feelings, or thoughts.

A strong argument clearly and logically lays out a claim, reasons to accept the claim, and sufficient **evidence**—relevant facts, statistics, quotations, examples, and expert opinions—to support those reasons.

As you read "The Automation Paradox," use a chart like this one to analyze the argument's claims, reasons, and evidence. Is the author's reasoning sound? How might you defend or challenge his claims?

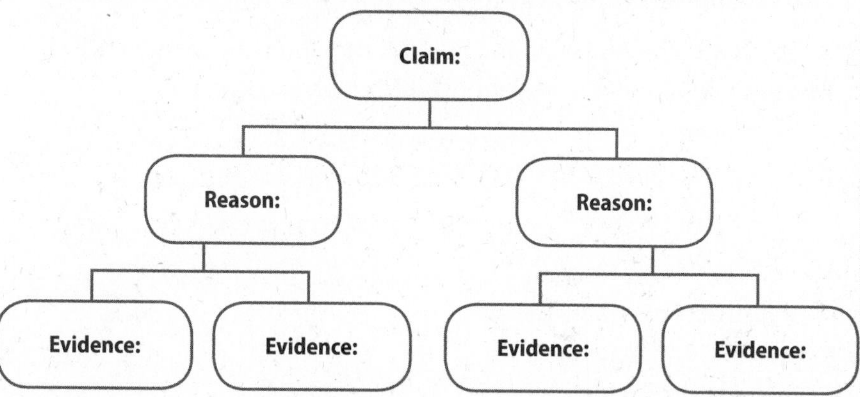

ANALYZE GRAPHIC FEATURES

A **graphic feature** is a design element such as a diagram, bar graph, or pie chart that visually represents information. Authors often use graphic features to show patterns and relationships between facts. As you read "The Automation Paradox," examine each graphic feature to see what it emphasizes. Ask yourself the following questions about each graphic feature:

- What information or evidence does the graph provide? What is the author's purpose, or reason, for including this visual?
- What conclusions can be drawn based on the information in the graph?

GENRE ELEMENTS: ARGUMENT

- states a claim and reasons to support the claim
- includes facts and other evidence to support reasons
- may note objections to claim and explain why they should be rejected
- takes many forms, such as editorials, feature articles, and essays

GET READY

CRITICAL VOCABULARY

redistribute	robustly	predominantly
relevant	expansive	collaborate

To see how many Critical Vocabulary words you already know, use them to complete the sentences.

1. The topic is too __________ to research, so I'm narrowing it down.
2. If we __________ on the project, we can all share the work.
3. Let's __________ the chores to divide the tasks more fairly.
4. At home, they __________ speak their native language, Spanish.
5. Evidence that is __________ clearly connects to a claim.
6. The vegetables grew __________, so we had a big harvest.

LANGUAGE CONVENTIONS

Transitional Words and Phrases Transitional words and phrases connect ideas and show how they are related. In the example below, the transition *but* connects two ideas and signals a contrast.

Yes, technology replaces workers, but it also creates new jobs.

As you read "The Automation Paradox," note transitional words and phrases that alert you to relationships between ideas.

NOTICE & NOTE 

ANNOTATION MODEL

As you read, note how the author presents his claim, reasons, and evidence. In the model, you can see one reader's notes about the introduction to "The Automation Paradox."

1 Automation isn't just for blue-collar workers anymore. Computers are now taking over tasks performed by professional workers, raising fears of massive unemployment. Some people, such as the MIT professors Erik Brynjolfsson and Andrew McAfee, identify automation as a cause of the slow recovery from the Great Recession and the "hollowing out of the middle class." Others see white-collar automation as causing a level of persistent technological unemployment that demands policies that would redistribute wealth. Robot panic is in full swing.

introduces the topic: impact of automation on employment

identifies two points of view that automation causes a negative impact

BACKGROUND

James Bessen *(b. 1958) is an economist and lecturer at Boston University whose interest in the impact of technology on innovation and jobs has paralleled the rise of personal computers in the workplace as well as the ongoing push to automate tasks with computer technology. His book* Learning by Doing: The Real Connection Between Innovation, Wages, and Wealth *looks at history to understand how new technologies affect wages and skills over the long term.*

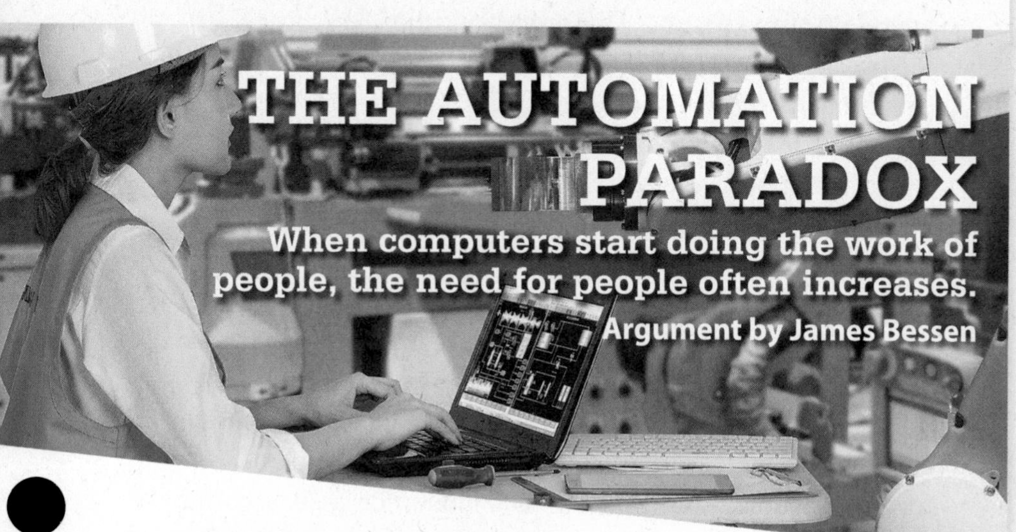

THE AUTOMATION PARADOX

When computers start doing the work of people, the need for people often increases.

Argument by James Bessen

PREPARE TO COMPARE

As you read, note viewpoints the writer identifies that oppose his claim and the evidence he provides to refute them. This will help you trace and evaluate the writer's argument.

Notice & Note

Use the side margins to notice and note signposts in the text.

1 Automation[1] isn't just for blue-collar[2] workers anymore. Computers are now taking over tasks performed by professional workers, raising fears of massive unemployment. Some people, such as the MIT professors Erik Brynjolfsson and Andrew McAfee, identify automation as a cause of the slow recovery from the Great Recession[3] and the "hollowing out of the middle class." Others see white-collar[4] automation as causing a level of persistent technological unemployment that demands policies that would **redistribute** wealth. Robot panic is in full swing.

redistribute
(rē´dĭ-strĭb´yo͞ot) *v.* To *redistribute* means to distribute again but differently.

[1] **automation:** the automatic operation of equipment, a process, or a system.

[2] **blue-collar:** relating to workers whose jobs are performed in work clothes and often involve manual labor.

[3] **Great Recession:** a period of economic decline from December 2007 to June 2009.

[4] **white-collar:** relating to workers whose work does not involve manual labor and who are often expected to dress with a degree of formality.

NOTICE & NOTE

ANALYZE CLAIM AND EVIDENCE

Annotate: In paragraph 2, mark the statement that best expresses the author's claim, or opinion, about the impact of automation on employment.

Analyze: A **paradox** is a statement that seems to contradict itself but may nonetheless be true. Why is the writer's claim about automation a paradox?

relevant
(rĕl´ə-vənt) *adj.* Something is *relevant* to a topic when it is related or important to that topic.

robustly
(rō-bŭst´lē) *adv. Robustly* means in a strong, healthy way.

NUMBERS AND STATS

Notice & Note: How do the results of the software study relate to the writer's claim? Circle or underline these results in the text.

Draw Conclusions: What conclusion can you draw based on this data?

ANALYZE GRAPHIC FEATURES

Annotate: On this bar graph, mark the text that tells you what, exactly, is represented by the height of each bar.

Analyze: How does the information in the graph support the writer's claim?

2 But these fears are misplaced—what's happening with automation is not so simple or obvious. It turns out that workers will have greater employment opportunities if their occupation undergoes some degree of computer automation. As long as they can learn to use the new tools, automation will be their friend.

3 Take the legal industry as an example. Computers are taking over some of the work of lawyers and paralegals, and they're doing a better job of it. For over a decade, computers have been used to sort through corporate documents to find those that are **relevant** to lawsuits. This process—called "discovery" in the profession—can run up millions of dollars in legal bills, but electronic methods can erase the vast majority of those costs. Moreover, the computers are often more accurate than humans: In one study, software correctly found 95 percent of the relevant documents, while humans identified only 51 percent.

4 But, perhaps surprisingly, electronic discovery software has not thrown paralegals and lawyers into unemployment lines. In fact, employment for paralegals and lawyers has grown **robustly.** While electronic discovery software has become a billion-dollar business since the late 1990s, jobs for paralegals and legal-support workers actually grew faster than the labor force as a whole, adding over 50,000 jobs since 2000, according to data from the U.S. Census Bureau. The number of lawyers increased by a quarter of a million.

5 Something similar happened when ATMs automated the tasks of bank tellers and when barcode scanners automated the work of cashiers: Rather than contributing to unemployment, the number of workers in these occupations grew. These are not special exceptions. On average, since 1980, occupations with above-average computer use have grown substantially faster (0.9 percent per year), as shown in this chart:

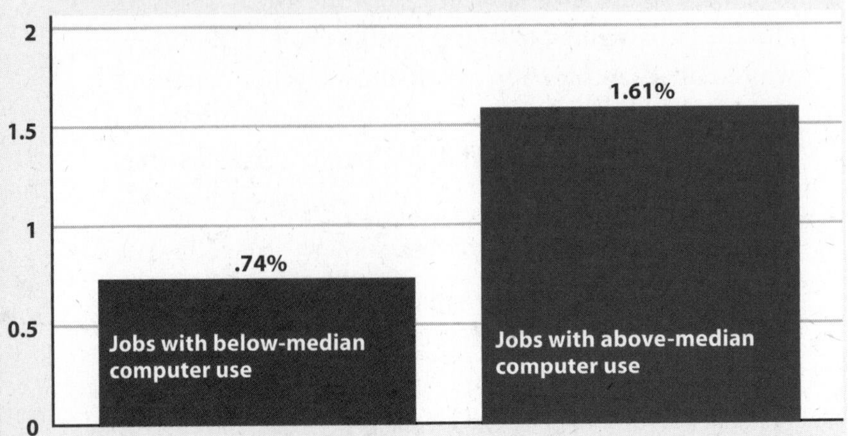

6 How can this be? It might seem a sure thing that automating a task would reduce employment in an occupation. But that logic ignores some basic economics: Automation reduces the cost of a product or service, and lower prices tend to attract more customers. Software made it cheaper and faster to trawl through legal documents, so law firms searched more documents and judges allowed more and more **expansive** discovery requests. Likewise, ATMs made it cheaper to operate bank branches, so banks dramatically increased their number of offices. So when demand increases enough in response to lower prices, employment goes up with automation, not down. And this is what has been happening with computer automation overall during the last three decades. It's also what happened during the Industrial Revolution when automation in textiles, steelmaking, and a whole range of other industries led to a major increase in manufacturing jobs.

7 But not all of the news about computer automation is good. Some of that growth in computer-using occupations has come at the expense of other occupations. As depicted in the chart below, desktop publishing systems have meant fewer jobs for typographers,[5] as graphic designers took over their work. Computerized phone lines meant fewer jobs for telephone operators, but more jobs for receptionists. These aren't examples of computers "stealing" jobs; they are cases where computers helped some workers take work from others. Workers with computers frequently substitute for workers in non-computerized jobs.

[5] **typographers:** people who set words into type.

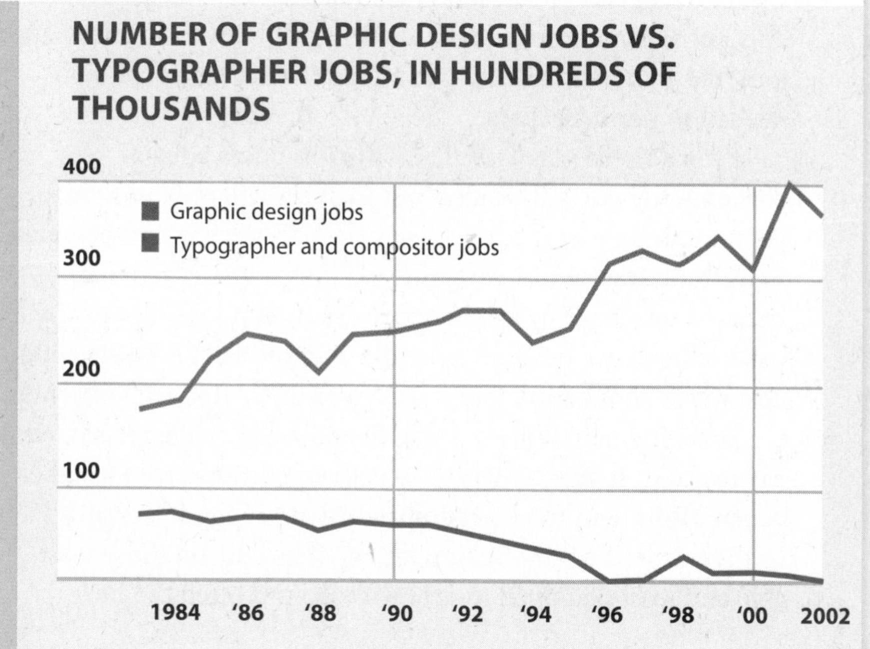

NOTICE & NOTE

LANGUAGE CONVENTIONS

Annotate: Transitional words and phrases can signal a comparison or contrast. Mark the transitions in paragraph 6.

Analyze: How does the writer use these transitions to connect ideas?

expansive
(ĭk-spăn´sĭv) *adj. Expansive* means broad in size, range, or degree of openness.

ANALYZE GRAPHIC FEATURES

Annotate: Mark the sentence in paragraph 7 that connects to the information in the graph.

Analyze: What relationship between graphic-design jobs and typographer jobs does the graph show? How does this information relate to the writer's claim?

NOTICE & NOTE

8 So, while computers create jobs in some occupations, they also reduce employment in others. The total effect on unemployment depends on which tendency is stronger. Some of my research shows that the net effect, across the economy, is a wash: Computers create about as many jobs as they eliminate. In other words, automation is not causing persistent unemployment.

9 That could change decades into the future, as new generations of software powered by artificial intelligence becomes ever more capable of advanced tasks. But in the near term, the story is much different. A new study by McKinsey & Company took a detailed look at work tasks that are likely to be automated and found that only about 5 percent of jobs are at risk of being completely automated in the near future. The main effect of automation for the time being will not be to eliminate jobs, but to redefine them—changing the tasks and the skills needed to perform them.

10 Even so, this means that automation poses a major challenge. There will be jobs, but workers will only be able to get them if they have the new sets of skills that computers make important. It's not just computer skills that are in demand, because automation can change the nature of jobs. For example, bank tellers have become more like marketing specialists, telling customers about bank loans, CDs, and other financial offerings.

11 Learning new skills is a significant social challenge as well. My research suggests that the jobs that get transferred to other occupations tend to be **predominantly** low-pay, low-skill jobs, so the burdens of automation fall most heavily on those least able and least equipped to deal with it. And often the new

NUMBERS AND STATS

Notice & Note: How do the results of the McKinsey & Company study relate to the writer's argument? Mark these results in the text.

Evaluate: Do you think this data is a strong or weak piece of evidence? Explain.

predominantly
(prĭ-dŏm´ə-nənt-lē) *adv.* *Predominantly* refers to the most important, obvious, or typical aspect(s) of something.

skills need to be learned on the job, so experience matters. To meet this challenge, some community colleges are **collaborating** with local employers to create work-study programs that allow trainees to learn on the job as well as in the classroom. Some trade groups are promoting skill-certification programs, which allow employers to recognize skills acquired through experience. These are the kinds of policies that can help overcome the real burden of automation. They deserve more attention than any panic about a supposed robot apocalypse.

collaborate
(kə-lăb´ə-rāt´) *v.* To *collaborate* means to work together.

CHECK YOUR UNDERSTANDING

Answer these questions before moving on to the **Analyze the Text** section on the following page.

1 Which sentence from the text best supports the writer's claim?

- **A** *Computers are now taking over tasks performed by professional workers, raising fears of massive unemployment.*
- **B** *But not all of the news about computer automation is good.*
- **C** *It might seem a sure thing that automating a task would reduce employment in an occupation.*
- **D** *It turns out that workers will have greater employment opportunities if their occupation undergoes some degree of computer automation.*

2 Based on the writer's argument, which word best describes the impact of automation on future employment?

- **F** insignificant
- **G** transformative
- **H** limited
- **J** devastating

3 Which of the following does the writer identify as an effect of automation that will have a positive impact on jobs?

- **A** more work space
- **B** slower production
- **C** increased demand
- **D** higher prices

RESPOND

ANALYZE THE TEXT

Support your responses with evidence from the text. NOTEBOOK

1. **Summarize** Reread paragraphs 1–2. Then, in your own words, restate the two viewpoints on automation that the writer says are fear-based and overly simplistic.
2. **Cause/Effect** Review paragraph 6. What explanation does the writer give to account for the fact that automation seems to have caused an increase in jobs in the legal and banking industries?
3. **Cite Evidence** The writer presents a counterargument to disprove the notion that computers are "stealing" jobs. Cite one piece of evidence from this counterargument. Then note what the writer says is happening instead.
4. **Evaluate** In paragraph 11, the writer states that "the jobs that get transferred to other occupations tend to be predominantly low-pay, low-skill jobs, so the burdens of automation fall most heavily on those least able and least equipped to deal with it." How does this information relate to the writer's claim?
5. **Notice & Note** How does the writer's use of statistical evidence, both in the text and in graphs, impact his argument? Cite evidence from the text to support your answer.

RESEARCH TIP
"The Automation Paradox" cites examples of the impact of automation on jobs in the banking and legal industries and on jobs that are already computerized. To broaden the scope of evidence, you might consider researching the potential impact of automation in other fields, such as the healthcare or service industries.

RESEARCH

Research additional evidence to support the writer's claim in "The Automation Paradox" that automation will create many new jobs. Try to locate different types of evidence, such as facts, statistics, quotations, and examples. Use the chart below to record the evidence and identify its connection to the claim.

EVIDENCE	CONNECTION

Connect Share your evidence with a small group. Discuss which pieces of evidence are most persuasive and why.

CREATE AND DISCUSS

Write a Persuasive Essay Based on the arguments you just read, write a short persuasive essay in which you support a claim of your own about the effects of increased automation on employment.

- ❑ Introduce the topic and state your claim about the impact of automation on future jobs.
- ❑ Give at least two reasons to support your claim. Defend or challenge the writers' claims about automation and cite evidence from the text and your research to support your argument.
- ❑ In your final paragraph, restate your claim. Conclude with a piece of advice or a call to action.

Go to **Writing Arguments** in the **Writing Studio** for help writing a persuasive essay.

Discuss with a Small Group Have a discussion about ways in which future workers might prepare for changes caused by increased automation. Make sure each group member gets equal time to speak.

- ❑ Review "The Automation Paradox" to identify ways in which the writer suggests automation will change or create future jobs. Take notes during your discussion and list types of skills and training that new or different jobs might require.
- ❑ Discuss steps workers might take to prepare for future changes in the job market and workplace. During the discussion, listen actively to help you ask questions and comment respectfully and thoughtfully on others' ideas.

Go to **Participating in Collaborative Discussions** in the **Speaking and Listening Studio** to learn more.

RESPOND TO THE ESSENTIAL QUESTION

? Does technology improve or control our lives?

Gather Information Review your annotations and notes on "The Automation Paradox." Then, add relevant details to your Response Log. To decide what information to include, think about:

- ways in which automation benefits the economy
- ways in which technology affects various occupations
- what workers will need to do to adapt to changes in job markets

At the end of the unit, you may use your notes to help you write an informational essay.

ACADEMIC VOCABULARY

As you write and discuss what you learned from the argument, be sure to use the Academic Vocabulary words. Check off each of the words that you use.

- ❑ **commentary**
- ❑ **occupation**
- ❑ **option**
- ❑ **speculate**
- ❑ **technology**

CRITICAL VOCABULARY

WORD BANK
redistribute
relevant
robustly
expansive
predominantly
collaborate

Practice and Apply Use your understanding of the Vocabulary words to answer each question.

1. Why would it be helpful to **collaborate** with a partner on a project?
2. What types of search terms produce more **expansive** results? Why?
3. Why have machines **predominantly** eliminated low-skill jobs?
4. What might cause a company's income to grow **robustly**?
5. Why might you want to **redistribute** items in a package?
6. How can you tell if a piece of evidence is **relevant**?

VOCABULARY STRATEGY: Use a Dictionary

Go to **Using Reference Sources** in the **Vocabulary Studio** for more on using a dictionary.

A **dictionary** is a reference work that provides information about words. Notice the parts of a dictionary entry:

syllabication | pronunciation | part of speech | forms of the word

rel•e•vant (rĕl´ə-vənt) *adj.* **relevance, relevantly**
1. Having a bearing on or connection with the matter at hand. **2.** Meaningful or purposeful in current society or culture: *thought that the traditional male role of breadwinner was no longer relevant.*

[Medieval Latin *relevāns, relevant-*, from Latin, present participle of *relevāre*, to relieve, raise up.]

precise meanings of word are numbered

example of usage

etymology or word origin

Practice and Apply Use a dictionary to look up the following words from "The Automation Paradox." Then fill out a chart like this one.

WORD	PRONUNCIATION	PART OF SPEECH	GUESSED DEFINITION	DICTIONARY DEFINITION
paralegal				
trawl				
net				
persistent				

LANGUAGE CONVENTIONS: Transitional Words and Phrases

Transitional words and phrases connect ideas and signal how those ideas are related. Transitions are often set off with commas. Read the following sentence from "The Automation Paradox":

Likewise, ATMs made it cheaper to operate bank branches, so banks dramatically increased their number of offices.

The word *likewise* signals a similarity, while the word *so* indicates an effect.

The chart below contains examples of transitional words and phrases based on specific purposes.

Go to **Writing Informative Texts: Organizing Ideas** in the **Writing Studio** for more on using transitional words and phrases.

COMMON TRANSITIONAL WORDS AND PHRASES

Purpose	Examples
compare or contrast ideas	but, however, although, on the other hand, while, similarly, likewise
indicate degree of importance	especially, significantly, most importantly, chiefly, notably, particularly
show time or sequence	first, second, finally, when, initially, next, while, before, after
add information	also, in addition, too, and, furthermore
introduce an example	for example, for instance, such as, this shows
indicate cause or effect	as a result, therefore, consequently, for this reason, so
indicate a conclusion	in conclusion, in summary, overall, to summarize

Practice and Apply Look back at the persuasive essay you wrote to support a claim about the impact of automation. Identify the transitions that you used and revise your essay to add more appropriate or stronger transitions. Then discuss with a partner how these transitions affect the flow of your essay and the connections between ideas.

ARGUMENT

HEADS UP, HUMANS

by **Claudia Alarcón**

pages 51–55

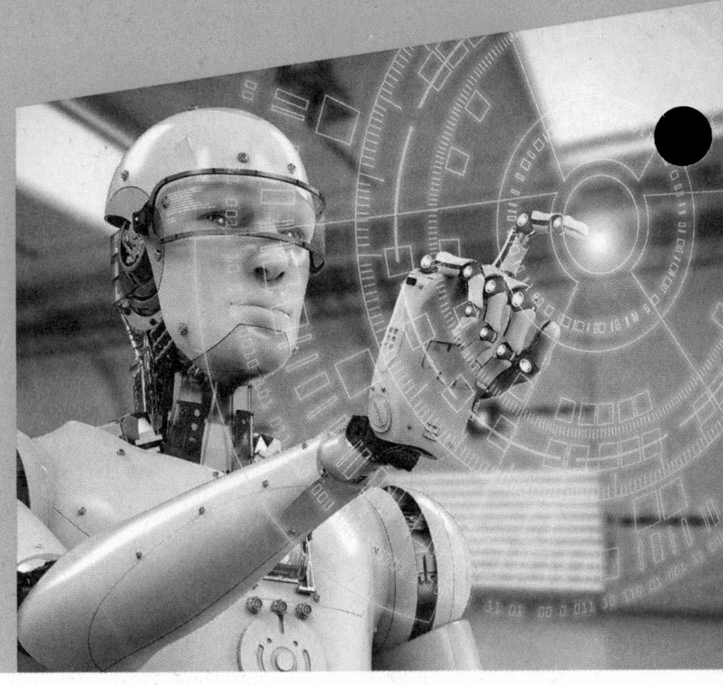

COMPARE ARGUMENTS

Now that you've read "The Automation Paradox," read "Heads Up, Humans" to analyze another argument about the future impact of automation on employment. As you read, think about how well the evidence in "Heads Up, Humans" supports the writer's claim. After you are finished, you will collaborate with a group on a final project that involves an analysis of both texts.

ESSENTIAL QUESTION:

Does technology improve or control our lives?

ARGUMENT

THE AUTOMATION PARADOX

by **James Bessen**

pages 39–43

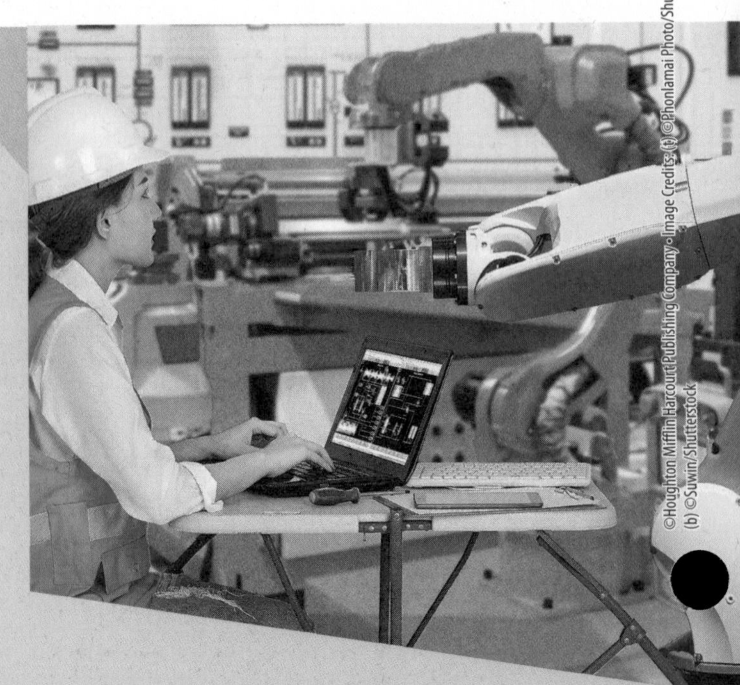

Heads Up, Humans

QUICK START

The argument you are about to read makes a claim about the impact of automation. Based on what you already know about the topic, list some effects you think automation will have on jobs and the economy.

EVALUATE EVIDENCE

Evidence is any information that helps prove a claim. Facts, quotations, examples, anecdotes, and statistics can all be used as evidence. When you analyze an author's argument, it's important to **evaluate** the evidence by determining whether it is valid, relevant, and sufficient.

- Valid evidence is based on reliable sources that use sound reasoning. Many texts include **endnotes**, which list sources of information. Credible sources can help you confirm whether the evidence is valid.
- Evidence is relevant if it supports the claim in a logical way. In a strong argument, the way it supports the claim should also be clear.
- Sufficient evidence is enough to support the claim. A thorough and balanced argument includes a convincing amount of information related to the claim, and it addresses opposing viewpoints.

As you read "Heads Up, Humans," identify the main claim and evaluate the evidence the writer uses to support it.

GENRE ELEMENTS: ARGUMENT

- makes a claim
- supports its claim with reasons and evidence
- takes into account other points of view
- for some topics, such as economics, may rely heavily on the analysis and interpretation of data

ANALYZE RHETORIC AND REASONING

Identifying the writer's intended **audience**, or the specific people to whom the argument is addressed, can help you analyze how and why the writer uses certain persuasive techniques, including rhetorical devices and logical fallacies.

Rhetorical devices are techniques writers use to enhance their arguments and communicate more effectively. Here are two examples:

RHETORICAL DEVICE	DEFINITION	EXAMPLE
Direct address	Talking directly to the reader, often using the pronoun *you*	If you're like most young people, you've probably embraced technology.
Rhetorical question	A question that has such an obvious answer that it requires no reply	Will all these people find some other source of employment?

Logical fallacies, such as bandwagon appeals, are misuses of logic or reasoning that can serve persuasive purposes in argumentative texts.

As you analyze "Heads Up, Humans," think about the writer's purposes for using any persuasive techniques you notice.

CRITICAL VOCABULARY

sector **scrutinize** **exotic** **renowned**

To see how many Critical Vocabulary words you already know, use them to complete the sentences.

1. __________ scientists are recognized as leading authorities in their fields of study.
2. The inspector will __________ the work to determine whether it has been done correctly.
3. The chef used __________ ingredients that we didn't recognize.
4. While certain positions will be eliminated, the overall demand for jobs in the financial __________ is expected to increase.

LANGUAGE CONVENTIONS

Active and Passive Voice In this lesson, you will learn about active and passive voice. **Active voice** shows that a subject performs the verb's action:

New technology made their jobs obsolete.

Passive voice shows that a subject is being acted upon:

Their jobs were made obsolete by new technology.

As you read "Heads Up, Humans," notice the writer's use of active and passive voice.

NOTICE & NOTE

ANNOTATION MODEL

As you read, mark up the text to trace and evaluate the writer's argument. In the model, you can see one reader's notes about "Heads Up, Humans."

1 If you're like most young people, you've probably embraced technology. You communicate with friends via videos and filters. You have vast numbers of songs and shows within reach. You can get items delivered to your home the same day you ordered them without leaving the house. These benefits of technology are easy to see.

The intended audience is young people.

The writer engages the audience and introduces the topic with examples that relate to young people's daily lives.

BACKGROUND

The potential future impact of automation on employment has been the subject of much heated debate. Such arguments rely on the analysis of historical data as well as economic forecasts that may be influenced by a variety of factors.

NOTICE & NOTE

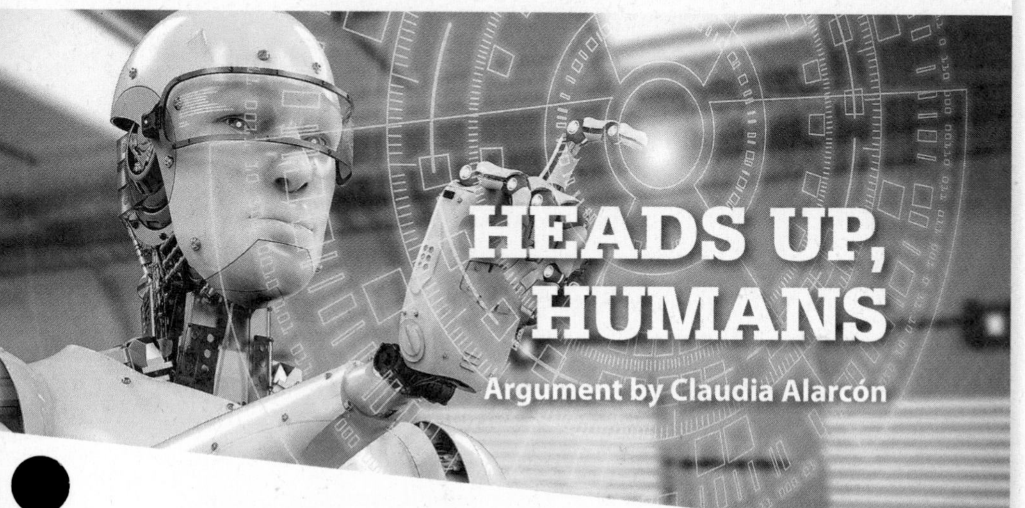

HEADS UP, HUMANS

Argument by Claudia Alarcón

PREPARE TO COMPARE

As you read, note evidence the writer uses to support her claims about the potential impact of automation. This will help you compare this argument with "The Automation Paradox."

Notice & Note

Use the side margins to notice and note signposts in the text.

1 If you're like most young people, you've probably embraced technology. You communicate with friends via videos and filters. You have vast numbers of songs and shows within reach. You can get items delivered to your home the same day you ordered them without leaving the house. These benefits of technology are easy to see.

2 Perhaps you take it further, and are one of those who believe that technology does not just add fun and convenience to our lives, but is actually the answer to most of our problems—even problems that are caused by technology itself. In the very near future, one of the biggest of these problems is likely to be that many jobs now held by humans will be done by some combination of artificial intelligence and automated machine. If you're tempted to shrug off concern about this phenomenon because you assume that the wonders of technology will somehow

LANGUAGE CONVENTIONS

Annotate: Mark instances of the subject *you* in paragraph 1.

Analyze: Does the subject perform or receive the action? How does this use of voice impact the writer's argument?

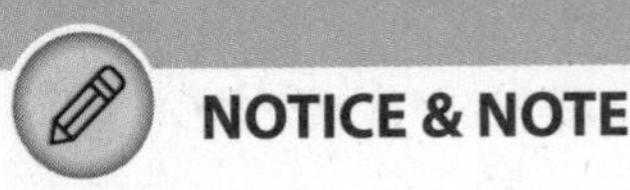

NUMBERS & STATS

Notice & Note: What data does the writer use as evidence in paragraph 3? Mark these details.

Draw Conclusions: How does this data connect to the writer's claim?

ANALYZE RHETORIC AND REASONING

Annotate: An **analogy** is a comparison between two things that are similar in some way but are otherwise dissimilar. Mark the two things the writer compares in paragraph 4.

Evaluate: Does this analogy strengthen the writer's argument? Explain.

sector
(sĕk′tər) *n.* A *sector* is a part or division, as of a city or a national economy.

EVALUATE EVIDENCE

Annotate: Identify the source of the evidence in paragraph 6.

Infer: Why does the writer include this evidence?

create new and better jobs, you should be aware that research tells another story. As part of the generation that will arguably be most affected by these changes, it's in your interest to stay informed rather than simply hope for the best.

3 There is no argument that many jobs now held by humans will be replaced by some form of advanced technology. According to a new report by a multi-national accounting and consulting firm based in London, 38% of U.S. jobs are at high risk of being replaced by robots and artificial intelligence over the next 15 years.[1] The report estimates the percentage of jobs lost to automation in Britain will be 30%, with 35% in Germany, and 21% in Japan.[2]

4 This change is already underway. Shipping companies have made headlines with self-driving trucks carrying cargo across the country. Ride share companies have been testing self-driving taxis in Pennsylvania and Arizona. Once more of our trucks and taxis drive themselves, what will happen to the people who held jobs as drivers? In the U.S., roughly 180,000 taxi drivers, 600,000 ride share drivers, and 3.5 million truck drivers could end up displaced.[3] This number is greater than the population of Houston, San Antonio, Dallas, Austin, and Fort Worth combined. Will all these people find some other source of employment? Or will the numbers of unemployed grow as the out-of-work drivers are joined by the millions of others who have been displaced by artificial intelligence and robots?

5 Technology fans claim that the fears that robots will lead to massive unemployment are unfounded. They say that people who are displaced from jobs will find new and better occupations that will be created by the economic shift. They suggest that a factory worker whose task on the assembly line is now completed by a machine might instead become someone who services the machine, for example. Or that there could be a rise in jobs in **sectors** that are harder to automate, such as healthcare.

6 "The last 200 years, we've had an incredible amount of automation," argues MIT economist David Autor. "We have tractors that do the work that horses and people used to do on farms. We don't dig ditches by hand anymore. We don't pound tools out of wrought iron. We don't do bookkeeping with books! But this has not in net reduced the amount of employment."[4]

7 However, there is plenty of evidence to suggest that it's going to be different going forward. The introduction of the

labor-saving tractor did indeed free up some farmers to plant more crops and others to take on different sorts of work. But the kind of automation combined with artificial intelligence being developed today doesn't just do the physical work of humans. It can do much of the high-level mental work too, faster and more effectively. In the past, newly freed laborers often went on to work in start-up industries that benefited from their availability. Today, the new industries are unlikely to need many human bodies or minds because technology can do the work for less cost.

8 Jerry Kaplan, an artificial intelligence expert who's founded multiple technology startups, has written a book called *Humans Need Not Apply*. In it, he lays out the risks of our new era. He explains what's cutting edge and poised to increase: systems that learn from experience and therefore don't need to be programmed, as we commonly understand the term. Not only will machines be able to do work that we think of as requiring human judgment and skill, such as fixing electrical problems, painting a house, or writing a news story, they will also be able to do work that people simply can't. "Unlike humans who are limited in the scope and scale of experiences they can absorb, these systems can **scrutinize** mountains of instructive examples at blinding speeds. They are capable of comprehending not only the visual, auditory, and written information familiar to us but also the more **exotic** forms of data that stream through computers and networks," he writes.[5]

9 Kaplan is mainly referring to the future he predicts based on his perspective as an expert in the tech world. But already, we can see the consequences. There is no evidence that recent advances in technology have so far offered the majority of workers better pay or positions. In fact, the opposite seems to be true. A report by the National Bureau of Economic Research found that between 1990 and 2007, automation lowered both the number of jobs available and the amount those jobs paid.

NOTICE & NOTE 

ANALYZE RHETORIC AND REASONING

Annotate: In a **juxtaposition,** a writer places two contrasting ideas or examples near each other to highlight the differences between them. Identify the juxtaposition in paragraph 7.

Analyze: How does this juxtaposition impact the writer's argument?

scrutinize
(skro͞ot´n-īz´) *v.* To *scrutinize* is to examine or inspect with great care.

exotic
(ĭg-zŏt´ĭk) *adj.* Something that is *exotic* is unusual or different.

NOTICE & NOTE

"We estimate large and robust negative effects of robots on employment and wages," write the authors of the study.[6]

renowned
(rĭ-nound´) *adj.* Someone or something that is *renowned* is famous.

10 **Renowned** theoretical physicist Stephen Hawking is concerned about massive job loss and how that could affect the stability of our society. "The automation of factories has already decimated jobs in traditional manufacturing," says Hawking. "The rise of artificial intelligence is likely to extend this job destruction deep into the middle classes, with only the most caring, creative, or supervisory roles remaining."[7] Hawking emphasizes that we live in a world where financial inequality is growing, not diminishing. He believes that many people can see their standard of living, and their ability to earn a living at all, disappearing.

11 This is a frightening scenario. It's tempting to avoid thinking about it, especially because solutions aren't obvious. But the first step toward avoiding the employment problems we might face is acknowledging them. As someone with your future on the line, don't let anyone tell you that technology is automatically going to create a healthy economy for everyone. If we don't want a bleak future for most of us, we have to prioritize human well-being even as we take advantage of what technology offers.

EVALUATE EVIDENCE

Annotate: Mark important details about the source in each citation.

Evaluate: Do these sources seem credible? Explain.

ENDNOTES

[1] Alanna Petroff, "U.S. workers face higher risk of being replaced by robots. Here's why," *CNNtech* 24 March 2017, 4 Dec. 2017 <http://money.cnn.com/2017/03/24/technology/robots-jobs-us-workers-uk/index.html>.

[2] Samantha Masunaga, "Robots could take over 38% of U.S. jobs within about 15 years, report says," *Los Angeles Times* 24 March 2017, 4 Dec. 2017 <http://http://www.latimes.com/business/la-fi-pwc-robotics-jobs-20170324-story.html>.

[3] David Pogue, "When the robots take over, will there be jobs left for us?," *CBS News* 9 April 2017, 4 Dec. 2017 <https://www.cbsnews.com/news/when-the-robots-take-over-will-there-be-jobs-left-for-us/>.

[4] Pogue, "When the robots take over."

[5] Jerry Kaplan, *Humans Need Not Apply: A Guide to Wealth and Work in the Age of Artificial Intelligence* (New Haven: Yale University Press, 2015).

[6] Daron Acemoglu and Pascual Restrepo, *Robots and Jobs: Evidence from US Labor Markets* (Cambridge, MA: National Bureau of Economic Research, 2017).

[7] Rob Price, "Stephen Hawking: This will be the impact of automation and AI on jobs," *World Economic Forum* 6 Dec. 2016, 4 Dec. 2017 <https://www.weforum.org/agenda/2016/12/stephen-hawking-this-will-be-the-impact-of-automation-and-ai-on-jobs>.

CHECK YOUR UNDERSTANDING

Answer these questions before moving on to the **Analyze the Text** section on the following page.

1 The writer supports the claim of the argument by —

A distinguishing the future of automation from historical trends

B explaining how machines impacted the farming and manufacturing industries

C showing how future changes in the job market will mirror past changes

D providing statistics that relate to many different employment sectors

2 The information in paragraph 4 suggests —

F a possible impact of automation on people who work as drivers

G a causal relationship between massive job loss and automation

H ways in which jobs might change as a result of automation

J ways in which automation might lead to growth in the shipping industry

3 Based on the text, more automation will cause an increase in —

A wages

B inequality

C the number of unskilled jobs

D the size of the middle class

RESPOND

ANALYZE THE TEXT

Support your responses with evidence from the text. NOTEBOOK

1. **Analyze** What persuasive techniques does the writer use to appeal to her intended audience? Cite evidence from the text to support your response.
2. **Critique** What is the purpose of the writer's questions in paragraph 4? How do these questions impact the writer's argument?
3. **Evaluate** Which two pieces of evidence in the argument do you find most convincing? Explain.
4. **Compare** How does the quotation from economist David Autor in paragraph 6 compare with the quotation from artificial intelligence expert Jerry Kaplan in paragraph 8?
5. **Notice & Note** What is the purpose of the data in paragraph 4? How does this evidence impact the writer's argument?

RESEARCH TIP
Web addresses ending in *.gov*, *.edu*, or *.org* often contain reliable information. For example, the National Bureau of Economic Research (nber.org) and the U.S. Bureau of Labor Statistics (bls.gov) gather data related to U.S. jobs and the economy.

RESEARCH

Research additional evidence to support the writer's claim in "Heads Up, Humans" that automation will eliminate many jobs. Try to locate different types of evidence, such as facts, statistics, quotations, and examples. Use the chart below to record the evidence and identify its connection to the claim. You will use the information you gather in a debate on the issue.

EVIDENCE	CONNECTION

Connect Share your evidence with a small group. Discuss the relevance and validity of each piece of evidence.

CREATE AND DISCUSS

Create a Public Service Announcement Use ideas from "Heads Up, Humans" to create a public service announcement to build awareness about the potential impact of automation on jobs in the future.

- ❑ Review the text to brainstorm ideas for your announcement. Decide on a slogan or a call to action to focus your message. Identify facts from the text or from additional research to support your message.
- ❑ Choose a format for your announcement, such as a poster or a video. Plan and create your announcement, combining text and visuals to effectively convey your message.

Go to the **Writing Studio** for help with creating a public service announcement.

Discuss with a Small Group Have a discussion about how governments and other organizations might prepare for the impact of automation. Make sure all group members are included.

- ❑ Review the text to identify issues and concerns related to the future impact of automation on employment and the economy.
- ❑ Discuss possible ways in which people might solve the problems presented by automation. What steps might government and private organizations take to plan for the future?
- ❑ Listen closely to your group members. Ask questions and respectfully comment on others' ideas. As a group, summarize the key points of the discussion and identify points of agreement.

Go to **Participating in Collaborative Discussions** in the **Speaking and Listening Studio** to learn more.

RESPOND TO THE ESSENTIAL QUESTION

Does technology improve or control our lives?

Gather Information Review your annotations and notes on "Heads Up, Humans." Then, add relevant details to your Response Log. As you determine which information to include, think about:

- the writer's claim about the impact of technology
- evidence that supports the writer's claim
- best opposing viewpoints the writer addresses

At the end of the unit, you may use your notes to help you write an informational essay.

ACADEMIC VOCABULARY

As you write and discuss what you learned from the argument, be sure to use the Academic Vocabulary words. Check off each of the words that you use.

- ❑ **commentary**
- ❑ **occupation**
- ❑ **option**
- ❑ **speculate**
- ❑ **technology**

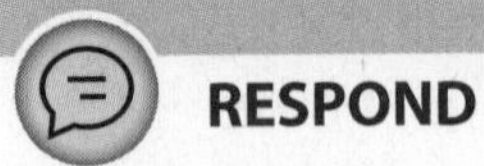

CRITICAL VOCABULARY

WORD BANK
sector
scrutinize
exotic
renowned

Practice and Apply Use your understanding of the Critical Vocabulary words to answer each question.

1. Which Vocabulary word goes with *examine*? Why?
2. Which Vocabulary word goes with *division*? Why?
3. Which Vocabulary word goes with *unusual*? Why?
4. Which Vocabulary word goes with *famous*? Why?

VOCABULARY STRATEGY: Greek Roots

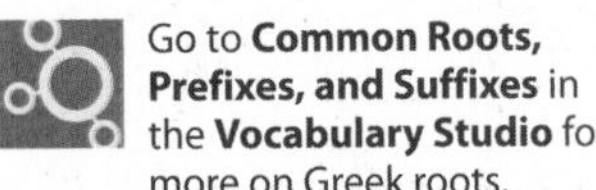

Go to **Common Roots, Prefixes, and Suffixes** in the **Vocabulary Studio** for more on Greek roots.

A **word root** is a word that forms the basis of a word's meaning. A root is combined with other word parts, such as a prefix or a suffix, to make a word. Many English words have a root that comes from Greek. Identifying word roots can help you understand a word's meaning. Look at this sentence from "Heads Up, Humans":

> **As part of the generation that will arguably be most affected by these changes, it's in your interest to stay informed rather than simply hope for the best.**

The word *generation* includes the Greek root *gen*, which means "to give birth." This can help you understand that *generation* means "the people born or living at the same time." Another way to use roots to help you determine the meaning of an unfamiliar word is to think of other words that include the same root. For example, *generation* relates to the word *generate*, which means "to come into being."

Practice and Apply Complete the word web with words that share the root *auto*, which means "self." Then tell how the meanings of the words are related.

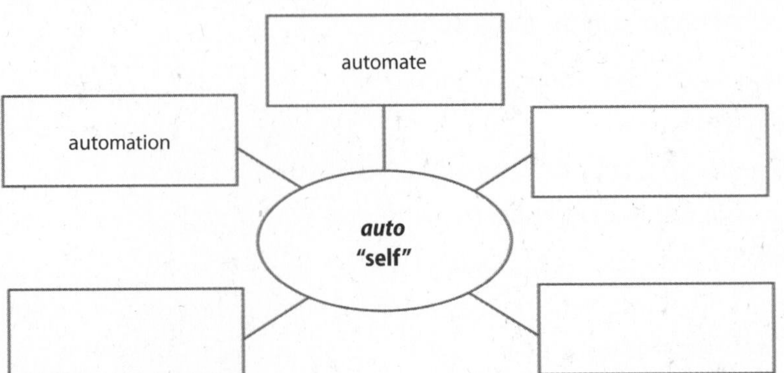

LANGUAGE CONVENTIONS:
Active and Passive Voice

The **voice of a verb** shows whether its subject performs or receives the action expressed by the verb. When the subject performs the action, the verb is in the **active voice**. When the subject is the receiver of the action, the verb is in the **passive voice**. Writers should take care to use active and passive voice consistently and should consider when each voice is most appropriate.

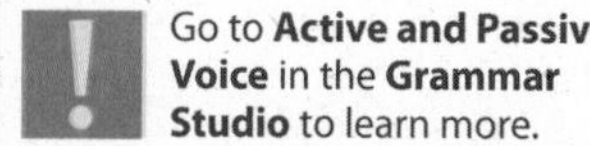
Go to **Active and Passive Voice** in the **Grammar Studio** to learn more.

	DEFINITION	EXAMPLE	USE TO . . .
Active Voice	• shows that a subject performs an action	• *The robot finished the job.*	• emphasize the subject or actor • keep writing lively
Passive Voice	• shows that a subject is acted upon • uses helping verbs	• *The job was finished.*	• emphasize the action • show that the doer is unknown or unimportant

In this sentence from "Heads Up, Humans," the writer uses the active voice appropriately to emphasize the impact of automation on the audience:

But already, we can see the consequences.

When the sentence is rewritten in the passive voice, the subject becomes unimportant:

But already, the consequences can be seen.

Practice and Apply Identify the voice of the verb in each sentence. Then rewrite the sentence in a different voice.

1. The manufacturing workers were affected by changes in technology.

   ____

2. Automation eliminated their jobs.

   ____

3. The study shows the impact on the healthcare industry.

   ____

4. Your generation will likely be most affected by these changes.

   ____

Collaborate & Compare

COMPARE ARGUMENTS

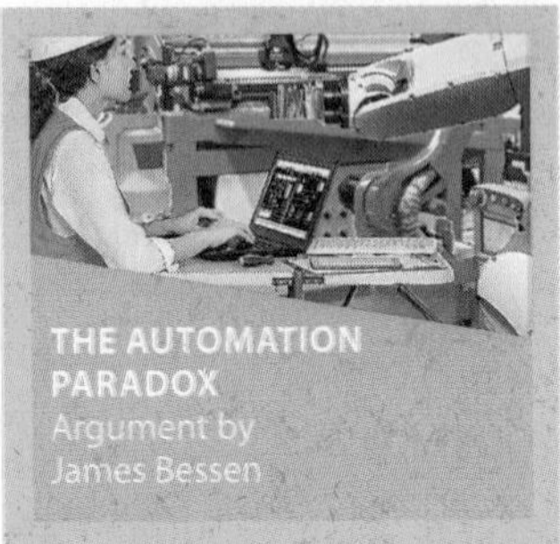
THE AUTOMATION PARADOX
Argument by James Bessen

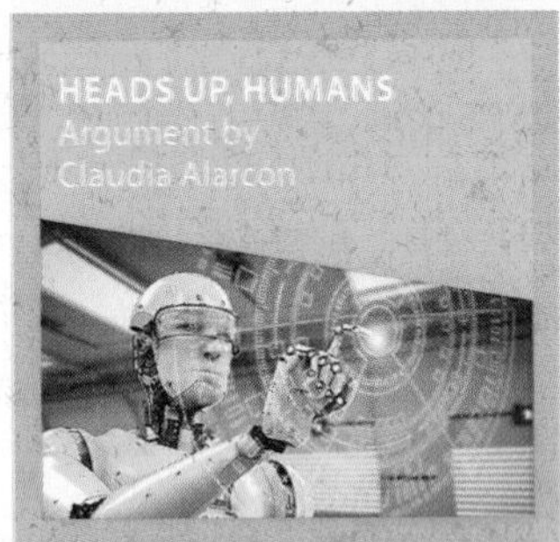
HEADS UP, HUMANS
Argument by Claudia Alarcon

When you **compare arguments,** you identify similarities and differences between the writers' claims, reasons, and evidence. As you review "The Automation Paradox" and "Heads Up, Humans" to compare the arguments, read carefully to identify each writer's central idea and the facts and interpretations used to support it. Identify where the texts disagree on matters of fact and interpretation.

Also be sure to consider how the two authors use counterarguments to respond to opposing claims. A **counterargument** is an argument made to address an alternative viewpoint or an objection. Good writers anticipate and acknowledge opposing views and objections to their arguments and refute them with counterarguments.

In a small group, complete the Venn diagram with similarities and differences between the two arguments.

"The Automation Paradox"

Both

"Heads Up, Humans"

ANALYZE THE TEXTS

Discuss these questions in your group.

1. **Compare** What are some points of agreement in both arguments?
2. **Connect** What pieces of evidence in each argument seem to contradict each other?
3. **Identify Patterns** What are some similarities and differences between the types of evidence used in each argument?
4. **Evaluate** Which argument is most convincing to you? Cite evidence from both texts to support your opinion.

DEBATE

Now your group can continue reflecting on the ideas in these texts and your responses to them by debating the impact of automation on employment. Follow these steps:

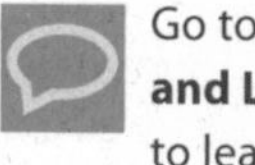

Go to the **Speaking and Listening Studio** to learn more about having a debate.

1. **Choose a Side** Working with a small group, decide which viewpoint you will argue. Will automation have a positive or negative impact on employment?

2. **Gather Information** Review the two arguments and use relevant text evidence to defend or challenge the writers' claims. List reasons from the texts and from your prior research that support your viewpoint.

Reason 1:
Evidence:
Reason 2:
Evidence:

3. **Prepare a Counterargument**
Anticipate the opposing team's claim, reasons, and evidence. List reasons and evidence you will cite to argue against the opposing team's position.

Opposing Team's Argument:	Counterargument:

4. **Conduct the Debate** Debate another group of students who have chosen the opposite position. Each group should be allowed to speak for a set amount of time. Use appropriate eye contact, speaking rate, volume, enunciation, and gestures to communicate your ideas effectively.

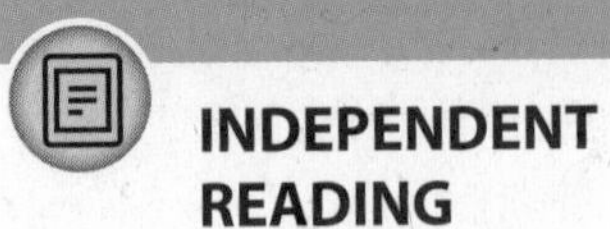

INDEPENDENT READING

? ESSENTIAL QUESTION:

Does technology improve or control our lives?

Reader's Choice

Setting a Purpose Select one or more of these options from your eBook to continue your exploration of the Essential Question.

- Read the descriptions to see which text grabs your interest.
- Think about which genres you enjoy reading.

Notice & Note

In this unit, you practiced noticing and noting three signposts: **Again and Again**, **Contrasts and Contradictions**, and **Aha Moment**. As you read independently, these signposts and others will aid your understanding. Below are the anchor questions to ask when you read literature and nonfiction.

Reading Literature: Stories, Poems, and Plays		
Signpost	**Anchor Question**	**Lesson**
Contrasts and Contradictions	Why did the character act that way?	p. 3
Aha Moment	How might this change things?	p. 3
Tough Questions	What does this make me wonder about?	p. 152
Words of the Wiser	What's the lesson for the character?	p. 406
Again and Again	Why might the author keep bringing this up?	p. 2
Memory Moment	Why is this memory important?	p. 153

Reading Nonfiction: Essays, Articles, and Arguments		
Signpost	**Anchor Question(s)**	**Lesson**
Big Questions	What surprised me? What did the author think I already knew? What challenged, changed, or confirmed what I already knew?	p. 77
Contrasts and Contradictions	What is the difference, and why does it matter?	p. 241
Extreme or Absolute Language	Why did the author use this language?	p. 76
Numbers and Stats	Why did the author use these numbers or amounts?	p. 325
Quoted Words	Why was this person quoted or cited, and what did this add?	p. 77
Word Gaps	Do I know this word from someplace else? Does it seem like technical talk for this topic? Do clues in the sentence help me understand the word?	p. 240

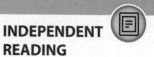

You can preview these texts in Unit 1 of your eBook.

Then, check off the text or texts that you select to read on your own.

POEM

- [ ] **If You Go into the Woods You Will Find It Has a Technology**
Heather Christle

If you look closely, you will see that nature is trying to communicate with us.

SCIENCE FICTION

- [ ] **Hallucination**
Isaac Asimov

A boy working in a planetary outpost realizes that things aren't what they seem.

SCIENCE FICTION

- [ ] **There Will Come Soft Rains**
Ray Bradbury

A vacant mechanized house is the only thing left standing in a ruined city.

NOVEL

- [ ] ***from* All the Light We Cannot See**
Anthony Doerr

The discovery of a radio brings the power of music to a young boy and girl.

Collaborate and Share Get with a partner to discuss what you learned from at least one of your independent readings.

- Give a brief synopsis or summary of the text.
- Describe any signposts that you noticed in the text and explain what they revealed to you.
- Describe what you most enjoyed or found most challenging about the text. Give specific examples.
- Decide if you would recommend the text to others. Why or why not?

Go to the **Reading Studio** for more resources on **Notice & Note.**

Write an Informational Essay

Go to the **Writing Studio** for help writing an informational essay.

This unit focuses on the ways technology can improve—and often control—our lives. For this writing task, you will write a short informational essay. You will tell someone unfamiliar with a new technology how it helped you and how to use it. For an example of a well-written informational text you can use as a mentor text, review "Are Bionic Superhumans on the Horizon?"

As you write your essay, use the notes from your Response Log, which you filled out after reading the texts in this unit.

Writing Prompt

Read the information in the box below.

This is the topic or context for your essay.

> **While the overall effects of technology on our lives can be debated, nearly everyone can identify at least one use of technology that makes something in their life easier, faster, better, or more fun.**

Think carefully about the following question.

This is the Essential Question for the unit. How would you answer this question, based on the texts in the unit?

> **Does technology improve or control our lives?**

Now mark the words that identify exactly what you are being asked to produce.

Write an essay explaining how a new technology helped you. Then explain how to use it to a person unfamiliar with the technology. For example, you might explain how to program a digital watch.

Be sure to—

Review these points as you write and again when you finish. Make any needed changes or edits.

- ❑ engage the reader and identify your purpose in your introduction
- ❑ list any necessary tools and materials
- ❑ present steps and details in a logical sequence
- ❑ use appropriate transitions between steps
- ❑ clearly express ideas
- ❑ use formatting to aid comprehension
- ❑ end by summarizing your main points and drawing a conclusion

1 Plan

Thorough planning will help you write an effective essay. The first step is to select a genre that is appropriate for your topic, purpose, and audience. For this writing task, you know that the genre will be an informational essay that includes instructions about how to use some type of technology. To identify and narrow your topic, brainstorm about technology with a partner or small group. Next, consider your purpose and audience—to explain a kind of technology to someone unfamiliar with it. As part of your planning process, you also might do some background reading or thinking about personal interests you have that relate to the topic. Use the table below to help you plan your draft.

Informational Essay Planning Table	
Genre	Informational essay with instructions
Topic	How one kind of technology is beneficial and instructions for using it
Purpose	
Audience	
Ideas from discussion with classmates	
Ideas from background reading	
Personal interests related to topic	

Background Reading Review the notes you have taken in your Response Log after reading the texts in this unit. These texts provide background reading that will help you formulate the key ideas you will include in your essay.

Go to **Writing Informative Texts: Developing a Topic** for help planning your essay.

Notice & Note

From Reading to Writing

As you plan your informative essay, apply what you've learned about signposts to your own writing. Remember that writers use common features, called signposts, to help convey their message to readers.

Think about how you can address any **Word Gaps** that might come up your essay.

Go to the **Reading Studio** for more resources on Notice & Note.

Use the notes from your Response Log as you plan your essay.

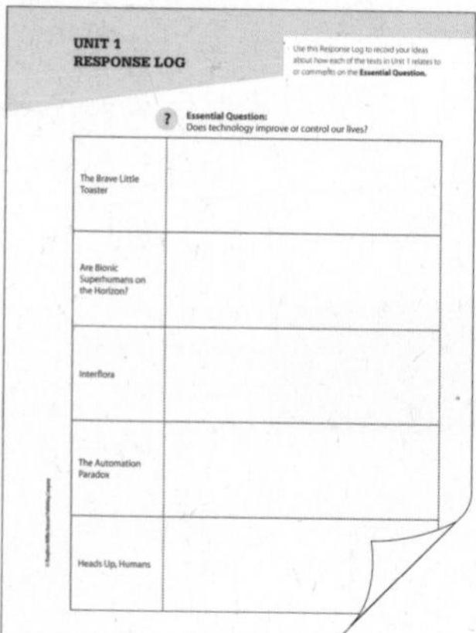

UNIT 1 RESPONSE LOG

Use this Response Log to record your ideas about how each of the texts in Unit 1 relates to or comments on the **Essential Question.**

Essential Question: Does technology improve or control our lives?

The Brave Little Toaster	
Are Bionic Superhumans on the Horizon?	
Interflora	
The Automation Paradox	
Heads Up, Humans	

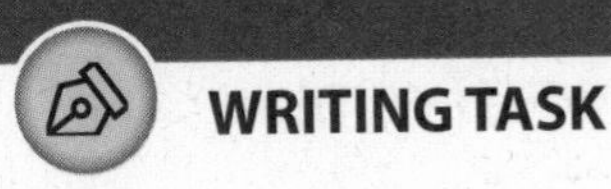

WRITING TASK

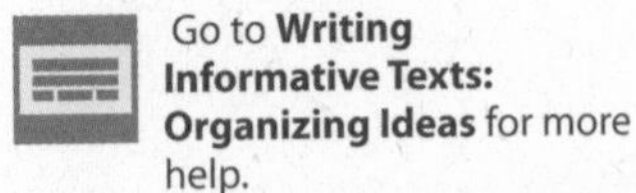

Go to **Writing Informative Texts: Organizing Ideas** for more help.

Organize Your Ideas Once you have identified your topic and other key elements of your essay, you need to organize your information and instructions in a way that will help you draft your essay. You can use the chart below to map out the steps required to use the technology you are describing. However, before you give instructions about how to use the technology, be sure to explain how it has benefited you.

Main Topic: How to Use One Kind of Technology	
Step 1	
Step 2	
Step 3	
Step 4	

You also may want to create an outline of your essay to serve as a kind of map that you can follow as you write. Use a Roman numeral for each paragraph in your essay. Use capital letters beneath each numeral to identify the contents of that paragraph.

2 Develop a Draft

You may prefer to draft your essay online.

Once you have completed planning your informational essay, you will be ready to begin drafting it. As you write your first draft, refer to the chart and outline you have created as well as any notes you took as you studied the unit texts. Be sure to explain how to complete the steps in the correct order. Using a word processor or online writing application makes it easier to move sentences around and make other changes later when you are ready to revise your first draft.

Use the Mentor Text

Author's Craft

Your introduction should include a statement or a question to capture the reader's attention. It also should include additional details about your topic to get your reader interested in reading your essay. Note the way the writer captures the reader's attention in "Are Bionic Superhumans on the Horizon?"

> **We're in the midst of a bionic revolution, yet most of us don't know it.**
>
> **Around 220,000 people worldwide already walk around with cochlear implants—devices worn around the ear that turn sound waves into electrical impulses shunted directly into the auditory nerve.**

The writer makes an intriguing statement about technology and adds a surprising fact, making the reader want to learn more about the topic.

Apply What You've Learned One way to capture your reader's attention in the introduction is to include a surprising fact or a personal anecdote related to the topic.

Genre Characteristics

Supporting details tell more about a central idea. Notice how the author of "Are Bionic Superhumans on the Horizon?" uses the following example to support a key idea about how bionic devices work.

> **She let researchers implant a small device in the part of her brain responsible for motor control. With that device, she is able to control an external robotic arm by thinking about it.**

The author provides an example as a supporting detail to describe how one type of bionic technology can be used.

Apply What You've Learned The details you include in your own informational essay should be clearly related to your explanation about how technology has benefited you. The step-by-step instructions should clearly show how to perform the task.

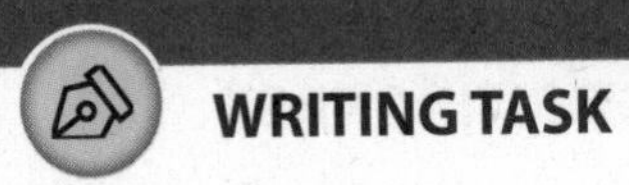

3 Revise

On Your Own Once you have written your draft, you'll want to go back and look for ways to improve your informational essay. Use the Revision Guide to evaluate and revise specific elements of your writing.

Go to **Writing Informative Texts: Precise Language and Vocabulary** for help revising your essay.

Revision Guide

Ask Yourself	Tips	Revision Techniques
1. Does my introduction grab the readers' attention?	**Highlight** the introduction.	**Add** an interesting fact or example to illustrate the topic.
2. Does my introduction clearly state the topic?	**Underline** the topic sentence.	**Add** a sentence that clearly states the topic.
3. Are all materials and tools listed in my introduction?	**Draw** a star next to any materials or tools you've noted.	**Add** any missing materials or tools to the list.
4. Are my instructions complete and arranged in a clear and sensible way?	**Underline** the steps and any transitions between them.	**Rearrange** or **add** steps and transitions as needed, being sure to move related details, too.
5. Do supporting details help to clarify the instructions?	**Underline** supporting details.	**Add** supporting details or clarifying prepositional phrases.
6. Does my format help to identify the steps and guide readers through them?	**Highlight** headings, numbers, or bulleted lists. **Circle** words that could be emphasized.	**Add** headings, numbers, or bullets to separate instructions into clear steps or parts.
7. Does my conclusion reinforce the reason(s) I gave for learning this type of technology?	**Highlight** the conclusion. **Underline** the reasons for learning the technology and your final advice to readers.	**Add** any missing reasons or a brief summary of them. **Add** some final advice or **recommend** a particular action.

ACADEMIC VOCABULARY

As you conduct your **peer review,** be sure to use these words.

- ❑ **commentary**
- ❑ **occupation**
- ❑ **option**
- ❑ **speculate**
- ❑ **technology**

With a Partner After working through the Revision Guide on your own, exchange papers with a partner and evaluate each other's draft in a **peer review**. Focus on suggesting revisions for at least three of the items mentioned in the chart. Explain why you think your partner's draft should be revised and your specific suggestions for revising it.

When receiving feedback from your partner, listen attentively and ask questions to make sure you fully understand the revision suggestions.

4 Edit

Once you have evaluated the organization, development, and flow of information in your essay and made necessary revisions, one important task remains. Don't let simple mistakes confuse your readers. Edit your final draft for the proper use of standard English conventions and be sure to correct any misspellings or errors in grammar or punctuation.

Language Conventions

Go to **Writing Informative Texts: Organizing Ideas** in the **Writing Studio** for more help with transitional words and phrases.

Transitional Words and Phrases When explaining how to perform a task with multiple steps, you can use transitional words and phrases to connect ideas and make the process clearer.

The chart below contains commonly used transitions.

Type of Transition	Examples
Sequence	*first, second, next, then, finally, when, before, later, while*
Degree of Importance	*mainly, more important, to begin with, then, last*
Compare	*also, and, another, just as, like, likewise, similarly*
Contrast	*although, but, however, yet, on the other hand*

Here are examples of transitions from "Are Bionic Superhumans on the Horizon?"

- **When** the implant was activated, it raised their scores by an average of 10 points on a 100-point scale.
- And **then**, one day, we'll wake up and realize that we're doing more than restoring lost function.

5 Publish

Finalize your essay and choose a way to share it with your audience. Consider these options:

- Produce a brochure for people who will find the instructions useful.
- Present your essay as a speech to the class.
- Post your essay as a blog on a classroom or school website.

WRITING TASK

Use the scoring guide to evaluate your essay.

Writing Task Scoring Guide: Informational Essay			
	Organization/ Progression	**Development of Ideas**	**Use of Language and Conventions**
4	• The organization is effective and appropriate for the purpose. • Ideas and steps are presented in a logical sequence. • Transitions clearly show the relationship among ideas and/or steps.	• The introduction catches the reader's attention, identifies the topic, and clearly states a thesis. • All materials, tools, and steps needed to perform the task are included and described in detail. • The thesis is clear and well developed with specific and relevant facts, details, examples, and quotations. • The conclusion summarizes the main points and either offers some final advice or recommends a next step or action.	• Language and word choice is purposeful and precise. • A variety of sentences is used to show how ideas are related. • Spelling, capitalization, and punctuation are correct. • Grammar and usage are correct. • Effective formatting aids comprehension.
3	• The organization is fairly effective and appropriate for the purpose. • Presentation of ideas and steps is logical, with only minor lapses. • A few more transitions are needed to show the relationship among ideas and/or steps.	• The introduction could be more engaging but presents a thesis. • Most materials and tools and all steps needed to perform the task are included. • The thesis is clear and fairly well developed with relevant facts, details, examples, and quotations. • The conclusion summarizes all the main points.	• Language is, for the most part, specific and clear. • Sentences vary somewhat in structure. • Some spelling, capitalization, and punctuation mistakes are present. • Some grammar and usage errors occur. • Some formatting is used to aid comprehension and does so fairly well.
2	• The organization is evident but not always appropriate for the purpose. • Notable gaps occur in the sequence of steps. • More transitions are needed to show the relationship among ideas and/or steps.	• The introduction suggests a topic but the thesis is unclear or missing. • A few key materials, tools, and/or steps needed to perform the task are unclear or missing. • The thesis is minimally and ineffectively developed because the writer uses vague, insufficient, or irrelevant facts, details, examples, and quotations. • The conclusion does not summarize all the main points.	• Language is often vague and general. • There is little variety in sentence structure. • Spelling, capitalization, and punctuation are often incorrect but do not make reading difficult. • Grammar and usage are often incorrect, but the writer's main points are still clear. • There is little formatting to aid comprehension and/or a few formatting inconsistencies or errors are present.
1	• Organization is absent, inconsistent, or not appropriate for purpose. • There is no discernible logical sequence to the ideas or steps presented. • No transitions are used, making the essay difficult to understand.	• The introduction is missing, confusing, or lacking a thesis. • Crucial materials, tools, or steps are omitted. • The development of ideas is weak. Supporting facts, details, examples, or quotations are unreliable, vague, or missing. • The conclusion is missing.	• Language is vague and confusing and, in some cases, inappropriate for the text. • There is no variety in sentence structure. • Many spelling, capitalization, and punctuation errors are present. • Many grammatical and usage errors make the writer's points or steps hard to follow. • Formatting is missing or very confusing.

Present and Respond to an Instructional Speech

You will now adapt your informational essay for presentation to your classmates. You will also listen to your classmates' speeches and then give feedback and ask questions that will help them improve their work.

Go to **Giving a Presentation** in the **Speaking and Listening Studio** to learn more.

1 Adapt Your Essay for Presentation

Review your informational essay and think about how to adapt it for an instructional speech. Keep in mind that listeners may have different needs than readers. How can you adjust the format and organization of your essay to work well as a speech? Use the chart below to guide you as you adapt your essay and create a script and presentation materials.

Presentation Planning Chart		
Title and Introduction	How might you revise your title and introduction to capture your listeners' attention? What do you want listeners to be able to do by the end of your speech?	
Audience	Does your audience already know something about your topic? If so, what information can you exclude? If not, what should you be sure to include or possibly add?	
Effective Language and Organization	Which parts of the instructions in your essay should be simplified? Where can you add transitions to clarify how to progress from one step to another?	
Visuals	What images or graphics would help clarify ideas or add interest? What text should appear on screen?	

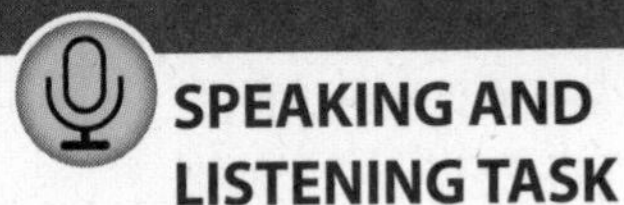

As you work to improve your presentations, be sure to follow discussion rules:

- ❑ **listen closely to each other**
- ❑ **don't interrupt**
- ❑ **stay on topic**
- ❑ **ask only helpful, relevant questions**
- ❑ **provide only clear, thoughtful, and direct answers**

2 Practice with a Partner or Group

Once you've completed a draft of your speech, practice with a partner or group to improve both your presentation and your delivery.

Practice Effective Verbal Techniques

- ❑ **Enunciation** Replace words that you stumble over, and rearrange or restructure sentences to make your delivery easy.
- ❑ **Voice Modulation and Pitch** Use your voice to display enthusiasm and emphasis.
- ❑ **Speaking Rate** Speak slowly enough that listeners understand you. Pause now and then to let them consider important points.
- ❑ **Volume** Remember that listeners at the back of the room need to hear you.

Practice Effective Nonverbal Techniques

- ❑ **Eye Contact** Try to let your eyes rest on each member of the audience at least once.
- ❑ **Facial Expression** Smile, frown, or raise an eyebrow to show your feelings or to emphasize points.
- ❑ **Gestures** Use gestures to emphasize key points or direct attention to visuals.

Provide and Consider Advice for Improvement

As a presenter, listen closely to questions and consider ways to revise your presentation to make sure your points are clear and the steps are logically sequenced. Provide additional information to clarify any misunderstandings. Remember to ask for suggestions about how you might change onscreen text or images to make your presentation clearer and more interesting.

As a listener, pay close attention. Take notes about points you want to remember or questions you want to ask the presenter. Refer to the visuals to help you follow the instructions given by the presenter. Think of ways that presenters can improve their presentations and more effectively use verbal and nonverbal techniques. Paraphrase and summarize each presenter's key ideas and main points to confirm your understanding, and ask questions to clarify any confusing ideas.

3 Deliver Your Presentation

Use the suggestions you received during practice to make final changes to your presentation. Then, using effective verbal and nonverbal techniques, present the speech to your classmates.

Reflect on the Unit

By completing your informational essay, you have created a writing product that pulls together and expresses your thoughts about the reading you have done in this unit. Now is a good time to reflect on what you have learned.

Reflect on the Essential Question

- How does technology improve and control our lives? How has your answer to this question changed since you first considered it at the start of this unit?
- What are some examples from the texts you've read that show how technology can improve and control our lives?

Reflect on Your Reading

- Which selections were the most interesting or surprising to you?
- From which selection did you learn the most about how technology improves and/or controls our lives?

Reflect on the Writing Task

- What difficulties did you encounter while working on your informational essay? How might you avoid them next time?
- Which parts of the essay were the easiest and hardest to write? Why?
- What improvements did you make to your essay as you were revising?

Reflect on the Speaking and Listening Task

- Which parts of your essay did you have to change or adapt for your presentation?
- What aspects of presenting your essay did you find most difficult?
- What are some techniques you could practice to make the task easier?

UNIT 1 SELECTIONS

- **"The Brave Little Toaster"**
- **"Are Bionic Superhumans on the Horizon?"**
- **"Interflora"**
- **"The Automation Paradox"**
- **"Heads Up, Humans"**

UNIT 2

THE THRILL OF HORROR

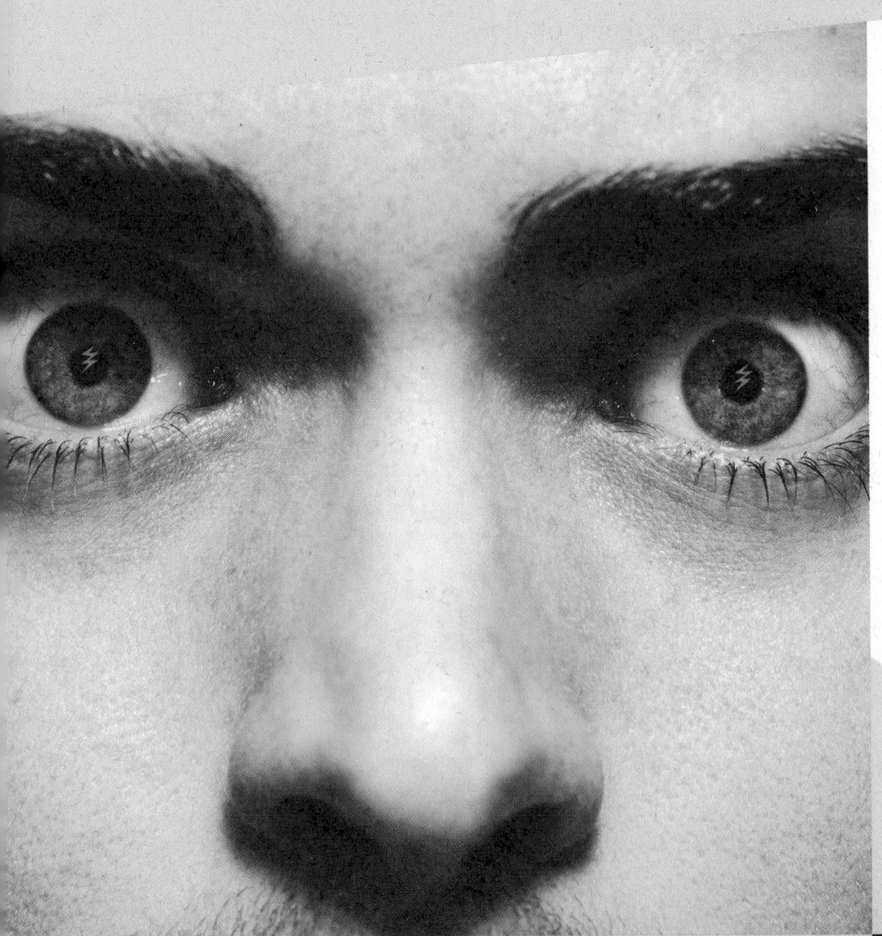

? **ESSENTIAL QUESTION:**

Why do we sometimes like to feel frightened?

> **"[A] horror story that is only two sentences long: The last man on Earth sat alone in a room. There was a knock at the door."**
>
> Fredric Brown

ACADEMIC VOCABULARY

Academic Vocabulary words are words you use when you discuss and write about texts. In this unit you will practice and learn five words.

☑ **convention** ☐ **predict** ☐ **psychology** ☐ **summary** ☐ **technique**

Study the Word Network to learn more about the word **convention**.

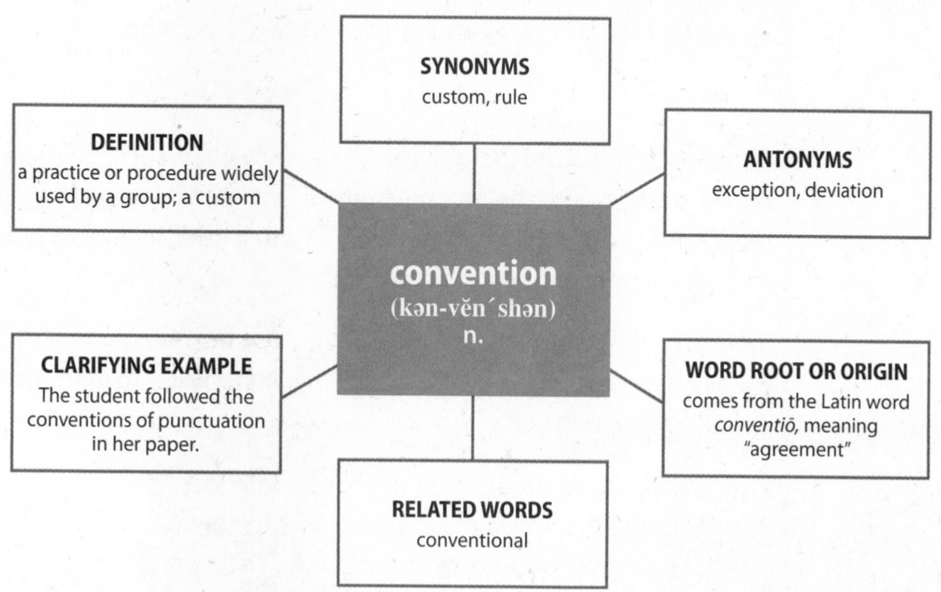

Write and Discuss Discuss the completed Word Network with a partner, making sure to talk through all of the boxes until you both understand the word, its synonyms, antonyms, and related forms. Then, fill out Word Networks for the remaining four words. Use a dictionary or online resource to help you complete the activity.

Go online to access the Word Networks.

RESPOND TO THE ESSENTIAL QUESTION

In this unit, you will encounter some scary stories and you will think about why so many people enjoy being frightened. As you read, you will revisit the **Essential Question** and gather your ideas about it in the **Response Log** that appears on page R2. At the end of the unit, you will have the opportunity to write a **literary analysis** of one of the stories and explain how it fits into the horror genre. Filling out the Response Log will help you prepare for this writing task.

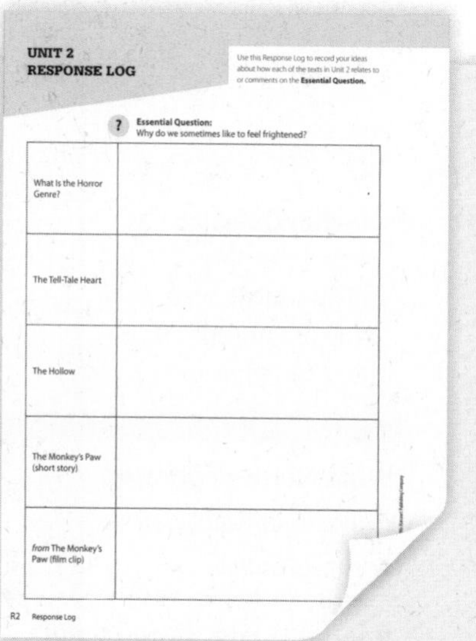

You can also go online to access the Response Log.

Notice & Note

READING MODEL

WHAT IS THE HORROR GENRE?

For more information on these and other signposts to Notice & Note, visit the **Reading Studio**.

You are about to read "What Is the Horror Genre?," a work of literary criticism. In it, you will notice and note signposts that will give you clues about the author's purpose. Here are three key signposts to look for as you read this essay and other works of nonfiction.

When you notice one of the following while reading, pause to see if it's an **Extreme or Absolute Language** signpost:

a word or phrase that indicates certainty or completeness, such as *all, none, everyone, no one, always, never, totally*

a phrase that expresses an uncompromising position, such as *We must all agree . . .* or *There's no way that . . .*

Extreme or Absolute Language Say your friend wants you to go see a movie, claiming it's "the *best* sci-fi movie *ever*" and "*everyone* is going to see it." Now, your friend may really think you'll love the movie. But she may also simply be trying to convince you to go with her.

Similarly, when authors use **Extreme or Absolute Language**, they usually have a purpose for doing so. Paying attention to Extreme or Absolute Language can

- provide clues to the author's purpose and biases
- point to the main idea the author wants to convey
- help you draw conclusions about the text's main points

The paragraph below shows a student's annotations on "What Is the Horror Genre?" and responses to a Notice and Note signpost.

1 Many people define horror by its subjects. We all think of creatures like Frankenstein's monster, Dracula, and the wolfman as monsters in the horror genre. Each one of these creatures has a history and developed over a period of time. But we also know that horror covers more than just these monsters. We could all make long lists of the kind of creatures we identify with horror, especially when we think of films as well as literature. The minute we would start to make such a list we would also realize that not all monsters are alike and that not all horror deals with monsters. The subject approach is not the clearest way to define this genre.

Anchor Question When you notice this signpost, ask: Why did the author use this language?

What words or phrases indicate certainty or completeness?	"We all" and "We could all"
Why might the author have used these phrases?	These words create a feeling of agreement between author and readers.

Quoted Words If you were writing a fiction story, you might use quotations to show the words your characters say. In nonfiction, writers often use **Quoted Words** to provide support for a point. Quoted Words might be the conclusions of an expert on a subject or the account of an eyewitness on an event. When you come across quoted words, ask yourself why the words were quoted and what they help you understand about the topic. Consider this example:

> There are good reasons why people flock to horror movies. As psychologist Irene Chen points out, "Like a good roller coaster ride, a scary film offers tremendous thrills, but it also offers safety."

Anchor Question
When you notice this signpost, ask: Why was this person quoted or cited, and what did this add?

What quoted words does the author use?	"Like a good roller coaster ride, a scary film offers tremendous thrills, but it also offers safety."
Why might the author have used this quote?	It gives an example of one good reason people might want to see a horror film.

Big Questions Have you ever listened to a friend tell a story and wondered if you had missed something? Sometimes, people assume you know something or have background knowledge that you don't.

Authors occasionally do the same thing. If you're reading a text and feel lost, stop and ask yourself: **What does the author think I already know?** This can help you clarify the point the author is making and determine what to look for as you continue to read. Here's an example:

When you start to feel lost or confused while reading, pause and ask yourself one or more of these **Big Questions**:

What does the author think I already know?

What surprised me?

What challenged, changed, or confirmed what I already knew?

> 6 We can also look at the kinds of themes common to horror. Many works concentrate on the conflict between good and evil. Works about the fantastic may deal with the search for forbidden knowledge that appears in much horror literature. Such quests are used as a way of examining our attitude toward knowledge. While society may believe that new knowledge is always good, the horror genre may question this assumption, examining how such advances affect the individual and society.

Which words or phrases are confusing?	"the search for forbidden knowledge that appears in much horror literature"
What does the author think I already know?	The author thinks I know some examples of horror works that deal with the search for forbidden knowledge.

ANALYZE & APPLY

WHAT IS THE HORROR GENRE?

Literary Criticism by **Sharon A. Russell**

? ESSENTIAL QUESTION:

Why do we sometimes like to feel frightened?

QUICK START

Before you read, think about some scary stories you know. What do they have in common? Discuss your ideas with a partner.

ANALYZE LITERARY CRITICISM

Literary criticism is writing that examines, analyzes, and interprets a particular work or an aspect of literature. The **author's purpose**—or reason for writing—is often to inform readers or to persuade them to adopt a particular opinion of the material. This opinion is the **controlling idea** around which the writing is organized. Whether stated directly or implied, the author supports it with evidence.

The chart shows some specific purposes an author might have when writing literary criticism.

PURPOSE	WHAT THE AUTHOR DOES
To define a genre	explains the characteristics of a type of writing using specific examples as evidence
To categorize works of literature	defines and classifies works of literature based on certain **criteria,** or standards
To examine the structure of a work of literature	analyzes the organization of a piece of literature
To analyze an author's technique	explains the effectiveness of literary techniques, such as suspense or flashbacks

As you read, look for clues that help you infer the author's purpose. To whom is she writing? What ideas does she want them to understand?

GENRE ELEMENTS: LITERARY CRITICISM

- often appears in the form of an essay with persuasive elements
- examines one or more works of literature
- contains specific examples and support from the literature and other sources
- may have the purpose of shaping how readers interpret a particular work

PARAPHRASE AND SUMMARIZE TEXT

A good way to check your comprehension of a text is to paraphrase or summarize it. These techniques are similar, but not the same.

- When you **paraphrase**, you restate all the information in the text using your own words. Paraphrasing is a helpful way to make sure you understand small, challenging sections of text.
- When you **summarize**, you briefly retell the text's central ideas and most important details in your own words. You must be careful not to change the author's meaning and to present ideas and details in the same order as the text. Summarizing helps you understand a larger section of text or the entire text.

As you read, use paraphrasing and summarizing to understand the author's ideas about the horror genre.

GET READY

CRITICAL VOCABULARY

intensify **justify** **parallel** **quest**

To see how many Critical Vocabulary words you already know, use them to complete the sentences.

1. I read a science fiction story about a(n) __________ world much like Earth but where computers have enslaved humans.
2. The trip is only two days, so I can't __________ bringing two bags.
3. We watch scary movies in the dark to __________ the experience.
4. How many restaurants have you visited in your __________ to find the perfect hamburger?

LANGUAGE CONVENTIONS

Commas In this lesson, you will learn about the effective use of commas in writing. Commas can make the meaning of sentences clearer by separating certain words, phrases, or clauses. Read aloud these two sentences from the selection and notice where you pause:

She does end up dead in the basement, a victim of the vampire.

This type of hesitation, when we almost believe, falls into the general category of the "fantastic."

How do the commas make the sentences easier to understand? As you read "What Is the Horror Genre?" notice other ways commas are used.

ANNOTATION MODEL

NOTICE & NOTE 

As you read, notice and note signposts, including **Extreme or Absolute Language** and **Quoted Words,** and ask **Big Questions.** Also note details that help you identify the controlling idea of "What Is the Horror Genre?" Here is how one student annotated the beginning of the selection.

Many people define horror by its subjects. We all think of creatures like Frankenstein's monster, Dracula, and the wolfman as monsters in the horror genre. Each one of these creatures has a history and developed over a period of time. But we also know that horror covers more than just these monsters. We could all make long lists of the kind of creatures we identify with horror, especially when we think of films as well as literature. . . .

"Many people" define horror this way. What does the author think?

subject = monsters

What other kinds of monsters are there?

BACKGROUND

Sharon A. Russell *(b. 1941) is a retired professor of Communication and Women's Studies at Indiana State University, where she taught courses on film and television. Russell has published extensively on horror film and literature and detective fiction. She is the author of* Stephen King: A Critical Companion, *a book that analyzes several of King's famous horror novels and in which this essay appears.*

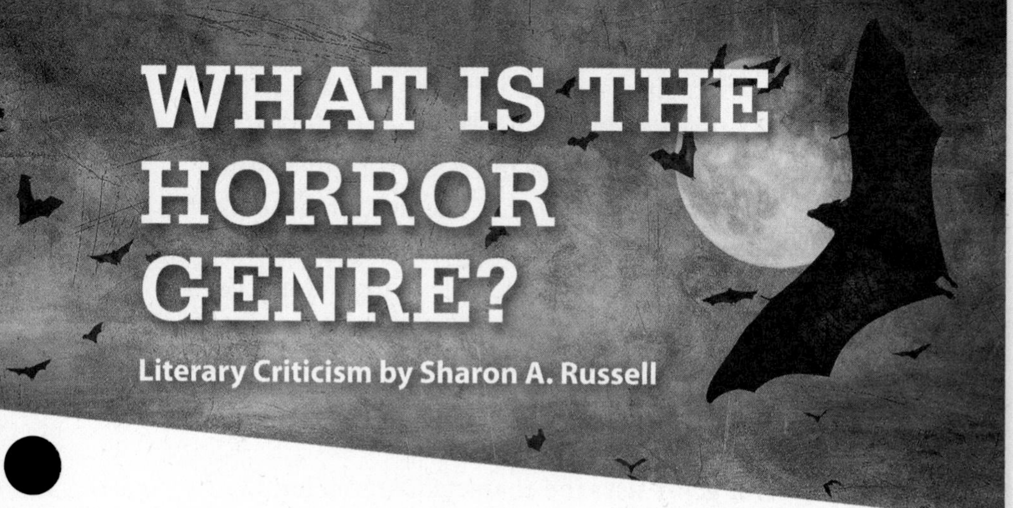

WHAT IS THE HORROR GENRE?

Literary Criticism by Sharon A. Russell

SETTING A PURPOSE

As you read, pay attention to the points the author makes about horror stories. Do her ideas make you think about horror stories in new ways?

1 Many people define horror by its subjects. We all think of creatures like Frankenstein's monster, Dracula, and the wolfman[1] as monsters in the horror genre. Each one of these creatures has a history and developed over a period of time. But we also know that horror covers more than just these monsters. We could all make long lists of the kind of creatures we identify with horror, especially when we think of films as well as literature. The minute we would start to make such a list we would also realize that not all monsters are alike and that not all horror deals with monsters. The subject approach is not the clearest way to define this genre.

Notice & Note

Use the side margins to notice and note signposts in the text.

BIG QUESTIONS

Notice & Note: Mark where Russell expects the reader to already know something.

Analyze: Why do you think she expects the reader to know this? Where did you look to get more information?

[1] **Frankenstein's monster, Dracula, and the wolfman:** legendary monsters. "Frankenstein's monster" is the creature created by Dr. Victor Frankenstein in Mary Shelley's novel; "Dracula" is the vampire in Bram Stoker's novel; in folklore, the wolfman is a man who can become a wolf.

NOTICE & NOTE

QUOTED WORDS

Notice & Note: Mark where Russell uses quoted words in paragraph 2.

Analyze: How does this quote support one of Russell's main ideas?

intensify
(ĭn-tĕn´sə-fī´) *v.* If you *intensify* something, you make it grow in strength.

justify
(jŭs´tə-fī´) *v.* If you *justify* something, you prove it is right or valid.

EXTREME OR ABSOLUTE LANGUAGE

Notice & Note: Mark where Russell makes an absolute statement in paragraph 3.

Evaluate: Is her statement justified, or do you think it is an exaggeration? Why?

2 Some students of this genre find that the best way to examine it is to deal with the way horror fiction is organized or structured. Examining the organization of a horror story shows that it shares certain traits with other types of fiction. Horror stories share the use of suspense as a tactic with many other kinds of literature. The tension we feel when a character goes into the attic, down into the basement, or just into the abandoned house is partially a result of suspense. We don't know what is going to happen. But that suspense is **intensified** by our knowledge of the genre. We know that characters involved in the world of horror always meet something awful when they go where they shouldn't. Part of the tension is created because they are doing something we know is going to get them in trouble. Stephen King refers directly to our anticipation of horror. In *Salem's Lot*[2] Susan approaches the house which is the source of evil. "She found herself thinking of those drive-in horror movie epics where the heroine goes venturing up the narrow attic stairs . . . or down into some dark, cobwebby cellar . . . and she . . . thinking: . . . *I'd never do that!*" Of course Susan's fears are **justified**. She does end up dead in the basement, a victim of the vampire.

3 If the horror genre uses the character's search for information to create suspense, it controls when and where we get our knowledge. Because we are outside of the situation we usually know more than the characters. Our advance knowledge creates suspense because we can anticipate what is going to happen. The author can play with those expectations by either confirming them or surprising us with a different outcome. When suspense is an important element in fiction we may often find that the plot is the most critical part of the story. We care more about what happens next than about who the characters are or where the story is set. But setting is often considered a part of the horror genre. If the genre has traditional monsters, it also has traditional settings. Only authors who want to challenge the tradition place events in bright, beautiful parks. We expect a connection between the setting and the events in this genre. We are not surprised to find old houses, abandoned castles, damp cellars, or dark forests as important elements in the horror story.

[2] ***Salem's Lot:*** a horror fiction novel written by Stephen King.

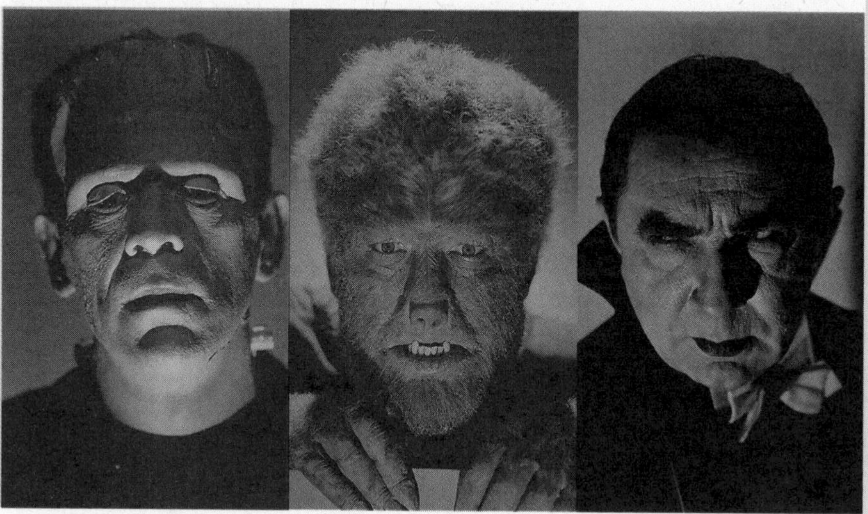

The actor Boris Karloff as the monster in the 1931 film *Frankenstein,* based on the novel

The actor Lon Chaney as a werewolf in the 1941 film *The Wolf Man*

The actor Bela Lugosi as Dracula in the 1931 film by the same name

4 Some people make further distinctions based on how the stories are organized. We can divide stories into different categories based on how we come to believe in the events related and how they are explained to us. Stories that deal with **parallel** worlds expect us to accept those worlds without question. We just believe Dorothy is in Oz; we accept Oz as a parallel world separate from ours. Other times events seem to be supernatural but turn out to have natural explanations: the ghosts turn out to be squirrels in the attic, or things that move mysteriously are part of a plot to drive someone crazy. Sometimes the supernatural is the result of the way the central character sees the world, as in stories told from the point of view of a crazy person. But at times we are not sure, and hesitate about believing in the possibility of the supernatural. When I first read Dracula I seriously considered hanging garlic on my windows because I believed that vampires could exist. This type of hesitation, when we almost believe, falls into the general category of the "fantastic" (Todorov 25).[3] Often horror has its greatest effect on us because we almost believe, or believe while we are reading the book or watching the film, that the events are possible.

[3] **Todorov 25:** the author is following MLA style to cite her source for the information just stated: page 25 of a work by an author named Todorov.

parallel
(păr′ə-lĕl′) *adj.* If things are *parallel*, they have comparable or similar parts.

ANALYZE LITERARY CRITICISM

Annotate: Review the purposes for writing literary criticism on page 79. Mark text in paragraph 4 that suggests the author has one of these purposes.

Infer: What is one of the author's purposes for writing this essay, based on the text you marked?

NOTICE & NOTE

LANGUAGE CONVENTIONS

Annotate: Mark the commas used by the author in paragraph 5.

Analyze: How does each comma help you understand the author's meaning in the sentence?

PARAPHRASE AND SUMMARIZE TEXT

Annotate: Underline a challenging sentence in paragraph 6. Circle words in the sentence that could be replaced with simpler ones.

Paraphrase: Restate the sentence in your own words.

5 Yet another way of categorizing works of horror is by the source of the horror. Some horror comes from inside the characters. Something goes wrong inside, and a person turns into a monster. Dr. Frankenstein's need for knowledge turns him into the kind of person who creates a monster. Dr. Jekyll also values his desire for information above all else, and creates Mr. Hyde.[4] In another kind of horror story the threat to the central character or characters comes from outside. An outside force may invade the character and then force the evil out again. The vampire attacks the victim, but then the victim becomes a vampire and attacks others. Stories of ghosts or demonic possession also fall into this category.

[4] **Dr. Jekyll . . . and . . . Mr. Hyde:** the good and evil sides of the same character in a novella by Robert Louis Stevenson.

NOTICE & NOTE

6 We can also look at the kinds of themes common to horror. Many works concentrate on the conflict between good and evil. Works about the fantastic may deal with the search for forbidden knowledge that appears in much horror literature. Such **quests** are used as a way of examining our attitude toward knowledge. While society may believe that new knowledge is always good, the horror genre may question this assumption, examining how such advances affect the individual and society.

quest
(kwĕst) *n.* A *quest* is a search.

ANALYZE LITERARY CRITCISM

Annotate: Mark the first sentence of each paragraph in this selection.

Analyze: Based on these topic sentences, what is the author's controlling idea, or thesis, about the horror genre? What evidence does she provide?

CHECK YOUR UNDERSTANDING

Answer these questions before moving on to the **Analyze the Text** section on the following page.

1 According to the author, what are the limitations of defining horror by its focus on monsters?

A People can think of many different kinds of monsters.

B Some horror stories do not have monsters at all.

C Our ideas about vampires have changed over time.

D The struggle between good and evil is more important.

2 The feeling of suspense in a horror story intensifies when —

F the story takes place in a cheerful setting

G the monsters in the story are unfamiliar to the reader

H the reader expects horrible events to occur

J the characters avoid going into places like basements

3 What is an example of horror that has its source inside a character?

A A woman knows she should not go into a basement but goes anyway.

B A vampire in a story inspires a reader to hang garlic on her windows.

C The squirrels in an attic cause people to think they hear ghosts.

D A scientist desires knowledge so intensely that he creates a monster.

ANALYZE THE TEXT

Support your responses with evidence from the text. NOTEBOOK

1. **Infer** Reread the first two paragraphs of the essay. What does the opening suggest about the author's purpose in writing this essay?
2. **Connect** In paragraph 2, the author states that in horror stories "suspense is intensified by our knowledge of the genre." What knowledge is the author referring to? Explain why it increases suspense.
3. **Summarize** How does the author answer the question in the title: "What Is the Horror Genre?" To answer, summarize the text.
4. **Analyze** Review the first sentences of each paragraph. How are ideas organized to support the author's controlling idea about the horror genre?
5. **Notice & Note** In paragraph 4, identify two examples of things that the author assumes readers already know. Why might she think her readers would be familiar with these things?

RESEARCH

In the selection, Russell discusses the novel *Salem's Lot* by "Master of Horror" Stephen King. Find three other famous Masters of Horror, including writers and directors. In the chart below, record their names and two works by each.

MASTER OF HORROR	TWO WORKS

Connect With a small group, share what you found. Consider whether you want to show images or a movie trailer along with each name. Then, using the categories Russell details in her essay, identify what makes each of the works a good example of the horror genre.

RESEARCH TIP

The Internet is full of lists of top authors and filmmakers in their genres. If you don't know the names of any famous horror writers or directors, think of a horror story or movie you enjoy, and then look up who made it.

CREATE AND DISCUSS

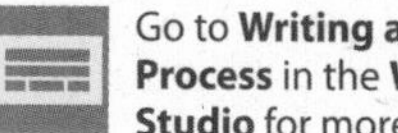

Go to **Writing as a Process** in the **Writing Studio** for more.

Write a Letter Have you ever seen a movie or show or played a video game that you thought was either too violent or rated too harshly? Write a three- to four-paragraph letter to the Motion Picture Association of America or to the Entertainment Software Rating Board in which you express a complaint about the rating of a movie, show, or game that includes horror content.

- ❑ Introduce yourself and the title of the movie, show, or game you are writing about.
- ❑ Explain why you think the rating is too restrictive or not restrictive enough, citing details.
- ❑ Be sure to keep a professional tone throughout your letter.

Go to **Participating in Collaborative Discussions** in the **Speaking and Listening Studio** for help.

Discuss with a Small Group Use the characteristics of the horror genre described in the essay to categorize the horror stories you have read and the horror films you have seen.

- ❑ Work with a small group to create a list of stories and films.
- ❑ Review the characters, setting, events, structure, and organization of the stories and films. Take notes on each.
- ❑ Decide how to categorize the stories and films. What creates the suspense in each one? Do they have similar themes or settings? Are the sources of horror alike in some way?
- ❑ Be prepared to explain your categories as you share your final list with the class or a small group.

RESPOND TO THE ESSENTIAL QUESTION

? Why do we sometimes like to feel frightened?

Gather Information Review your annotations and notes on "What Is the Horror Genre?" Then, add relevant details to your Response Log. As you determine which information to include, think about:

- how we categorize horror
- how our knowledge of the genre shapes how we read it

At the end of the unit, you can use your notes to help you write a literary analysis.

ACADEMIC VOCABULARY

As you write and discuss what you learned from the selection, be sure to use the Academic Vocabulary words. Check off each of the words that you use.

- ❑ **convention**
- ❑ **predict**
- ❑ **psychology**
- ❑ **summary**
- ❑ **technique**

RESPOND

CRITICAL VOCABULARY

WORD BANK
intensify
justify
parallel
quest

Practice and Apply Write the best answer for each question. Then, explain your response.

1. Which Vocabulary word goes with *similar*? Why?
2. Which Vocabulary word goes with *strengthen*? Why?
3. Which Vocabulary word goes with *search*? Why?
4. Which Vocabulary word goes with *defend*? Why?

VOCABULARY STRATEGY: Use Suffixes

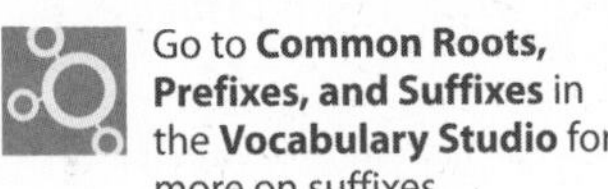

Go to **Common Roots, Prefixes, and Suffixes** in the **Vocabulary Studio** for more on suffixes.

A **suffix** is a word part that is added to the end of a root or base word. For example, the suffix *-d* or *-ed* may be added to a verb to change it to a past form, like *scared* or *screamed*. Sometimes when *-d* or *-ed* is added, spelling changes are also made to the base word.

> **But that suspense is intensified by our knowledge of the genre. Of course Susan's fears are justified.**

In the two sentences above from "What Is the Horror Genre?," the *y* at the end of each verb form was changed to *i* before the *-ed* suffix was added; that's because in each case, the *y* follows a consonant. This table summarizes patterns that will help you use base words and the suffixes *-d* and *-ed* to identify unfamiliar words:

EXAMPLE	PATTERN TO REMEMBER
abandon**ed**	Add *-ed* to most verbs to create past forms.
reliev**ed**	If a verb ends in *-e*, only *-d* is added.
horrifi**ed**	If a verb ends in consonant + *y*, the *y* is changed to *i*, then *-ed* is added.
occurr**ed**	If a verb ends in a vowel + consonant and has more than one syllable, the consonant is doubled only if the verb is accented on the last syllable, then *-ed* is added.

Practice and Apply Read the sentences. Change each verb in parentheses to the past tense by adding *-d* or *-ed*.

1. The main character (stop) for gas in a small town.
2. She was (mystify) when the pump was empty.
3. She (glance) around the town but it was deserted.
4. Suddenly, she heard a scream that (petrify) her.
5. Now, she was (worry) that she was not alone.

LANGUAGE CONVENTIONS: Commas

A writer's use of punctuation not only helps readers understand the message, but also signals how the writer wants the text to be read. In your writing, you can use commas to signal a break or a pause to the reader. When you write, read your sentences out loud, noticing where you pause. The places where you pause probably need to be punctuated by a comma.

Go to the **Grammar Studio: Punctuation** for more on commas.

Look at these examples of how Sharon A. Russell uses commas in "What Is the Horror Genre?"

PURPOSE OF COMMA	EXAMPLE
To signal a break in thought or an additional thought	"Often horror has its greatest effect on us because we almost believe, or believe while we are reading the book or watching the film, that the events are possible."
To signal a pause between phrases or clauses	"If the genre has traditional monsters, it also has traditional settings."
To set off a phrase or clause that provides extra information that is not essential to the sentence's meaning	"She does end up dead in the basement, a victim of the vampire."

Practice and Apply These sentences include words, phrases, and clauses that need to be punctuated with commas. Rewrite the sentences, inserting the needed punctuation. If you get stuck, try reading the sentence aloud.

1. Yes I absolutely love horror stories.
2. You know of course that the main purpose of horror stories is to inspire fear and dread.
3. If Frankenstein is frightening he is also sympathetic.
4. The long movie was terrifying so much so that several times I just closed my eyes and blocked my ears.
5. Writing a horror story a big dream of mine will take a lot of thought and hard work.

THE TELL-TALE HEART

Short Story by **Edgar Allan Poe**

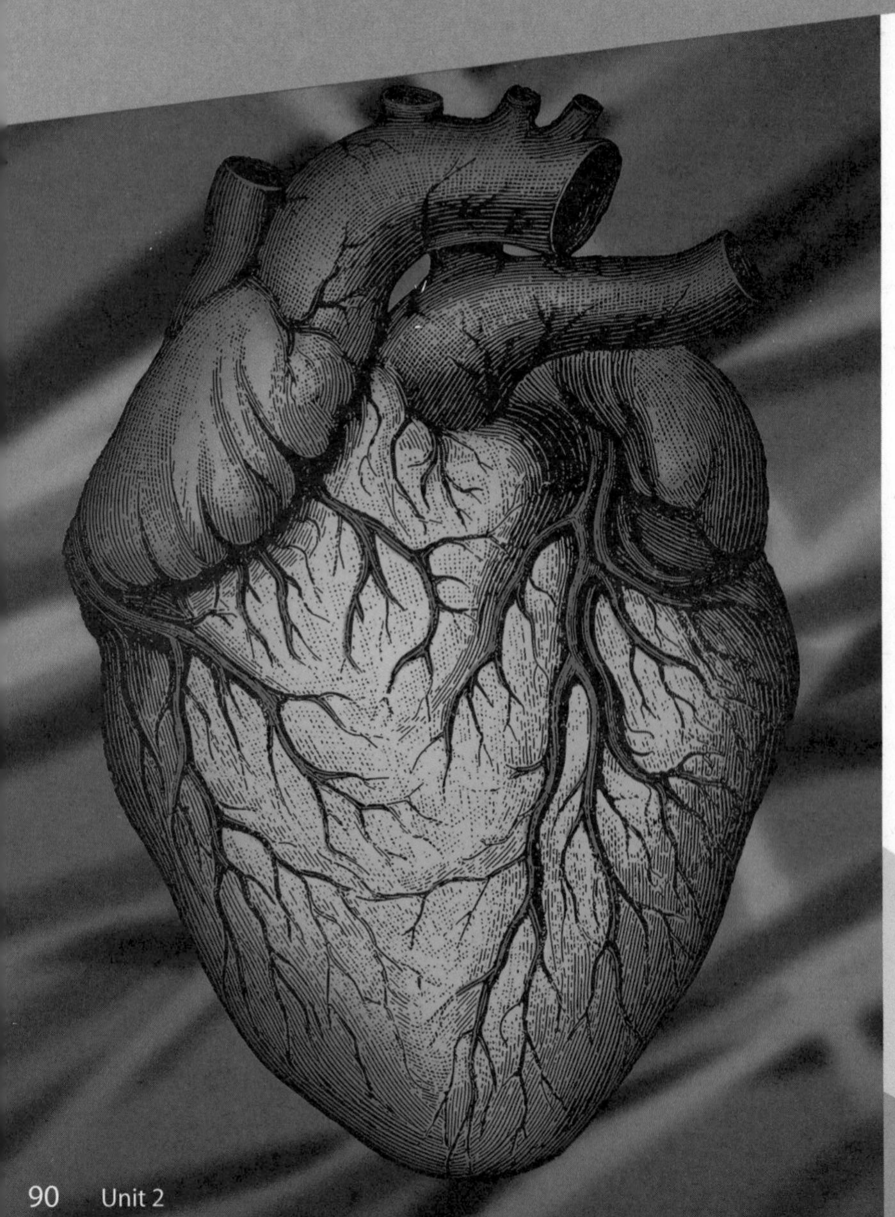

? ***ESSENTIAL QUESTION:***

Why do we sometimes like to feel frightened?

QUICK START

How can you tell when someone is nervous? List some of the tell-tale signs, including how the person might act and speak.

ANALYZE POINT OF VIEW

Point of view is the method of narration used in a short story, novel, narrative poem, or work of nonfiction. In a story told from the **third-person point of view,** the **narrator**, or the voice that tells the story, is an outside observer. In a story told from the **first-person point of view**, the narrator is a character and uses the pronouns *I, me,* and *we.*

Just as you can't believe everything everyone tells you, you can't always believe everything you learn from a first-person narrator. An **unreliable narrator** is a narrator whose assessment of events cannot be trusted for some reason—he or she might be purposefully lying, mentally unstable, or too young or unsophisticated to fully understand events. To determine whether or not a narrator is reliable, consider his or her actions, attitudes, and statements, and then decide whether he or she is generally trustworthy.

As you read "The Tell-Tale Heart," look for clues that tell you whether the narrator is reliable or unreliable.

GENRE ELEMENTS: SHORT STORY

- includes the basic elements of fiction—setting, characters, plot, conflict, and theme
- centers on one particular moment or event in the main character's life
- can be read in one sitting

ANALYZE SUSPENSE

Suspense is the sense of growing tension, fear, and excitement felt by the reader. When a story is suspenseful, the reader becomes increasingly curious about what will happen next. Writers use different techniques to create suspense in fiction. Some of these are listed in the chart below. Fill in the chart with examples of these techniques as you read "The Tell-Tale Heart."

TECHNIQUE	EXAMPLE
Describing a character's anxiety or fear	
Using vivid words to describe dramatic sights, sounds, or feelings	
Repeating words, phrases, or characters' actions	

GET READY

CRITICAL VOCABULARY

conceive	**stifle**	**audacity**	**derision**
vex	**crevice**	**vehemently**	**hypocritical**

To see how many Critical Vocabulary words you already know, use them to complete the sentences.

1. Expressing an unpopular opinion often leads to __________.
2. It's difficult to __________ that someone could be so cruel.
3. My brother loves to __________ me whenever he gets a chance.
4. A(n) __________ person says one thing and does another.
5. __________ is a characteristic of people who take risks.
6. I wanted to shout out in fear, but I had to __________ my reaction.
7. The convict __________ denied committing the crime.
8. My keys fell into a deep __________ while I was rock climbing.

LANGUAGE CONVENTIONS

Phrases and Clauses In this lesson, you will learn about one way of using phrases and clauses in writing. Edgar Allan Poe often separates a phrase or a clause from the rest of a sentence by using dashes:

You should have seen how wisely I proceeded—with what caution—with what foresight—with what dissimulation I went to work!

As you read, note how Poe uses dashes to set off phrases and clauses.

ANNOTATION MODEL

NOTICE & NOTE 

As you read, note how the author's use of point of view and suspense builds tension. Also mark up evidence that supports your own ideas. In the model, you can see one reader's notes about "The Tell-Tale Heart."

1 True!—nervous—very, very dreadfully nervous I had been and am! but why *will* you say that I am mad? The disease had sharpened my senses—not destroyed—not dulled them. Above all was the sense of hearing acute. I heard all things in the heaven and in the earth. I heard many things in hell. How, then, am I mad? . . .

POV: The person telling the story is very nervous.

I already feel the suspense. Why is he nervous? Who says he is mad?

NOTICE & NOTE

BACKGROUND

Edgar Allan Poe *(1809–1849) was born in Boston to parents who were traveling actors. Orphaned by the time he was three, he moved to Virginia, where friends of his family raised him. As a young man, Poe worked as a journalist while writing the stories and poems that would earn him the title "father of the modern mystery." After his young wife died, Poe fell into despair. He passed away two years later. His dark and sometimes horrifying works perhaps mirror the darkness and sadness of his own short life.*

THE TELL-TALE HEART

Short Story by Edgar Allan Poe

SETTING A PURPOSE

As you read, pay attention to the way the narrator describes himself. What makes him unusual?

1 True!—nervous—very, very dreadfully nervous I had been and am! but why *will* you say that I am mad? The disease had sharpened my senses—not destroyed—not dulled them. Above all was the sense of hearing acute. I heard all things in the heaven and in the earth. I heard many things in hell. How, then, am I mad? Hearken! and observe how healthily—how calmly I can tell you the whole story.

2 It is impossible to say how first the idea entered my brain; but once **conceived,** it haunted me day and night. Object there was none. Passion there was none. I loved the old man. He had never wronged me. He had never given me insult. For his gold I had no desire. I think it was his eye! yes, it was this! He had the eye of a vulture—a pale blue eye, with a film over it. Whenever it fell upon me, my blood ran cold; and so by degrees—very gradually—I made up my

Notice & Note

Use the side margins to notice and note signposts in the text.

CONTRASTS AND CONTRADICTIONS

Notice & Note: In paragraphs 1–2, mark details that contradict each other or that contrast with your normal expectations.

Critique: Do these details make you want to keep reading, or are they merely confusing? Explain.

conceive
(kən-sēv´) *v.* When you *conceive* an idea, you think of it.

mind to take the life of the old man, and thus rid myself of the eye forever.

3 Now this is the point. You fancy me mad. Madmen know nothing. But you should have seen *me*. You should have seen how wisely I proceeded—with what caution—with what foresight—with what dissimulation[1] I went to work!

AGAIN AND AGAIN

Notice & Note: In paragraph 4, mark details or ideas that the narrator keeps repeating as he tells his story.

Infer: Why do you think the narrator repeats these ideas again and again?

4 I was never kinder to the old man than during the whole week before I killed him. And every night, about midnight, I turned the latch of his door and opened it—oh, so gently! And then, when I had made an opening sufficient for my head, I put in a dark lantern, all closed, closed, so that no light shone out, and then I thrust in my head. Oh, you would have laughed to see how cunningly I thrust it in! I moved it slowly—very, very slowly, so that I might not disturb the old man's sleep. It took me an hour to place my whole head within the opening so far that I could see him as he lay upon his bed. Ha!—would a madman have been so wise as this? And then, when my head was well in the room, I undid the lantern cautiously—oh, so cautiously—cautiously (for the hinges creaked)—I undid it just so much that a single thin ray fell upon the vulture eye. And this I did for seven long nights—every night just at midnight—but I found the eye always closed; and so it was impossible to do the work; for it was not the old man who **vexed** me, but his Evil Eye. And every morning, when the day broke, I went boldly into the chamber, and spoke courageously to him, calling him by name in a hearty tone, and inquiring how he had passed the night. So you see he would have been a very profound old man, indeed, to suspect that every night, just at twelve, I looked in upon him while he slept.

vex
(vĕks) *v.* If you *vex* someone, you annoy that person.

ANALYZE POINT OF VIEW

Annotate: In paragraph 5, mark details that suggest whether the narrator can or cannot be trusted to describe events as they truly are.

Infer: Is the narrator reliable or unreliable? Explain why you think so.

5 Upon the eighth night I was more than usually cautious in opening the door. A watch's minute hand moves more quickly than did mine. Never before that night had I *felt* the extent of my own powers—of my sagacity.[2] I could scarcely contain my feelings of triumph. To think that there I was, opening the door, little by little, and he not even to dream of my secret deeds or thoughts. I fairly chuckled at the idea; and perhaps he heard me; for he moved on the bed suddenly, as if startled. Now you may think that I drew back—but no. His room was as black as pitch

[1] **dissimulation** (dĭ-sĭm´yə-lā´shən): a hiding of one's true feelings.

[2] **sagacity** (sə-găs´ĭ-tē): sound judgment.

with the thick darkness (for the shutters were close fastened, through fear of robbers), and so I knew that he could not see the opening of the door, and I kept pushing it on steadily, steadily.

6 I had my head in, and was about to open the lantern, when my thumb slipped upon the tin fastening, and the old man sprang up in the bed, crying out—"Who's there?"

7 I kept quite still and said nothing. For a whole hour I did not move a muscle, and in the meantime I did not hear him lie down. He was still sitting up in the bed listening,—just as I have done, night after night, hearkening to the death watches[3] in the wall.

8 Presently I heard a slight groan, and I knew it was the groan of mortal terror. It was not a groan of pain or grief—oh, no!—it was the low, **stifled** sound that arises from the bottom of the soul when overcharged with awe. I knew the sound well. Many a night, just at midnight, when all the world slept, it has welled up from my own bosom, deepening, with its dreadful echo, the terrors that distracted me. I say I knew it well. I knew what the old man felt, and pitied him, although I chuckled at heart. I knew that he had been lying awake ever since the first slight noise, when he had turned in the bed. His fears had been ever since growing upon him. He had been trying to fancy them causeless, but could not. He had been saying to himself—"It is nothing but the wind in the chimney—it is only a mouse crossing the floor," or "it is merely a cricket which has made a single chirp." Yes, he has been trying to comfort himself with these suppositions; but he had found all in vain. *All in vain;* because Death, in approaching him, had stalked with his black shadow before him, and enveloped the victim. And it was the mournful influence of the unperceived shadow that caused him to feel—although he neither saw nor heard—to *feel* the presence of my head within the room.

9 When I had waited a long time, very patiently, without hearing him lie down, I resolved to open a little—a very, very little **crevice** in the lantern. So I opened it—you cannot imagine how stealthily, stealthily—until, at length, a single dim ray, like the thread of the spider, shot from out the crevice and fell full upon the vulture eye.

[3] **death watches**: deathwatch beetles—insects that make a tapping sound with their heads.

stifle
(stī´fəl) *v.* If you *stifle* something, you smother it.

LANGUAGE CONVENTIONS

Annotate: In the first four sentences of paragraph 8, underline each clause (a group of words containing a subject and verb). Circle each phrase set off by commas or dashes.

Evaluate: Does Poe's use of different sentence structures make his writing more interesting to read? Why?

crevice
(krĕv´ĭs) *n.* A *crevice* is a narrow crack.

NOTICE & NOTE

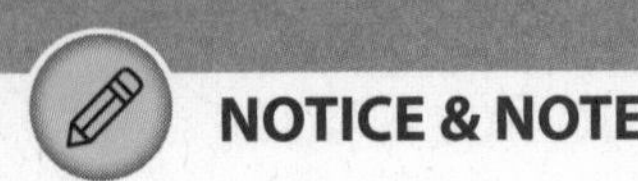

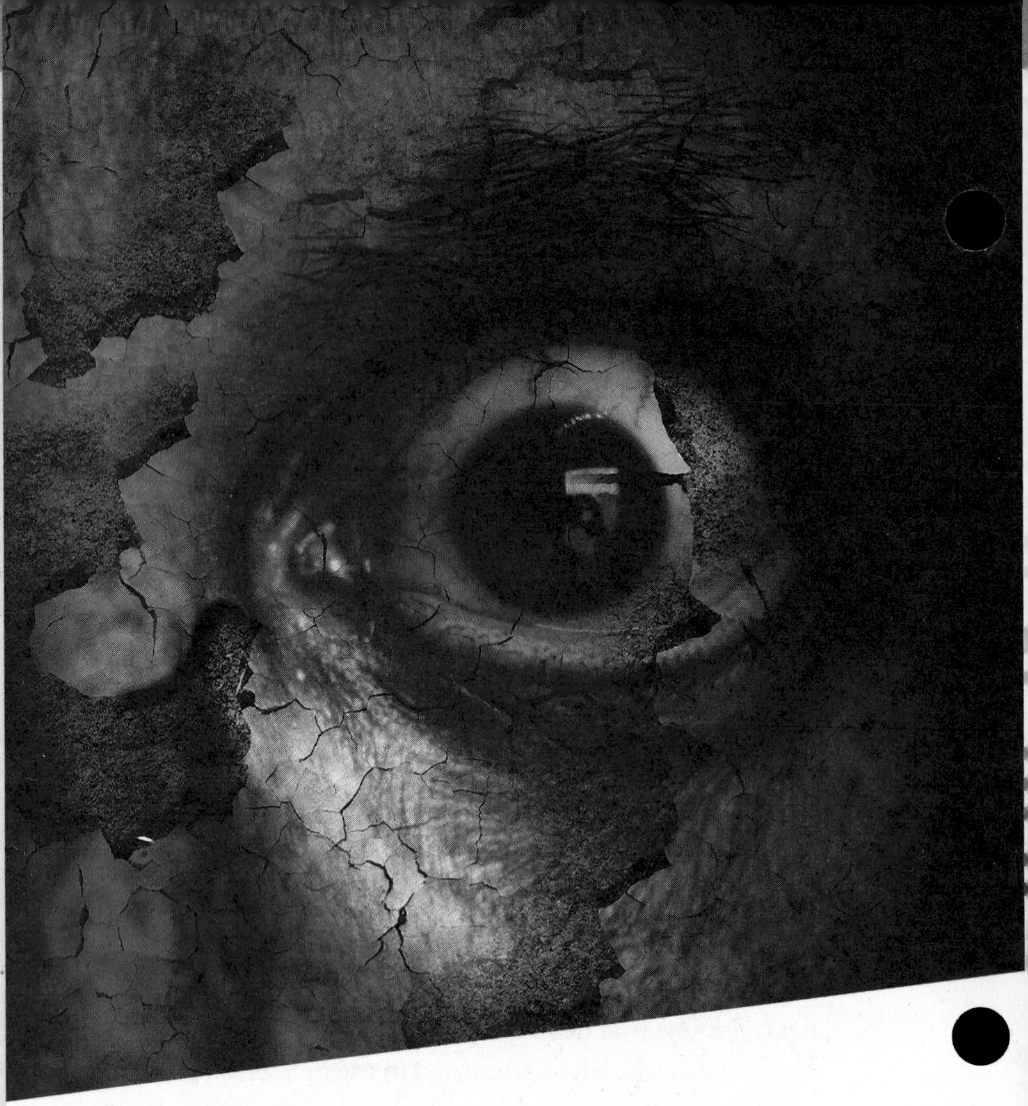

10 It was open—wide, wide open—and I grew furious as I gazed upon it. I saw it with perfect distinctness—all a dull blue, with a hideous veil over it that chilled the very marrow in my bones; but I could see nothing else of the old man's face or person: for I had directed the ray as if by instinct, precisely upon the damned spot.

ANALYZE SUSPENSE

Annotate: Mark words and phrases in paragraphs 11–12 that Poe uses to create suspense.

Analyze: Why do these details create suspense?

11 And now have I not told you that what you mistake for madness is but over-acuteness of the senses?—now, I say, there came to my ears a low, dull, quick sound, such as a watch makes when enveloped in cotton. I knew *that* sound well too. It was the beating of the old man's heart. It increased my fury, as the beating of a drum stimulates the soldier into courage.

12 But even yet I refrained and kept still. I scarcely breathed. I held the lantern motionless. I tried how steadily I could maintain the ray upon the eye. Meantime the hellish tattoo[4] of the heart increased. It grew quicker and quicker, and louder and louder every instant. The old man's terror *must* have been

[4] **hellish tattoo:** awful drumming.

extreme! It grew louder, I say, louder every moment!—do you mark me well? I have told you that I am nervous: so I am. And now at the dead hour of the night, amid the dreadful silence of that old house, so strange a noise as this excited me to uncontrollable terror. Yet, for some minutes longer I refrained and stood still. But the beating grew louder, louder! I thought the heart must burst. And now a new anxiety seized me—the sound would be heard by a neighbor! The old man's hour had come! With a loud yell, I threw open the lantern and leaped into the room. He shrieked once—once only. In an instant I dragged him to the floor, and pulled the heavy bed over him. I then smiled gaily, to find the deed so far done. But, for many minutes, the heart beat on with a muffled sound. This, however, did not vex me; it would not be heard through the wall. At length it ceased. The old man was dead. I removed the bed and examined the corpse. Yes, he was stone, stone dead. I placed my hand upon the heart and held it there many minutes. There was no pulsation. He was stone dead. His eye would trouble me no more.

13 If still you think me mad, you will think so no longer when I describe the wise precautions I took for the concealment of the body. The night waned, and I worked hastily, but in silence. First of all I dismembered the corpse. I cut off the head and the arms and the legs.

14 I then took up three planks from the flooring of the chamber, and deposited all between the scantlings.[5] I then replaced the boards so cleverly, so cunningly, that no human eye—not even *his*—could have detected anything wrong. There was nothing to wash out—no stain of any kind—no blood-spot whatever. I had been too wary for that. A tub had caught all—ha! ha!

15 When I made an end of these labors, it was four o'clock—still dark as midnight. As the bell sounded the hour, there came a knocking at the street door. I went down to open it with a light heart,—for what had I *now* to fear? There entered three men, who introduced themselves, with perfect suavity,[6] as officers of the police. A shriek had been heard by a neighbor during the night: suspicion of foul play had been aroused; information had been lodged at the police office, and they (the officers) had been deputed to search the premises.

ANALYZE POINT OF VIEW

Annotate: In paragraphs 13–14, mark details that show how the narrator tries to convince readers that he is sane and reliable.

Evaluate: What effect do the narrator's explanations have on the reader?

[5] **scantlings:** small wooden beams supporting the floor.

[6] **suavity** (swä´vĭ-tē): graceful politeness.

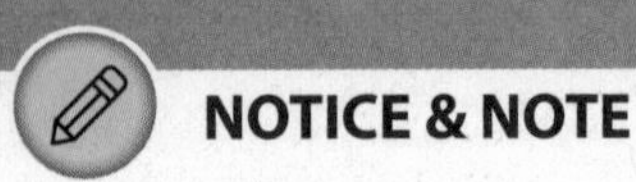

16 I smiled,—for *what* had I to fear? I bade the gentlemen welcome. The shriek, I said, was my own in a dream. The old man, I mentioned, was absent in the country. I took my visitors all over the house. I bade them search—search *well*. I led them, at length, to *his* chamber. I showed them his treasures, secure, undisturbed. In the enthusiasm of my confidence, I brought chairs into the room, and desired them here to rest from their fatigues, while I myself, in the wild **audacity** of my perfect triumph, placed my own seat upon the very spot beneath which reposed the corpse of the victim.

audacity
(ô-dăs´ĭ-tē) *n. Audacity* is shameless daring or boldness.

17 The officers were satisfied. My *manner* had convinced them. I was singularly at ease. They sat, and while I answered cheerily, they chatted of familiar things. But, ere long, I felt myself getting pale and wished them gone. My head ached, and I fancied a ringing in my ears: but still they sat and still chatted. The ringing became more distinct:—it continued and became more distinct: I talked more freely to get rid of the feeling: but it continued and gained definitiveness—until at length, I found that the noise was *not* within my ears.

CONTRASTS AND CONTRADICTIONS

Notice & Note: Mark details that show the contrast between the narrator's perception of the noise and the police officers'.

Draw Conclusions: What conclusion can you draw about this noise?

18 No doubt I now grew *very* pale;—but I talked more fluently, and with a heightened voice. Yet the sound increased—and what could I do? It was *a low, dull, quick sound—much such a sound as a watch makes when enveloped in cotton.* I gasped for breath—and yet the officers heard it not. I talked more quickly—more **vehemently**; but the noise steadily increased. I arose and argued about trifles, in a high key and with violent gesticulations,[7] but the noise steadily increased. Why *would* they not be gone? I paced the floor to and fro with heavy strides, as if excited to fury by the observation of the men—but the noise steadily increased. What *could* I do? I foamed—I raved—I swore. I swung the chair upon which I had been sitting, and grated it upon the boards, but the noise arose over all and continually increased. It grew louder—louder—*louder!* And still the men chatted pleasantly, and smiled. Was it possible they heard not?—no, no! They heard!—they suspected!—they *knew!*—they were making a *mockery* of my horror!—this I thought, and this I think. But anything was better than this agony! Anything was more tolerable than this **derision**! I could bear those **hypocritical** smiles no longer! I felt that I must scream or die!—and now—again!—hark! louder! louder! *louder!*—

vehemently
(vē´ə-mənt-lē) *adv.* If you do something *vehemently,* you do it with intense emotion.

derision
(dĭ-rĭzh´ən) *n. Derision* is jeering laughter or ridicule.

hypocritical
(hĭp´ə-krĭt´ĭ-kəl) *adj.* If someone is *hypocritical,* the person is false or deceptive.

[7] **gesticulations** (jĕ-stĭk´yə-lā´shəns): energetic gestures of the hands or arms.

19 "Villains!" I shrieked, "dissemble[8] no more! I admit the deed!—tear up the planks!—here, here!—it is the beating of his hideous heart!"

[8] **dissemble:** pretend.

CHECK YOUR UNDERSTANDING

Answer these questions before moving on to the **Analyze the Text** section on the following page.

1 What is the narrator's reason for killing the old man?

A The old man has insulted the narrator many times.

B The narrator cannot bear to hear the beating of the old man's heart.

C The old man's eye reminds the narrator of a vulture's.

D The narrator hopes to inherit the old man's treasures.

2 To prove he is not mad, the narrator —

F describes how cunning and cautious he is

G waits until the eighth night to kill the old man

H says he pities the old man but laughs in his heart

J hides the old man's body under the floor boards

3 The police officers cannot hear the old man's heart because —

A the narrator is talking too loudly

B they are sitting too far away from the body

C their senses are not as acute as the narrator's

D the heart is not actually beating

ANALYZE THE TEXT

Support your responses with evidence from the text. NOTEBOOK

1. **Infer** Does the narrator's opinion of himself in paragraphs 1–2 make him seem more reliable, or less? Explain your choice.
2. **Analyze** What prevents the narrator from killing the old man during the first seven nights? Explain how his inaction contributes to the story's suspense.
3. **Draw Conclusions** Reread paragraphs 9–11. What do readers learn from this first-person narration about the narrator's subjective, or personal, experience?
4. **Evaluate** Does the reader's inability to trust the narrator increase the suspense in this story? Explain your answer.
5. **Notice & Note** In what way does the repeated image of the "eye of a vulture" help to create suspense?

RESEARCH TIP
Just as a narrator can be unreliable, so can a website. Be sure to assess the quality of any online sources you use. Personal websites may provide inaccurate information. They may be **biased**, or unfairly slanted toward one side. The websites of museums, universities, and well-known encyclopedias are more likely to be reliable.

RESEARCH

Want to learn more about the writer who created the "very, very dreadfully nervous"—and very murderous—narrator in "The Tell-Tale Heart"? Use various sources to research answers to the following questions about Edgar Allan Poe's career.

QUESTION	ANSWER
What was Poe's first published work?	
What different kinds of writing did Poe do?	
What are some of Poe's most famous works?	

Extend Locate one of Poe's famous poems. Practice reading it aloud, using your voice to convey the mood or feeling of the poem. Then get together with a partner and read your poems to each other.

CREATE AND DRAMATIZE

Write a Scene Rewrite a scene from "The Tell-Tale Heart" from the point of view of a reliable narrator.

- ❑ Review the story to find a brief scene. Identify specific details that a reliable narrator would describe differently.
- ❑ Decide whether you will write from the first-person or the third-person point of view.
- ❑ Write the scene from the perspective of your reliable narrator.

Dramatize a Scene Working alone or with one or more partners, act out an especially suspenseful scene from "The Tell-Tale Heart."

- ❑ Review your notes to identify a scene in which Poe uses point of view and other literary devices to create suspense.
- ❑ Decide how many characters your scene needs and who will play them. Write dialogue for each character.
- ❑ Practice your scene. Then perform it for the class.

Go to the **Writing Studio: Writing Narratives** for more on writing a fictional scene.

RESPOND TO THE ESSENTIAL QUESTION

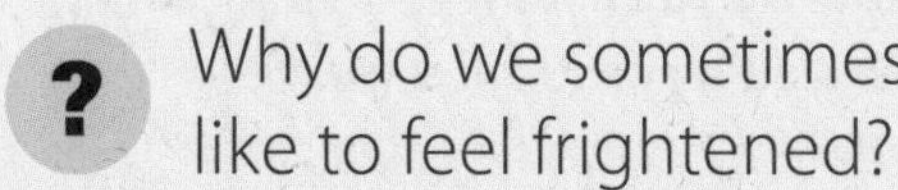

? Why do we sometimes like to feel frightened?

Gather Information Review your annotations and notes on "The Tell-Tale Heart." Then, add relevant details to your Response Log. As you determine which information to include, think about:

- the elements of a classic horror story
- why people might enjoy being spooked by Poe's suspenseful story
- whether Poe's unreliable narrator is like other characters in the unit

At the end of the unit, you can use your notes to help you write a literary analysis.

ACADEMIC VOCABULARY

As you write and discuss what you learned from the story, be sure to use the Academic Vocabulary words. Check off each of the words that you use.

- ❑ **convention**
- ❑ **predict**
- ❑ **psychology**
- ❑ **summary**
- ❑ **technique**

RESPOND

CRITICAL VOCABULARY

WORD BANK
conceive
vex
stifle
crevice
audacity
vehemently
derision
hypocritical

Practice and Apply Use what you know about the Vocabulary words to answer these questions.

1. Would it **vex** you if someone were **hypocritical**? Why?
2. Why does it take **audacity** to **vehemently** deny that you told a lie?
3. What method can you **conceive** to get something out of a **crevice**?
4. What can you do to **stifle derision** of another student?

VOCABULARY STRATEGY: Use a Dictionary

Go to **Using Reference Sources** in the **Vocabulary Studio** for more on using a dictionary.

A **dictionary** is a reference work that provides an alphabetical list of words with their meanings and pronunciations. It also may describe each word's **etymology**, or the history and origin of the word. Some dictionaries are books, while others are electronic or online resources.

Notice the parts of this dictionary entry for the word *wary*.

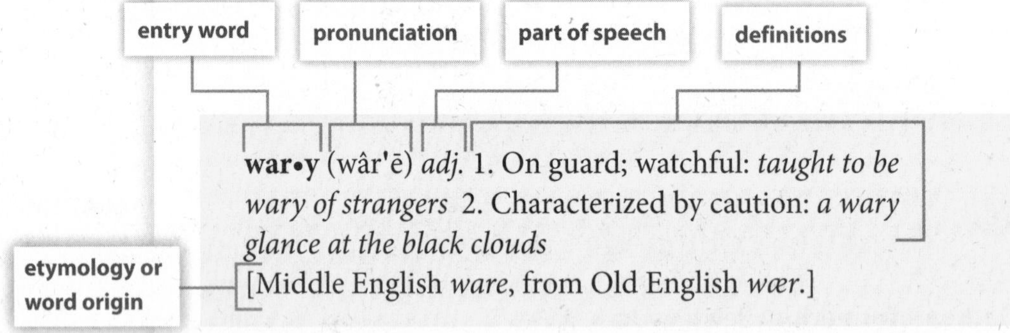

war•y (wâr'ē) *adj.* 1. On guard; watchful: *taught to be wary of strangers* 2. Characterized by caution: *a wary glance at the black clouds* [Middle English *ware*, from Old English *wær*.]

Practice and Apply Use a dictionary to answer these questions about the Academic Vocabulary words for this unit.

1. What are two different meanings for *convention*?
2. What part of speech is *predict*?
3. What definition of *psychology* fits in the sentence *Our track team has a very successful psychology*?
4. What language does *summary* originally come from?
5. Which syllable is stressed when you pronounce the word *technique*?

LANGUAGE CONVENTIONS: Phrases and Clauses

Sentences are built from words, phrases, and clauses. A **phrase** is a group of related words that does not contain a subject and a predicate but functions as a single part of speech. A **clause** is a group of words that contains a subject and a predicate.

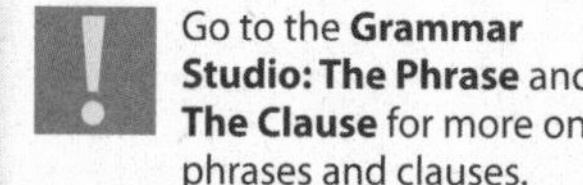

Go to the **Grammar Studio: The Phrase** and **The Clause** for more on phrases and clauses.

Both phrases and clauses can be either restrictive or nonrestrictive. A **restrictive** phrase or clause provides information that is necessary to understand the meaning of the sentence. Here is an example of a restrictive phrase from "The Tell-Tale Heart":

> **And then, when I had made an opening sufficient for my head, I put in a dark lantern, all closed, closed, so that no light shone out, and then I thrust in my head.**

A **nonrestrictive** phrase or clause provides additional information in a sentence whose meaning is already clear. Nonrestrictive phrases and clauses are typically set off from the rest of the sentence with commas. However, Poe often uses dashes instead of commas for dramatic effect, as he does with the following nonrestrictive clause:

> **So I opened it—you cannot imagine how stealthily, stealthily—until, at length, a single dim ray, like the thread of the spider, shot from out the crevice and fell full upon the vulture eye.**

Practice and Apply In each sentence from "The Tell-Tale Heart" below, identify the underlined text as a phrase or a clause and as restrictive or nonrestrictive.

1. I knew that he had been lying awake ever since the first slight noise, when he had turned in the bed.
2. It was open—wide, wide open—and I grew furious as I gazed upon it.
3. There entered three men, who introduced themselves, with perfect suavity, as officers of the police.
4. . . . I myself, in the wild audacity of my perfect triumph, placed my own seat upon the very spot beneath which reposed the corpse of the victim.

THE HOLLOW

Poem by **Kelly Deschler**

? ESSENTIAL QUESTION:

Why do we sometimes like to feel frightened?

QUICK START

The poem you are about to read uses **imagery**, a type of figurative language that draws on sensory details, to describe the sights and sounds of a cold October night. Use the graphic organizer below to write or draw about a time when you quietly observed your surroundings and how it made you feel.

What I Saw or Heard	How It Made Me Feel

MAKE CONNECTIONS

When you relate the content of literature to your own experience and prior knowledge, you **make connections** with what you read. Making connections can help you deepen and enrich your understanding of texts and gain insights into your life and the lives of others.

Many written works contain **allusions**, or references to famous people, places, events, or works of literature. The poem "The Hollow," for example, is inspired by the characters and setting of the short story "The Legend of Sleepy Hollow" by Washington Irving. Read this excerpt from the short story.

> In the dead hush of midnight he could even hear the barking of the watchdog from the opposite shore of the Hudson; but it was so vague and faint as only to give an idea of his distance from this faithful companion of man. Now and then, too, the long-drawn crowing of a cock, accidentally awakened, would sound far, far off, from some farmhouse away in the hills—but it was like a dreaming sound in his ear. No signs of life occurred near him, but occasionally the melancholy chirp of a cricket, or perhaps the guttural twang of a bull-frog from a neighboring marsh, as if sleeping uncomfortably and turning suddenly in his bed.

As you read "The Hollow," make connections between the vivid descriptions in the story and in the poem.

GENRE ELEMENTS: LYRIC POETRY

- usually short to convey emotional intensity
- written using first-person point of view to express the speaker's thoughts and feelings
- often uses repetition and rhyme to create a melodic quality
- includes many forms, such as sonnets, odes, and elegies

GET READY

ANALYZE RHYME SCHEME

"The Hollow" is a **lyric poem**. In a lyric poem, a single speaker expresses his or her personal ideas and feelings. Lyric poetry has a variety of forms and covers many subjects, from love and death to everyday experiences.

The **rhyme scheme** in any type of poetry is the pattern of rhyming words at the end of a poem's lines. You can use letters to identify a poem's rhyme scheme. Write the letter *a* next to the first rhyming line and all the lines that rhyme with it. Then write the letter *b* next to the second rhyming line, and so on. As you read "The Hollow," note the rhyme scheme and consider its impact on readers.

LINES FROM THE POEM

The October night was dark and cold, a
As the autumn sun was going down, b
When I recalled the legends I had been told, a
About this sleepy, little town. b

There were tales about the haunted woods— c

ANNOTATION MODEL

NOTICE & NOTE 

As you read, make notes about connections between the poem and "The Legend of Sleepy Hollow." This model shows one reader's notes about the beginning of "The Hollow."

The October night was dark and cold,
As the autumn sun was going down,
When I recalled the legends I had been told,
About this sleepy, little town.

The poem's title, "The Hollow," and the words legends and sleepy make it clear that the poem is about "The Legend of Sleepy Hollow."

The description of the cold, dark night in the poem reminds me of the "dead hush of midnight" in the story.

BACKGROUND

One of the first short stories in American literature and an early example of the horror genre, "The Legend of Sleepy Hollow" by Washington Irving (1783–1859) has inspired numerous adaptations since it was first published in1819. The setting of Sleepy Hollow in 18th-century New York's Hudson River Valley is described in the story as "one of the quietest places in the whole world," where "a drowsy, dreamy influence seems to hang over the land, and pervade the very atmosphere." Tales of a headless horseman who haunts the community both intrigue and terrify main character Ichabod Crane, who arrives from Connecticut for a short-lived stint as the new village schoolmaster.

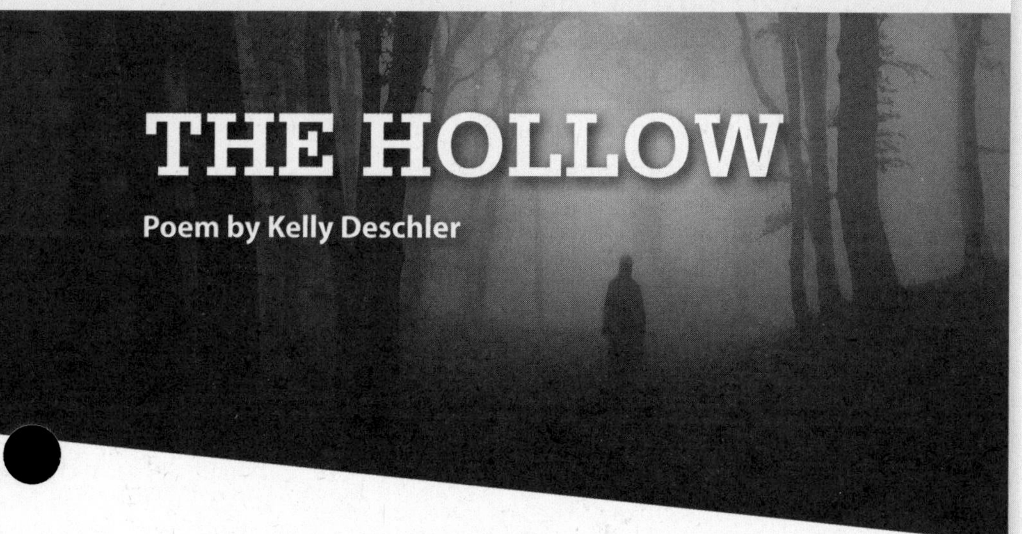

THE HOLLOW

Poem by Kelly Deschler

SETTING A PURPOSE

As you read, make connections between the poem, your own prior knowledge, and what you have learned about "The Legend of Sleepy Hollow" to help you make inferences about the poem's speaker.

The October night was dark and cold,
As the autumn sun was going down,
When I recalled the legends I had been told,
About this sleepy, little town.

There were tales about the haunted woods—
They say the wind seems to call your name.
I was going where no one should,
And if I survived, I'd never be the same.

NOTICE & NOTE

Notice & Note

Use the side margins to notice and note signposts in the text.

MAKE CONNECTIONS

Annotate: In lines 1–12, mark words and phrases that connect to the characters and setting of "The Legend of Sleepy Hollow."

Connect: What can you infer about the poem's speaker based on the details about "The Legend of Sleepy Hollow"?

NOTICE & NOTE

ANALYZE RHYME SCHEME

Annotate: Mark the rhyme scheme of the poem.

Analyze: Read several stanzas, or the whole poem, out loud. How does the regular pattern of rhyme affect you as a reader and as a listener?

MAKE CONNECTIONS

Annotate: Underline what the speaker tells herself.

Describe: When have you ever told yourself something similar? What was your motivation for it?

I walked through the covered bridge,
As the harvest moon rose into the sky.
I had made it around the darkened ridge,
Just as I heard a lone wolf's cry.

I walked the path of the dark, gnarled thicket,
Through the fallen leaves of maple and oak.
I heard the chirping of a cricket,
Near the hollow, where the bullfrogs croak.

Then, I heard the "hoot" of an owl in a tree,
And the "caw" of a raven on its perch.
The headless horseman I hoped not to see,
As I passed the graveyard near the church.

I told myself I would be all right,
Just as I heard the hooves of a horse.
But I knew I would make it home tonight,
Because there are no ghosts, of course.

CHECK YOUR UNDERSTANDING

Answer these questions before moving on to the **Analyze the Text** section on the following page.

1 Which words from the poem add tension to the mood?

A *haunted* and *darkened*

B *autumn* and *harvest*

C *sleepy* and *little*

D *maple* and *oak*

2 The sensory language in lines 1–20 helps the reader understand that the speaker is —

F familiar with the sleepy town

G enjoying a long walk

H alone in the dark

J ready to journey home

3 Lines 21–24 reveal that the speaker —

A enjoys spending time in nature

B will not return home that night

C is uncertain about the future

D rejects beliefs about the haunted woods

RESPOND

ANALYZE THE TEXT

Support your responses with evidence from the text. NOTEBOOK

1. **Infer** Review lines 5–8 and lines 21–24. Based on lines 5–8, what can you infer about the speaker? Do lines 21–24 change your inference, or confirm it? Explain.
2. **Connect** Based on details in the Background note and the poem, how does the speaker of "The Hollow" compare to Ichabod Crane, the main character of "The Legend of Sleepy Hollow"?
3. **Interpret** How does the poem's rhyme scheme affect the **mood,** or the feeling or atmosphere that the poet creates? Cite evidence from the poem to support your interpretation.
4. **Analyze** Trace the poem's shift in mood. Which section of the poem brings a change in mood, and how does the poet accomplish this?
5. **Critique** How do the details about darkness affect the poem's meaning? Use evidence from the poem to support your answer.

RESEARCH TIP
When you research works that have been adapted to many versions, include the full title and author name in your search to locate information about the original version.

RESEARCH

Research "The Legend of Sleepy Hollow" to help you make additional connections between the story and the poem. Use the chart to note details about the story and the connections you make to the poem.

DETAIL	CONNECTION

Extend With your partner, find examples of illustrations of "The Legend of Sleepy Hollow." Share your findings with a small group. Then discuss possible illustrations that might be a good fit for the poem "The Hollow." Support your opinions with details from the poem.

CREATE AND PRESENT

Write a Poem Write a poem inspired by a favorite story, movie, or character.

- ❑ Consider how the poem will relate to the story, movie, or character. List details that the poem will include.
- ❑ Decide on a mood for the poem, such as funny or serious.
- ❑ Choose a structure for your poem. If your poem will use rhyme, decide whether you will use an alternate rhyme scheme (*abab*) as in "The Hollow," couplets (*aa bb*), or another rhyme scheme.

Present a Poem Read aloud a poem you wrote or another poem that you choose.

- ❑ Practice reading the poem aloud. Use appropriate volume and rate.
- ❑ Read your poem aloud to the class. Make eye contact with your audience. Use facial expressions and natural gestures to convey the meaning of the poem.

Go to **Giving a Presentation: Delivering Your Presentation** in the **Speaking and Listening Studio** for help.

RESPOND TO THE ESSENTIAL QUESTION

? Why do we sometimes like to feel frightened?

Gather Information Review your annotations and notes on "The Hollow." Then, add relevant details to your Response Log. As you determine which information to include, think about:

- details in the poem
- connections between the poem and "The Legend of Sleepy Hollow"
- your inferences and response to the poem

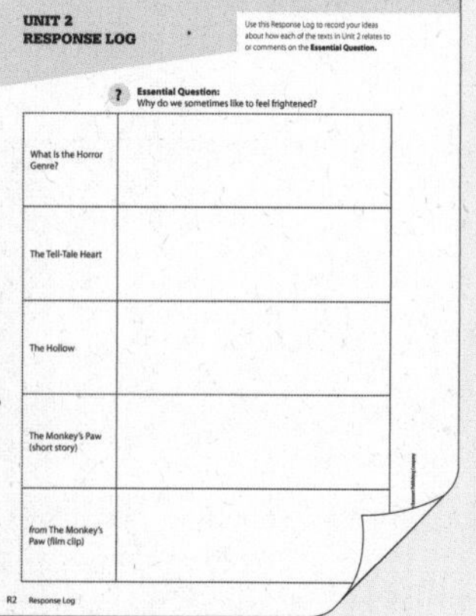

UNIT 2 RESPONSE LOG

Use this Response Log to record your ideas about how each of the texts in Unit 2 relates to or comments on the **Essential Question.**

? **Essential Question:** Why do we sometimes like to feel frightened?

What Is the Horror Genre?	
The Tell-Tale Heart	
The Hollow	
The Monkey's Paw (short story)	
from The Monkey's Paw (film clip)	

R2 Response Log

At the end of the unit, you can use your notes to help you write a literary analysis.

ACADEMIC VOCABULARY

As you write about and discuss your response to the poem, be sure to use the Academic Vocabulary words. Check off each of the words that you use.

- ❑ **convention**
- ❑ **predict**
- ❑ **psychology**
- ❑ **summary**
- ❑ **technique**

SHORT STORY

THE MONKEY'S PAW

by **W. W. Jacobs**

pages 115–127

COMPARE VERSIONS

As you read, notice key details about the story's characters, setting, and plot events. Then, examine how these elements are adapted in a film version of the story's ending. After you read the story and view the film clip, you will collaborate with a small group on a final project.

? ***ESSENTIAL QUESTION:***

Why do we sometimes like to feel frightened?

FILM CLIP

from THE MONKEY'S PAW

by **Ricky Lewis Jr.**

page 135

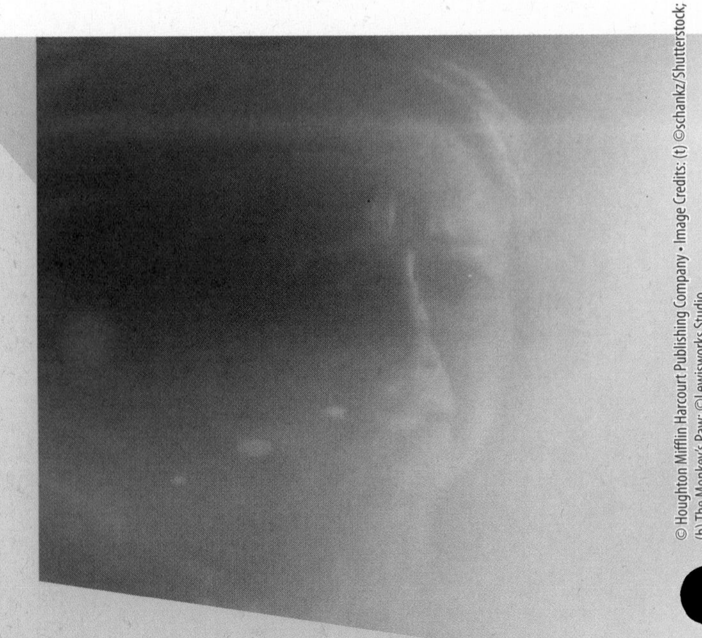

The Monkey's Paw

QUICK START

The story you will read is about a monkey's paw that grants wishes. Write a brief paragraph about something you might want to change, and describe the possible effects of having your wish granted.

ANALYZE THEME

One reason people read literature is to learn how to avoid or understand common problems. Literature conveys lessons through **themes,** the messages about life or human nature that writers share with readers.

- In some stories, the theme is **explicit,** or stated directly in the text.
- In most cases, the theme is **implicit,** or not stated directly. Readers must **infer,** or make an educated guess about, the theme based on clues in the text.
- Clues in the text can include the ways that characters interact with each other. For instance, who treats whom lovingly?
- Clues can also include the events in the text. Do the events benefit the characters or harm them? Do the characters do anything to cause the events?

As you read "The Monkey's Paw," pay attention to details that show how the main characters change, and consider the messages about life or human nature that these changes might suggest.

GENRE ELEMENTS: SHORT STORY

- is a work of fiction
- contains a plot, characters, setting, and theme
- is a popular format for horror stories
- if it is a horror story, often includes supernatural elements

ANALYZE FORESHADOWING

Foreshadowing occurs when a writer provides hints that suggest future events in a story. Writers use this technique to encourage readers to make predictions about what will happen next and to add suspense. Clues about future events may appear in **dialogue** (written conversation between characters), descriptions of events, or **imagery** (descriptive words and phrases that appeal to the senses). Consider how the first example in the chart foreshadows events to come. As you read "The Monkey's Paw," use the chart to note examples of dialogue, events, or imagery that foreshadow what will occur later in the story.

Dialogue	"I did have some idea of selling it, but I don't think I will. It has caused enough mischief already."
Event	
Imagery	

GET READY

CRITICAL VOCABULARY

peril	**grimace**	**credulity**	**compensation**
condole	**fate**	**prosaic**	**resignation**

To see how many Critical Vocabulary words you already know, answer these questions.

1. What **perils** might you face while hiking in the forest?
2. How could you **condole** with a friend who lost a pet?
3. What emotion is expressed by a **grimace**?
4. Why might a person believe that **fate** controls his life?
5. What effect might being lied to have on your **credulity**?
6. Why would you be unlikely to remember a **prosaic** day?
7. What **compensation** do people get for doing their jobs?
8. If you met a request with **resignation,** what might you be feeling?

LANGUAGE CONVENTIONS

Verb Tenses This lesson shows how to use **verb tenses** correctly to indicate the time that an action or condition takes place. "The Monkey's Paw" is narrated in the past tense:

There was another knock, and another. The old woman with a sudden wrench broke free and ran from the room.

As you read, note how the author uses verb tenses consistently. The verb tense should change only when an action or condition happens at a different time.

NOTICE & NOTE

ANNOTATION MODEL

As you read, notice details that establish the setting and the mood. You can also mark up evidence that supports your own ideas. In the model, you can see one reader's notes about "The Monkey's Paw."

1 Without, the night was cold and wet, but in the small parlor of Laburnum Villa the blinds were drawn and the fire burned brightly. Father and son were at chess; the former, who possessed ideas about the game involving radical changes, putting his king into such sharp and unnecessary perils that it even provoked comment from the white-haired old lady knitting placidly by the fire.

The author contrasts the cold, stormy weather outside with the warm, cozy feeling inside.

BACKGROUND

__William Wymark Jacobs__ (1863–1943) grew up in London near the waterfront wharfs. As a boy, Jacobs absorbed the tales of strange, distant lands told by passing sailors. As a young man, Jacobs worked at a bank—a job that he hated—and wrote stories in his spare time. He eventually became a popular writer of humor. Ironically, his best-known work, "The Monkey's Paw," became a classic of the horror genre.

THE MONKEY'S PAW

Short Story by W. W. Jacobs

PREPARE TO COMPARE

As you read, pay attention to the details Sergeant-Major Morris shares about the monkey's paw and the different ways in which the paw affects the members of the White family. This will help you compare the story's ending to a film version of the ending, which you will view after you read the story.

1 Without, the night was cold and wet, but in the small parlor of Laburnum Villa the blinds were drawn and the fire burned brightly. Father and son were at chess; the former, who possessed ideas about the game involving radical changes, putting his king into such sharp and unnecessary **perils** that it even provoked comment from the white-haired old lady knitting placidly by the fire.

2 "Hark at the wind," said Mr. White, who, having seen a fatal mistake after it was too late, was amiably desirous of preventing his son from seeing it.

3 "I'm listening," said the latter, grimly surveying the board as he stretched out his hand. "Check."

Notice & Note

Use the side margins to notice and note signposts in the text.

ANALYZE FORESHADOWING

Annotate: Mark details in paragraph 1 that reveal the father's personality.

Analyze: What might the details about the father hint about future events in the plot?

peril

(pĕr´əl) *n.* A *peril* is something that is dangerous.

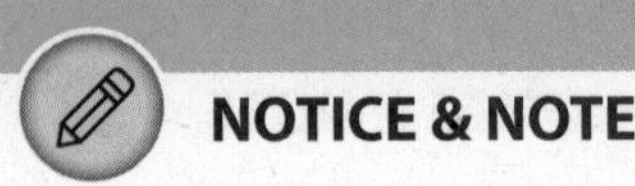

NOTICE & NOTE

4 "I should hardly think that he'd come tonight," said his father, with his hand poised over the board.

5 "Mate," replied the son.

6 "That's the worst of living so far out," bawled Mr. White, with sudden and unlooked-for violence; "of all the beastly, slushy, out-of-the-way places to live in, this is the worst. Pathway's a bog,[1] and the road's a torrent.[2] I don't know what people are thinking about. I suppose because only two houses in the road are let,[3] they think it doesn't matter."

7 "Never mind, dear," said his wife soothingly; "perhaps you'll win the next one."

8 Mr. White looked up sharply, just in time to intercept a knowing glance between mother and son. The words died away on his lips, and he hid a guilty grin in his thin gray beard.

9 "There he is," said Herbert White, as the gate banged loudly and heavy footsteps came toward the door.

condole
(kən-dōl´) *v.* If you *condole* with someone, you express sympathy or sorrow.

10 The old man rose with hospitable haste, and opening the door, was heard **condoling** with the new arrival. The new arrival also condoled with himself, so that Mrs. White said, "Tut, tut!" and coughed gently as her husband entered the room, followed by a tall, burly man, beady of eye and rubicund of visage.[4]

11 "Sergeant-Major Morris," he said, introducing him.

12 The sergeant-major shook hands, and taking the proffered seat by the fire, watched contentedly while his host brought out drinks and stood a small copper kettle on the fire.

ANALYZE FORESHADOWING

Annotate: Mark details in paragraph 13 that tell about Sergeant-Major Morris.

Analyze: How does this information about the Whites' guest help build suspense?

13 He began to talk, the little family circle regarding with eager interest this visitor from distant parts, as he squared his broad shoulders in the chair and spoke of wild scenes and doughty[5] deeds; of wars and plagues and strange peoples.

14 "Twenty-one years of it," said Mr. White, nodding at his wife and son. "When he went away, he was a slip of a youth in the warehouse. Now look at him."

15 "He don't look to have taken much harm," said Mrs. White politely.

16 "I'd like to go to India myself," said the old man, "just to look round a bit, you know."

---

[1] **bog:** a swamp.

[2] **torrent** (tôr´ənt): a swift-flowing stream.

[3] **let:** rented.

[4] **rubicund** (ro͞o´bĭ-kənd) **of visage** (vĭz´ĭj): with a ruddy complexion.

[5] **doughty** (dou´tē): brave.

17 "Better where you are," said the sergeant-major, shaking his head. He put down the empty glass, and sighing softly, shook it again.

18 "I should like to see those old temples and fakirs and jugglers," said the old man. "What was that you started telling me the other day about a monkey's paw or something, Morris?"

19 "Nothing," said the soldier hastily. "Leastways nothing worth hearing."

20 "Monkey's paw?" said Mrs. White curiously.

21 "Well, it's just a bit of what you might call magic, perhaps," said the sergeant-major off-handedly.

22 His three listeners leaned forward eagerly. The visitor absent-mindedly put his empty glass to his lips and then set it down again. His host filled it for him.

23 "To look at," said the sergeant-major, fumbling in his pocket, "it's just an ordinary little paw, dried to a mummy."

24 He took something out of his pocket and proffered it. Mrs. White drew back with a **grimace**, but her son, taking it, examined it curiously.

grimace
(grĭm´ĭs) *n.* A *grimace* is a facial expression of pain or disgust.

25 "And what is there special about it?" inquired Mr. White as he took it from his son, and having examined it, placed it upon the table.

26 "It had a spell put on it by an old fakir," said the sergeant-major, "a very holy man. He wanted to show that **fate** ruled people's lives, and that those who interfered with it did so to their sorrow. He put a spell on it so that three separate men could each have three wishes from it."

fate
(fāt) *n. Fate* is a power that is thought to determine the course of events.

ANALYZE THEME

Annotate: In paragraph 26, underline the lesson that the old fakir wanted to teach people.

Infer: What does this lesson suggest about the story's theme?

27 His manner was so impressive that his hearers were conscious that their light laughter jarred somewhat.

28 "Well, why don't you have three, sir?" said Herbert White cleverly.

29 The soldier regarded him in the way that middle age is wont to regard presumptuous youth. "I have," he said quietly, and his blotchy face whitened.

30 "And did you really have the three wishes granted?" asked Mrs. White.

31 "I did," said the sergeant-major, and his glass tapped against his strong teeth.

32 "And has anybody else wished?" persisted the old lady

33 "The first man had his three wishes. Yes," was the reply; "I don't know what the first two were, but the third was for death. That's how I got the paw."

34 His tones were so grave that a hush fell upon the group.

NOTICE & NOTE

ANALYZE THEME

Annotate: Underline evidence in paragraphs 35–44 that suggests the paw will cause the Whites harm.

Predict: How do you think the paw might affect the main characters' relationships? Cite evidence from the text to support your prediction.

WORDS OF THE WISER

Notice & Note: What words of advice about the paw does Sergeant-Major Morris share with the Whites in paragraph 47?

Infer: How does the sergeant-major's advice suggest a lesson the Whites might learn?

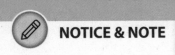

35 "If you've had your three wishes, it's no good to you now, then, Morris," said the old man at last. "What do you keep it for?"

36 The soldier shook his head. "Fancy, I suppose," he said slowly. "I did have some idea of selling it, but I don't think I will. It has caused enough mischief already. Besides, people won't buy. They think it's a fairy tale, some of them; and those who do think anything of it want to try it first and pay me afterward."

37 "If you could have another three wishes," said the old man, eyeing him keenly, "would you have them?"

38 "I don't know," said the other. "I don't know."

39 He took the paw, and dangling it between his forefinger and thumb, suddenly threw it upon the fire. White, with a slight cry, stooped down and snatched it off.

40 "Better let it burn," said the soldier solemnly.

41 "If you don't want it, Morris," said the other, "give it to me."

42 "I won't," said his friend doggedly. "I threw it on the fire. If you keep it, don't blame me for what happens. Pitch it on the fire again like a sensible man."

43 The other shook his head and examined his new possession closely. "How do you do it?" he inquired.

44 "Hold it up in your right hand and wish aloud," said the sergeant-major, "but I warn you of the consequences."

45 "Sounds like the *Arabian Nights*,"[6] said Mrs. White, as she rose and began to set the supper. "Don't you think you might wish for four pairs of hands for me?"

46 Her husband drew the talisman[7] from his pocket, and then all three burst into laughter as the sergeant-major, with a look of alarm on his face, caught him by the arm.

47 "If you must wish," he said gruffly, "wish for something sensible."

48 Mr. White dropped it back in his pocket, and placing chairs, motioned his friend to the table. In the business of supper the talisman was partly forgotten, and afterward the three sat listening in an enthralled fashion to a second installment of the soldier's adventures in India.

49 "If the tale about the monkey's paw is not more truthful than those he has been telling us," said Herbert, as the door closed behind their guest, just in time for him to catch the last train, "we shan't make much out of it."

[6] ***Arabian Nights***: a famous collection of Asian stories.

[7] **talisman** (tăl´ĭs-mən): an object thought to have magical powers.

50 "Did you give him anything for it, Father?" inquired Mrs. White, regarding her husband closely.

51 "A trifle," said he, coloring slightly. "He didn't want it, but I made him take it. And he pressed me again to throw it away."

52 "Likely," said Herbert, with pretended horror. "Why, we're going to be rich, and famous, and happy. Wish to be an emperor, Father, to begin with; then you can't be henpecked."

53 He darted round the table, pursued by the maligned Mrs. White armed with an antimacassar.[8]

54 Mr. White took the paw from his pocket and eyed it dubiously. "I don't know what to wish for, and that's a fact," he said slowly. "It seems to me I've got all I want."

55 "If you only cleared the house, you'd be quite happy, wouldn't you?" said Herbert, with his hand on his shoulder. "Well, wish for two hundred pounds, then; that'll just do it."

56 His father, smiling shamefacedly at his own **credulity,** held up the talisman, as his son, with a solemn face, somewhat marred by a wink at his mother, sat down at the piano and struck a few impressive chords.

credulity
(krĭ-do͞o´lĭ-tē) *n. Credulity* is a tendency to believe too readily.

57 "I wish for two hundred pounds," said the old man distinctly.

58 A fine crash from the piano greeted the words, interrupted by a shuddering cry from the old man. His wife and son ran toward him.

59 "It moved," he cried, with a glance of disgust at the object as it lay on the floor. "As I wished, it twisted in my hand like a snake."

60 "Well, I don't see the money," said his son, as he picked it up and placed it on the table, "and I bet I never shall."

61 "It must have been your fancy, father," said his wife, regarding him anxiously.

ANALYZE THEME

Annotate: Mark details in paragraphs 58–61 that show the main characters' attitudes toward the paw.

Compare: How have the Whites' views of the paw changed? How do you think these changing views relate to the story's theme?

62 He shook his head. "Never mind, though; there's no harm done, but it gave me a shock all the same."

63 They sat down by the fire again. Outside, the wind was higher than ever, and the old man started nervously at the sound of a door banging upstairs. A silence unusual and depressing settled upon all three, which lasted until the old couple rose to retire for the night.

64 "I expect you'll find the cash tied up in a big bag in the middle of your bed," said Herbert, as he bade them goodnight, "and something horrible squatting up on top of the wardrobe watching you as you pocket your ill-gotten gains."

[8] **antimacassar** (ăn´tĭ-mə-kăs´ər): a cloth placed over an arm or the back of a chair.

65 He sat alone in the darkness, gazing at the dying fire, and seeing faces in it. The last face was so horrible and so simian[9] that he gazed at it in amazement. It got so vivid that, with a little uneasy laugh, he felt on the table for a glass containing a little water to throw over it. His hand grasped the monkey's paw, and with a little shiver he wiped his hand on his coat and went up to bed.

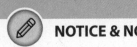

Part II

66 In the brightness of the wintry sun next morning as it streamed over the breakfast table he laughed at his fears. There was an air of **prosaic** wholesomeness about the room which it had lacked on the previous night, and the dirty, shriveled little paw was pitched on the sideboard[10] with a carelessness which betokened no great belief in its virtues.[11]

prosaic
(prō-zā′ĭk) *adj.* If something is *prosaic*, it is dull or ordinary.

67 "I suppose all old soldiers are the same," said Mrs. White. "The idea of our listening to such nonsense! How could wishes be granted in these days? And if they could, how could two hundred pounds hurt you, father?"

68 "Might drop on his head from the sky," said the frivolous[12] Herbert.

69 "Morris said the things happened so naturally," said his father, "that you might if you so wished attribute it to coincidence."

70 "Well, don't break into the money before I come back," said Herbert as he rose from the table. "I'm afraid it'll turn you into a mean, avaricious[13] man, and we shall have to disown you."

71 His mother laughed, and following him to the door, watched him down the road; and returning to the breakfast table, was very happy at the expense of her husband's credulity. All of which did not prevent her from scurrying to the door at the postman's knock, when she found that the post brought a tailor's bill.

72 "Herbert will have some more of his funny remarks, I expect, when he comes home," she said, as they sat at dinner.

73 "I dare say," said Mr. White, "but for all that, the thing moved in my hand; that I'll swear to."

74 "You thought it did," said the old lady soothingly.

[9] **simian** (sĭm′ē-ən): monkey- or ape-like.
[10] **sideboard:** a piece of furniture used to store linens and dishes.
[11] **virtues:** powers.
[12] **frivolous** (frĭv′ə-ləs): inappropriately silly.
[13] **avaricious** (ăv′ə-rĭsh′əs): greedy.

75 "I say it did," replied the other. "There was no thought about it; I had just—What's the matter?"

76 His wife made no reply. She was watching the mysterious movements of a man outside, who, peering in an undecided fashion at the house, appeared to be trying to make up his mind to enter. In mental connection with the two hundred pounds, she noticed that the stranger was well dressed, and wore a silk hat of glossy newness. Three times he paused at the gate, and then walked on again. The fourth time he stood with his hand upon it, and then with sudden resolution flung it open and walked up the path. Mrs. White at the same moment placed her hands behind her, and hurriedly unfastening the strings of her apron, put that useful article of apparel beneath the cushion of her chair.

77 She brought the stranger, who seemed ill at ease, into the room. He gazed at her furtively, and listened in a preoccupied fashion as the old lady apologized for the appearance of the room, and her husband's coat, a garment which he usually reserved for the garden. She then waited patiently for him to broach his business, but he was at first strangely silent.

78 "I—was asked to call," he said at last, and stooped and picked a piece of cotton from his trousers. "I come from Maw and Meggins."

79 The old lady started. "Is anything the matter?" she asked breathlessly. "Has anything happened to Herbert? What is it? What is it?"

80 Her husband interposed. "There, there, mother," he said hastily. "Sit down, and don't jump to conclusions. You've not brought bad news, I'm sure, sir;" and he eyed the other wistfully.

81 "I'm sorry—" began the visitor.

82 "Is he hurt?" demanded the mother wildly.

83 The visitor bowed in assent. "Badly hurt," he said quietly, "but he is not in any pain."

84 "Oh!" said the old woman, clasping her hands. "Thank goodness for that! Thank—"

85 She broke off suddenly as the sinister meaning of the assurance dawned upon her and she saw the awful confirmation of her fears in the other's averted face. She caught her breath, and turning to her slower-witted husband, laid her trembling old hand upon his. There was a long silence.

NOTICE & NOTE

ANALYZE FORESHADOWING

Annotate: Mark details in paragraph 76 that describe the man outside.

Infer: What are some possible causes of the man's behavior? How does this example of foreshadowing propel the story's action?

AHA MOMENT

Notice & Note: What "sinister meaning of the assurance" does Mrs. White realize?

Draw Conclusions: What might this realization cause the Whites to believe?

86 "He was caught in the machinery," said the visitor at length in a low voice.

87 "Caught in the machinery," repeated Mr. White, in a dazed fashion, "yes."

88 He sat staring blankly out at the window, and taking his wife's hand between his own, pressed it as he had been wont to do in their old courting days nearly forty years before.

89 "He was the only one left to us," he said, turning gently to the visitor. "It is hard."

90 The other coughed, and rising, walked slowly to the window. "The firm wished me to convey their sincere sympathy with you in your great loss," he said, without looking round. "I beg that you will understand I am only their servant and merely obeying orders."

91 There was no reply; the old woman's face was white, her eyes staring, and her breath inaudible; on the husband's face was a look such as his friend the sergeant might have carried into his first action.

92 "I was to say that Maw and Meggins disclaim all responsibility," continued the other. "They admit no liability at all, but in consideration of your son's services, they wish to present you with a certain sum as **compensation**."

compensation
(kŏm´pən-sā´shən) *n.* *Compensation* is something, such as money, that is received as payment.

93 Mr. White dropped his wife's hand, and rising to his feet, gazed with a look of horror at his visitor. His dry lips shaped the words, "How much?"

94 "Two hundred pounds," was the answer.

95 Unconscious of his wife's shriek, the old man smiled faintly, put out his hands like a sightless man, and dropped, a senseless heap, to the floor.

Part III

96 In the huge new cemetery, some two miles distant, the old people buried their dead, and came back to a house steeped in shadow and silence. It was all over so quickly that at first they could hardly realize it, and remained in a state of expectation as though of something else to happen— something else which was to lighten this load, too heavy for old hearts to bear.

97 But the days passed, and expectation gave place to **resignation**—the hopeless resignation of the old, sometimes miscalled apathy. Sometimes they hardly exchanged a word, for now they had nothing to talk about, and their days were long to weariness.

resignation

(rĕz´ĭg-nā´shən) *n. Resignation* is the acceptance of something that is inescapable.

98 It was about a week after that the old man, waking suddenly in the night, stretched out his hand and found himself alone. The room was in darkness, and the sound of subdued weeping came from the window. He raised himself in bed and listened.

ANALYZE FORESHADOWING

Annotate: Mark details in paragraphs 96–100 that describe the Whites' feelings following their son's burial.

Evaluate: Why do you think the author includes this description? Cite evidence to support your ideas.

99 "Come back," he said tenderly. "You will be cold."

100 "It is colder for my son," said the old woman, and wept afresh.

101 The sound of her sobs died away on his ears. The bed was warm, and his eyes heavy with sleep. He dozed fitfully, and then slept until a sudden wild cry from his wife awoke him with a start.

102 "*The paw!*" she cried wildly. "The monkey's paw!"

103 He started up in alarm. "Where? Where is it? What's the matter?"

NOTICE & NOTE

104 She came stumbling across the room toward him. "I want it," she said quietly. "You've not destroyed it?"

105 "It's in the parlor, on the bracket," he replied, marveling. "Why?"

106 She cried and laughed together, and bending over, kissed his cheek.

107 "I only just thought of it," she said hysterically. "Why didn't I think of it before? Why didn't *you* think of it?"

108 "Think of what?" he questioned.

109 "The other two wishes," she replied rapidly. "We've only had one."

AHA MOMENT

Notice & Note: What sudden realization causes Mrs. White to become excited in paragraphs 101–111?

Predict: What do you think will happen if Mr. White carries out his wife's orders?

110 "Was not that enough?" he demanded fiercely.

111 "No," she cried triumphantly; "we'll have one more. Go down and get it quickly, and wish our boy alive again."

112 The man sat up in bed and flung the bedclothes from his quaking limbs. "You are mad!" he cried, aghast.

113 "Get it," she panted; "get it quickly, and wish—Oh, my boy, my boy!"

114 Her husband struck a match and lit the candle. "Get back to bed," he said unsteadily. "You don't know what you are saying."

115 "We had the first wish granted," said the old woman feverishly; "why not the second?"

116 "A coincidence," stammered the old man.

117 "Go and get it and wish," cried his wife, quivering with excitement.

118 He went down in the darkness, and felt his way to the parlor, and then to the mantelpiece. The talisman was in its place, and a horrible fear that the unspoken wish might bring his mutilated son before him ere he could escape from the room seized upon him, and he caught his breath as he found that he had lost the direction of the door. His brow cold with sweat, he felt his way round the table, and groped along the wall until he found himself in the small passage with the unwholesome thing in his hand.

119 Even his wife's face seemed changed as he entered the room. It was white and expectant, and to his fears seemed to have an unnatural look upon it. He was afraid of her.

LANGUAGE CONVENTIONS

As in many stories, the events in this story are narrated in the past tense, while the dialogue spoken by the characters is in the present tense. Why does putting dialogue in the present tense make sense?

120 "*Wish!*" she cried, in a strong voice.

121 "It is foolish and wicked," he faltered.

122 "*Wish!*" repeated his wife.

123 He raised his hand. "I wish my son alive again."

124 The talisman fell to the floor, and he regarded it fearfully. Then he sank trembling into a chair as the old woman, with burning eyes, walked to the window and raised the blind.

NOTICE & NOTE 

125 He sat until he was chilled with the cold, glancing occasionally at the figure of the old woman peering through the window. The candle-end, which had burned below the rim of the china candlestick, was throwing pulsating shadows on the ceiling and walls, until, with a flicker larger than the rest, it expired. The old man, with an unspeakable sense of relief at the failure of the talisman, crept back to his bed, and a minute or two afterward the old woman came silently and apathetically beside him.

126 Neither spoke, but lay silently listening to the ticking of the clock. A stair creaked, and a squeaky mouse scurried noisily through the wall. The darkness was oppressive, and after lying

for some time gathering up his courage, he took the box of matches, and striking one, went downstairs for a candle.

127 At the foot of the stairs the match went out, and he paused to strike another; and at the same moment a knock, so quiet and stealthy as to be scarcely audible, sounded on the front door.

128 The matches fell from his hand. He stood motionless, his breath suspended until the knock was repeated. Then he turned and fled swiftly back to his room, and closed the door behind him. A third knock sounded through the house.

129 "*What's that?*" cried the old woman, starting up.

130 "A rat," said the old man in shaking tones—"a rat. It passed me on the stairs."

131 His wife sat up in bed listening. A loud knock resounded through the house.

132 "It's Herbert!" she screamed. "It's Herbert!"

133 She ran to the door, but her husband was before her, and catching her by the arm, held her tightly.

ANALYZE THEME

Annotate: In paragraphs 134–138, circle Mr. White's dialogue and underline Mrs. White's.

Infer: What lesson, if any, might each character have learned?

134 "What are you going to do?" he whispered hoarsely.

135 "It's my boy; it's Herbert!" she cried, struggling mechanically. "I forgot it was two miles away. What are you holding me for? Let go. I must open the door."

136 "Don't let it in," cried the old man, trembling.

137 "You're afraid of your own son," she cried, struggling.

138 "Let me go. I'm coming, Herbert; I'm coming."

139 There was another knock, and another. The old woman with a sudden wrench broke free and ran from the room. Her husband followed to the landing, and called after her appealingly as she hurried downstairs. He heard the chain rattle back and the bottom bolt drawn slowly and stiffly from the socket. Then the old woman's voice, strained and panting.

140 "The bolt," she cried loudly. "Come down. I can't reach it."

141 But her husband was on his hands and knees groping wildly on the floor in search of the paw. If he could only find it before the thing outside got in. A perfect fusillade[14] of knocks reverberated through the house, and he heard the scraping of a chair as his wife put it down in the passage against the door. He heard the creaking of the bolt as it came slowly back, and at the same moment he found the monkey's paw, and frantically breathed his third and last wish.

[14] **fusillade** (fyo͞o′sə-läd′): discharge from many guns; a rapid outburst.

142 The knocking ceased suddenly, although the echoes of it were still in the house. He heard the chair drawn back, and the door opened. A cold wind rushed up the staircase, and a long loud wail of disappointment and misery from his wife gave him courage to run down to her side, and then to the gate beyond. The streetlamp flickering opposite shone on a quiet and deserted road.

CHECK YOUR UNDERSTANDING

Answer these questions before moving on to the **Analyze the Text** section on the following page.

1 Mr. White first shows fear of the paw because it —

A makes his friend anxious

B scratches the mantelpiece

C moves in his hand

D has had a spell put on it

2 The dialogue in paragraphs 67–68 indicates that Mrs. White and Herbert are —

F disagreeing about the possible results of their wish

G mocking the idea that the paw is magic

H happy that they wished for something sensible

J nervous about the harm that the paw might cause

3 Based on Mr. White's reaction to the knock on the door in paragraphs 130–136, the reader can conclude that he —

A wants his wife to go downstairs

B realizes he ought to make a third wish

C hopes it will stop if he ignores it

D thinks it is a rat trying to get into his room

RESPOND

ANALYZE THE TEXT

Support your responses with evidence from the text. NOTEBOOK

1. **Analyze** Review paragraphs 1–6. What details about the setting seem to foreshadow later events?

2. **Draw Conclusions** Reread paragraphs 45–49. Identify the allusion, or reference to a well-known work, that Mrs. White makes. What does the allusion suggest about Mrs. White's view of the paw?

3. **Compare** What do the actions of Mr. and Mrs. White at the end of the story reveal about their different expectations for wishes made on the monkey's paw? Identify what hopes or fears these expectations reveal.

4. **Analyze** What **theme** is suggested by "The Monkey's Paw"? Provide examples that show how the author develops the theme through the characters and plot.

5. **Notice & Note** Review paragraphs 92–95. What do the Whites realize about the two hundred pounds they will receive "as compensation"?

RESEARCH TIP

When you conduct online research, be sure to evaluate the **credibility,** or trustworthiness, of websites. Credible sites are known for not omitting crucial information and for guarding against bias, or preference toward a certain view. Web addresses ending in *.gov, .edu,* or *.org* may have more reliable information than other sites. British government and nonprofit Web addresses often end in *.gov.uk* or *.org.uk,* while academic domains use the ending *.ac.uk.*

RESEARCH

Review paragraphs 13–18. What ideas and attitudes about India are expressed here? Do research to learn more about the historical relationship between Britain and India. Record what you learn in the chart.

QUESTION	ANSWER
What was the British East India Company?	
How did Britain come to rule India?	
What attitudes did Indians and the British have toward one another during British rule?	

Connect With a small group, discuss the ways in which the attitudes in the story reflect the historical context.

CREATE AND DISCUSS

Personal Response Write a personal response to each of the three sections of "The Monkey's Paw." Then write a paragraph that reflects on your responses and connections to the text.

- ❑ Review your annotations and notes about Parts I–III of the story. Write a one-paragraph response to each of the three sections. Cite evidence from the text to support your reactions.
- ❑ Review your responses. Note similarities and differences between your reactions to each section.
- ❑ Write a paragraph that describes how your reactions changed over the course of the story.

Share and Discuss Ideas Are you familiar with the fairy tales "The Three Little Pigs," "Three Billy Goats Gruff," and "The Three Wishes"? These tales and many other traditional stories are structured around three important events or characters. Discuss connections between "The Monkey's Paw" and other familiar stories that follow this "rule of three" pattern.

- ❑ Identify how the "rule of three" structure is used in "The Monkey's Paw" and two other stories with which you are familiar. Note your ideas about the similarities and differences between the stories.
- ❑ Share and discuss your ideas with your group. Ask clarifying questions to make sure you understand others' views.
- ❑ Conclude your discussion by summarizing the main points that were raised and reflecting on new understandings.

Go to **Participating in Collaborative Discussions** in the **Speaking and Listening Studio** to learn more.

RESPOND TO THE ESSENTIAL QUESTION

? Why do we sometimes like to feel frightened?

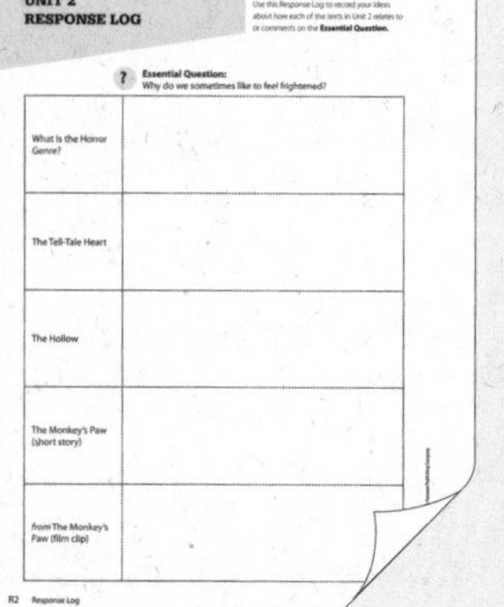

UNIT 2 RESPONSE LOG

Use this Response Log to record your ideas about how each of the texts in Unit 2 relates to or comments on the **Essential Question.**

? **Essential Question:** Why do we sometimes like to feel frightened?

What Is the Horror Genre?	
The Tell-Tale Heart	
The Hollow	
The Monkey's Paw (short story)	
from The Monkey's Paw (film clip)	

R2 Response Log

Gather Information Review your annotations and notes on "The Monkey's Paw." Then, add relevant details to your Response Log. As you determine which information to include, think about:

- the structure of the plot
- supernatural elements of the story
- ways in which the author builds suspense

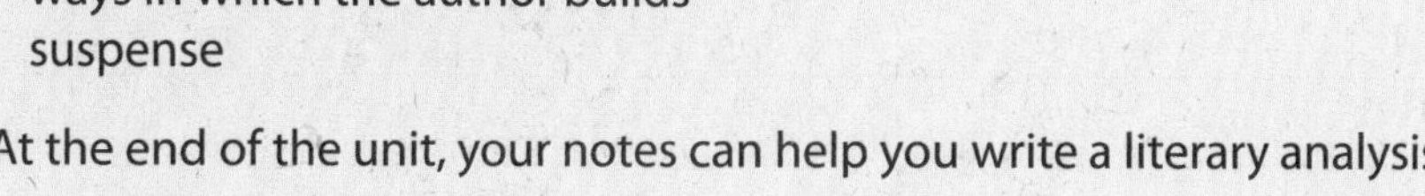

At the end of the unit, your notes can help you write a literary analysis.

ACADEMIC VOCABULARY

As you write and discuss what you learned from the story, be sure to use the Academic Vocabulary words. Check off each of the words that you use.

- ❑ **convention**
- ❑ **predict**
- ❑ **psychology**
- ❑ **summary**
- ❑ **technique**

RESPOND

WORD BANK

peril	**credulity**
condole	**prosaic**
grimace	**compensation**
fate	**resignation**

Go to **Common Roots, Prefixes, and Suffixes** in the **Vocabulary Studio** to learn more about Latin roots.

CRITICAL VOCABULARY

Practice and Apply Explain what is alike and different about the meanings of the words in each pair.

1. peril/risk
2. grimace/frown
3. compensation/wages
4. fate/outcome
5. credulity/trust
6. resignation/acceptance
7. condole/courage
8. prosaic/dull

VOCABULARY STRATEGY: Latin Roots

A **word root** is a word part that contains the core meaning of a word. A root is combined with other word parts, such as a prefix or a suffix, to form a word. The roots of many English words come from Latin. Read this sentence from "The Monkey's Paw."

His mother laughed, and following him to the door, watched him down the road; and returning to the breakfast table, was very happy at the expense of her husband's credulity.

The word *credulity* includes the Latin root *cred*, which means "believe" or "trust." You can use the meaning of the root *cred* to figure out that *credulity* means "a disposition to believe too readily."

Practice and Apply Find the word in each sentence that includes the Latin root *cred*. Use context and the meaning of the root to help you write the definition of the word. Then verify each of your definitions by finding the word's precise meaning in a print or digital dictionary.

1. Herbert was incredulous when he heard the sergeant-major's tale.

   ____

2. A person must have the proper credentials to enter a foreign country.

   ____

3. Mrs. White didn't give any credence to the notion that the monkey's paw moved.

   ____

4. Were the sergeant-major's stories about India credible?

   ____

5. One witness may discredit the story that another person tells.

   ____

LANGUAGE CONVENTIONS: Verb Tenses

Correct verb tenses tell the reader when an action happened—in the past, present, or future. As you write, it's important to use the same tense between sentences and across paragraphs to describe actions that take place at the same time and to change tenses when shifting from one time period to another. In general, use the present tense when writing about the action in a story, movie, or book—unless you are describing events that happened before the start of the main action. To describe events that preceded the main action in a story, movie, or book, use the past tense.

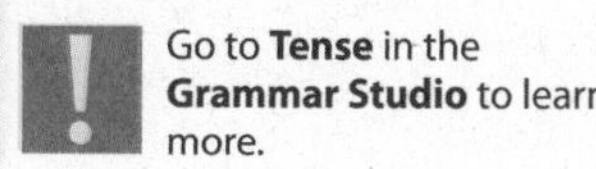
Go to **Tense** in the **Grammar Studio** to learn more.

ORIGINAL	REVISED
Last night I watch a movie about a sea monster that terrorized the people of a small fishing village. In one scene, the monster jumps up and surprised a fisherman. When this happened, I jump up too and spill all of my popcorn. (*The first sentence uses the present tense to describe a past event but uses the past tense to describe the action in a movie. The second and third sentences use the present and past tenses inconsistently.*)	Last night I watched a movie about a sea monster that terrorizes the people of a small fishing village. In one scene, the monster jumps up and surprises a fisherman. When this happened, I jumped up too and spilled all of my popcorn. (*The first sentence uses the present tense to describe the action in the movie but uses the past tense to describe an event that occurred in the past. The second sentence uses the present tense to describe the action of the movie. The third sentence uses the past tense to describe the viewer's reaction.*)

Practice and Apply Read the following paragraph. For each choice in parentheses, choose the verb with the correct tense.

> The short story "The Monkey's Paw" by W. W. Jacobs (was, is) set in the English countryside during the late 19th century. At the beginning of the story, Sergeant-Major Morris, a friend of the White family who recently (returned, returns) from India, (arrived, arrives) at the White home for a visit. Morris tells the Whites about a magical monkey's paw that he (obtained, obtains) on his travels. After explaining how the paw (brought, brings) misfortune on himself and another man who (used, uses) it, he reluctantly (gave, gives) the paw to the Whites.

Write a one-paragraph review of "The Monkey's Paw." Tell how the story begins, whether you recommend it, and how you think others will react to it. Then edit your paragraph for appropriate use of verb tenses.

FILM CLIP

from THE MONKEY'S PAW

by **Ricky Lewis Jr.**

page 135

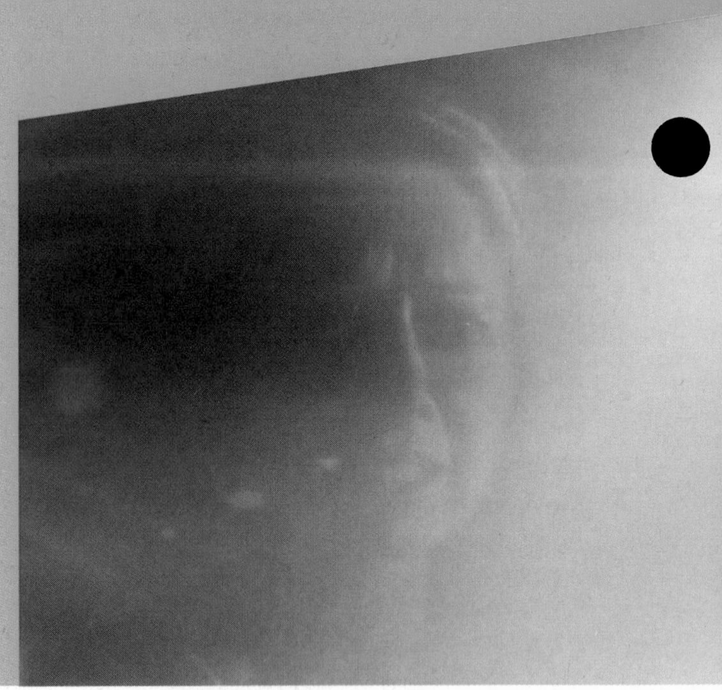

COMPARE VERSIONS

Now that you've read "The Monkey's Paw," view the film clip based on the short story's ending. As you do, think about similarities and differences between the short story and the film adaptation. After you are finished, you will collaborate with a small group on a final project that involves an analysis of both works.

? *ESSENTIAL QUESTION:*

Why do we sometimes like to feel frightened?

SHORT STORY

THE MONKEY'S PAW

by **W. W. Jacobs**

pages 115–127

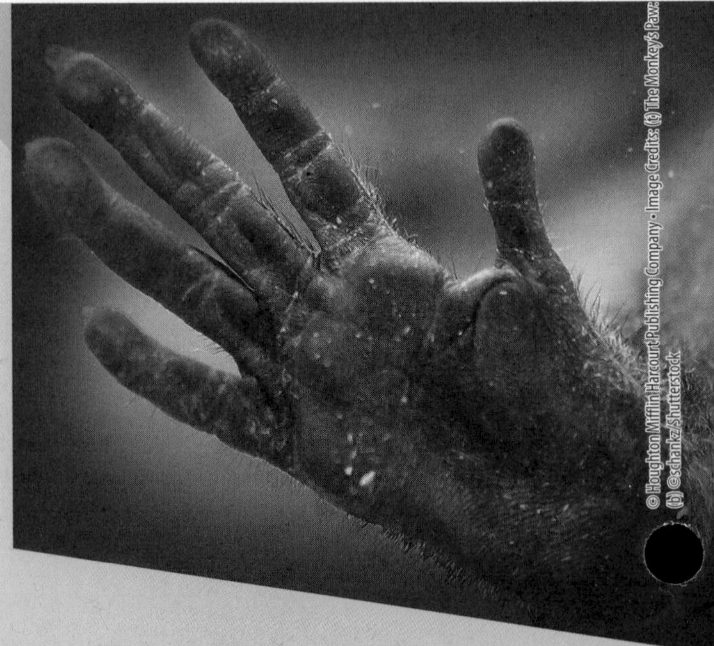

from The Monkey's Paw

QUICK START

Think back to a suspenseful scene in a movie. How did you feel as you watched the scene? With a partner, describe the scene and your reaction to it.

ANALYZE FILM

Like many movies, the film *The Monkey's Paw* is based on a written work. Writers and directors use different techniques to create suspense and tell a story.

- Writers use words to describe the rising action or the characters' struggles.
- Directors use a combination of visual and sound techniques.

Directors may use different camera shots to convey ideas, to track characters' emotions, or to show a situation from a character's viewpoint.

GENRE ELEMENTS: FILM

- combines images and sound to tell a story or convey information
- uses visual and sound techniques such as camera shots, lighting, music, and sound effects
- often includes actors who play the roles of characters

CAMERA SHOT	WHAT IT IS	WHY IT IS USED
Close-up shot	a shot that focuses on a character's face	to convey a character's emotions or thoughts
Low-angle shot	a shot in which the camera looks up at a subject	to create the impression of height or distance; to make a subject look more menacing
High-angle shot	a shot in which the camera looks down at a subject	to show a character in relation to his or her surroundings; to make a subject look unprotected or exposed
Point-of-view shot	a shot that is filmed from the character's point of view	to show viewers what the character is seeing

ANALYZE FILM *(continued)*

Directors may also use other visual and sound techniques to convey mood, to build suspense, and to focus viewers' attention on characters and events.

- **Lighting** can create moods that are gloomy, mysterious, or scary. Suspenseful movies often have minimal lighting with frequent use of shadows.
- **Camera filters** are glass or plastic dishes that are inserted in front of a camera lens. These filters can change the way images appear, making them clearer, brighter, darker, or fuzzier.
- **Sound effects** may include action noises or nature sounds. The sound of a loud bang or heavy rain, for example, might contribute to a threatening or dreary mood.
- **Music** can signal dramatic events or tense moments. Music sometimes foreshadows, or hints at, what is going to happen.

As you view the film clip, use a chart like this to help you analyze the different film techniques the director uses.

TECHNIQUE	PART IN THE FILM	EFFECT
1.		
2.		
3.		
4.		

When a director makes a movie of a written story, he or she has to make choices about how closely to follow the written work. Will the film

- include all of the same characters?
- have the same setting?
- add or cut a scene?

As you view the film clip, think about how the director's choices affect the content of the film version of "The Monkey's Paw."

BACKGROUND

The film The Monkey's Paw *is an adaptation of the short story of the same name. The film's writer and director, Ricky Lewis Jr., read the story as a child. He decided to make it into a movie because his "morbid curiosity wanted to see it." While other film adaptations of the story had modernized it, Lewis thought it was important that the film be set in the past, "when odd things were sure to happen." He chose to "let a little darkness" into his film to create its gloomy, sometimes spooky mood.*

PREPARE TO COMPARE

As you view the film clip, note important details about each scene. This will help you identify similarities and differences between the short story and the film adaptation. **NOTEBOOK**

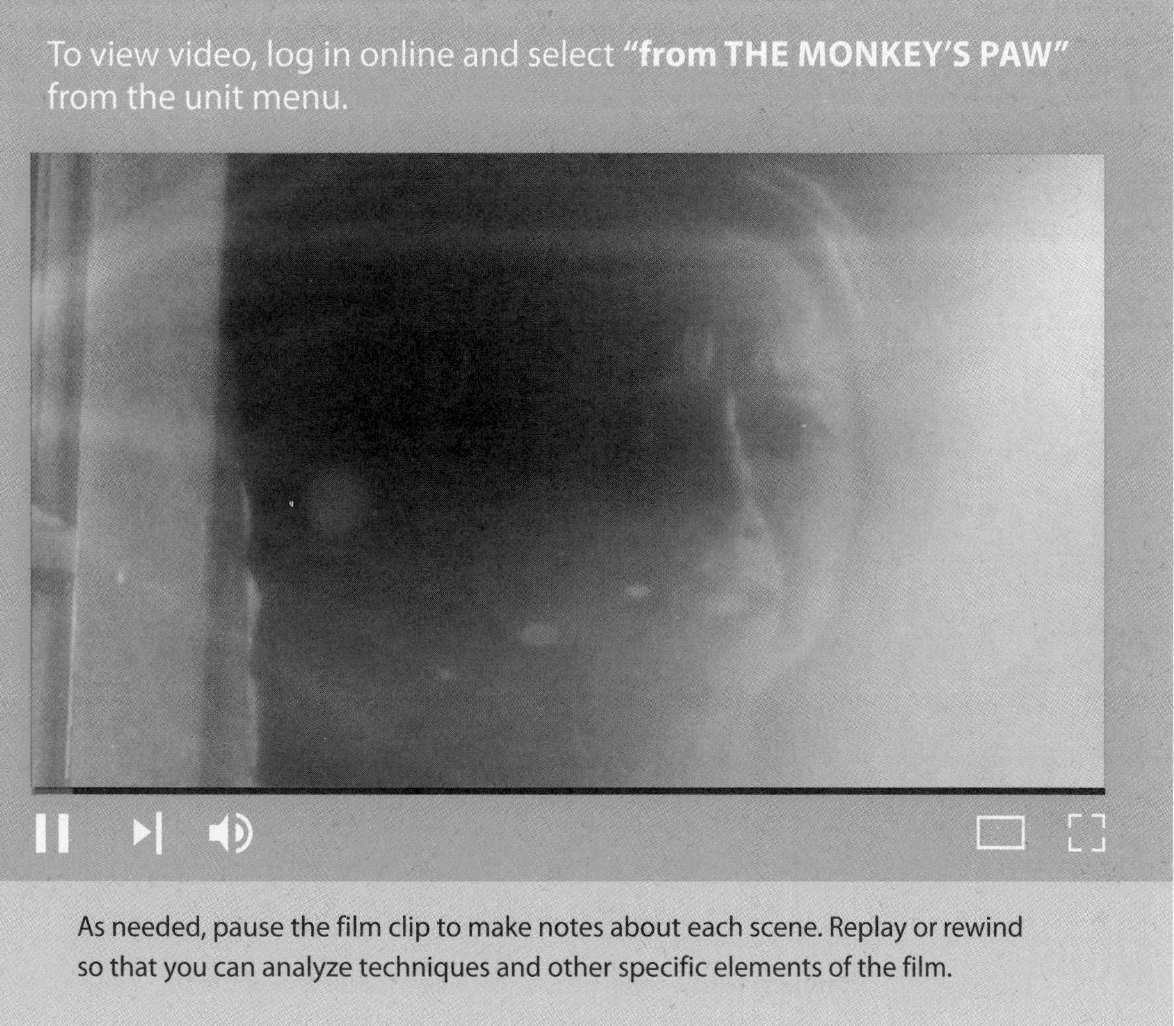

To view video, log in online and select **"from THE MONKEY'S PAW"** from the unit menu.

As needed, pause the film clip to make notes about each scene. Replay or rewind so that you can analyze techniques and other specific elements of the film.

ANALYZE MEDIA

Support your responses with evidence from the film clip. NOTEBOOK

1. **Summarize** The film clip shows several scenes from the short story "The Monkey's Paw." Summarize the events shown and described in the film.
2. **Analyze** Consider the ways the director uses lighting in the film. What is the effect of the lighting in the scene in which Herbert returns to the house?
3. **Interpret** Why do you think the music changes as Mr. White makes his second and third wishes?
4. **Analyze** How do the camera angles and camera filters that the director uses affect the mood of the film? How do they affect the impact of the final scenes at the cemetery?
5. **Compare** Identify two ways in which the director uses sound effects in the film. In what ways do these effects impact the mood?

RESEARCH TIP

As you begin research, you can start with a general search and use the results to help you narrow your search. For example, you might start with the search terms *filming techniques* or *cinematography*; the results of these searches might lead you to focus your search on particular lighting or camera movement techniques.

RESEARCH

On pages 133–134, you learned about various film techniques that film directors use to achieve particular effects. Research additional filming techniques to learn more. Record your findings in the chart.

TECHNIQUE	WHAT IT IS

Connect With a small group, discuss whether any of the techniques you researched appeared in the film clip. Then discuss effective examples of the techniques in other films. If possible, practice some of the techniques yourself.

CREATE AND DISCUSS

Discuss Ideas Have a group discussion about adapting a scene in "The Monkey's Paw" to create a film version.

- ❑ Review the story and the film clip. Think about the techniques the film director uses in the adaptation of the story's ending.
- ❑ Share your ideas about which scene you would choose to adapt to create a film version and why. Cite details from the story and the film clip to support your ideas.
- ❑ As a group, discuss whether you think a film adaptation should stay true to the text or vary. Support your reasoning with examples.

Create a Storyboard With your group, create a storyboard for a film retelling of a scene from "The Monkey's Paw." A **storyboard** is a device filmmakers use to plan the shooting of a movie. It serves as a map that includes images and descriptions.

- ❑ Discuss whether you will stay faithful to the text or make changes. Take a vote to determine your path.
- ❑ Draw a series of several frames. Sketch the characters and scene for each frame.
- ❑ Underneath each frame, write a description of the shot—such as close-up, medium, or distance shot—and write a line of dialogue or a description of the action.
- ❑ Decide what kind of music or sound effects you will add, and write where you'll include them.

Go to the **Speaking and Listening Studio** for help with having a group discussion.

RESPOND TO THE ESSENTIAL QUESTION

? Why do we sometimes like to feel frightened?

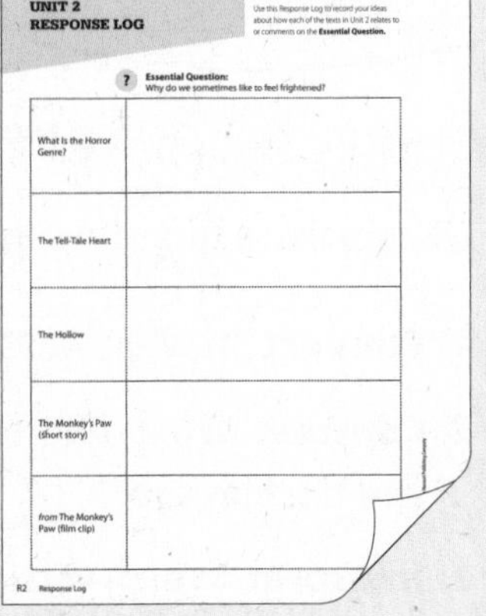

UNIT 2 RESPONSE LOG

Use this Response Log to record your ideas about how each of the texts in Unit 2 relates to or comments on the **Essential Question.**

? **Essential Question:** Why do we sometimes like to feel frightened?

What Is the Horror Genre?	
The Tell-Tale Heart	
The Hollow	
The Monkey's Paw (short story)	
from The Monkey's Paw (film clip)	

R2 Response Log

Gather Information Review your annotations and notes on the film clip. Then, add relevant details to your Response Log. As you determine which information to include, think about:

- ways in which visual and sound techniques affect the mood of the film
- aspects of the film that elicit a strong reaction

At the end of the unit, you can use your notes to help you write a literary analysis.

ACADEMIC VOCABULARY

As you write and discuss what you learned from the film clip, be sure to use the Academic Vocabulary words. Check off each of the words that you use.

- ❑ **convention**
- ❑ **predict**
- ❑ **psychology**
- ❑ **summary**
- ❑ **technique**

Collaborate & Compare

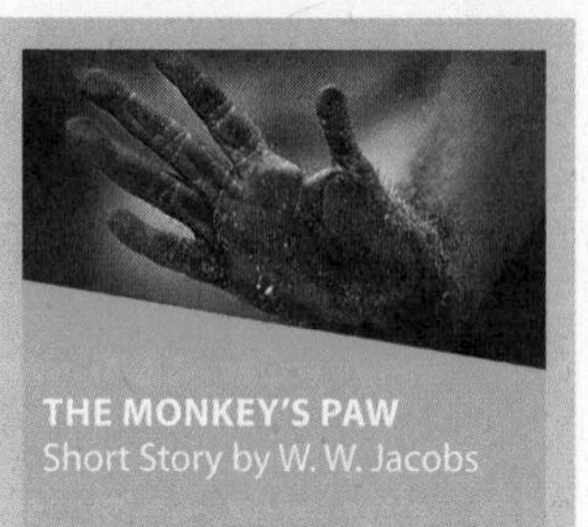

THE MONKEY'S PAW
Short Story by W. W. Jacobs

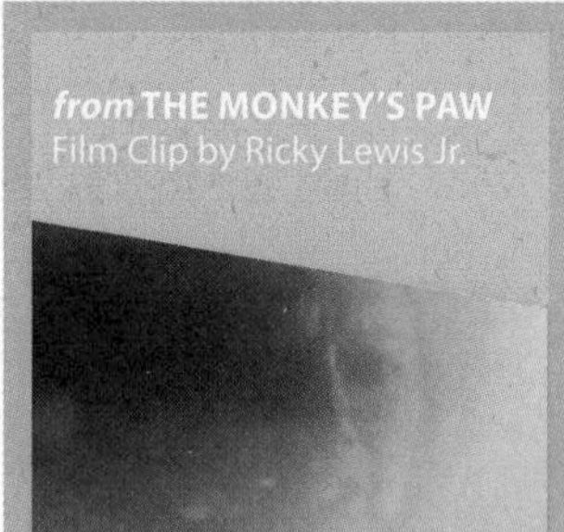

COMPARE VERSIONS

While authors use language to tell stories, film directors rely on visual and sound techniques to help bring stories to life. When directors decide to make a movie based on a written story or novel, they make choices about what to include and what to omit. For example, they might cut a scene that's hard to portray visually or isn't necessary to move the plot forward. Or they might add a scene to help show what a character is experiencing. In a small group, complete the Venn diagram with similarities and differences between the story's ending and the film clip. Then write a response summarizing your findings.

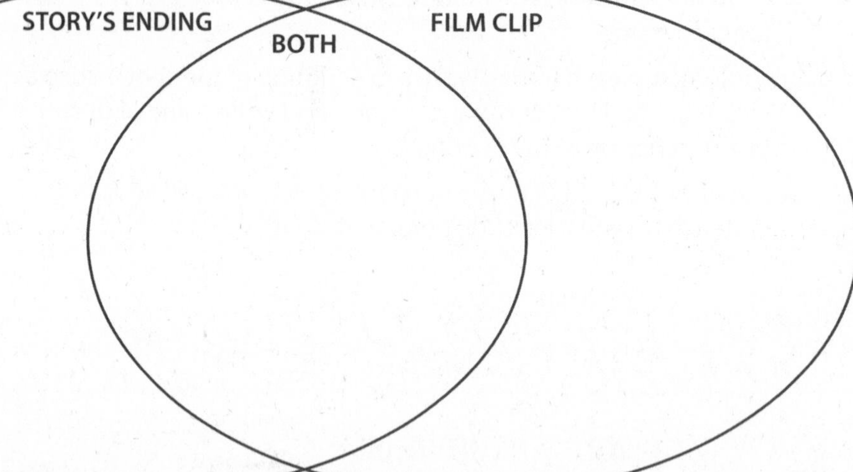

ANALYZE THE TEXT AND FILM CLIP

Discuss these questions in your group.

1. **Connect** In what ways does the film clip stay true to the story?
2. **Contrast** What differences are there between the story's ending and the film clip?
3. **Interpret** Which version helps you better understand how the characters feel? Cite evidence from the versions in your discussion.
4. **Evaluate** Which do you find more frightening, the film version or the story? Which do you find more tragic? Cite evidence to support your ideas.

DISCUSS AND PRESENT

Now, your group can continue comparing the story's ending and the film clip by exploring the reasons for the director's choices and evaluating the advantages of each version.

1. **Decide on the Most Important Details** With your group, review your diagram to identify similarities and differences between the story's ending and the film clip. What are the most important details in each version?

2. **Discuss the Director's Choices** Consider the similarities and differences you identified. Discuss possible reasons why the director might have chosen to stay true to some parts of the story and to tell some parts differently. You can use this chart to record supporting evidence.

Go to **Participating in Collaborative Discussions** in the **Speaking and Listening Studio** for help.

	POSSIBLE REASON FOR DIRECTOR'S CHOICE
Setting	
Characters	
Events	

3. **Evaluate Advantages of Each Version** With your group, discuss advantages of the story and film versions. Record your ideas in the chart.

	ADVANTAGES
Story	
Film	

4. **Present to the Class** Now it is time to share your ideas. Clearly state your inferences about the reasons for the director's choices. Provide examples to support your opinions about the advantages of each version. Adapt the charts you created or create other visuals to help convey your ideas to the class.

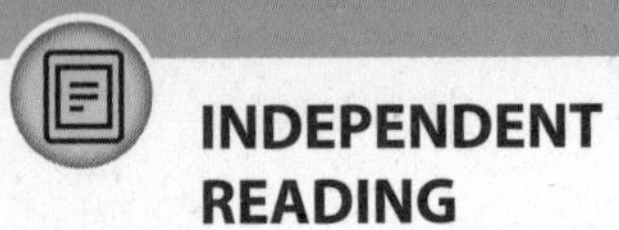

INDEPENDENT READING

Reader's Choice

? ***ESSENTIAL QUESTION:***

Why do we sometimes like to feel frightened?

Setting a Purpose Select one or more of these options from your eBook to continue your exploration of the Essential Question.

- Read the descriptions to see which text grabs your interest.
- Think about which genres you enjoy reading.

Notice & Note

In this unit, you practiced asking **Big Questions** and noticing and noting two signposts: **Extreme or Absolute Language** and **Quoted Words.** As you read independently, these signposts and others will aid your understanding. Below are the anchor questions to ask when you read literature and nonfiction.

Reading Literature: Stories, Poems, and Plays		
Signpost	**Anchor Question**	Lesson
Contrasts and Contradictions	Why did the character act that way?	p. 3
Aha Moment	How might this change things?	p. 3
Tough Questions	What does this make me wonder about?	p. 152
Words of the Wiser	What's the lesson for the character?	p. 406
Again and Again	Why might the author keep bringing this up?	p. 2
Memory Moment	Why is this memory important?	p. 153

Reading Nonfiction: Essays, Articles, and Arguments		
Signpost	**Anchor Question(s)**	Lesson
Big Questions	What surprised me? What did the author think I already knew? What challenged, changed, or confirmed what I already knew?	p. 77
Contrasts and Contradictions	What is the difference, and why does it matter?	p. 241
Extreme or Absolute Language	Why did the author use this language?	p. 76
Numbers and Stats	Why did the author use these numbers or amounts?	p. 325
Quoted Words	Why was this person quoted or cited, and what did this add?	p. 77
Word Gaps	Do I know this word from someplace else? Does it seem like technical talk for this topic? Do clues in the sentence help me understand the word?	p. 240

INDEPENDENT READING

You can preview these texts in Unit 2 of your eBook.

Then, check off the text or texts that you select to read on your own.

POEM

Frankenstein
Edward Field

Frankenstein's monster encounters kindness for the first time.

POEM

beware: do not read this poem
Ishmael Reed

Prepare to be devoured by poetry.

SHORT STORY

Blood
Zdravka Evitmova

A generous impulse has unintended consequences.

SHORT STORY

The Outsider
H. P. Lovecraft

A narrator makes a shocking discovery when he escapes from his home, a dark and lonely castle.

ESSAY

Scary Tales
Jackie Torrence

A storyteller follows in her grandfather's footsteps.

Collaborate and Share Meet with a partner to discuss what you learned from at least one of your independent readings.

- Give a brief synopsis or summary of the text.
- Describe any signposts that you noticed in the text and explain what they revealed to you.
- Describe what you most enjoyed or found most challenging about the text. Give specific examples.
- Decide if you would recommend the text to others. Why or why not?

Go to the **Reading Studio** for more resources on **Notice & Note.**

Write a Literary Analysis

Go to the **Writing Studio** for help writing your literary analysis.

In this unit, you have read some scary stories and you have discussed the horror genre and what makes it enjoyable for many people. For this writing task, you will write a literary analysis in which you analyze and interpret one of the stories in this unit. For an example of a well-written literary analysis you can use as a mentor text, review "What Is the Horror Genre?" You can also use the notes from your Response Log that you recorded after reading the texts in this unit.

Writing Prompt

Read the information in the box below.

This is the topic or context for your literary analysis.

> As Sharon A. Russell points out in "What Is the Horror Genre?," various elements may be used to define and categorize horror stories, including suspense, plot, setting, theme, and the source of threats to the characters.

Think carefully about the following question.

This is the Essential Question for the unit. Answering this question may offer insights into the horror genre.

> Why do we sometimes like to feel frightened?

Now mark the words that identify exactly what you are being asked to produce.

Write a literary analysis of one of the stories in this unit. Refer to the examples given in the selection "What Is the Horror Genre?" to explain how the story fits into the horror genre.

Be sure to —

Review these points as you write and again when you finish. Make any needed changes or edits.

- ❑ provide an introduction that catches the reader's attention and includes a clear controlling idea about the story you are analyzing
- ❑ develop support for your controlling idea by including examples and quotations from the story
- ❑ logically organize main ideas and supporting evidence
- ❑ use appropriate transitions to connect ideas
- ❑ use appropriate word choice and sentence variety
- ❑ end by summarizing ideas or drawing an overall conclusion

1 Plan

In order to plan the content and organization of your literary analysis, the first thing you need to do is select a story. With a partner, review the stories you read in this unit and identify which elements of horror they include. Use the planning table below to assist you.

Go to **Writing as a Process: Planning and Drafting** for help planning your literary analysis.

Horror Elements	"The Tell-Tale Heart"	"The Monkey's Paw"	"Blood"	"The Outsider"
Subjects	guilty murderer	normal family	pet-shop owner	normal guy, ghouls
Suspense				
Setting				
Plot				
Supernatural events				
Source of threat				
Theme				

Choose a Story Review the table and decide which story you would like to analyze. Consider how interested you were in the story and also how many elements of the horror genre it will allow you to write about in your literary analysis.

Background Reading Review the notes you took in your Response Log after reading each horror story. They may provide some valuable insights into the story or horror genre that you could include in your literary analysis. You may also wish to reread "What Is the Horror Genre?" to review what Sharon A. Russell wrote about the various elements of horror.

Use the notes from your Response Log as you plan your literary analysis.

Go to **Writing as a Process: Planning and Drafting** for help organizing your ideas.

Notice & Note

From Reading to Writing

As you plan your analysis, apply what you learned about signposts to your own writing.

Go to the **Reading Studio** for more resources on Notice & Note.

Organize Your Ideas After you have selected a story that meets the horror criteria, you will need to come up with a controlling idea for your analysis. Begin by choosing the elements you want to write about. You can draw from those listed in the table on page 143 and include others of your own. Then review the story as well as what you wrote about it in your Response Log. You can use the chart below to collect examples and notes that support your points.

Elements of the Horror Genre in (story title) ______________

Horror Elements	Supporting Examples and Quotations from the Story
Element 1:	
Element 2:	
Element 3:	

2 Develop a Draft

You might prefer to draft your essay online.

Once you have completed your planning activities, you will be ready to begin drafting your literary analysis. Refer to your completed chart; it may serve as a kind of map for you to follow as you write. Start with an introduction that includes your controlling idea and previews the elements you'll be talking about. In the body of your analysis, devote a paragraph to each element you previewed. Finish with a conclusion that summarizes your main points.

Use the Mentor Text

ANALYZE & APPLY
WHAT IS THE HORROR GENRE?
Literary Criticism by Sharon A. Russell
ESSENTIAL QUESTION:
Why do we sometimes like to feel frightened?

Author's Craft

Your introduction is your first chance to grab the reader's attention. In addition to your controlling idea or thesis statement, your introduction should include something that gets your reader interested in reading your essay. Note the way the writer captures the reader's attention in "What Is the Horror Genre?"

Many people define horror by its subjects. We all think of creatures like Frankenstein's monster, Dracula, and the wolfman as monsters in the horror genre. Each one of these creatures has a history and developed over a period of time. But we also know that horror covers more than just these monsters.

The writer grabs the reader's attention by naming monsters, then introduces the controlling idea—horror involves other elements besides monsters.

Apply What You've Learned To capture your reader's attention, you might include a surprising fact, a famous quotation, or a personal anecdote related to the topic.

Genre Characteristics

In a literary analysis, each main idea is supported by examples and quotations from the story being analyzed. Notice how the author of "What Is the Horror Genre?" supports a key idea about how Stephen King builds suspense. Also notice how she cites her source.

. . . Stephen King refers directly to our anticipation of horror. In *Salem's Lot* Susan approaches the house which is the source of evil. "She found herself thinking of those drive-in horror movie epics where the heroine goes venturing up the narrow attic stairs . . . or down into some dark, cobwebby cellar . . . and she . . . thinking: . . . *I'd never do that!*" Of course Susan's fears are justified.

The author provides an example and cites her source. She then includes a quotation to provide more vivid details. The example and quotation support her point that anticipation builds suspense.

Apply What You've Learned Each point you make about an element of the horror genre should be supported by examples and quotations. Be sure to identify the author and title of the story the first time you cite evidence from the story.

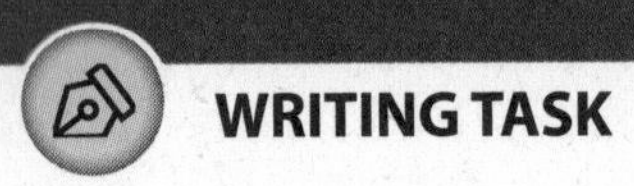

3 Revise

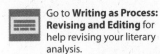

Go to **Writing as Process: Revising and Editing** for help revising your literary analysis.

On Your Own Once you've written a first draft of your literary analysis, you'll want to go back and look for ways to improve it. As you reread and revise, think about whether you have achieved your purpose. The Revision Guide will help you focus on specific elements to make your writing stronger.

Revision Guide

Ask Yourself	Tips	Revision Techniques
1. Does my introduction grab readers' attention?	**Highlight** the introduction.	**Add** an interesting fact, example, or quotation that illustrates the topic.
2. Is my controlling idea clear?	**Underline** the controlling idea.	**Add** a controlling idea or make an existing one clearer.
3. Are ideas organized logically? Is there coherence within and across paragraphs? Do transitions connect ideas?	**Highlight** main ideas. **Underline** the transitional words and phrases that connect them.	**Rearrange** paragraphs or sentences within paragraphs to organize ideas logically and create coherence. **Add** transitions to clarify connections.
4. Do I support each main idea with evidence?	**Underline** each supporting example or quotation.	**Add** more examples or quotations to support ideas.
5. Do I include phrases and clauses to add details and link ideas?	**Circle** phrases that add details. **Underline** clauses that add details or show connections.	**Add** some phrases or clauses if you need more details to develop your ideas.
6. Does my conclusion summarize the topic and support the information presented?	**Underline** the summary, if one is present.	**Add** a statement that summarizes the main ideas.

ACADEMIC VOCABULARY

As you conduct your **peer review,** be sure to use these words.

- ❑ **convention**
- ❑ **predict**
- ❑ **psychology**
- ❑ **summary**
- ❑ **technique**

With a Partner Once you have worked through the Revision Guide on your own, exchange papers with a partner and evaluate each other's draft in a **peer review**. Focus on providing revision suggestions for at least three of the items mentioned in the chart. Explain why you think your partner's draft should be revised and what your specific suggestions are.

When receiving feedback from your partner, listen attentively and ask questions to make sure you fully understand the revision suggestions.

4 Edit

Once you have revised your literary analysis, you can address the finer points of your draft. Edit for the proper use of standard English conventions, and make sure to correct any misspellings or grammatical errors.

Language Conventions

Phrases and Clauses You can use phrases and clauses to add details that help you develop your ideas and to create sentence variety.

- A **phrase** is a group of words that functions as a single part of speech. It does not contain a verb and its subject. A phrase often modifies a noun or adjective, adding more detail about it.
- A **clause** is a group of words that contains a verb and its subject. Both phrases and clauses can be either restrictive or nonrestrictive.

Go to the **Grammar Studio** to learn more about phrases and clauses.

A **restrictive** phrase or clause provides information that is necessary to understand the sentence. It is therefore not set off with commas, as shown in these examples from "What Is the Horror Genre?"

- "Stories of ghosts or demonic possession also fall into this category."
- "We don't know what is going to happen."

A **nonrestrictive** phrase or clause provides additional information in a sentence whose meaning is already clear. Nonrestrictive phrases and clauses are typically set off from the rest of the sentence with commas:

- "She does end up dead in the basement, a victim of the vampire."
- "This type of hesitation, when we almost believe, falls into the general category of the 'fantastic' (Todorov 25)."

Review your first draft and check that you have set off nonrestrictive phrases and clauses with commas.

5 Publish

Finalize your literary analysis and choose a way to share it with your audience. Consider these options:

- Present your literary analysis as a speech to the class.
- Post your literary analysis as a blog on a classroom or school website.

WRITING TASK

Use the scoring guide to evaluate your literary analysis.

Writing Task Scoring Guide: Literary Analysis

	Organization/Progression	Development of Ideas	Use of Language and Conventions
4	• The organization is very effective and appropriate to the purpose. • The controlling idea is stated very clearly. • Body paragraphs clearly relate to the controlling idea, and ideas within each body paragraph follow a logical order. • There are very clear transitions between paragraphs.	• The introduction grabs the reader's attention and states a compelling controlling idea. • The analysis offers insightful interpretations of the chosen text. • The analysis contains clear main ideas supported by well-chosen examples and quotations. • The conclusion effectively summarizes the analysis.	• Language and word choice is purposeful and precise. • Sources are correctly cited. • Sentences include a variety of phrases and clauses. • Grammar, spelling, capitalization, punctuation, and usage are correct.
3	• The organization is effective and appropriate to the purpose. • The controlling idea is stated clearly. • Body paragraphs relate to the controlling idea, and ideas within each body paragraph are mostly easy to follow. • There are clear transitions between paragraphs.	• The introduction could be more engaging, but it states a controlling idea. • The analysis offers reasonable interpretations of the text. • The analysis is developed with clear main ideas supported by mostly relevant examples and quotations. • The conclusion summarizes the analysis.	• Language and word choice is somewhat purposeful and precise. • Sources are mentioned but may not be correctly cited. • Sentences include a variety of phrases and clauses, and most are punctuated correctly. • Grammar, spelling, capitalization, punctuation, and usage are mostly correct.
2	• The organization is somewhat confusing or lacking in purpose. • The controlling idea is not stated very clearly. • It is unclear how ideas within body paragraphs are related. • More transitions are needed to show connections between paragraphs.	• The introduction is not engaging; the controlling idea is unclear or missing. • The interpretations of the text are unclear or questionable. • The analysis is minimally developed. Main ideas are unclear or lack appropriate examples and quotations to support them. • The conclusion only partially summarizes the analysis.	• Language is often vague and general. • Sources are not correctly cited. • Some phrases or clauses are punctuated incorrectly. • There are errors in grammar, spelling, capitalization, punctuation, and usage, but they do not make reading difficult.
1	• The organization is not appropriate to the purpose. • The controlling idea is missing. • The order of paragraphs or ideas within paragraphs is confusing. • There are no transitions between paragraphs.	• The introduction is missing or confusing. • The analysis offers no clear interpretations of the text. • The analysis is poorly developed. Examples and quotations are irrelevant or missing. • The conclusion is missing.	• Language is inappropriate, vague, or confusing. • No sources are mentioned. • Phrases and clauses are punctuated incorrectly. • There are many errors in grammar, usage, and mechanics that make the analysis difficult to follow.

Reflect on the Unit

In the literary analysis you created, you analyzed a story from the unit and explained the elements that make it fit within the horror genre. Now is a good time to reflect on what you have learned in this unit.

Reflect on the Essential Question

- Why do we sometimes like to feel frightened? Has your answer to this question changed since you first considered it when you started this unit? If so, in what way?

- How do authors make stories frightening and enjoyable to read?

Reflect on Your Reading

- Which selections most interested or surprised you?

- From which selection did you learn the most about why people sometimes like to feel frightened?

Reflect on the Writing Task

- What difficulties did you encounter while working on your literary analysis? How might you avoid them next time?

- What parts of the literary analysis were the easiest and hardest to write? Why?

- What improvements did you make to your literary analysis during the revising stage?

UNIT 2 SELECTIONS

- "What Is the Horror Genre?"
- "The Tell-Tale Heart"
- "The Hollow"
- "The Monkey's Paw" (short story)
- from *The Monkey's Paw* (film clip)

UNIT 3

PLACES WE CALL HOME

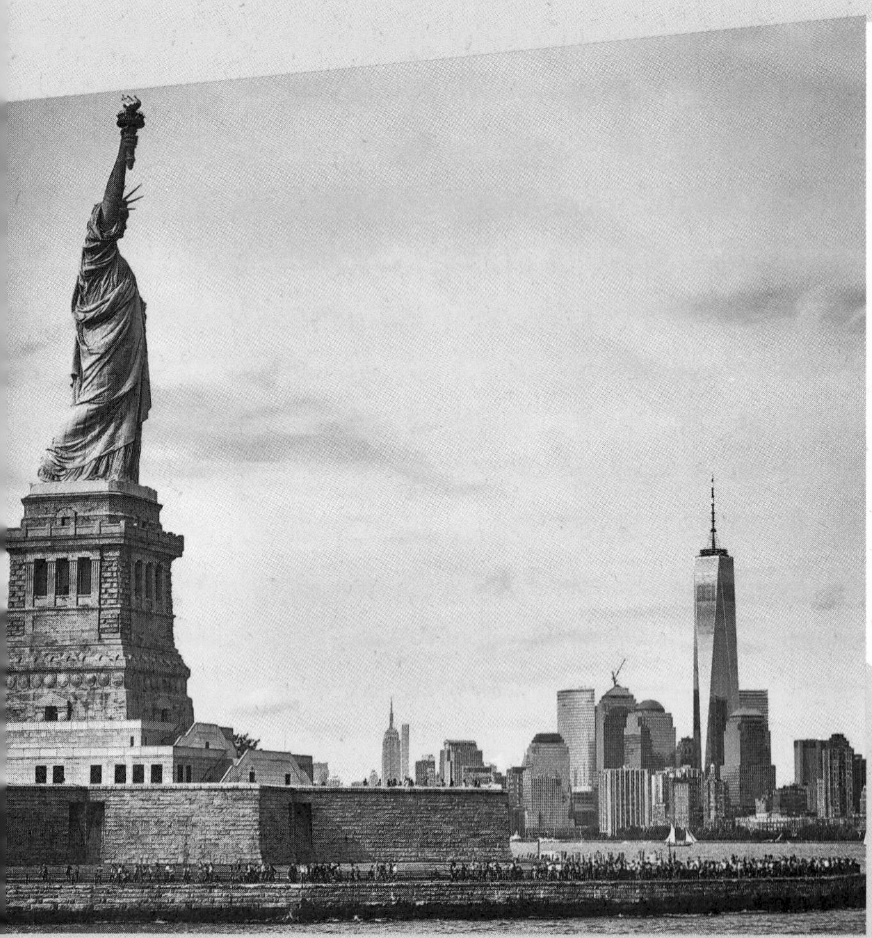

? **ESSENTIAL QUESTION:**

What are the places that shape who you are?

> **You can have more than one home. You can carry your roots with you, and decide where they grow.**
>
> Henning Mankel

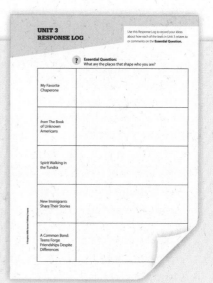

ACADEMIC VOCABULARY

Academic Vocabulary words are words you use when you discuss and write about texts. In this unit you will practice and learn five words.

☑ **contribute** ☐ **immigrate** ☐ **reaction** ☐ **relocate** ☐ **shifting**

Study the Word Network to learn more about the word **contribute**.

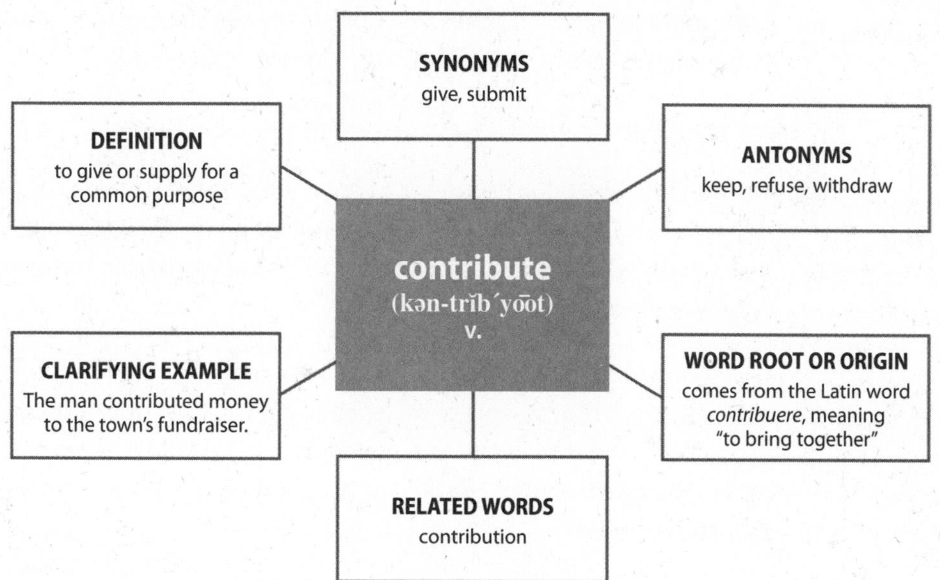

Write and Discuss Discuss the completed Word Network with a partner, making sure to talk through all of the boxes until you both understand the word, its synonyms, antonyms, and related forms. Then, fill out Word Networks for the four remaining words. Use a dictionary or online resource to help you complete the activity.

Go online to access the Word Networks.

RESPOND TO THE ESSENTIAL QUESTION

In this unit, you will explore how places can shape the way people are. As you read, you will revisit the **Essential Question** and gather your ideas about it in the **Response Log** that appears on page R3. At the end of the unit, you will have the opportunity to write a **short story**. Filling out the Response Log will help you prepare for this writing task.

You can also go online to access the Response Log.

UNIT 3
RESPONSE LOG

Essential Question:
What are the places that shape who you are?

My Favorite Chaperone	
from The Book of Unknown Americans	
Spirit Walking in the Tundra	
New Immigrants Share Their Stories	
A Common Bond: Teens Forge Friendships Despite Differences	

MY FAVORITE CHAPERONE

For more information on these and other signposts to Notice & Note, visit the **Reading Studio**.

You are about to read the short story "My Favorite Chaperone." In it, you will notice and note signposts that will give you clues about the story's plot, characters, and themes. Here are three key signposts to look for as you read this short story and other works of fiction.

When you notice one of the following phrases while reading, pause to see if it's a **Tough Questions** signpost:

"What could I possibly do to . . . ?"

"I couldn't imagine how I could cope with . . ."

"Why would she [or he] . . . ?"

Tough Questions If a friend began a sentence with "How in the world will I ever . . . ," you would get the signal that he or she was feeling overwhelmed and was asking for help. So, you would listen closely to what your friend said next.

It's a good idea to take the same approach while reading a story. When characters ask themselves or other characters tough questions, pay attention to what they ask. The question may reveal an important inner struggle, a central conflict, or even a theme. Noticing **Tough Questions** can:

- help you recognize the plot's central conflict
- provide clues to the story's theme or lesson
- reveal a character's traits or motivations

The paragraph below illustrates a student's annotation within "My Favorite Chaperone" and a response to a Tough Questions signpost.

1 In homeroom when Mr. Horswill handed out the permission slip for the Spring Fling, the all-school dance, I almost didn't take one. Why should I bother when I was sure the answer would be the same? Even though I'm in ninth grade now, it would still be the same. No. *Nyet* is what they say, and I don't want to hear this again. . . .

Anchor Question
When you notice this signpost, ask: What does this make me wonder about?

What tough question is the character asking herself?	"Why should I bother when I was sure the answer would be the same?"
What clues does the question provide about the character and the plot?	The narrator wants to go to the dance but thinks she won't be allowed. This suggests a conflict between her and her parents.

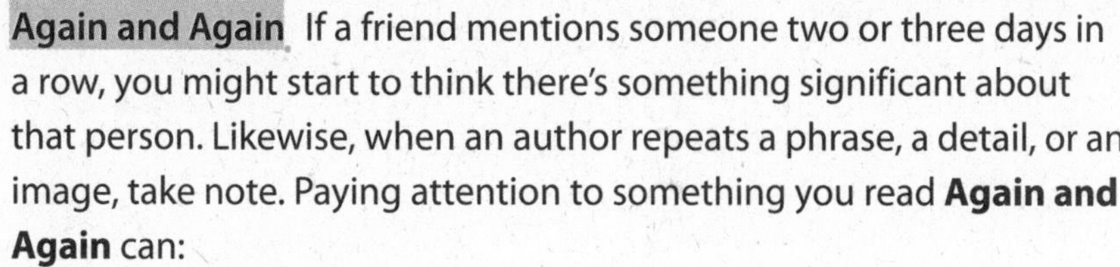

Again and Again If a friend mentions someone two or three days in a row, you might start to think there's something significant about that person. Likewise, when an author repeats a phrase, a detail, or an image, take note. Paying attention to something you read **Again and Again** can:

- reveal a symbol, or something that stands for something else
- provide an important insight into a character
- point to a significant idea or theme in the story

Here, a student marked an example of Again and Again.

> 137 . . . The door slammed. Papa stood like a huge bull in his dark leather jacket and flung open the back door of the cab.
>
> 141 . . . Papa roared in front of me, and as he charged toward the door in his glistening dark leather jacket, he again seemed transformed to a creature that was half man and half bull.

When you notice one of the following while reading, pause to see if it's an **Again and Again** signpost:

a second or third appearance of an object

a word or phrase that you think you may have read earlier in the story

a similar pattern to events or actions

Anchor Question
When you notice this signpost, ask: Why might the author keep bringing this up?

What image is repeated?	the image of Papa looking like a bull
Why might the author have used this image twice?	The author repeats the comparison of Maya's father to a bull as a way of emphasizing that he is angry and threatening.

Memory Moment In life, when a memory suddenly comes to mind, it's usually triggered for a reason. In a story, when the flow of the narrative is interrupted by a memory, there's usually a reason, too. A **Memory Moment** may help reveal:

- what one or more characters are feeling
- why a character is acting or feeling a certain way
- a connection between past and present events
- how the characters came to be in their current situation

In this example, a student marked a Memory Moment.

> 57 . . . "That kid Ossie Nishizono was teasing Nurzhan something fierce. Telling him he could never be a real American, making fun of the way he talked." He bent down and picked up a candy wrapper. "Reminded me of how this bully used to treat me when my family came after the revolution."

When you see a phrase like one of these, pause to see if it's signaling a **Memory Moment:**

"I remember when . . ."

"That reminds me of . . ."

"Once, when I was . . ."

"Did I ever tell you about the time . . ."

Anchor Question
When you notice this signpost, ask: Why is this memory important?

What word(s) introduce the recollection?	"Reminded me of how"
What does this memory reveal about Ossie and Nurzhan?	Mr. Zabornik's memory suggests that there have always been bullies who pick on kids who are different.

ANALYZE & APPLY

MY FAVORITE CHAPERONE

Short Story by **Jean Davies Okimoto**

ESSENTIAL QUESTION:

What are the places that shape who you are?

QUICK START

In this story, the main character struggles against her parents' rules. With a partner, share rules you must observe and your reactions to them.

ANALYZE PLOT

Most stories contain a **plot,** a series of events that occur in stages of development. Most story plots focus on a **conflict,** or a problem faced by the main character. These are the five stages of plot development:

- **exposition,** which introduces characters, setting, and conflict
- **rising action,** in which the main character takes steps to solve the problem even while complications might be introduced
- **climax,** the point of greatest tension in the story, in which the conflict begins to be resolved
- **falling action,** in which effects of the climax become clear
- **resolution,** in which the final outcome is revealed

Most plots are **linear**—events proceed in chronological order. But some stories have **non-linear** plots—events are told out of order.

GENRE ELEMENTS: REALISTIC FICTION

- includes the basic elements of fiction—setting, characters, plot, conflict, and theme
- features events and characters that could exist in real life
- contains natural-sounding dialogue and realistic interactions between characters
- often has a linear plot—story events are presented in chronological order

ANALYZE CHARACTER

Characterization is the way an author reveals the traits and personalities of characters. Like real people, characters have **motivations**—needs, wants, and impulses that cause them to behave as they do. Authors reveal their characters' motivations through

- direct comments made by the narrator
- the characters' own thoughts, speech, and actions
- the thoughts, speech, and actions of other characters

Characters' motivations and behaviors influence story events and even how the conflict is resolved. Read the following **dialogue,** or conversation. What can you infer about Maya's motivation as she translates the words of Mr. Shanaman, her brother's principal, for Papa?

DIALOGUE	INFERENCES
"We have asked Maya to translate, Mr. Alazova." "Yes." Papa nodded. When he heard my name, he understood what Mr. Shanaman meant. "Your son, Nurzhan, was involved in quite a nasty fight." Papa looked at me, and I said to him in Russian, "Nurzhan was in little fight."	

GET READY

CRITICAL VOCABULARY

sponsor **stun** **dispatcher** **scuffle** **whimper**

To see how many Critical Vocabulary words you already know, answer these questions.

1. If someone were to **sponsor** you, would you be annoyed, or grateful? Why?
2. Which would be more likely to **stun** you: getting a homework assignment, or getting a special award? Why?
3. If you were a **dispatcher,** would you need to speak to people, or write to them? Why?
4. Would people be more likely to have a **scuffle** if they were angry, or if they were lost? Why?
5. If you heard someone **whimper,** would you think the person was feeling lucky, or scared? Why?

LANGUAGE CONVENTIONS

Subject-Verb Agreement Verbs must agree with their subjects in number. This is true even when a prepositional phrase (beginning with a preposition such as *at, for, from, in, of, to,* or *with*) lies between the subject and its verb. To determine whether a subject modified by a prepositional phrase is singular or plural, ignore the phrase.

Their parents are unhappy because the punishment for both boys is a two-day suspension.

(This sentence has two subjects and two verbs. The second subject is *punishment,* not *boys,* so the verb needs to be singular: *is.*)

ANNOTATION MODEL

NOTICE & NOTE

As you read, note and notice signposts, such as **Tough Questions, Again and Again,** and **Memory Moments.** Here are one reader's notes about the beginning of "My Favorite Chaperone."

1 In homeroom when Mr. Horswill handed out the permission slip for the Spring Fling, the all-school dance, I almost didn't take one. Why should I bother when I was sure the answer would be the same? Even though I'm in ninth grade now, it would still be the same. No. *Nyet* is what they say, and I don't want to hear this again. But I took a permission slip anyway. . . .

The narrator remembers times in the past when her parents said "nyet." Could be an important clue to their relationship.

BACKGROUND

In addition to being the author of more than a dozen novels for young adults, ***Jean Davies Okimoto*** *(b. 1942) is a therapist. Perhaps that is why she has such insight into the characters that she portrays. Okimoto typically writes about the everyday problems and challenges faced by teenagers like Maya, the main character in "My Favorite Chaperone." Maya and her family have come to the United States from Kazakhstan, a country in Central Asia that used to be part of the Soviet Union.*

MY FAVORITE CHAPERONE

Short Story by Jean Davies Okimoto

SETTING A PURPOSE

As you read, pay attention to Maya's interactions with her family and her friends. How do these interactions help you to understand the challenges of being an immigrant in a new country?

1 In homeroom when Mr. Horswill handed out the permission slip for the Spring Fling, the all-school dance, I almost didn't take one. Why should I bother when I was sure the answer would be the same? Even though I'm in ninth grade now, it would still be the same. No. *Nyet* is what they say, and I don't want to hear this again. But I took a permission slip anyway. I don't know why I didn't just shake my head when this very popular girl Marcia Egness was handing them out. And even after I took one, I don't know why I didn't throw it away. Maybe I just couldn't give up hope. It's like that in America. It's a place where things can change for people, and many people always seem to have hope. At least that's how it seems to me. Maybe I was beginning to think this way, too, although my hope was very small.

Notice & Note

Use the side margins to notice and note signposts in the text.

ANALYZE CHARACTER

Annotate: In paragraph 1, mark details that reveal something about Maya.

Infer: In a few sentences, summarize what you can infer about Maya from these details.

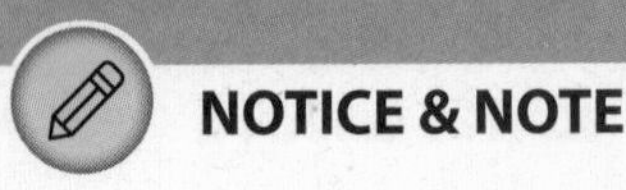

NOTICE & NOTE

MEMORY MOMENT

Notice & Note: Mark the sentences in paragraph 2 that help you realize that Maya is interrupting her story to recall events from an earlier time.

Analyze: What do the events described in paragraphs 2–7 help you understand about Mama and about Maya's family?

2 We came to America through an international dating magazine. I don't mean that our whole family was in the magazine looking for dates, just Madina Zhamejakova, my aunt. Aunt Madina came after Kazakhstan broke away from the Soviet Union and things got very hard. Everyone's pay was cut and the *tenge*, our money, was worth less and less. Then my grandmother died. That was the worst part. She was the head of our family, and without her everything fell apart. That's when Aunt Madina started reading international dating magazines.

3 The next thing we knew, she had a beautiful photo taken of herself wearing her best outfit, a black dress with a scoop neck and a red silk band around the neck. Aunt Madina is very pretty. Mama says she looks like an old American movie star we saw on TV named Natalie Wood, except Aunt Madina looks more Kazakh with her dark, beautiful Asian eyes. She sent the photo to one of these magazines, and in a very short time a man from Seattle saw her picture. He started calling her, and they would talk on the phone for hours. I guess he had plenty of money for these calls, which Aunt Madina thought was a good sign. After about six months, he asked her to marry him.

4 His name was Bob Campbell and he'd been in the navy. He told Aunt Madina he never had a chance to meet anyone because he traveled so much. Maybe that was true, but Mama was worried.

5 "Madina, something must be wrong with this man if he has to find a wife through a magazine."

6 Mama was afraid for her, but Aunt Madina went to America anyway and married Mr. Bob Campbell. She phoned us a lot from America, and Mama admitted she sounded okay. Madina said Bob was a lot older and had less hair than in the picture he had sent her. He was also fatter than in the picture, but he was very nice. She sounded so good, Mama stopped worrying about Aunt Madina, but then things got so bad in Kazakhstan that she worried all the time about us. Papa and Mama lost their teaching jobs because the government was running out of money. Mama had to go to the market and sell many of our things: clothes, dishes, even some furniture. When Aunt Madina asked us to come to America for the hundredth time, we were running out of things to sell and my parents finally agreed. Aunt Madina **sponsored** us, and not long after we got here, Papa got a job driving a cab, and Mama worked cleaning people's houses. It was hard for them not to have the respect they were used to from holding government teaching jobs, but

sponsor
(spŏn′sər) *v.* If you *sponsor* someone, you support his or her admission into a group.

they had high regard for the food they could now easily buy at the store.

7 Six months after we got here, the Boeing Company moved to Chicago and Mr. Bob Campbell got transferred there. When Aunt Madina left with him, it broke Mama's heart. Aunt Madina was the only person we knew from Kazakhstan, and it felt like our family just huddled together on a tiny island in the middle of a great American sea.

8 I looked at the permission slip, wishing there were some special words I could say to get Mama and Papa to sign it. Around me, everyone in my homeroom was talking excitedly about the Spring Fling. Mama says she thinks the school is strange to have parties and events after school when students should be doing their homework. Ever since I've been at Beacon Junior High, the only slip they signed was for the gymnastics team. Papa loves sports. (I think he told Mama that giving permission for this activity was important for my education.) I can't find words to say how grateful I was he signed that slip. The gymnastics team is a fine, good thing in my life. I compete in all the events: vault, beam, floor exercise, and my favorite: the uneven bars. I love to swing up and up, higher and higher, and as I fly through the air, a wonderful thing happens and suddenly I have no worries and no responsibilities. I'm free!

9 But there's another reason why I love gymnastics. Shannon Lui is on the team. We became friends when she was a teaching assistant in my ESL class. We're the same age,

ANALYZE PLOT
Annotate: Mark details in paragraph 8 that reveal the story's main conflict.

Summarize: Describe the story's conflict in one sentence.

ANALYZE CHARACTER
Annotate: Mark the reasons Maya gives in paragraph 8 for loving the gymnastics team.

Infer: What does her description of swinging on the uneven bars reveal about her?

but she says I'm like her little sister. Her grandparents came from China, and her parents speak perfect English. Everything about Shannon's family is very American. Her mother has a red coat with gold buttons from Nordstrom, and her father cooks and sometimes even washes dishes! (I couldn't believe this when I first saw it; no Kazakh man would do kitchen work.) Shannon encouraged me to try out for the gymnastics team, and the team has meant even more to me this year since I got put in the mainstream and had to leave ESL. Since I left ESL, I often feel like I'm in the middle of a game where I don't know the players, the rules, or even the object of the game.

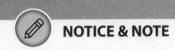

10 In my next class, Language Arts, even though I knew it was foolish, I was dreaming of the Spring Fling. I really like Language Arts. Ms. Coe, our teacher, is also the gymnastics coach, and there's a guy in the class, Daniel Klein, who was my partner for a research project last semester. He encouraged me to talk and listened to what I had to say (he's also a very handsome guy), and I always look forward to this class so I can see him. I was trying to think of some ideas to convince Mama and Papa to give permission (and also sneaking glances at Daniel Klein) when Mr. Walsh, the vice-principal, came into our class. He whispered something to Ms. Coe and she nodded. And then I was **stunned** because she nodded and pointed to me!

stun
(stŭn) *v.* To *stun* someone is to make him or her feel shocked or dazed.

11 "Maya, you're wanted in the office," Ms. Coe said. "You can go now with Mr. Walsh."

12 My fingers tingled with fear. What was wrong? What had I done? Mr. Walsh only comes for people when there's trouble.

13 Like a robot, I gathered my books and followed Mr. Walsh. As he closed the classroom door behind us, my heart began to bang and I felt like I needed to go to the bathroom. In the hallway he told me Ms. Johnson, the school counselor, wanted to speak with me.

ANALYZE CHARACTER

Annotate: Mark words and phrases in paragraphs 11–17 that show how Maya is feeling.

Infer: What do her feelings reveal about her?

14 "What is wrong?" My voice came out as a whisper. I felt such terror I could barely speak.

15 "What's that?" Mr. Walsh couldn't hear my whisper.

16 "What is wrong?" I tried to speak more loudly.

17 "She didn't say. She just asked me to find you since I was heading down the hall anyway."

18 I suddenly remembered Sunstar Sysavath, who was in my ESL class last year. Her family came from Cambodia, and on her first day at Beacon she was in the wrong line in the

lunchroom. Mr. Walsh went to help her, and he tapped her on her shoulder to get her attention. When she felt the tap and saw him, she lifted her hands in the air as if she were being arrested and about to be shot. People who saw this in the lunchroom laughed, but it wasn't a joke. Sunstar was filled with terror.

19 I knew I wouldn't be shot, but walking with Mr. Walsh to the office seemed like one of the longest walks of my life. I often fill my mind with nice things, such as imagining myself at the Olympics winning a gold medal for the U.S.A.—especially on days like today, when we have a gymnastics meet after school. But now my mind was filled with nothing. It was empty, like a dry riverbed where there is only cracked, baked earth and nothing lives.

20 I walked into the main office, where Ms. Johnson was waiting for me. "Come with me, Maya." Ms. Johnson smiled at Mr. Walsh. "Thanks, Tom."

21 Like a person made from wood, a puppet, I followed Ms. Johnson through the main office down the hall to her office across from the principal's. She showed me in and closed the door behind us.

22 "Sit down, dear."

23 I sat in a chair across from her desk and clutched my books to my chest. I'd never been in her office before. She had many nice green plants in front of the window and a small fish tank in one corner. I stared at the brightly colored fish swimming back and forth, back and forth. Then Ms. Johnson spoke.

24 "I received a call from Mr. Shanaman, the principal at Evergreen Elementary, and your brother's been suspended for fighting."

25 "Nurzhan?"

26 "Yes. Nurzhan Alazova." She read his name from a pink message slip. "They haven't been able to locate your mother, so they called over here to see if you could help."

27 "Is Nurzhan all right?"

28 "Yes. And I believe the other boy wasn't seriously hurt."

29 "Who did Nurzhan fight?" It was a foolish question—I was sure of the answer. Ms. Johnson hesitated, so I just said, "Ossie Nishizono," and she nodded.

30 "What must I do?" I asked.

31 "The school policy on suspension requires that the parent or guardian must have a conference at school within twenty-four hours of the suspension. Can you help us locate your mother or your father?"

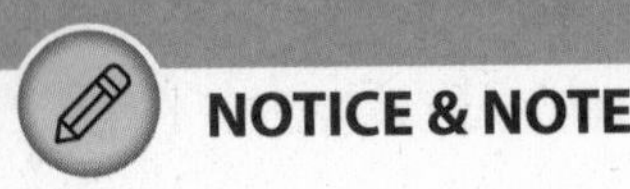

ANALYZE PLOT

Annotate: Nurzhan's suspension creates a complication in the plot. Mark the reason that Ms. Johnson wants Maya to attend the meeting about Nurzhan.

Infer: What can you infer about Maya's role in her family?

dispatcher
(dĭs-păch´ər) *n.* A *dispatcher* is a person who sends out vehicles according to a schedule.

32 "Yes. I can do that."

33 "Do your parents speak English, Maya?"

34 "Just a little."

35 "Then perhaps you could attend the meeting and translate for them."

36 "Yes. I must always do this for my parents—at the store, at the doctor, things like that."

37 "Here's the phone. I'll step out to give you some privacy."

38 Ms. Johnson left the office, quietly closing the door behind her. I looked at the nameplate on her desk. CATHERINE JOHNSON, it said. Outside her window, the sky was gray and it had started to rain. I stared at the phone, wishing I didn't have to be the messenger with this bad news. Then I called the Northwest Cab Company and asked them to contact my father.

39 "Aibek Alazova. Cab 191. I'm his daughter, and there is a family problem I must speak with him about."

40 I stayed on the line while the **dispatcher** radioed Papa. I looked at the clock and felt my heart grow heavy. In a minute the bell would ring, school would be out, and the gymnastics meet would begin.

41 "Maya!" Papa's voice was alarmed. "What is wrong?"

42 "Nurzhan has been in a fight with another boy." Then I explained in Russian what had happened, and Papa said he had to drop his passenger at the Four Seasons Hotel downtown and then he'd come straight to Nurzhan's school. He'd be there about three-thirty.

43 Ms. Johnson came back into the office as I hung up the phone. "Did you get your mother?"

44 "I don't have the number where she works today, but I got my father. He will come to the school."

45 "Good."

46 "Ms. Johnson?"

47 "Yes?"

48 "I will leave now for Evergreen. Will you tell Ms. Coe I have a family problem and I cannot attend the gymnastics meet?"

49 "Of course. And I'll call Mr. Shanaman at Evergreen now and let him know that you and your father will be there."

50 I went to my locker, got my coat, then walked quickly down the hall to the south door that opens onto the play field that joins our school with Evergreen. Poor Nurzhan, getting in such big trouble. I couldn't fault him for fighting with Ossie Nishizono. Such a mean boy—he'd been teasing Nurzhan

without mercy for not speaking well and mispronouncing things. I hoped Nurzhan had given him a hard punch. But why did he have to make this fight today! I felt angry that I had to miss the meet because of Nurzhan. Would Ms. Coe still want me on the team? Would she think I wasn't reliable?

51 But as I neared Nurzhan's school—my old school—I only worried about Papa. Even though he didn't shout at me on the phone, that didn't mean he wasn't angry. He had a person in his cab and the dispatcher might have been hearing us. Probably the dispatcher didn't know Russian, but Papa wouldn't show his anger in the cab anyway. But Papa could be very, very angry—not just with Nurzhan but with me, too. He and Mama think it's my duty to watch out for Nurzhan and keep him out of trouble.

52 As I walked up to the front door, Mr. Zabornik, the custodian, waved to me. He was picking up papers and litter around the bushes next to the front walk. It was still raining lightly, and Mr. Zabornik's wet gray hair was pasted against his forehead.

53 "Hi, Maya."

54 "Hello, Mr. Zabornik."

55 "Here about your brother, I suppose."

56 "How did you know?"

57 "I was fixing the drainpipe when it happened." He pointed to the corner of the building by the edge of the play field. "That kid Ossie Nishizono was teasing Nurzhan something fierce. Telling him he could never be a real American, making fun of the way he talked." He bent down and picked up a candy wrapper. "Reminded me of how this bully used to treat me when my family came after the revolution."

58 "Oh." I think Mr. Zabornik could tell I didn't know what revolution this was.

TOUGH QUESTIONS

Notice & Note: Mark the tough questions Maya asks herself in paragraph 50.

Infer: What do these questions suggest about Maya's traits and motivations?

scuffle
(skŭf′əl) *n.* A *scuffle* is a disorderly fight.

59 "The Hungarian revolution, in 1956." He looked out over the play field and folded his arms across his chest. "Guess some things never change."

60 "Nurzhan's going to be suspended."

61 "Sorry to hear that. 'Course, the school can't allow fights, and this was no **scuffle**. But I can sure see how your brother lost his temper." Then he went back to picking up the litter. "Good luck."

62 "Thank you, Mr. Zabornik."

63 I went to the front office, where Ms. Illo, the head secretary, spoke to me in a very kind way. "Maya, Mr. Shanaman is waiting for you in his office. You can go right in."

64 Mr. Shanaman was behind his big desk, and Nurzhan was sitting on a chair in the corner. He looked like a rabbit caught in a trap. He had scrapes on his hands and on his cheek, and his eyes were puffed up. I couldn't tell if that was from crying or being hit.

65 "I understand your father will be coming. Is that right, Maya?"

66 I nodded.

67 "Just take a seat by your brother. Ms. Illo will bring your father in when he gets here."

68 Then Mr. Shanaman read some papers on his desk and I sat down next to Nurzhan and spoke quietly to him in Russian.

69 "*Neechevo, Nurzhan. Ya vas ne veenu.*" It's okay, Nurzhan. I don't blame you, is what I said.

70 Nurzhan's eyes were wet with tears as he nodded to me.

71 I stared out the principal's window. Across the street, the bare branches of the trees were black against the cement gray sky. The rain came down in a steady drizzle, and after a few minutes, I saw Papa's cab turn the corner. His cab is green, the color of a lime, and he always washes and shines it. I watched Papa park and get out of the cab. His shoulders are very broad underneath his brown leather jacket, and Papa has a powerful walk, like a large, strong horse that plows fields. He walked briskly, and as he came up the steps of the school, he removed his driver cap.

72 It seemed like one thousand years, but it was only a minute before Ms. Illo brought Papa into the office. Nurzhan and I stood up when he entered, but he didn't look at us, only at Mr. Shanaman, who shook hands with him and motioned for him to have a seat.

73 Papa sat across the desk from Mr. Shanaman and placed his driver cap in his lap.

74 "We have asked Maya to translate, Mr. Alazova."

75 "Yes." Papa nodded. When he heard my name, he understood what Mr. Shanaman meant.

76 "Your son, Nurzhan, was involved in quite a nasty fight."

77 Papa looked at me, and I said to him in Russian, "Nurzhan was in little fight."

78 Mr. Shanaman continued. "The other boy, Ossie Nishizono, needed two stitches at the hospital."

79 "The other boy, Ossie Nishizono, was a little hurt," I told Papa.

80 Nurzhan's eyes became wide as he listened to my translation.

81 "We have a policy that anyone who fights must be suspended from school. Both boys will receive a two-day suspension."

82 "The other boy, who is very bad," I translated for Papa, "is not allowed to come to school for two days and his parents must punish him. Nurzhan must stay home, too. But he should not be punished so much."

83 Papa nodded.

84 Then Mr. Shanaman said, "We've been told the other boy was teasing your son. We'd like you to help Nurzhan find ways to handle this situation without resorting to violence. We're working with the other boy to help him show respect for all students."

85 I looked at Papa and translated: "The other boy was teasing Nurzhan in a violent manner. This boy will be punished and must learn to respect all students. We understand how Nurzhan became so angry, and we ask that you punish him by not allowing him to watch television."

86 "Yes, I will punish my son as you suggest," Papa said in Russian.

87 I looked at Mr. Shanaman. "My father says he will teach Nurzhan not to fight by giving him a very serious punishment."

88 "We are glad you understand the serious nature of this situation," Mr. Shanaman said. Then I told Papa in Russian the exact words of Mr. Shanaman.

89 Mr. Shanaman held out a form on a clipboard. "We require you to sign this to show that we've discussed the suspension and you'll keep Nurzhan at home until Monday."

ANALYZE CHARACTER

Annotate: Mark the details in paragraphs 76–90 that indicate Nurzhan's reaction to Maya's translations.

Connect: When people react like this, what are they usually thinking and feeling? Why might Nurzhan be having this reaction?

NOTICE & NOTE

AGAIN AND AGAIN

Notice & Note: In paragraph 91, mark the details that Maya focuses on and how she tries to calm herself.

Compare: Recall another time when Maya tried to do something similar. What insights into Maya's character can you gain by comparing these instances?

MEMORY MOMENT

Notice & Note: Mark the brief Memory Moment in paragraph 92.

Infer: Why might Maya be recalling this now?

ANALYZE CHARACTER

Annotate: Mark details that indicate the role that Maya plays in Nurzhan's life.

Draw Conclusions: What does Maya want Nurzhan to understand about the events of the day and her feelings about what happened?

90 Again, I told Papa exactly what Mr. Shanaman said, and Papa signed the form.

91 We said nothing as we left the school and followed Papa to his cab. Nurzhan and I sat in the back, not daring to speak. There was a small rip in the leather of the seat and I poked my finger in it. The cab smelled of perfume; maybe Papa's last ride was a lady who wore a lot of it. It smelled like some kind of flower, but I couldn't name it. I wished so much I was in a beautiful meadow right then, surrounded by sweet-smelling flowers, lying in the soft grass, looking up at the clouds. I tried to calm myself by thinking about this meadow, but I just kept feeling scared—scared Papa might somehow find out I'd changed what Mr. Shanaman said.

92 Maybe I should've felt bad about changing Mr. Shanaman's words, but I didn't. I only felt afraid. I don't mean that I think changing words like that is okay; I have to admit it's sort of like telling lies. But I think maybe some lies are okay, like in the play we read last semester about Anne Frank and how the people who were hiding her family lied and said no one was in the attic when they really were. They lied to save Anne's family from the Nazis. Maybe I wasn't saving Nurzhan from death, but I was sure scared to death of what Papa might have done if I hadn't changed the words. I stared at the back of Papa's thick neck. It was very red, and he drove in silence until he pulled up in front of our building. Papa shut off the engine. Then he put his arm across the top of the seat and turned his face to us, craning his neck.

93 His dark eyes narrowed and his voice was severe. "I am ashamed of this! To come to this school and find you in trouble, Nurzhan! This does not seem like much punishment to me, this no watching television. You will go to bed tonight without dinner." He clenched his teeth. "I have lost money today because of you. And Maya, you must keep your brother out of trouble!" Then he waved us away furiously, like shooing away bugs. "Go now! Go!"

94 We went in the house, and Nurzhan marched straight to the table in the kitchen with his books. He seemed to be in such a hurry to do his work, he didn't even take off his jacket.

95 "Take off your jacket and hang it up, Nurzhan."

96 "Okay."

97 I began peeling potatoes for dinner, while Nurzhan hung up his jacket. Then he sat back down at the table.

98 "Maya, I—"

99 "Don't talk. Do your work."

100 "But I—"

101 "I missed the gymnastics meet because of you!"

102 "Watch the knife!" Nurzhan looked scared.

103 I glanced at my hand. I was holding the knife and I'd been waving it without realizing it.

104 "I wasn't going to stab you, stupid boy."

105 "I was only going to say thank you." Nurzhan looked glumly at his book.

106 I went back to peeling the potatoes. I'd had enough of him and his troubles.

107 "For changing what Mr. Shanaman said when you told Papa," he said in a timid voice, like a little chick peeping.

108 "It's okay, Nurzhan." I sighed. "Just do your work."

109 A few minutes before six, we heard Mama get home. She came straight to the kitchen, and when she saw Nurzhan sitting there doing his work, a smile came over her tired face.

110 "Oh, what a good boy, doing his work."

111 "Not so good, Mama. Nurzhan got in trouble." I didn't mind having to tell her this bad news too much (not like when I had to call Papa). Then I explained about the fight and how Papa had to come to the school.

112 "Oh, my poor little one!" Mama rushed to Nurzhan and examined his hands. Tenderly, she touched his face where it had been cut. Then she turned sharply toward me.

113 "Maya! How could you let this happen?"

114 "Me! I wasn't even there."

115 "On the bus, when this boy is so bad to Nurzhan. You must make this boy stop."

116 "No, Mama," Nurzhan explained. "He would tease me more if my sister spoke for me."

117 "I don't understand this. In Kazakhstan, if someone insults you, they have insulted everyone in the family. And everyone must respond."

118 "It's different here, Mama."

119 Mama looked sad. She sighed deeply. Then the phone rang and she told me to answer it. Mama always wants me to answer because she is shy about speaking English. When her work calls, I always speak on the phone to the women whose houses she cleans and then translate for Mama. (I translate their exact words, not like with Mr. Shanaman.)

120 But it wasn't for Mama. It was Shannon, and her voice was filled with worry.

TOUGH QUESTIONS

Notice & Note: Mark the tough question that prompts the heated dialogue between Mama and her children in paragraphs 113–119.

Analyze: What differences between Kazakh and U.S. culture does this dialogue reveal?

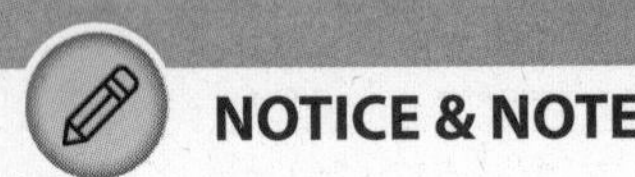

NOTICE & NOTE

121 "Maya, why weren't you at the meet? Is everything all right?"

122 "Everything's okay. It was just Nurzhan." Then I explained to her about what had happened. "I hope I can still be on the team."

123 "Ms. Coe is cool. Don't worry, it won't mess anything up."

124 Shannon was right. The next day at practice Ms. Coe was very understanding. Practice was so much fun I forgot all about Nurzhan, and Shannon and I were very excited because Ms. Coe said we were going to get new team leotards.

125 After practice we were waiting for the activity bus, talking about the kind of leotards we wanted, when two guys from the wrestling team joined us. One was David Pfeiffer, a guy who Shannon talked about all the time. She always said he was so cute, that he was "awesome" and "incredible" and things like that. She was often laughing and talking to him after our practice, and I think she really liked him. And today he was with Daniel Klein!

126 "Hey, Maya! How was practice?"

127 "Hi." I smiled at Daniel, but then I glanced away, pretending to look for the bus because talking to guys outside class always made me feel embarrassed and shy.

128 The guys came right up to us. David smiled at Shannon. "Wrestling practice was great! We worked on takedowns and escapes, and then lifted weights. How was your practice?"

129 "Fun! We spent most of it on the beam."

130 "I'm still pumped from weight training!" David grinned and picked up a metal trash can by the gym door. He paraded around with the can, then set it down with a bang right next to Shannon. Everyone was laughing, and then David bent his knees and bounced up and down on his heels and said, "Check this out, Daniel! Am I strong or what?" The next thing we knew, David had one arm under Shannon's knees and one arm under her back and he scooped her up. Shannon squealed and laughed, and I was laughing watching them, when all of a sudden Daniel scooped me up too!

131 "*Chort*!" I shouted, as he lifted me. I grabbed him around his neck to hang on, and my head was squished against his shoulder. He strutted around in a circle before he let me down. I could feel that my face was the color of borscht, and I flamed

AGAIN AND AGAIN

Notice & Note: Do you recall having recently read the word *shy*? Mark the word in paragraph 127 and in the earlier paragraph where it appears.

Analyze: What does this repetition cause you to notice? Why might the author have wanted to draw your attention to this?

with excitement and embarrassment and couldn't stop laughing from both joy and nervousness.

132 "That's nothing, man." David crouched like a weight lifter while he was still holding Shannon and lifted her as high as his shoulders.

133 It was exciting and crazy: Daniel and David showing each other how strong they were, first picking up Shannon and me, then putting us down, then picking us up and lifting us higher, as if Shannon and I were weights. After a few times, whenever Daniel picked me up, I was easily putting my arms around his neck, and I loved being his pretend weight, even though Shannon and I were both yelling for them to put us down. (We didn't really mean it. Shannon is a strong girl, and if she didn't like being lifted up and held by David, there was no way it would be happening.) I couldn't believe it, but I began to relax in Daniel's arms, and I laughed each time as he slowly turned in a circle.

134 Then Shannon and I tried to pick them up, and it was hilarious. Every time we tried to grab them, they did wrestling moves on us and we ended up on the grass in a big heap, like a litter of playful puppies. I couldn't remember a time in my life that had been so fun and so exciting. We lay on the grass laughing, and then David and Daniel jumped up and picked Shannon and me up again.

135 But this time when we turned, as my face was pressed against Daniel's shoulder, I saw something coming toward the school that made me tremble with fear.

136 "Daniel, please. Put me down!" My voice cracked as my breath caught in my throat.

137 But Daniel didn't hear. Everyone was shouting and laughing, and he lifted me up even more as the lime green cab came to a halt in front of the school. The door slammed. Papa stood like a huge bull in his dark leather jacket and flung open the back door of the cab.

138 "MAYA ALAZOVA!" His voice roared across the parking lot. He pointed at me the way one might identify a criminal. "*EDEE SUDA*!" he shouted in Russian. COME HERE!

139 Daniel dropped me and I ran to the cab, **whimpering** and trembling inside like a dog caught stealing a chicken.

140 Papa didn't speak. His silence filled every corner of the cab like a dark cloud, slowly suffocating me with its poisonous rage. Papa's neck was deep red, and the skin on the back of my hands tingled with fear. I lay my head back against the seat and closed

ANALYZE CHARACTER

Annotate: A simile is a comparison that uses the word *like* or *as*. Mark the similes that help you visualize the scene that unfolds in paragraphs 137–140.

Analyze: What do these similes reveal about Papa and Maya?

whimper
(hwĭm´pər) *v.* To *whimper* is to sob or let out a soft cry.

my eyes, squeezing them shut, and took myself far away until I was safe on the bars at a beautiful gymnastics meet in the sky. I swung back and forth, higher and higher, and then I released and flew to the next bar through fluffy white clouds as soft as goose feathers, while the air around me was sweet and warm, and my teammates cheered for me, their voices filled with love.

141 We screeched to a stop in front of our building. My head slammed back against the seat. When I struggled from the taxi, it was as though I had fallen from the bars, crashing down onto the street, where I splintered into a million pieces. And as hard as I tried, I couldn't get back on the bars any more than I could stop the hot tears that spilled from my eyes. Papa roared in front of me, and as he charged toward the door in his glistening dark leather jacket, he again seemed transformed to a creature that was half man and half bull.

ANALYZE PLOT

Annotate: Review paragraphs 137–150. Mark evidence of Maya's parents' reactions to finding her in the arms of an American boy.

Predict: What impact might this complication have on Maya's ability to resolve the story's main conflict?

142 "Gulnara!" He flung open the door, shouting for Mama, his voice filled with anger and blame.

143 "Why are you here? What has happened, Aibek?" Mama came from the kitchen as Nurzhan darted to the doorway and peeked around like a little squirrel.

144 I closed the front door and leaned against it with my wet palms flat against the wood, like a prisoner about to be shot.

145 "Is this how you raise your daughter! Is this what you teach her? Lessons to be a toy for American boys!" Papa spat out the words.

146 The color rose in Mama's face like a flame turned up on the stove, and she spun toward me, her eyes flashing. "What have you done?"

147 "Your daughter was in the arms of an American boy."

148 Mama looked shocked. "When? H-how can this be?" she stammered.

149 "Outside the school as I drove by, I found them at this. Don't you teach her anything?"

150 "Who let her stay after school? Who gives permission for all these things? You are the one, Aibek. If you left it to me, she would come home every day. She would not have this permission!"

151 Mama and Papa didn't notice that I went to the bathroom and locked the door. I huddled by the sink and heard their angry voices rise and fall like the pounding of thunder, and then I heard a bang, so fierce that the light bulb hanging from the ceiling swayed with its force. Papa slamming the front door. Then I heard the engine of the cab and a sharp squeal of tires as he sped away.

152 I imagined running away. I would run like the wind, behind the mini-mart, sailing past the E-Z Dry Cleaner, past the bus stop in an easy gallop through the crosswalk. As I ran, each traffic light I came to would turn green, until there would be a string of green lights glowing like a necklace of emeralds strung all down the street. And then I would be at the Luis' house. Mrs. Lui would greet me in her red Nordstrom coat with the gold buttons. She would hug me and hold me close. Then Mr. Lui would say, "Hi, honey," and make hamburgers. "Want to use the phone, Maya?" Mrs. Lui would say. "Talk as long as you want—we have an extra line for the kids."

153 "Oh, by the way," Mr. Lui would say, "Shannon is having David and some other kids over Friday night for pizza and videos. It's fine if there's a guy you want to invite, too."

154 "Maya! Open this door. Do you want more trouble?" Mama rattled the doorknob so hard I thought she'd rip it off.

155 "I'm coming." My voice caught in my throat. I felt dizzy as I unlocked the door and held my stomach, afraid I would be sick.

156 "You have brought shame to your father and to this family." Mama glared at me.

157 "Mama, it was just kids joking. Guys from the wrestling team pretending some of us were weights."

158 "I don't know this weights."

159 "It was nothing, Mama!"

160 "Do not tell me 'nothing' when your father saw you!" she screamed.

161 The next morning Papa was gone when I woke up. And even though Mama hadn't yet left for work, it was like she was gone, too. She didn't speak to me and didn't even look at me, except once when she came in the kitchen. I was getting *kasha*, and she stared at me like I was a stranger to her. Then she turned

NOTICE & NOTE

AGAIN AND AGAIN

Notice & Note: Maya imagines nice things time and again during emotionally difficult moments. Mark the fantasy she describes in paragraphs 152–153.

Contrast: What differences between Kazakh and U.S. culture do the details in Maya's fantasy highlight?

and left. Not only was Mama not speaking to me, but she didn't speak to Nurzhan, either. This never happens. Even when he was punished for the fight with Ossie Nishizono and had to stay home, Mama still spoke to him. But as I was getting dressed in my room, I heard Nurzhan try to talk to her. I put my ear to the door to listen.

162 "It's different here, Mama. I'm sure Maya and those guys were playing. Joking, like in a game."

163 "Quiet, boy! You know nothing of these things!"

164 I was shocked. Mama hardly ever says a harsh word to her precious boy. Then I heard her rush by, and then *bam*! The door slammed. The *kamcha* that hung by the door trembled with the force. We brought our *kamcha* when we came to America. It looks like a riding crop with a carved wooden handle and a leather cord, decorated with some horsehair. It's an old Kazakh tradition to put the *kamcha* inside the house next to the door because it's believed to bring good fortune and happiness. But our *kamcha* was not bringing us good fortune today. Mama left without a word of goodbye to either one of us.

165 I came out of my room and Nurzhan and I just looked at each other. I didn't feel happy that Nurzhan got yelled at; I felt bad about the whole thing.

166 "Did you hear?"

167 I nodded.

168 "She won't listen."

169 "Thank you for trying, Nurzhan."

170 "It did no good," he said with sadness. "They don't know about things here, only their own ways. They are like stone."

ANALYZE CHARACTER

Annotate: In paragraph 171, mark Maya's description of how and why her family's relationships become "almost calm" again.

Analyze: What does this description emphasize about how Maya's family is affected by their being recent immigrants?

171 I wondered how long this tension and anger would stay in our home. I was afraid it might be a long time, because Mama and Papa were so upset. But gradually, in the way that winter becomes spring, there was a slight thaw each day. Perhaps because we huddled together like a tiny Kazakh island in the middle of the great American sea, we couldn't allow our winter to go on and on, and by the next week, things in my family were almost calm.

172 But it was not to last. On Wednesday afternoon of the following week, Mama was waiting to talk to me when I got home from school. I was afraid when I saw her. Her ankle was taped up, and she sat on the couch with her leg up on a chair. Next to it was a pair of crutches!

173 "Mama, what happened?"

174 "I fell at work. Mrs. Hormann took me to the emergency room. I can't work for six weeks until it heals. I must keep my foot up as much as possible."

175 "I'll start dinner." My eyes filled with tears, I felt so bad for her. And I felt bad that I'd made them so upset when my father saw me and Daniel. Even though I knew I hadn't done anything wrong, it still bothered me that I'd been the cause of such trouble in our house.

176 It was decided that I'd take Mama's jobs for her while she couldn't work. I wouldn't go to gymnastics practice; instead, right after school I'd go straight to the houses Mama cleaned. The people Mama worked for agreed to this, and I worked at each house from three-thirty until six-thirty, when Papa came to pick me up. I wasn't able to clean their entire houses in this amount of time, but they told me which rooms were the most important, and I was able to clean those. Bathrooms were on the list at every house.

177 I didn't mind doing Mama's jobs. Although I did get very tired, and I was scared sometimes that I might break something when I dusted (especially at Mrs. Hathaway's house, because she had a lot of glass vases and some small glass birds), but I didn't mind vacuuming, mopping, dusting, cleaning cupboards, counters, stoves, and refrigerators. I didn't even mind cleaning toilets. It was as if all the work I did at Mama's jobs was to make up for the problems I'd caused. And besides, our family needed the money.

178 When I finished working for Mama, as soon as I got home I had to make dinner for everyone. Each day I got more tired, and on Friday, when I was peeling potatoes, I cut my finger. I thought it was just a little cut, so I washed it off and continued to peel.

179 Nurzhan looked up from the table, where he was doing his work. "What's wrong with the potatoes?"

180 "Nothing," I said automatically, with my eyes half-closed.

181 "They're red!"

182 "What?"

183 "The potatoes, Maya. They look like you painted them with red streaks."

184 I looked down and saw my finger bleeding on the potatoes, and it scared me to be so tired that I hadn't seen this. "It's just blood, Nurzhan. I cut myself. It'll wash off."

185 "Oh, yuck."

186 "Quiet, boy! I said I would wash it off."

NOTICE & NOTE

ANALYZE PLOT

Annotate: Mark the event that results in more responsibilities and sacrifices for Maya.

Analyze: What stage of the plot do this event and its results fall into? Explain why.

187 That night at dinner, Nurzhan refused to eat the potatoes, even though there was no sign of blood on them, and I wanted to take the whole dish and dump them on his head.

188 The next week I was so tired after going to school and cleaning Mrs. Hathaway's house that I burned the chicken. After I put it in the oven, I sat at the table with Nurzhan to do my homework. I rested my head on my book for just a minute, and the next thing I knew, Nurzhan was pounding on my arm.

189 "Maya! The oven!" he shouted.

190 I woke to see smoke seeping from the oven. "Oh, no!"

191 I leaped up and grabbed a dishtowel and pulled the pan from the oven. The chicken was very dark but not black, although all the juice at the bottom of the pan had burned and was smoking. "It's okay, Nurzhan. We can still eat it."

192 "Good."

ANALYZE CHARACTER

Annotate: In paragraphs 193–196, mark what Mama says and Maya's reaction to it.

Cause/Effect: What is the impact of Mama's statement on Maya?

193 Nurzhan didn't mind the almost-burned chicken that night, but Papa did.

194 "This tastes like my shoe!" Papa grumbled.

195 "Aibek, I have to keep my foot up, and Maya is doing the best she can. It is not easy. She must go to school, then do my work, then cook for us. She is just a young girl."

196 I looked at Mama and felt tears in my eyes. I couldn't remember another time when Mama spoke on my behalf, and my tears were the kind you have when you know someone is on your side.

197 The next evening as dinner was cooking, I sat with Nurzhan at the kitchen table and helped him with his spelling words. While I waited for him to think how to spell *admire*, I took the permission slip for the Spring Fling from my notebook and stared at it. I'd never thrown it away.

ANALYZE CHARACTER

Annotate: In the dialogue between Maya and Nurzhan, mark the statements that suggest Nurzhan is going to attempt to resolve the main conflict of the story.

Analyze: What do these statements suggest about how Nurzhan has developed or changed?

198 "A-D-M-I-E-R."

199 "Almost, Nurzhan. It's this," I said as I wrote the correct spelling on the top of the permission slip and turned it for him to see.

200 "A-D-M-I-R-E," he spelled. Then he looked closely at the slip. "What's this for?"

201 "It's a permission slip for the Spring Fling, the all-school dance, but it is only good for scratch paper to help you with spelling. Papa will never let me go. I don't know why I trouble myself to keep such a thing."

202 Nurzhan took the slip and put it in his notebook.

203 "What are you doing with it?"

204 "Let me try."

205 "Try what?"

206 "Let me try to get permission for you from Papa."

207 I laughed. "Oh, Nurzhan. Don't be foolish. You waste your time. Papa will never change his thinking because of you."

208 "I will try anyway. When he comes home tonight, I will speak to him myself. I have a plan."

209 I could only smile a sad smile at the idea of little Nurzhan trying to change the mind of Papa, who is a man like a boulder.

210 After dinner I went to my room to study, leaving Nurzhan to talk with Mama and Papa. I was afraid to really hope that any good thing could come from Nurzhan's plan. To hope and then be disappointed seemed to be worse. It was better not to hope and to live my dreams through Shannon. I could at least hear every little detail of her experience at the dance and be happy for her, giving up the idea that I'd ever be the one who goes to the dance, too.

211 But I comforted myself thinking about the dream in my life that really had come true—the gymnastics team. I still had that, and I was warming my heart with thoughts of the team when Nurzhan burst into the room.

212 "Maya! You can go!" Nurzhan jumped up and down like a little monkey, and I stared at him in disbelief.

213 "Don't joke with me about such a thing, boy!" I snapped.

214 "No! It's true. Look!" He waved the permission slip in front of my face.

215 I stared at the slip, still in disbelief. *Aibek Alazova* . . . Papa's name and Papa's writing. *It was true!* I was still staring at the slip, still afraid to completely believe that such a thing could be true, when Mama and Papa came in.

216 "We give permission for this, Maya, because Nurzhan will go, too," Mama said.

217 "He will not leave your side," Papa announced in a most serious tone. "He is your *capravazhdieuushee*."

218 "Chaperone." I said the English word. I knew this word because the parents who help the teachers supervise the kids at school activities are called this. But I hadn't heard of a little boy being a chaperone.

219 "Thank you, Mama. Thank you, Papa."

220 "It is Nurzhan you must thank," Mama said.

221 I thanked Nurzhan, too, and Mama and Papa left our room. Then I heard the front door close and I knew Papa had left for work.

ANALYZE PLOT

Annotate: Mark the part of the story that appears to be the climax—the point of greatest tension—when the conflict begins to be resolved.

Cite Evidence: What story events and details support your conclusion?

NOTICE & NOTE

222 That night Nurzhan and I whispered in our beds after Mama had gone to sleep.

223 "Nurzhan, what will I tell my friends when you come to the dance?"

224 "Don't worry. I thought about that problem. You will tell them you must baby-sit for me."

225 "But at a dance?"

226 "I think it will work. At least it is better than to say I am your chaperone."

227 "That is true."

228 I watched the orange light of the mini-mart sign blink on and off, and I heard Nurzhan's slow breathing as he fell asleep.

229 "Thank you, Nurzhan," I whispered as I began to dream of the dance.

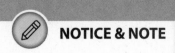

ANALYZE CHARACTER

Annotate: Mark the parts of the whispered conversation between Nurzhan and Maya that best show his growth as a character.

Infer: Based on these details, in what ways has Nurzhan grown?

230 The morning of the dance, Mama came into the kitchen while Nurzhan and I were eating *kasha.* Mama still had a wrap on her ankle, but she was walking without her crutches now. She was happier, and I could tell she felt better. It was better for me, too. When Mama was happier, I didn't feel so worried about her.

231 "Maya, I have something for you." Mama came to the table and put a small package wrapped in tissue paper in front of me. "Open." She pointed at the package.

232 I looked up at her, my face full of surprise.

233 "Open."

234 Carefully, I unfolded the tissue paper and let out a gasp when I saw a small gold bracelet lying on the folds of the thin paper.

235 "You wear this to the dance." Mama patted my shoulder.

236 "Oh, Mama." I wanted to hug her like we hug on the gymnastics team, but I was too shy. We don't hug in our family.

237 "I forget sometimes when there is so much work that you are just a young girl. This bracelet my mother gave to me when

ANALYZE PLOT

Annotate: The events following a story's climax are the falling action. Mark the most important dialogue that is spoken during the falling action described in paragraphs 230–237.

Connect: Reread the first paragraph of the story. How do Mama's words connect with Maya's earlier thoughts?

NOTICE & NOTE

I was sixteen. Girls and boys dance younger here, Maya. So you wear this now."

238 "Thank you, Mama. I will be careful with it."

239 "I know. You're a good girl. And Nurzhan will be right there. Always by your side."

240 "Yes, Mama." Nurzhan nodded.

241 Shannon and I met in the bathroom after school, and she loaned me her peach lip-gloss. I can't remember ever being so excited about anything, and so nervous, too.

242 Nurzhan was waiting by the gym door when we got out of the bathroom. Shannon and I said hi to him, and he followed us into the gym. Nurzhan found a chair next to the door and waved to us while we joined Leslie Shattuck and her sister Tina and Faith Reeves from the gymnastics team. The gym got more and more crowded, and everywhere you looked there were flocks of boys and flocks of girls, but no boys and girls together, as if they were birds that only stayed with their own kind.

243 Then a few ninth-grade guys and girls danced together. They were very cool and everyone watched them, except some seventh-grade boys who were pushing each other around in an empty garbage can.

244 Shannon and I were laughing at those silly boys when Daniel and David came up to us. I was so happy to see Daniel, even though I was embarrassed about my face, which I knew was once again the deepest red, like borscht. But the next thing I knew, Daniel had asked me to dance, and Shannon was dancing with David!

245 Daniel held my hand and put his arm around my waist, and I put my hand on his shoulder just the way Shannon and I had practiced so many times. It was a slow dance, and Mama's bracelet gleamed on my wrist as it lay on Daniel's shoulder.

246 "My little brother's here. I had to baby-sit."

247 "Want to check on him?" Daniel asked.

248 "Sure."

249 We danced over near Nurzhan, who sat on the chair like a tiny mouse in the corner, and I introduced him to Daniel.

250 "Are you doing okay?" I asked Nurzhan.

251 "Yes. It's a little boring though."

252 "I'm sorry you have to be here."

253 "It's not that bad. The boys in the garbage can are fun to watch. I would enjoy doing that if I came to this dance."

LANGUAGE CONVENTIONS

Annotate: In paragraph 253, circle the prepositional phrase that might cause confusion about which noun is the subject of the sentence. Then underline the subject and verb in the sentence.

Evaluate: If the author had left out the prepositional phrase, would the sentence's meaning be more clear, or less so? Why?

NOTICE & NOTE

254 Then we danced away and danced even more slowly, and Daniel moved a little closer to me. I looked over, afraid that Nurzhan was watching, but all I saw was an empty chair. And then we danced closer.

255 Daniel and I danced four more times that afternoon (two fast and two *very* slow), and each time Nurzhan's chair was empty and he seemed to have disappeared. I didn't think too much about Nurzhan during the rest of the dance, and on the bus going home, while Shannon and I talked and talked, reliving every wonderful moment, I almost forgot he was there.

256 But that night when Nurzhan and I were going to sleep and I was thinking about how that day had been the best day of my life, I thanked him for making it possible for me to go to the dance.

257 "There's just one thing I wondered about," I whispered as the mini-mart sign blinked on and off.

258 "What's that?"

259 "Where did you go when I danced with Daniel?"

260 "To the bathroom."

261 "The bathroom?"

262 "Yes."

263 "You are an excellent chaperone."

264 Nurzhan and I giggled so loud that Mama came in and told us to be quiet. "Shhh, Nurzhan, Maya. Go to sleep!" She spoke sharply to both of us.

265 After she left, Nurzhan fell asleep right away like he usually does. But I lay awake for a while and I looked over at Nurzhan and was struck by how much things had changed. I looked at the table by my bed and saw the gold bracelet shining in the blinking light of the mini-mart sign, and I imagined Mama

AGAIN AND AGAIN

Notice & Note: Mark the statement Maya recalls in paragraph 265.

Analyze: Why might the author have repeated these words?

wearing it when she was sixteen, and I treasured what she'd said as much as the bracelet: "Girls and boys dance younger here, Maya. So you wear this now."

266 And I thought of Daniel, who I think is quite a special boy with a good heart. *Kak horosho.* How wonderful. Thinking of him made me smile inside. Then I closed my eyes, hoping very much that Nurzhan would like to chaperone at the next dance.

CHECK YOUR UNDERSTANDING

Answer these questions before moving on to the **Analyze the Text** section on the following page.

1 What does paragraph 1 reveal about Maya and her conflict?

A She wants to go to the all-school dance, but she isn't sure she should attend because she can't dance.

B She wants to go to the all-school dance, but she thinks her parents are unlikely to give her permission.

C She didn't take a permission slip for the all-school dance, so now she has to figure out how to get one.

D She took a permission slip for the all-school dance, but she will have to confront the popular girl to go.

2 What do Maya's thoughts, feelings, and actions in response to her mother's injury reveal about her traits and motivations?

F She is caring, obedient, and wants to help her family.

G She cares about her brother and wants him to help her out.

H She can't cook and cleans slowly but wants to improve.

J She is self-centered and wants to win in gymnastics.

3 The conflict in the story is resolved when —

A Nurzhan promises to stop fighting Ossie at school

B Maya agrees to quit gymnastics if she can go to the dance

C Nurzhan offers to be Maya's chaperone at the dance

D Maya's father agrees to be her chaperone at the dance

ANALYZE THE TEXT

Support your responses with evidence from the text. NOTEBOOK

1. **Infer** In paragraph 18, Maya tells a story about a student from Cambodia. How does this story enhance the plot's rising action?
2. **Draw Conclusions** Reread paragraph 85. Complete this chart to show how Maya's translation changes the meaning of what the principal says. Why does she make these changes?

PRINCIPAL'S WORDS	MAYA'S TRANSLATION	EFFECT

3. **Compare** Reread the dialogue in paragraphs 109–119. What does this dialogue reveal about how the mother's relationship with Maya differs from her relationship with Nurzhan?
4. **Analyze** A character's motivations can play a role in the resolution of a story's conflict. Whose motivations affect the resolution of this story, and what are those motivations? Support your answer.
5. **Notice & Note** Find the reference to a door in paragraph 151, and then review the story for similar references. What ideas might doors represent or symbolize in this story?

RESEARCH TIP
Online encyclopedias are great resources for information about countries and cultures. Also good are sites that are run by the countries themselves or by other credible authorities on culture who do not have a personal bias or agenda.

RESEARCH

The behavior expected of Maya by her parents reflects their Kazakhstani roots. Learn about Kazakhstani culture by researching answers to these questions.

QUESTION	ANSWER
What roles do gender and age play in Kazakhstani society? Explain.	
What is one example of a Kazakhstani custom?	
How free are Kazakhstani young people to choose their marriage partners?	

Connect Is the author's portrayal of the Alazova family's rules and expectations realistic? Discuss this in a small group.

CREATE AND DISCUSS

Write a Summary Write a summary of "My Favorite Chaperone." To do this, you will briefly retell the plot of the story in your own words.

- ❑ Introduce the major characters and state the conflict.
- ❑ Convey the major events that occur during the rising action. Maintain the author's meaning and the logical order of events.
- ❑ Identify the climax of the story. Then describe the resolution of the conflict and the story's final outcome.

Discuss with a Small Group Did Maya handle the situation in the principal's office appropriately? Discuss this question with a group.

- ❑ Reread paragraphs 74–90. Discuss Maya's translations and their outcome. Look for clues as to why she chose to handle the situation in this way.
- ❑ Discuss what you would have done in Maya's place and whether any of these options would have been better, considering their likely impact on Maya and Nurzhan. Support your ideas.
- ❑ Together, decide whether Maya's handling of events was appropriate. Be prepared to support your conclusion.

Go to **Using Textual Evidence: Summarizing, Paraphrasing, and Quoting** in the **Writing Studio** for more on writing a summary.

Go to **Participating in Collaborative Discussions** in the **Speaking and Listening Studio** for help.

RESPOND TO THE ESSENTIAL QUESTION

What are the places that shape who you are?

Gather Information Review your annotations and notes on "My Favorite Chaperone." Then, add relevant details to your Response Log. As you determine which details to include, think about:

- the Alazova family's rules, expectations, and ways of interacting
- Maya's thoughts, actions, and feelings and what they suggest about her beliefs and values
- the differences Maya notices between the Lui family and hers

At the end of the unit, you can use your notes to help you write a short story.

ACADEMIC VOCABULARY

As you write and discuss what you learned from the story, be sure to use the Academic Vocabulary words. Check off each of the words that you use.

- ❑ **contribute**
- ❑ **immigrate**
- ❑ **reaction**
- ❑ **relocate**
- ❑ **shifting**

CRITICAL VOCABULARY

WORD BANK
sponsor
stun
dispatcher
scuffle
whimper

Practice and Apply To demonstrate that you understand the Critical Vocabulary words, complete each sentence in a way that makes sense.

1. When Maya becomes a U.S. citizen, she may want to **sponsor** . . .
2. When Nurzhan is Maya's chaperone, he **stuns** her by . . .
3. The cab driver needed to have his **dispatcher** . . .
4. The sounds of a **scuffle** alerted me to the fact that . . .
5. At a gymnastics meet, Maya might **whimper** if she . . .

VOCABULARY STRATEGY: Context Clues

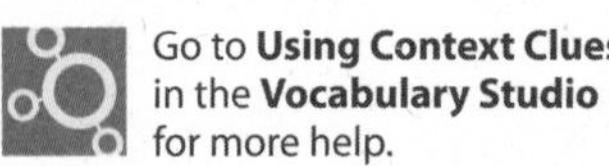
Go to **Using Context Clues** in the **Vocabulary Studio** for more help.

The **context** of a word is made up of the punctuation marks, words, sentences, and paragraphs that surround the word. When you encounter an unfamiliar or ambiguous word or one with multiple meanings, its context may provide you with clues that can help you understand its meaning. Look at the following example:

> **Mr. Walsh, the vice-principal, came into our class. He whispered something to Ms. Coe and she nodded. And then I was stunned because she nodded and pointed to me!**

The exclamation point suggests that Maya did not expect that Mr. Walsh had come to get her. Feeling stunned probably means feeling surprised or shocked. If you knew the other meaning of *stunned,* "dazed by a blow or a loud noise," this context would help you know that it doesn't apply here.

Practice and Apply Review "My Favorite Chaperone" to find the following words. Then complete this chart.

WORD	CONTEXT CLUES	MY GUESSED DEFINITION	DICTIONARY DEFINITION
huddled (paragraph 7)			
mispronouncing (paragraph 50)			
drizzle (paragraph 71)			

LANGUAGE CONVENTIONS:
Subject-Verb Agreement

The subject and verb in a sentence or clause must agree in number. **Agreement** means that if the subject is singular, the verb must also be singular; if the subject is plural, the verb must also be plural. In this sentence from "My Favorite Chaperone," both the subject and the verb are singular.

Nurzhan has been in a fight with another boy.

Notice how the verb changes when the subject is plural:

Nurzhan and Ossie have been in a fight.

Sometimes a **prepositional phrase**—which consists of a preposition, its object, and any modifiers of the object—comes between the subject and the verb. In that case, you must ignore the phrase and identify the sentence's true subject. The subject is never found within a prepositional phrase. In the example below, note how the prepositional phrase *in Maya's class* ends with a singular noun. However, the subject of the sentence is *kids*, which requires the plural noun *were*.

The kids in Maya's class were nice.

The agreement rule is true for all sentence types. Consider the following **complex sentence**, which consists of a main clause and a subordinate clause. The prepositional phrase *on the gymnastics team* ends with a singular noun, but the subject of the clause is *girls*, which requires the plural noun *were*.

While she cleaned houses, the other girls on the gymnastics team were practicing.

Practice and Apply Choose the verb form that agrees with the subject in each sentence or clause.

1. A stack of permission slips (was, were) lying on the teacher's desk.
2. Students on the gymnastics team (practices, practice) after school.
3. The boys in the fight (shoves, shove) each other hard, while a teacher and a custodian in the yard (runs, run) over to stop them.
4. Boys and girls at the Spring Fling (dances, dance) to the music.

Go to **Agreement of Subject and Verb** in the **Grammar Studio** for more on subject-verb agreement.

from THE BOOK OF UNKNOWN AMERICANS

Novel by **Cristina Henríquez**

? ***ESSENTIAL QUESTION:***

What are the places that shape who you are?

QUICK START

If you moved to another state or country, what would you remember most about where you live now? How would you want to spend your time if you returned for a brief visit? Write down your thoughts.

ANALYZE NARRATIVE STRUCTURE

The **structure** of a work of literature is the way in which it is put together. The excerpt from *The Book of Unknown Americans* spans a stretch of time from the narrator's early childhood until the present, revealing how the characters change over time. Many of these changes occur gradually: One event brings about, or causes, another, and that event in turn causes yet another. Thus, both the short-term and long-term consequences of small events become apparent. As you read the novel excerpt, note these cause-effect relationships between events.

GENRE ELEMENTS: NOVEL

- is a long work of fiction
- tells a story from the writer's imagination
- can develop characters and conflict more thoroughly than a short story
- often develops more than one plot and/or contains subplots

Cause →	Effect
Panama was ravaged by war.	The narrator's family moved to the United States.
Cause →	**Effect**
Cause →	**Effect**

ANALYZE THEME

A **theme** is a message about life or human nature that's shared by a writer. Here are some ways to find and analyze themes:

- Look for **explicit** textual statements of the characters' ideas about life or people. Pay particular attention to statements characters make about lessons they have learned over the course of events.
- Look for details that **implicitly** convey, or imply, what a character believes about life or human nature. For instance, how a character reacts to a **conflict,** or problem, and the results of his or her behavior may hold a message the author wants to convey.

One important theme of *The Book of Unknown Americans* is related to the challenges immigrants face in adapting to life in a new culture. As you read the novel excerpt, consider how events in the story affect the characters' sense of their cultural identity. Also consider how details about places in Panama and other settings influence the narrator's values and beliefs about himself.

CRITICAL VOCABULARY

reminisce	ravage	froth	convene
assure	melodrama	confer	

To see how many Critical Vocabulary words you already know, use them to complete the sentences.

1. When we met to __________, the __________ created by people who personally disliked each other interfered with our ability to reach an agreement about the issue.
2. Officials planned to __________ at City Hall to discuss responses for the storm that is expected to __________ the area.
3. I __________ you that our region is not in the path of the storm.
4. He was in a(n) __________ over the long lines at the store.
5. The two old friends would often __________ about their childhood.

LANGUAGE CONVENTIONS

Pronouns A **pronoun** is a word used in place of a noun or another pronoun. In this example, the pronoun *he* refers back to *my dad:*

Besides, my dad never wanted to take time off from his job. He probably could've asked for a few days of vacation time. . . .

As you read the excerpt from *The Book of Unknown Americans,* pay attention to the author's use of pronouns and note how the pronouns differ when they serve as subjects or as objects.

ANNOTATION MODEL

NOTICE & NOTE

As you read, note how the characters respond to events. Also mark up evidence that supports your own ideas. In the model, you can see one reader's notes about *The Book of Unknown Americans.*

1 I was less than a year old when my parents brought my brother and me to the United States. Enrique was four. He used to tell me things about Panamá that I couldn't possibly have remembered—like about the scorpions in our backyard and the cement utility sink where my mom used to give us baths. He reminisced about walking down the street with my mom to the Super 99, the dust blowing up everywhere, the heat pounding down, and about looking for crabs between the rocks along the bay.

cause: The narrator was brought to the U.S. as a baby.

effect: He does not remember anything about Panama.

BACKGROUND

The Book of Unknown Americans *is told from the points of view of different immigrants who all reside in an apartment building in Delaware. Author* **Cristina Henríquez** *(b. 1977) grew up in Delaware and currently resides in Illinois. Her father emigrated from Panama in 1971, and she spent many childhood summer vacations visiting family there. This excerpt is narrated by Mayor, a boy who came to the United States with his family after the United States invaded Panama in 1989 in order to remove that country's military leader, Manuel Noriega, from power.*

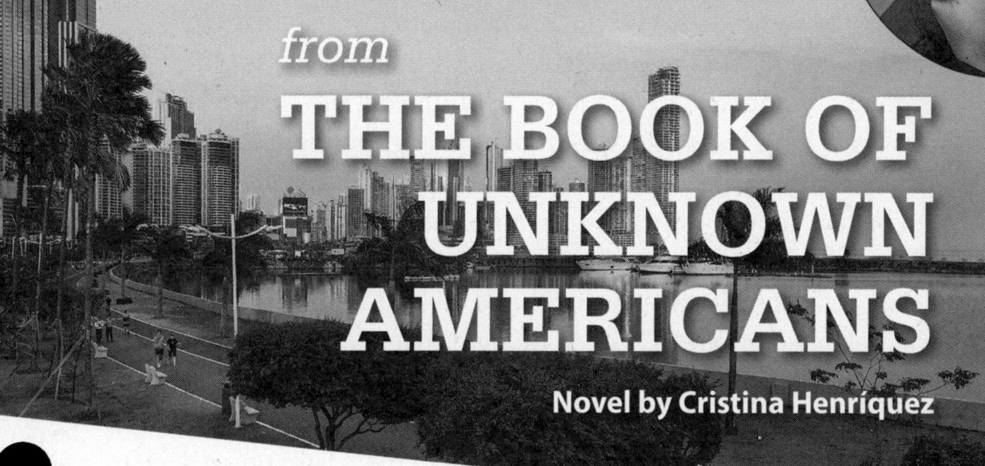

from

THE BOOK OF UNKNOWN AMERICANS

Novel by Cristina Henríquez

SETTING A PURPOSE

As you read, pay attention to details that show how the characters feel about their current home and the home they left.

1 I was less than a year old when my parents brought my brother and me to the United States. Enrique was four. He used to tell me things about Panamá that I couldn't possibly have remembered—like about the scorpions in our backyard and the cement utility sink where my mom used to give us baths. He **reminisced** about walking down the street with my mom to the Super 99, the dust blowing up everywhere, the heat pounding down, and about looking for crabs between the rocks along the bay.

2 "It's in you," my dad **assured** me once. "You were born in Panamá. It's in your bones."

3 I spent a lot of time trying to find it in me, but usually I couldn't. I felt more American than anything, but even that was up for debate according to the kids at school who'd taunted me over the years, asking me if I was related to

Notice & Note

Use the side margins to notice and note signposts in the text.

reminisce
(rĕm′ə-nĭs′) *v.* When you *reminisce,* you think or talk about past experiences.

assure
(ə-shŏŏr′) *v.* To *assure* is to state something positively, so as to remove doubt about it.

Noriega, telling me to go back through the canal. The truth was that I didn't know which I was. I wasn't allowed to claim the thing I felt and I didn't feel the thing I was supposed to claim.

4 The first time I heard my parents tell the story about leaving Panamá, my mom said, "Our hearts kept breaking each time we walked out the door." They tried to give it time. They assumed conditions would improve. But the country was so **ravaged** that their hearts never stopped breaking. Eventually they sold almost everything they owned and used the money to buy plane tickets to somewhere else, somewhere better, which to them had always meant the United States. A while after I was old enough to understand this story, I pointed out how backwards it was to have fled to the nation that had driven them out of theirs, but they never copped to the irony of it. They needed to believe they'd done the right thing and that it made sense. They were torn between wanting to look back and wanting to exist absolutely in the new life they'd created. At one point, they had planned to return. They'd thought that with enough time, Panamá would be rebuilt and that their hearts, I guess, would heal. But while they waited for that day, they started making friends. My dad got a job as a busboy and then, later on, as a dishwasher. Years passed. Enrique was in school, and I started, too. My dad was promoted to line cook. More years slid by. And before they knew it, we had a life here. They had left their lives once before. They didn't want to do it again.

ravage
(răv´ĭj) *v.* To *ravage* is to cause serious damage or destruction.

ANALYZE NARRATIVE STRUCTURE

Annotate: Mark words and phrases in paragraph 4 that show the passage of time.

Interpret: How do the narrator's parents' attitudes about their homeland change as time passes?

5 So they applied for U.S. citizenship, sitting up at night reading the Constitution, a dictionary by their side, and studying for the exam. They contacted someone at the Panamanian consulate[1] in Philadelphia who helped them navigate the paperwork. Then they woke up one morning, got dressed in their best clothes, caught a bus to the courthouse, and, while my mom held me in her arms and my dad rested his hand on Enrique's shoulder, took an oath along with a group of other men and women who had made living in the United States a dream. We became Americans.

AGAIN AND AGAIN

Notice & Note: Mark details in paragraph 5 that tell how the family "became Americans."

Analyze: How does the description of the family becoming Americans in paragraph 5 relate to the ideas the narrator expresses about feeling American in paragraph 3?

6 We never went back to Panamá, not even for a visit. It would have taken us forever to save enough money for plane tickets. Besides, my dad never wanted to take time off from his

[1] **consulate** (kŏn´sə-lĭt): a representative office of a foreign government located within another nation's borders.

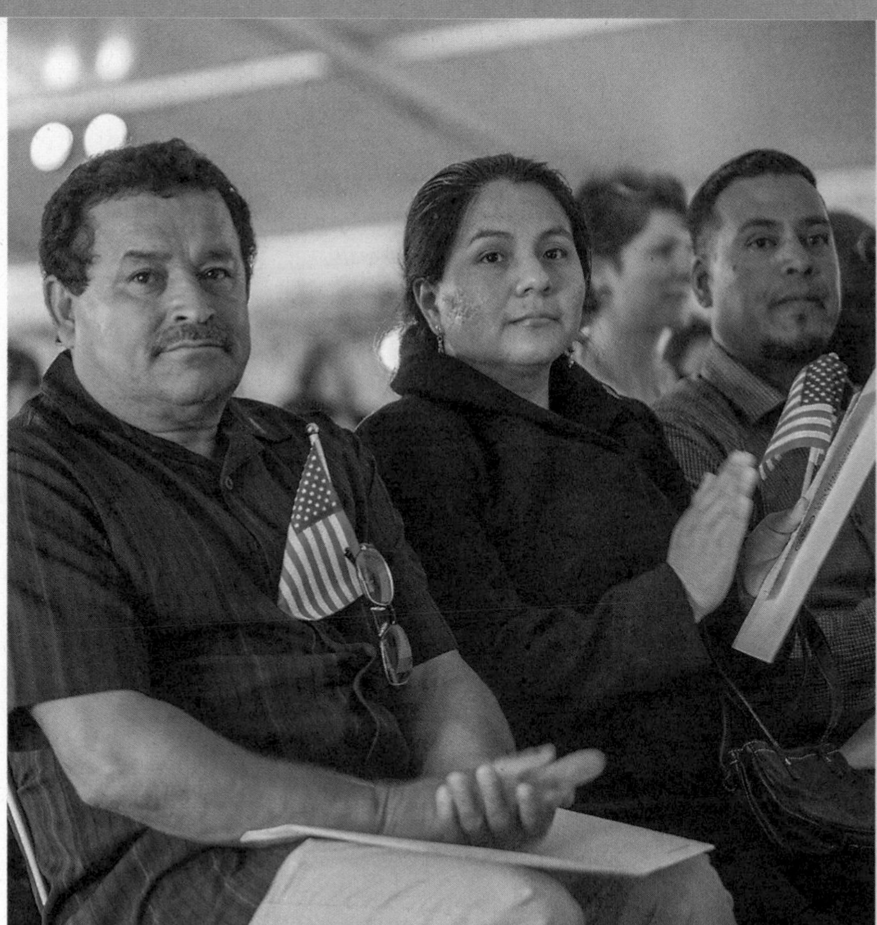

job. He probably could've asked for a few days of vacation time, but even after years of being there, making omelets and flipping pancakes, he knew—we all knew—that he was on the low end of the food chain. He could be replaced in a heartbeat. He didn't want to risk it.

7 Because of that, we'd missed my tía Gloria's wedding, which she'd had on a hillside in Boquete. She told my mom that she'd convinced her new husband, Esteban, to dance and that therefore the whole event was a success. We had my aunt on speakerphone and my mom had said, "Take it from me, hermanita,[2] they dance at the wedding and then they never do it again." My dad had said, "That's what you think?" and clutched my mom by the wrist, sending her into a small spin in the middle of the kitchen. She squealed with delight while he swayed with her for a few beats and then he broke out into some goofy merengue[3] moves, kicking his leg up at the end and shouting "¡Olé!" My aunt started yelling through the phone, "Are you still there? Celia! Rafael!" And my parents laughed

[2] **hermanita** (ûr-mə-nē´tə): the Spanish word for "little sister."

[3] **merengue** (mə-rĕng´gā): a dance of Dominican and Haitian folk origin, characterized by a sliding step.

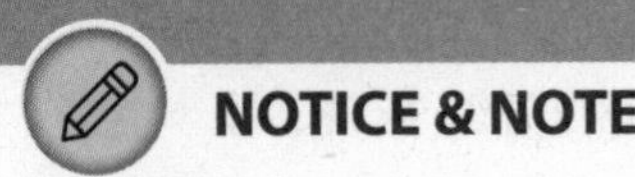

NOTICE & NOTE

until my mom dabbed the corners of her eyes with the back of her hand. I'd never seen them so happy with each other, even though it was just for those few seconds.

8 We almost went back for my dad's high school reunion, which my dad somehow got into his head that he didn't want to miss. The reunion was on a Friday, so maybe, he told us, he could fix his work schedule so that he was off on Friday. We could fly there, go to the reunion, and then fly back Saturday night. He was usually off on Sundays, but if he took off Friday instead, he'd have to be back and work Sunday to make up for it. So one night would be the longest we could stay, but one night would be enough. He had decided. And it looked like we were going to try.

ANALYZE THEME

Annotate: Mark places in paragraph 9 that show Celia's feelings about the trip to Panama.

Infer: What do the narrator's descriptive details suggest about Celia?

9 My mom was as excited about the trip as I don't know what. She went to Sears to buy a new dress and had giddy phone conversations with my aunt about seeing each other again and what they would be able to pack into our eighteen hours on the ground. She started laying out her clothes weeks in advance even though my dad kept telling her she only needed two outfits—one to go and one to come home. "And why do you have ten pairs of shoes here?" he asked, pointing to the sandals and leather high heels my mom had lined up along the baseboard in the bedroom. "Ten!" my mom scoffed. "I don't even own ten pairs of shoes." My father counted them. "Fine. Seven. That's still six too many." He told her that he intended to take only a duffel bag for our things because that would make it easier to get through customs. My mom said, "I'll check my own bag, then." My dad kicked the row of shoes my mom had lined up and sent them flying into the wall. He walked right up to my mom and held his index finger in front of her face. "One bag, Celia. One! For all four of us. Don't talk to me about it again."

LANGUAGE CONVENTIONS

The word or phrase to which a pronoun refers is called its **antecedent.** Circle the uses of the pronoun *he* in paragraph 10 and underline its antecedent in each case.

10 A few weeks before the reunion, my dad called the number on the invitation to RSVP. The guy who answered had been the class president. He and my dad joked around for a minute and then my dad told the guy we were coming. According to what my dad told us later, the guy said, "We'll roll out the red carpet, then." When my dad asked him what he meant by that, the guy said that my dad would have to forgive him if the party wasn't up to my dad's standards. "We didn't

know the gringo[4] royalty was coming. We'll have to get the place repainted before you arrive." When my dad asked again what the guy was talking about, the guy said he hoped my dad didn't expect them all to kiss his feet now and reminded my dad how humble Panamá was. It didn't take long for my dad to slam the phone down. He stormed over to my mom, who was washing dishes, and said, "We're not going. If that's what they think, then we're not going."

11 My mom said, "What?"

12 "They think we're Americans now. And maybe we are! Maybe we don't belong there anymore after all." My dad went out on the balcony, which he did whenever he was really upset.

13 My mom stood in the kitchen, a soapy pot in her hand, and looked at me, baffled. "What just happened?" she asked.

14 When I told her everything I'd been able to gather, she walked out to the balcony and closed the door behind her. At the commotion, Enrique came out of his room.

15 "We're not going anymore," I told him.

16 "Huh?"

17 "On the trip."

18 "Are you serious?" Enrique asked.

19 My brother and I huddled together, listening through the front door. I heard my mom say, "Please, Rafa. He doesn't know anything about us. We can still go. You'll see. Once we get there . . . All your friends . . . And everyone will love you." I imagined her reaching out to touch his shoulder, the way she did sometimes when she was asking for something. "Don't you miss it?" she asked. "Can't you imagine landing there, being there again? You know how it smells? The air there. And seeing everyone again. Please, Rafa."

20 But my dad wasn't swayed.

21 The following year, we talked about going back, too. My dad's anger over being cast as a holier-than-thou gringo had finally simmered down, and my mom, who couldn't bring herself to return the new dress she'd bought and who hadn't gotten over the disappointment of not being able to see her sister after all, had been dropping hints ever since that she would still like to go even if the trip was only for one night again. She'd become a genius at turning any and every

ANALYZE NARRATIVE STRUCTURE

Annotate: Mark details in paragraph 21 that show the Toros still want to visit Panama.

Draw Conclusions: How do these details advance the story's plot?

[4] **gringo** (grĭng´gō): a foreigner in Latin America, especially an American or English person; the term is often considered offensive.

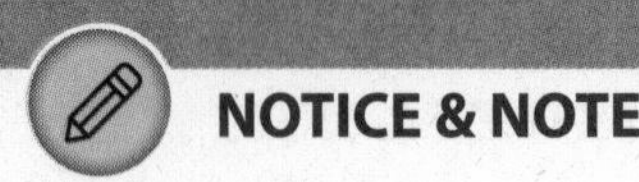

little thing into a way to talk about Panamá. She would get a mosquito bite on her ankle and point out the welt to us, reminiscing about the bites she used to get in Panamá and wondering aloud "what the mosquitoes there looked like now," as if they were old friends. She would make rice and start talking about the gallo pinto at El Trapiche, which was her favorite restaurant, saying things like "I wonder how Cristóbal—wasn't that the owner's name?—is doing. Wouldn't it be nice to find out?" We would drive over a bridge and suddenly she was talking about the Bridge of the Americas near the canal. "Do you remember, Enrique? That time we took the ferry back from Taboga at night and it was all lit up? It was so beautiful. Mayor, I wish you could have seen it." She sighed. "Maybe one day." And my dad would sometimes shake his head at her **melodrama** and other times would just stay quiet, like he'd fallen into the haze of a particular memory himself.

melodrama (mĕl´ə-drä´mə) *n. Melodrama* is behavior characterized by exaggerated emotions.

22 My mom's birthday was September 22, so my dad finally gave in and made plans for us to go to Panamá. The Toro Family! One night only! Put it in lights! My mom worked herself into a **froth** all over again, **conferring** with my tía Gloria on the phone. My aunt apparently said she wanted to take my mom to the new mall and for a drive through Costa del Este, which used to be a garbage dump but now had been transformed into an up-and-coming area of the city, and out for sushi on the causeway, and afterwards they could hit the clubs along Calle Uruguay and yes, she realized they weren't twenty anymore but it would be so much fun! Besides, she and my tío Esteban weren't doing so well, she told my mom. He was never home. He spent the night at friends' apartments. So she could use some distraction and someone to talk to. "Not a divorce!" my mom gasped. To her, there could be nothing worse. "No," my aunt assured her. "Just problems."

froth (frôth) *n.* A *froth* is a fit of frustration or excitement.

confer (kən-fûr´) *v.* To *confer* is to share ideas or make a decision with one or more other people.

23 Then, less than two weeks before we were scheduled to go, two planes flew into the World Trade Center in New York City and another one into the Pentagon in Washington, D.C. The country went into shock and we went right along with it. My dad called my mom from the diner, where, on the television above the counter, he had just seen the second plane hit the second tower. "They're blowing it up!" he apparently told her. "It's just like El Chorrillo.[5] They're destroying it!" And my mom, in her nightgown, rushed to the set and stood in front of

ANALYZE NARRATIVE STRUCTURE

Annotate: Mark words and phrases in paragraphs 23–25 that relate to time.

Compare: How does the passage of time in this section of the narrative compare with the passage of time in paragraphs 10–20? What is the impact of this structure on the story's plot?

[5] **El Chorrillo** (ĕl chô-rē´yō): a neighborhood in Panama City that suffered heavy damage during the 1989 U.S. invasion of Panama.

it, watching with her hand over her mouth. I had been eating cereal in the kitchen. I carried my bowl over and stood next to her and kept eating, which, when I thought about it later, seemed kind of messed up, but at the time we didn't know what was happening. The world hadn't stopped—just stopped—like it would later that day and for days after. Everything was still just unfolding in front of our eyes and we had no idea what to make of it.

24 It didn't take long before everyone in our building was knocking on each other's doors and **convening** out on the balcony, standing around stunned and shaking with fear. Nelia Zafón just kept repeating, "What is happening? What is happening? What is happening?" I heard my mom say to someone, "We moved here because it was supposed to be safer! Where can we go after this?" All day long she kept herself no more than an arm's length from me and my brother, hugging us against her and then letting us go, like she wanted to assure herself that we were still there and that we were okay. Enrique, who was old enough by then that he usually squirmed away from my mom's embraces, must have known the situation was serious, because he let her do it. I let her, too, even though every time she did, instead of comforting me, it only made me more scared.

convene
(kən-vēn′) *v.* To *convene* is to come together for a purpose.

25 By evening, everyone's front doors were open and people were roaming in and out of each other's units, watching each other's televisions as if a different set would deliver different news, checking to see if anyone had heard anything new, getting tedious translations. Benny Quinto led prayer circles in his living room. Micho Alvarez paced up and down the balcony, talking on his cell phone and jotting things in his notebook. Gustavo Milhojas, who was half-Mexican and half-Guatemalan, wrote a letter to the army telling them that as of that day he was 100 percent American and that he was ready to serve the country and kill the cowards who had murdered his fellow paisanos.[6] At the end he wrote, "And here is a list of people who are willing to join me." He drew a few blank lines and spent the afternoon trying to recruit everyone in the building. When my mom saw what it was, she said, "More killing? That's what you want? *More?*" And Gustavo said, "Not killing. Justice."

26 That year around the holidays we were all miserable. Holidays were always bad—my mom in particular got homesick

[6] **paisanos** (pī-zä′nōs): countrymen.

NOTICE & NOTE

ANALYZE THEME

Annotate: Mark places in paragraphs 26–27 that show Celia's attitude toward her home in Panama and her home in the United States.

Infer: Why do you think the holiday season is a particularly difficult time of year for the Toros?

sometimes like it was a genuine illness—but that Christmas was the worst. We were depressed and on edge, still shaken up about September 11, and then re-shaken when someone tried to blow up another plane by hiding a bomb in his shoes two days before Christmas Eve.

27 My aunt called, which cheered my mom up for a while, but once that wore off, she was more down than ever, shuffling around the house in her slippers, no makeup, her hair a disaster. She carried tissues in the pocket of her bathrobe and made a big show of dabbing her nose with them every so often. Eventually, my dad came up with an idea. "You want Panamá?" he said. "A beach is the closest thing you're going to get." He hustled us out the door and down the street, where we took a chain of buses for an hour and a half to Cape Henlopen in southern Delaware. It was snowing when we arrived—Enrique kept complaining that the snow was going to mess up his beloved Adidas sneakers—and everything was so colorless and barren that it looked like the moon. I had to hand it to my dad, though. With the water and the sand, my mom said it almost *was* like a little piece of Panamá. The waves roared in toward us and then silently pulled back again, slipping over the shore. Even with the falling snow, the air had the sting of salt water, and we crunched broken seashells under our shoes. But one beach isn't every beach. And one home isn't every home. And I think we all sensed, standing there, just how far we were from where we had come, in ways both good and bad. "It's beautiful," my mom said, staring out at the ocean. She sighed and shook her head. "This country."

CHECK YOUR UNDERSTANDING

Answer these questions before moving on to the **Analyze the Text** section on the following page.

1 Rafa cancels a trip to attend his high school reunion in Panama because he is —

- **A** worried about losing his job if he takes too much time off from work
- **B** afraid that someone tried to blow up a plane two days before he was supposed to leave
- **C** angry about a conversation he had with a former classmate about his plans
- **D** upset that the neighborhood in his home city has been destroyed

2 The novel's title, *The Book of Unknown Americans,* emphasizes the idea in the excerpt that the characters struggle to —

- **F** find out about their past
- **G** locate their other family members
- **H** fit in with their new culture
- **J** return to their former home

3 Which character in the story shows the strongest desire to visit Panama?

- **A** Mayor
- **B** Enrique
- **C** Celia
- **D** Rafa

RESPOND

ANALYZE THE TEXT

Support your responses with evidence from the text. NOTEBOOK

1. **Analyze** State one theme the author develops in this excerpt. Cite evidence from the text to support your analysis.
2. **Draw Conclusions** In paragraph 7, the narrator states, "And my parents laughed until my mom dabbed the corners of her eyes with the back of her hand." What can you conclude about Celia based on this statement? Cite text evidence to support your conclusion.
3. **Cause and Effect** What are the effects of the two canceled trips to Panama on the course of the story?
4. **Analyze** How is the narrator's identity, or sense of himself, affected by his surroundings? Cite text evidence to support your answer.
5. **Notice & Note** How do the statements Rafa makes about being American in paragraph 12 relate to other ideas about American identity expressed elsewhere in the text?

RESEARCH TIP
Some websites are more reliable than others. In your research, try to use websites that have reliable and verified information, such as those of institutions dedicated to fact-checking their information.

RESEARCH

The Book of Unknown Americans references real people, places, and events related to the history of Panama. Conduct research to learn more about Panama's history. Record your findings in the chart.

QUESTION	ANSWER
What is the Panama Canal? When was it built?	
How did the United States gain control of the Panama Canal? When did Panama gain complete control of the canal?	
Who was Manuel Noriega?	
Why did the United States invade Panama in 1989?	

Connect In paragraph 4, the narrator says of his parents' decision to emigrate to the United States, "I pointed out how backwards it was to have fled to the nation that had driven them out of theirs, but they never copped to the irony of it." In a small group, discuss how your research about Panama's history helps you understand this statement.

CREATE AND PRESENT

Write a Paragraph Choose a character from *The Book of Unknown Americans* and write a paragraph from that character's point of view explaining how he or she feels about the place(s) he or she calls home.

- ❑ Review the text for implicit and explicit details that help you make inferences about the character's thoughts and feelings.
- ❑ Describe the connections the character feels to his or her home(s) and why. Be sure to write from the point of view of the character.
- ❑ Make sure you include details that clearly identify the character. Convey the voice of the character by using language that allows your reader to "hear" his or her personality.

Go to **Writing Narratives** in the **Writing Studio** for more help with writing from a character's point of view.

Act Out a Scene In a small group, choose a scene to act out that's described by the narrator in *The Book of Unknown Americans*.

- ❑ As a group, review the text and discuss which scenes would be best to perform. Take a vote to decide on a scene. How many actors will you need? How does the scene relate to the themes of the novel excerpt? Take notes to record your group's ideas.
- ❑ As a group, write a script. Next, cast the characters. Rehearse your scene. Assemble any props you may need.
- ❑ Finally, perform your scene for the class. Listen attentively as you watch other groups' scenes. Ask questions about the choices each group made in planning and performing their scenes.

Go to **Participating in Collaborative Discussions** in the **Speaking and Listening Studio** for more.

RESPOND TO THE ESSENTIAL QUESTION

What are the places that shape who you are?

Gather Information Review your annotations and notes on *The Book of Unknown Americans*. Then, add relevant details to your Response Log. To decide what to include, think about:

- where a person calls home after he or she has moved
- why a person can call more than one place home
- how where we live or where we are from affects others' opinions of us

At the end of the unit, you may use your notes to help you write a short story.

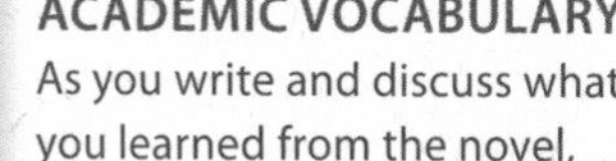

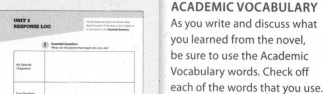

ACADEMIC VOCABULARY

As you write and discuss what you learned from the novel, be sure to use the Academic Vocabulary words. Check off each of the words that you use.

- ❑ **contribute**
- ❑ **immigrate**
- ❑ **reaction**
- ❑ **relocate**
- ❑ **shifting**

RESPOND

CRITICAL VOCABULARY

WORD BANK
reminisce
assure
ravage
melodrama
froth
confer
convene

Practice and Apply Write a short answer to show that you understand each of the Critical Vocabulary words.

1. Write about a time in your life you like to **reminisce** about.
2. Write a sentence using the word **ravage.**
3. Share an example of a **melodrama.**
4. Write a sentence using the word **froth.**
5. Describe something two people might **confer** about.
6. Describe how someone might **assure** you of something.
7. Give a reason why a group of people might **convene.**

VOCABULARY STRATEGY: Use a Dictionary

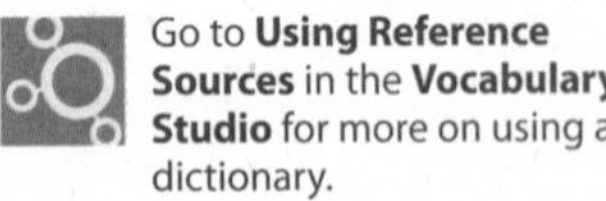

Go to **Using Reference Sources** in the **Vocabulary Studio** for more on using a dictionary.

While you can use online search engines to look up a word's spelling or meaning, it is important to evaluate the source you use. A reliable print or online dictionary will tell you not only a word's correct spelling and definition but also its pronunciation, syllabication, part of speech, and word origin. Note the word *copped* in paragraph 4 of the excerpt from *The Book of Unknown Americans.* You can use context, or the words and sentences around the word, to infer its meaning. If you look the word up in the dictionary to confirm its precise meaning, you might find these definitions for the transitive verb form of *cop:*

> **cop** (kŏp) *tr. v. Slang* **1.** To get hold of; gain or win. **2.** To take unlawfully or without permission; steal. **3.** To plead guilty; admit. [Probably variant of *cap*, to catch, from Old French *caper*, from Latin *capere.*]

Definition **3** best matches the meaning of *copped* in the sentence.

Practice and Apply Find the words below in the excerpt from *The Book of Unknown Americans.* Use a print or online dictionary to identify the definition that matches the word's meaning in context and its part of speech. Then use the pronunciation to say the word.

WORD	PART OF SPEECH	MEANING
utility (paragraph 1)		
taunted (paragraph 3)		
recruit (paragraph 25)		

LANGUAGE CONVENTIONS: Pronouns

It's important to know how to use subject pronouns and object pronouns correctly in formal writing and speech. A **subject pronoun** is used as a subject in a sentence. An **object pronoun** is used as a direct object, an indirect object, or the object of a preposition.

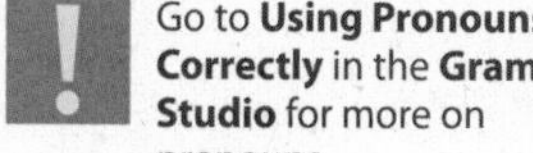

Go to **Using Pronouns Correctly** in the **Grammar Studio** for more on pronouns.

SUBJECT PRONOUNS	OBJECT PRONOUNS
I, we	**me, us**
you	**you**
he, she, it, they	**him, her, it, them**

SUBJECT OBJECT

We will give them to her.

OBJECT OF PREPOSITION

Sometimes a pronoun is part of a **compound,** which means that more than one subject or object is joined by the conjunction *or* or *and.* Study these examples from *The Book of Unknown Americans:*

> **My brother and I huddled together, listening through the front door.**

In this sentence, notice how "I huddled" still sounds correct without the compound part *My brother and,* but "me huddled" would not sound correct.

> **All day long she kept herself no more than an arm's length from me and my brother.**

In this sentence, the preposition *from* and the compound object *me and my brother* form a **prepositional phrase.** Note that "an arm's length from me" sounds correct, but "an arm's length from I" would not.

Practice and Apply Choose the correct personal pronoun in each sentence.

1. You should give the paper to him or (her/she).
2. My teacher asked my classmate and (me/I) to help hand out papers.
3. When they are finished, you and (I/me) will take a turn.
4. After we present our work, (they/them) will give their presentation.

SPIRIT WALKING IN THE TUNDRA

Poem by **Joy Harjo**

? ESSENTIAL QUESTION:

What are the places that shape who you are?

QUICK START

The poem you are about to read describes a place that is important to the speaker's sense of identity. Think about a place that is significant to your own identity. Then take notes about it.

Place	Why It Is Significant

ANALYZE LINE LENGTH

The **form** of a poem is the way it is laid out on the page. A **line** is the core unit of a poem. The place where a line ends is called a **line break**. Sometimes a complete line as written by the poet cannot fit on the page or screen. When that happens, the words that spill over to the next line are indented, or pushed in slightly to the right, to show they are not intended to be read as line breaks. Notice the line breaks in these five lines from "Spirit Walking in the Tundra."

All the way to Nome, I trace the shadow of the plane as it
    walks
Over turquoise lakes made by late spring breakup
Of the Bering Sea.
The plane is so heavy with cargo load it vibrates our bones.
Like the pressure made by light cracking ice.

Line length is an essential element of a poem's meaning and rhythm. What else do you need to know about line breaks?

- They do not always signal the end of a sentence or thought.
- A line break can occur in the middle of a sentence or phrase to create a meaningful pause or emphasis.
- Poets use a variety of line breaks to convey a wide range of effects, such as pace, mood, rhythm, and tone.

As you read the poem, think about why the poet breaks lines where she does. Is it to create a dramatic pause, to encourage the reader to stop and think, to focus on a particular word, or for some other reason?

GENRE ELEMENTS: POETRY

- can convey emotional intensity in relatively few words
- is sometimes written using first-person point of view to express the speaker's thoughts and feelings
- often uses repetition to emphasize important ideas
- may include rhyming words or may be written in free verse, with no regular pattern of rhyme

GET READY

ANALYZE LITERARY DEVICES

Each word in a poem contributes to its overall meaning and effect. One way poets create meaning is through the use of **imagery**, descriptions that appeal to the senses of sight, hearing, smell, taste, and touch and help a reader create mental images.

Poets also convey meaning through **allusions**, which are connections to ideas in other texts and society. Allusions may refer to people, places, events, or works of literature. In "Spirit Walking in the Tundra," Joy Harjo alludes to places and traditions that are important in Alaska Native cultures. As you read the poem, use a chart like this one to help you analyze imagery and allusions.

EXAMPLE OF IMAGERY OR ALLUSION	OVERALL MEANING AND EFFECT
Allusion: "late spring breakup / Of the Bering Sea."	
Imagery: "We are refreshed by small winds."	

The poet also uses **situational irony**, which is a contrast between what the reader expects and what actually happens. As you read, consider what some readers might find unexpected or ironic about the speaker's interaction with her friend's son.

ANNOTATION MODEL

NOTICE & NOTE 

As you read, notice the allusions and imagery in the poem. This model shows one reader's notes about the beginning of "Spirit Walking in the Tundra."

All the way to Nome, I trace the shadow of the plane as it
    walks
Over turquoise lakes made by late spring breakup
Of the Bering Sea.
The plane is so heavy with cargo load it vibrates our bones.
Like the pressure made by light cracking ice.

Allusions to Nome and the Bering Sea establish that the poem is set in Alaska.

Strong use of imagery helps the reader imagine the speaker's experience.

BACKGROUND

Born in Tulsa, Oklahoma, award-winning poet, musician, and author ***Joy Harjo*** *(b. 1951) is a member of the Mvskoke (Muscogee) Nation. Although many of her poems are set in the American Southwest, Harjo also explores the landscapes and native cultures of Alaska. The "tundra" in the poem's title refers to the flat, treeless regions in northern Alaska where the subsoil is permanently frozen.*

SPIRIT WALKING IN THE TUNDRA

Poem by Joy Harjo

SETTING A PURPOSE

As you read, pay attention to the details Harjo includes in the poem. What do these details suggest about her thoughts and feelings regarding the place and the people she is visiting?

All the way to Nome, I trace the shadow of the plane as it
    walks
Over turquoise lakes made by late spring breakup
Of the Bering Sea.
The plane is so heavy with cargo load it vibrates our bones.
Like the pressure made by light cracking ice.

Below I see pockets of marrow where seabirds nest.
Mothers are so protective they will dive humans.

Notice & Note

Use the side margins to notice and note signposts in the text.

ANALYZE LITERARY DEVICES

Annotate: Mark the image in line 1.

Analyze: What effect does this image have on the reader's understanding of the poem?

NOTICE & NOTE

I walk from the tarmac and am met by an old friend.
We drive to the launching place
And see walrus hunters set out toward the sea.
We swing to the summer camps where seal hangs on
drying frames.
She takes me home.
I watch her son play video games on break from the
university.

CONTRASTS AND CONTRADICTIONS

Notice & Note: In line 13, mark the text that contrasts with the other details included in the second stanza.

Analyze: What might the poet be suggesting by mentioning this unexpected detail?

This is what it feels like, says her son, as we walk up tundra,
Toward a herd of musk ox, *when you spirit walk.*
There is a shaking, and then you are in mystery.

Little purple flowers come up from the permafrost.
A newborn musk ox staggers around its mother's legs.

I smell the approach of someone with clean thoughts.
She is wearing designs like flowers, and a fur of ice.
She carries a basket and digging implements.
Her smell is sweet like blossoms coming up through the
snow.
The spirit of the tundra stands with us, and we collect
sunlight together,
We are refreshed by small winds.

We do not need history in books to tell us who we are
Or where we come from, I remind him.
Up here, we are near the opening in the Earth's head, the
place where the spirit leaves and returns.
Up here, the edge between life and death is thinner than
dried animal bladder.

(FOR ANUQSRAAQ AND QITUVITUAQ)

NOME, ALASKA, 2011

NOTICE & NOTE

ANALYZE LINE LENGTH

Annotate: Mark the lines in the final stanza that are longer than most of the other lines in the poem.

Analyze: Why do you think the poet made these lines longer than the others?

CHECK YOUR UNDERSTANDING

Answer these questions before moving on to the **Analyze the Text** section on the following page.

1 The speaker travels to Alaska in order to —

A observe the ocean ice breaking apart

B visit an old friend and her family

C hunt for walrus and seal

D explain her beliefs to a young man

2 The line "Her smell is sweet like blossoms coming up through the snow" emphasizes —

F the woman's physical beauty

G the powerful odor of the tundra flowers

H the woman's connection to the natural world

J the extreme coldness of the environment

3 Which of the following is an important idea in the poem?

A Air travel can be uncomfortable.

B Technology can help people relax.

C Cultural change can cause serious problems.

D Places can remind people of who they are.

RESPOND

ANALYZE THE TEXT

Support your responses with evidence from the text. NOTEBOOK

1. **Infer** The title of the poem makes an allusion to the Native American tradition of the spirit walk. Based on the events in the poem, how do you think the speaker of the poem would define the phrase "spirit walk"?

2. **Evaluate** Read aloud lines 1–3. Notice that the first two line breaks do not come at the end of a sentence. What effect do the line breaks have on the poem's rhythm, mood, or tone? Why do you think the poet chose to break the lines where she did?

3. **Interpret** Identify the imagery in lines 4 and 5. To what senses does it appeal? Explain what this imagery suggests about the speaker's feelings during her flight to Alaska.

4. **Draw Conclusions** In lines 7 and 18, the speaker refers to animal mothers and their young. How are these lines related to the rest of the poem?

5. **Notice & Note** Reread lines 12–16. Explain the situational irony of the speaker's encounter with her friend's son.

RESEARCH TIP

When you research a cultural or ethnic group online, think about possible biases that the sites' creators may have. Make sure that some of your sources are created or endorsed by members of that group, who have the greatest authority to speak on it.

RESEARCH

With a partner, research Alaska Natives. Use the questions in the chart to guide your investigation and to note the answers.

QUESTION	ANSWER
How many major groups of Alaska Natives are there? How are the groups defined?	
What is the climate like where Alaska Natives live? How has that influenced their lifestyle?	
What is the role of wildlife in the cultures and economies of Alaska Natives?	

Connect In a small group, present your results. Discuss how your research affected your understanding of the poem. Identify the lines and images in the poem that have greater meaning to you now, and explain why.

CREATE AND DEBATE

Write a Poem Write a poem that describes a time you took a walk with a friend. Use these guidelines to help you plan and draft your poem.

- ❑ Decide if you want your poem to be serious or funny.
- ❑ Use a free-verse structure, and think about where and why you will break lines.
- ❑ Use strong imagery that creates clear mental pictures for your reader.

Hold a Debate Do you learn more about yourself and your identity by traveling, or by staying close to home? Debate this issue.

- ❑ With your group, decide who will represent each side.
- ❑ Identify sources to help support your position. What have writers or thinkers said about the topic? What reasons or examples can you provide to defend your point of view?
- ❑ As you present your side's argument, make eye contact with audience members, speak clearly and loudly, and make natural hand gestures to emphasize your points.

Go to **Participating in Collaborative Discussions** in the **Speaking and Listening Studio** for more help with holding a debate.

RESPOND TO THE ESSENTIAL QUESTION

? What are the places that shape who you are?

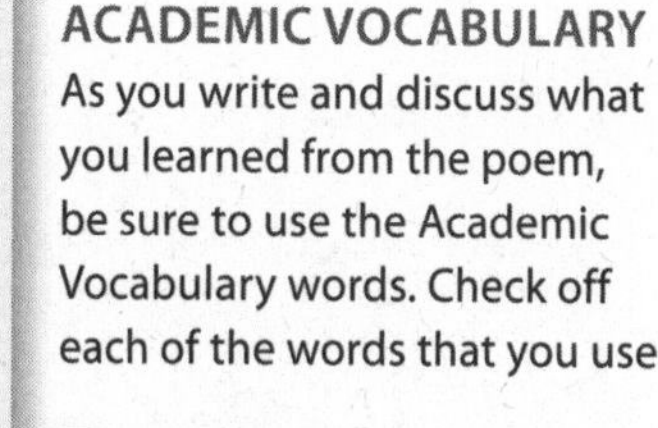

UNIT 3
RESPONSE LOG
Essential Question:
What are the places that shape who you are?
My Favorite Chaperone
from The Book of Unknown Americans
Spirit Walking in the Tundra
New Immigrants Share Their Stories
A Common Bond: Teens Forge Friendships Despite Differences

Gather Information Review your annotations and notes on "Spirit Walking in the Tundra." Then, add relevant details to your Response Log. As you determine which information to include, think about:

- how allusions to real places can enrich a poem
- how vivid imagery can capture a reader's attention
- why people often feel attached to the places that shape who they are

At the end of the unit, you may use your notes to help you write a short story.

ACADEMIC VOCABULARY

As you write and discuss what you learned from the poem, be sure to use the Academic Vocabulary words. Check off each of the words that you use.

- ❑ **contribute**
- ❑ **immigrate**
- ❑ **reaction**
- ❑ **relocate**
- ❑ **shifting**

DOCUMENTARY

NEW IMMIGRANTS SHARE THEIR STORIES

directed by **Lisa Gossels**

page 211

COMPARE PURPOSES

As you view the documentary and read the text that follows it, think about how each author achieves her purpose by using the unique elements of film or text to convey ideas. After you view and read the selections, you will collaborate with a group on a final project.

ESSENTIAL QUESTION:

What are the places that shape who you are?

INFORMATIONAL TEXT

A COMMON BOND

Teens Forge Friendships Despite Differences

by **Brooke Hauser**

pages 212–221

QUICK START

Many families have dramatic stories to tell about how and why the first family members came to the United States. In a small group, take turns sharing immigration stories about your own family or someone else's.

ANALYZE A DOCUMENTARY

New Immigrants Share Their Stories is a **documentary,** a nonfiction film that presents, or documents, information about people or events. A documentary's **purpose** is the reason it is made: to inform, entertain, persuade, or express feelings or opinions. The opinion, claim, or idea a filmmaker wants to convey is the film's **message.** Documentary filmmakers usually have a **motive,** or a reason why they feel the story is worth telling. Here are some examples of motives and clues that can help you identify a motive based on the film's emphasis, or focus:

MOTIVE	FOCUS OF FILM / CLUES TO MOTIVE
Social	human interactions, changing behaviors or attitudes
Commercial	a product that viewers are encouraged to buy
Political	support for or opposition to government or laws

Documentary filmmakers combine visual and sound techniques to present information. These techniques can include:

- **Voice-over**—the voice of an unseen commentator or narrator. The narrator explains or clarifies images and provides important new information. *New Immigrants Share Their Stories* uses several narrators, including a commentator, teachers, and students.
- **Stills**—images that are motionless, such as illustrations or photographs. In this film, the students' video diaries include photographs from their years growing up in other countries.
- **Animation**—images that appear to move and seem alive. For example, *New Immigrants Share Their Stories* includes an animated graphic of travel across the globe.

To **evaluate** a documentary, you examine its techniques and content to judge its impact. Ask yourself these questions:

- How well does the film achieve its main purpose?
- What is the film's main message, and is it conveyed effectively?
- What techniques caught my interest? Why?
- What kind of motive did the filmmaker most likely have?

GENRE ELEMENTS: DOCUMENTARY

- provides factual information
- may investigate or tell a true story
- employs the basic elements of film, such as live footage, narration, music, animation, and on-screen text
- often includes interviews with experts or other people involved with the topic

GET READY

GENRE ELEMENTS: INFORMATIONAL TEXT

- provides factual information
- often includes graphic features
- typically makes use of text elements such as subheadings, boldfacing, sidebars, and footnotes

ANALYZE TEXT ELEMENTS

Text elements are print and graphic features that authors use to structure texts. As you read "A Common Bond," notice how these elements help guide your reading and achieve specific purposes.

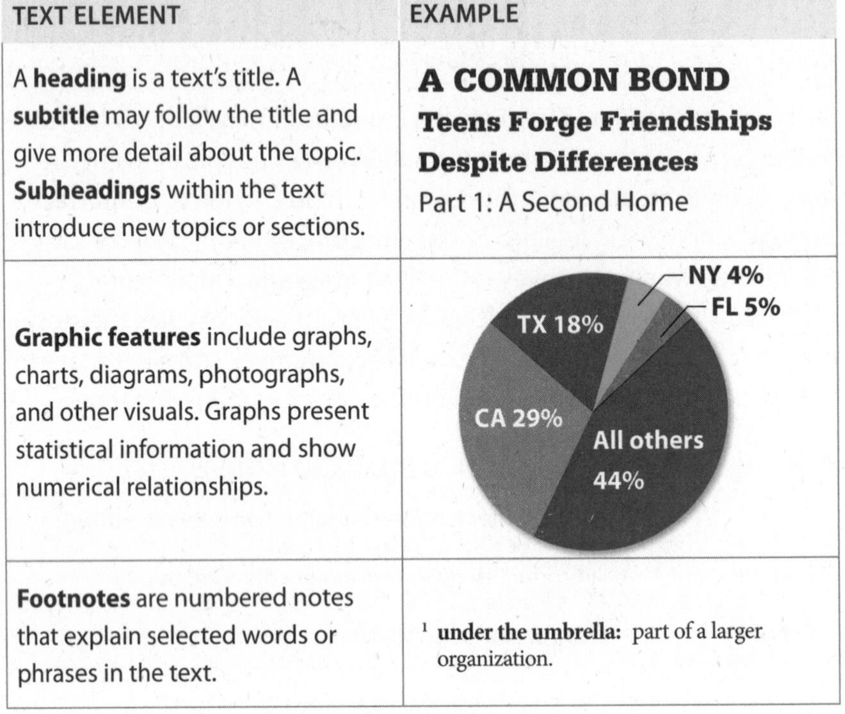

TEXT ELEMENT	EXAMPLE
A **heading** is a text's title. A **subtitle** may follow the title and give more detail about the topic. **Subheadings** within the text introduce new topics or sections.	**A COMMON BOND** **Teens Forge Friendships Despite Differences** Part 1: A Second Home
Graphic features include graphs, charts, diagrams, photographs, and other visuals. Graphs present statistical information and show numerical relationships.	NY 4% FL 5% TX 18% CA 29% All others 44%
Footnotes are numbered notes that explain selected words or phrases in the text.	[1] **under the umbrella:** part of a larger organization.

CRITICAL VOCABULARY

eligible **assimilate** **embrace** **capitalize** **unrest**

To see how many Critical Vocabulary words you already know, answer each question and explain your answer.

1. If you were **eligible** for an award, would you be happy or scared?
2. To **assimilate** into U.S. culture, would immigrants more likely need to learn to speak English or become good at sports?
3. If you **embraced** a new fashion, would you wear it often or rarely?
4. Should people want to **capitalize** on their strengths?
5. Would **unrest** in your hometown make you sleepy or anxious?

LANGUAGE CONVENTIONS: Semicolons, Colons, and Parentheses

In this lesson, you will learn how to correctly use semicolons, colons, and parentheses to punctuate sentences. For example, notice how the author uses a **semicolon** to separate two clauses in a compound sentence or a **colon** to introduce a list. **Parentheses** set off extra information that does not change the overall meaning of a sentence.

BACKGROUND

The Building Bridges project is a collaboration between two very different New York schools. Through letter writing, video diaries, and interviews, the English language learners from Newcomers High School in Queens, New York, tell their personal immigration stories to their "buddies" from St. Luke's, a private middle school in Manhattan. Together, students from both schools hope to change stereotyped ideas about immigrants. The documentary New Immigrants Share Their Stories *chronicles the students' project.*

PREPARE TO COMPARE

As you view the film, pay attention to the interviews between the immigrant students and their "buddies." Listen to the questions asked and the answers given. Also watch the facial expressions and gestures of the individuals. Think about what you learn about the two groups from these conversations. Write down any questions you have as you view the film. **NOTEBOOK**

To view the video, log in online and select **"NEW IMMIGRANTS SHARE THEIR STORIES"** from the unit menu.

As needed, pause the video to make notes about what impresses you or about ideas you might want to talk about later. Replay or rewind so that you can clarify anything you do not understand.

BACKGROUND

*Longtime journalist **Brooke Hauser** has profiled a wide array of subjects, from Chinese beauty queens to former U.S. Secretary of State Colin Powell. However, in her first book,* The New Kids: Big Dreams and Brave Journeys at a High School for Immigrant Teens, *she chronicled the experiences of people who don't normally take center stage: recent immigrants who attend the International High School at Prospect Heights. The following text is informed by what she learned and whom she got to know while writing that award-winning book.*

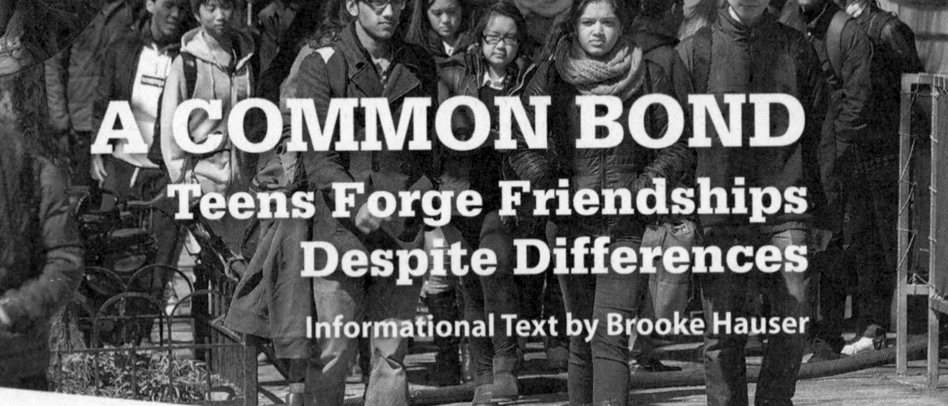

A COMMON BOND

Teens Forge Friendships Despite Differences

Informational Text by Brooke Hauser

Notice & Note

Use the side margins to notice and note signposts in the text.

PREPARE TO COMPARE

As you read this article, take note of the surprising facts and statistics you learn about students who have recently immigrated to the United States. Also keep track of all the individuals you get to hear from.

ANALYZE TEXT ELEMENTS

Annotate: Mark the first subheading in the article.

Predict: Based on this subheading, what can you predict about the overall structure of the article?

Part 1: A Second Home

1 Have you ever been the new kid at school? Or maybe you've known the new kid at school? Either way, if you answered yes, then you might have a little glimpse into the experiences of the students at the International High School at Prospect Heights in Brooklyn, New York. Started in 2004, the school serves recent immigrants and refugees to the United States. How recent? Well, some of the students come to America just months or weeks before the first day of school in September each year.

2 According to a book about the school written by the author of this article, *The New Kids: Big Dreams and Brave Journeys at a High School for Immigrant Teens,* the students hail from 40-plus different countries and speak nearly 30

languages: Spanish, Creole, Arabic, Fulani, and Tibetan, to name just a few. Imagine walking down those halls: They're noisy! In many ways, they're also a reflection of our country and what's special about America, which has always been home to newcomers.

3 Spend a few hours at the International High School, and you'll quickly realize that students here represent a range of backgrounds and beliefs. Some are Christian or Jewish, others Buddhist or Muslim. But despite their differences, all of the students share one very important thing in common: They are all learning English together. In fact, to be **eligible** for enrollment, students must have failed an English language assessment test and be relatively new to the country, says Joe Luft, Executive Director of the Internationals Network for Public Schools, which oversees the school in Prospect Heights and others like it around New York City, and beyond: "All of the students in our schools are recently arrived immigrant youth who are new to learning English. Generally, they've been in this country for less than four years, although the majority have been here for less than a year or two."

eligible
(ĕl´ĭ-jə-bəl) *adj. Eligible* means qualified to be selected.

4 Maybe you've heard the term ESL, which stands for "English as a second language." The funny thing is, for many of these students, English isn't their second language: In some cases, it's their third, fourth, or fifth.

5 Take Nourou Sow, a rising senior at the International High School who immigrated from Guinea in West Africa when she was 12, along with her mother, older brother, and little sister. In her native country, Nourou grew up speaking Fulani, as well as Susu and Mandinka. So technically, English is her *fourth* language, but we don't have a term for that, like "EFL." The better term for these students is "ELL" for English language learner.

6 Learning a new language is hard enough, but English is just one part of what these students must conquer as new immigrants in America. They are adapting to a new way of life, too. Every once in a while, there's a student who has never been to *any* school before the International High School. Some students have fled from their homes in countries damaged by war, political strife, or famine. Some have spent time in refugee camps, where a formal education isn't an option. Many students grew up in rural places, such as on farms or in the mountains, and they can experience major culture shock when they arrive in New York City: They have to take a bus or subway to school, navigating new routes through the city, which can be a scary

NOTICE & NOTE

prospect when you don't speak the language. A good number of students also work after school, some in restaurants or nail salons, to help provide for their families. Others help out with housework and childcare, cooking and cleaning, and looking after younger siblings.

7 For many students, the International High School at Prospect Heights is kind of like a second home in the city. "What makes our school a welcoming place and feel like home is in the importance we put on relationships: You can only develop a relationship with a people if you spend time with them and do things together," says the school principal, Nedda de Castro. Students and teachers get to know each other in small groups and different settings both inside and outside of school, on field trips, for instance. "Even though they come from all over the world and may be very different from each other," she says, "they are all in the same boat and have much in common in their journey to becoming a new American."

QUOTED WORDS

Notice & Note: Mark the quoted words in paragraph 7.

Evaluate: The author could have paraphrased what the principal said, or restated the ideas in her own words. What is the effect of including the principal's exact words?

8 You may have heard the term "melting pot" to describe America as a place where people from different cultures and backgrounds mix together and **assimilate** into the whole, to create a new culture. At the International High Schools, there's another metaphor that students **embrace**, according to Luft. "The thing that I hear more than any other idea is the school as a family, in all its complexity," he says. "Everybody doesn't always get along, but ultimately they feel this very strong connection to each other and care about each other."

assimilate
(ə-sĭm´ə-lāt´) *v.* To *assimilate* means to blend into or become similar to the prevailing culture.

embrace
(ĕm-brās´) *v.* To *embrace* an idea means to accept and support it.

Part 2: A New Identity

9 Indeed, most of the students are learning a new culture, all the while honoring traditions from their home countries. When the school's first-ever graduating class wanted to organize their senior prom, first they had to figure out exactly what a prom *was*. The prom committee, made up of mostly African and Haitian girls, watched Hollywood prom movies as research. When the big night arrived, the girls and boys who went embraced many American prom customs, like buying corsages for their dates and getting their hair done at the beauty salon, but they also incorporated their own international touches. For instance, a girl from Bangladesh opted to wear a sari as her prom dress, and all the students danced to music from around the world.

10 For Lobsang Jampa, who's originally from Tibet, that was the best part: "The disco," he says and laughs. "The teachers

QUOTED WORDS

Notice & Note: Mark the quoted words in paragraph 10.

Evaluate: Is the quotation essential to understanding the main ideas of the text? Why do you think the author included it?

also danced, and they showed some funny moves that I had never seen, never expected."

11 While every culture has its specific traits, being a teenager can be challenging whether you're from Tibet or Texas. And as Nedda de Castro points out, an American teenager from another part of the country might actually share more in common with one of her immigrant students than with a native New Yorker. "For instance, a young person who lives on a farm in the United States could have more in common with one of my immigrant students who came from a farming community in their native country," she says. "You may not speak the same language, wear the same clothes, or even have the same religion, but there may be ways in which you understand each other very well and have the same values."

12 Like most kids, International High School students worry about what to wear on the first day of school and where to sit in the cafeteria and how to talk to someone they have a crush on. They also worry about getting good grades and getting into college. Nourou, the girl from Guinea, dreams of being a doctor.

13 Her classmate Daniel Coradin, a rising senior originally from the Dominican Republic, wants to be a professional baseball player like his idol, Derek Jeter. "My dream since I was 11 years is to sign with the Yankees," says Daniel, who moved to New York when he was ten.

14 Finally, Lobsang is determined to become a film director. His favorite movie? "*Forrest Gump,*" says Lobsang, who recently graduated high school and plans to study theater at college in the fall. "I love the story. It's not just one story, there's many different stories."

15 The same could be said about the high school. It's amazing how many different stories are inside of one school—around 415, in fact.

ANALYZE TEXT ELEMENTS

Annotate: Mark the phrase in paragraph 16 that has a footnote.

Infer: What does the footnote help you understand about the International High School at Prospect Heights?

16 The International High School at Prospect Heights in Brooklyn is one of many schools of its kind popping up around the nation, from Bowling Green, Kentucky, to San Francisco, California. Many are under the umbrella[1] of the Internationals Network of Public Schools, which oversees 27 schools and academies with more than 9,000 students. In New York City alone, there are around 15 of these schools, serving newcomers who are learning English. At last count, the New York schools, combined, had students representing nearly 120 countries and more than 90 different languages.

[1] **under the umbrella:** part of a larger organization.

PERCENTAGE OF ENGLISH LANGUAGE LEARNERS IN PUBLIC SCHOOLS ACROSS THE UNITED STATES

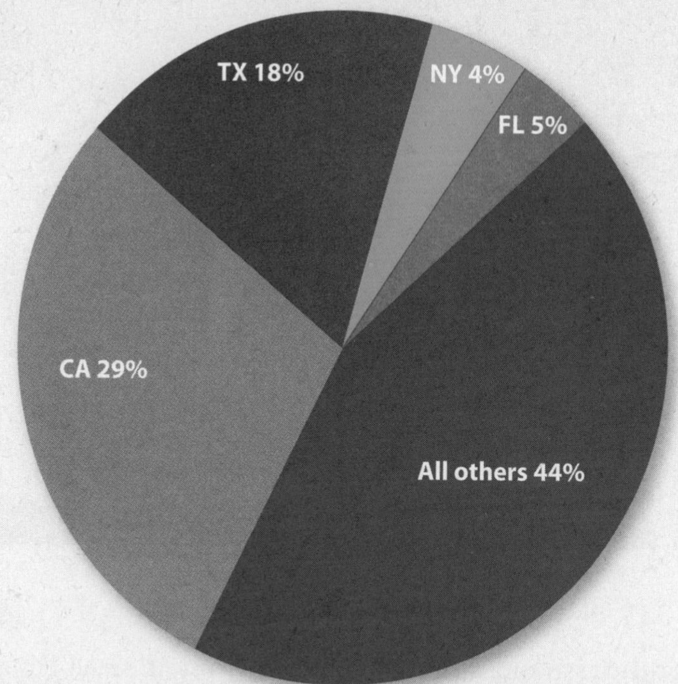

In 2014–15, there were nearly 5 million students who were English language learners (ELLs) in public schools across the United States. That's approximately 1 in 10 students. Most of these students live in five states, although every state has some population of students who participate in language assistance programs. Note: Not all ELLs are immigrants (some students born here grew up speaking a different primary language at home), just as not all immigrants are ELLs (many newcomers from England or Jamaica, for example, speak English as their native language).

17 New York City is very diverse. Any public high school is likely to have some newcomers, so some people wonder why there is a high school just for immigrants learning English in the first place. Wouldn't they be better off mixing with other students born here? But one idea behind these "international" schools and academies is that English language learners (ELLs) benefit from incorporating their native cultures and languages into the classroom.

18 "Biculturalism is something that we celebrate because when our students arrive in this country, they immediately begin a process of developing a new identity," says the principal, Nedda de Castro. "They bring all of the richness of their languages and culture from their own countries, and then, as soon as they arrive, they begin to develop an identity that includes the new experiences they have in the United States.

19 "Coming to a new place changes you," she adds, "but it does not mean that you leave everything behind or erase your past."

LANGUAGE CONVENTIONS

Annotate: In paragraph 17, mark the use of parentheses.

Analyze: Does the sentence make sense without the parenthetical information? Why do you think the author included it?

NOTICE & NOTE

Part 3: A Global Perspective

20 In the classroom, students frequently work in small groups, along with students who speak other languages. Sometimes, students are paired together with friends from their home country who speak the same native language and are able to translate words and ideas into English. All of the students mingle with classmates from a range of other countries throughout the day, whether they're learning math, playing basketball in the gym, eating lunch in the cafeteria, or attending a meeting of one of the many after-school clubs. ("I was in chess club, photography club, magazine club, dance club, and fashion club," says Lobsang. "I was a male model.") In the process, they learn English in addition to picking up bits and pieces of other languages and cultures.

ANALYZE TEXT ELEMENTS

Annotate: In paragraph 22, mark the information that is also represented by the bar graph.

Analyze: What does showing this information graphically help the author to emphasize? Explain.

capitalize
(kăp´ĭ-tl-īz´) *v.* To *capitalize* on something means to use it to one's advantage.

21 "Our belief is that language and content cannot be separated and therefore you have to teach them together," says Luft. "There's a myth that students can't learn meaningful content until they learn English, and we think that's not true. Teenage immigrants know a lot about life and academics from their home country. We should think about ways to **capitalize** on that."

22 This approach shows positive results: According to a recent study looking at English language learners over four years in New York City, International High School students graduate at a higher percentage than ELL students at other schools in the area (74% compared to approximately 31%).

23 "You want students to use all of the tools they have; that's part of what education should teach you, how to use every tool and source at your disposal," Luft says. "Think of a carpenter trying to bang in a nail," he adds: "You wouldn't tell a carpenter to build something and take the hammer away, and say, 'OK, do the job without your most important tool.' So the whole idea of telling a student, 'Don't use your language,' or that it's not important… It's how they think, and it's often a part of how they express their emotions. It's an integral part of who they are as a person. You should always try to capitalize on all aspects of who you are as a person and extend that into learning."

NOTICE & NOTE

BIG QUESTIONS

Notice & Note: One question you should ask yourself when reading nonfiction text is "What challenged, changed, or confirmed what I already knew?" Mark any details in the bar graph that help you answer this question.

Summarize: How does the information in the graph connect with what you already knew or believed to be true about graduation rates?

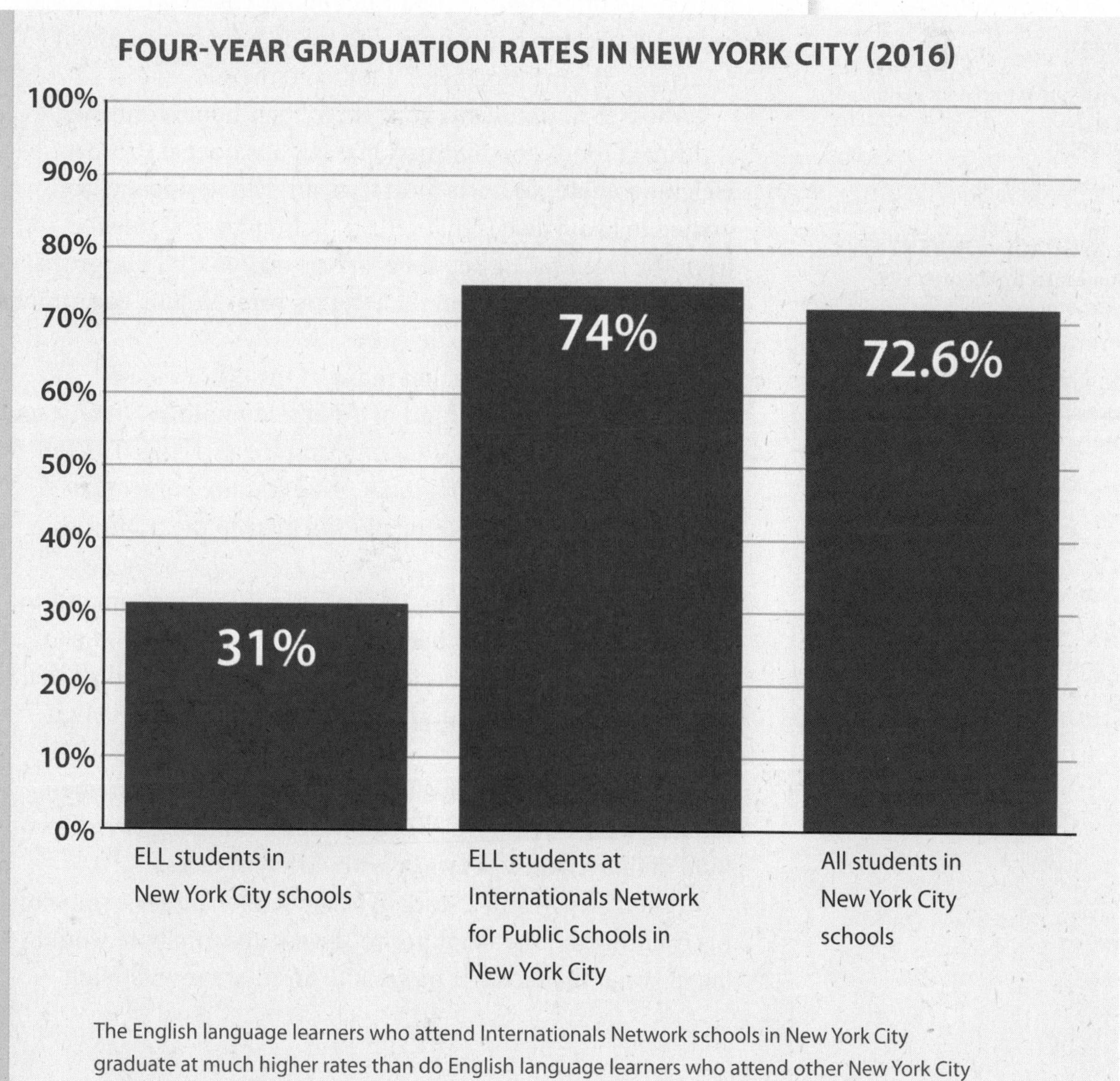

The English language learners who attend Internationals Network schools in New York City graduate at much higher rates than do English language learners who attend other New York City public high schools.

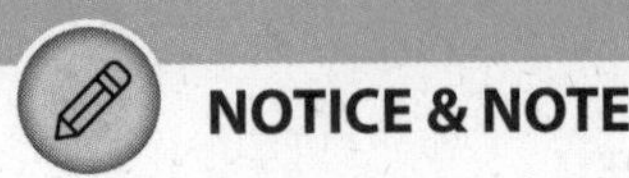

24 For some students, their native language *is* their identity. Take Lobsang, for example. His family left Tibet because they weren't allowed to live freely there under Chinese rule. Before coming to the U.S., he says, "We had to immigrate to Nepal to live the way we want." In America, Lobsang and his family are free to speak their language and honor their culture in a variety of ways. "Right now, I live in Queens, so I think of myself as an American New Yorker," says Lobsang, who embraces his Tibetan identity at the same time. "We still practice celebrations like the Tibetan New Year," he says. Nourou, from Guinea, honors her culture by attending West African weddings in the city. She also celebrates religious holidays such as Eid al-Fitr, which marks the end of Ramadan, when Muslims fast for a month. It's important to honor her culture here, she says, partly because **unrest** in her country has made her nervous about returning. "I can't remember a lot from there."

unrest
(ŭn-rĕst´) *n. Unrest* refers to an unstable or turbulent condition that is often marked by protests or riots.

25 Another way students connect to their home countries is through food. The International High School at Prospect Heights sometimes hosts food festivals, where students are invited to bring dishes that reflect their culture. Daniel, from the Dominican Republic, brings mangú. "It's like green plantain; you mash it, and then put on some salami, egg, onions and cheese," he says. "It's delicious."

LANGUAGE CONVENTIONS

Annotate: In paragraph 25, mark the sentence that uses a semicolon.

Analyze: Explain why a semicolon is needed in this sentence instead of a comma.

26 Meanwhile, Lobsang and many of the other Tibetan students enjoy *momo*, a kind of Tibetan dumpling. "In Queens, there's a lot of Tibetan restaurants, and we also cook Tibetan food," he says. "Even though the pizza and the burger taste delicious, we still eat traditional food to keep the tradition alive."

27 Now that he has graduated, Lobsang is looking forward to college and his dream of becoming a filmmaker. But he also took some time to look back at the past four years and all that he accomplished and experienced at the International High School.

28 "I made a lot of friends from different countries: Yemen, Mexico, Pakistan, I have African friends," Lobsang says. "It's kind of like a family; a family with different races."

29 When he was still a student at the school, he says, some of his friends from the neighborhood who grew up here would laugh about the fact that he went to an International High

School. "They called it 'immigrant high school,' " he says, "but they don't know how helpful the school is.

"If you are in a school with people from different countries, they share their problems, and it gives you more information to understand the world better," he continues. "If everyone is from same country and go to same school, then they don't have a lot of stories to share. Here, there are a lot of interesting stories."

CHECK YOUR UNDERSTANDING

Answer these questions before moving on to the **Analyze Media and Text** section on the following page.

1 Which of the following best expresses the focus of Part 2 of the text?

A The purpose and organization of international schools

B How and why immigrant students form new identities

C Who benefits from going to international schools and why

D The origins of most immigrants and the languages they speak

2 Which claim from the text does the bar graph best support?

F *International High School students graduate at a higher percentage than ELL students at other schools in the area.*

G *There's a myth that students can't learn meaningful content until they learn English, and we think that's not true.*

H *Indeed, most of the students are learning a new culture, all the while honoring traditions from their home countries.*

J *For many students, the International High School at Prospect Heights is kind of like a second home in the city.*

3 About which person do you learn the most from the text?

A Nourou Sow

B Nedda de Castro

C Daniel Coradin

D Lobsang Jampa

ANALYZE MEDIA AND TEXT

Support your responses with evidence from the documentary and the text. NOTEBOOK

1. **Summarize** Reread paragraph 6. Then, briefly restate the challenges many immigrants must deal with besides learning English and why they may face these difficulties.

2. **Analyze** Identify an example from the documentary of each technique in the chart and note what it emphasizes.

TECHNIQUE	SCENE FROM FILM	WHAT IT EMPHASIZES
Voice-over		
Stills		
Animation		

3. **Analyze** Review the subheadings in the text. What purposes do they serve?

4. **Synthesize** Choose one of the two graphic features from the informational text and explain what it contributes to the text.

5. **Notice & Note** What is the author's purpose for including quoted words in paragraph 21?

RESEARCH TIP

To begin your research, review *New Immigrants Share Their Stories* and "A Common Bond" to identify useful search terms such as school names and locations as well as the names of organizations, experts, and administrators. Use these as starting points for online research. Then, follow links from your results to discover other similar schools and related information.

RESEARCH

Research high schools that specifically serve recent immigrants. Use the chart below to record what you learn.

HIGH SCHOOL	FACTS & STATISTICS	SIGNIFICANT SIMILARITIES	SIGNIFICANT DIFFERENCES

Connect Share your discoveries with a small group. Discuss which similarities and differences are most significant and why.

CREATE AND DISCUSS

Write a Letter Write a three- to four-paragraph letter to one of the high schools you discovered in your research. In your letter, request information that will help you determine whether the school is one that you would recommend to recent immigrants.

- ❑ Provide the date, your return address, the name and address of the recipient, and a salutation in correct letter format.
- ❑ Begin the body of your letter by explaining who you are and why you are writing. Then ask for the information you are seeking.
- ❑ Thank the recipient for his or her time. End with an appropriate closing, such as "Sincerely," or "Yours truly," and your signature.

Discuss with a Small Group Have a discussion about what makes you feel welcome at your school and what gives you a sense of belonging there.

- ❑ Review the text to identify ways in which the students form bonds with one another. Then consider whether you do anything similar.
- ❑ Identify school-sponsored activities at your school that help foster a sense of school spirit, unity, and belonging. During the discussion, listen actively to ask questions and comment respectfully on others' ideas.

Go to **Participating in Collaborative Discussions** in the **Speaking and Listening Studio** for more.

RESPOND TO THE ESSENTIAL QUESTION

? What are the places that shape who you are?

Gather Information Review your notes on the two selections. Then, add relevant details to your Response Log. As you determine which information to include, think about:

- factors that shaped the students' early identities
- current challenges students face and how these affect them
- what the students themselves say about identity

At the end of the unit, you can use your notes to help you write a short story.

ACADEMIC VOCABULARY

As you write and discuss what you learned from the text and video, be sure to use the Academic Vocabulary words. Check off each of the words that you use.

- ❑ **contribute**
- ❑ **immigrate**
- ❑ **reaction**
- ❑ **relocate**
- ❑ **shifting**

RESPOND

CRITICAL VOCABULARY

WORD BANK
eligible
assimilate
embrace
capitalize
unrest

Practice and Apply Select the best answer to each question. Then explain your response. If a word has more than one meaning, use the meaning that it has in the selection.

1. Which of the following would be a sign of **unrest**?
   a. a cold   **b.** a rebellion
2. Which should make a baseball player **eligible** to play on the team?
   a. showing up to every practice   **b.** showering every day
3. Which is a way to **capitalize** on hot weather?
   a. selling misting fans   **b.** closing a store early
4. What is one reason to try to **assimilate**?
   a. to honor old traditions   **b.** to connect with others
5. Which would you be more likely to **embrace**?
   a. more free time   **b.** extra chores

VOCABULARY STRATEGY: Multiple-Meaning Words

Go to **Words with Multiple Meanings** in the **Vocabulary Studio** for more.

Many words have more than one meaning. To determine the meaning of a **multiple-meaning word**, you can use clues from its **context**—the words, sentences, paragraphs, and punctuation surrounding it. In the example below from "A Common Bond," learning a language is identified as something new immigrants conquer. One meaning of *conquer* is "to defeat in war," but the context helps you understand that the intended meaning in this sentence is "to overcome."

> **Learning a new language is hard enough, but English is just one part of what these students must conquer as new immigrants in America.**

Practice and Apply Select the best meaning of each boldfaced word.

1. Lederhosen and dirndls are perfect clothes to wear in Switzerland, but to **assimilate** here, you will need to wear blue jeans.
   a. to absorb into the mind   **b.** to blend into the main group
2. Ellie's friends all wanted to **capitalize** on her new job at the ice cream parlor by getting her to give them extra toppings.
   a. take advantage of   **b.** invest funds in

LANGUAGE CONVENTIONS:
Semicolons, Colons, and Parentheses

Writers use punctuation to make the meaning of a sentence clear. Some punctuation marks, such as periods and exclamation points, indicate the end of a sentence and the end of a complete thought. Other marks occur in the middle of a sentence and help separate one idea from the next. The chart explains how semicolons (;), colons (:), and parentheses are used.

Go to **Punctuation I** in the **Grammar Studio** for more on semicolons, colons, and parentheses.

PUNCTUATION MARK	WHAT IT DOES	EXAMPLES
Semicolon	separates parts of a compound sentence with no coordinating conjunction	"You want students to use all of the tools they have**;** that's part of what education should teach you, how to use every tool and source at your disposal."
	separates items in a series that contain commas	There are schools for recent immigrants in Brooklyn, New York**;** Bowling Green, Kentucky**;** and San Francisco, California.
Colon	introduces a list	"I made a lot of friends from different countries**:** Yemen, Mexico, Pakistan. . . ."
	introduces a long quotation	Joe Luft explained that eligible students must have failed an English language assessment test**:** "All of the students in our schools are recently arrived immigrant youth who are new to learning English."
	follows the salutation of a business letter	To Whom It May Concern**:** Dear Mr. Luft**:**
Parentheses	set off extra information that explains or expands upon an idea in the sentence	"International High School students graduate at a higher rate than ELL students at other schools in the area **(**74% compared with approximately 31%**)**."

Practice and Apply With the help of a partner, review the letter you wrote. Look for sentences that could be improved or clarified by using one of the punctuation marks in the chart. Consider the following:

- ❑ Can I use a semicolon to combine two simple sentences with closely related meanings?
- ❑ Can I use a colon to add a list of examples or introduce a quotation from "A Common Bond"?
- ❑ Can I use parentheses to add an extra detail about one of my ideas?

Collaborate & Compare

COMPARE PURPOSES

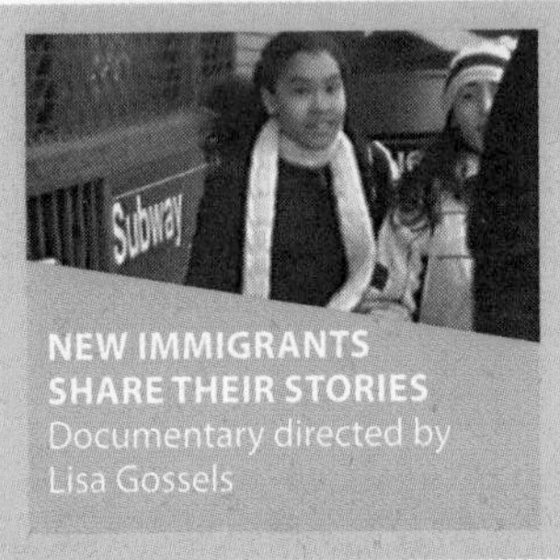

NEW IMMIGRANTS SHARE THEIR STORIES
Documentary directed by Lisa Gossels

A COMMON BOND
Informational Text by Brooke Hauser

When you compare the information in two or more sources on the same topic, you also synthesize that information, making connections, expanding on key ideas, and even developing new questions. In a small group, compare and contrast the purposes of *New Immigrants Share Their Stories* and "A Common Bond." Remember, each selection may have been made to fulfill one or more of the following purposes: to inform, to entertain, to persuade, or to express the feelings or opinions of its creator. Complete the Venn diagram with similarities and differences in each selection's purpose and how effectively you think the purpose is achieved. One example is completed for you.

New Immigrants Share Their Stories	Both	"A Common Bond"
	To inform people about challenges immigrants face	

ANALYZE MEDIA AND TEXT

Discuss these questions in your group.

1. **Connect** What similarities do you see between the immigrants' stories in the documentary and those mentioned in the text?
2. **Infer** Based on the focus of the documentary, what possible motives did the filmmakers have in creating it?
3. **Contrast** In what ways do the filmmakers' purpose and the writer's purpose differ?
4. **Synthesize** What do both sources reveal about the challenges recent teen immigrants face and how best to overcome them?

CREATE AND PRESENT

Now your group can continue unearthing the kinds of stories and information you learned about in the documentary and the informational text. Follow these steps:

1. **Choose a brief personal story to tell.** In your group, tell a brief personal story that you would feel comfortable sharing in an interview. The story you share might be a family immigration story, or it could be a story about another important event in your life.
2. **Choose a "buddy" to interview.** After everyone has shared a story, choose a "buddy" in the group whose story interests you.
3. **Prepare for the interview.** Use the chart to jot down details or aspects of the story that sparked your interest. Then list questions that can help you learn more. Use the interview questions from *New Immigrants Share Their Stories* as a guide. Keep your questions general and open-ended.

INTERESTING DETAIL OR ASPECT OF STORY	INTERVIEW QUESTION ABOUT IT

4. **Record your interviews.** Modeling the techniques you saw used in the documentary, take turns interviewing your buddies and recording one another's interviews.

VIDEOGRAPHY TIP

If you can use more than one camera angle to record each interview, that will give you the best opportunity to create an effective film. With different camera angles you can capture

- both people together from a middle distance
- the interviewee's facial reactions and verbal responses to questions
- the interviewer's reactions to what he or she hears and sees

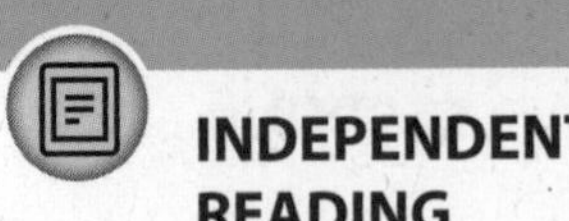

INDEPENDENT READING

? *ESSENTIAL QUESTION:*

What are the places that shape who you are?

Reader's Choice

Setting a Purpose Select one or more of these options from your eBook to continue your exploration of the Essential Question.

- Read the descriptions to see which text grabs your interest.
- Think about which genres you enjoy reading.

Notice & Note

In this unit, you practiced noticing and noting three signposts: **Tough Questions, Again and Again,** and **Memory Moments.** As you read independently, these signposts and others will aid your understanding. Below are the anchor questions to ask when you read literature and nonfiction.

Reading Literature: Stories, Poems, and Plays		
Signpost	**Anchor Question**	**Lesson**
Contrasts and Contradictions	Why did the character act that way?	p. 3
Aha Moment	How might this change things?	p. 3
Tough Questions	What does this make me wonder about?	p. 152
Words of the Wiser	What's the lesson for the character?	p. 406
Again and Again	Why might the author keep bringing this up?	p. 2
Memory Moment	Why is this memory important?	p. 153

Reading Nonfiction: Essays, Articles, and Arguments		
Signpost	**Anchor Question(s)**	**Lesson**
Big Questions	What surprised me? What did the author think I already knew? What challenged, changed, or confirmed what I already knew?	p. 77
Contrasts and Contradictions	What is the difference, and why does it matter?	p. 241
Extreme or Absolute Language	Why did the author use this language?	p. 76
Numbers and Stats	Why did the author use these numbers or amounts?	p. 325
Quoted Words	Why was this person quoted or cited, and what did this add?	p. 77
Word Gaps	Do I know this word from someplace else? Does it seem like technical talk for this topic? Do clues in the sentence help me understand the word?	p. 240

You can preview these texts in Unit 3 of your eBook.

Then, check off the text or texts that you select to read on your own.

☐ POEM

My Father and the Figtree
Naomi Shihab Nye

For one girl's father, no house could truly be a home without a figtree growing in the yard.

☐ SHORT STORY

Golden Glass
Alma Luz Villanueva

How can sleeping in a fort in the woods help heal a broken heart?

☐ MEMOIR

***from* The Latehomecomer**
Kao Kalia Yang

An immigrant family from a war-torn country adapts to American life, while a daughter struggles to survive.

☐ RESEARCH STUDY

A Place to Call Home
Scott Bittle and Jonathan Rochkind

Life in America is not the way many immigrants imagined it would be.

☐ MYTH

Salmon Boy
Michael J. Caduto and Joseph Bruchac

A young boy who does not respect the ways of his people pays a high price.

Collaborate and Share With a partner, discuss what you learned from at least one of your independent readings.

- Give a brief synopsis or summary of the text.
- Describe any signposts that you noticed in the text and explain what they revealed to you.
- Describe what you most enjoyed or found most challenging about the text. Give specific examples.
- Decide if you would recommend the text to others. Why or why not?

Go to the **Reading Studio** for more resources on **Notice & Note.**

Write a Short Story

Go to the **Writing Studio** for help writing your short story.

In this unit, you read about how places shape people's lives. For this writing task, you will write a short story about a character who is struggling with an obstacle in relation to a place. For an example of a well-written story you can use as a mentor text, review the excerpt from *The Book of Unknown Americans.*

As you write your short story, you can use the notes from your Response Log, which you filled out after reading and viewing the selections in this unit.

Writing Prompt

Read the information in the box below.

This is the context for your short story.

> Where we come from affects who we are. Everything about a place—people and their culture, land, and history—contributes to our identity, our relationships, and our choices.

This is the Essential Question for the unit. How might some of the people and characters from the unit answer it?

Think carefully about the following question.

> What are the places that shape who you are?

Now circle the word or words that tell what your short story should be about.

Write a short story about how a character is shaped by an important place.

Review these points as you write and again when you finish. Make any needed changes or edits.

Be sure to—

- ❑ establish, develop, and resolve a conflict
- ❑ introduce and develop characters and a setting
- ❑ create a plot with a well-structured sequence of events
- ❑ use transitions to show sequence
- ❑ use dialogue, pacing, descriptive details, and reflection to develop characters and events
- ❑ provide a resolution that reflects a theme, or message, about life or human nature

1 Plan

Short stories include made-up characters and events, many of which could exist or happen in real life. Before you start writing, plan how you want your story to be structured and what its main events will be.

Writers of novels, short stories, and narratives consider the following elements of fiction as they plan their work. Think about these questions as you begin planning your story.

Short Story Planning Table	
Characters Who is your main character, and what is he or she like? Who are the other characters in the story?	
Point of View Who tells the story? Decide if it will be a character in the story (first-person point of view) or a voice outside the story (third-person point of view).	
Setting What place is important to the character? What details can you use to describe the place vividly?	
Conflict What does the main character want? What obstacles does he or she need to overcome to achieve that goal?	

Background Reading Review the notes you have taken in your Response Log after reading the texts in this unit. These texts provide background reading that may give you some ideas you can use when planning your short story.

Go to **Writing Narratives** for help planning your short story.

Notice & Note

From Reading to Writing

As you plan your short story, apply what you've learned about signposts to your own writing. Remember that writers use common features, called signposts, to help convey their message to readers.

Think about how you can incorporate **Tough Questions** into your story.

Go to the **Reading Studio** for more resources on Notice & Note.

Use the notes from your Response Log as you plan your short story.

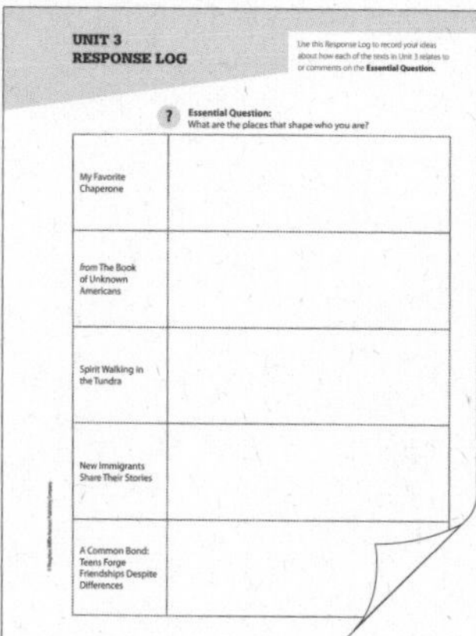

UNIT 3
RESPONSE LOG

Use this Response Log to record your ideas about how each of the texts in Unit 3 relates to or comments on the **Essential Question.**

Essential Question:
What are the places that shape who you are?

My Favorite Chaperone	
from The Book of Unknown Americans	
Spirit Walking in the Tundra	
New Immigrants Share Their Stories	
A Common Bond: Teens Forge Friendships Despite Differences	

WRITING TASK

Go to **Writing Narratives: Narrative Structure** for help organizing your short story.

Organize Your Ideas Before drafting your short story, you need to organize all the ideas you have generated about your characters, point of view, setting, and conflict. Placing the main events of your story on a plot diagram will help you see the "big picture."

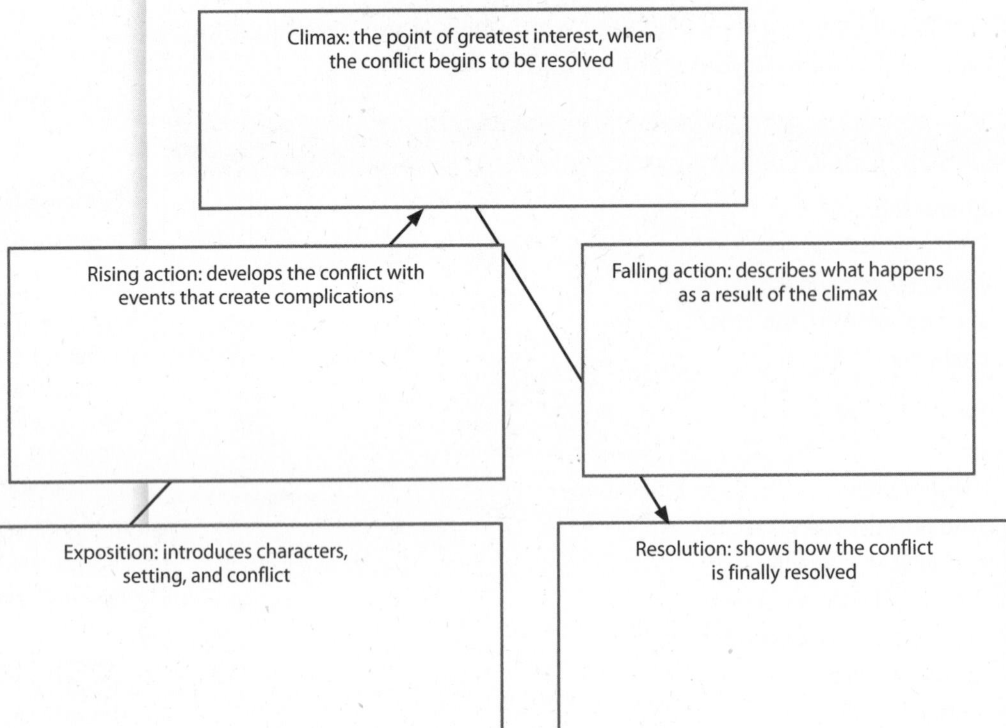
PLOT DIAGRAM
Climax: the point of greatest interest, when the conflict begins to be resolved
Rising action: develops the conflict with events that create complications
Falling action: describes what happens as a result of the climax
Exposition: introduces characters, setting, and conflict
Resolution: shows how the conflict is finally resolved

2 Develop a Draft

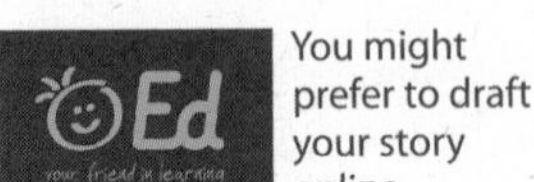

You might prefer to draft your story online.

Once you have completed your planning activities, you are ready to begin drafting your short story. Refer to your Planning Table and the plot diagram you created, as well as any notes you took as you studied the texts in the unit.

- Introduce the main character, setting, and conflict.
- Establish the point of view.
- Create a sequence of events, using transition words.
- Use precise words and sensory language to create vivid pictures.
- Build tension as your story approaches its climax.
- Tell how the conflict is resolved.
- Leave the reader with a theme on which to reflect.

Using a word processor or online writing application makes it easier to make changes later, when you are ready to revise your first draft.

Use the Mentor Text

from
THE BOOK OF UNKNOWN AMERICANS
ESSENTIAL QUESTION:
What are the places that shape who you are?

Author's Craft

Your task in the exposition is to capture the reader's attention. Your first paragraph should include something intriguing, such as dialogue or a description, that gets your reader interested in reading your short story. Note the way the writer captures the reader's attention in this paragraph from *The Book of Unknown Americans*.

I was less than a year old when my parents brought my brother and me to the United States. Enrique was four. He used to tell me things about Panamá that I couldn't possibly have remembered—like about the scorpions in our backyard and the cement utility sink where my mom used to give us baths. He reminisced about walking down the street with my mom to the Super 99, the dust blowing up everywhere, the heat pounding down, and about looking for crabs between the rocks along the bay.

The reader knows right away that the story will be told by a first-person narrator. The narrator provides vivid sensory details that describe an important setting.

Apply What You've Learned To capture your reader's attention, you might include details of setting, introduce an interesting character, or establish the point of view with a distinctive voice.

Genre Characteristics

Fiction writers give information about characters by describing what they say and how they act. Notice how the author of *The Book of Unknown Americans* describes a character's words and actions.

She'd become a genius at turning any and every little thing into a way to talk about Panamá. She would get a mosquito bite on her ankle and point out the welt to us, reminiscing about the bites she used to get in Panamá and wondering aloud "what the mosquitoes there looked like now," as if they were old friends.

The narrator's mother attempts to persuade her husband to visit Panamá by evoking memories of their life there. Sensory details contribute to our understanding of this character.

Apply What You've Learned The descriptions of important characters in your story should include how they speak and act. Dialogue and sensory details make the characters seem real.

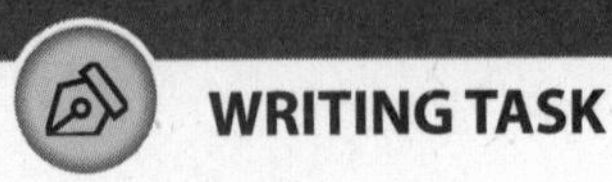

WRITING TASK

3 Revise

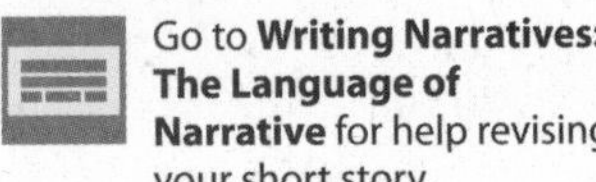

Go to **Writing Narratives: The Language of Narrative** for help revising your short story.

On Your Own Once you have written your draft, you'll want to go back and look for ways to improve your short story. As you reread and revise, think about whether you have achieved your purpose. The Revision Guide will help you focus on specific elements to make your writing stronger.

Revision Guide		
Ask Yourself	**Tips**	**Revision Techniques**
1. Does my exposition grab my readers' attention?	**Highlight** the exposition.	**Introduce** a character. **Add** dialogue and specific, vivid details of the setting.
2. Are my characters believable and well-developed?	**Underline** examples of characters' authentic speech and actions.	**Add** speech and actions that are original and unique to the characters.
3. How well does the setting affect characters and help shape the plot?	**Highlight** details of setting. **Underline** details that affect characters and help shape the plot.	**Add** sensory details to descriptions of setting. **Show** their impact on the characters and story events.
4. Is the conflict in the story clear? Do events build to a climax?	**Circle** details about the conflict. **Highlight** the climax.	**Add** details that make it clear how the conflict is developing. **Add** a strong climax.
5. Does the pacing keep the action moving, building interest and suspense?	**Underline** events that build interest and suspense.	**Delete** any unnecessary events. **Add** some foreshadowing.
6. Does my resolution reflect a theme, or message, about life or human nature?	**Highlight** the resolution. **Underline** phrases or sentences that reflect the theme.	**Insert** phrases or sentences that clearly reflect and/or state the theme.

ACADEMIC VOCABULARY

As you conduct your **peer review,** be sure to use these words.

- ❑ **contribute**
- ❑ **immigrate**
- ❑ **reaction**
- ❑ **relocate**
- ❑ **shifting**

With a Partner Once you and your partner have worked through the Revision Guide on your own, exchange drafts and evaluate each other's stories in a **peer review.** Focus on providing revision suggestions for at least three of the items mentioned in the guide. Explain why you think your partner's draft should be revised and what your specific suggestions are.

When receiving feedback from your partner, listen attentively and ask questions to make sure you fully understand the revision suggestions.

4 Edit

Once you have made the necessary revisions to your short story, you can consider how to improve the language in your draft. Edit for the proper use of standard English conventions, and make sure to correct any misspellings or grammatical errors.

Language Conventions

Pronouns and Prepositions A **pronoun** is a word used in place of one or more nouns. Personal pronouns change their form to express person, number, gender, and case. A **subject pronoun** is used as the subject of a sentence. An **object pronoun** is used as the object of a verb or of a preposition.

Go to **Using Pronouns Correctly** in the **Grammar Studio** to learn more.

	Subject Pronouns	Object Pronouns
Singular		
First Person	I	me
Second Person	you	you
Third Person	she, he, it	her, him, it
Plural		
First Person	we	us
Second Person	you	you
Third Person	they	them

In your writing, make sure to use the objective case in prepositional phrases. In other words, use only object pronouns as the objects of prepositions.

INCORRECT: Keep this a secret between **you and I.**

CORRECT: Keep this a secret between **you and me.**

To check whether to use *I* or *me* in a sentence like the one above, try reading the preposition with each pronoun separately. "Between you" and "between me" sound correct. "Between I" does not.

5 Publish

Finalize your short story and choose a way to share it with your audience. Consider these options:

- Read your story aloud to the class.
- Post your short story on a classroom or school website.

WRITING TASK

Use the scoring guide to evaluate your short story.

Writing Task Scoring Guide: Short Story

	Organization/Progression	Development of Ideas	Use of Language and Conventions
4	• The event sequence is smooth and well structured, building to a satisfying climax and resolution. • The pacing is effective. • Transitions clearly signal shifts between settings. • The resolution clearly reflects a theme, or message about life.	• A conflict is skillfully introduced, developed, and resolved. • A vividly described setting shapes the characters and plot. • Characters are well developed, compelling, and believable. • Dialogue and descriptions are used successfully.	• A consistent point of view is maintained. • Vivid, precise words and sensory language describe the setting and the characters. • Spelling, capitalization, and punctuation are correct. • Grammar and usage are correct.
3	• The event sequence is well structured, but it includes some extraneous events. • Pacing is somewhat uneven and confusing. • Transition words are used sporadically. • The resolution does not present the theme clearly.	• A conflict is introduced, developed, and resolved. • The setting somewhat affects the characters and the conflict. • Characters are interesting and have some believable traits. • Dialogue and descriptions are not consistently effective.	• The point of view is mostly consistent. • Some descriptive words and phrases are used, but there could be more sensory details. • Spelling, capitalization, and punctuation are correct. • Some grammatical and usage errors occur in the story.
2	• Some of the story's events are out of order or structured poorly, making the plot hard to follow at times. • Pacing is choppy or distracting. • Transition words are used ineffectively, if at all. • The resolution does not reflect a theme about life.	• The conflict is introduced but not developed or resolved. • The setting is not clearly established and does not impact the story. • Characters are not adequately developed. • The story lacks sufficient dialogue and descriptions.	• The point of view is inconsistent. • The story lacks precise words and sensory language. • Spelling, capitalization, and punctuation are unreliable. • There are some grammar and usage errors, but the ideas are still clear.
1	• The story does not have a clear sequence of events or plot. • There is no evidence of pacing. • Transition words are not used. • The resolution is inappropriate to the story or missing.	• The story has no identifiable conflict. • The setting is vague. • Characters are underdeveloped or not believable. • Dialogue and descriptions are missing.	• A clear point of view is not established. • The language is vague. • Many spelling, capitalization, and punctuation errors occur. • Many grammatical and usage errors obscure the meaning.

Reflect on the Unit

By completing your short story, you have created a writing product that expresses ideas related to those you have read about in this unit. Now is a good time to reflect on what you have learned.

Reflect on the Essential Question

- What are the places that shape who you are? How has your answer to this question changed since you first considered it when you started this unit?
- What are some examples from the texts you've read about the way places shape people?

Reflect on Your Reading

- Which selections were the most interesting or surprising to you?
- From which selection did you learn the most about how people interact with places—both new places and places from their past?

Reflect on the Writing Task

- What challenges did you encounter while working on your short story? How might you deal with them next time?
- How did analyzing the mentor text help you craft your own story?
- Which part of your short story was the easiest to write? Which was the hardest? Why?
- How did you improve your short story as you were revising?

UNIT 3 SELECTIONS

- **"My Favorite Chaperone"**
- ***The Book of Unknown Americans***
- **"The Powwow at the End of the World"**
- ***New Immigrants Share Their Stories***
- **"A Common Bond: Teens Forge Friendships Despite Differences"**

UNIT 4

THE FIGHT FOR FREEDOM

? **ESSENTIAL QUESTION:**

What will people risk to be free?

> "I should fight for liberty as long as my strength lasted."
>
> Harriet Tubman

ACADEMIC VOCABULARY

Academic Vocabulary words are words you use when you discuss and write about texts. In this unit you will practice and learn five words.

☑ **access** ☐ **civil** ☐ **demonstrate** ☐ **document** ☐ **symbolize**

Study the Word Network to learn more about the word **access.**

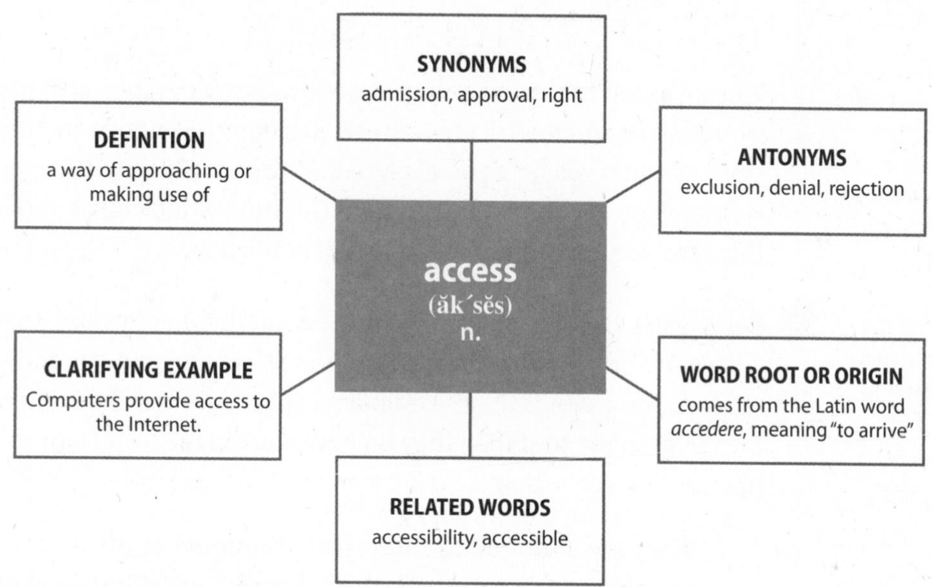

Write and Discuss Discuss the completed Word Network with a partner, making sure to talk through all of the boxes until you both understand the word and its synonyms, antonyms, and related forms. Then, fill out Word Networks for the remaining four words. Use a dictionary or online resource to help you complete the activity.

Go online to access the Word Networks.

RESPOND TO THE ESSENTIAL QUESTION

In this unit, you will meet people who sacrificed for freedom. As you read, you will revisit the **Essential Question** and gather your ideas about it in the **Response Log** that appears on page R4. At the end of the unit, you will have the opportunity to write a **research report** on a topic related to the abolition movement in the United States. Filling out the Response Log will help you prepare for this writing task.

You can also go online to access the Response Log.

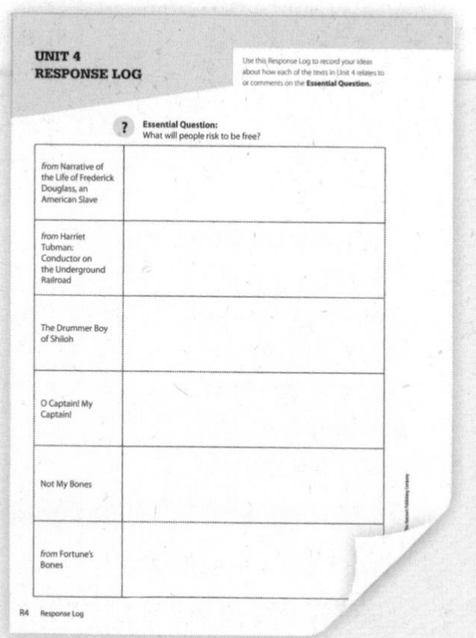

from NARRATIVE OF THE LIFE OF FREDERICK DOUGLASS, AN AMERICAN SLAVE

For more information on these and other signposts to Notice & Note, visit the **Reading Studio**.

You are about to read an excerpt from the autobiography of Frederick Douglass. As you read it, you will ask questions and notice and note signposts that will help you analyze the author's purpose and message. Here are two key signposts and a Big Question to look for as you read this autobiography and other works of nonfiction.

When you notice one of the following while reading, pause to see if it's a **Word Gaps** signpost:

unfamiliar vocabulary

familiar words used in unexpected ways

phrases that seem awkward or unclear

words in italic or boldfaced type, which may be specialized or technical terms

Word Gaps Because Douglass wrote his autobiography more than 170 years ago, some of his language can be challenging for modern readers. Some words might be unfamiliar because they had different meanings in the past than they do now. You may also encounter phrases that seem clumsy or unclear, as in this example:

> **They gave tongue to interesting thoughts of my own soul, which had frequently flashed through my mind, and died away for want of utterance.**

The underlined phrases may seem strange to you. We usually think of *tongue* as the thing that helps us eat and *want* as desire; however, in this context, those words have other meanings. Context clues can help us figure that out: *thoughts* and *flashed through my mind* suggest that both underlined phrases have to do with expressing ideas, or speaking. In this example a student underlined a Word Gap:

> 1 I lived in Master Hugh's family about seven years. During this time, I succeeded in learning to read and write. In accomplishing this, I was compelled to resort to various stratagems. I had no regular teacher. My mistress, who had kindly commenced to instruct me, had, in compliance with the advice and direction of her husband, not only ceased to instruct, but had set her face against my being instructed by any one else. . . .

Anchor Question When you notice this signpost, ask: Do clues in the sentence help me understand the word or phrase?

What does the phrase "compelled to resort to various stratagems" mean? What clues help you find the meaning?	Stratagems looks like the word strategy. The context reveals that Douglass wanted to learn to read and write. He didn't have a real teacher, so he had to figure out another way to learn.

Contrasts and Contradictions When something unexpected happens, our first reaction is usually surprise. Upon further reflection, however, we might ask ourselves whether the event was truly unusual or our expectations were just unrealistic.

Noticing similar **Contrasts and Contradictions** while reading can help deepen your understanding of the topic you are reading about. An author might point out an interesting contrast, using signal words and phrases such as *however* and *on the other hand.* Or, something you read might contradict your own expectations. If the latter is the case, pause to see how the new information fits in with your previous knowledge. The following sentence from *Narrative of the Life of Frederick Douglass* could be an example of Contrasts and Contradictions:

Slavery proved as injurious to her as it did to me.

Anchor Question
When you notice this signpost, ask: What is the difference, and why does it matter?

What expectation does this sentence contradict?	The sentence suggests that slavery can cause harm to both slaveholders and enslaved people. This contradicts the expectation that slavery is harmful only to the people who are enslaved.

Big Questions Suppose you watch a TV show about a foreign country. What will you share with your friends the next day? Most likely, you'll talk about the things that surprised you—such as strange foods and unusual clothing. They are the most interesting new facts you learned.

When you read a nonfiction text, pause now and then to ask yourself: **What surprised me?** This question can help you identify the new information you are learning. It can also help you recognize any incorrect ideas you had before you read the text.

Notice how a student answered Big Questions about the following passage:

2 Nothing seemed to make her more angry than to see me with a newspaper. She seemed to think that here lay the danger. I have had her rush at me with a face made all up of fury, and snatch from me a newspaper, in a manner that fully revealed her apprehension [fear].

Remember to ask **Big Questions** when you read nonfiction text. Pause to ask yourself these questions:

- What surprised me?
- Why was it surprising?
- Does the new information challenge my previous ideas or beliefs about the topic?

What surprised you in this passage?	Douglass's mistress seems to be angry when she sees him with a newspaper, but she's actually afraid.
What new information did you learn?	Slaveholders were afraid of what would happen if enslaved children learned to read.

from

NARRATIVE OF THE LIFE OF FREDERICK DOUGLASS, AN AMERICAN SLAVE

Autobiography by **Frederick Douglass**

? **ESSENTIAL QUESTION:**

What will people risk to be free?

QUICK START

How did you learn to read? In what ways would your life be different if you couldn't read? Discuss these questions with your classmates.

ANALYZE AUTOBIOGRAPHY

Narrative of the Life of Frederick Douglass, an American Slave is an **autobiography,** which is an account of the writer's own life.

Authors of autobiography often have a **purpose,** or reason for writing, beyond informing readers about events in their own lives. For example, writers might also want to shed light on the time period in which they have lived, or share a message about an issue that has shaped their lives as well as the lives of others. Sometimes writers state their purpose directly, but often you must infer it from the details the author chooses to share and comment on.

As you read, try to identify Frederick Douglass's main purpose in this section of his autobiography.

GENRE ELEMENTS: AUTOBIOGRAPHY

- gives an account of the writer's own life, told from the first-person point of view
- describes events in chronological order
- provides interesting details and anecdotes
- has a tone that reveals the author's attitude toward people and events

ANALYZE STRUCTURE

In an autobiography, authors often choose to focus on events that are related by **cause and effect,** which means that one event brings about another event or creates a change in attitude. Paragraphs may be structured to show these cause-and-effect relationships, even in narratives told in chronological order.

For example, Douglass states that his mistress was "a kind and tender-hearted woman," and he gives examples to support his statement. Then he explains how slavery caused her to change. "Under its influence, the tender heart became stone, and the lamblike disposition gave way to one of tigerlike fierceness." He supports this description of slavery's effects by giving examples: "I have had her rush at me with a face made all up of fury, and snatch from me a newspaper."

As you read, note how the cause-and-effect structure helps Douglass achieve his purpose. Use a chart like this.

CAUSE		EFFECT
Slavery		A kind woman turns angry and cruel.

GET READY

CRITICAL VOCABULARY

commence **prudence** **denunciation**
apprehension **unabated** **vindication**

To see how many Critical Vocabulary words you already know, use them to complete the sentences.

1. You might feel __________ about moving to another country.

2. The fierce argument continued __________ for hours.

3. The convict received __________ of his innocence and was freed.

4. Did you __________ watching the TV series with the first episode, or did you start watching it later?

5. Saving some of your money instead of spending it all is an example of __________.

6. The entire school united in its __________ of the arsonist who burned down the library.

LANGUAGE CONVENTIONS

Pronoun-Antecedent Agreement In this lesson, you will learn how writers use pronouns to refer to their antecedents correctly. In the following sentence, notice how Douglass uses the plural pronoun *they* to refer back to a plural antecedent, *fellows*.

It is enough to say of the dear little fellows, that they lived on Philpot Street. . . .

ANNOTATION MODEL

NOTICE & NOTE

As you read, notice and note signposts, such as **Word Gaps** and **Contrasts and Contradictions,** and pause to ask yourself **Big Questions.** In the model, you can see one reader's notes about *Narrative of the Life of Frederick Douglass, an American Slave.*

1 I lived in Master Hugh's family about seven years. During this time, I succeeded in learning to read and write. In accomplishing this, I was compelled to resort to various stratagems. I had no regular teacher. My mistress, who had kindly commenced to instruct me, had, in compliance with the advice and direction of her husband, not only ceased to instruct, but had set her face against my being instructed by any one else. . . .

It's surprising that Douglass's mistress started to teach him but later made sure no one did. Was it just her husband that changed her?

BACKGROUND

Frederick Douglass *(1818–1895) was born into enslavement in Maryland at a time when slavery was still legal in many states in the Union. As Douglass grew up, he tried to escape several times. Finally, in 1838, he succeeded. Douglass went on to become a famous speaker and writer, fighting to abolish, or end, slavery. His autobiography,* Narrative of the Life of Frederick Douglass, an American Slave, *became a best seller in the United States and Europe.*

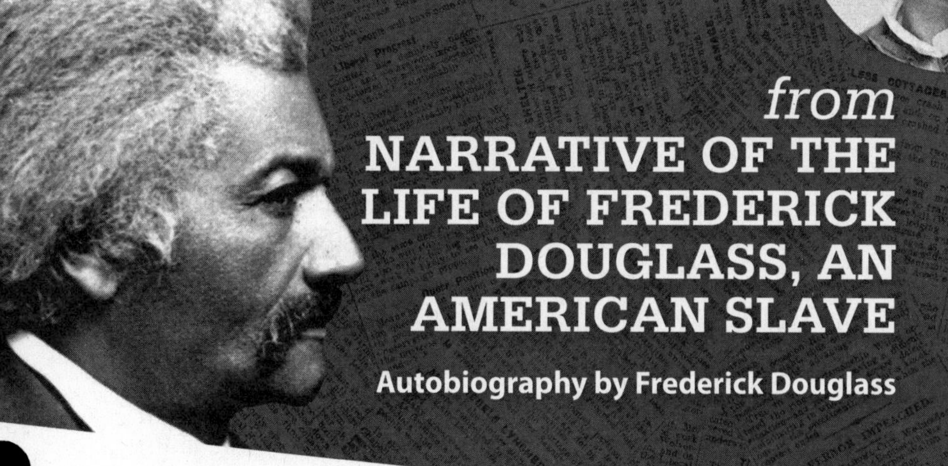

from NARRATIVE OF THE LIFE OF FREDERICK DOUGLASS, AN AMERICAN SLAVE

Autobiography by Frederick Douglass

SETTING A PURPOSE

As you read, consider why Frederick Douglass chose these particular events to write about. Think about what his focus on these events reveals about his character and his struggle for freedom.

Notice & Note

Use the side margins to notice and note signposts in the text.

1 I lived in Master Hugh's family about seven years. During this time, I succeeded in learning to read and write. In accomplishing this, I was compelled to resort to various stratagems. I had no regular teacher. My mistress, who had kindly commenced to instruct me, had, in compliance with the advice and direction of her husband, not only ceased to instruct, but had set her face against my being instructed by any one else. It is due, however, to my mistress to say of her, that she did not adopt this course of treatment immediately. She at first lacked the depravity[1] indispensable to shutting me up in mental darkness. It was at least necessary for her to have some training in the exercise of irresponsible power, to make her equal to the task of treating me as though I were a brute.

LANGUAGE CONVENTIONS

Annotate: Mark the antecedent of the pronoun *her* in the fifth sentence of paragraph 1.

Analyze: How does correct pronoun-antecedent agreement make the meaning of this sentence clear?

[1] **depravity** (dĭ-prăv′ĭ-tē): moral corruption.

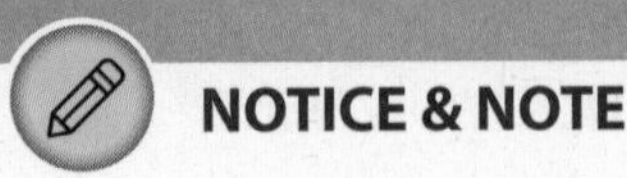

commence
(kə-mĕns´) *v.* When things *commence,* they begin or start.

ANALYZE AUTOBIOGRAPHY

Annotate: Mark details in paragraph 2 that describe Douglass's mistress.

Infer: What might Douglass's purpose be in devoting so much space to describing his mistress?

BIG QUESTIONS

Notice & Note: Mark details in paragraphs 2–3 that are surprising when compared to the lives of most young people today.

Synthesize: What is surprising about these details of Douglass's life?

apprehension
(ăp´rĭ-hĕn´shən) *n. Apprehension* is the fear or dread of the future.

2 My mistress was, as I have said, a kind and tender-hearted woman; and in the simplicity of her soul she **commenced,** when I first went to live with her, to treat me as she supposed one human being ought to treat another. In entering upon the duties of a slaveholder, she did not seem to perceive that I sustained to her the relation of a mere chattel,[2] and that for her to treat me as a human being was not only wrong, but dangerously so. Slavery proved as injurious to her as it did to me. When I went there, she was a pious, warm, and tender-hearted woman. There was no sorrow or suffering for which she had not a tear. She had bread for the hungry, clothes for the naked, and comfort for every mourner that came within her reach. Slavery soon proved its ability to divest her of these heavenly qualities. Under its influence, the tender heart became stone, and the lamblike disposition gave way to one of tigerlike fierceness. The first step in her downward course was in her ceasing to instruct me. She now commenced to practise her husband's precepts.[3] She finally became even more violent in her opposition than her husband himself. She was not satisfied with simply doing as well as he had commanded; she seemed anxious to do better. Nothing seemed to make her more angry than to see me with a newspaper. She seemed to think that here lay the danger. I have had her rush at me with a face made all up of fury, and snatch from me a newspaper, in a manner that fully revealed her **apprehension.** She was an apt woman; and a little experience soon demonstrated, to her satisfaction, that education and slavery were incompatible with each other.

3 From this time I was most narrowly watched. If I was in a separate room any considerable length of time, I was sure to be suspected of having a book, and was at once called to give an account of myself. All this, however, was too late. The first step had been taken. Mistress, in teaching me the alphabet, had given me the inch, and no precaution could prevent me from taking the *ell.*

4 The plan which I adopted, and the one by which I was most successful, was that of making friends of all the little white boys whom I met in the street. As many of these as I could, I converted into teachers. With their kindly aid, obtained at different times and in different places, I finally succeeded in learning to read. When I was sent of errands, I always took my book with me, and by going one part of my errand quickly,

[2] **chattel** (chăt´l): a property or slave.

[3] **precepts** (prē´sĕpts´): rules or principles regarding action or conduct.

I found time to get a lesson before my return. I used also to carry bread with me, enough of which was always in the house, and to which I was always welcome; for I was much better off in this regard than many of the poor white children in our neighborhood. This bread I used to bestow upon the hungry little urchins, who, in return, would give me that more valuable bread of knowledge. I am strongly tempted to give the names of two or three of those little boys, as a testimonial of the gratitude and affection I bear them; but **prudence** forbids;—not that it would injure me, but it might embarrass them; for it is almost an unpardonable offence to teach slaves to read in this Christian country. It is enough to say of the dear little fellows, that they lived on Philpot Street, very near Durgin and Bailey's ship-yard. I used to talk this matter of slavery over with them. I would sometimes say to them, I wished I could be as free as they would be when they got to be men. "You will be free as soon as you are twenty-one, *but I am a slave for life!* Have not I as good a right to be free as you have?" These words used to trouble them; they would express for me the liveliest sympathy, and console me with the hope that something would occur by which I might be free.

5 I was now about twelve years old, and the thought of being *a slave for life* began to bear heavily upon my heart. Just about this time, I got hold of a book entitled "The Columbian Orator."[4] Every opportunity I got, I used to read this book. Among much of other interesting matter, I found in it a dialogue between a master and his slave. The slave was represented as having run away from his master three times. The dialogue represented the conversation which took place between them, when the slave was retaken the third time. In this dialogue, the whole argument in behalf of slavery was brought forward by the master, all of which was disposed of by the slave. The slave was made to say some very smart as well as impressive things in reply to his master—things which had the desired though unexpected effect; for the conversation resulted in the voluntary emancipation of the slave on the part of the master.

6 In the same book, I met with one of Sheridan's mighty speeches on and in behalf of Catholic emancipation.[5] These were choice documents to me. I read them over and over

ANALYZE AUTOBIOGRAPHY

Annotate: In paragraph 4, circle words and phrases that describe the boys' attitude toward Douglass. Underline text that tells how Douglass feels about them.

Infer: What message about people does Douglass convey by describing his interactions with these boys?

prudence
(pro͞od´ns) *n. Prudence* is the wise handling of practical matters.

ANALYZE STRUCTURE

Annotate: In paragraphs 5 and 6, mark details about the texts Douglass read at age 12 that were especially important to him.

Cause/Effect: What effect did reading these texts have on Douglass?

[4] **"The Columbian Orator":** a collection of political essays, poems, and dialogues that were used to teach reading and speaking at the beginning of the 19th century.

[5] **one of Sheridan's mighty speeches on and in behalf of Catholic emancipation:** Richard Brinsley Sheridan (1751–1816) was an Irish playwright and politician who made speeches about the rights of Roman Catholics in Britain and Ireland.

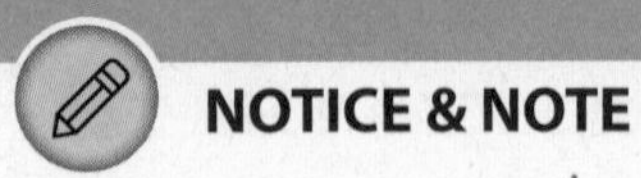

unabated
(ŭn´ə-bā´tĭd) *adj.* If something is *unabated,* it keeps its full force without decreasing.

denunciation
(dĭ-nŭn´sē-ā´shən) *n.* A *denunciation* is the public condemnation of something as wrong or evil.

vindication
(vĭn´dĭ-kā´shən) *n. Vindication* is the evidence or proof that someone's claim is correct.

CONTRASTS AND CONTRADICTIONS

Notice & Note: Douglass went to great lengths to teach himself how to read. In paragraph 6, mark the feelings he had after learning to read.

Infer: Why did Douglass feel that learning to read was "a curse rather than a blessing"?

WORD GAPS

Notice & Note: Mark words and phrases on this page that signal the fact that Douglass was writing in the 1800s rather than today.

Infer: Use context clues to infer the meanings of the words and phrases you marked.

again with **unabated** interest. They gave tongue to interesting thoughts of my own soul, which had frequently flashed through my mind, and died away for want of utterance. The moral which I gained from the dialogue was the power of truth over the conscience of even a slaveholder. What I got from Sheridan was a bold **denunciation** of slavery, and a powerful **vindication** of human rights. The reading of these documents enabled me to utter my thoughts, and to meet the arguments brought forward to sustain slavery; but while they relieved me of one difficulty, they brought on another even more painful than the one of which I was relieved. The more I read, the more I was led to abhor and detest my enslavers. I could regard them in no other light than a band of successful robbers, who had left their homes, and gone to Africa, and stolen us from our homes, and in a strange land reduced us to slavery. I loathed them as being the meanest as well as the most wicked of men. As I read and contemplated the subject, behold! that very discontentment which Master Hugh had predicted would follow my learning to read had already come, to torment and sting my soul to unutterable anguish. As I writhed under it, I would at times feel that learning to read had been a curse rather than a blessing. It had given me a view of my wretched condition, without the remedy. It opened my eyes to the horrible pit, but to no ladder upon which to get out. In moments of agony, I envied my fellow-slaves for their stupidity. I have often wished myself a beast. I preferred the condition of the meanest reptile to my own. Anything, no matter what, to get rid of thinking! It was this everlasting thinking of my condition that tormented me. There was no getting rid of it. It was pressed upon me by every object within sight or hearing, animate or inanimate. The silver trump of freedom had roused my soul to eternal wakefulness. Freedom now appeared, to disappear no more forever. It was heard in every sound, and seen in every thing. It was ever present to torment me with a sense of my wretched condition. I saw nothing without seeing it, I heard nothing without hearing it, and felt nothing without feeling it. It looked from every star, it smiled in every calm, breathed in every wind, and moved in every storm.

CHECK YOUR UNDERSTANDING

Answer these questions before moving on to the **Analyze the Text** section on the following page.

1 Through the experiences described in this excerpt, Douglass gained —

A gratitude for his master's and mistress's actions

B a belief that people are not to be trusted

C more knowledge about the problem of slavery

D pleasure in spending time with his white friends

2 Which sentence from the excerpt best demonstrates Douglass's feelings about reading after he learned about slavery?

F *In the same book, I met with one of Sheridan's mighty speeches on and in behalf of Catholic emancipation.*

G *In moments of agony, I envied my fellow-slaves for their stupidity.*

H *It was pressed upon me by every object within sight or hearing, animate or inanimate.*

J *I heard nothing without hearing it, and felt nothing without feeling it.*

3 Why does Douglass first describe his mistress as "a kind and tender-hearted woman"?

A To contrast with her later, cruel behavior

B To show how much he wanted to learn to read

C To prove that some slaveholders were caring

D To emphasize his good fortune

ANALYZE THE TEXT

Support your responses with evidence from the text. NOTEBOOK

1. **Cause/Effect** Reread paragraphs 2 and 3. Did the mistress's initial kindness or her eventual cruelty have a greater effect on Frederick Douglass? Explain.
2. **Interpret** When describing how he paid his child tutors, Douglass says, "This bread I used to bestow upon the hungry little urchins, who, in return, would give me that more valuable bread of knowledge." In what way is knowledge "bread"?
3. **Evaluate** Reread paragraph 6. What words reveal Douglass's perspective on, or view of, slaveholders?
4. **Analyze** What is Douglass's purpose for writing? Identify three passages that help him achieve his goal, and explain why.
5. **Notice & Note** In paragraph 6, Douglass says, "I have often wished myself a beast." What does the word *beast* mean in other contexts? What point do you think Douglass is making when he uses it here?

RESEARCH TIP

The best search terms are very specific. Along with the name Frederick Douglass, you will want to include a word such as *slavery* or *abolitionist* to make sure you get the information you need.

RESEARCH

You have read about how Frederick Douglass learned to read in spite of the limitations placed upon him as an enslaved person. Research more details about the significant events in Douglass's life. You might focus on what his life was like as an enslaved person, how he gained his freedom, and how he fought for an end to slavery. Record what you learn in the chart. Then share what you learn with a small group.

PARTS OF DOUGLASS'S LIFE	HIS EXPERIENCES
Childhood	
Freedom	
The Fight Against Slavery	

Extend Find another passage from Douglass's autobiography. Take turns reading it aloud with members of a small group. Discuss the feelings and ideas stirred by Douglass's language and the events he describes.

CREATE AND DISCUSS

Write a Literary Analysis In one to three paragraphs, explain how the tone of Douglass's autobiography helps him achieve his purpose and communicate his message.

- ❑ Think about the author's purpose for writing.
- ❑ Identify the **tone**—the writer's attitude toward his subject. Find examples where Douglass's choice of words helps establish the tone.
- ❑ When you write, begin by stating your view. Then support that view with evidence from the text.

Go to **Writing Informative Texts** in the **Writing Studio** for more help.

Discuss with a Small Group In paragraph 6, Douglass says, "I would at times feel that learning to read had been a curse rather than a blessing."

- ❑ With a small group, discuss Douglass's statement and examine whether people today might share his attitude.
- ❑ Be sure to support your views with evidence from the autobiography.
- ❑ During your discussion, listen closely and respectfully to all ideas.

Go to the **Speaking and Listening Studio** for help with having a group discussion.

RESPOND TO THE ESSENTIAL QUESTION

What will people risk to be free?

UNIT 4 RESPONSE LOG

Use this Response Log to record your ideas about how each of the texts in Unit 4 relates to or comments on the **Essential Question.**

? **Essential Question:** What will people risk to be free?

from Narrative of the Life of Frederick Douglass, an American Slave	
from Harriet Tubman: Conductor on the Underground Railroad	
The Drummer Boy of Shiloh	
O Captain! My Captain!	
Not My Bones	
from Fortune's Bones	

R4 Response Log

Gather Information Review your annotations and notes on the excerpt from *Narrative of the Life of Frederick Douglass, an American Slave*. Then, add relevant details to your Response Log. As you determine which information to include, think about:

- the obstacles that Douglass faced
- the risks he took to learn how to read
- how knowledge both liberated and frightened him

At the end of the unit, you can use your notes to help you write a research report.

ACADEMIC VOCABULARY

As you write and discuss what you learned from the autobiography, be sure to use the Academic Vocabulary words. Check off each of the words that you use.

- ❑ **access**
- ❑ **civil**
- ❑ **demonstrate**
- ❑ **document**
- ❑ **symbolize**

RESPOND

CRITICAL VOCABULARY

WORD BANK
commence
apprehension
prudence
unabated
denunciation
vindication

Practice and Apply Use what you know about the vocabulary words to answer the following questions.

1. If an innocent convict receives **vindication,** will he feel relieved or upset?
2. Which demonstrates **prudence,** studying a little each day or waiting until the night before the test to begin studying?
3. To **commence** baking a cake, would you stir the batter or study the recipe?
4. Which is a type of **denunciation,** praise or criticism?
5. Would you feel **apprehension** about taking a test or getting an A?
6. If your interest in Frederick Douglass is **unabated,** will you read many books about him or just one?

VOCABULARY STRATEGY: Latin Roots

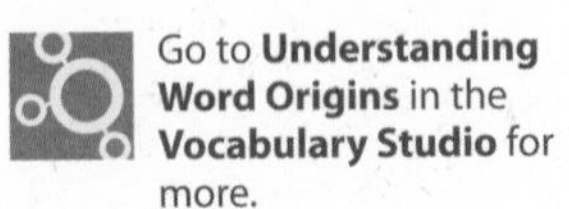

Go to **Understanding Word Origins** in the **Vocabulary Studio** for more.

A **word root** is a word part that contains the core meaning of a word. A root is combined with other word parts, such as a prefix or a suffix, to form a word. The roots of many English words come from Latin. Read this sentence from Frederick Douglass's autobiography.

> **She was not satisfied with simply doing as well as he had commanded; she seemed anxious to do better.**

The word *commanded* includes the Latin root *mand,* which means "to entrust." You can use the meaning of the root *mand* as a clue to figure out that *commanded* means "entrusted someone to carry out an order."

Practice and Apply Find the word in each sentence that includes the Latin root *dict,* which means "to say." Use context and the meaning of the root to help you write a definition of the word. Then verify each of your definitions by finding the word's precise meaning in a print or digital dictionary.

1. Douglass probably did not have access to a dictionary as he learned how to read.
2. Douglass's cruel master and mistress were like dictators.
3. He did not contradict his master's view of the dangers of reading.
4. No one could dictate to him not to follow his desires.
5. The verdict for Douglass's "crime" of reading is "not guilty."

LANGUAGE CONVENTIONS: Pronoun-Antecedent Agreement

A **pronoun** is a word used in place of a noun or another pronoun. The word or phrase to which the pronoun refers is called its **antecedent.** For example, in the following sentence, the pronoun *their* refers to the antecedent *they*: ***They** took **their** seats at the restaurant.*

Go to **Pronoun-Antecedent Agreement** in the **Grammar Studio** for more.

For **agreement in number,** use singular pronouns with singular antecedents and plural pronouns with plural antecedents.

- *Incorrect:* Douglass was grateful to **their** friends for teaching **them** how to read.
- *Revised:* Douglass was grateful to **his** friends for teaching **him** how to read.

For **agreement in gender,** masculine pronouns (*he, his, him*) refer to male antecedents, and feminine pronouns (*she, her*) refer to female antecedents.

- *Incorrect:* Douglass was grateful to **her** friends.
- *Revised:* Douglass was grateful to **his** friends.

For **agreement in person,** a pronoun in the first-, second-, or third-person form must match the person of its antecedent.

- *Incorrect:* You were grateful to **their** friends.
- *Revised:* You were grateful to **your** friends.

Practice and Apply Rewrite each sentence to correct the pronoun-antecedent error.

1. Following his husband's example, Douglass's mistress became cruel.

2. The boys taught her friend Douglass how to read.

3. The library acquired another book by Douglass for their history collection.

4. Douglass was angry when they read about slavery.

5. Douglass gave many speeches about their experiences with slavery.

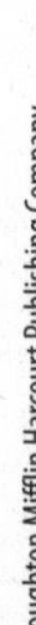

from HARRIET TUBMAN: CONDUCTOR ON THE UNDERGROUND RAILROAD

Biography by **Ann Petry**

? *ESSENTIAL QUESTION:*

What will people risk to be free?

QUICK START

Imagine being led on a difficult or dangerous journey. What qualities would you want the leader of this journey to have? List the top three.

ANALYZE CHARACTERIZATION

A **biography** is a form of nonfiction in which a writer provides a true account of another person's life. In a strong biography, the writer not only recounts the most significant events of the subject's life but also provides insights about the subject's traits and motivations. The way a biographer creates and develops the subject's character is called **characterization.** There are four main methods of characterization. As you read Petry's biography of Tubman, look for the following:

- Direct comments about Tubman—what the author states about Tubman's hopes, thoughts, and worries
- Descriptions of Tubman's physical appearance
- Tubman's own thoughts, speech, and actions and her possible **motivations,** or reasons for her actions
- How others behave toward Tubman and what you can infer about her from their thoughts, speech, and actions toward her

GENRE ELEMENTS: BIOGRAPHY

- presents a true and balanced account of a person's life
- is based on multiple credible sources
- is told from the third-person point of view

ANALYZE AUTHOR'S CRAFT

Author's craft refers to how an author uses literary techniques and narrative elements. **Mood** is the feeling or atmosphere that an author creates for the reader. **Tone** is the author's attitude toward his or her subject. **Voice** refers to the author's unique use of language that allows a reader to "hear" the author's personality behind the words. Study the examples below to see how Petry uses literary techniques to convey Tubman's story and establish mood, tone, and voice. Then, as you read, look for additional examples of each technique.

TECHNIQUE	DEFINITION	EXAMPLES
word choice	the author's use of specific words	The man who stood in the doorway looked at her coldly, looked with unconcealed astonishment and fear. . . .
sentence variety; punctuation variations	variations in sentence length; use of punctuation for dramatic effect	She had never used it—except as a threat.
parallelism	the use of similar grammatical constructions to express ideas that are related or equal in importance	When she knocked on the door of a farmhouse, a place where she and her parties of runaways had always been welcome, always been given shelter. . . .
syntax	the arrangement of words and phrases in sentences	Sometimes the masters thought they had heard the cry of a hoot owl, repeated, . . .

GET READY

CRITICAL VOCABULARY

disheveled	dispel	sullen	cajole
instill	linger	eloquence	evoke

To see how many Critical Vocabulary words you already know, answer the following questions.

1. Would you **linger** at a party if you were **disheveled**? Why or why not?
2. Could someone **instill eloquence** in you? Why or why not?
3. What might someone do to **evoke** a **sullen** response?
4. Would you **cajole** a friend to **dispel** a bad mood? Why or why not?

LANGUAGE CONVENTIONS

Run-on Sentences In this lesson, you will learn about run-on sentences and how to avoid them. A run-on sentence is made up of two or more **independent clauses**—a group of words that contains a subject and predicate and that can stand alone as a sentence—that are run together as a single sentence. In the sentence below, the author uses a comma and the conjunction *but* to create a **compound sentence** and avoid a run-on.

He was a big man and strong, but he had never used his strength to harm anyone, always to help people.

Throughout *Harriet Tubman: Conductor on the Underground Railroad,* notice the way the author uses punctuation and conjunctions to avoid run-on sentences.

ANNOTATION MODEL

NOTICE & NOTE

As you read, pay attention to the author's characterization of Harriet Tubman and the techniques she uses in her writing. You can also mark up evidence that supports your own ideas. In the model, you can see one reader's notes about *Harriet Tubman: Conductor on the Underground Railroad.*

5 Harriet Tubman could have told them that there was far more involved in this matter of running off slaves than signaling the would-be runaways by imitating the call of a whippoorwill, or a hoot owl, far more involved than a matter of waiting for a clear night when the North Star was visible.

The author's use of parallelism emphasizes the idea that Tubman's work was difficult and involved careful preparations.

BACKGROUND

Ann Lane Petry *(1908–1997) grew up in a small town in Connecticut, where she and her family were the only African American residents. Much of her writing focuses on the important contributions of African Americans. Before the Civil War, many enslaved people fled north to freedom along the Underground Railroad, a secret network of safe houses. One of the Underground Railroad's most famous "conductors" was Harriet Tubman.*

from HARRIET TUBMAN: CONDUCTOR ON THE UNDERGROUND RAILROAD

Biography by Ann Petry

SETTING A PURPOSE

As you read, look for clues about the kind of person Harriet Tubman was.

The Railroad Runs to Canada

1 Along the Eastern Shore of Maryland, in Dorchester County, in Caroline County, the masters kept hearing whispers about the man named Moses, who was running off slaves. At first they did not believe in his existence. The stories about him were fantastic, unbelievable. Yet they watched for him. They offered rewards for his capture.

2 They never saw him. Now and then they heard whispered rumors to the effect that he was in the neighborhood. The woods were searched. The roads were watched. There was never anything to indicate his whereabouts. But a few days afterward, a goodly number of slaves would be gone from the plantation. Neither the master nor the overseer had heard or seen anything unusual

Notice & Note

Use the side margins to notice and note signposts in the text.

ANALYZE AUTHOR'S CRAFT

Annotate: A **simple sentence** contains a single independent clause. In paragraph 2, mark two simple sentences with very similar structures that appear in a row.

Analyze: What effect does the author create by expressing these two ideas in separate but parallel sentences?

in the quarter.[1] Sometimes one or the other would vaguely remember having heard a whippoorwill call somewhere in the woods, close by, late at night. Though it was the wrong season for whippoorwills.

3 Sometimes the masters thought they had heard the cry of a hoot owl, repeated, and would remember having thought that the intervals between the low moaning cry were wrong, that it had been repeated four times in succession instead of three. There was never anything more than that to suggest that all was not well in the quarter. Yet when morning came, they invariably discovered that a group of the finest slaves had taken to their heels.

4 Unfortunately, the discovery was almost always made on a Sunday. Thus a whole day was lost before the machinery of pursuit could be set in motion. The posters offering rewards for the fugitives could not be printed until Monday. The men who made a living hunting for runaway slaves were out of reach, off in the woods with their dogs and their guns, in pursuit of four-footed game, or they were in camp meetings saying their prayers with their wives and families beside them.

ANALYZE CHARACTERIZATION

Annotate: Mark details in paragraphs 5–7 that reveal Harriet Tubman's character.

Draw Conclusions: How does the information in these paragraphs differ from the details about "the man named Moses" in paragraphs 1–4? What do these differences suggest about the sources each may have been based on?

5 Harriet Tubman could have told them that there was far more involved in this matter of running off slaves than signaling the would-be runaways by imitating the call of a whippoorwill, or a hoot owl, far more involved than a matter of waiting for a clear night when the North Star was visible.

6 In December, 1851, when she started out with the band of fugitives that she planned to take to Canada, she had been in the vicinity of the plantation for days, planning the trip, carefully selecting the slaves that she would take with her.

7 She had announced her arrival in the quarter by singing the forbidden spiritual—"Go down, Moses, 'way down to Egypt Land"[2]—singing it softly outside the door of a slave cabin, late at night. The husky voice was beautiful even when it was barely more than a murmur borne[3] on the wind.

8 Once she had made her presence known, word of her coming spread from cabin to cabin. The slaves whispered to each other, ear to mouth, mouth to ear, "Moses is here." "Moses has come." "Get ready. Moses is back again." The ones who had agreed to go North with her put ashcake and salt herring in

[1] **quarter:** the area in which enslaved people lived.

[2] **"Go down, Moses, 'way down to Egypt Land":** a line from an African American folk song. In the Bible, Moses led the Israelite slaves in Egypt to freedom.

[3] **borne:** carried.

an old bandanna, hastily tied it into a bundle, and then waited patiently for the signal that meant it was time to start.

9 There were eleven in this party, including one of her brothers and his wife. It was the largest group that she had ever conducted, but she was determined that more and more slaves should know what freedom was like.

10 She had to take them all the way to Canada. The Fugitive Slave Law[4] was no longer a great many incomprehensible words written down on the country's lawbooks. The new law had become a reality. It was Thomas Sims, a boy, picked up on the streets of Boston at night and shipped back to Georgia. It was Jerry and Shadrach, arrested and jailed with no warning.

ANALYZE AUTHOR'S CRAFT

Annotate: Mark the language the author uses to describe the effects of the Fugitive Slave Law in paragraph 10.

Interpret: What does the author's word choice and syntax help her convey about the law?

11 She had never been in Canada. The route beyond Philadelphia was strange to her. But she could not let the runaways who accompanied her know this. As they walked along she told them stories of her own first flight, she kept painting vivid word pictures of what it would be like to be free.

12 But there were so many of them this time. She knew moments of doubt when she was half-afraid, and kept looking back over her shoulder, imagining that she heard the sound of pursuit. They would certainly be pursued. Eleven of them. Eleven thousand dollars' worth of flesh and bone and muscle that belonged to Maryland planters. If they were caught, the eleven runaways would be whipped and sold South, but she—she would probably be hanged.

13 They tried to sleep during the day but they never could wholly relax into sleep. She could tell by the positions they assumed, by their restless movements. And they walked at night. Their progress was slow. It took them three nights of walking to reach the first stop. She had told them about the place where they would stay, promising warmth and good food, holding these things out to them as an incentive to keep going.

14 When she knocked on the door of a farmhouse, a place where she and her parties of runaways had always been welcome, always been given shelter and plenty to eat, there was no answer. She knocked again, softly. A voice from within said, "Who is it?" There was fear in the voice.

15 She knew instantly from the sound of the voice that there was something wrong. She said, "A friend with friends," the password on the Underground Railroad.

16 The door opened, slowly. The man who stood in the doorway looked at her coldly, looked with unconcealed

[4] **Fugitive Slave Law:** a law by which enslaved people who escaped could be recovered by their owners.

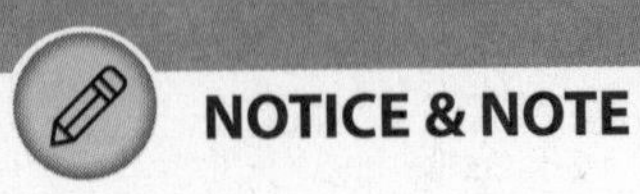

disheveled
(dĭ-shĕv´əld) *adj.* When something is *disheveled,* it is messy or untidy.

ANALYZE AUTHOR'S CRAFT
Annotate: Find and mark an example of parallelism in paragraph 17.

Evaluate: Explain the effect of that technique in the example.

instill
(ĭn-stĭl´) *v.* When you *instill* something, you establish or implant it gradually.

dispel
(dĭ-spĕl´) *v.* When you *dispel* something, you drive it away.

ANALYZE CHARACTERIZATION
Annotate: Mark details the author uses to show Tubman's view of Thomas Garrett in paragraphs 20–21.

Predict: Why might the author have included this information?

astonishment and fear at the eleven **disheveled** runaways who were standing near her. Then he shouted, "Too many, too many. It's not safe. My place was searched last week. It's not safe!" and slammed the door in her face.

17 She turned away from the house, frowning. She had promised her passengers food and rest and warmth, and instead of that, there would be hunger and cold and more walking over the frozen ground. Somehow she would have to **instill** courage into these eleven people, most of them strangers, would have to feed them on hope and bright dreams of freedom instead of the fried pork and corn bread and milk she had promised them.

18 They stumbled along behind her, half-dead for sleep, and she urged them on, though she was as tired and as discouraged as they were. She had never been in Canada but she kept painting wondrous word pictures of what it would be like. She managed to **dispel** their fear of pursuit, so that they would not become hysterical, panic-stricken. Then she had to bring some of the fear back, so that they would stay awake and keep walking though they drooped with sleep.

19 Yet during the day, when they lay down deep in a thicket, they never really slept, because if a twig snapped or the wind sighed in the branches of a pine tree, they jumped to their feet, afraid of their own shadows, shivering and shaking. It was very cold, but they dared not make fires because someone would see the smoke and wonder about it.

20 She kept thinking, eleven of them. Eleven thousand dollars' worth of slaves. And she had to take them all the way to Canada. Sometimes she told them about Thomas Garrett, in Wilmington. She said he was their friend even though he did not know them. He was the friend of all fugitives. He called them God's poor. He was a Quaker[5] and his speech was a little different from that of other people. His clothing was different, too. He wore the wide-brimmed hat that the Quakers wear.

21 She said that he had thick white hair, soft, almost like a baby's, and the kindest eyes she had ever seen. He was a big man and strong, but he had never used his strength to harm anyone, always to help people. He would give all of them a new pair of shoes. Everybody. He always did. Once they reached his house in Wilmington, they would be safe. He would see to it that they were.

22 She described the house where he lived, told them about the store where he sold shoes. She said he kept a pail of milk and a loaf of bread in the drawer of his desk so that he would have

[5] **Quaker:** a member of a religious group called the Society of Friends.

food ready at hand for any of God's poor who should suddenly appear before him, fainting with hunger. There was a hidden room in the store. A whole wall swung open, and behind it was a room where he could hide fugitives. On the wall there were shelves filled with small boxes—boxes of shoes—so that you would never guess that the wall actually opened.

23 While she talked, she kept watching them. They did not believe her. She could tell by their expressions. They were thinking, New shoes, Thomas Garrett, Quaker, Wilmington—what foolishness was this? Who knew if she told the truth? Where was she taking them anyway?

24 That night they reached the next stop—a farm that belonged to a German. She made the runaways take shelter behind trees at the edge of the fields before she knocked at the door. She hesitated before she approached the door, thinking, suppose that he, too, should refuse shelter, suppose— Then she thought, Lord, I'm going to hold steady on to You and You've got to see me through—and knocked softly.

25 She heard the familiar guttural voice say, "Who's there?"

26 She answered quickly, "A friend with friends."

27 He opened the door and greeted her warmly. "How many this time?" he asked.

28 "Eleven," she said and waited, doubting, wondering.

29 He said, "Good. Bring them in."

30 He and his wife fed them in the lamplit kitchen, their faces glowing, as they offered food and more food, urging them to eat, saying there was plenty for everybody, have more milk, have more bread, have more meat.

LANGUAGE CONVENTIONS

Annotate: Mark the author's use of dashes in paragraphs 22–24.

Analyze: Which sentences would become run-ons if the dashes were not used?

A stop on the Underground Railroad

NOTICE & NOTE

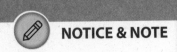

31 They spent the night in the warm kitchen. They really slept, all that night and until dusk the next day. When they left, it was with reluctance. They had all been warm and safe and well-fed. It was hard to exchange the security offered by that clean warm kitchen for the darkness and the cold of a December night.

"Go On or Die"

32 Harriet had found it hard to leave the warmth and friendliness, too. But she urged them on. For a while, as they walked, they seemed to carry in them a measure of contentment; some of the serenity and the cleanliness of that big warm kitchen **lingered** on inside them. But as they walked farther and farther away from the warmth and the light, the cold and the darkness entered into them. They fell silent, **sullen**, suspicious. She waited for the moment when some one of them would turn mutinous. It did not happen that night.

linger
(lĭng´gər) *v.* To *linger* is to remain or stay longer.

sullen
(sŭl´ən) *adj. Sullen* people show silent resentment.

33 Two nights later she was aware that the feet behind her were moving slower and slower. She heard the irritability in their voices, knew that soon someone would refuse to go on.

34 She started talking about William Still and the Philadelphia Vigilance Committee.[6] No one commented. No one asked any questions. She told them the story of William and Ellen Craft and how they escaped from Georgia. Ellen was so fair that she looked as though she were white, and so she dressed up in a man's clothing and she looked like a wealthy young planter. Her husband, William, who was dark, played the role of her slave. Thus they traveled from Macon, Georgia, to Philadelphia, riding on the trains, staying at the finest hotels. Ellen pretended to be very ill—her right arm was in a sling, and her right hand was bandaged, because she was supposed to have rheumatism. Thus she avoided having to sign the register at the hotels for she could not read or write. They finally arrived safely in Philadelphia, and then went on to Boston.

ANALYZE AUTHOR'S CRAFT

Annotate: Mark the author's use of parallelism in paragraph 37.

Interpret: What words are repeated? Explain the effects of this repeated grammatical construction and word choice.

35 No one said anything. Not one of them seemed to have heard her.

36 She told them about Frederick Douglass, the most famous of the escaped slaves, of his **eloquence**, of his magnificent appearance. Then she told them of her own first vain effort at running away, **evoking** the memory of that miserable life she had led as a child, reliving it for a moment in the telling.

eloquence
(ĕl´ə-kwəns) *n. Eloquence* is the ability to speak powerfully and persuasively.

evoke
(ĭ-vōk´) *v.* When you *evoke* something, you bring it to mind.

37 But they had been tired too long, hungry too long, afraid too long, footsore too long. One of them suddenly cried out in

[6] **Philadelphia Vigilance Committee:** a fundraising organization that helped people who had escaped enslavement.

despair, "Let me go back. It is better to be a slave than to suffer like this in order to be free."

38 She carried a gun with her on these trips. She had never used it—except as a threat. Now as she aimed it, she experienced a feeling of guilt, remembering that time, years ago, when she had prayed for the death of Edward Brodas, the Master, and then not too long afterward had heard that great wailing cry that came from the throats of the field hands, and knew from the sound that the Master was dead.

39 One of the runaways said, again, "Let me go back. Let me go back," and stood still, and then turned around and said, over his shoulder, "I am going back."

40 She lifted the gun, aimed it at the despairing slave. She said, "Go on with us or die." The husky low-pitched voice was grim.

41 He hesitated for a moment and then he joined the others. They started walking again. She tried to explain to them why none of them could go back to the plantation. If a runaway returned, he would turn traitor, the master and the overseer would force him to turn traitor. The returned slave would disclose the stopping places, the hiding places, the cornstacks they had used with the full knowledge of the owner of the farm, the name of the German farmer who had fed them and sheltered them. These people who had risked their own security to help runaways would be ruined, fined, imprisoned.

42 She said, "We got to go free or die. And freedom's not bought with dust."

43 This time she told them about the long agony of the Middle Passage[7] on the old slave ships, about the black horror of the holds, about the chains and the whips. They too knew these stories. But she wanted to remind them of the long hard way they had come, about the long hard way they had yet to go. She told them about Thomas Sims, the boy picked up on the streets of Boston and sent back to Georgia. She said when they got him back to Savannah, got him in prison there, they whipped him until a doctor who was standing by watching said, "You will kill him if you strike him again!" His master said, "Let him die!"

44 Thus she forced them to go on. Sometimes she thought she had become nothing but a voice speaking in the darkness, **cajoling**, urging, threatening. Sometimes she told them things to make them laugh, sometimes she sang to them, and heard the eleven voices behind her blending softly with hers, and then she knew that for the moment all was well with them.

[7] **Middle Passage:** a sea route along which enslaved Africans were transported to the Americas.

BIG QUESTIONS

Notice & Note: Mark anything that surprises you in paragraph 38. If nothing surprises you, mark details that confirm what you already knew.

Analyze: Why might the author have included the facts you marked?

cajole
(kə-jōl´) *v.* When you *cajole*, you coax or urge gently.

NOTICE & NOTE

ANALYZE CHARACTERIZATION

Annotate: Mark details in paragraph 46 that tell how the people in Tubman's group felt about her.

Infer: What do the details about the group members' actions suggest about Tubman?

45 She gave the impression of being a short, muscular, indomitable woman who could never be defeated. Yet at any moment she was liable to be seized by one of those curious fits of sleep, which might last for a few minutes or for hours.

46 Even on this trip, she suddenly fell asleep in the woods. The runaways, ragged, dirty, hungry, cold, did not steal the gun as they might have, and set off by themselves, or turn back. They sat on the ground near her and waited patiently until she awakened. They had come to trust her implicitly, totally. They, too, had come to believe her repeated statement, "We got to go free or die." She was leading them into freedom, and so they waited until she was ready to go on.

47 Finally, they reached Thomas Garrett's house in Wilmington, Delaware. Just as Harriet had promised, Garrett gave them all new shoes, and provided carriages to take them on to the next stop.

48 By slow stages they reached Philadelphia, where William Still hastily recorded their names, and the plantations whence

 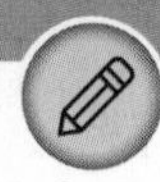

they had come, and something of the life they had led in slavery. Then he carefully hid what he had written, for fear it might be discovered. In 1872 he published this record in book form and called it *The Underground Railroad*. In the foreword to his book he said: "While I knew the danger of keeping strict records, and while I did not then dream that in my day slavery would be blotted out, or that the time would come when I could publish these records, it used to afford me great satisfaction to take them down, fresh from the lips of fugitives on the way to freedom, and to preserve them as they had given them."

49 William Still, who was familiar with all the station stops on the Underground Railroad, supplied Harriet with money and sent her and her eleven fugitives on to Burlington, New Jersey.

50 Harriet felt safer now, though there were danger spots ahead. But the biggest part of her job was over. As they went farther and farther north, it grew colder; she was aware of the wind on the Jersey ferry and aware of the cold damp in New

NOTICE & NOTE

York. From New York they went on to Syracuse, where the temperature was even lower.

51 In Syracuse she met the Reverend J. W. Loguen, known as "Jarm" Loguen. This was the beginning of a lifelong friendship. Both Harriet and Jarm Loguen were to become friends and supporters of Old John Brown.[8]

QUOTED WORDS

Notice & Note: Mark the details that the author uses to introduce the quotation in paragraph 52.

Connect: How does the information in the quote relate to the information the author provides about Douglass? Why might the author have chosen to include this quote?

52 From Syracuse they went north again, into a colder, snowier city—Rochester. Here they almost certainly stayed with Frederick Douglass, for he wrote in his autobiography:

> On one occasion I had eleven fugitives at the same time under my roof, and it was necessary for them to remain with me until I could collect sufficient money to get them to Canada. It was the largest number I ever had at any one time, and I had some difficulty in providing so many with food and shelter, but, as may well be imagined, they were not very fastidious in either direction, and were well content with very plain food, and a strip of carpet on the floor for a bed, or a place on the straw in the barnloft.

53 Late in December, 1851, Harriet arrived in St. Catharines, Canada West (now Ontario), with the eleven fugitives. It had taken almost a month to complete this journey; most of the time had been spent getting out of Maryland.

ANALYZE CHARACTERIZATION

Annotate: Mark details in paragraph 54 that describe Tubman's actions after she arrives in Canada.

Infer: What do these details reveal about Tubman's character?

54 That first winter in St. Catharines was a terrible one. Canada was a strange frozen land, snow everywhere, ice everywhere, and a bone-biting cold the like of which none of them had ever experienced before. Harriet rented a small frame house in the town and set to work to make a home. The fugitives boarded with her. They worked in the forests, felling trees, and so did she. Sometimes she took other jobs, cooking or cleaning house for people in the town. She cheered on these newly arrived fugitives, working herself, finding work for them, finding food for them, praying for them, sometimes begging for them.

55 Often she found herself thinking of the beauty of Maryland, the mellowness of the soil, the richness of the plant life there.

[8] **Old John Brown:** an anti-slavery leader who was executed.

Harriet Tubman is honored in this bronze statue, titled *Step on Board*, by sculptor Fern Cunningham. Located at the entrance to Harriet Tubman Park in Boston, Massachusetts, the statue shows Tubman holding a Bible as she leads a group northward to freedom.

The climate itself made for an ease of living that could never be duplicated in this bleak, barren countryside.

56 In spite of the severe cold, the hard work, she came to love St. Catharines, and the other towns and cities in Canada where black men lived. She discovered that freedom meant more than the right to change jobs at will, more than the right to keep the money that one earned. It was the right to vote and to sit on juries. It was the right to be elected to office. In Canada there were black men who were county officials and members of school boards. St. Catharines had a large colony of ex-slaves, and they owned their own homes, kept them neat and clean and in good repair. They lived in whatever part of town they chose and sent their children to the schools.

57 When spring came she decided that she would make this small Canadian city her home—as much as any place could be said to be home to a woman who traveled from Canada to the Eastern Shore of Maryland as often as she did.

58 In the spring of 1852, she went back to Cape May, New Jersey. She spent the summer there, cooking in a hotel. That fall she returned, as usual, to Dorchester County, and brought out nine more slaves, conducting them all the way to St. Catharines, in Canada West, to the bone-biting cold, the snow-covered forests—and freedom.

59 She continued to live in this fashion, spending the winter in Canada, and the spring and summer working in Cape May, New Jersey, or in Philadelphia. She made two trips a year into slave territory, one in the fall and another in the spring. She now had a definite crystallized purpose, and in carrying it out, her life fell into a pattern which remained unchanged for the next six years.

CHECK YOUR UNDERSTANDING

Answer these questions before moving on to the **Analyze the Text** section on the following page.

1 What was significant about the group Tubman led to escape slavery in December 1851?

A It was the largest number of people she had ever taken.

B It traveled deeper into the swamp than ever before.

C It journeyed farther south than previous groups.

D It included eleven members of the same family.

2 Read this sentence from paragraph 12.

If they were caught, the eleven runaways would be whipped and sold South, but she—she would probably be hanged.

The author includes this sentence most likely to emphasize that Tubman —

F felt that she needed to look out for herself more than others

G thought that the risks of danger on her journey were unlikely

H wanted to turn back and lead the travelers into slavery again

J continued bravely despite her own fears and doubts

3 What can you conclude about the travelers based on the details in paragraph 19?

A They were afraid of getting caught.

B They were thankful to be journeying north.

C They slept a lot to restore their energy.

D They knew the most difficult part of the journey was over.

RESPOND

ANALYZE THE TEXT

Support your responses with evidence from the text. NOTEBOOK

1. **Infer** Reread paragraphs 1–2. What does the description suggest about the qualities of the person called Moses?
2. **Interpret** Identify the parallelism in paragraph 8. What does this technique help to evoke?
3. **Infer** In paragraphs 10–11, the author describes the difficulty of the task facing Harriet Tubman. What is Tubman's response? Explain what her words and actions reveal about her.
4. **Analyze** Why might the author have included details from the stories Tubman likely told while leading the slaves to freedom?
5. **Notice & Note** Identify a fact or detail in this selection that surprised or impressed you. Then explain why it was surprising or impressive and how it affected your view of Harriet Tubman.

RESEARCH TIP
Instead of searching for each question individually, try finding a short biographical summary of each subject's life. Searching for both individuals might help you find out about ways in which the two leaders interacted.

RESEARCH

In this selection, not only does Tubman tell her band of fugitives about Frederick Douglass, they eventually meet him. Conduct research to learn more about Tubman and Douglass. Record what you learn below.

QUESTION	ANSWER
What did Tubman and Douglass have in common?	
How did Tubman and Douglass differ in their fight against slavery?	
What interactions did the two leaders have with each other?	

Extend Tubman and Douglass took different approaches to winning slaves' freedom. Was one approach better or more necessary than the other? Take a position on this matter and present it to a small group, using evidence from your research to back up your claim.

CREATE AND PRESENT

Write a Speech Prepare a persuasive speech to convince the board of a museum that Harriet Tubman should be included in a "Heroes Hall of Fame" exhibit. The following tips will help you.

- ❑ Remember, this speech is an argument. Form a claim, and state it in early in your speech, along with an attention-grabbing example of Tubman's heroism.
- ❑ Support your claim with reasons, and each reason with strong, relevant evidence. Consider quoting an historian's opinion of Tubman's impact on the quest for freedom prior to the Civil War.
- ❑ Use transitional words and phrases to help listeners follow how your claim, reasons, and evidence are related.
- ❑ Utilize persuasive devices to be as convincing as possible.
- ❑ Close by summarizing your main points.

Go to the **Writing Studio** for more on writing an argument.

Present a Speech Practice delivering your speech with the following in mind:

- ❑ Mark the points you want to emphasize and try out different ways of emphasizing them. For instance, you might pause to scan faces, raise your volume, slow your pace, or pound your fist.
- ❑ Speak clearly, and talk at a pace your audience can follow.
- ❑ If you have planned to include charts, graphs, or other visual aids, practice showing these items until you can do so smoothly.

Go to the **Speaking and Listening Studio** for help with giving a presentation.

RESPOND TO THE ESSENTIAL QUESTION

? What will people risk to be free?

Gather Information Review your annotations and notes on *Harriet Tubman: Conductor on the Underground Railroad.* Then, add relevant details to your Response Log. To determine which information to include, think about:

- what people have risked to be free
- what it means to be free
- what kinds of qualities a person would need to be willing to risk her life to obtain freedom for others

At the end of the unit, you can use your notes to help you write a research report.

ACADEMIC VOCABULARY

As you write and discuss what you learned from the biography, be sure to use the Academic Vocabulary words. Check off each of the words that you use.

- ❑ **access**
- ❑ **civil**
- ❑ **demonstrate**
- ❑ **document**
- ❑ **symbolize**

CRITICAL VOCABULARY

WORD BANK
disheveled
instill
dispel
linger
sullen
eloquence
evoke
cajole

Practice and Apply Circle the letter of the best answer to each question. Then, explain your response.

1. Which of the following would **instill** a sense of responsibility?
   a. having a child care for a plant **b.** giving a child fresh flowers

2. Which of the following would be **disheveled**?
   a. a car that was just washed **b.** a person who just woke up

3. Which of the following would require **eloquence**?
   a. cheering at a football game **b.** giving a speech

4. Which of the following exemplifies what it means to **cajole**?
   a. worrying about losing **b.** giving someone a pep talk

5. Which of the following exemplifies what it means to **evoke**?
   a. getting sympathy from others by looking sad **b.** getting removed from someone else's property

6. Which of the following exemplifies what it means to **dispel**?
   a. walking off into the sunset **b.** proving a rumor isn't true

7. Which of the following exemplifies what it means to **linger**?
   a. staying seated after a movie to watch the credits **b.** making eye contact as you walk down the street

8. Which of the following would you describe as **sullen**?
   a. an angry mob **b.** an unhappy loser

VOCABULARY STRATEGY: Latin Roots

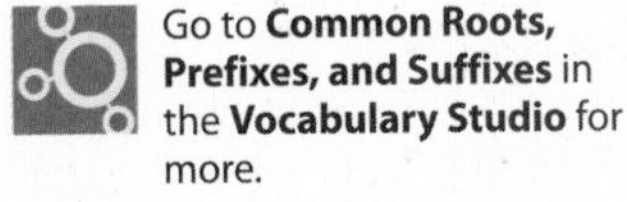

Go to **Common Roots, Prefixes, and Suffixes** in the **Vocabulary Studio** for more.

Recognizing **word roots** can help you determine the meanings of unfamiliar words. For example, the word *conducted* includes the Latin root *duc* or *duct*, which means "to lead." This information can help you infer that *conducted* in the sentence below means "led or guided together." Similarly, a *conductor* is "a person who leads."

> **It was the largest group that she had ever <u>conducted</u>, but she was determined that more and more slaves should know what freedom was like.**

Practice and Apply Use online or print resources to find four additional examples of words that use the Latin root *duc* or *duct*. Use your knowledge of the root's meaning to write a definition for each word. Then consult a dictionary to confirm each word's meaning.

LANGUAGE CONVENTIONS:
Run-on Sentences

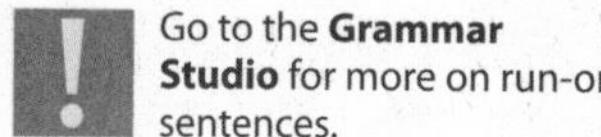

Go to the **Grammar Studio** for more on run-on sentences.

A **run-on sentence** is made up of two or more sentences written as though they were one. Knowing how to construct and punctuate different types of sentences can help you avoid run-ons. For example, to join the two independent clauses that make up a **compound sentence,** you could use a comma and a coordinating conjunction such as *and, but, or, for, so, yet,* or *nor.*

> **Run-on:** They were too tired to walk any farther they stopped to rest.
>
> **Correct:** They were too tired to walk any farther, so they stopped to rest.

Similarly, in a complex sentence you would use a comma between the independent and subordinate clauses. As you may recall, a **complex sentence** is a sentence made up of an independent clause—that is, one that could stand alone as a sentence—and one or more subordinate clauses. **Subordinate clauses** express incomplete thoughts and contain subordinating conjunctions such as *although, after, while,* or *because.* Here is a complex sentence from the selection.

> **While she talked,** she kept watching them.

The underlined part of the sentence is an independent clause. The part in boldface type is a subordinate clause. Without the comma, the sentence would not be a run-on, but the meaning would be less clear.

In a **compound-complex sentence,** which is one that has at least one subordinate clause and at least two independent clauses, you would also use commas and conjunctions to avoid creating a run-on. For example, look at this sentence from the selection.

> They stumbled along behind her, half-dead for sleep, and she urged them on, **though she was as tired and as discouraged as they were.**

The underlined part consists of two independent clauses joined by a comma and the coordinating conjunction *and*. The part in boldface type is a subordinate clause. If a comma and *and* did not separate the two independent clauses, this sentence would be a run-on.

Practice and Apply Write three sentences about a journey. Make one sentence complex, another compound, and another compound-complex. Be sure to use commas and conjunctions appropriately to avoid creating run-ons.

ANALYZE & APPLY

THE DRUMMER BOY OF SHILOH

Historical Fiction by **Ray Bradbury**

? ***ESSENTIAL QUESTION:***

What will people risk to be free?

QUICK START

What do you know about drummer boys in the Civil War? For example, how old were they? What role did they play in battles? Discuss your ideas with a partner.

ANALYZE SETTING

Every story has a **setting,** the time and place in which the action occurs. In historical fiction such as "The Drummer Boy of Shiloh," the setting is usually a key aspect of the work.

Historical fiction is set in the past and includes real places and events from the time period. Like other works of historical fiction, Ray Bradbury's story involves characters that may be based on real people, plot developments that reflect real events, and details that are historically accurate. The story feels realistic because his characters hold beliefs and values that real people in the historical period would have had.

As you read, pay attention to details about the setting, and consider how the setting influences the characters' beliefs and values.

GENRE ELEMENTS: HISTORICAL FICTION

- includes the basic elements of fiction—setting, characters, plot, conflict, and theme
- is set in the past
- includes real places and historical events, along with events from the author's imagination
- has characters based on real people from history

ANALYZE MOOD

When you get a general sense of anxiety, sadness, giddiness, or some other emotion as you read a story, you are responding to the work's **mood,** the feeling or atmosphere that the author creates for readers. Writers use language and literary elements to create a mood.

ELEMENTS	HOW THEY CREATE MOOD
Setting, where and when the events take place	The writer's choice of setting and the words he or she uses to describe it can create a mood.
Imagery, language that appeals to the five senses	What we see, hear, or otherwise sense can make us feel frightened, cheerful, or many other things.
Symbol, a person, place, object, or activity that stands for something beyond itself	The emotions evoked by a symbol or what happens to it can affect the overall feeling of a piece. For example, a wounded bird might contribute to a mood of vulnerability.
Allusion, or reference to a famous person, place, event, or work of literature	An allusion to a serious person can help set a somber mood, just as an allusion to a fanciful place can contribute to a whimsical mood.

Look for language and literary elements that help create different moods in "The Drummer Boy of Shiloh."

GET READY

CRITICAL VOCABULARY

solemn	**strew**	**resolute**
askew	**legitimately**	**muted**

To see how many Critical Vocabulary words you already know, answer these questions.

1. Which of these is a **solemn** occasion?
   a. a funeral **b.** a birthday party

2. Which could you describe as **askew**?
   a. a door shut tight **b.** a picture hanging crookedly

3. What might you **strew** across a front yard?
   a. grass seeds **b.** a rake

4. Which action is done **legitimately**?
   a. registering to vote **b.** stealing a pack of gum

5. Which gesture makes someone appear **resolute**?
   a. standing up straight **b.** shrugging the shoulders

6. What makes a **muted** sound?
   a. a car's horn **b.** a kitten under a blanket

LANGUAGE CONVENTIONS

Sentence Fragments In this lesson, you will learn about complete sentences and fragments. The story's dialogue includes fragments because people often use them in speaking. As you read, observe how Ray Bradbury uses fragments to create realistic-sounding dialogue.

God's truth. Thinking of everything ahead. Both sides figuring the other side will just give up, and soon, and the war done. . . .

ANNOTATION MODEL

NOTICE & NOTE

As you read, note how the author describes the setting and creates mood. You can also mark up evidence to support your own ideas. The model shows one reader's notes about "The Drummer Boy of Shiloh."

1 In the April night, more than once, blossoms fell from the orchard trees and lit with rustling taps on the drumskin. At midnight a peach stone left miraculously on a branch through winter, flicked by a bird, fell swift and unseen, struck once, like panic, which jerked the boy upright. . . .

setting—in an orchard during the spring

mood—a little spooky, since it's midnight. Will the boy be safe?

NOTICE & NOTE

BACKGROUND

*Though **Ray Bradbury** (1920–2012) is best known as a science fiction writer, he's also written plays, mysteries, fantasies, realistic stories, and novels. In this story, Bradbury tells about a drummer boy on the night before the Battle of Shiloh in the Civil War. This two-day battle began on April 6, 1862, near the southwestern Tennessee church from which the bloody clash takes its name. More than 23,000 soldiers died during those two days. At that time, it was the bloodiest battle in American history.*

THE DRUMMER BOY OF SHILOH

Historical Fiction by Ray Bradbury

SETTING A PURPOSE

As you read, pay attention to the details the author provides about the scene of the battle and about the men who were preparing to fight. What do the details suggest about the realities of war?

1 In the April night, more than once, blossoms fell from the orchard trees and lit with rustling taps on the drumskin. At midnight a peach stone left miraculously on a branch through winter, flicked by a bird, fell swift and unseen, struck once, like panic, which jerked the boy upright. In silence he listened to his own heart ruffle away, away, at last gone from his ears and back in his chest again.

2 After that, he turned the drum on its side, where its great lunar[1] face peered at him whenever he opened his eyes.

3 His face, alert or at rest, was **solemn**. It was indeed a solemn time and a solemn night for a boy just turned fourteen in the peach field near the Owl Creek not far from the church at Shiloh.

[1] **lunar** (lo͞o′nər): of or relating to the moon.

Notice & Note

Use the side margins to notice and note signposts in the text.

ANALYZE SETTING

Annotate: Mark words the author uses to describe the story's setting in paragraphs 1–3.

Compare: How do these details compare or contrast with what you already know about the historical setting of this story?

solemn
(sŏl′əm) *adj.* If an event is *solemn*, it is deeply serious.

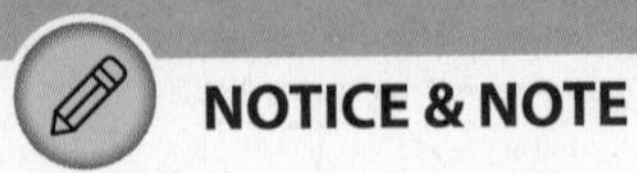

NOTICE & NOTE

askew
(ə-skyo͞o´) *adj.* When something is *askew,* it is off center.

strew
(stro͞o) *v.* If you *strew* something, you spread it here and there, or scatter it.

ANALYZE MOOD
Annotate: Mark language in paragraphs 7–10 that reveals the atmosphere in the camp on the night before the battle.

Analyze: What mood do these details create?

ANALYZE SETTING
Annotate: Mark text in paragraph 12 that describes what the young men and boys did before their first battle.

Infer: What values inspired these men and boys, and how do those values reflect the story's Civil War setting?

4 ". . . thirty-one, thirty-two, thirty-three . . ."

5 Unable to see, he stopped counting.

6 Beyond the thirty-three familiar shadows, forty thousand men, exhausted by nervous expectation, unable to sleep for romantic dreams of battles yet unfought, lay crazily **askew** in their uniforms. A mile yet farther on, another army was **strewn** helter-skelter, turning slow, basting themselves with the thought of what they would do when the time came: a leap, a yell, a blind plunge their strategy, raw youth their protection and benediction.[2]

7 Now and again the boy heard a vast wind come up, that gently stirred the air. But he knew what it was, the army here, the army there, whispering to itself in the dark. Some men talking to others, others murmuring to themselves, and all so quiet it was like a natural element arisen from south or north with the motion of the earth toward dawn.

8 What the men whispered the boy could only guess, and he guessed that it was: Me, I'm the one, I'm the one of all the rest won't die. I'll live through it. I'll go home. The band will play. And I'll be there to hear it.

9 Yes, thought the boy, that's all very well for them, they can give as good as they get!

10 For with the careless bones of the young men harvested by night and bindled[3] around campfires were the similarly strewn steel bones of their rifles, with bayonets fixed like eternal lightning lost in the orchard grass.

11 Me, thought the boy, I got only a drum, two sticks to beat it, and no shield.

12 There wasn't a man-boy on this ground tonight did not have a shield he cast, riveted or carved himself on his way to his first attack, compounded of remote but nonetheless firm and fiery family devotion, flag-blown patriotism and cocksure immortality strengthened by the touchstone of very real gunpowder, ramrod, minnieball and flint.[4] But without these last the boy felt his family move yet farther off away in the dark, as if one of those great prairie-burning trains had chanted them away never to return, leaving him with this drum which was worse than a toy in the game to be played tomorrow or some day much too soon.

13 The boy turned on his side. A moth brushed his face, but it was peach blossom. A peach blossom flicked him, but it was a

---

[2] **benediction** (bĕn´ĭ-dĭk´shən): a blessing.

[3] **bindled:** fastened or wrapped by encircling, as with a belt.

[4] **ramrod, minnieball, and flint:** items used to fire a rifle.

NOTICE & NOTE

moth. Nothing stayed put. Nothing had a name. Nothing was as it once was.

14 If he lay very still, when the dawn came up and the soldiers put on their bravery with their caps, perhaps they might go away, the war with them, and not notice him lying small here, no more than a toy himself.

15 "Well, by God, now," said a voice.

16 The boy shut up his eyes, to hide inside himself, but it was too late. Someone, walking by in the night, stood over him.

17 "Well," said the voice quietly, "here's a soldier crying *before* the fight. Good. Get it over. Won't be time once it all starts."

18 And the voice was about to move on when the boy, startled, touched the drum at his elbow. The man above, hearing this, stopped. The boy could feel his eyes, sense him slowly bending near. A hand must have come down out of the night, for there was a little rat-tat as the fingernails brushed and the man's breath fanned his face.

19 "Why, it's the drummer boy, isn't it?"

20 The boy nodded, not knowing if his nod was seen. "Sir, is that *you?*" he said.

21 "I assume it is." The man's knees cracked as he bent still closer.

22 He smelled as all fathers should smell, of salt sweat, ginger tobacco, horse and boot leather, and the earth he walked upon. He had many eyes. No, not eyes, brass buttons that watched the boy.

23 He could only be, and was, the General.

24 "What's your name, boy?" he asked.

25 "Joby," whispered the boy, starting to sit up.

26 "All right, Joby, don't stir." A hand pressed his chest gently, and the boy relaxed. "How long you been with us, Joby?"

27 "Three weeks, sir."

28 "Run off from home or joined **legitimately,** boy?"

29 Silence.

30 "Damn-fool question," said the General. "Do you shave yet, boy? Even more of a damn-fool. There's your cheek, fell right off the tree overhead. And the others here not much older. Raw, raw, damn raw, the lot of you. You ready for tomorrow or the next day, Joby?"

31 "I think so, sir."

32 "You want to cry some more, go on ahead. I did the same last night."

33 "*You,* sir?"

LANGUAGE CONVENTIONS

Annotate: As you read the dialogue in paragraphs 15–30, mark the sentences that are fragments—meaning they lack either a subject or a verb.

Evaluate: Does the author's use of fragments make the dialogue seem more realistic? Explain.

legitimately
(lə-jĭt´ə-mĭt-lē) *adv.* When you do something *legitimately,* you do it lawfully.

NOTICE & NOTE

34 "God's truth. Thinking of everything ahead. Both sides figuring the other side will just give up, and soon, and the war done in weeks, and us all home. Well, that's not how it's going to be. And maybe that's why I cried."

35 "Yes, sir," said Joby.

36 The General must have taken out a cigar now, for the dark was suddenly filled with the Indian smell of tobacco unlit as yet, but chewed as the man thought what next to say.

37 "It's going to be a crazy time," said the General. "Counting both sides, there's a hundred thousand men, give or take a few thousand out there tonight, not one as can spit a sparrow off a tree, or knows a horse clod from a minnieball. Stand up, bare the breast, ask to be a target, thank them and sit down, that's us, that's them. We should turn tail and train four months, they should do the same. But here we are, taken with spring fever and thinking it blood lust, taking our sulphur

with cannons instead of with molasses[5] as it should be, going to be a hero, going to live forever. And I can see all of them over there nodding agreement, save the other way around. It's wrong, boy, it's wrong as a head put on hind side front and a man marching backward through life. It will be a double massacre if one of their itchy generals decides to picnic his lads on our grass. More innocents will get shot out of pure Cherokee enthusiasm than ever got shot before. Owl Creek was full of boys splashing around in the noonday sun just a few hours ago. I fear it will be full of boys again, just floating, at sundown tomorrow, not caring where the tide takes them."

38 The General stopped and made a little pile of winter leaves and twigs in the darkness, as if he might at any moment strike fire to them to see his way through the coming days when the sun might not show its face because of what was happening here and just beyond.

39 The boy watched the hand stirring the leaves and opened his lips to say something, but did not say it. The General heard the boy's breath and spoke himself.

40 "Why am I telling you this? That's what you wanted to ask, eh? Well, when you got a bunch of wild horses on a loose rein somewhere, somehow you got to bring order, rein them in. These lads, fresh out of the milkshed, don't know what I know, and I can't tell them: men actually die, in war. So each is his own army. I got to make *one* army of them. And for that, boy, I need you."

41 "Me!" The boy's lips barely twitched.

42 "Now, boy," said the General quietly, "you are the heart of the army. Think of that. You're the heart of the army. Listen, now."

43 And, lying there, Joby listened.

44 And the General spoke on.

45 If he, Joby, beat slow tomorrow, the heart would beat slow in the men. They would lag by the wayside.[6] They would drowse in the fields on their muskets. They would sleep forever, after that, in those same fields, their hearts slowed by a drummer boy and stopped by enemy lead.

46 But if he beat a sure, steady, ever faster rhythm, then, then their knees would come up in a long line down over that hill, one knee after the other, like a wave on the ocean shore! Had

[5] **taking our sulphur with cannons instead of with molasses:** Sulphur was an ingredient in gunpowder that was used to fire cannons; at that time sulphur was also used as a tonic or medical treatment. Molasses is a thick, brown syrup, used to mask the unpleasant taste of medicines.

[6] **lag by the wayside:** fall behind.

ANALYZE MOOD

Annotate: In paragraph 38, mark the thing that may be a symbol, standing for something beyond itself.

Synthesize: What might this object symbolize?

WORDS OF THE WISER

Notice & Note: Read paragraphs 42–52. Then mark the main ideas in the advice that the General gives Joby.

Analyze: How does the General's advice help Joby overcome a problem?

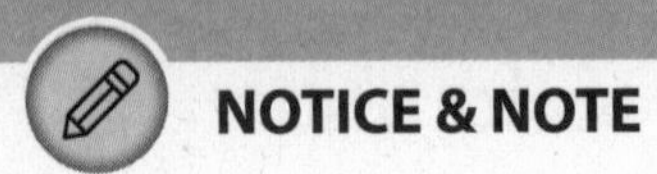

NOTICE & NOTE

resolute
(rĕz´ə-lo͞ot´) *adj.* If you are *resolute,* you are firm or determined.

he seen the ocean ever? Seen the waves rolling in like a well-ordered cavalry charge to the sand? Well, that was it, that's what he wanted, that's what was needed! Joby was his right hand and his left. He gave the orders, but Joby set the pace!

47 So bring the right knee up and the right foot out and the left knee up and the left foot out. One following the other in good time, in brisk time. Move the blood up the body and make the head proud and the spine stiff and the jaw **resolute.** Focus the eye and set the teeth, flare the nostrils and tighten the hands, put steel armor all over the men, for blood moving fast in them does indeed make men feel as if they'd put on steel. He must keep at it, at it! Long and steady, steady and long! Then, even though shot or torn, those wounds got in hot blood—in blood he'd helped stir—would feel less pain. If their blood was cold, it would be more than slaughter, it would be murderous nightmare and pain best not told and no one to guess.

48 The General spoke and stopped, letting his breath slack off. Then, after a moment, he said, "So there you are, that's it. Will you do that, boy? Do you know now you're general of the army when the General's left behind?"

49 The boy nodded mutely.

50 "You'll run them through for me then, boy?"

51 "Yes, sir."

52 "Good. And, God willing, many nights from tonight, many years from now, when you're as old or far much older than me, when they ask you what you did in this awful time, you will tell them—one part humble and one part proud—'I was the drummer boy at the battle of Owl Creek,' or the Tennessee River, or maybe they'll just name it after the church there. 'I was the drummer boy at Shiloh.' Good grief, that has a beat and sound to it fitting for Mr. Longfellow. 'I was the drummer boy at Shiloh.' Who will ever hear those words and not know you, boy, or what you thought this night, or what you'll think tomorrow or the next day when we must get up on our legs and *move!*"

53 The general stood up. "Well, then. God bless you, boy. Good night."

54 "Good night, sir."

55 And, tobacco, brass, boot polish, salt sweat and leather, the man moved away through the grass.

56 Joby lay for a moment, staring but unable to see where the man had gone.

57 He swallowed. He wiped his eyes. He cleared his throat. He settled himself. Then, at last, very slowly and firmly, he turned the drum so that it faced up toward the sky.

ANALYZE MOOD

Annotate: Read paragraphs 56–58. Mark words and phrases that indicate a change in the mood compared to the beginning of the story.

Analyze: How would you describe the mood at the end of the story?

58 He lay next to it, his arm around it, feeling the tremor, the touch, the **muted** thunder as, all the rest of the April night in the year 1862, near the Tennessee River, not far from the Owl Creek, very close to the church named Shiloh, the peach blossoms fell on the drum.

muted
(myo͞o´tĭd) *adj.* When something is *muted,* it is softened or muffled.

CHECK YOUR UNDERSTANDING

Answer these questions before moving on to the **Analyze the Text** section on the following page.

1 The "vast wind" that Joby hears in paragraph 7 indicates that —

A April weather in Tennessee is windy and cold

B Joby is frightened to be alone in the darkness

C the battle is likely to begin at any moment

D the two armies are camped very close together

2 The General says Joby is "the heart of the army" because —

F Joby has more training than the other soldiers

G Joby's drumbeat sets the pace for the battle

H Joby gives the orders for the soldiers to march

J Joby's battle position is in the middle of the action

3 How does Joby feel at the end of the story?

A He misses his father even more than before.

B He feels ready to face the next battle.

C He is overwhelmed by the task before him.

D He is confident that he is the most important soldier.

ANALYZE THE TEXT

Support your responses with evidence from the text. NOTEBOOK

1. **Cite Evidence** What descriptive details does the author provide about the General in paragraph 22? What is the effect of such details in a work of historical fiction?
2. **Infer** The General asks Joby if he has "run off from home or joined legitimately." What is the answer to this question, and what do Joby's actions reveal about his values?
3. **Interpret** What do the peach blossoms symbolize in this story? Explain how this symbol contributes to the overall mood.
4. **Analyze** Henry Wadsworth Longfellow was a popular American author who wrote "Paul Revere's Ride" and other works immortalizing early American history. Locate the allusion to him in paragraph 52. What mood does this allusion help create?
5. **Notice & Note** How does the General's advice to Joby about his role in the next day's battle affect Joby?

RESEARCH TIP
Online encyclopedias can be a great place to start your research. The first paragraph of an article often gives a summary of the topic. If you need more in-depth information, scan the headings in the rest of the article to zero in on the precise facts you need.

RESEARCH

Want to learn more about the historical events that inspired Ray Bradbury to write "The Drummer Boy of Shiloh"? Research the Battle of Shiloh and its historical importance.

QUESTION	ANSWER
What did the Union army hope to achieve by fighting this battle in Tennessee?	
Why did the battle begin sooner than the army expected?	
How were the Union and Confederate armies affected by the battle's outcome?	

Extend Plan a visit to the Shiloh National Military Park. Find out what there is to see and do, and create a schedule of your activities. Then ask some friends to join you, either by writing to them, talking to them, or showing them some images. Choose the method you think will convince them.

CREATE AND DRAMATIZE

Write a Report Use your research about the Battle of Shiloh to write a report about how the General's beliefs and values would have been influenced by the historical setting in which he lived.

- ❑ Review your research notes and conduct additional research as needed about soldiers' experiences fighting battles during the Civil War.
- ❑ Make inferences about how the General's beliefs and values would have been affected by his experiences.
- ❑ Write a report that combines historical facts with your inferences about the General.

Dramatize a Scene Working with a partner, act out the scene in which the General discusses Joby's fears and his role in the coming battle.

- ❑ Discuss the General's motivation for the conversation, and draw conclusions about how that might affect the way he speaks.
- ❑ Make a script with the dialogue each character will speak. Note movements, gestures, and facial expressions that will bring the scene to life.
- ❑ Practice your scene. Then perform it for the class.

Go to the **Writing Studio** for more on conducting research and writing informative texts.

RESPOND TO THE ESSENTIAL QUESTION

What will people risk to be free?

Gather Information Review your annotations and notes on "The Drummer Boy of Shiloh." Then, add relevant details to your Response Log. As you determine which information to include, think about:

- elements of the story that make it historical fiction
- how the setting influences the characters' beliefs and values
- details that contribute to the story's mood

At the end of the unit, you can use your notes to help you write a research report.

ACADEMIC VOCABULARY

As you write and discuss what you learned from the story, be sure to use the Academic Vocabulary words. Check off each of the words that you use.

- ❑ **access**
- ❑ **civil**
- ❑ **demonstrate**
- ❑ **document**
- ❑ **symbolize**

CRITICAL VOCABULARY

WORD BANK
solemn
askew
strew
legitimately
resolute
muted

Practice and Apply Use what you know about the Vocabulary words to answer these questions.

1. When did you have to act in a **resolute** way to face a challenge?
2. When did you **legitimately** claim that someone owed you something?
3. When might you **strew** things across a room? Why might you do that?
4. When would you need to be **solemn** in a group of people?
5. When has your response to news been **muted?**
6. When has your hat been **askew** on your head?

VOCABULARY STRATEGY: Interpret Figures of Speech

Go to **Using Context Clues** in the **Vocabulary Studio** for more on figures of speech.

A **figure of speech** is a word or phrase that communicates meanings beyond the literal definition of the words. **Idioms,** or expressions in which the entire phrase means something different from the words in it, are one kind of figure of speech. Consider this idiom from the story.

> **These lads, fresh out of the milkshed, don't know what I know, and I can't tell them.**

You can use nearby words and phrases, or **context,** to help you understand that "fresh out of the milkshed" implies that not long ago these lads were farm hands milking cows. The phrase "don't know what I know" helps you understand that the General is using a figure of speech to express concern that his soldiers lack battle experience.

Practice and Apply Use context to explain the meaning of each underlined figure of speech below.

1. "Yes, thought the boy, that's all very well for them, they can give as good as they get! . . . Me, thought the boy, I got only a drum, two sticks to beat it, and no shield."
2. "There's a hundred thousand men, . . . not one as can spit a sparrow off a tree, or knows a horse clod from a minnieball. . . . We should turn tail and train four months."
3. "He might at any moment strike fire to them to see his way through the coming days when the sun might not show its face."

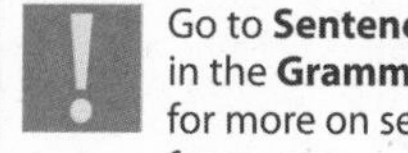

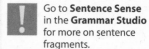

LANGUAGE CONVENTIONS: Sentence Fragments

A **complete sentence** contains a subject and a predicate. The **subject** is a noun, pronoun, or noun phrase—all the words that identify the person, place, thing, or idea that the sentence is about. The **predicate** includes a verb and all the words that tell about the subject.

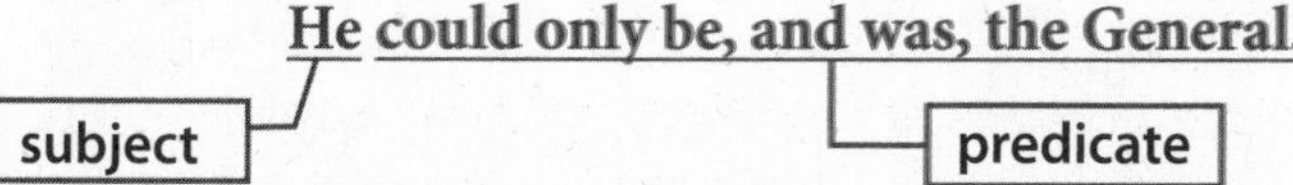
He could only be, and was, the General.
subject
predicate

Writers usually use complete sentences to make their meaning clear. However, they may sometimes include **fragments,** or incomplete sentences that lack either a subject or a predicate. Fragments may be used to create a particular style of writing or to imitate the way people speak. Notice the underlined fragments in the following dialogue:

> **"Damn-fool question," said the General. "Do you shave yet, boy? Even more of a damn-fool. There's your cheek, fell right off the tree overhead. And the others here not much older. Raw, raw, damn raw, the lot of you. . ."**

Go to **Sentence Sense** in the **Grammar Studio** for more on sentence fragments.

Practice and Apply For each fragment, identify whether the subject or predicate is missing. Then rewrite the fragment as a complete sentence.

FRAGMENT	MISSING PART	COMPLETE SENTENCE
1. Gathered around the campfire.		
2. Joby, a drummer boy.		
3. Thousands of soldiers, dreaming of glory in battle.		
4. Inspired Joby by telling him about his important role in the battle.		

O CAPTAIN! MY CAPTAIN!

Poem by **Walt Whitman**

ESSENTIAL QUESTION:

What will people risk to be free?

QUICK START

The poem you are about to read mourns the passing of a great leader. Make notes about people who inspire you—either real or fictional—and their admirable qualities. After you read the poem, you'll write your own poem about someone you admire.

Person or Character	**Admirable Qualities**

ANALYZE FIGURATIVE LANGUAGE

One way poets can help readers understand things in new ways is by using **figurative language,** or imaginative descriptions that are not literally true. A **metaphor** is a type of figurative language in which an author compares two things that are basically dissimilar but have some quality or qualities in common. Unlike a simile, a metaphor does not use the word *like* or *as.* In an **extended metaphor,** this comparison between two things is developed at some length and in different ways.

An extended metaphor may continue, or extend, through several lines or stanzas or throughout the entire poem. In "O Captain! My Captain!" Whitman uses an extended metaphor to express his feelings about President Lincoln and the Civil War.

Read the poem to determine what is being compared. Also consider the poet's purpose in using the extended metaphor. Use a chart like this to record your ideas.

GENRE ELEMENTS: LYRIC POETRY

- is usually short and conveys strong emotions
- uses first-person point of view to express the speaker's thoughts and feelings
- often uses repetition and rhyme to create a melodic quality
- includes many forms, such as sonnets, odes, and elegies

QUESTIONS	ANSWERS AND TEXT EVIDENCE
What two things are compared in the extended metaphor?	
What effect does the extended metaphor have?	

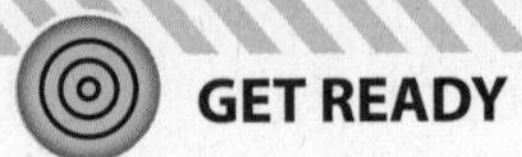

GET READY

ANALYZE GENRE: POETRY

Certain forms of poetry are associated with particular topics. For example, sonnets are often associated with love, and limericks are often associated with humor. "O Captain! My Captain!" is an elegy. An **elegy** is a poem in which the speaker reflects on death. In contrast to other forms of poetry, elegies often pay tribute to people who have recently died.

Most elegies use formal, dignified language that contributes to a serious **tone,** which is the writer's attitude toward the subject. Elegies may also express

- sorrow and grief
- praise for the person who has died
- comforting thoughts or ideas

Punctuation, such as exclamation points, can help communicate emotion and tone. In these lines from "O Captain! My Captain!" Whitman expresses his shock and sorrow.

But O heart! heart! heart!
O the bleeding drops of red,
Where on the deck my Captain lies,
Fallen cold and dead.

As you read "O Captain! My Captain!," identify words, phrases, and punctuation that pay tribute to Lincoln's greatness and express emotions related to his death.

ANNOTATION MODEL

NOTICE & NOTE 

As you read, note details that develop an extended metaphor involving Abraham Lincoln, as well as language that expresses the speaker's tone. You can also record your own thoughts on the poem. This model shows one reader's notes about the beginning of "O Captain! My Captain!"

O Captain! my Captain! our fearful trip is done,
The ship has weather'd every rack, the prize we sought is won,
The port is near, the bells I hear, the people all exulting,
While follow eyes the steady keel, the vessel grim and daring:

Is the poem really about a ship? What could be compared to a "fearful trip"?

"bells" and "exulting" sound like a celebration

BACKGROUND

On April 14, 1865, only five days after the Civil War ended, President Abraham Lincoln was assassinated at the Ford Theater in Washington, D.C., where he was watching a performance. Lincoln was shot by John Wilkes Booth, a famous actor and a Confederate sympathizer. Although Booth initially escaped, he was discovered days later by Union soldiers. Booth was killed while trying to avoid capture.

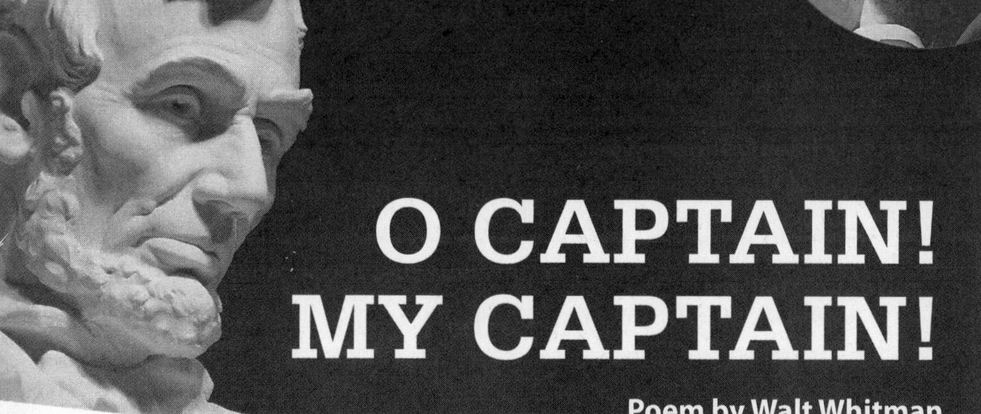

O CAPTAIN! MY CAPTAIN!

Poem by Walt Whitman

Walt Whitman *(1819–1892) was a great admirer of President Lincoln. After the president was assassinated, Whitman wrote "O Captain! My Captain!" to capture the sense of tragedy that descended upon the country. Largely unknown to the public when he wrote this poem, Whitman eventually gained a reputation as one of the greatest American writers. "O Captain! My Captain!" is among his most famous works, and his book of poems,* Leaves of Grass, *is considered one of the masterpieces of American literature.*

SETTING A PURPOSE

As you read, look for evidence of Whitman's feelings about Abraham Lincoln. Do others seem to share his feelings? Write down any questions you have as you read.

Notice & Note

Use the side margins to notice and note signposts in the text.

NOTICE & NOTE

ANALYZE GENRE: POETRY

Annotate: In lines 1–16, underline words and phrases that evoke either sorrow or joy. Circle punctuation that conveys strong emotion.

Analyze: What is the overall effect on the reader of the language in this elegy?

ANALYZE FIGURATIVE LANGUAGE

Annotate: After reading the poem once, go back and mark details in lines 17–24 that are part of the extended metaphor of a ship's voyage and return.

Draw Conclusions: In the extended metaphor, who is the "Captain," and what is the "fearful trip"?

O Captain! My Captain!

O Captain! my Captain! our fearful trip is done,
The ship has weather'd every rack,[1] the prize we sought[2] is won,
The port is near, the bells I hear, the people all exulting,
While follow eyes the steady keel,[3] the vessel grim and daring:
But O heart! heart! heart!
O the bleeding drops of red,
Where on the deck my Captain lies,
Fallen cold and dead.

O Captain! my Captain! rise up and hear the bells;
Rise up—for you the flag is flung[4]—for you the bugle trills,
For you bouquets and ribbon'd wreaths—for you the shores a-crowding,
For you they call, the swaying mass, their eager faces turning;
Here Captain! dear father!
This arm beneath your head!
It is some dream that on the deck,
You've fallen cold and dead.

My Captain does not answer, his lips are pale and still,
My father does not feel my arm, he has no pulse nor will,
The ship is anchor'd safe and sound, its voyage closed and done,
From fearful trip the victor ship comes in with object won;
Exult O shores, and ring O bells!
But I with mournful tread,[5]
Walk the deck my Captain lies,
Fallen cold and dead.

[1] **rack:** a mass of wind-driven clouds.
[2] **sought** (sôt): searched for; tried to gain.
[3] **keel:** the main part of a ship's structure.
[4] **flung:** suddenly put out.
[5] **tread** (trĕd): footsteps.

The funeral procession of President Abraham Lincoln

NOTICE & NOTE

CHECK YOUR UNDERSTANDING

Answer these questions before moving on to the **Analyze the Text** section on the following page.

1 Why are the people "all exulting" in line 3?

A The ship has returned with "the prize . . . won."

B The ringing of the bells signals a celebration.

C They don't see that the ship is "grim and daring."

D They are relieved that the Captain is dead.

2 In the poem's extended metaphor, the "fearful trip" is —

F the speaker's grief

G the Captain's death

H the Civil War

J the election of Abraham Lincoln

3 In lines 13 and 18, the speaker calls the Captain his "father" most likely to —

A suggest that the poem is really about Whitman's father

B reveal that the speaker is the Captain's son

C create doubt about the poem's subject

D show the speaker's respect and love for the Captain

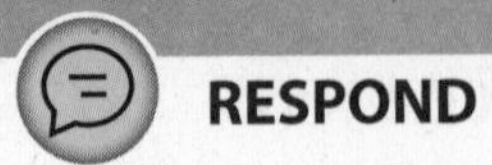

RESPOND

ANALYZE THE TEXT

Support your responses with evidence from the text. NOTEBOOK

1. **Interpret** Reread lines 1–3. In Whitman's metaphor, what are the "fearful trip," the "ship," and the "prize" that was won? What is the "port"? Express your response in a chart like the one shown.

ELEMENT	WHAT IT REPRESENTS
fearful trip	
ship	
prize	
port	

2. **Summarize** Describe the grand celebration that Whitman tells about in lines 3–12. Why are the crowds rejoicing?

3. **Evaluate** When there is a contrast between appearance and reality, **irony** results. Why is it ironic that the crowds in this poem are celebrating?

4. **Cite Evidence** How does Whitman express his own grief about Lincoln's death? Cite three specific examples from the poem.

5. **Analyze** Reread lines 19–20. What is the meaning of these lines in terms of Whitman's extended metaphor?

RESEARCH

Walt Whitman's "O Captain! My Captain!" was first published the year Abraham Lincoln was assassinated. Use a variety of sources to research significant events of this period and use them to construct a timeline.

EVENT	DATE
End of the Civil War	
Assassination of Abraham Lincoln	
Lincoln's funeral and burial	
Publication of "O Captain! My Captain!"	

RESEARCH TIP
Timelines are a popular visual aid in reference books as well as on educational websites. In addition to the events listed in the chart, try to find information about other significant events that happened during the same time period. You might be surprised how this will expand your understanding of history.

Connect Get together with a partner and compare your timelines. Then review the poem and discuss whether knowing more about the historical context affects the poem's impact on you.

CREATE AND RECITE

Write a Poem Write a poem in which you pay tribute to someone you respect or admire, either real or imaginary. Review your notes from the Quick Start activity before you begin.

- ❑ Decide if you want your poem to be an elegy, a limerick, a sonnet, or some other form.
- ❑ Consider creating an extended metaphor that connects to your subject in multiple ways.
- ❑ Draft your poem and then read it aloud to find places where you can sharpen the language or improve the rhythm.

Choral Reading Work with a small group to present a choral reading of "O Captain! My Captain!"

- ❑ Reread the poem carefully. As a group, decide how each line should be read. Do the words express sorrow? praise? comfort?
- ❑ Decide who will read each line or part of a line. Should some words be read by one speaker? two speakers? the entire group?
- ❑ The choices you make should reflect your analysis of the poem. Be prepared to explain your choices.

RESPOND TO THE ESSENTIAL QUESTION

What will people risk to be free?

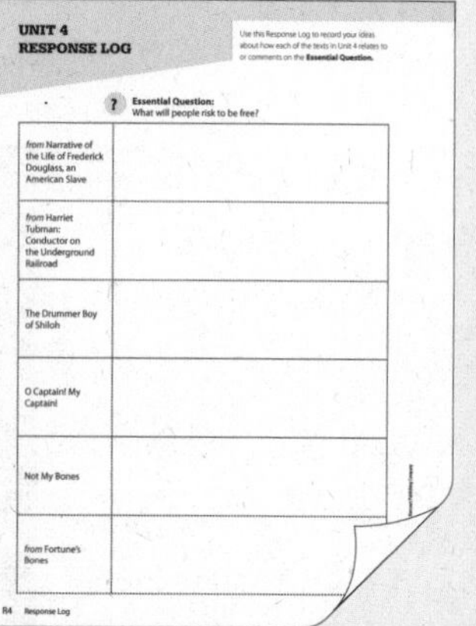

UNIT 4 RESPONSE LOG

Use this Response Log to record your ideas about how each of the texts in Unit 4 relates to or comments on the **Essential Question.**

? **Essential Question:** What will people risk to be free?

from Narrative of the Life of Frederick Douglass, an American Slave	
from Harriet Tubman: Conductor on the Underground Railroad	
The Drummer Boy of Shiloh	
O Captain! My Captain!	
Not My Bones	
from Fortune's Bones	

R4 Response Log

Gather Information Review your annotations and notes on "O Captain! My Captain!" Then, add relevant details to your Response Log. As you determine which information to include, think about:

- what Abraham Lincoln and others risked during the Civil War
- the role of heroes and leaders in the fight for freedom
- what this poem says about sacrifice

At the end of the unit, you can use your notes to help you write a research report.

ACADEMIC VOCABULARY

As you write and discuss what you learned from the poem, be sure to use the Academic Vocabulary words. Check off each of the words that you use.

- ❑ **access**
- ❑ **civil**
- ❑ **demonstrate**
- ❑ **document**
- ❑ **symbolize**

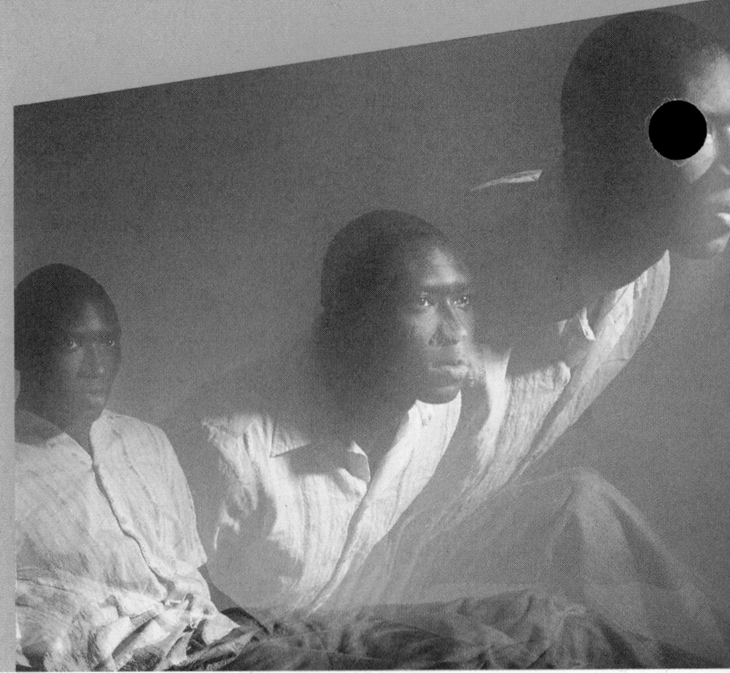

POEM

NOT MY BONES

by **Marilyn Nelson**

pages 299–301

COMPARE TREATMENTS

The poem and nonfiction text you are about to read share the same topic. As you read, notice how each writer uses the elements of her chosen genre to explore the topic, and how each treatment helps you understand different aspects of the topic. After reading, you will collaborate with a small group on a final project.

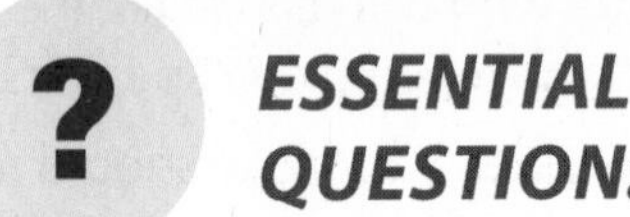

ESSENTIAL QUESTION:

What will people risk to be free?

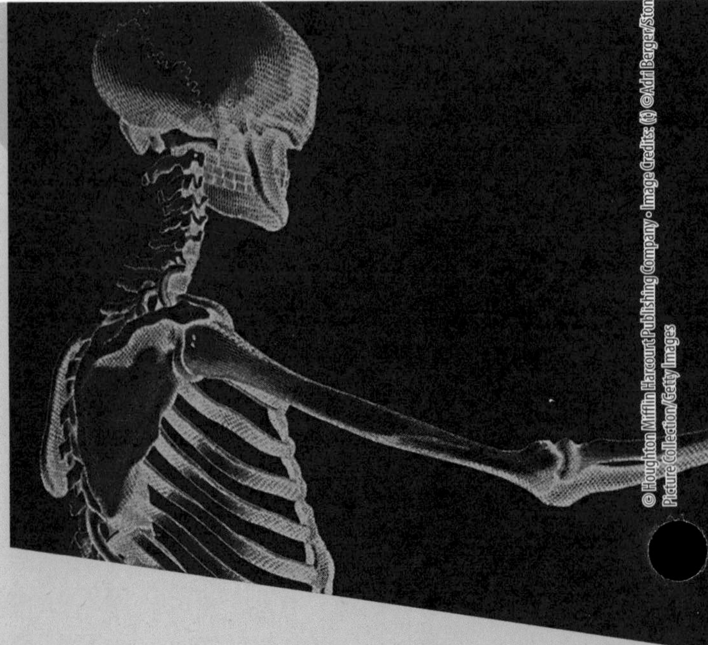

HISTORY WRITING

from FORTUNE'S BONES

by **Pamela Espeland**

pages 302–305

QUICK START

What makes you *you*? Is it your physical body or something inside you that determines the person you are? Write down your thoughts. Then share them with a partner or a small group.

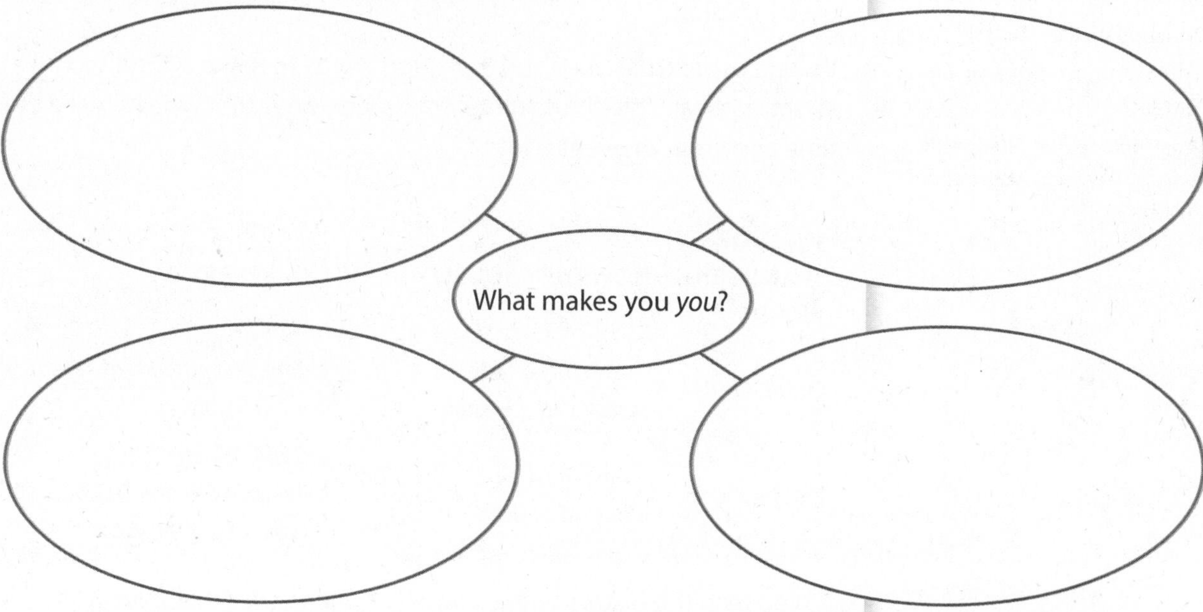

PARAPHRASE POETRY

As you read, make sure you **monitor your comprehension,** or notice how well you understand the meaning of the poem or text. One way to do so is to see if you can **paraphrase** a passage, or restate it in your own words. A paraphrase should be about as long as the original text. It should use simpler language and explain any figurative language in more literal terms.

If you find you don't understand a passage well enough to paraphrase it, go back and reread it. Annotate the parts that are confusing to you, and ask questions as needed. You can seek answers by asking others, using reference sources, or drawing on your own background knowledge until you have a better understanding. Then try to paraphrase the passage again. It should be easier this time.

Monitor your comprehension of "Not My Bones" by paraphrasing the sections that are hard to understand. The chart shows an example of how two lines from the first stanza can be paraphrased.

ORIGINAL	PARAPHRASE
Elementary molecules converged for a breath, / then danced on beyond my individual death.	While I was alive, my body was composed of tiny particles, but when I died, these elements were released from my body.

GENRE ELEMENTS: POETRY

- uses imagery and figurative language to convey meaning and mood
- uses sound devices such as rhythm and repetition to unify the poem and create emphasis
- expresses a theme, or a message about life or human nature
- includes a speaker who "talks" to the reader, like a narrator in fiction; the speaker is not necessarily the poet

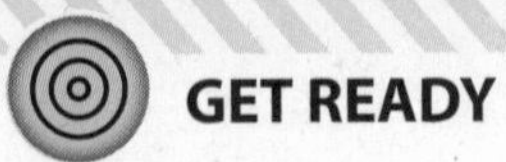

GENRE ELEMENTS: HISTORY WRITING

- uses chronological structure
- relates facts about important events from history or from an individual's life
- is most often written to inform or teach
- may include domain-specific vocabulary (e.g., words about slavery)

ANALYZE CHRONOLOGICAL STRUCTURE

Chronological structure is the arrangement of events by their order of occurrence, or the order in which they happen. This organizational pattern is used in biography, autobiography, and other history writing, such as the notes you will read from *Fortune's Bones*. It is also often used in fiction.

Writers use textual clues and transition words to make a chronological structure clear. This chart summarizes some ways that writers make the time and order of events clear:

TYPES OF TRANSITION WORDS	HOW THEY'RE USED	EXAMPLES
Order words	to show the order or sequence of events	*before, first, afterward, then, during, finally*
Time words	to specify a date, a time, or a period of time	*in 1784, the late 1700s, between 1798 and 1933, for 25 years, over the years*

As you read the history writing from *Fortune's Bones* that follows the poem "Not My Bones," note the words and phrases the author uses to signal the order of events and when events take place. Consider how the chronological structure helps the author achieve her purpose.

ANNOTATION MODEL

NOTICE & NOTE

As you read, you can paraphrase difficult passages in the side margin. The model shows one reader's notes about the first stanza of "Not My Bones."

I was not this body,
I was not these bones.
This skeleton was just my
temporary home.
Elementary molecules converged for a breath,
then danced on beyond my individual death.
And I am not my body,
I am not my body.

Paraphrase: This body and these bones weren't all I was. My physical body was just a shelter for my being.

great image—like molecules gathered for a meeting

"danced" is a happy word

BACKGROUND

The poem "Not My Bones" comes from the book Fortune's Bones: The Manumission Requiem. *The author,* **Marilyn Nelson,** *is a former poet laureate of Connecticut and the winner of many awards, including the Newbery Honor and the Coretta Scott King Honor. She wrote* Fortune's Bones *to honor the memory of Fortune, an enslaved person who died in 1798. Nelson was commissioned to write the book by the Mattatuck Museum of Connecticut, where Fortune's skeleton had been displayed after descendants of the man who owned Fortune donated it to the museum.*

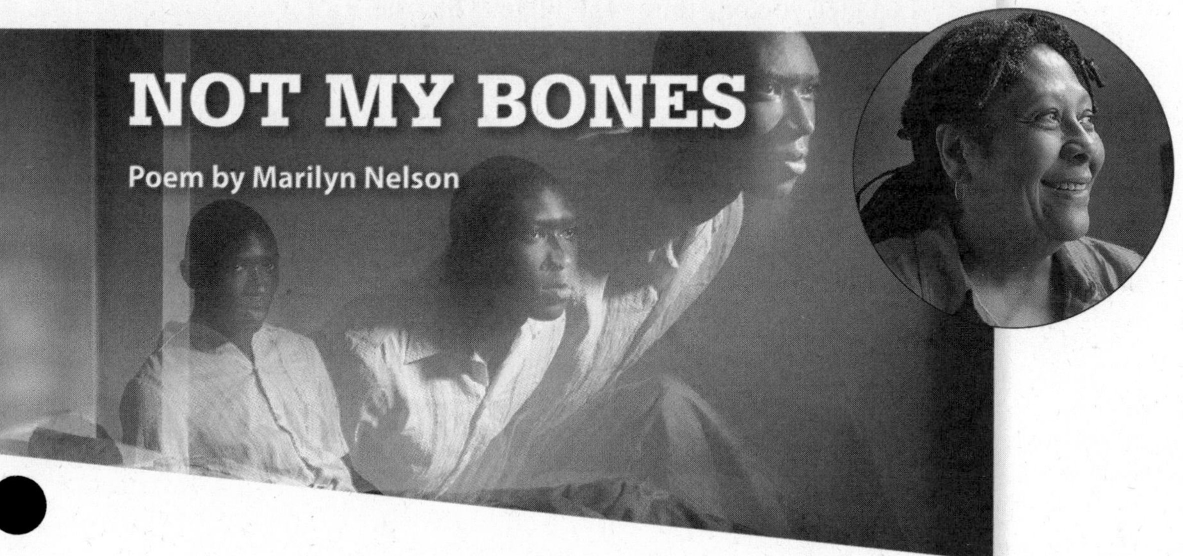

NOT MY BONES

Poem by Marilyn Nelson

PREPARE TO COMPARE

As you read the poem, look for how the poet uses language to create images, communicate ideas, and convey mood.

I was not this body,
I was not these bones.
This skeleton was just my
temporary home.
Elementary molecules[1] converged[2] for a breath,
then danced on beyond my individual death.
And I am not my body,
I am not my body.

We are brief incarnations,[3]
we are clouds in clothes.
We are water respirators,
we are how earth knows.

[1] **elementary molecules:** the smallest, most basic particles of substances.
[2] **converged:** came together in one place; met.
[3] **incarnations:** bodily forms.

Notice & Note

Use the side margins to notice and note signposts in the text.

PARAPHRASE POETRY

Annotate: Circle the word *incarnations* in the poem. Underline its definition in the footnotes.

Interpret: Restate lines 9–12 in your own words. Do not quote directly from the text in your paraphrase.

I bore[4] light passed on from an original flame;
while it was in my hands it was called by my name.
But I am not my body,
I am not my body.

You can own a man's body,
but you can't own his mind.
That's like making a bridle
to ride on the wind.
I will tell you one thing, and I'll tell you true:
Life's the best thing that can happen to you.
But you are not your body,
you are not your body.

You can own someone's body,
but the soul runs free.
It roams the night sky's
mute geometry.
You can murder hope, you can pound faith flat,
but like weeds and wildflowers, they grow right back.
For you are not your body,
you are not your body.

You are not your body,
you are not your bones.
What's essential[5] about you

PARAPHRASE POETRY

Annotate: Reread lines 29–30. Mark examples of figurative language.

Interpret: Restate those lines in your own words.

[4] **bore:** carried; transported.

[5] **essential:** having the qualities that give something its true identity.

is what can't be owned.
What's essential in you is your longing to raise
your itty-bitty voice in the cosmic[6] praise.
For you are not your body,
you are not your body.

Well, I woke up this morning just so glad to be free,
glad to be free, glad to be free.
I woke up this morning in restful peace.
For I am not my body,
I am not my bones.
I am not my body,
glory hallelujah, not my bones,
I am not my bones.

[6] **cosmic:** universal; infinitely large.

PARAPHRASE POETRY
Annotate: In the last stanza, mark the lines that describe how the speaker felt upon waking.

Interpret: Paraphrase those lines. What idea might they be conveying?

CHECK YOUR UNDERSTANDING

Answer these questions about "Not My Bones" before moving on to the next selection.

1 The speaker in the poem is most likely —

A the author of the poem, Marilyn Nelson

B one of Dr. Porter's descendants

C Fortune or another formerly enslaved person

D one of Fortune's ancestors or descendants

2 Which of the following is an example of personification?

F *You can murder hope*

G *you can pound faith flat*

H *We are water respirators*

J *You can own someone's body*

3 The primary message in "Not My Bones" is that —

A a person's most important qualities can't be owned

B a person's remains should be treated with respect

C Dr. Porter's descendants were wrong to use Fortune's skeleton

D people should not own or control other people

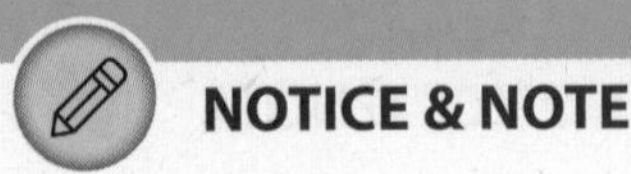

NOTICE & NOTE

BACKGROUND

Along with "Not My Bones" and five other poems by Marilyn Nelson, Fortune's Bones *includes history writing and primary source documents and illustrations that tell Fortune's story. Some of the historical notes written by Pamela Espeland are included here. Read these notes to learn facts and additional information about Fortune's life and about what happened to his bones after he died.*

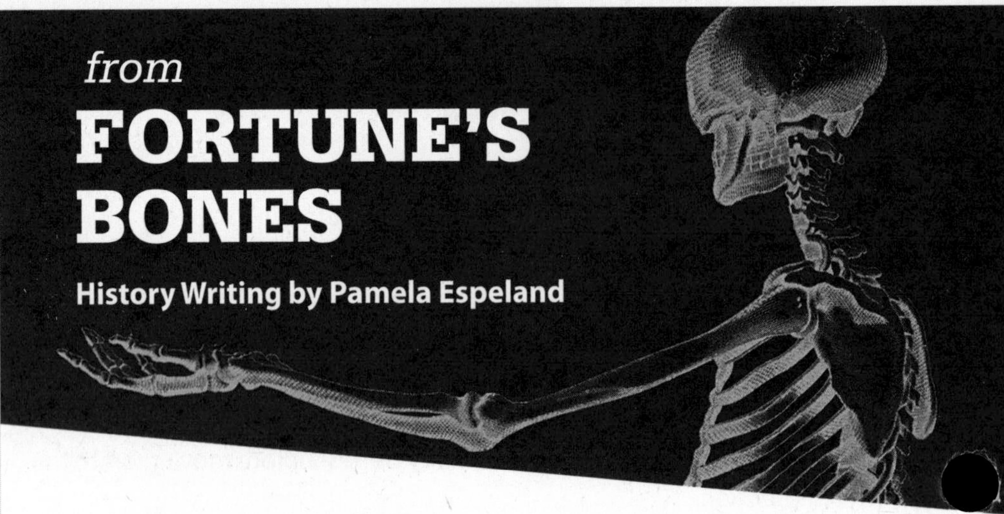

from

FORTUNE'S BONES

History Writing by Pamela Espeland

PREPARE TO COMPARE

As you read this history writing, think about how the writer uses a chronological structure to relate key moments during and after Fortune's life. Think about how this selection compares to the poem "Not My Bones" and how it adds to your understanding of the topic.

ANALYZE CHRONOLOGICAL STRUCTURE

Annotate: Mark the word that signals sequence in the first paragraph.

Predict: What does this first sentence tell you about how the text will be organized?

1 Before Fortune was bones in a Connecticut museum, he was a husband, a father, a baptized Christian, and a slave.

2 His wife's name was Dinah. His sons were Africa and Jacob. His daughters were Mira and Roxa. He was baptized in an Episcopal church, which did not make him free. His master was Dr. Preserved Porter, a physician who specialized in setting broken bones.

3 They lived in Waterbury, Connecticut, in the late 1700s. Dr. Porter had a 75-acre farm, which Fortune probably ran. He planted and harvested corn, rye, potatoes, onions, apples, buckwheat, oats, and hay. He cared for the cattle and hogs.

4 Unlike many slaves, who owned little or nothing and were often separated from their families, Fortune owned a small house near Dr. Porter's home. He and Dinah and their children lived together.

5 When Dr. Porter died in 1803, he left an estate that was worth about $7,000—a lot of money for the time. The estate included Fortune's widow, Dinah, and their son Jacob. Fortune had died in 1798.

6 According to Connecticut's Act of Gradual Emancipation, children born to enslaved parents after March 1, 1784, were to be freed when they reached age 21. Jacob was 18. By law, he could be enslaved for another three years.

7 In Dr. Porter's will, he left Dinah to his wife, Lydia. He gave Jacob to his daughter Hannah.

8 No one knows what happened to Africa, Mira, and Roxa.

9 Most slaves who died in Waterbury in the 1700s were buried in one of the town's cemeteries. When Fortune died, he wasn't buried. Instead, Dr. Porter preserved Fortune's skeleton to further the study of human anatomy.[1]

10 Dr. Porter had been a bonesetter for many years, but he'd never had a skeleton to study. He had two sons who were also doctors. They could learn from the skeleton, too.

11 Fortune was about 60 at the time of his death and, in spite of his injuries, in relatively good health. His skeleton was sturdy and complete.

12 Four more generations of Porters became physicians, and the skeleton stayed in the family. Porter children, grandchildren, and great-grandchildren used it to learn the names of the bones. This was their earliest medical training.

13 Sally Porter Law McGlannan, the last Porter doctor, remembered playing with the skeleton as a young girl. . . . Another family member, Leander Law, once brought part of Fortune's skeleton to a college physiology class.

14 At some point—no one knows exactly when—"Larry" was written on the skull. Fortune's name was forgotten for nearly a century.

15 Over the years, the skeleton was lost and found. It was boarded up[2] in an attic, then discovered by a crew of workers hired to renovate an old building.

16 In 1933, Sally Porter Law McGlannan gave the bones to the Mattatuck Museum. The museum sent the bones to Europe

ANALYZE CHRONOLOGICAL STRUCTURE

Annotate: Mark the time words in paragraphs 5–8.

Draw Conclusions: In what year was Fortune's son Jacob probably emancipated?

CONTRASTS AND CONTRADICTIONS

Notice & Note: Review paragraphs 12–14. Underline how the Porter family made use of Fortune's skeleton. Circle the name someone gave it.

Interpret: What is ironic and perhaps shocking about this contradiction?

[1] **anatomy:** the structure and parts of the body.

[2] **boarded up:** packed away.

A sculptor used information about Fortune's bones to create this reconstruction of Fortune's face.

ANALYZE CHRONOLOGICAL STRUCTURE

Annotate: In paragraphs 12–16, mark time and order words that help you follow what happened to Fortune's skeleton.

Summarize: What had become of Fortune's skeleton before Sally Porter Law McGlannan gave it to the Mattatuck Museum?

to be assembled for display. The skeleton hung in a glass case in the museum for decades, fascinating adults and frightening children.

17 Many stories were invented about the skeleton. Some said that "Larry" was a Revolutionary War hero—maybe even George Washington. Some said he fell to his death. Some said he drowned. Some said he was killed trying to escape. Some thought he had been hanged.

18 One Waterbury resident remembers, "Larry was the thing to see when you go to the museum. I don't think anybody ever envisioned[3] that this was truly a human being."

19 In 1970, the skeleton, still called "Larry," was taken out of its case and put into storage. Times had changed. The museum now believed that displaying the skeleton was disrespectful. It wasn't just a bunch of bones. It was the remains of someone's son, maybe someone's father.

[3] **envisioned:** imagined.

 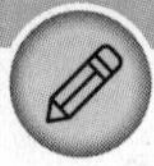

20 The skeleton rested for more than 25 years. Then, in the 1990s, historians searched local records and found a slave named Fortune. Archaeologists and anthropologists studied the bones, which started giving up their secrets. The bones told how Fortune labored, suffered, and died: A quick, sudden injury, like whiplash, may have snapped a vertebra[4] in his neck. He did not drown or fall from a cliff. He was not hanged.

21 But he was free.

[4] **vertebra:** a piece of bone that makes up the spinal column.

BIG QUESTIONS

Notice & Note: In paragraph 20, mark a fact that raises the question of whether or not Fortune's death was accidental.

Analyze: What does the author expect you to know or to wonder about whiplash? Where could you look to get more information?

CHECK YOUR UNDERSTANDING

Answer these questions before moving on to the **Analyze the Text** section on the following page.

1 Which of the following is not one of the reasons we know about Fortune today?

A Historians searched local records and found information about him.

B Archaeologists and anthropologists studied his bones.

C Marilyn Nelson was commissioned to write poems about him.

D Sally Porter Law McGlannan asked the museum to research his bones.

2 For what period of time were Fortune's bones displayed in the Mattatuck Museum?

F From 1798 to 1970

G From 1803 to 1970

H From 1933 to 1970

J From 1933 to the 1990s

3 The last line, "But he was free," emphasizes that —

A Fortune and his family were freed after Dr. Porter died

B Fortune managed to escape from slavery before he died

C Fortune's family reclaimed his bones from the museum

D Fortune could no longer be owned after his death

ANALYZE THE TEXTS

Support your responses with evidence from the texts. NOTEBOOK

1. **Identify Patterns** Review "Not My Bones." Which lines in the poem are most often repeated? How might that repetition help underscore the message of the poem?
2. **Connect** Paraphrase lines 25–28 of "Not My Bones." How is this idea related to the imagery in lines 37–38?
3. **Analyze** Reread paragraph 18 of the notes from *Fortune's Bones*. What do the Waterbury resident's observations reveal about people's feelings and behavior toward Fortune? Cite evidence in your response.
4. **Evaluate** How does the chronological structure of the history writing from *Fortune's Bones* help the author achieve her purpose?
5. **Notice & Note** State in your own words why the museum put Fortune's skeleton in storage. How does this attitude contrast with the attitude of the museum and its visitors in 1933?

RESEARCH

The man called Fortune was held in slavery on a farm in Connecticut until his death in 1798. After reading these selections, what do you know want to know about slavery in the northern states? With your group, note research questions in the chart below. One question has been provided for you. Research to find the answers.

QUESTION	ANSWER
In what year did Connecticut abolish slavery?	

RESEARCH TIP
Remember that when you do research, you need to keep track of where you find information. For print sources, make a note of the title, author, publisher, publication date, and page number. For online sources, make a note of the website, URL, article title, author, and access date. Keep in mind that it's often wise to verify each fact you find in a second source. For example, if you used an online encyclopedia to find out which northern states were free states in 1861, then you might confirm that information by looking in a second online source, or in a print encyclopedia or history book.

Extend With your group, share your research findings with the class. Then discuss what surprised you or what you found most interesting or noteworthy. Identify one or two questions that you still have that you would like to explore.

CREATE AND RECITE

Express Ideas Visually Create a visual work of some kind—such as a painting, drawing, or video—that is inspired by details you learned about Fortune's life.

- ❑ As a group, decide what kind of visual work you will create.
- ❑ Reread the poem and the history notes. Draw on imagery in the poem and details in the history writing to form mental images about Fortune's story.
- ❑ Create your part of the group's work.
- ❑ As a group, present your work. Explain the aspects of Fortune's life or story that it focuses on or was inspired by.

Recite a Poem With your group, recite part of "Not My Bones" aloud for the class.

- ❑ Work with your group to select one stanza of the poem.
- ❑ Discuss how you will recite it. Will you recite it together chorally? Will you sing it like a song? Will different members of your group speak different lines? Will you accompany the words with movements or gestures?
- ❑ Memorize your lines and rehearse them a few times with your group.
- ❑ Present the poem to the class, using appropriate volume, phrasing, and expression.

RESPOND TO THE ESSENTIAL QUESTION

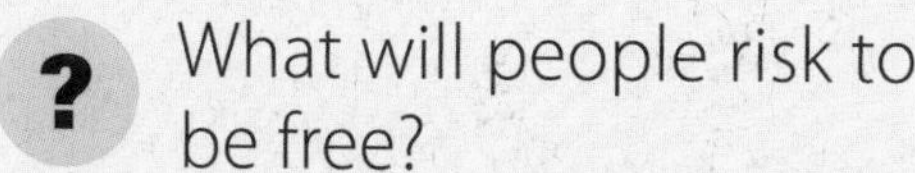

? What will people risk to be free?

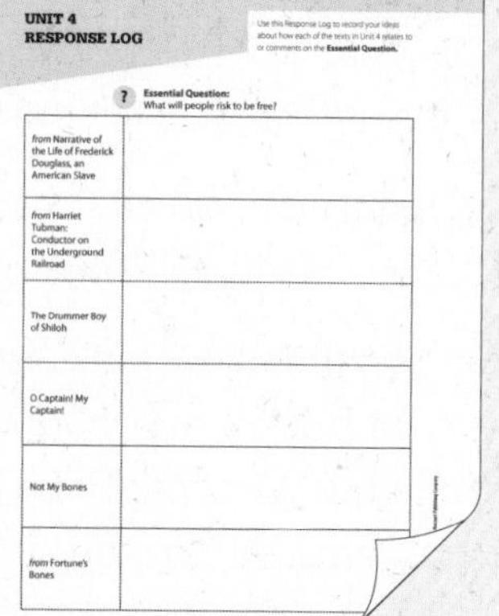

UNIT 4 RESPONSE LOG

Use this Response Log to record your ideas about how each of the texts in Unit 4 relates to or comments on the **Essential Question.**

? **Essential Question:** What will people risk to be free?

from Narrative of the Life of Frederick Douglass, an American Slave	
from Harriet Tubman: Conductor on the Underground Railroad	
The Drummer Boy of Shiloh	
O Captain! My Captain!	
Not My Bones	
from Fortune's Bones	

R4 Response Log

Gather Information Review your annotations and notes on "Not My Bones" and *Fortune's Bones*. Then, add relevant details to your Response Log. As you determine which information to include, think about:

- information you learned about Fortune and what became of his bones
- what it means to be free
- how each writer treats the topic of freedom

At the end of the unit, you can use your notes to help you write a research report.

ACADEMIC VOCABULARY

As you write and discuss what you learned from the two selections, be sure to use the Academic Vocabulary words. Check off each of the words that you use.

- ❑ **access**
- ❑ **civil**
- ❑ **demonstrate**
- ❑ **document**
- ❑ **symbolize**

from FORTUNE'S BONES
History Writing by
Pamela Espeland

Collaborate & Compare

COMPARE TREATMENTS

Marilyn Nelson and Pamela Espeland both wrote on the same topic—Fortune's bones—but they handled the topic differently. The way a topic is handled is called its **treatment.** In order to identify a writer's treatment, ask yourself the following questions:

- ❑ What form does the writing take? For example, is it a poem, a biography, a blog post, or a newspaper article?
- ❑ For what primary purpose was the selection written? Was it mostly written to entertain, to express ideas and feelings, to inform, or to persuade?
- ❑ What is the writer's **tone,** or attitude toward the subject?

In a small group, identify similarities and differences in the treatment of each selection. Record your thoughts in the chart.

	"Not My Bones"	from *Fortune's Bones*
Form of writing		
Primary purpose		
Tone		
Description of the writing		

ANALYZE THE TEXTS

Discuss these questions in your group.

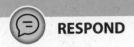

1. **Connect** Which text uses more figurative language and imagery? Cite examples. What purpose does it serve?
2. **Synthesize** Think about the understanding of Fortune that you get from "Not My Bones" and from the *Fortune's Bones* historical notes. What might be the strengths of a book that combines poems with historical notes?
3. **Evaluate** Think about how the poem and the historical notes were written. Which type of writing allows more freedom in its treatment? Why do you think that is?
4. **Critique** The full title of Marilyn Nelson's book is *Fortune's Bones: The Manumission Requiem.* (*Manumission* means being freed from slavery, and a *requiem* is music written to honor the dead.) Do you think that is a good title for the book? Why? Draw on information from both selections to support your answer.

DECIDE AND DISCUSS

Now, you can continue exploring the ideas in these texts by discussing with classmates which treatment of Fortune's life and death is more effective. Follow these steps:

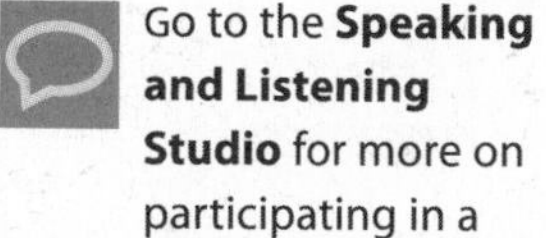

Go to the **Speaking and Listening Studio** for more on participating in a collaborative discussion and on giving a presentation.

1. **Choose a Position** Decide for yourself which treatment of Fortune's bones is the most effective or powerful. Ask:
   - ❏ Which treats the topic more comprehensively, or fully?
   - ❏ Which gives readers a better sense of the man and the issue of slavery in the United States?
   - ❏ Which evokes stronger feelings?
   - ❏ Which conveys a more universal message?
2. **Gather Information** Form a group with others who share the same opinion. Working together, support that opinion with examples from the text.

What I Learned or Understood Better	Support from the Text

3. **Select Information** As a group, select three of the strongest examples to present to the class.
4. **Share Your Views** With your group, present your views to the class. Cite text evidence from both the poem and the historical notes to support your ideas. Listen to what others have to say, ask questions to request and clarify information, and build on the ideas of others as you discuss this topic.

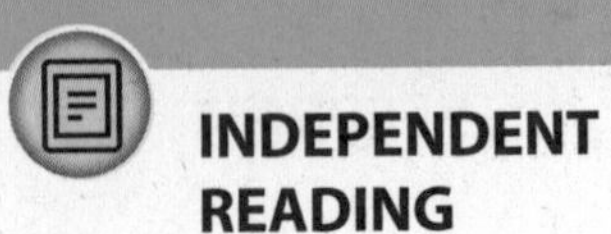
INDEPENDENT READING

? ESSENTIAL QUESTION:

What will people risk to be free?

Reader's Choice

Setting a Purpose Select one or more of these options from your eBook to continue your exploration of the Essential Question.

- Read the descriptions to see which text grabs your interest.
- Think about which genres you enjoy reading.

Notice & Note

In this unit, you practiced asking **Big Questions** and noticing and noting two signposts: **Word Gaps** and **Contrasts and Contradictions.** As you read independently, these signposts and others will aid your understanding. Below are the anchor questions to ask when you read literature and nonfiction.

Reading Literature: Stories, Poems, and Plays		
Signpost	**Anchor Question**	**Lesson**
Contrasts and Contradictions	Why did the character act that way?	p. 3
Aha Moment	How might this change things?	p. 3
Tough Questions	What does this make me wonder about?	p. 152
Words of the Wiser	What's the lesson for the character?	p. 406
Again and Again	Why might the author keep bringing this up?	p. 2
Memory Moment	Why is this memory important?	p. 153

Reading Nonfiction: Essays, Articles, and Arguments		
Signpost	**Anchor Question(s)**	**Lesson**
Big Questions	What surprised me? What did the author think I already knew? What challenged, changed, or confirmed what I already knew?	p. 77
Contrasts and Contradictions	What is the difference, and why does it matter?	p. 241
Extreme or Absolute Language	Why did the author use this language?	p. 76
Numbers and Stats	Why did the author use these numbers or amounts?	p. 325
Quoted Words	Why was this person quoted or cited, and what did this add?	p. 77
Word Gaps	Do I know this word from someplace else? Does it seem like technical talk for this topic? Do clues in the sentence help me understand the word?	p. 240

You can preview these texts in Unit 4 of your eBook.

Then, check off the text or texts that you select to read on your own.

POEM

I Saw Old General at Bay
Walt Whitman

What kind of leader makes soldiers feel honored to risk their lives?

SHORT STORY

A Mystery of Heroism
Stephen Crane

A soldier struggles with the true meaning of heroism.

HISTORY WRITING

***from* Bloody Times: The Funeral of Abraham Lincoln and the Manhunt for Jefferson Davis**
James L. Swanson

As the city of Richmond burns, one president escapes while another is welcomed like a king.

BIOGRAPHY

My Friend Douglass
Russell Freedman

Discover why Abraham Lincoln was so eager to speak with Frederick Douglass after his second inauguration.

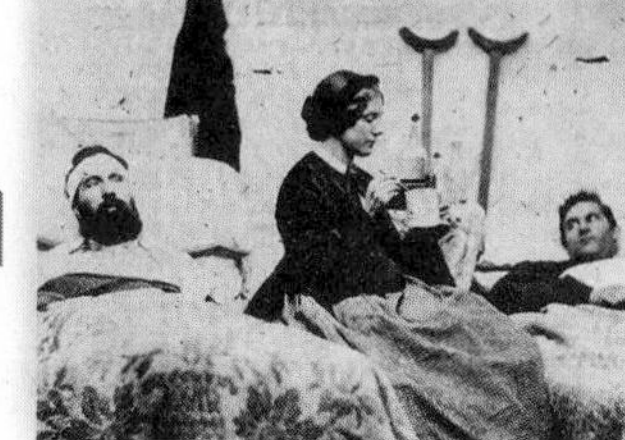

JOURNAL

Civil War Journal
Louisa May Alcott

Alcott reflects on her experiences as a nurse during the Civil War.

Collaborate and Share With a partner, discuss what you learned from at least one of your independent readings.

- Give a brief synopsis or summary of the text.
- Describe any signposts that you noticed in the text and explain what they revealed to you.
- Describe what you most enjoyed or found most challenging about the text. Give specific examples.
- Decide if you would recommend the text to others. Why or why not?

Go to the **Reading Studio** for more resources on **Notice & Note.**

WRITING TASK

Go to the **Writing Studio** for help writing your research report.

Write a Research Report

This unit focuses on the struggle against slavery before, during, and after the Civil War. For this writing task, you will research and write a report about an aspect of the abolition movement in the United States. A research report is a type of informational text that uses information from a variety of sources to support a thesis or answer a question. For an example of a well-written informational text that you can use as a mentor text, review *Fortune's Bones*. As you plan your report, you can also use any relevant notes from your Response Log.

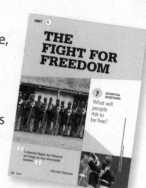

Writing Prompt

Read the information in the box below.

This is the context for your research report.

> The movement to end slavery in the United States was a long process that took many years.

Think carefully about the following question.

This is the Essential Question for the unit. How would you answer this question, based on the texts in the unit?

> What will people risk to be free?

Research and write a report about an aspect of the abolition movement in the United States.

Be sure to —

Review these points as you write and again when you finish. Make any needed changes and edits.

- ❑ provide an engaging introduction that catches the reader's attention, clearly states the topic, and includes a thesis statement
- ❑ develop the topic and support the thesis by synthesizing facts, definitions, and examples from multiple sources
- ❑ accurately quote and paraphrase source material and document each source of information
- ❑ clearly organize ideas and use transitions to connect ideas
- ❑ create coherence within and across paragraphs
- ❑ provide a conclusion that summarizes main points and restates the thesis or answers the original question

1 Plan

The first thing you need to do is take the broad topic of abolition and narrow it. Will you discuss the efforts of one abolitionist? Will you trace milestones in the movement to end slavery?

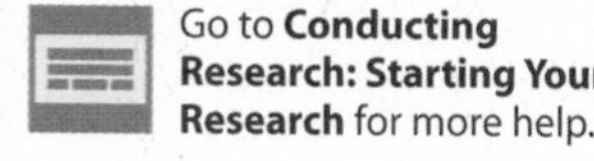

Go to **Conducting Research: Starting Your Research** for more help.

Develop Research Questions A good way to narrow a topic is to ask questions about it. For example, you might begin by asking "Who were famous abolitionists?" Based on your preliminary research, you may realize that you need to refine, or change, your research questions in order to narrow your topic further or find something more interesting to write about. For example, a question that begins with *how* or *why* will usually generate more to write about than one that begins with *who* or *where*. Use the table below, or one like it, to record questions and take notes that will help you narrow or refine your topic.

Preliminary and Refined Research Questions	
(initial question) **Who started the abolition movement in the U.S.?**	William Lloyd Garrison founded the American Anti-Slavery Society in 1833. (Encyclopædia Britannica)
(refined question) **How did the abolition movement grow and spread?**	

Research Your Report Once you've refined your question, search for both digital and print sources to help you answer it. Your report will be more interesting if you include **primary sources**—materials that were created by people who witnessed events, such as the autobiography *Narrative of the Life of Frederick Douglass*. Also consult **secondary sources,** which are those created by people who were not involved with the event, such as the biography *Harriet Tubman: Conductor on the Underground Railroad.* Take notes on what you learn. As you research, you might find that you want to revise your plan in response to the information you're finding. If that happens, follow your interests.

Use any relevant notes from your Response Log as you plan your report.

Evaluate and Document Your Sources Evaluate the sources you locate—particularly online sources—to ensure that they are reliable, credible, unbiased, and do not include loaded language or faulty reasoning. Avoid commercial, political, and personal websites. Keep a list of your sources; this will make them easier to cite and document later.

Go to **Writing Informational Texts: Organizing Ideas** for help with creating an outline.

Organize Your Ideas The answer to your research question is likely to be your thesis. To support it thoroughly, you will need to **synthesize,** or combine information from multiple sources. Create an outline to guide your writing. For each paragraph of the body, group related ideas together and organize them by central ideas and supporting information. This will help create coherence within paragraphs. Also, check that all paragraphs support your thesis statement; this will help create coherence across paragraphs. This example outline shows you how you might group your ideas:

Notice & Note

From Reading to Writing

As you draft your research report, apply what you've learned about signposts to your own writing.

Think about how you can incorporate **Quoted Words** into your essay.

Go to the **Reading Studio** for more resources on Notice & Note.

Outline for Research Report

I. Introduction with thesis statement
II. Body
   A. Subtopic
      1. Supporting facts and details
      2. Supporting facts and details
   B. Subtopic
      1. Supporting facts and details
      2. Supporting facts and details
III. Conclusion with summary and reworded thesis statement

2 Develop a Draft

You might prefer to draft your research report online.

Refer to your outline as you draft your report.

- State your thesis clearly in your introduction. Include a fact, quote, or anecdote to interest the reader in your topic.
- Group your ideas and information into paragraphs. Support each point with relevant and specific details, facts, and examples. These may include quotations, paraphrases, or summaries of source material.
- Create a formal style by using complete sentences with precise language. Avoid contractions and pronouns such as *I* and *you*.
- Include transition words and phrases such as *because, also, in addition,* and *finally* to clarify the relationships between ideas.
- Write a conclusion that follows from and supports your thesis.

Go to **Using Textual Evidence: Summarizing, Paraphrasing, and Quoting** for help.

Cite Your Sources As you write, be careful to avoid plagiarizing your sources. **Plagiarizing** means using other people's words or ideas without giving them credit. One way to avoid plagiarizing is to place the source's exact words in quotation marks. Another way is to write a good **paraphrase,** in which you restate the author's ideas in your own words. In either case, you should always identify the author and the title of the work you are quoting or paraphrasing.

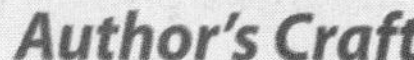

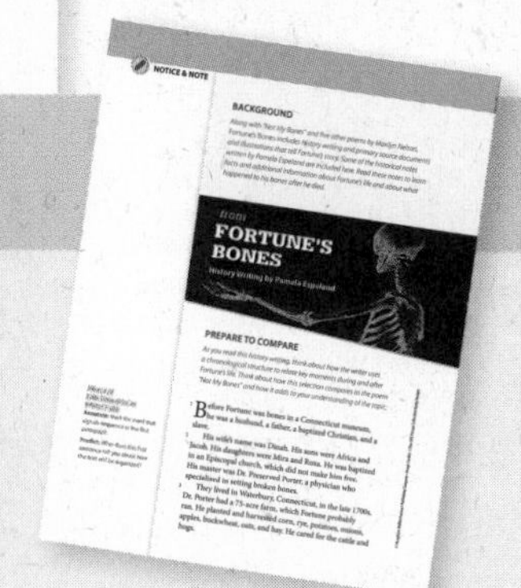

Use the Mentor Text

Author's Craft

In the introduction of your research report, you should express your thesis statement, or controlling idea. You should also include something that gets your reader interested in reading your report. Notice the way the writer captures the reader's attention in this opening sentence from *Fortune's Bones.*

Before Fortune was bones in a Connecticut museum, he was a husband, a father, a baptized Christian, and a slave.

The writer grabs the audience's attention by making a connection between a real person and his remains in a museum.

Apply What You've Learned To capture your reader's attention, you might include a surprising fact, a famous quotation, or an anecdote related to the topic.

Genre Characteristics

Writers of informational texts often include quotations to provide supporting evidence for their main points—and if they do so, they must cite their sources. In this example, notice how the writer uses a quotation and cites her source to support an idea in *Fortune's Bones*. In this case, the person quoted may have preferred to be unnamed.

One Waterbury resident remembers, "Larry was the thing to see when you go to the museum. I don't think anybody ever envisioned that this was truly a human being."

The writer provides a quotation to support her idea that the display of Fortune's bones was dehumanizing. She cites the source of her quote.

Apply What You've Learned To develop and support your ideas, you will want to include quotations, facts, and examples from sources. Cite each source of information so readers know where it came from.

3 Revise

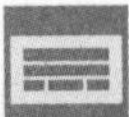

Go to **Writing Informative Texts: Precise Language and Vocabulary** for help revising your research report.

On Your Own Once you have written your draft, you'll want to go back and look for ways to improve your report. As you reread and revise, think about whether you have achieved your purpose. The Revision Guide will help you focus on specific elements to make your writing stronger.

Revision Guide

Ask Yourself	Tips	Revision Techniques
1. Is the thesis statement clear?	**Underline** the thesis statement.	**Add** a thesis statement. **Revise** a vague thesis to make it stronger.
2. Does each paragraph have a main point related to the thesis?	**Highlight** the main point of each paragraph.	**Add** a main point if one is missing. **Rewrite** any main points that are unclear.
3. Are there relevant supporting details for each point?	**Underline** facts, statistics, examples, and quotations that support your points.	**Delete** unrelated ideas. **Add** more facts, statistics, examples, and quotations from your notes.
4. Are ideas organized logically? Do transitions clearly connect ideas? Is there coherence within and across paragraphs?	**Highlight** transitional words and phrases within and between paragraphs.	**Rearrange** sentences and paragraphs to organize ideas logically. **Add** transitions to connect ideas and create coherence.
5. Is information gathered from a variety of sources, and are those sources cited correctly?	**Underline** references to sources.	**Add** more sources for variety. **Cite** all sources correctly.
6. Does the conclusion summarize the topic and support the information presented?	**Underline** the summary. **Highlight** sentences that support information in the report.	**Add** a statement that summarizes the main ideas. **Insert** supporting sentences.

ACADEMIC VOCABULARY

As you conduct your **peer review,** be sure to use these words.

- ❑ **access**
- ❑ **civil**
- ❑ **demonstrate**
- ❑ **document**
- ❑ **symbolize**

With a Partner After working through the Revision Guide on your own, exchange papers with a partner and evaluate each other's drafts in a **peer review**. Take turns reading or listening to each other's reports and use the Revision Guide to offer suggestions to make the reports more effective. Provide revision suggestions for any points mentioned in the chart that might improve your partner's report. Remember to be positive and respectful. When receiving feedback from your partner, listen attentively and ask questions to make sure you fully understand the revision suggestions.

 Edit

Once you have addressed the organization, development, and flow of ideas in your research report, you can improve the language of your draft. Edit for the proper use of standard English conventions, such as correct punctuation. Be sure to correct any misspellings or grammatical errors.

Language Conventions

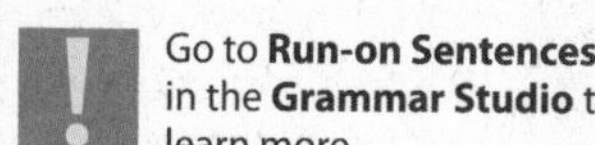
Go to **Run-on Sentences** in the **Grammar Studio** to learn more.

Run-On Sentences A **run-on sentence** is made up of two or more sentences that have been run together as if they were one thought. This can be confusing to readers, especially in informational texts that contain many facts and examples. Consider the following example of a run-on sentence. The corrected sentence is from *Fortune's Bones:*

EXAMPLE:

> **Run-on sentence:** The museum now believed that displaying the skeleton was disrespectful it wasn't just a bunch of bones it was the remains of someone's son, maybe someone's father.
>
> **Corrected example:** The museum now believed that displaying the skeleton was disrespectful. It wasn't just a bunch of bones. It was the remains of someone's son, maybe someone's father.

To correct run-on sentences, do the following:

- Divide the sentence into separate sentences. Mark the end of each idea with a period (as in the above example), a question mark, or an exclamation point. Begin each sentence with a capital letter.
- If the two sentences are very closely related, use a conjunction, such as *and* or *but* (and a comma, if necessary) to combine them into a compound or complex sentence. Or, you may use a semicolon to join the two sentences.

5 Publish

Create a final version of your research report and choose a way to share it with your audience. Consider these options:

- Present your report as a speech to the class.
- Post your report on a school website.
- Produce a multi-modal presentation of your report.

WRITING TASK

Use the scoring guide to evaluate your research report.

Writing Task Scoring Guide: Research Report

	Organization/Progression	Development of Ideas	Use of Language and Conventions
4	• The organization is effective and logical throughout the report. • Transitions clearly show the relationship among ideas from one paragraph to another. • There is very strong coherence within and across paragraphs.	• The thesis statement is clear, and the introduction is appealing and informative. • The topic is well developed with relevant facts, concrete details, interesting quotations, and examples from reliable sources. • The conclusion effectively summarizes the information presented and repeats the thesis statement.	• The writing maintains a formal style throughout. • Language is strong and precise. • Ideas have been combined to create detailed sentences. • Spelling, grammar, usage, and mechanics are correct. • Research sources are cited correctly.
3	• The organization is mostly effective and logical but may be confusing in a couple places. • A few more transitions are needed to connect related ideas. • There is coherence within and across paragraphs.	• The introduction contains a thesis statement, but the introduction does not create interest in the topic. • Some key points need more support from relevant facts, concrete details, quotations, and examples from reliable sources. • The conclusion summarizes the information presented and includes the thesis statement.	• The style is inconsistent in a few places. • Language is not always precise. • Some ideas have been combined to add detail to sentences; there may be one or two run-ons. • There are a few errors in spelling, grammar, usage, and mechanics. • Sources are not cited consistently.
2	• The organization is logical in some places but often doesn't follow a pattern. • More transitions are needed throughout to connect ideas. • There is little coherence within and across paragraphs.	• The thesis statement is confusing. The introduction is not very informative or engaging. • The development of ideas is minimal. The writer uses facts, details, and examples that are inappropriate or ineffectively presented. • The conclusion does not include a complete summary or a rewording of the thesis statement.	• The style is informal in many places. • The language is often overly general. • There are several run-on sentences. • There are many spelling, grammar, usage, and mechanics errors, but they do not obscure meaning. • Only one or two research sources are cited, and the format is incorrect.
1	• A logical organization is not used; information is presented randomly. • Transitions are not used, making the writing difficult to understand. • There is no coherence within and across paragraphs.	• The thesis statement is missing. The introduction is not engaging and does not prepare the reader for the content of the report. • There are few, if any, facts, details, quotations, and examples. Or, they are from unreliable sources. • There is no conclusion.	• The style is inappropriate for the report. • Language is too general to convey meaningful information. • There are many run-on sentences. • There are many errors in spelling, grammar, usage, and mechanics that obscure meaning. • Research sources are not cited.

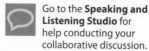

Participate in a Collaborative Discussion

This unit, "The Fight for Freedom," focuses on the Civil War and the struggle against slavery. Imagine you are invited to design a new unit that addresses the same essential question: "What will people risk to be free?" Work collaboratively with group members to choose a topic for such a unit, select materials you would use to teach it, and then present your ideas to the class.

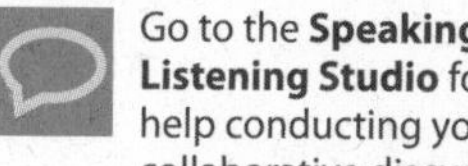

Go to the **Speaking and Listening Studio** for help conducting your collaborative discussion.

1 Make a Plan

Brainstorm With your group, assign a notetaker and moderator. Then brainstorm a list of other fights for freedom you know about. Consider these types of struggles:

- periods of war or unrest, such as the Revolutionary War
- political movements, such as the fight for civil rights or the fight against apartheid
- efforts to escape oppression or preserve democracy

Vote Discuss the pros and cons of designing a Fight for Freedom unit around each idea on your list. Then vote on which topic to focus on. You can vote by a show of hands, or by a secret ballot.

Set an Agenda and Identify Action Items With group members, analyze the task and create an **agenda,** or a list of things the group must discuss, agree upon, and do in order to design a unit to present to the class. One item on your agenda should be to create a list of **action items,** or tasks that must be done before the next meeting. Decide together who will do each one.

Create a Schedule Keeping in mind the final deadline date, set progress deadlines by which each task must be completed. Make sure deadlines are realistic; for example, researching a topic will require more time than practicing for the final presentation. You may find it helpful to use an online calendar and collaborative workspace to help keep everyone on track. Reconvene as necessary to report on progress and make adjustments to your plan.

As you work collaboratively, follow these rules of polite discussion:

- ❑ **listen closely to one another**
- ❑ **value contributions of all group members**
- ❑ **stay on topic**
- ❑ **express disagreement politely and respectfully**
- ❑ **ask only helpful, relevant questions**
- ❑ **provide only clear, thoughtful, and direct answers**

2 Prepare to Present

Once you have decided what your unit will focus on and include, prepare to present your proposal to the class. Everyone in the group should have a role. Practice for each other to improve your performance. Below are some other guidelines on presenting and giving feedback.

Provide and Consider Advice for Improvement

As a presenter, use the techniques below to help make your points clear. Then, listen to feedback and consider ways to revise your work.

- Effective **verbal techniques** include clearly enunciating words, speaking slowly enough so that listeners can understand you, and speaking at an appropriate volume.
- Effective **nonverbal techniques** include making eye contact, varying facial expressions, and using meaningful gestures.

As a listener, pay close attention. Suggest ways that presenters can improve their presentations. Ask questions to clarify any confusing ideas and provide feedback.

3 Present the Unit

Based on the practice session, make any final changes as you get ready for your presentation. Then, groups should take turns presenting their units to the whole class:

- As group members present their unit, they may refer briefly to their notes to recall main points, but they should speak directly to the audience.
- Audience members should listen closely and take notes.
- After each presentation, groups should invite the audience to ask questions about their unit.

Reflect on the Unit

By completing your research report and engaging in a collaborative discussion, you have expressed your thoughts about the reading you have done in this unit as well as the information you discovered in your research. Now is a good time to reflect on what you have learned.

Reflect on the Essential Question

- What will people risk to be free? How has your answer changed since you first considered this question at the beginning of the unit?
- What are some examples you've read in the unit, and in other sources, of people taking risks to be free?

Reflect on Your Reading

- Which selections were the most interesting or surprising to you?
- Which selection or selections made you want to learn more about the topic?
- From which selection did you learn the most about what people will risk to be free?

Reflect on the Writing Task

- What difficulties did you encounter while working on your research report? How might you avoid them next time?
- Which part of the report was the easiest to write? Which was the hardest? Why?
- What improvements did you make to your report as you were revising?

Reflect on the Speaking and Listening Task

- What did you learn from creating and presenting your unit?
- In what ways was your collaboration on developing and presenting the material successful? How could you improve the process the next time?

UNIT 4 SELECTIONS

- *Narrative of the Life of Frederick Douglass, an American Slave*
- *Harriet Tubman: Conductor on the Underground Railroad*
- "The Drummer Boy of Shiloh"
- "O Captain! My Captain!"
- "Not My Bones"
- *Fortune's Bones*

UNIT 5

FINDING YOUR PATH

? **ESSENTIAL QUESTION:**

How do your teenage years prepare you for adulthood?

"When you become a teenager, you step onto a bridge. . . . The opposite shore is adulthood."

Gail Carson Levine

ACADEMIC VOCABULARY

Academic Vocabulary words are words you use when you discuss and write about texts. In this unit you will practice and learn five words.

☑ **debate** ❑ **deduce** ❑ **license** ❑ **sufficient** ❑ **trend**

Study the Word Network to learn more about the word **debate.**

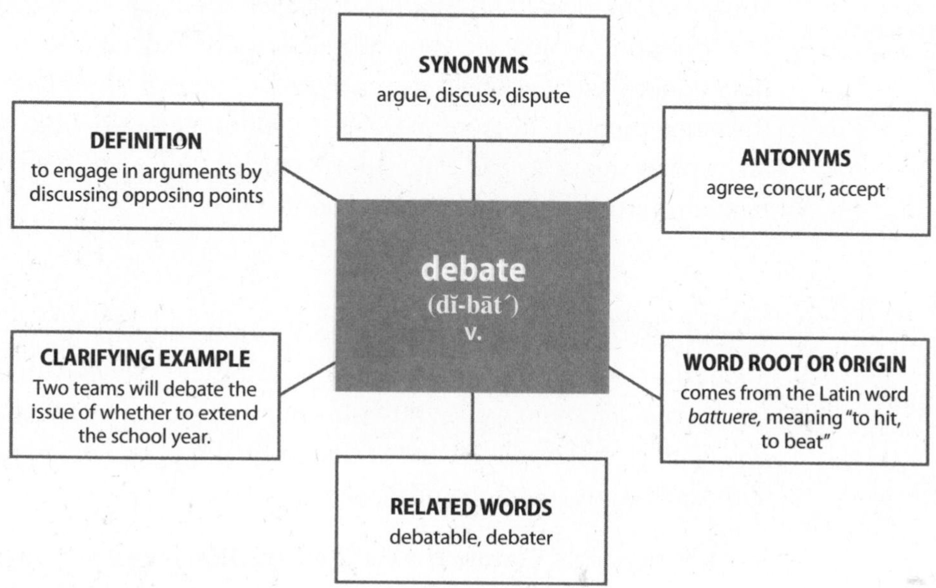

Write and Discuss Discuss the completed Word Network with a partner, making sure to talk through all of the boxes until you both understand the word, its synonyms, antonyms, and related forms. Then, fill out Word Networks for each of the remaining four words. Use a dictionary or online resource to help you complete the activity.

Go online to access the Word Networks.

RESPOND TO THE ESSENTIAL QUESTION

In this unit, you will explore the teenage years as a unique stage of life between childhood and adulthood. As you read, you will revisit the **Essential Question** and gather your ideas about it in the **Response Log** that appears on page R5. At the end of the unit, you will have the opportunity to write an **argument** about the impact of technology on teen friendships. Filling out the Response Log will help you prepare for this writing task.

You can also go online to access the Response Log.

UNIT 5 RESPONSE LOG

Use this Response Log to record your ideas about how each of the texts in Unit 5 relates to or comments on the **Essential Question.**

? **Essential Question:** How do your teenage years prepare you for adulthood?

The Debt We Owe to the Adolescent Brain	
from Bronx Masquerade	
Hanging Fire	
Summer of His Fourteenth Year	
from It's Complicated: The Social Lives of Networked Teens	
Outsmart Your Smartphone	

THE DEBT WE OWE TO THE ADOLESCENT BRAIN

For more information on these and other signposts to Notice & Note, visit the **Reading Studio**.

You are about to read the informational text "The Debt We Owe to the Adolescent Brain." In it, you will ask questions and notice and note signposts that will help you analyze the author's purpose and the organizational structure she uses to support her main ideas. Here are two key signposts and a Big Question to look for as you read this magazine article and other works of nonfiction.

When you read and encounter phrases like these, pause to see if it's a **Contrasts and Contradictions** signpost:

"on the other hand, . . ."

"by contrast, . . ."

"however, . . ."

"another viewpoint . . ."

Contrasts and Contradictions If you ask an older student to tell you about the classes he is taking, he might contrast his classes with those in your grade by naming ways they are more difficult. If he said that one of his classes was much easier than yours, however, you might be surprised by this contradiction in what you expected to hear.

In nonfiction texts, **Contrasts and Contradictions** can help you better understand main ideas and supporting details. Contrasts can reveal the unique qualities of a subject in comparison to others that seemed to be similar. Contradictions may highlight sharp or startling contrasts between what we expect and what we observe.

Read this paragraph from "The Debt We Owe to the Adolescent Brain" to see a student's annotation of Contrasts and Contradictions:

1 Polar bears can live above the Arctic Circle but they can't live at the Equator. Gorillas can live at the Equator but they can't live above the Arctic Circle. Humans, however, can live in the Arctic or they can live in the tropics. Why is our species so adaptable? We can thank our long period of adolescence for that.

Anchor Question
When you notice this signpost, ask: What is the difference, and why does it matter?

What does the author contrast in the example?	The author contrasts the adaptability of humans with that of polar bears and gorillas.
Why does the author point out this contrast?	The author wants to emphasize that humans are unusual by contrasting them with other animals.

Big Questions When you tell a friend about a movie that only you have seen, you might share some basic information about the plot and your overall reaction. When you and a friend talk about a movie you've both seen, you might discuss details about specific parts of the movie.

Authors have an intended audience when they write. Asking the Big Question **What does the author think I already know?** can help you make inferences about the author's reasons for including or leaving out certain facts, details, and examples. Here's an example of a student identifying and marking this Big Question in the text:

> 3 Dr. Jay Giedd, professor of psychiatry at the University of California at San Diego, says, "Nothing is even close to humans in terms of how long we're dependent on caregivers."

What does the author think I already know about animals?	Animals are more independent from their parents at younger ages than humans.
Why doesn't the author provide more details about the differences between humans and animals?	She thinks her audience knows enough to understand her point: that humans depend on their parents for an unusually long time.

Remember to apply the **Big Questions** strategy when you read nonfiction text. Pause to ask yourself these questions:

- Who is the author's intended audience?
- What prior knowledge does the author think the audience has?
- What experiences does the author think the audience can relate to?

Numbers and Stats For what purposes might you count or measure something? Authors often use **Numbers and Stats** as evidence to support their main ideas. They might cite, track, or compare specific quantities or sizes to support an idea, identify a pattern, or point out a change over time. Paying attention to Numbers and Stats can help you:

- analyze an author's use of evidence
- understand an author's message and purpose
- identify author bias or faulty reasoning

Here's an example of a student underlining some Numbers and Stats:

> 13 . . . It's a sad paradox that, relative to children, people in their late adolescence, who are generally the strongest and healthiest they'll ever be, face a 200 percent increase in the chance of dying.

How does the author use numbers to compare children and adolescents?	The risk of death in adolescence is 200 percent higher than in childhood.
Why might this number be important to the author's message?	There might be something about the adolescent brain that increases the risk of death.

When you see words and phrases like these, pause to see if it's a **Numbers and Stats** signpost:

"amount"

"increase"

"greater/less than"

"60 percent"

"three times as many as"

"one out of every four"

Anchor Question
When you notice this signpost, ask: Do these numbers help prove a point?

THE DEBT WE OWE TO THE ADOLESCENT BRAIN

Informational Text by **Jeanne Miller**

? ESSENTIAL QUESTION:

How do your teenage years prepare you for adulthood?

QUICK START

What might be special about the brains of teenagers? Make a list of questions about the adolescent brain that you'd like the text to answer.

ANALYZE STRUCTURE

The **structure** of a text is the way in which it is put together. In "The Debt We Owe to the Adolescent Brain," the author uses **headings** to divide the article into sections. Previewing the article by skimming the headings can help you predict the text's structure and its **pattern(s) of organization,** or arrangement of ideas and information.

Pattern	What It Highlights	Signal Words
main-idea-and-details order	evidence that supports a key idea	*for example, experts say, others agree that*
cause-and-effect order	relationships between causes and effects	*because, so, as a result, therefore*
compare-and-contrast order	ways in which subjects are alike and different	*all, most, similarly, by contrast, but, however*

A pattern of organization may be used to organize an entire piece of writing or single paragraphs or sections within a work. As you read, note the pattern of organization in each section of the article.

ANALYZE AUTHOR'S PURPOSE

An **author's purpose** is his or her main reason for writing. In an informational text, the author's purpose is usually to inform or explain. An author's **message** is the main idea he or she wants to convey. To analyze how the author of this article achieves her purpose and to infer what her message is, complete the chart below as you read.

SECTION	KEY IDEAS
Introduction (paragraphs 1–2)	
"Brain Under Construction" (paragraphs 3–5)	
"Moving On from Childhood" (paragraphs 6–11)	
"Stone Age Impulses in the Modern World" (paragraphs 12–14)	
Author's Purpose and Message:	

GENRE ELEMENTS: INFORMATIONAL TEXT

- provides factual information
- may include headings and subheadings to help readers navigate the text
- uses organizational patterns such as main idea and details to present information clearly
- may appear in a variety of formats, including magazine articles—brief pieces that report on current events or topics

GET READY

CRITICAL VOCABULARY

adaptable	**insulate**	**lethal**
dependent	**deplete**	**paradox**

To see how many Critical Vocabulary words you already know, use them to complete these sentences.

1. Due to the dry conditions, too much water use will __________ the town's supply of water.
2. Certain bacteria can cause __________ illness.
3. Infants are __________ on caregivers to feed and clothe them.
4. An extra layer of clothing helps __________ you from the cold.
5. It felt like a(n) __________ that the team scored only one goal but still won the game.
6. A highly __________ species is able to grow and thrive in extreme conditions.

LANGUAGE CONVENTIONS

Pronoun-Antecedent Agreement In this lesson, you will see that pronouns agree with their antecedents and learn how to check them in your own writing. In this example, note that the speaker uses the plural pronoun *they* to refer back to a plural antecedent, *adolescents:*

"Adolescents are dealing with a lot," Casey says, "but they should remember they have greater potential for change now than at any other time."

As you read the text, notice the author's correct use of pronouns.

ANNOTATION MODEL

NOTICE & NOTE

As you read, notice and note signposts, such as **Contrasts and Contradictions** and **Numbers and Stats,** and pause to ask yourself **Big Questions.** In the model, you can see one reader's notes about "The Debt We Owe to the Adolescent Brain."

2 Most mammals have a period of adolescence. But as soon as they're able to reproduce, they begin bearing and caring for children. By contrast, humans, under the protection of their families, take many years to develop and grow into adulthood.

Difference: other mammals have a shorter period of adolescence than humans.

NOTICE & NOTE

BACKGROUND

Jeanne Miller *grew up in northwestern Pennsylvania but later settled in Berkeley, California. She writes children's and young adult magazine articles on a variety of science topics. Her book* Food Science *informs young readers about food chemistry, the movement to promote local and traditional foods, and the future of food.*

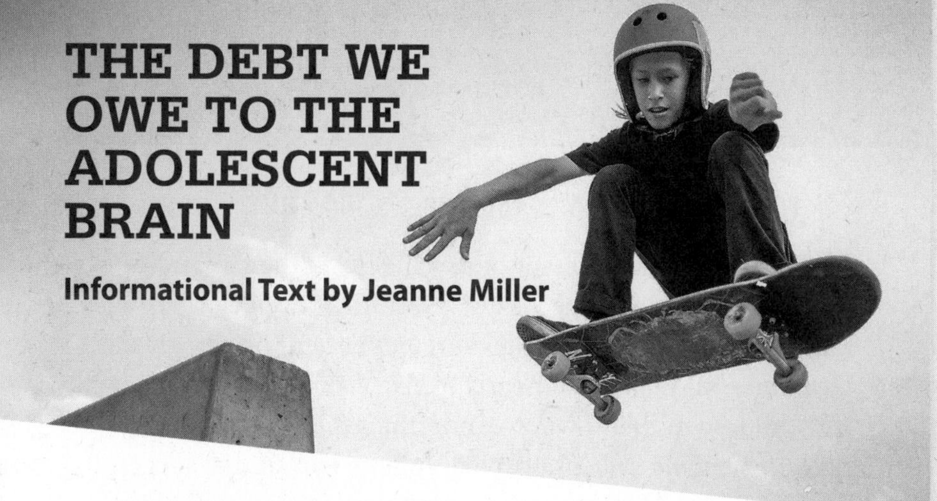

THE DEBT WE OWE TO THE ADOLESCENT BRAIN

Informational Text by Jeanne Miller

SETTING A PURPOSE

As you read, pay attention to details that reveal the author's purpose and message.

1 Polar bears can live above the Arctic Circle but they can't live at the Equator. Gorillas can live at the Equator but they can't live above the Arctic Circle. Humans, however, can live in the Arctic or they can live in the tropics. Why is our species so **adaptable**? We can thank our long period of adolescence for that.

2 Most mammals have a period of adolescence. But as soon as they're able to reproduce, they begin bearing and caring for children. By contrast, humans, under the protection of their families, take many years to develop and grow into adulthood.

Notice & Note

Use the side margins to notice and note signposts in the text.

adaptable
(ə-dăp´tə-bəl) *adj. Adaptable* means able to survive under certain conditions.

LANGUAGE CONVENTIONS

Annotate: In paragraph 2, underline all the pronouns. Then circle the two antecedents—the nouns to which the pronouns refer.

Analyze: Could the author have used the pronoun *our* instead of *their* in the last sentence? Explain.

NOTICE & NOTE

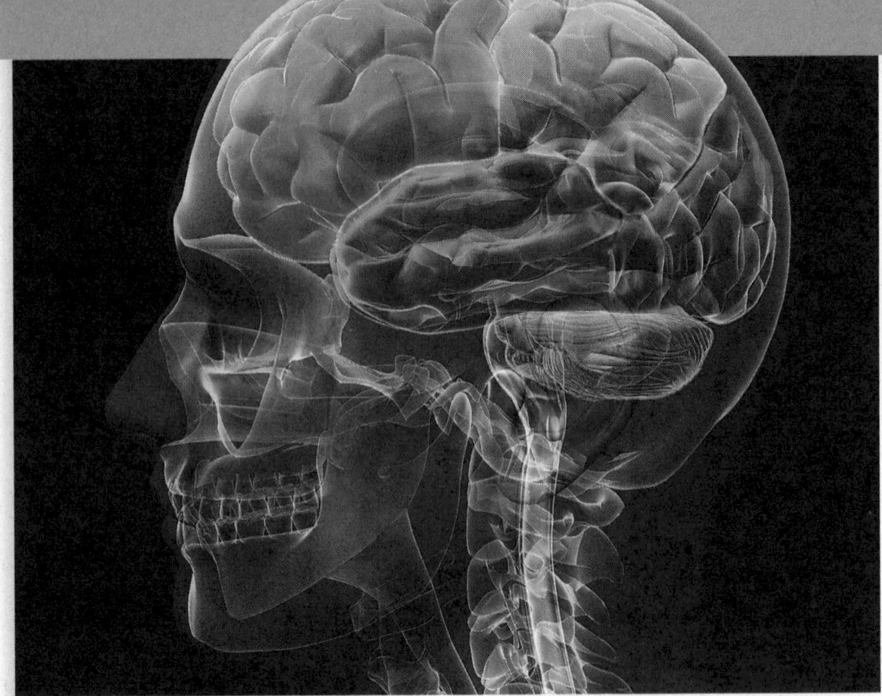

Brain Under Construction

3 Dr. Jay Giedd, professor of psychiatry[1] at the University of California at San Diego, says, "Nothing is even close to humans in terms of how long we're **dependent** on caregivers." He points out that in their early teens, Neanderthals[2] already had children of their own. Neanderthals died out, but our ancestors, *Homo sapiens*, thrived. A large part of that success comes from our brain's taking a long time to mature. This extended period of development lets us build exactly the brain we need in our circumstances. Giedd says, "All the brain's parts have their periods of rapid explosive growth and then rapid pruning back. You have overproduction—more connections than can possibly survive—and then they fight it out. The ones that are used and lead to positive outcomes stay, and those that aren't used, or are used and lead to bad outcomes, are eliminated."

dependent
(dĭ-pĕn´dənt) *adj. Dependent* means relying on or requiring the aid or support of another.

ANALYZE STRUCTURE

Annotate: Mark signal words and phrases that show relationships between ideas in paragraphs 1–3.

Analyze: What is the author's pattern of organization in these paragraphs? How does this pattern help the author introduce and develop main ideas?

4 We lose "gray matter" and gain "white matter": myelin, which forms an **insulating** sheath around nerve fibers. "We get more and more myelin, which speeds up the communication between nerve cells, as we go through adolescence," says Giedd. "We learn what we need to do and be good at and then the process streamlines that." But the price we pay is that, as myelin is laid down, flexibility diminishes. Adolescence is a kind of golden age when, as Giedd puts it, "You're asking your brain, 'What do I need to be good at? What do I need to do to make it in this world?' Every choice you make trains your brain."

insulate
(ĭn´sə-lāt´) *v.* To *insulate* means to surround or cover to prevent the passage of heat, electricity, or sound.

[1] **psychiatry** (sĭ-kī´ə-trē): the branch of medicine that deals with the diagnosis, treatment, and prevention of mental and emotional disorders.

[2] **Neanderthals** (nē-ăn´dər-thôlz´): an extinct human species or subspecies.

5 This lets us adjust to our surroundings. Giedd points out, "We all had ancestors that were good at adapting to change. Neanderthals had brains that were about 13 percent bigger than ours and they lived in pretty tough conditions and harsh climates, but they didn't adapt."

Moving On from Childhood

6 Dr. B. J. Casey is a professor of psychology at Weill Cornell Medical College. Her focus on adolescent brains includes those of humans and mice. "There is evidence," she says, "that even adolescent rodents tend to hang out with same-aged peers and tend to have more fights with their parents." Sound familiar? These behaviors—sensitivity to influence from peers, taking risks, and pulling away from parents—are hallmarks of human adolescence. They have their roots in the hunter-gatherer world of our early ancestors, where success meant surviving and reproducing.

7 Finding a mate and passing on your genes means leaving the comfort of your home. Casey says, "If you're getting all your needs met, why in the world would you leave? There needs to be some push-pull tension in evolution to get you to leave that home. Otherwise you'll **deplete** all the resources and it will be difficult to find a mate to partner with."

8 Going out into the world can involve risks, but the adolescent brain is wired for that. Giedd points out that "high risk equals high reward at times." And, compared to children or adults, teens are much more sensitive to rewards.

9 A study in Casey's lab demonstrated that fact when researchers put teenagers in a brain-scanning machine and asked them to complete a simple task. Successfully completing it earned them a lot of money. The resulting brain scans showed

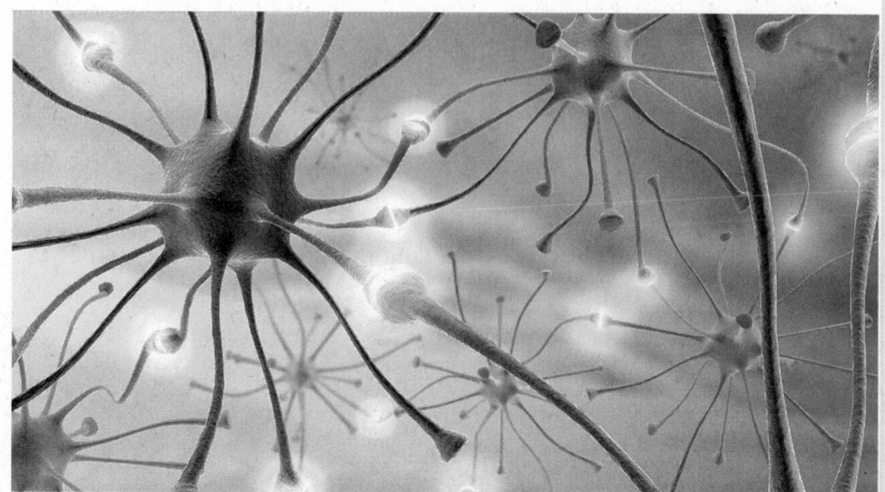

NOTICE & NOTE 

NUMBERS AND STATS

Notice & Note: In paragraph 5, what comparison does the author make using a percentage number? Circle this statistic in the text.

Infer: What purpose does this number serve in this context?

BIG QUESTIONS

Notice & Note: A **rhetorical question** has such an obvious answer that it does not require a reply. Underline the rhetorical question in paragraph 6. Why do you think the author poses this question?

Infer: What prior knowledge or experience does the author's rhetorical question assume?

deplete
(dĭ-plēt´) *v.* To *deplete* means to use up or to reduce to a very small amount.

CONTRASTS AND CONTRADICTIONS

Notice & Note: What evidence does the author provide in paragraphs 8–9 to contrast adolescents with children and adults? Mark these details.

Analyze: Why does the author point out these differences?

NOTICE & NOTE

an exaggerated response in the reward center of the teens' brains, but only a moderate response in children and adults.

ANALYZE AUTHOR'S PURPOSE

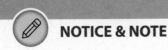

Annotate: Circle the heading of the last section. Consider its meaning and make a prediction about how this section helps the author achieve her purpose. Then, underline possible effects of "Stone Age impulses in the modern world" in paragraphs 12–14.

Analyze: After reading the last section, confirm or correct the prediction you made previously. What overall message does the information in this section help support?

10 Sometimes the reward might be approval by their peers, who will be important to a teenager's future. In another study, Casey's group showed that, unlike children and adults, adolescents found smiling faces to be almost irresistible. She says, "When your peers are smiling it means they're accepting you."

11 Giedd says, "The peer group is the one that will help protect you, who will be your teammates, and who will supply resources. Job one for adolescents is navigating their social world."

Stone Age Impulses in the Modern World

12 In hunter-gatherer societies, success in a risk-taking activity might result in a supply of food, in securing a mate, or in finding new territory. Of course, it can sometimes result in being killed by a predator. Taking certain risks can also pay off for modern teens. Giedd says, "As long as it's not **lethal**—as in the case of foolish risk-taking—it can lead to innovation and creativity."

lethal
(lē´thəl) *adj. Lethal* means causing or capable of causing death.

13 The dangers today's teens face are different from those our early ancestors faced. It's a sad **paradox** that, relative to children, people in their late adolescence, who are generally the strongest and healthiest they'll ever be, face a 200 percent increase in the chance of dying. The main cause is accidents, with one-third of those being automobile crashes. Reckless driving and other dangerous behaviors put teenagers at risk, but young people also face threats to their health from the considerable stresses of growing up in the 21st century. "Adolescents are dealing with a lot," Casey says, "but they

paradox
(păr´ə-dŏks´) *n.* A *paradox* is a person, thing, or situation that is contradictory.

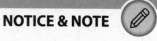

should remember they have greater potential for change now than at any other time. There will be many opportunities for them to change behaviors that they don't want to engage in and to become what they want to be."

14 Giedd agrees. "The challenges adolescents present to their brains now will have effects for decades," he says. The potential for mastering new skills and honing their abilities is phenomenal. "We never lose it completely," Giedd says, "but it's never going to be as good as it is when we're adolescents."

CHECK YOUR UNDERSTANDING

Answer these questions before moving on to the **Analyze the Text** section on the following page.

1 The word pruning in paragraph 3 means —

A connecting

B overproducing

C growing

D eliminating

2 What idea does the evidence in paragraph 9 support?

F The adolescent brain is highly efficient in completing simple tasks.

G The adolescent brain is wired to seek safety.

H Adolescents do not want to leave home if all of their needs are met.

J Adolescents are more sensitive to rewards than children or adults.

3 What is the author's main purpose in "The Debt We Owe to the Adolescent Brain"?

A to entertain

B to persuade

C to inform or explain

D to express thoughts or feelings

RESPOND

ANALYZE THE TEXT

Support your responses with evidence from the text. NOTEBOOK

1. **Analyze** What is the author's main purpose for writing this article? How do the text's structure, headings, and patterns of organization help the author to achieve this purpose?
2. **Infer** Why does the author compare humans to Neanderthals? Cite evidence to support your answer.
3. **Cause/Effect** What cause-effect relationship does the author identify in the section "Moving On from Childhood"? How does this information relate to the author's main message?
4. **Analyze** What patterns of organization does the author use to convey information in this article? For each pattern you identify, cite an example and give a reason why she might have used it.
5. **Notice & Note** What paradox does the author point out in paragraph 13? How does this contradiction relate to the author's message?

RESEARCH TIP
When you research science topics, look for sources that include diagrams and charts to help you interpret complex information.

RESEARCH

In "The Debt We Owe to the Adolescent Brain," you learned about ways in which adolescents' brains are unique. Conduct research to find out more about the brain's structure and characteristics. Record what you learn in the chart.

QUESTION	ANSWER
What is the cerebral cortex?	
What is the function of each lobe of the cerebral cortex?	
What is the difference between the cerebral cortex of an adult and that of an adolescent?	

Connect Consider what you have learned from your research about the brain. How does this information help support key ideas in "The Debt We Owe to the Adolescent Brain"? Discuss your ideas with a partner.

CREATE AND DISCUSS

Write a Letter Write a friendly letter to an adult in your life using research on the adolescent brain to explain the evolutionary purpose of some aspect of your behavior.

- ❑ Format your letter with an appropriate heading, a salutation, and a closing.
- ❑ Identify an aspect of your behavior that might be explained by current research on brain changes that occur during adolescence.
- ❑ Cite evidence from the text to support your ideas about the evolutionary purpose of your behavior.

Go to **Writing as a Process** in the **Writing Studio** for more.

Discuss with a Small Group Have a discussion about how information in "The Debt We Owe to the Adolescent Brain" can help you navigate school and life.

- ❑ With a small group, discuss practical ways in which your understanding of adolescent brain changes might influence choices you make or goals that you set at school and at home.
- ❑ Be sure to support your views with evidence from the article.
- ❑ During your discussion, listen closely and respectfully to all ideas.

Go to **Participating in Collaborative Discussions** in the **Speaking and Listening Studio** for more help.

RESPOND TO THE ESSENTIAL QUESTION

? How do your teenage years prepare you for adulthood?

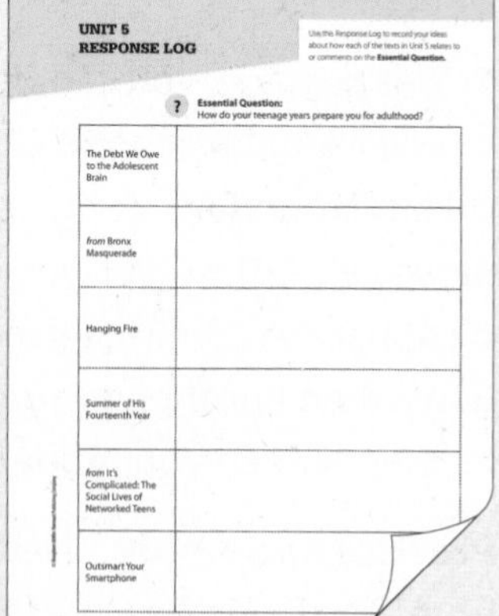
UNIT 5 RESPONSE LOG

Use this Response Log to record your ideas about how each of the texts in Unit 5 relates to or comments on the **Essential Question.**

? **Essential Question:** How do your teenage years prepare you for adulthood?

The Debt We Owe to the Adolescent Brain	
from Bronx Masquerade	
Hanging Fire	
Summer of His Fourteenth Year	
from It's Complicated: The Social Lives of Networked Teens	
Outsmart Your Smartphone	

Gather Information Review your annotations and notes on "The Debt We Owe to the Adolescent Brain." Then, add relevant details to your Response Log. As you determine which information to include, think about:

- brain changes that happen during adolescence
- ways in which the adolescent brain is unique
- dangers today's teens face

At the end of the unit, you can use your notes to help you write an argument.

ACADEMIC VOCABULARY

As you write and discuss what you learned from the article, be sure to use the Academic Vocabulary words. Check off each of the words that you use.

- ❑ **debate**
- ❑ **deduce**
- ❑ **license**
- ❑ **sufficient**
- ❑ **trend**

RESPOND

CRITICAL VOCABULARY

WORD BANK
adaptable
dependent
insulate
deplete
lethal
paradox

Practice and Apply Use what you know about the Vocabulary words to answer the following questions.

1. Are you **dependent** on anyone for help with your homework? Why or why not?
2. What would **insulate** a swimmer, a wetsuit or a life jacket? Why?
3. What might **deplete** your energy, a good night's rest or a long soccer practice? Why?
4. Is a **paradox** more of a contradiction or an affirmation? Why?
5. If a species is highly **adaptable**, will a change in its environment likely be **lethal**? Why or why not?

VOCABULARY STRATEGY: Use Resources

Go to **Using Reference Sources** in the **Vocabulary Studio** for more.

When reading an informational text such as a science article, looking up technical or cross-curricular terms in print or digital resources such as dictionaries or glossaries can help you better understand the ideas.

Read this passage from "The Debt We Owe to the Adolescent Brain."

> **We lose "gray matter" and gain "white matter": myelin, which forms an insulating sheath around nerve fibers. "We get more and more myelin, which speeds up the communication between nerve cells, as we go through adolescence," says Giedd.**

In that passage, you can determine the meaning of the technical term *myelin* from the context clues "white matter," "forms an insulating sheath around nerve fibers," and "speeds up communication between nerve cells." However, you can also look up the word *myelin* in a dictionary to confirm its meaning and determine its pronunciation. Consulting another resource, such as a science reference book, will further deepen your understanding.

Practice and Apply Use context clues to define the following terms from "The Debt We Owe to the Adolescent Brain." Then use a resource such as a dictionary, glossary, or science reference book to confirm that your definition is correct.

TERM	GUESSED DEFINITION	RESOURCE DEFINITION
nerve cell (paragraph 4)		
psychology (paragraph 6)		
gene (paragraph 7)		

LANGUAGE CONVENTIONS:
Pronoun-Antecedent Agreement

A pronoun must agree with its antecedent in number, gender, and person.

- A **pronoun** is a word used in the place of one or more nouns or pronouns.
- An **antecedent** is the noun or pronoun to which a pronoun refers.

Go to **Pronoun-Antecedent Agreement** in the **Grammar Studio** for more.

Read these sentences from "The Debt We Owe to the Adolescent Brain":

> **Dr. B. J. Casey is a professor of psychology at Weill Cornell Medical College. Her focus on adolescent brains includes those of humans and mice.**

The third-person singular pronoun *her* agrees with the antecedent *Dr. B. J. Casey*. Since the author used a feminine pronoun, readers can assume that Casey's gender must be female.

Indefinite pronouns do not refer to specific persons or things. The chart explains how to use indefinite pronouns and antecedents.

IF THE ANTECEDENT IS ...	THE PRONOUN SHOULD BE ...	EXAMPLE
a singular indefinite pronoun such as *each*, *either*, or *everything*	singular	Either is fine; just make sure you identify **it** in your notes.
a plural indefinite pronoun such as *both*, *many*, *several*, or *few*	plural	Both of the sources were relevant, but **they** didn't seem reliable.
an indefinite pronoun such as *all*, *some*, *none*, or *most* modified by a **prepositional phrase**, when the object of the preposition refers to a quantity or one part of something	singular	I thought I put all of my homework in my folder, but **it** isn't there now.
an indefinite pronoun such as *all*, *some*, *none*, or *most* modified by a **prepositional phrase**, when the object of the preposition refers to numbers of individual things	plural	Some of my library books are overdue, so I need to return **them** immediately.

Practice and Apply Correct the pronoun-antecedent error in each sentence and, where necessary, revise the verb to match in number.

1. All of the teens showed that she could adapt.
2. I dropped my phone, and now they won't work.
3. Everything is served and ready, but now they are getting cold.
4. I knew that all of the research was valid because they came from a reliable source.

from

BRONX MASQUERADE

Novel by **Nikki Grimes**

? ***ESSENTIAL QUESTION:***

How do your teenage years prepare you for adulthood?

QUICK START

Have you ever taken part in or attended a poetry reading? Discuss with your group what you do or do not like about reading, writing, or listening to poetry.

ANALYZE STRUCTURE

In a novel, **structure** involves the writer's arrangement of plot elements to tell a story. A **linear plot structure** tells the story in chronological order, following one or more protagonists, or main characters, as they deal with conflict. Some realistic fiction uses a **non-linear plot structure** in which the narrative jumps back and forth in time, using multiple protagonists, flashbacks, foreshadowing, parallel plot structures, or subplots. *Bronx Masquerade* has a non-linear plot structure and multiple first-person narrators. It includes both poetry and prose. The narration proceeds along parallel lines, with some time jumps. As you read, notice how each narrator provides his or her unique point of view.

GENRE ELEMENTS: NOVEL

- is a long work of fiction
- has a plot, or series of events, centered on a conflict that characters try to solve
- has a setting, or time and place of the action, that may affect the characters
- depicts characters who develop and change over time
- develops one or more themes, or messages about life

ANALYZE CHARACTERIZATION

The way a writer creates and develops characters is known as **characterization.** In *Bronx Masquerade*, the school setting influences the characters' values and beliefs and has an important effect on their growth and development. The characters are encouraged to see and understand one another in new ways and to examine their own goals and aspirations.

To understand the characters' conflicts, challenges, and goals, pay attention to the clues the author provides about them. Here are some examples from *Bronx Masquerade*.

CHARACTER CLUES	EXAMPLE
A character's own thoughts, speech, and actions	I refuse to give them new reasons to laugh at me. The Jolly Green Giant jokes are bad enough.
Thoughts, speech, and actions of other characters	Talk about nervous! Diondra's hands were shaking the whole time she was holding that poem. She sure spooks easy for somebody so tall. "Yo!" I said. "Take a deep breath. Ain't nobody going to hurt you here."
Description of a character's physical appearance	I've got good height and good hands, and that's a fact.

As you read *Bronx Masquerade*, think about ways in which the author uses characterization to convey meaning.

CRITICAL VOCABULARY

tirade **hunker** **snicker** **confide**

To see how many Critical Vocabulary words you already know, use them to complete the sentences.

1. When you __________ in a trusted friend, he or she can often help you understand how to deal with problems.
2. When I finished reading my poem, I was afraid that instead of applause, I would hear a __________ coming from the audience.
3. When Coach caught us making fun of the other team, she launched into a long __________ about sportsmanship.
4. If you want to be successful at something, you need to __________ down and work at it.

LANGUAGE CONVENTIONS

Modifiers Adjectives and adverbs are **modifiers** that can be used to show comparisons. Modifiers have **comparative** and **superlative** forms. The **comparative form** is used to compare two things, groups, or actions. The **superlative form** is used to compare more than two things, groups, or actions. Study these examples from *Bronx Masquerade*.

Comparative: "It's not much better at home."

Superlative: "I hate always being the tallest girl in school."

As you read, note how Nikki Grimes uses modifiers to show comparisons.

ANNOTATION MODEL

NOTICE & NOTE 

As you read *Bronx Masquerade,* note how the author uses different first-person points of view to reveal characters' conflicts, goals, relationships, and values. Also note your observations about characters, events, and setting. In the model, you can see one reader's notes about *Bronx Masquerade.*

1 If only I was as bold as Raul. The other day, he left one of his paintings out on Mr. Ward's desk where anybody could see it. Which was the point. He sometimes works at Mr. Ward's desk during lunch. The wet paintbrushes sticking up out of the jar are always a sign that he's been at it again. So of course, anybody who glances over in that direction will be tempted to stop by and look.

Diondra admires Raul's confidence. Is she jealous of his artistic talent?

BACKGROUND

Nikki Grimes *(b. 1950) was born in Harlem and spent some of her younger years in foster homes. At age 13, she gave her first public poetry reading at a local library named after the poet Countee Cullen. She was already steeped in the works of Cullen and other black poets of the era known as the Harlem Renaissance. These poets, she says, have been the primary influences in her work. Grimes has written prose and poetry for adults, children, and young adults, winning many honors and awards for her work.*

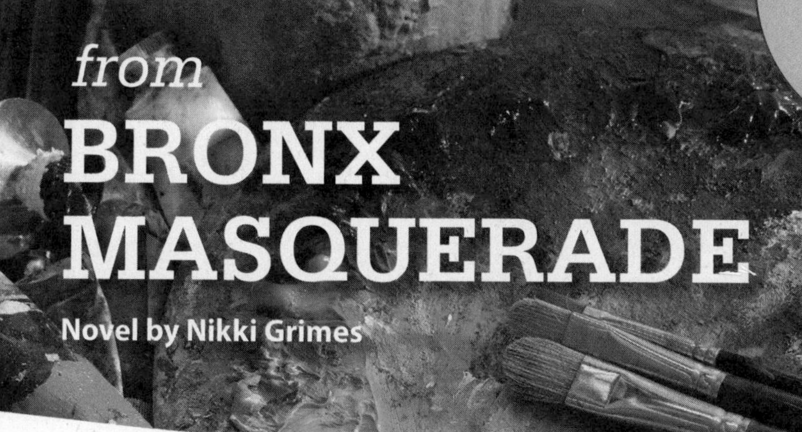

from BRONX MASQUERADE

Novel by Nikki Grimes

SETTING A PURPOSE

As you read, pay attention to ways in which the novel's setting influences the characters.

Diondra Jordan

1 If only I was as bold as Raul. The other day, he left one of his paintings out on Mr. Ward's desk where anybody could see it. Which was the point. He sometimes works at Mr. Ward's desk during lunch. The wet paintbrushes sticking up out of the jar are always a sign that he's been at it again. So of course, anybody who glances over in that direction will be tempted to stop by and look.

2 This particular painting was rough, but anyone could tell it was Raul. A self-portrait. He'll probably hang it in class. Back in September, Mr. Ward covered two of the classroom walls with black construction paper and then scattered paper frames up and down the walls, each one a different size and color. Now half the room looks sort of like an art gallery, which was the idea. We're supposed to use the paper frames for our work. Whether we put up poems or photographs or even paintings is up to us, so

Notice & Note

Use the side margins to notice and note signposts in the text.

ANALYZE CHARACTERIZATION

Annotate: Mark the words and phrases in paragraphs 1–2 that suggest Diondra's view of Raul.

Infer: What is Diondra's opinion of Raul?

long as the work is ours and we can tie it in with our study of the Harlem Renaissance.[1] I guess Raul's self-portrait fits, since we've been talking a lot about identity. He'll probably put it up next to his poem. You should have seen him hang that thing. You'd think he was handling a million-dollar masterpiece the way he took his time placing it just so. If you look close, you can see the smudges where he erased a word or two and rewrote it. Mr. Ward must be in shock. He can never get Raul to rewrite a lick of homework or anything else. And don't even talk to him about checking his spelling! He'll launch into a **tirade** on you in a minute. "What?" he'll snap. "You think Puerto Ricans can't spell?" Forget it. Anyway, I dare you to find one misspelled word in that poem of his! Maybe it's a visual thing. Maybe he wants his poem to look as good as his self-portrait. And it is good.

tirade
(tī´rād) *n.* A *tirade* is a long, angry speech.

3 I've never tried doing a self-portrait, but why not? I could maybe do one in charcoal. I like drawing faces in charcoal. I've been drawing since I can't remember when. Not that anyone here knows that, except Tanisha, and she found out by accident when she came to my house to study once and saw a couple of drawings hanging in my room. Mom loves my watercolors and she hung one in the living room, but it isn't signed. Nobody

ANALYZE CHARACTERIZATION
Annotate: Mark details in paragraphs 3–4 that help you understand Diondra's character.
Interpret: Why doesn't Diondra want her schoolmates to know about the art she creates?

[1] **Harlem Renaissance:** Between the end of World War I and the 1930s, black writers, artists, scholars, and musicians fled the repression of the Jim Crow South and moved to Harlem in New York City. The influential literary and cultural movement that began there is known as the Harlem Renaissance.

NOTICE & NOTE

ever mentions it, especially not my father. He's not too wild about my art. Mostly, he's disappointed, first off that I wasn't born a boy, and second that I won't play ball like one. I'm six feet tall, almost as tall as he, and he figures the height is wasted on me since I don't share his dreams of me going to the WNBA. I keep telling him not to hold his breath.

4 I hate always being the tallest girl in school. Everybody expects me to play basketball, so they pick me for their team, throw me the ball, and wait for me to shoot. Big mistake. I fumble it every time. Then they have the nerve to get mad at me, like I did it on purpose! But basketball is not my game. I have no game. I'm an artist, like Raul. The difference is, I don't tell anybody. I refuse to give them new reasons to laugh at me. The Jolly Green Giant jokes are bad enough.

5 Yeah, it's definitely time to try a self-portrait. I think I'll paint myself in front of an easel. With a basketball jersey sticking up out of the trash. Then I could hang it in Mr. Ward's class. See if anybody notices.

LANGUAGE CONVENTIONS

Annotate: Mark the superlative modifier in paragraph 4 that shows a comparison.

Analyze: How does the modifier help explain why Diondra resents the expectations people have of her?

NOTICE & NOTE

ANALYZE STRUCTURE

Annotate: Mark the repeated words and phrases in the poem.

Analyze: How does repetition in the poem emphasize the feelings Diondra described about poetry and art as a narrator?

ANALYZE CHARACTERIZATION

Annotate: Mark the words and phrases that show what Tyrone thinks about the readers.

Draw Conclusions: What do Tyrone's comments about Diondra and the other readers reveal about his personality?

OPEN MIKE

If

By Diondra Jordan

6 *If I stood on tiptoe*
reached up and sculpted
mountains from clouds
would you laugh out loud?

7 *If I dipped my brush in starlight*
painted a ribbon of night
on your windowsill
would you still laugh?

8 *If I drew you adrift*
in a pen and ink sea
in a raging storm
would you laugh at me?

9 *If I planted watercolor roses*
in your garden
would you laugh then?
Or would you breathe deep
to sample their scent?
I wonder.

Tyrone

10 If the sista read any faster, I'd be looking for her Supergirl cape. Talk about nervous! Diondra's hands were shaking the whole time she was holding that poem. She sure spooks easy for somebody so tall.

11 "Yo!" I said. "Take a deep breath. Ain't nobody going to hurt you here." She smiled a little and tried to slow down. But I swear that girl burned rubber getting back to her seat when she was through. I guess she's not exactly used to the limelight.

12 She's got plenty of company. Four more kids read their poetry for the first time today. They were shaking in their boots, but it was all good. I only had to tell one of them to loosen up. Guess you could call that progress!

Devon Hope

13 Jump Shot. What kind of name is that? Not mine, but try telling that to the brothers at school. That's all they ever call me.

14 You'd think it was written somewhere. Tall guys must be jocks. No. Make that tall *people,* 'cause Diondra's got the same problem. Everybody expects her to shoot hoops. The difference is, she's got no talent in that direction. Ask me, she's got no business playing b-ball. That's my game.

15 I've got good height and good hands, and that's a fact. But what about the rest of me? Forget who I really am, who I really want to be. The law is be cool, be tough, play ball, and use books for weight training—not reading. Otherwise, everybody gives you grief. Don't ask me why I care, especially when the grief is coming from a punk like Wesley. Judging from the company he keeps, he's a gangsta in sheep's clothing. I don't even know why he and Tyrone bother coming to school. It's clear they don't take it seriously, although maybe they're starting to. That's according to Sterling, who believes in praying for everybody and giving them the benefit of the doubt. I love the preacher-man, but I think he may be giving these brothers too much credit. Anyway, when I hang around after school and any of the guys ask me: "Yo, Devon, where you going?" I tell them I'm heading for the gym to meet Coach and work on my layup. Then once they're out the door, I cut upstairs to the library to sneak a read.

ANALYZE STRUCTURE

Annotate: Mark thoughts and ideas Devon expresses in paragraphs 13–15 that are similar to those that Diondra expresses.

Analyze: How is Devon's comparison of his situation with Diondra's an example of parallel plot structure?

NOTICE & NOTE

ANALYZE CHARACTERIZATION

Annotate: Mark details about setting in paragraph 19.

Infer: What do the descriptions of the library and the books of poetry reveal about Devon's character?

hunker
(hŭng´kər) *v.* To *hunker* down means to stay in a place and focus on a task for a period of time.

snicker
(snĭk´ər) *n.* A *snicker* is a superior, partially suppressed laugh.

AHA MOMENT

Notice & Note: In paragraphs 19–20, mark words and phrases that show a change in Devon's attitude.

Predict: How might this realization change things for Devon?

16 It's not much better at home. My older brother's always after me to hit the streets with him, calls me a girly man for loving books and jazz.

17 Don't get me wrong. B-ball is all right. Girls like you, for one thing. But it's not *you* they like. It's Mr. Basketball. And if that's not who you are inside, then it's not you they're liking. So what's the point? Still, I don't mind playing, just not all the time.

18 This year is looking better. My English teacher has got us studying the Harlem Renaissance, which means we have to read a lot of poetry. That suits me just fine, gives me a reason to drag around my beat-up volumes of Langston Hughes and Claude McKay. Whenever anybody bugs me about it, all I have to say is "Homework." Even so, I'd rather the brothers not catch me with my head in a book.

19 The other day, I duck into the library, snare a corner table, and **hunker** down with *3000 Years of Black Poetry*. Raynard sees me, but it's not like he's going to tell anybody. He hardly speaks, and he never hangs with any of the brothers I know. So I breathe easy. I'm sure no one else has spotted me until a head pops up from behind the stacks. It's Janelle Battle from my English class. I freeze and wait for the **snickers** I'm used to. Wait for her to say something like: "What? Coach got you *reading* now? Afraid you're gonna flunk out and drop off the team?" But all she does is smile and wave. Like it's no big deal for me to be in a library reading. Like I have a right to be there if I want. Then she pads over, slips a copy of *The Panther & the Lash* on my table, and walks away without saying a word. It's one of my favorite books by Langston Hughes. How could she know? Seems like she's noticed me in the library more often than I thought.

20 Janelle is all right. So what if she's a little plump? At least when you turn the light on upstairs, somebody's at home. She's smart, and she doesn't try hiding it. Which gets me thinking. Maybe it's time I quit sneaking in and out of the library like some thief. Maybe it's time I just started being who I am.

NOTICE & NOTE 

OPEN MIKE

Bronx Masquerade

By Devon Hope

21 *I woke up this morning*
exhausted from hiding
the me of me
so I stand here ***confiding***
there's more to Devon
than jump shot and rim.
I'm more than tall
and lengthy of limb.
I dare you to peep
behind these eyes,
discover the poet
in tough-guy disguise.
Don't call me Jump Shot.
My name is Surprise.

confide
(kən-fīd´) *v.* To *confide* means to share private or secret information.

CHECK YOUR UNDERSTANDING

Answer these questions before moving on to the **Analyze the Text** section on the following page.

1 Diondra secretly —

A is excited to present her poem

B is proud of her basketball skills

C sees herself as an artist

D enjoys being very tall

2 Devon secretly —

F hates being tall

G loves reading poetry

H feels jealous of Wesley

J wants to be friends with Tyrone

3 When Devon first sees Janelle Battle, he —

A worries she will tease him

B encourages her to read his poem

C reminds her they are in a class together

D feels relieved she does not recognize him

RESPOND

ANALYZE THE TEXT

Support your responses with evidence from the text. NOTEBOOK

1. **Evaluate** What do the various settings reveal about the characters? How do the settings influence the values and beliefs of the characters?
2. **Analyze** Reread Diondra's poem "If" and Devon's poem "Bronx Masquerade." What does the tone, or attitude, of each poem reveal about its writer's search for identity?
3. **Critique** What does Tyrone's perspective add to the plot development? Explain.
4. **Analyze** A masquerade is a costume party at which people wear masks. How does the author use the idea of a masquerade to pull together the different perspectives in the story?
5. **Notice & Note** What does the classroom project help Diondra and Devon realize about themselves and others in their struggle for self-expression? Cite examples to support your answer.

RESEARCH TIP

Be sure to assess the quality of any online sources you use. Personal websites may provide inaccurate or misleading information. The websites of museums, universities, and well-known encyclopedias are more likely to be reliable.

RESEARCH

Can writing to express your deepest feelings impact your physical and mental health? Research answers to the following questions about the relationship between expressive writing and health. Record what you learn in the chart.

QUESTION	ANSWER
How can expressive writing impact health?	
What are some specific possible effects of expressive writing?	

Extend In *Bronx Masquerade,* the students who share their writing experience social benefits as well as emotional benefits. Discuss with your group how poetry readings can help create understanding and a sense of community.

CREATE AND PRESENT

Write a Poem Write a poem about identity or the search for identity that you might perform at a poetry reading.

- ❑ Review the poems in the story for inspiration, and decide on the message you want to convey in your own poem.
- ❑ Think about the form and tone that will best suit your message.
- ❑ Consider using repetition to emphasize the most important idea.
- ❑ Have a partner read your poem and give you feedback. Make revisions, if necessary.

Present a Poem Recite your poem aloud for the class.

- ❑ With a partner, rehearse reading your poem aloud.
- ❑ Decide whether you will accompany the words with movement or gestures.
- ❑ Present your poem to the class, using appropriate volume, phrasing, and expression.

Go to the **Speaking and Listening Studio** for help giving presentations.

RESPOND TO THE ESSENTIAL QUESTION

? How do your teenage years prepare you for adulthood?

Gather Information Review your annotations and notes on *Bronx Masquerade*. Then add relevant details to your Response Log. As you determine which information to include, think about:

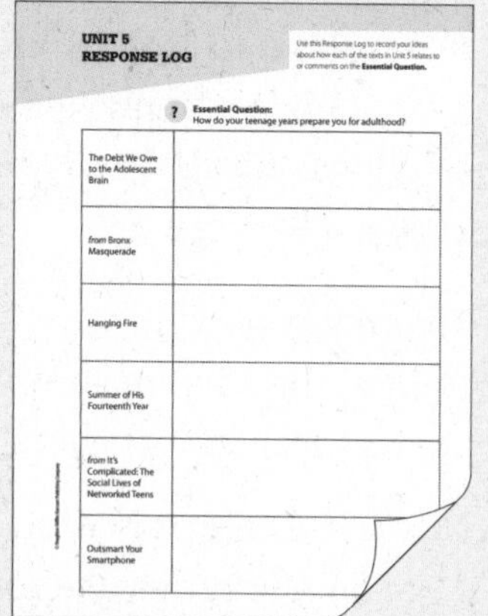
UNIT 5 RESPONSE LOG

Use this Response Log to record your ideas about how each of the texts in Unit 5 relates to or comments on the **Essential Question.**

? **Essential Question:** How do your teenage years prepare you for adulthood?

The Debt We Owe to the Adolescent Brain	
from Bronx Masquerade	
Hanging Fire	
Summer of His Fourteenth Year	
from It's Complicated: The Social Lives of Networked Teens	
Outsmart Your Smartphone	

- elements of *Bronx Masquerade* that make it realistic fiction
- how the story connects the perspectives of different characters
- the importance of resisting stereotypes and the value of self-expression

At the end of the unit, you may use your notes to help you write an argument.

ACADEMIC VOCABULARY

As you write and discuss what you learned from the selection, be sure to use the Academic Vocabulary words. Check off each of the words that you use.

- ❑ **debate**
- ❑ **deduce**
- ❑ **license**
- ❑ **sufficient**
- ❑ **trend**

CRITICAL VOCABULARY

WORD BANK
tirade
hunker
snicker
confide

Practice and Apply Use your understanding of the Vocabulary words to complete each sentence.

1. A basketball fan might launch into a **tirade** if . . .
2. A serious writer hates to hear **snickers** from the audience during a poetry reading because . . .
3. If you **confide** in a trusted friend, you are . . .
4. When you **hunker** down with a good book, you are . . .

VOCABULARY STRATEGY: Use Context Clues

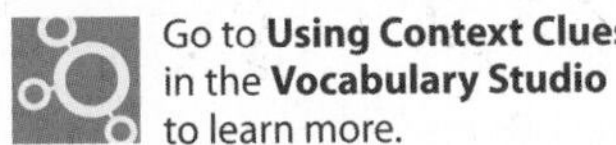
Go to **Using Context Clues** in the **Vocabulary Studio** to learn more.

Context clues can help you clarify the meaning of unfamiliar or ambiguous words. Some words have more than one meaning, and using context clues can help you determine which meaning of a multiple-meaning word is correct for the sentence. To use context clues, look at surrounding words and phrases to find hints about a word's meaning. Note this example of a multiple-meaning word from *Bronx Masquerade:*

So of course, anybody who glances over in that direction will be tempted to stop by and look.

This particular painting was rough, but anyone could tell it was Raul. A self-portrait. He'll probably hang it in class.

The context clues help you understand that the narrator is referring to what the painting looks like, not how it feels. You can tell from the context that *rough* means "unpolished," not "coarse to the touch."

Practice and Apply Find the following words in paragraphs 2, 4, and 15 of *Bronx Masquerade.* Identify context clues to each word's meaning, and write your guessed definition in the chart. Then look up each word in a dictionary to check your definition.

WORD	CONTEXT CLUES	GUESSED DEFINITION
gallery		
smudge		
launch		
fumble		
credit		

Go to **Using Modifiers Correctly** in the **Grammar Studio** for more help.

LANGUAGE CONVENTIONS: Modifiers

Modifiers are words or groups of words that change or limit the meanings of other words. Adjectives and adverbs are common modifiers. Modifiers can be used to compare two or more things. The form of a modifier shows the degree of comparison.

- The **comparative form** is used to compare two things, groups, or actions.
- The **superlative form** is used to compare more than two things, groups, or actions.

Regular forms of comparative modifiers are often preceded by the word "more" or "less" or end in *-er*. Superlative modifiers are often preceded by the word "most" or "least" or end in *-est*. There are also some irregular forms of comparative and superlative modifiers.

The chart shows some examples of each kind of modifier.

TYPE OF MODIFIER	EXAMPLE	COMPARATIVE FORM	SUPERLATIVE FORM
One syllable	tall fast	taller faster	tallest fastest
More than one syllable	graceful happy	more graceful happier	most graceful happiest
Irregular	good bad	better worse	best worst

Practice and Apply In their search for identity, the characters in *Bronx Masquerade* often compare themselves to others or to the expectations of others. Write a paragraph using the first-person point of view that describes the thoughts and feelings of a narrator. Use at least one comparative and one superlative modifier.

POEM

HANGING FIRE

by **Audre Lorde**

pages 355–357

COMPARE POEMS

The free verse poems you are about to read share the same topic. As you read, notice how each writer uses the elements of poetry to express the speaker's thoughts and feelings. After reading, you will collaborate with a small group on a final project.

ESSENTIAL QUESTION:

How do your teenage years prepare you for adulthood?

POEM

SUMMER OF HIS FOURTEENTH YEAR

by **Gloria Amescua**

pages 358–359

QUICK START

What pressures, emotions, and concerns make the teenage years challenging? Think about your own experience and write down your thoughts. Then share them with a partner or a small group.

ANALYZE FREE VERSE POETRY

Free verse is poetry that does not have regular patterns of rhythm or rhyme. The lines in free verse often flow more naturally than lines in rhymed, metrical poems; they may have a rhythm more like that of everyday speech. Although free verse does not have conventional meter, it may contain a variety of rhythmic and sound effects, such as repetition of syllables or words.

In free verse poetry, poets often create different effects by using a variety of line lengths and unexpected line breaks, playing with sense, grammar, and syntax. Line length is an essential element of the poem's meaning and rhythm. Lines may or may not break, or end, at the ends of sentences or grammatical units. A line break in the middle of a grammatical unit can create a meaningful pause or provide emphasis. Punctuation (such as dashes) or a lack of punctuation within or at the ends of sentences can help to convey the speaker's state of mind or emotions.

This chart summarizes some elements of free verse poetry:

ELEMENT	FREE VERSE	EFFECT
Meter	Lacks conventional meter	Flows like everyday speech
Line length	Uses a variety of line lengths; may follow no set pattern	Suggests pauses or emphasis; creates rhythm, drama, or other effects
Punctuation	May be omitted or used for emphasis	Omission of commas or periods suggests anxiety or fear; use of dashes provides emphasis

As you read "Hanging Fire" and "Summer of His Fourteenth Year," analyze how the poets use meter, line breaks, and punctuation to convey each speaker's feelings.

GENRE ELEMENTS: FREE VERSE

- like other poetic forms, uses imagery and figurative language to convey meaning and mood
- may use sound devices such as rhythm and repetition
- sounds like everyday speech, with no regular patterns of rhythm or rhyme
- expresses a theme, or a message about life
- includes a speaker who "talks" to the reader

GET READY

MAKE INFERENCES

Both "Hanging Fire" and "Summer of His Fourteenth Year" are poems about adolescence, but they offer starkly different points of view—in part because the speakers in the poems are quite different. In poetry, the **speaker** is the voice that "talks" to the reader and shares his or her point of view, similar to the narrator in a story. A poem's speaker may or may not be the poet.

Often readers must make an **inference,** or logical guess based on clues and their own knowledge and experience, in order to identify a poem's speaker. For example, text clues in "Hanging Fire" help readers figure out that the speaker is a teenager, and text clues in "Summer of His Fourteenth Year" help readers figure out that the speaker is an adult.

TEXT CLUES	WHAT YOU KNOW FROM EXPERIENCE	INFERENCE ABOUT THE SPEAKER
I am fourteen / and my skin has betrayed me / . . . and momma's in the bedroom / with the door closed. —from "Hanging Fire"	Many teens are dissatisfied with their appearance and feel they can't communicate with their parents.	a teen who feels unsettled and would like to be reassured by her mother
He tears at the seams / that hold us together / and sees in mother only ties to childhood —from "Summer of His Fourteenth Year"	Teens often challenge their parents as they begin to assert their independence.	a mother who is struggling with her son's growth into adulthood

As you read the two poems, think about what text-based inferences you can make about each speaker and her point of view.

ANNOTATION MODEL

NOTICE & NOTE

As you read each poem, you can mark details and make notes about the speaker in the side margin. The model shows one reader's notes about the first few lines of "Hanging Fire."

I am fourteen
and my skin has betrayed me
<u>the boy I cannot live without</u>
<u>still sucks his thumb</u>
in secret

I'm fourteen too, and my skin is breaking out.

This detail shows that the speaker feels more mature than the boy she likes.

BACKGROUND

Audre Lorde *(1934–1992) was born in New York City and found early success as a poet. One of her poems was published in a popular magazine while she was still in high school. In addition to poetry, Lorde went on to write acclaimed essays and novels. She won many important awards for her writing and worked to support several social causes close to her heart. Toward the end of her life, Lorde took the African name Gamba Adisa, which is believed to mean "she who makes her meaning clear."*

HANGING FIRE

Poem by Audre Lorde

PREPARE TO COMPARE

As you read the poem, look for details that help you understand the speaker's point of view.

I am fourteen
and my skin has betrayed me
the boy I cannot live without
still sucks his thumb
in secret
how come my knees are
always so ashy
what if I die
before morning
and momma's in the bedroom
with the door closed.

Notice & Note

Use the side margins to notice and note signposts in the text.

ANALYZE FREE VERSE POETRY

Annotate: Mark the first stanza with punctuation to show each separate thought.

Analyze: What effect does the poet create by omitting punctuation throughout the poem?

I have to learn how to dance
in time for the next party
my room is too small for me
suppose I die before graduation
they will sing sad melodies
but finally
tell the truth about me
There is nothing I want to do
and too much
that has to be done
and momma's in the bedroom
with the door closed.

Nobody even stops to think
about my side of it
I should have been on Math Team
my marks were better than his
why do I have to be
the one
wearing braces
I have nothing to wear tomorrow
will I live long enough
to grow up
and momma's in the bedroom
with the door closed.

MAKE INFERENCES

Annotate: In the last stanza, mark the phrases that describe the speaker's complaints. Then number the complaints.

Infer: What can you infer about the speaker based on the complaints she expresses?

CHECK YOUR UNDERSTANDING

Answer these questions about "Hanging Fire" before moving on to the next selection.

1 The speaker in the poem feels —

A proud to be a teenager

B dissatisfied with many aspects of her life

C optimistic about her future

D annoyed by her mother's strict rules

2 Which of the following is an example of personification?

F *my skin has betrayed me*

G *my room is too small for me*

H *they will sing sad melodies*

J *I should have been on Math Team*

3 The image of the closed bedroom door suggests that the speaker —

A is determined to be independent

B feels frustrated by her math scores

C craves attention from her mother

D has closed the door on her problems

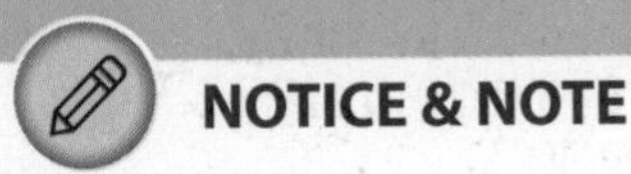

NOTICE & NOTE

BACKGROUND

__Gloria Amescua__ has been writing poems and stories since she was a child. Born in Austin, Texas, of Mexican American heritage, she became an inaugural member of Canto Mundo, a national Latino poetry community. Amescua has received numerous awards for her work, including the 2016 New Voices Award Honor. Much of her poetry revolves around the importance of family and community.

SUMMER OF HIS FOURTEENTH YEAR

Poem by Gloria Amescua

PREPARE TO COMPARE

As you read the poem, look for details that help you understand the speaker's point of view.

A deep, resonant voice answers when I call home.
My child is gone—
In his place is someone who resembles him,
only taller, size ten shoes.

Empty sneakers and dirty socks mark his passage down vacant halls.
He wanders aimlessly, flexing against walls grown too narrow,
as tensely strung as the tennis racket he grips,
as easily punctured as the deflated hand of the batting glove—
his passions are flung across the hours.

He leaves a trail of teenage hunger—
half empty Coke cans, stale chips in an unclosed bag.
Intermittent impulses, quickly sated,
rarely fill his emptiness,
never end his searching.

Notice & Note

Use the side margins to notice and note signposts in the text.

ANALYZE FREE VERSE POETRY

Annotate: Mark the end of the longest line. Notice that from this point the stanzas taper down to the shortest lines at the end of the poem.

Analyze: What does the shape of the poem on the page suggest about the boy's turbulent journey through adolescence to adulthood?

NOTICE & NOTE

Wailing guitars weave a cocoon
as he sits cross legged in a recess of his room,
his teeming emotions playing on a muted keyboard.

He tears at the seams
that hold us together
and sees in mother only ties to childhood
Choking him with nagging chores,
Cloying protection,
Closed doors.

Surliness is his knife
Cutting away the bonds.

Silence is his distance
Murmuring goodbye.

WORDS OF THE WISER

Notice & Note: In lines 18–23, mark a comment that reveals an important insight about the teen's behavior.

Analyze: What does this comment suggest the speaker understands about her son?

CHECK YOUR UNDERSTANDING

Answer these questions about "Summer of His Fourteenth Year" before moving on to the **Analyze the Text** section on the following page.

1 In "Summer of His Fourteenth Year," the speaker —

A is angry because her son misbehaves

B doesn't understand why her son is so restless

C is filled with grief because her son has died

D accepts that change is part of growing up

2 Which of the following is an example of simile?

F *as tensely strung as the tennis racket he grips*

G *Intermittent impulses, quickly sated*

H *Wailing guitars weave a cocoon*

J *Surliness is his knife*

3 An important message in "Summer of His Fourteenth Year" is that —

A teenagers are messy and inconsiderate

B it's impossible to communicate with a surly teenager

C leaving childhood behind is hard for parents and teens

D parents of teens are too nagging and protective

RESPOND

RESEARCH TIP

Remember that when you do research, you need to keep track of where you find information. For print sources, make a note of the title, author, publisher, publication date, and page number. For online sources, make a note of the website, URL, article title, author, and access date. Keep in mind that it's often wise to verify each fact you find in a second source. For example, if you used an online health website for teens, then you might confirm that information by looking in a second online source or in a print book.

ANALYZE THE TEXT

Support your responses with evidence from the texts. NOTEBOOK

1. **Infer** The figure of speech in which human qualities are given to an object, idea, or animal is called **personification.** What does the speaker's use of personification in the first stanza of "Hanging Fire" reveal about her self-image and her personality?
2. **Analyze** How does the use of repetition at the end of each stanza in "Hanging Fire" relate to the message of the poem?
3. **Analyze** Read stanzas 1–3 of "Summer of His Fourteenth Year" aloud. What effect does the author create by using dashes in these stanzas?
4. **Analyze** Reread lines 10–17 of "Summer of His Fourteenth Year." What effect is created by the poet's use of alliteration and rhyme in these two stanzas?
5. **Notice & Note** Reread lines 18–27 of "Summer of His Fourteenth Year." What does the insight in line 20 suggest about the mother's point of view on her son's "surliness" and "silence"?

RESEARCH

The teens in both poems suffer from mood swings and anxiety that are common during adolescence. Work in small groups to research causes of teenage mood swings and ways to cope with them. Locate the answers to the questions below and generate other questions to research and answer with your group.

QUESTION	ANSWER
What causes teenage mood swings?	
Does exercise help to prevent mood swings? If so, how?	
What are some good coping techniques for teens?	
How do sleep patterns affect mood?	

Extend With your group, select an appropriate method of sharing your research findings with the class. Then discuss what surprised you or what you found most interesting or noteworthy. Present the highlights of your research to the class.

CREATE AND PRESENT

Write a Response to Literature How do the poems connect to your own experiences? Capture your thoughts and feelings by freewriting about being a teenager. Then use ideas from your writing to decide what feelings and emotions you want to convey in a dramatic reading of one of the poems.

- ❑ Set a time limit of 10 or 15 minutes for your writing.
- ❑ Write without stopping to check spelling or grammar.
- ❑ At the end of your time limit, read what you wrote and underline all the ideas you would like to convey in a dramatic poetry reading.
- ❑ If your freewriting doesn't yield any useful ideas, try another session.

Go to the **Writing Studio** for more on writing a response to literature.

Give a Dramatic Reading Work with a partner to create a dramatic reading of one of the poems.

- ❑ Begin by discussing the impact of the poet's word choices.
- ❑ Practice reading each line of your chosen poem in a way that conveys your personal connection to the poem's meaning.
- ❑ Consider how you will accompany the words with movements or gestures.
- ❑ Take turns rehearsing with a partner, giving and receiving feedback.
- ❑ Present your dramatic reading to the class, using appropriate volume, phrasing, and expression.

Go to the **Speaking and Listening Studio** for more on reciting a poem.

RESPOND TO THE ESSENTIAL QUESTION

How do your teenage years prepare you for adulthood?

Gather Information Review your annotations and notes on "Hanging Fire" and "Summer of His Fourteenth Year." Then add relevant details to your Response Log. As you determine which information to include, think about:

- the fears and challenges that seem to overwhelm the teens in the poems
- what it means to become an adult
- how each writer treats the topic of adolescence

At the end of the unit, you can use your notes to help you write an argument.

ACADEMIC VOCABULARY

As you write and discuss what you learned from the two poems, be sure to use the Academic Vocabulary words. Check off each of the words that you use.

- ❑ **debate**
- ❑ **deduce**
- ❑ **license**
- ❑ **sufficient**
- ❑ **trend**

Collaborate & Compare

COMPARE POEMS

Both "Hanging Fire" and "Summer of His Fourteenth Year" are free verse poems about the problems and changes teenagers are going through. Although the poems are about the same topic, they differ in a number of ways. Ask yourself the following questions to compare the poems.

- ❑ How does the speaker's point of view affect the poem's theme?
- ❑ What effect does the form of the poem, or the arrangement of lines on the page, create for the reader?
- ❑ What do style elements such as word choice, syntax, and imagery contribute to the overall mood or tone?

In a small group, identify similarities and differences between the two poems. Record your thoughts in the chart.

	"Hanging Fire"	"Summer of His Fourteenth Year"
Point of View		
Form		
Impact of Style Elements		

ANALYZE THE TEXTS

Discuss these questions in your group.

1. **Compare** Which poem makes more effective use of figurative language and imagery? Cite text evidence in your discussion.
2. **Synthesize** Think about the different points of view in the poems. How do these different perspectives help the reader form a fuller understanding of the trials of adolescence?
3. **Cite Evidence** Both poems include the image of a closed door. Discuss what the closed door represents to the teen in each poem. Cite text evidence in your discussion.
4. **Connect** Discuss quotations or images from each poem that reflect feelings, worries, or problems that you have experienced or have observed in others. How does making these connections add to your understanding and appreciation of the poems?

CREATE AND PRESENT

Now your group can continue exploring these poems by comparing their styles and considering how each poem appeals to teen readers.

Go to the **Speaking and Listening Studio** for more on participating in a collaborative discussion and on making a presentation.

1. **Decide on the Most Important Style Elements** Think about the elements of each poem that appeal to you. Ask:
   - ❑ Which evokes stronger feelings?
   - ❑ Which style elements best connect with the reader?
   - ❑ What insights does each speaker offer?
   - ❑ What message about teenage years does each poem convey?
2. **Gather Information** With your group, discuss and list the examples of the most important style elements of each poem.

"Hanging Fire"	"Summer of His Fourteenth Year"

3. **Compare Styles** As a group, select two of the strongest style examples for each poem. Discuss how each style choice helps to convey the message of the poem.
4. **Present to the Class** Now present your views to the class. Cite text evidence from the poems to support your ideas. Discuss what each poem adds to your understanding about why teenage years can be so difficult. You may use charts or other visuals to help convey information to the class.

COLLABORATE & COMPARE

ARGUMENT

from IT'S COMPLICATED: The Social Lives of Networked Teens

by **danah boyd**

pages 367–371

COMPARE ARGUMENTS

As you read the next two selections, look for the main claim in each argument and the reasons and evidence given to support it. Then, consider whether your opinion of teens' media use has changed at all as a consequence of reading these arguments. After you read both selections, you will collaborate on a final project.

ESSENTIAL QUESTION:

How do your teenage years prepare you for adulthood?

ARGUMENT

OUTSMART YOUR SMARTPHONE

by **Catherine Steiner-Adair**

pages 379–385

It's Complicated

QUICK START

Poll a small group of friends or classmates to find out how many belong to social media networks. Discuss whether using social media creates a "complicated" social life, and why.

ANALYZE CLAIM AND EVIDENCE

A strong argument clearly states a **claim,** or position on an issue, and reasons to accept the claim. It provides sufficient relevant evidence to support those reasons. **Evidence** consists of the specific facts, examples, statistics, and expert opinions that support a claim.

Evidence is **relevant** if it supports the claim in a logical way. If it isn't based on sound reasoning and isn't clearly connected to the claim, then it is irrelevant. When you analyze an argument, watch out for irrelevant facts that don't actually support the claim.

Also watch out for **opinions,** or personal beliefs, that are stated without proof or facts to support them. The author should provide **citations**—references to research studies, books, and other sources—to back up his or her assertions. A citation may be provided directly in the text where the assertion is made. In other cases, the author may use numbered **footnotes** that cite sources at the bottom of each page, or **endnotes** that list sources at the end of the text.

GENRE ELEMENTS: ARGUMENT

- states a claim and reasons to support the claim
- includes facts and other evidence to support reasons
- may note objections to the claim or alternative viewpoints and explain why they should be dismissed
- takes many forms, such as editorials, feature articles, and essays

IDENTIFY COUNTERARGUMENT

A **counterargument** is an argument made to oppose another argument. Good writers understand the viewpoints of their intended audience or reader, and anticipate possible objections and alternative viewpoints and provide counterarguments for them. By doing so, they can show how weak an opposing viewpoint is, and they can clear the way for the reader to accept their position without reservations.

In the selection from *It's Complicated,* the author first introduces common parental concerns about teens' media use. Then she presents her own counterargument: she explains why adults really don't need to worry so much about these things. As you read, notice how the author does this and note relevant examples in a chart like this one.

PARENTS' CONCERNS ABOUT SOCIAL MEDIA USE	THE AUTHOR'S COUNTERARGUMENTS
"Why are my kids tethered to their cell phones or perpetually texting with friends even when they are in the same room?"	"Most teens are not compelled by gadgetry as such—they are compelled by friendship."

GET READY

CRITICAL VOCABULARY

relish **dynamic** **appease** **intimacy**

To see how many Critical Vocabulary words you already know, use them to complete the sentences.

1. The family __________ can make for some tense car rides.
2. Spending time alone with someone can create a feeling of __________.
3. After a fight with his sister, Jamie had to __________ her by letting her choose the movie.
4. Ana loves to travel, so she will __________ her upcoming trip.

LANGUAGE CONVENTIONS

Compound Sentences In a compound sentence like the following one, the clauses are joined with a conjunction to avoid producing a run-on sentence, and a comma is placed before the conjunction.

Some teens may reject the messages of adulthood that they hear or see, <u>but</u> they still learn from all of the signals around them.

As you read *It's Complicated,* notice other compound sentences in which the author uses a conjunction preceded by a comma.

ANNOTATION MODEL

NOTICE & NOTE

As you read, note the main claim on which the author's argument is based and how she supports it. In the model, you can see the notes one reader made while reading the first paragraph.

1 Developing meaningful friendships is a key component of the coming of age process. Friends offer many things—advice, support, entertainment, and a connection that combats loneliness. And in doing so, they enable the transition to adulthood by providing a context beyond that of family and home. Though family is still important, many teens relish the opportunity to create relationships that are not simply given but chosen.

"coming of age" = the transition to adulthood

I can relate to this. My friends are very important to me.

NOTICE & NOTE

BACKGROUND

When **danah boyd** *(b. 1977) was born, her mother named her "danah michele mattas." Her name was later changed and properly capitalized. As an adult, however, she legally renamed herself "danah boyd," taking her grandfather's last name, honoring her mother's original lowercase spelling, and satisfying her own "political irritation at the importance of capitalization." A Principal Researcher at Microsoft Research and a visiting professor at New York University, she has spent years researching how young people use social media.*

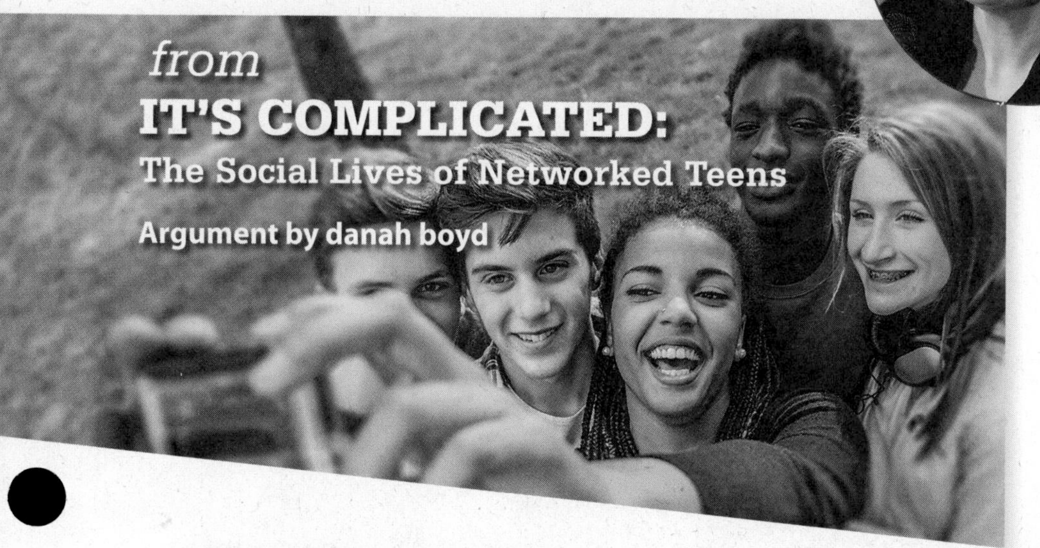

from IT'S COMPLICATED: The Social Lives of Networked Teens

Argument by danah boyd

PREPARE TO COMPARE

As you read boyd's argument, notice her tone, choice of language, and way of expressing herself to readers. Paying attention to these aspects of her writing will allow you to compare her style to that of Catherine Steiner-Adair, the author of the second argument.

1 Developing meaningful friendships is a key component of the coming of age process. Friends offer many things—advice, support, entertainment, and a connection that combats loneliness. And in doing so, they enable the transition to adulthood by providing a context[1] beyond that of family and home. Though family is still important, many teens **relish** the opportunity to create relationships that are not simply given but chosen.

2 The importance of friends in social and moral development is well documented. But the fears that surround teens' use of social media overlook this fundamental desire for social connection. All too often,

[1] **context:** setting or environment.

Notice & Note

Use the side margins to notice and note signposts in the text.

relish
(rĕl′ĭsh) *v.* To *relish* is to take great joy or pleasure in something.

ANALYZE CLAIM AND EVIDENCE

Annotate: In paragraph 2, mark the sentence that summarizes the main idea of this paragraph.

Infer: Might this be boyd's claim? If so, what should the rest of the argument show or prove?

parents project their values onto their children, failing to recognize that school is often not the most pressing concern for most teens. Many parents wonder: Why are my kids tethered to their cell phones or perpetually texting with friends even when they are in the same room? Why do they seem compelled to check Facebook hundreds of times a day? Are they addicted to technology or simply wasting time? How will they get into college if they are constantly distracted? I encounter these questions from concerned adults whenever I give public lectures, and these attitudes figure prominently in parenting guides and in journalistic accounts of teens' engagement with social media.

IDENTIFY COUNTER ARGUMENT

Annotate: In paragraph 3, mark all the statements that address the worries the author noted in paragraph 2.

Evaluate: Might a worried parent reading paragraph 3 be convinced by what she says here? Explain.

3 Yet these questions seem far less urgent and difficult when we acknowledge teens' underlying social motivations. Most teens are not compelled by gadgetry as such—they are compelled by friendship. The gadgets are interesting to them primarily as a means to a social end. Furthermore, social interactions may be a distraction from school, but they are

often not a distraction from learning. Keeping this basic social **dynamic** firmly in view makes networked teens suddenly much less worrisome and strange.

4 Consider, for example, the widespread concern over internet addiction. Are there teens who have an unhealthy relationship with technology? Certainly. But most of those who are "addicted" to their phones or computers are actually focused on staying connected to friends in a culture where getting together in person is highly constrained.[2] Teens' preoccupation[3] with their friends dovetails[4] with their desire to enter the public spaces that are freely accessible[5] to adults. The ability to access public spaces for sociable purposes is a critical component of the coming of age process, and yet many of the public spaces where adults gather—bars, clubs, and restaurants—are inaccessible to teens.

[2] **constrained:** limited.
[3] **preoccupation:** mental absorption or sole focus of attention.
[4] **dovetails:** fits together well, unites, or joins.
[5] **accessible:** open and available.

dynamic
(dī-năm´ĭk) *n.* A *dynamic* is a system in which conflicting or competing forces are at work.

LANGUAGE CONVENTIONS

Annotate: Mark the compound sentence in paragraph 4 that is joined by two conjunctions preceded by a comma.

Analyze: Is the word *and* necessary in this sentence? Explain what it adds, if anything.

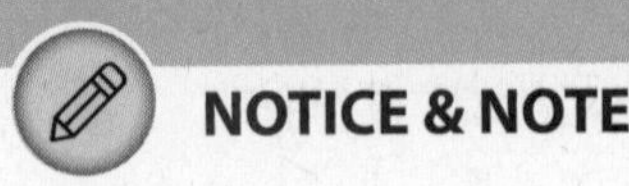

NOTICE & NOTE

IDENTIFY COUNTERARGUMENT

Annotate: In paragraph 5, mark the clues that help reveal what concern boyd is answering here.

Infer: Use these clues to infer the concern she is addressing in this paragraph. Then write this concern in the form of a question posed by a concerned parent.

appease
(ə-pēz´) *v.* To *appease* means to pacify or lessen the anger of, usually by making concessions.

CONTRASTS AND CONTRADICTIONS

Notice & Note: Mark the word in paragraph 7 that suggests the information boyd is about to share may come as a surprise to her readers.

Infer: Who would not already know this? What does this suggest about who boyd's intended readers are?

intimacy
(ĭn´tə-mə-sē) *n.* *Intimacy* refers to a state of personal closeness that is usually experienced in privacy.

5 As teens transition from childhood, they try to understand how they fit into the larger world. They want to inhabit public spaces, but they also look to adults, including public figures, to understand what it means to be grown-up. They watch their parents and other adults in their communities for models of adulthood. But they also track celebrities like Kanye West and Kim Kardashian to imagine the freedoms they would have if they were famous. For better or worse, media narratives also help construct broader narratives for how public life works. "Reality" TV shows like *Jersey Shore* signal the potential fun that can be had by young adults who don't need to **appease** parents and teachers.

6 Some teens may reject the messages of adulthood that they hear or see, but they still learn from all of the signals around them. As they start to envision themselves as young adults, they begin experimenting with the boundaries of various freedoms, pushing for access to cars or later curfews. Teens' determination to set their own agenda can be nerve-racking for some parents, particularly those who want to protect their children from every possible danger. Coming of age is rife with self-determination, risk taking, and tough decision-making.

7 Teens often want to be with friends on their own terms, without adult supervision, and in public. Paradoxically, the networked publics they inhabit allow them a measure of privacy and autonomy that is not possible at home where parents and siblings are often listening in. Recognizing this is important to understanding teens' relationship to social media. Although many adults think otherwise, teens' engagement with public life through social media is not a rejection of privacy. Teens may wish to enjoy the benefits of participating in public, but they also relish **intimacy** and the ability to have control over their social situation. Their ability to achieve privacy is often undermined by nosy adults—notably their parents and teachers—but teens go to great lengths to develop innovative strategies for managing privacy in networked publics.

8 Social media enables a type of youth-centric[6] public space that is often otherwise inaccessible. But because that space is highly visible, it can often provoke concerns among adults who are watching teens as they try to find their way.

[6] **youth-centric:** focused on young people's needs, concerns, and interests.

CHECK YOUR UNDERSTANDING

Answer these questions before moving on to the **Analyze the Text** section on the following page.

1 What is the author's main claim in paragraph 1?

A Coming of age is a lonely and difficult process.

B Friends offer one another advice, support, and fun.

C Teens have a profound need to make deep friendships.

D Family members become unimportant to teenagers.

2 In paragraph 7, the author encourages readers to recognize that —

F teens reject privacy in favor of socializing with their friends in a public space

G social media sites offer teens more privacy and autonomy than their homes do

H the nosiness of adults and siblings at home forces teens to rebel

J teens are better at using and manipulating social media than adults are

3 Which statement best characterizes the author's main message to people who worry about teens' use of social media?

A Instead of worrying about your teens, you should worry about developing your own life more fully.

B You need to recognize that it's safer for teens to meet online than it is to get together in person these days.

C Teens' use of social media is not so worrisome if you take into account how much they need friends at this age.

D The real danger of teens using social media is that it makes them want to live like celebrities who have lots of freedom.

ANALYZE THE TEXT

Support your responses with evidence from the text. NOTEBOOK

1. **Interpret** In paragraph 8, what reason does boyd give to explain why adults may be so worried about teenagers' use of social media?
2. **Analyze** Review paragraph 6. Why might the author have chosen to provide this information? Is it relevant to her argument or not? Explain.
3. **Analyze** Reread the last sentence in paragraph 5. Is this statement relevant to the author's argument? Explain.
4. **Evaluate** Does boyd provide sufficient relevant reasons and evidence to support her position? Cite evidence to support your response.
5. **Notice & Note** In paragraph 7, identify the two seemingly contradictory things that teens want. How does this idea counter the assumption that many adults make about social media use?

RESEARCH TIP

When investigating a field of study such as psychology, in which ongoing research constantly prompts experts to revise older ideas and propose new ones, only the most recent information may be currently accepted as true. Therefore, when doing such research, check the date of your sources to make sure they are as current as possible.

RESEARCH

Research social media use to learn more about the amount of time teens and adults spend online and the effects of doing so, if any. Try to locate different types of evidence, such as facts, statistics, research studies, and quotes from experts. Use the chart below to record the evidence and, if it's related to boyd's argument, explain whether it supports or contradicts her argument.

EVIDENCE	SUPPORTS OR CONTRADICTS BOYD'S ARGUMENT?

Extend Share your evidence with a small group. Discuss which pieces of evidence are the most persuasive and why. Then, develop a claim about social media use that you could support with this evidence.

CREATE AND PRESENT

Write an Opinion Piece Write a one- or two-paragraph opinion piece in which you take a position regarding social media use at school. Use evidence from *It's Complicated* and your own research to support your points.

- ❑ Introduce the topic, state your position on it, and give one good reason to accept your viewpoint. Also state an opposing viewpoint and make a strong counterargument.
- ❑ Alternatively, begin by introducing the topic and the prevailing viewpoint that differs from your own. Present a reason to reject or modify that viewpoint, and conclude by stating your position.
- ❑ Use facts, quotations, and other relevant evidence from the text and your research to support your opinions.
- ❑ In your conclusion, tell readers what you think they should believe, why they should believe it, and what to do because they now hold this belief.

Go to **Writing Arguments** in the **Writing Studio** for help with writing an opinion piece.

Advocate a Position Deliver a multimodal presentation of your argument to the class by adding an illustration, a poster, a software demonstration, or sound effects to more effectively convey your message. Use appropriate eye contact, speaking rate, volume, enunciation, and gestures to communicate your argument effectively. After giving your presentation, respond to any questions or comments your classmates may have.

Go to **Using Media in a Presentation** in the **Speaking and Listening Studio** for more help.

RESPOND TO THE ESSENTIAL QUESTION

How do your teenage years prepare you for adulthood?

Gather Information Review your annotations and notes on *It's Complicated*. Then, add relevant details to your Response Log. To decide what to include, think about:

- the author's information about how teens develop into adults
- what the author says matters most to teens and why
- what you have learned about the process of "coming of age" through research and firsthand observation

At the end of the unit, use your notes to help you write an argument.

ACADEMIC VOCABULARY

As you write and discuss what you learned from the argument, be sure to use the Academic Vocabulary words. Check off each of the words that you use.

- ❑ **debate**
- ❑ **deduce**
- ❑ **license**
- ❑ **sufficient**
- ❑ **trend**

RESPOND

CRITICAL VOCABULARY

WORD BANK
relish
dynamic
appease
intimacy

Practice and Apply Demonstrate your understanding of the Critical Vocabulary words by answering the following questions.

1. What would be more likely to **appease** a coach's irritation with you, showing up to practice sessions early or arriving late? Why?
2. If you **relish** a song, are you more likely to want to learn it or forget it? Why?
3. What **dynamic** does boyd think parents ought to keep in mind when evaluating their teens' use of social media? Why?
4. Would **intimacy** be more or less likely to strengthen a relationship? Why?

VOCABULARY STRATEGY: Context Clues

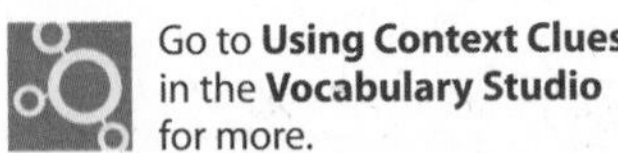
Go to **Using Context Clues** in the **Vocabulary Studio** for more.

You know that a word's **context,** or the text that comes before and after it, can help you figure out its meaning. But did you know that some of the clearest context clues are **synonyms**—words with the same meaning as the unfamiliar word—and **antonyms**—words with the opposite meaning? When one of these turns up in a sentence, it can immediately help you clarify the meaning of a word that is unfamiliar or that has multiple meanings. The chart shows an example.

Any of the following words can be a clue to the presence of a synonym: *similarly, as, like, or.* These words and phrases can signal the presence of an antonym: *but actually, whereas, on the other hand, by contrast.*

CONTEXT SENTENCE	ANALYSIS
Teens may wish to enjoy the benefits of participating in public, but they also relish intimacy and the ability to have control over their social situation.	*In public* and *intimacy* are antonyms, as signaled by the word *but.* Since *in public* means "open to the knowledge or judgment of all," you can infer that *intimacy* is the opposite of that, and means something like "privacy."

Practice and Apply Imagine you need to explain social media and smartphones to a younger person unfamiliar with the technology. Write four sentences that you might use in your explanation. In each sentence, use a synonym or an antonym to clarify the meaning of one unfamiliar or difficult word. You may use these sentence frames if you like:

- ❑ The [unfamiliar word], or [synonym], is something that ___________.
- ❑ You might think that [clause containing unfamiliar word], but actually [clause containing antonym of unfamiliar word].

LANGUAGE CONVENTIONS: Compound Sentences

A **clause** is a group of words that contains a subject and a predicate. A **compound sentence** consists of two or more **independent clauses,** or clauses that can each stand alone as a sentence. There are two ways to correctly form and punctuate a compound sentence.

Go to **The Sentence** in the **Grammar Studio** for more on punctuating compound sentences.

You may join independent clauses by using a coordinating conjunction (*and, but, or, nor, yet, for,* or *so*) preceded by a comma (,).

> **Furthermore, social interactions may be a distraction from school, but they are often not a distraction from learning.**

You may also join two independent clauses with a semicolon (;).

> **Furthermore, social interactions may be a distraction from school; they are often not a distraction from learning.**

If you do not join clauses correctly, you will have a **run-on sentence,** which is a grammatical error. Using only a comma between the two clauses, without a coordinating conjunction, creates a run-on error called a **comma splice.**

Practice and Apply Rewrite the following sentences to correct run-ons and add any missing punctuation. Then look back at the opinion piece you wrote to find and fix any comma splices and run-on sentences you may have created.

1. You may be preoccupied by social media but you aren't necessarily addicted to it.
2. The sleek smartphones are alluring, they glow, *ping,* and provide access to movies, music, games, and friends.
3. The two friends were constantly connected on social media they even stayed connected while they were asleep.
4. Theresa's mother watches TV all the time but she criticizes Theresa for being online for more than an hour.
5. Raj keeps his social network open on his computer he hides it with the screen containing his homework.

COLLABORATE & COMPARE

ARGUMENT

OUTSMART YOUR SMARTPHONE

by **Catherine Steiner-Adair**

pages 379–385

COMPARE ARGUMENTS

Now that you've read *It's Complicated,* read an argument that takes the opposite position. As you read, pay attention to how well the evidence in "Outsmart Your Smartphone" supports the writer's claim. Also notice whether the evidence ever causes you to question your opinion on this matter. After you are finished, you will collaborate on a final project that involves analyzing both texts.

ESSENTIAL QUESTION:

How do your teenage years prepare you for adulthood?

ARGUMENT

from

IT'S COMPLICATED: The Social Lives of Networked Teens

by **danah boyd**

pages 367–371

Outsmart Your Smartphone

QUICK START

Do you ever feel that technology and social media are having a negative impact on your life? Make a list of some possible drawbacks.

ANALYZE STRUCTURE

All arguments take a position on an issue—that is, they make a **claim.** Writers almost always state their claims early in their arguments. However, they may present their reasons and evidence to support the claim in a variety of ways. In "Outsmart Your Smartphone," the author uses a cause-effect structure. Specifically, she tries to convince readers that five kinds of effects result from social media use. She introduces each with a transition such as *first, second,* and *third*. As you read, look for these transitions and the cause-effect relationships they introduce.

GENRE ELEMENTS: ARGUMENT

- makes a claim
- supports claim with reasons and evidence
- notes counter claims and provides counterarguments to disprove them
- for topics involving society or psychology, may cite scientific studies as evidence

ANALYZE RHETORICAL DEVICES

Rhetorical devices are techniques writers use to enhance their arguments and communicate effectively. Several of these techniques are defined in the chart. As you read "Outsmart Your Smartphone," add more examples from the text. Then consider why the author might have used these devices. What audience is she trying to reach?

RHETORICAL DEVICE	DEFINITION	EXAMPLE
Analogy	A point-by-point comparison between two things that are alike in some respect	Paragraph 11: The author compares learning conversation skills to learning to drive.
Direct address	Talking directly to the reader, often using the pronoun *you*	Paragraph 2: "You can use smartphones and social media to build healthy relationships and a sense of belonging."
Juxtaposition	The placement of two or more things side by side to show their similarities and/or differences	
Rhetorical question	A question that has such an obvious answer that it requires no reply	

Being aware of rhetorical devices helps you recognize how the author is trying to persuade you. Watching out for **logical fallacies,** or misuses of logic, helps you decide whether the argument is sound. One kind of fallacy is **circular reasoning,** which is supporting a statement simply by repeating it in different words.

GET READY

CRITICAL VOCABULARY

perspective	**deliberate**	**impulsive**
stimulant	**anonymous**	**inhibited**

To see how many Critical Vocabulary words you already know, answer the following questions.

1. What does asking for someone's **perspective** on a topic mean you want to know? Why?
2. If someone took a **stimulant,** would he or she be likely to fall asleep immediately? Why?
3. Why might a **deliberate** comment that's hurtful be worse than an **impulsive** one?
4. If you wanted to be an **anonymous** source for a news article, how might you react to seeing your full name in the article? Why?
5. Which is more likely to make you feel **inhibited:** a stern look from your teacher or a kind smile? Why?

LANGUAGE CONVENTIONS

Correct Capitalization In this lesson, you will learn to correctly capitalize proper nouns, such as the names of organizations, and hyphenated words that begin sentences. The author models proper capitalization in sentences such as this one:

Twenty-four percent of them say they are online "almost constantly," according to a 2015 study by the Pew Research Center.

ANNOTATION MODEL

NOTICE & NOTE 

As you read "Outsmart Your Smartphone," mark the text to trace the writer's argument. This model shows one reader's notes.

1 Adolescence has always been a hero's journey of growing independence, exploration, and self-discovery. When smartphones swept onto the scene in 2008, teenagers used them for familiar purposes—to connect to each other and share interests out of adults' view. [But was the technology itself significantly changing the landscape of teen life?] At first, people took sides on this issue based on their own gut feelings. Now with more than a decade of experience, it's possible to hold a more informed perspective on the effects of engaging with social media and life online. . . .

Will the argument give the author's answer to this question?

She may provide scientific evidence to replace "gut feelings."

BACKGROUND

Catherine Steiner-Adair *is an internationally recognized clinical psychologist, consultant, and speaker and the author of the award-winning book* The Big Disconnect. *She has a different perspective on teenagers and technology than danah boyd in* It's Complicated. *In this argument, Steiner-Adair explores problems associated with teenagers' use of social media and smartphones.*

OUTSMART YOUR SMARTPHONE

Argument by Catherine Steiner-Adair

PREPARE TO COMPARE

As you read, analyze both the author's style and the argument she makes. Do all the reasons given by the author support her claim? Is there sufficient relevant evidence to support her position?

1 Adolescence has always been a hero's journey of growing independence, exploration, and self-discovery. When smartphones swept onto the scene in 2008, teenagers used them for familiar purposes—to connect to each other and share interests out of adults' view. But was the technology itself significantly changing the landscape of teen life? At first, people took sides on this issue based on their own gut feelings. Now with more than a decade of experience, it's possible to hold a more informed **perspective** on the effects of engaging with social media and life online. In writing my book *The Big Disconnect: Protecting Childhood and Family Relationships in the Digital Age,* I studied the current research and interviewed hundreds of teenagers around the country. I can say without hesitation that though social media is a useful and enticing tool, it poses unique risks to adolescent well-being.

Notice & Note

Use the side margins to notice and note signposts in the text.

ANALYZE RHETORICAL DEVICES

Annotate: In paragraph 1, mark two ways the author identifies for arriving at an opinion on an issue.

Infer: What might be the author's purpose for using this juxtaposition?

perspective
(pər-spĕk′tĭv) *n.* A *perspective* is a viewpoint on or understanding of something.

NOTICE & NOTE

ANALYZE STRUCTURE

Annotate: Mark all the positive effects of using social media listed in paragraph 2.

Infer: How might identifying these benefits at the beginning of her argument help the author achieve her purpose?

CONTRASTS AND CONTRADICTIONS

Notice & Note: Mark the two sentences in paragraph 3 that introduce a sharp contrast or contradiction.

Connect: What earlier juxtaposition is the author echoing and expanding upon here? Explain.

2 The benefits of social media are obvious. You can use smartphones and social media to build healthy relationships and a sense of belonging. You can partner with others to help, share, volunteer, collaborate. Never before have middle school students been able to take a class with students in China. You can get in touch with total strangers who like the same rock band, write fan fiction together with people anywhere in the world, or join an online gaming group. Texting and social networking sites make it easier to connect with kids right where you are, too. Social networking lets you get together with friends where your parents aren't around. Expressing yourself, figuring out who you are and developing a sense of self and identity that's separate from your parents and family are important parts of adolescent development.

3 But there's more to the story. While it's tempting to believe that social media is just a new version of what's always been, with the same dangers and benefits, studies suggest that's just not true. A growing body of scientific evidence and everyday experience show that social media is not simply a natural and healthy extension of teens' social lives and development. It can negatively affect the brain and behavior in ways that mimic addiction, adversely affect learning, distort normal aspects of social and emotional development, and increase anxiety. There is too much research and too much everyday evidence now for us to ignore the risks. You have to approach social media with restraint and caution if you want to avoid harm.

4 How and how often you use social media matters. Ninety-two percent of teens report going online daily. Twenty-four percent of them say they are online "almost constantly," according to a 2015 study by the Pew Research Center. More than half (fifty-six percent) of teens, ages thirteen to seventeen, go online several times a day. Most use mobile devices and three-quarters of the teens say they have access to a smartphone. The more time you spend texting or online, the greater the risks of harm. This is especially concerning in

adolescence. It's a critical window of time for brain growth, physical development, and social and emotional development.

5 Social media is a **stimulant** to the brain. Texting and other use triggers release of dopamine, a natural chemical that produces a pleasurable sensation that most brains crave to repeat. But the more you use social media, the more you want to use it, and that impulse can override the **deliberate** decision-making activity of the part of the brain called the prefrontal cortex. It also creates a sense of urgency. You feel compelled to react or respond right away and hit send.

6 The combination of the stimulants to the brain and the fact that you feel **anonymous** or at a distance from the person you're communicating with can lead you to behave differently than you would face to face. You become **impulsive,** quick to act and react, even when it carries a risk. You feel less **inhibited,** more likely to say mean or careless things without a thought to the impact of your words, or the consequences. It's easy to say things you later wish you hadn't. On the receiving (or waiting) end, you feel anxious when someone doesn't respond right away, or you feel antsy or bored when there's a lull in communication. Every ping, buzz, or text you send or receive keeps you hooked.

7 A false sense of privacy can trick you into thinking it's safe to share anything—or text or post private or inflammatory[1] things. Plenty of teens have found themselves entangled in social drama made worse when posts went viral. At the most tragic extreme, social media has provided a platform for cyberbullying. In a study of teens and social media use, nine out of ten teens reported that they had seen bullying online.

8 Bullying gets a lot of attention and for good reason, but let's look at other common social media behaviors or beliefs with negative consequences.

9 First, texting is easier than talking and seems like the same thing, but it isn't. Social media is no substitute for face-to-face conversation or hanging out, a handshake or comforting hug, shared laughter or even shared quiet time. Texting, tweeting, email and other text-only forms of messaging eliminate two essential aspects of human communication: the power of voice and the ability to see the impact of your words.

10 Tone of voice gives meaning to our words. You might use the phrase "I hate you!" jokingly to mean "I'm so jealous of you!" but what if that's not clear? Even a simple text like "sorry" can be difficult to decipher—are you being snarky or sincere?

[1] **inflammatory:** provocative; likely to provoke a strong reaction.

NOTICE & NOTE 

stimulant
(stĭm´yə-lənt) *n.* A *stimulant* is an agent that excites or temporarily speeds up mental and/or physical functions.

deliberate
(dĭ-lĭb´ər-ĭt) *adj. Deliberate* decision-making activity is the process of making a choice only after carefully considering its likely effects.

anonymous
(ə-nŏn´ə-məs) *adj.* To be *anonymous* means to be unknown or unidentified by name.

impulsive
(ĭm-pŭl´sĭv) *adj.* To be *impulsive* means to act quickly, before thinking about the consequences.

inhibited
(ĭn-hĭb´ĭt-əd) *adj.* If you feel *inhibited,* you feel restrained, held back, or self-conscious.

ANALYZE RHETORICAL DEVICES

Annotate: Review paragraphs 5 and 6. Mark the sentences in which the author uses direct address.

Analyze: What is the impact of using direct address to convey this particular information?

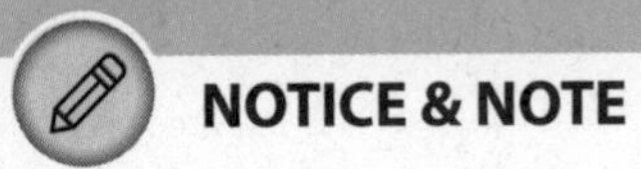

NOTICE & NOTE

ANALYZE RHETORICAL DEVICES

Annotate: Mark the analogy in paragraph 11.

Infer: Think about who would be able to relate to this analogy. For what audience is the author most likely writing? Explain.

ANALYZE STRUCTURE

Annotate: In paragraph 13, underline the effect of "constant connectivity," according to the author. Then circle what that, in turn, can cause.

Evaluate: Does this cause-effect relationship help the author support her argument? Explain.

LANGUAGE CONVENTIONS

Annotate: Mark the capitalized proper nouns in paragraph 14.

Infer: Why is it incorrect to capitalize words such as *of* in the name of an institution?

Distanced from the impact your words have on others, you can't see their reaction or correct a misunderstanding.

11 Also, when texting takes the place of face-to-face talking, you don't get the real-time practice of conversation skills and the confidence that goes with it. You can't get a driver's license just by passing an online test. You have to log hours of actual driving time to develop the real-time, real life skills to drive. The same in-real-life practice is required for the social and emotional skills you need to navigate life. Direct communication is one of the most important.

12 Second, social media expands social networks, but not necessarily the deeper stuff of meaningful friendship. Research and life experience tell us that "likes" and casual online "friends" are no substitute for friendship. Friendship includes a deeper knowing of one another, shared respect and trust, and acceptance. It's easy to think that your "street smarts"—your ability to assess if someone is trustworthy or not—work just as well on social media sites as in real life, but research tells us that we tend to trust too easily online. Social media was designed to be a way to connect people. But it also has put a crimp in teens' ability to connect in deep and meaningful ways. Some find it harder to be emotionally vulnerable and emotionally honest with one another. Emotional growth and learning how to be a partner in relationship are hard work, and part of natural development that emerges in adolescence. But it takes time and practice to develop that natural capacity. The default text of *hey what's up?* mutes those moments for more textured conversations. You might find it easier to say things that are serious and important to you by texting, where you don't feel as vulnerable as you might face to face. Ultimately, though, it's important in life to be able to say directly to people what's on your mind and what's in your heart, and have difficult conversations. That takes practice.

13 Third, the "everywhere, always on" presence of social media and life online creates new kinds of psychological issues. The constant connectivity can create psychological dependence. This can cause anxiety when you're separated from your phone or unable to go online. Some teens experience a form of separation anxiety if they don't have their phone, or if an adult takes it away.

14 If you are "always on," the fear of missing out often creates anxiety with no relief. On social media, like never before, you can see every party, every event, every "inside joke" that you are not a part of. You see the endless stream of nasty comments or trending gossip and might start to quietly fear you'll become

the target of it. A growing number of studies have also found that looking at "perfect" photos of other people may increase anxiety and make people feel bad about themselves. A 2016 study by researchers at the University of Cologne in Germany described so-called Facebook envy and depression as a serious concern, echoing other studies of social media's negative effects on mental health. Students often tell me that class outings or summer camp where cell phones weren't allowed were "the best ever." Why? Because after a short withdrawal period, classmates enjoyed the freedom from the pressures of social media and the fun of being together.

15 Fourth, social media distraction has a negative effect on learning and on grades. When you multitask on different devices or online activities your brain makes you feel really powerful. It makes you think you can multitask

effectively. That's one reason it's so hard to listen to teachers or parents when they say don't do it. But actually, in your brain, multitasking on digital devices takes away from your attention to any one thing with a continuous stream of mini-interruptions.

16 Studies show that multitasking with social media makes homework take longer. It also weakens short-term and long-term memory. Students who used social networking scored twenty percent lower on tests, and had lower grades compared to those that stayed off social media until their work was done. Even when users just go on social media for a "quick" break, the average amount of time off their task is typically twenty to twenty-five minutes. That increases the time it takes to complete a two-hour task by thirty percent. A study conducted by scientists at University of Texas-Austin in 2017 found that just having your smartphone nearby reduces cognitive performance—how well your brain can think and learn—even when the phone is silent or out of sight.

NOTICE & NOTE

ANALYZE STRUCTURE

Annotate: In paragraph 14, mark the sentences that present scholarly research.

Analyze: Which point does this evidence support?

ANALYZE RHETORICAL DEVICES

Annotate: Underline the effect the author introduces in paragraph 15, and circle the information she provides to support it.

Analyze: Has the author provided sufficient evidence to support her point, or does the paragraph use circular reasoning? Explain.

NOTICE & NOTE

17 Fifth, the distraction of social media can pull you away from your best self, drawing you into the online culture where it's cool to be cruel or disingenuous,[2] and where snarky, mean posts get lots of "likes." This dark side of social networking is not just about meanness. It's that social media cultivates an image-based value system that creates unrealistic expectations and rewards shallowness. As shaming, hate-talk, and other destructive behaviors online get worse, social media becomes increasingly antisocial.

18 A generation ago, parents worried about their kids watching too much TV, which was also seen as spreading poor values. Today's "screen time" is even more problematic. While TV and online entertainment both use screens, our brains don't connect with them in the same ways. TV is at a distance, compared to the close-up visual stimulation on a smartphone or computer screen. Think of how different it feels to binge-watch on the big TV screen versus on your smartphone. TV also tends to be a more social activity. You watch with other people, share the experience, and perhaps talk as you do so.

19 All of this does not mean we must abandon social media entirely, along with those prosocial benefits it does have. But you need self-awareness so that you use this tool to be your best self, make the most of your education, and protect your brain and your own well being. It's important not to let any new app, virtual reality, or whatever the next tech innovation is delete what science has told us for years and still stands true: As a species, we thrive in the context of healthy relationships. We need to manage our use of social media to create supportive connections for learning and life.

20 For example, you don't have to be part of every social media stream your friends are. Be conscious of how much time you're online and limit yourself. Take breaks. Take off one day a week or at mealtimes. Even when it seems easier to stay home and text with your friends, make an effort to get together somewhere and see them instead. If your school allows

ANALYZE RHETORICAL DEVICES

Annotate: An imperative sentence is a direct command, instruction, or request. Mark the imperative sentences In paragraph 20.

Analyze: What rhetorical device are these sentences examples of?

[2] **disingenuous** (dĭs´ĭn-jĕn´yo͞o-əs): insincere, false.

students to use phones, exercise restraint. Resist the temptation to multitask when you need to have singular focus on your homework. Educate your peers—remember that just having your phone on your desk or in your backpack interferes with your attention.

21 Adolescents have always been the pioneers in evolving cultures, and today's teens are, too. Given the information and education needed to make sound choices, you'll learn to master the social media tool and be able to share tips with the generations before you and after you, as well.

CHECK YOUR UNDERSTANDING

Answer these questions before moving on to the **Analyze the Text** section on the following page.

1 Which is the writer's main claim in "Outsmart Your Smartphone"?

A *As a species, we thrive in the context of healthy relationships.*

B *Social media . . . poses unique risks to adolescent well-being.*

C *The constant connectivity can create psychological dependence.*

D *You might find it easier to say things that are serious . . . by texting.*

2 The author uses the statistics in paragraph 4 to suggest that —

F almost all teens use or have access to social media in their daily lives and are therefore affected by it

G adolescence is a time when people develop mentally, physically, socially, and emotionally

H a significant percentage of teenagers overestimate the amount of time they spend online each day

J teens can become physically addicted to social media because it triggers the release of dopamine

3 In paragraph 18, the author suggests that although TV and online entertainment both use screens —

A watching TV is a more dangerous habit than going online

B going online doesn't result in the acquisition of poor values

C dramas on big screens feel more real than those on smartphones

D watching TV is not as engaging or as isolating as being online

RESPOND

ANALYZE THE TEXT

Support your responses with evidence from the text. NOTEBOOK

1. **Identify** What is the author's main claim about social media? How does the information in paragraph 2 relate to the claim?
2. **Analyze** Are the statistics in paragraph 4 relevant to the author's claim? Explain.
3. **Cause/Effect** In your own words, explain the cause-effect relationship the author describes in paragraph 5.
4. **Compare** How does the author's use of direct address in paragraphs 5–6 differ from her use of that same rhetorical device in paragraph 20?
5. **Notice & Note** What contradiction does the author explore in paragraph 12, and why is it important?

RESEARCH TIP

When researching online, you may quickly find information on a wiki—a website published collaboratively by online users. While it may be a place to begin exploring a subject, a wiki is not a source you should rely upon. It is not credible because anyone can write or edit the articles there—including people with a bias or personal agenda, vandals with malicious intent, and individuals who lack accurate information. Always verify information in multiple credible sources before accepting it as true.

RESEARCH

What topics mentioned in this argument intrigued you? Smartphones, social media sites, the effects of social network addiction? Research one of these or a related topic. Use the chart to note your findings. Be sure to use credible sources and note those sources for your records.

TOPIC	FACTS	SOURCES
Smartphones		
Social Networking Sites		
Social Network Addiction		

Connect In a small group, share what you've learned from your research. If group members' facts conflict, use the credibility of sources to decide which facts to believe. As you discuss, note what you learn for later use in a critique of the argument.

CREATE AND DISCUSS

Write a Letter Write a letter to the owner or administrator of a social media site that you believe has negatively affected you or someone you know.

- ❑ Provide the date, your address, the name and address of the recipient, and a salutation in correct letter format.
- ❑ In the body of your letter, explain the nature of the negative impact that you have experienced or witnessed. Be sure to support your position with facts, examples, or other relevant evidence.
- ❑ In your final paragraph, make a constructive suggestion for how the site owners might help prevent this problem from occurring again. Close with "Sincerely," and your signature.

Go to **Writing as a Process** in the **Writing Studio** for help.

Critique as a Class Critique the argument presented in "Outsmart Your Smartphone" to decide whether it is convincing enough to accept as valid.

- ❑ Review the text and your notes to identify flaws or fallacies, such as circular reasoning. Also look for strengths, such as well-used rhetorical devices. Discuss your observations.
- ❑ Share what you learned about the topic from your research. Discuss how this information confirms or contradicts Steiner-Adair's evidence and conclusions.
- ❑ As a class, identify points of agreement and draw a conclusion about the effectiveness and soundness of the author's argument.

Go to **Participating in Collaborative Discussions** in the **Speaking and Listening Studio** for more help.

RESPOND TO THE ESSENTIAL QUESTION

? How do your teenage years prepare you for adulthood?

Gather Information Review your annotations and notes on "Outsmart Your Smartphone." Then, add relevant details to your Response Log. To decide what to include, think about:

- the writer's main points
- her recommendations and the reasons she gives for them
- what you have learned from your research and discussions

At the end of the unit, use your notes to help you write an argument.

ACADEMIC VOCABULARY

As you write and discuss what you learned from the argument, be sure to use the Academic Vocabulary words. Check off each of the words that you use.

- ❑ **debate**
- ❑ **deduce**
- ❑ **license**
- ❑ **sufficient**
- ❑ **trend**

CRITICAL VOCABULARY

WORD BANK
perspective
stimulant
deliberate
anonymous
impulsive
inhibited

Practice and Apply Explain how the meanings of the words in each pair are related.

1. stimulant/sedative
2. perspective/bias
3. inhibited/impulsive
4. deliberate/thoughtless
5. anonymous/renowned

VOCABULARY STRATEGY: Word Families

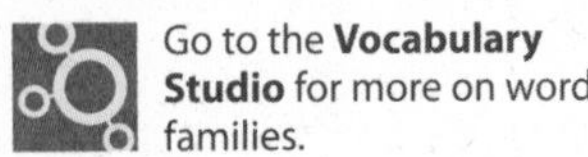

Go to the **Vocabulary Studio** for more on word families.

You can use word families to figure out the meanings of unfamiliar words. A **word family** consists of words that have the same root and, thus, related meanings. However, their meanings may be altered by different **affixes**—word parts that are attached before or after the root. For example, the word *perspective* is derived from the Latin root *specere,* meaning "to look at," and the prefix *per-*, meaning "through." Can you see how the meanings of words with this root are similar?

LATIN ROOT	WORD FAMILY
specere: to look at	**inspect:** to examine carefully **perspective:** a viewpoint on or understanding of something **speculate:** to engage in reasoning based on incomplete evidence

Practice and Apply Complete the word web with words that share the Latin root *ductus*, meaning "to lead." Define each related word. Then infer the meaning of *conducted* as it is used in this sentence from the selection:

> **A study conducted by scientists at University of Texas-Austin in 2017 found that just having your smartphone nearby reduces cognitive performance—how well your brain can think and learn—even when the phone is silent or out of sight.**

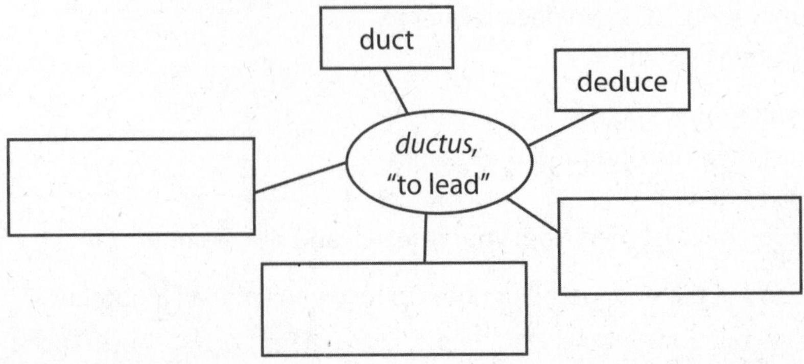

LANGUAGE CONVENTIONS: Correct Capitalization

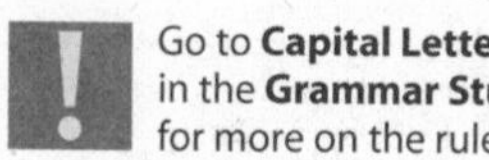

Go to **Capital Letters** in the **Grammar Studio** for more on the rules of capitalization.

Capitalize the first letters of all the important words in the names of organizations and institutions. However, do not capitalize words such as *hospital, school, college, university, center,* or even *research center* when they are not used as parts of the official names.

Incorrect: Studies conducted by the Pew research center show that many teens are online frequently.

Correct: Studies conducted by the Pew Research Center show that many teens are online frequently.

Incorrect: Psychologists at the Research Center conduct studies daily.

Correct: Psychologists at the research center conduct studies daily.

The first word in a sentence is always capitalized. However, when a hyphenated word begins a sentence, capitalize only the first word in the compound—that is, the one that comes before the first hyphen.

Incorrect: Ninety-Two percent of teens report going online daily.

Correct: Ninety-two percent of teens report going online daily.

Practice and Apply Review the letter you wrote to the owner or administrator of a social media site, checking it for errors in capitalization. Then trade letters with a classmate and peer edit one another's work. Discuss the reasons for any recommended corrections to capitalization before fixing those errors.

RESPOND

Collaborate & Compare

from IT'S COMPLICATED: THE SOCIAL LIVES OF NETWORKED TEENS
Argument by danah boyd

OUTSMART YOUR SMARTPHONE
Argument by Catherine Steiner-Adair

COMPARE ARGUMENTS

When you **compare arguments,** you identify similarities and differences between important aspects of each, using examples from the texts to make your points. You might compare and contrast the claims, reasons, and evidence in each. Alternatively, you might focus more deeply on an analysis of one of the following:

- ❑ **Evidence:** Is the evidence relevant, credible, current, sufficient, impressive, and/or accurate?
- ❑ **Use of facts and opinions:** Does the argument depend mostly on facts or on opinions? What are the sources of each?
- ❑ **Audience:** Whom is the piece meant to persuade? How does the intended audience affect the argument?
- ❑ **Objections and/or differing viewpoints:** Are the most important or popular objections raised and addressed?
- ❑ **Counterarguments:** Are opposing claims disproved with effective reasons and evidence?
- ❑ **Overall quality of writing:** Are rhetorical devices used effectively? Does the writing contain any logical fallacies?

In a small group, choose what you would like to focus on as you compare. Complete a chart like this one, adjusting the headings in the left column as necessary to reflect your particular focus. Then, review the texts to find examples of each similarity and difference you note.

Evidence	*It's Complicated*	Both	"Outsmart Your Smartphone"
Credibility			
Relevancy			
Currency			

ANALYZE THE TEXTS

Discuss these questions in your group.

1. **Compare** What do both arguments have in common?
2. **Connect** For what audience is each piece written, and how does this affect each argument?
3. **Analyze** What kind of support does each author rely upon most?
4. **Critique** Which argument exhibits the best overall quality of writing? Cite evidence from both texts to support your opinion.

CREATE AND PRESENT

With a partner, play the role of an adult and a teenager in a discussion about social media use. The adult may be a parent, a teacher, or someone who is an expert on the topic. However, the adult and teen should take opposing viewpoints. Follow these steps:

1. **Choose a Role and a Position** With your partner, decide who will play the adult and who will play the teenager. Also choose the viewpoint you each plan to promote. This may mean that one of you must adopt a viewpoint that does not match your own.
2. **Gather Information** List reasons and evidence from the texts and from your prior research that support your chosen viewpoint.

Reason 1:
Evidence:
Reason 2:
Evidence:

3. **Prepare Your Counterargument** Anticipate the other person's claim as well as his or her objections to your points. List reasons and evidence you will cite to challenge the opposing viewpoint.

Other's Claims and/or Objections	Your Counterargument

4. **Role-play the Discussion** In your chosen roles, have a conversation with your partner in which each of you tries to convince the other to adopt your position. Be on the lookout for errors in one another's reasoning, and point them out as appropriate. Also, as your partner presents evidence to support his or her position, reflect on your own argument and think about how you might adjust your approach to the issue in response. Consider beginning your argument by acknowledging the other's position and its merits and then countering it.

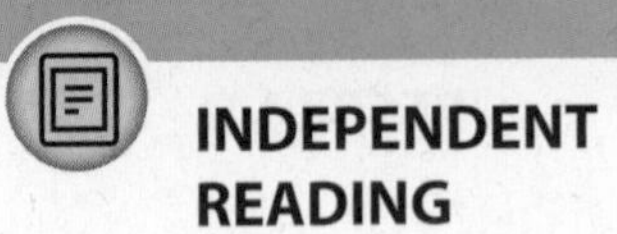

INDEPENDENT READING

Reader's Choice

? ESSENTIAL QUESTION:

How do your teenage years prepare you for adulthood?

Setting a Purpose Select one or more of these options from your eBook to continue your exploration of the Essential Question.

- Read the descriptions to see which text grabs your interest.
- Think about which genres you enjoy reading.

Notice & Note

In this unit, you practiced asking **Big Questions** and noticing and noting two signposts: **Contrasts and Contradictions** and **Numbers and Stats.** As you read independently, these signposts and others will aid your understanding. Below are the anchor questions to ask when you read literature and nonfiction.

Reading Literature: Stories, Poems, and Plays

Signpost	Anchor Question	Lesson
Contrasts and Contradictions	Why did the character act that way?	p. 3
Aha Moment	How might this change things?	p. 3
Tough Questions	What does this make me wonder about?	p. 152
Words of the Wiser	What's the lesson for the character?	p. 406
Again and Again	Why might the author keep bringing this up?	p. 2
Memory Moment	Why is this memory important?	p. 153

Reading Nonfiction: Essays, Articles, and Arguments

Signpost	Anchor Question(s)	Lesson
Big Questions	What surprised me? What did the author think I already knew? What challenged, changed, or confirmed what I already knew?	p. 77
Contrasts and Contradictions	What is the difference, and why does it matter?	p. 241
Extreme or Absolute Language	Why did the author use this language?	p. 76
Numbers and Stats	Why did the author use these numbers or amounts?	p. 325
Quoted Words	Why was this person quoted or cited, and what did this add?	p. 77
Word Gaps	Do I know this word from someplace else? Does it seem like technical talk for this topic? Do clues in the sentence help me understand the word?	p. 240

You can preview these texts in Unit 5 of your eBook.

Then, check off the text or texts that you select to read on your own.

☐ POEM

Teenagers
Pat Mora

Parents and teenagers living in the same house feel like strangers behind closed doors.

☐ POEM

Identity
Julio Noboa Polanco

A young poet imagines being free from society's rules.

☐ POEM

Hard on the Gas
Janet S. Wong

Doing things his own way, a grandfather challenges a teen's expectations.

☐ SHORT STORY

Marigolds
Eugenia Collier

The impulsive actions of a young girl change her life forever.

☐ ESSAY

My Summer of Scooping Ice Cream
Shonda Rhimes

A teenager gets more than a paycheck from her summer job.

Collaborate and Share With a partner, discuss what you learned from at least one of your independent readings.

- Share a brief synopsis or summary of the text.
- Describe any signposts that you noticed in the text and explain what they revealed to you.
- Describe what you most enjoyed or found most challenging about the text. Give specific examples.
- Decide if you would recommend the text to others. Why or why not?

Go to the **Reading Studio** for more resources on **Notice & Note.**

Write an Argument

Go to the **Writing Studio** for help writing an argument.

This unit focuses on the challenges faced by teenagers as they move toward adulthood. For this writing task, you will write an argument on a topic related to teenagers. In a writing context, an argument is not a conflict or disagreement. It is a carefully stated claim that is supported by reasons and evidence. For a well-written argument you can use as a mentor text, review the selection from *It's Complicated: The Social Lives of Networked Teens.*

As you write your argument, you can use the notes from your Response Log, which you filled out after reading the texts in this unit.

Writing Prompt

Read the information in the box below.

This is the topic or context for your argument.

> **As they move toward being adults, teenagers encounter many obstacles in their struggles for identity and independence.**

This is the Essential Question for the unit. How would you answer this question based on the texts in the unit?

Think carefully about the following question.

> **How do your teenage years prepare you for adulthood?**

Now mark the words that identify exactly what you are being asked to produce.

Write an argument about whether or not technology and social media are obstacles to friendship.

Be sure to —

Review these points as you write and again when you finish. Make any needed changes or edits.

- ❑ provide an engaging introduction that establishes your claim
- ❑ support the claim with valid reasons and evidence, including facts, details, and examples from credible sources
- ❑ logically organize your reasons and evidence
- ❑ use transitional words and phrases to clarify relationships among your claim, reasons, and evidence
- ❑ establish and maintain a formal style
- ❑ summarize your main points in an effective conclusion

 Plan

Before you start writing, you need to plan your argument. The first step is to choose a position you can defend. Use a range of strategies as you identify your position in response to the prompt. Begin by reviewing the notes you have taken in your Response Log for this unit. What other reading have you done about this topic? Think about this background reading as you formulate the key ideas you will include in your argument. Discuss the topic with your classmates and consider any personal interests you have that relate to the topic.

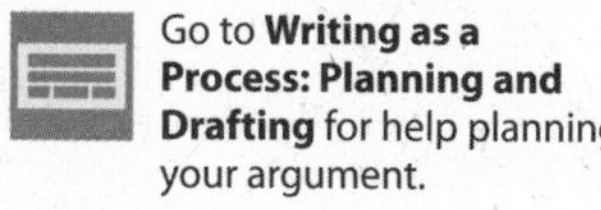

Go to **Writing as a Process: Planning and Drafting** for help planning your argument.

Use the table below as you determine your position in response to the prompt.

Argument Planning Table	
Topic	
Ideas from background reading	
Discussion with classmates	
Personal interest in the topic	
Position/Claim	

Gather Support Once you have determined your position and stated your claim, the next step is to gather support. Consider the reasons you have for your position. Then conduct research online and in print sources to gather evidence—facts, statistics, and examples—that backs up these reasons. Next, anticipate alternative or opposing views and consider how you might refute them. Incorporating counterarguments to disprove opposing views will make your own argument stronger.

Consider Your Purpose and Audience Keep your purpose and audience in mind. Do you want to persuade your classmates? Your friends? A group of adults? The reasons and evidence you will use to support your claim—and the tone you will use to convey your argument—may vary according to who that audience is.

Use the notes from your Response Log as you plan your argument.

WRITING TASK

Go to **Writing Arguments: Support: Reasons and Evidence** in the **Writing Studio** for help organizing your ideas.

Notice & Note

From Reading to Writing

Remember that writers use common features, called signposts, to help convey their message to readers.

Go to the **Reading Studio** for more resources on Notice & Note.

Organize Your Ideas After you have gathered ideas and evidence, you need to organize the information in a way that will help you draft your argument. You can use this graphic organizer to make an outline of your argument. Place your claim in the top box, your reasons in the next row of boxes, and your evidence in the bottom row.

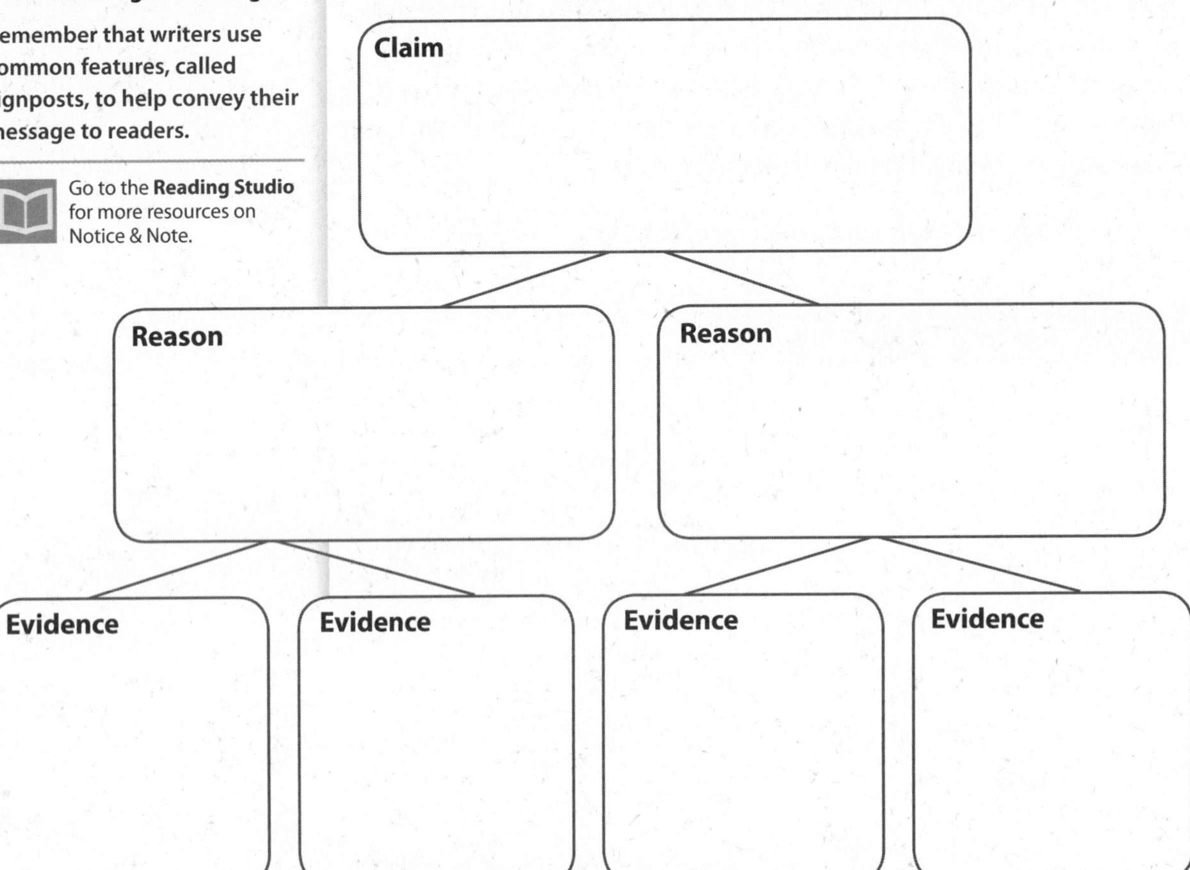

2 Develop a Draft

Once you have completed your planning activities, you can begin drafting your argument. Refer to your notes and your completed graphic organizer as you begin your draft. You might devote a paragraph to each reason or, if you have a great deal of supporting evidence to share, you might devote separate paragraphs to the evidence that supports a reason. Whatever you choose to do, sequence your reasons and evidence logically. Decide whether to begin or end with your strongest reason. Use transition words and phrases such as *because, therefore,* and *for this reason* to clarify relationships between ideas. Vary the length and structure of your sentences as you write.

Using a word processor or online writing application makes it easier to make changes or move sentences around later when you are ready to revise your first draft.

You might prefer to draft your argument online.

Use the Mentor Text

Author's Craft

Use your introduction to get your reader interested in your topic. Sometimes you can do this by making a bold statement. Another way is to begin with an accepted idea upon which you can build your argument. Note the way the writer begins the excerpt from *It's Complicated: The Social Lives of Networked Teens.*

Developing meaningful friendships is a key component of the coming of age process. Friends offer many things—advice, support, entertainment, and a connection that combats loneliness. And in doing so, they enable the transition to adulthood by providing a context beyond that of family and home. Though family is still important, many teens relish the opportunity to create relationships that are not simply given but chosen.

The first sentence states an accepted idea and proceeds to develop that idea into the claim that teens want to develop social relationships in their own way.

Apply What You've Learned To lay the foundation for your argument, you might begin with some facts or ideas that your audience is likely to agree with. Then you can state your claim within this shared context.

Genre Characteristics

An argument uses reasons and evidence to support a claim and to argue against anticipated objections and opposing views. Evidence can include facts, statistics, and examples. Notice how the author of *It's Complicated* uses the following example to support her claim.

Most teens are not compelled by gadgetry as such—they are compelled by friendship. The gadgets are interesting to them primarily as a means to a social end.

The author provides an example to support her claim: most teens use their phones to nurture their relationships with others.

Apply What You've Learned The evidence you include to support your argument should be clearly related to your claim. Some types of details you can use to support your ideas are facts, examples, and statistics.

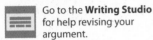

WRITING TASK

Go to the **Writing Studio** for help revising your argument.

3 Revise

On Your Own Once you have written your draft, you'll want to go back and look for ways to improve your argument. As you reread and revise, think about whether you have achieved your purpose. The Revision Guide will help you focus on specific elements to make your writing stronger.

Revision Guide		
Ask Yourself	**Tips**	**Revision Techniques**
1. Does my introduction contain a clear claim?	**Highlight** the sentences that state the issue and the claim.	**Add** a claim, or **revise** an existing claim for clarity.
2. Is my claim supported by solid reasons and evidence?	**Highlight** each reason, and **underline** the evidence that supports it.	**Add** reasons, or **insert** evidence. **Elaborate** to clarify evidence or how it relates to a given reason.
3. Do I address counter claims?	**Underline** where you mention opposing claims. **Highlight** sentences that address them.	**Add** possible opposing claims and persuasive responses to answer them.
4. Do I use and maintain a formal style?	**Highlight** contractions, slang, or informal language.	**Reword** contractions and **replace** informal language with precise, formal vocabulary.
5. Does the conclusion restate my claim?	**Underline** the restatement of the claim.	**Add** a sentence that restates the claim.

ACADEMIC VOCABULARY

As you conduct your **peer review,** be sure to use these words.

- ❑ **debate**
- ❑ **deduce**
- ❑ **license**
- ❑ **sufficient**
- ❑ **trend**

With a Partner Once you and your partner have worked through the Revision Guide on your own, exchange papers and evaluate each other's draft in a **peer review**. Focus on providing revision suggestions for at least three of the items mentioned in the chart. Explain why you think your partner's draft should be revised and what your specific suggestions are.

When receiving feedback from your partner, listen attentively and ask questions to make sure you fully understand the revision suggestions.

4 Edit

Once you are satisfied with your argument, you'll want to proofread and edit it to find and correct any errors in grammar, usage, or mechanics.

Language Conventions

Modifiers A modifier gives information about another word. When a modifier is used in a comparison, the form of the modifier shows the degree of comparison—that is, whether it is comparative or superlative.

Go to **Using Modifiers Correctly** in the **Grammar Studio** to learn more.

The **comparative** form compares two things, groups, or actions.

> Most teenagers are **more skilled** than adults, who have been **slower** to use social media.

The **superlative** form compares more than two things, groups, or actions.

> The **most popular** smartphones have the **newest** features.

To form comparatives and superlatives of most one- and some two-syllable modifiers, add *-er* and *-est*. To properly use most two-syllable and all three-syllable modifiers in comparisons, just add *more* or *most*.

REGULAR COMPARISONS		
Modifier	**Comparative**	**Superlative**
tall	taller	tallest
curious	more curious	most curious

IRREGULAR COMPARISONS		
Modifier	**Comparative**	**Superlative**
bad	worse	worst
much	more	most

5 Publish

Finalize your argument and choose a way to share it with your audience. Consider these options:

- Adapt your argument as an opinion letter to a local newspaper.
- Post your argument as a blog on a classroom or school website.
- Hold a debate with someone with an opposing position.

WRITING TASK

Use the scoring guide to evaluate your argument.

Writing Task Scoring Guide: Argument			
	Organization/Progression	**Development of Ideas**	**Use of Language and Conventions**
4	• Reasons and evidence are organized logically and consistently throughout the argument. • Transitions effectively connect reasons and evidence to the writer's claim.	• The introduction is attention-getting and states the writer's position. • Logical reasons and relevant evidence support the writer's claim. • Opposing or alternate claims are acknowledged and addressed. • The conclusion effectively summarizes the claim.	• A formal style is maintained. • Sentence variety creates a rhythmic flow. • Comparative and superlative modifiers are formed and used correctly. • Spelling, grammar, mechanics, and usage are correct.
3	• The organization of reasons and evidence is confusing in a few places. • A few more transitions are needed to connect reasons and evidence to the writer's claim.	• The introduction could be more engaging; the claim states a position. • Reasons and evidence support the claim, but they could be stronger. • Opposing or alternate claims are acknowledged, but the responses need to be better developed. • The conclusion restates the claim.	• The style becomes informal in a few places. • There could be more sentence variety. • Most comparative and superlative modifiers are used correctly. • Some errors in spelling, grammar, mechanics, and usage are made.
2	• The organization of reasons and evidence is logical in some places, but the writing lacks focus. • Many more transitions are needed to connect reasons and evidence to the writer's claim.	• The introduction is uninteresting; the introduction identifies an issue, but the writer's position is not clearly stated. • Reasons and evidence are not always logical or relevant. • Opposing or alternate claims are acknowledged but not always addressed or countered logically. • The conclusion provides an incomplete summary of the claim.	• The style becomes informal in many places. • There is little or no sentence variety. • There are a few errors with comparative and superlative modifiers. • Spelling, grammar, mechanics, and usage errors are distracting to the reader.
1	• The organization is not logical. Reasons and evidence are presented randomly. • The lack of any transitions makes the argument difficult to understand.	• The introduction is confusing; no claim is made. • Reasons are unconvincing and the evidence is not relevant. • Opposing or alternate claims are neither acknowledged nor addressed. • The conclusion is missing.	• The style is informal and inappropriate. • Poorly or incorrectly formed sentences make the argument hard to follow. • Modifiers are missing or used incorrectly. • Spelling, grammar, mechanics, and usage errors obscure the writer's meaning.

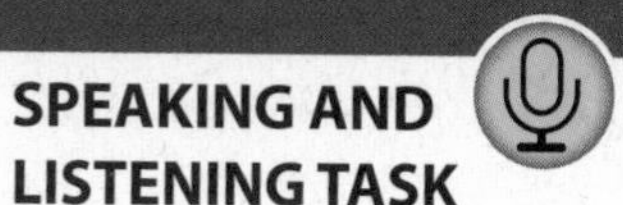

Present an Argument

You will now adapt your argument for presentation to your classmates. You also will listen to their presentations, ask questions to better understand their ideas, and make suggestions to help them improve their work.

Go to **Giving a Presentation** in the **Speaking and Listening Studio** for help.

1 Adapt Your Argument for Presentation

Use the chart below to plan how you will adapt the key elements of your argument in order to create a script and other presentation materials.

Presentation Planning Chart		
Title and Introduction	How will you revise your title and introduction to capture the listener's attention? Is there a more concise way to state your claim?	
Audience	What tone will be most persuasive in an oral presentation? To what specific vocabulary will your audience respond most positively?	
Effective Language and Organization	Which parts of your argument could be clearer? Where can you add transitions to better connect reasons and evidence back to your claim?	
Visuals	What images or graphics would help clarify your claim, reasons, and evidence? How can you add interest? What text should appear on screen?	

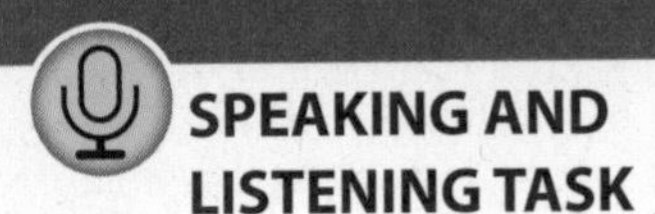

2 Practice with a Partner or Group

Once you've completed your draft, practice with a partner or group to improve both the presentation and your delivery. Keep in mind that even when an argument is well written, an oral presentation of the argument won't be as effective if the delivery is weak.

As you work to improve your presentations, be sure to follow discussion rules:

- ❑ **listen closely to each other**
- ❑ **don't interrupt**
- ❑ **stay on topic**
- ❑ **ask only helpful, relevant questions**
- ❑ **provide only clear, thoughtful, and direct answers**

Practice Effective Verbal Techniques

- ❑ **Enunciation** Replace words that you stumble over, and rearrange sentences so that your delivery is smooth.
- ❑ **Voice Modulation and Pitch** Use your voice to display enthusiasm and emphasis.
- ❑ **Speaking Rate** Speak slowly enough that listeners understand you. Pause now and then to let them consider important points.
- ❑ **Volume** Remember that listeners at the back of the room need to hear you.

Practice Effective Nonverbal Techniques

- ❑ **Eye Contact** Try to let your eyes rest on each member of the audience at least once.
- ❑ **Facial Expression** Smile, frown, or raise an eyebrow to show your feelings or to emphasize points.
- ❑ **Gestures** Stand tall and relaxed, and use natural gestures—shrugs, nods, or shakes of your head—to add meaning and interest to your presentation.

Provide and Consider Advice for Improvement

As a listener, pay close attention. Take notes about ways that presenters can improve their presentations and more effectively use verbal and nonverbal techniques. Paraphrase and summarize each presenter's claim and reasons to confirm your understanding, and ask questions to clarify any confusing ideas.

As a presenter, listen closely to questions and consider ways to revise your presentation to make sure your points are clear and logically sequenced. Remember to ask for suggestions about how you might change onscreen text or images to make your presentation clearer and more interesting.

3 Deliver Your Presentation

Use the advice you received during practice to make final changes to your presentation. Then, using effective verbal and nonverbal techniques, present it to your classmates.

Reflect on the Unit

In writing your argument, you have formulated and expressed your thoughts about the reading you have done in this unit. Now is a good time to reflect on what you have learned.

Reflect on the Essential Question

- How do your teenage years prepare you for adulthood? How has your answer to this question changed since you first considered it when you started this unit?
- What are some examples from the texts you read that show how teens can prepare for the transition into adulthood?

Reflect on Your Reading

- Which selections were the most interesting or surprising to you?
- From which selection did you learn the most about the challenges teenagers face as they move toward becoming adults?

Reflect on the Writing Task

- Which part of the argument was the easiest to write? Which was the hardest? Why?
- How could you have made your argument more convincing?

Reflect on the Speaking and Listening Task

- Did your delivery make your argument more effective? Why or why not?
- What kinds of ideas about how to revise your presentation did your listeners' reactions and feedback give you?

UNIT 5 SELECTIONS

- **"The Debt We Owe to the Adolescent Brain"**
- ***Bronx Masquerade***
- **"Hanging Fire"**
- **"Summer of His Fourteenth Year"**
- ***It's Complicated: The Social Lives of Networked Teens***
- **"Outsmart Your Smartphone"**

UNIT 6

THE LEGACY OF ANNE FRANK

? **ESSENTIAL QUESTION:**

What can we learn from Anne Frank?

"I don't want to have lived in vain like most people . . . I want to go on living even after my death!"

Anne Frank

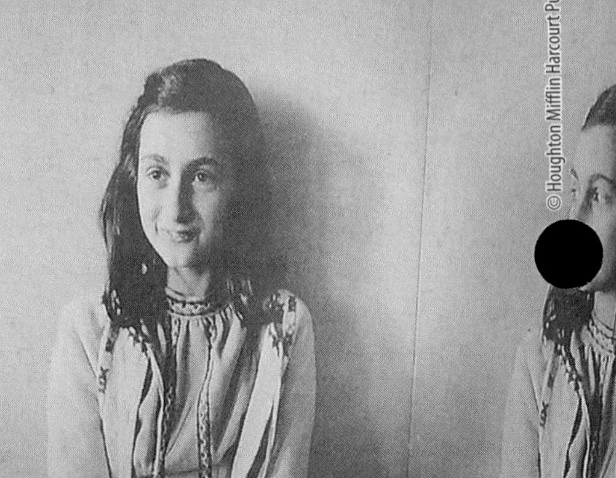

ACADEMIC VOCABULARY

Academic Vocabulary words are words you use when you discuss and write about texts. In this unit you will practice and learn five words.

- [x] communicate
- [ ] draft
- [ ] liberation
- [ ] philosophy
- [ ] publish

Study the Word Network to learn more about the word **communicate.**

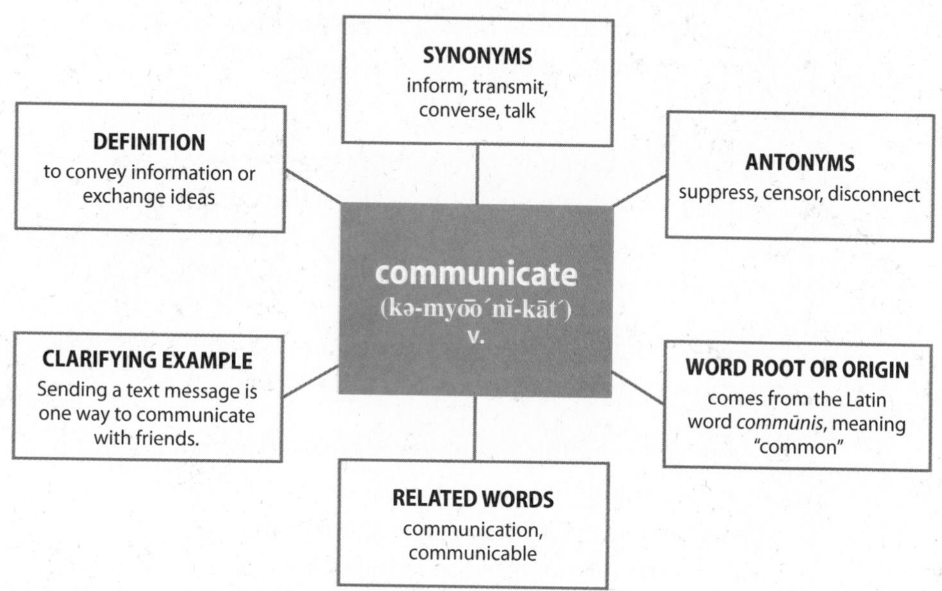

Write and Discuss Discuss the completed Word Network with a partner, making sure to talk through all of the boxes until you both understand the word and its synonyms, antonyms, and related forms. Then, fill out Word Networks for the remaining four words. Use a dictionary or online resource to help you complete the activity.

Go online to access the Word Networks.

RESPOND TO THE ESSENTIAL QUESTION

In this unit, you will consider the lessons to be learned from tragic events such as the Holocaust. As you read, you will revisit the **Essential Question** and gather your ideas about it in the **Response Log** that appears on page R6. At the end of the unit, you will have the opportunity to write a **personal narrative** similar to the diary entries written by Anne Frank. Filling out the Response Log will help you prepare for this writing task.

You can also go online to access the Response Log.

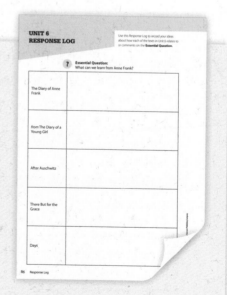

UNIT 6 RESPONSE LOG

Use this Response Log to record your ideas about how each of the texts in Unit 6 relates to or comments on the **Essential Question.**

? Essential Question: What can we learn from Anne Frank?

The Diary of Anne Frank	
from The Diary of a Young Girl	
After Auschwitz	
There But for the Grace	
Days	

R6 Response Log

Notice & Note

READING MODEL

THE DIARY OF ANNE FRANK

For more information on these and other signposts to Notice & Note, visit the **Reading Studio**.

You are about to read a drama called *The Diary of Anne Frank*. In it, you will notice and note signposts that will give you clues about the play's characters and themes. Here are three key signposts to look for as you read this drama and other works of fiction.

Words of the Wiser To whom do you turn when you need help figuring something out? As in real life, characters in literature sometimes benefit from the wisdom and guidance of another—often a character who is older and wiser than they are.

When a character speaks helpful or inspiring words, stop and think. Paying attention to **Words of the Wiser** can:

- highlight something a character needs to learn
- reveal a solution to a problem a character is facing
- explain or provide insight into a situation
- hint at the theme or lesson of the story

The passage below illustrates a student's annotation in *The Diary of Anne Frank* and a response to a Words of the Wiser signpost.

165 **Mr. Frank.** Never. I am sorry, Anneke. It isn't safe. No, you must never go beyond that door.

166 *(For the first time Anne realizes what "going into hiding" means.)*

167 **Anne.** I see.

168 **Mr. Frank.** It'll be hard, I know. But always remember this, Anneke. There are no walls, there are no bolts, no locks that anyone can put on your mind.

Anchor Question
When you notice this signpost, ask: What's the life lesson, and how might it affect the character?

What wise words does Mr. Frank share with his daughter?	He says that her mind will always be free—even if she must live in hiding for a time.
Why might Mr. Frank want Anne to know this?	He wants her to remember something encouraging even if life becomes very difficult in their small space.

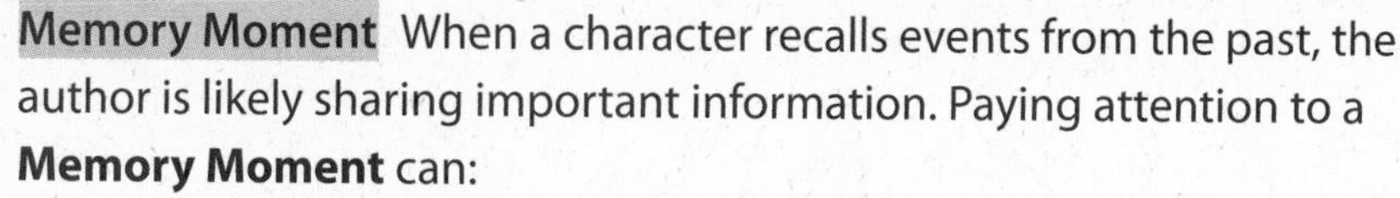

Memory Moment When a character recalls events from the past, the author is likely sharing important information. Paying attention to a **Memory Moment** can:

- provide historical context for a story or play
- provide background that relates to the current situation
- reveal details about characters' lives or relationships
- show what motivates or drives a character's actions

When you encounter a phrase like these while reading, pause to see if it's a **Memory Moment** signpost:

"Only three years ago . . ."

"that reminded him of . . ."

"It was just like when . . ."

"I remember when . . ."

"when we were little . . ."

Here, a student marked a Memory Moment.

> 31 **Mr. Frank** (*quietly*). Anne's diary. (*He opens the diary and begins to read.*) "Monday, the sixth of July, nineteen forty-two." (*to* Miep) Nineteen forty-two. Is it possible, Miep? . . . Only three years ago. . . .

Anchor Question When you notice this signpost, ask: Why might this memory be important?

What memory is introduced at the beginning of the play?	the memory of his daughter Anne, writing in the diary three years earlier
Why might this memory be important to the story?	It provides a transition into the three-year-old story, which focuses on Anne.

Contrasts and Contradictions When a character acts in a way that clashes with what you would expect, take the time to figure out what it means. **Contrasts and Contradictions** often give you a deeper insight into a character or a situation. In this example, a student underlined details that show Contrasts and Contradictions.

> 19 **Miep.** Mr. Frank, you can't leave here! This is your home! Amsterdam is your home. Your business is here, waiting for you . . . You're needed here . . . Now that the war is over, there are things that . . .
>
> 20 **Mr. Frank.** I can't stay in Amsterdam, Miep. It has too many memories for me.

Anchor Question When you notice this signpost, ask: Why did the character act (or feel) that way?

What makes Mr. Frank's choice an unexpected one?	It's surprising that he wants to leave his home, a place where he has a business.
Why might Mr. Frank wish to leave a place with many memories?	The memories are of sad events in that place and of loved ones who now are dead.

THE DIARY OF ANNE FRANK

Drama by **Frances Goodrich** and **Albert Hackett**

? ***ESSENTIAL QUESTION:***

What can we learn from Anne Frank?

QUICK START

Do you agree or disagree with the view that most people are basically good at heart? Briefly share your views and reasons with a partner.

ANALYZE DRAMA

A **drama,** or play, is a form of literature meant to be performed by actors for an audience. The author is called a **playwright,** and the text of the drama is the **script.** The script includes these elements:

- The **cast of characters** is a list of all the characters in the play.
- **Stage directions,** which often are italicized and in parentheses, are mostly instructions about how to perform the drama. Some stage directions describe the setting and the characters.
- **Dialogue** is the written conversation between characters.
- A drama is often divided into acts and scenes. An **act** is a major division within a play, similar to a chapter in a book. Each act may be divided into smaller sections, called **scenes.**

As you read Act One of this drama, note differences between Scene 1 and Scene 2. What do these differences help you understand?

GENRE ELEMENTS: DRAMA

- is written to be performed by actors in front of an audience
- tells a story through characters' words and actions
- includes stage directions with important details that explain what's happening
- may be divided into acts, which are in turn divided into scenes
- may show that the time or place of the action has changed by starting a new act or scene

SCENE	WHERE?	WHEN?	KEY EVENTS
Scene 1			
Scene 2			

ANALYZE PLOT DEVELOPMENT

Each scene in a drama presents an episode of the play's **plot,** or story line. To analyze a drama's plot development, consider these factors:

- Most plays have a **linear plot,** with events presented in the order in which they occur. However, some plays have a **nonlinear plot,** in which events are told out of order.
- The plot may include one or more subplots. A **subplot** is an additional, or secondary, plot that contains its own conflict.
- When an author interrupts the chronological order by describing something that took place at an earlier time, it is called a **flashback.** A flashback can help readers better understand a current situation.
- The playwright may provide hints to suggest future events. This is called **foreshadowing.** Foreshadowing creates suspense and makes readers eager to find out what will happen.

As you analyze the plot of *The Diary of Anne Frank,* think about how certain events cause others to happen. Also note the playwrights' use of subplot, flashback, and foreshadowing.

CRITICAL VOCABULARY

conspicuous **indignantly** **appalled**
loathe **ostentatiously** **inarticulate**

To see how many Critical Vocabulary words you already know, use them to complete the sentences.

1. Maya __________ washed the dishes that her brother had left in the sink.
2. The bicyclist was __________ with her bright yellow reflectors.
3. The mayor arrived __________ in a long black limousine.
4. Binh used to __________ math, but now he loves it.
5. She was shy and __________ around strangers but very talkative among friends.
6. People were __________ by all the storm damage.

LANGUAGE CONVENTIONS

Correct Capitalization In this lesson, you will learn which types of words need to be capitalized.

As my family is Jewish, we emigrated to Holland when Hitler came to power.

In the above example, words that name an ethnicity, a country, and a person are capitalized. As you read *The Diary of Anne Frank,* note which words the playwrights capitalized, and why they did so.

ANNOTATION MODEL

NOTICE & NOTE 

As you read, notice and note signposts, including **Words of the Wiser, Memory Moments,** and **Contrasts and Contradictions.** In the model, you can see one reader's notes about *The Diary of Anne Frank.*

33 **Mr. Frank and Anne.** "My father started a business, importing spice and herbs. Things went well for us until nineteen forty. Then the war came, and the Dutch capitulation, followed by the arrival of the Germans. Then things got very bad for the Jews."	memories of life before hiding
34 (Mr. Frank's Voice *dies out.* Anne's Voice *continues alone. The lights dim slowly to darkness. The curtain falls on the scene.*)	
35 **Anne's Voice.** You could not do this and you could not do that. They forced Father out of his business. We had to wear yellow stars. I had to turn in my bike. I couldn't go to a Dutch school any more. . . .	This contradicts what decent people would do.

NOTICE & NOTE

Frances Goodrich *(1890–1984) and* ***Albert Hackett*** *(1900–1995) were a married couple who worked together to write screenplays for movies. They wrote the play called* The Diary of Anne Frank *based on Anne's actual diary entries. Although the play differs from the diary in many ways, Anne's father, who survived the Holocaust, believed that it captured the essence of his daughter's diary. The play won the 1956 Pulitzer Prize for drama. It was later made into an Oscar-winning movie, for which Goodrich and Hackett also wrote the screenplay.*

THE DIARY OF ANNE FRANK

Drama by Frances Goodrich and Albert Hackett

BACKGROUND

Anne Frank and her family were Jewish citizens of Germany. After the Nazi Party, led by Adolf Hitler, came to power in 1933, the Franks moved to the Netherlands to escape persecution. However, the Nazis invaded that country in 1940. In order to survive, Anne's family went into hiding when she was 13 years old. They hid in attic rooms behind Mr. Frank's office, and several other Jews joined them. In this "Secret Annex," Anne kept a diary about her life in hiding. More than two years later, the group's worst fears came true when the Nazis found them. Everyone who had been living there was sent to concentration camps. Anne's diary was discovered later.

SETTING A PURPOSE

As you read, think about what the play reveals about Anne Frank's philosophy of life. How are her thoughts communicated?

Notice & Note

Use the side margins to notice and note signposts in the text.

NOTICE & NOTE

ANALYZE DRAMA
Annotate: Review the cast of characters. Circle four members of one family. Underline three members of another.

Analyze: What two families live in the Secret Annex? What other characters are in the play?

CHARACTERS

SECRET ANNEX RESIDENTS

Anne Frank	Peter Van Daan
Margot Frank	Mr. Van Daan
Mr. Frank	Mrs. Van Daan
Mrs. Frank	Mr. Dussel

WORKERS IN MR. FRANK'S BUSINESS

Miep Gies (mēp gēs) Mr. Kraler (krä´lər)

ANALYZE DRAMA
Annotate: In paragraphs 3–5, mark details that describe what this scene looks like and sounds like.

Analyze: Why do you think the stage directions include a description of the sounds outside the Annex?

1 **The Time.** *July 1942–August 1944, November 1945*

2 **The Place.** *Amsterdam, the Netherlands*

3 *The scene remains the same throughout the play. It is the top floor of a warehouse and office building in Amsterdam, Holland. The sharply peaked roof of the building is outlined against a sea of other rooftops, stretching away into the distance. Nearby is the belfry of a church tower, the Westertoren, whose carillon rings out the hours. Occasionally faint sounds float up from below: the voices of children playing in the street, the tramp of marching feet, a boat whistle from the canal.*

4 *The three rooms of the top floor and a small attic space above are exposed to our view. The largest of the rooms is in the center, with two small rooms, slightly raised, on either side. On the right is a bathroom, out of sight. A narrow steep flight of stairs at the back leads up to the attic. The rooms are sparsely furnished with a few chairs, cots, a table or two. The windows are painted over, or covered with makeshift blackout curtains. In the main room there is a sink, a gas ring for cooking and a wood-burning stove for warmth.*

5 *The room on the left is hardly more than a closet. There is a skylight in the sloping ceiling. Directly under this room is a small steep stairwell, with steps leading down to a door. This is the only entrance from the building below. When the door is opened we see that it has been concealed on the outer side by a bookcase attached to it.*

ACT ONE

Scene 1

6 *The curtain rises on an empty stage. It is late afternoon November, 1945.*

7 *The rooms are dusty, the curtains in rags. Chairs and tables are overturned.*

8 *The door at the foot of the small stairwell swings open.* Mr. Frank *comes up the steps into view. He is a gentle, cultured European in his middle years. There is still a trace of a German accent in his speech.*

9 *He stands looking slowly around, making a supreme effort at self-control. He is weak, ill. His clothes are threadbare.*

ANALYZE DRAMA
Annotate: In paragraphs 8–9, mark details that describe the character of Mr. Frank.

Infer: What details do the stage directions provide about Mr. Frank? What does the description suggest about him?

10 *After a second he drops his rucksack on the couch and moves slowly about. He opens the door to one of the smaller rooms, and then abruptly closes it again, turning away. He goes to the window at the back, looking off at the Westertoren as its carillon strikes the hour of six, then he moves restlessly on.*

11 *From the street below we hear the sound of a barrel organ and children's voices at play. There is a many-colored scarf hanging from a nail.* Mr. Frank *takes it, putting it around his neck. As he starts back for his rucksack, his eye is caught by something lying on the floor. It is a woman's white glove. He holds it in his hand and suddenly all of his self-control is gone. He breaks down, crying.*

12 *We hear footsteps on the stairs.* Miep Gies *comes up, looking for* Mr. Frank. *Miep is a Dutch girl of about twenty-two. She wears a coat and hat, ready to go home. She is pregnant. Her attitude toward* Mr. Frank *is protective, compassionate.*

ANALYZE DRAMA
Annotate: Review the stage directions in paragraphs 11–12 and the first lines of dialogue in paragraphs 13–16. Mark the lines that describe how seeing the glove affects Mr. Frank.

Analyze: Why has Mr. Frank returned to the Secret Annex? Why does he have that reaction to the glove?

13 **Miep.** Are you all right, Mr. Frank?

14 **Mr. Frank** (*quickly controlling himself*). Yes, Miep, yes.

15 **Miep.** Everyone in the office has gone home . . . It's after six. (*then pleading*) Don't stay up here, Mr. Frank. What's the use of torturing yourself like this?

NOTICE & NOTE

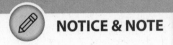

16 **Mr. Frank.** I've come to say goodbye . . . I'm leaving here, Miep.

17 **Miep.** What do you mean? Where are you going? Where?

18 **Mr. Frank.** I don't know yet. I haven't decided.

19 **Miep.** Mr. Frank, you can't leave here! This is your home! Amsterdam is your home. Your business is here, waiting for you . . . You're needed here . . . Now that the war is over, there are things that . . .

20 **Mr. Frank.** I can't stay in Amsterdam, Miep. It has too many memories for me. Everywhere there's something . . . the house we lived in . . . the school . . . that street organ playing out there . . . I'm not the person you used to know, Miep. I'm a bitter old man. (*breaking off*) Forgive me. I shouldn't speak to you like this . . . after all that you did for us . . . the suffering . . .

21 **Miep.** No. No. It wasn't suffering. You can't say we suffered. (*As she speaks, she straightens a chair which is overturned.*)

22 **Mr. Frank.** I know what you went through, you and Mr. Kraler. I'll remember it as long as I live. (*He gives one last look around.*) Come, Miep.

23 (*He starts for the steps, then remembers his rucksack, going back to get it.*)

24 **Miep** (*hurrying up to a cupboard*). Mr. Frank, did you see? There are some of your papers here. (*She brings a bundle of papers to him.*) We found them in a heap of rubbish on the floor after . . . after you left.

25 **Mr. Frank.** Burn them.

26 (*He opens his rucksack to put the glove in it.*)

27 **Miep.** But, Mr. Frank, there are letters, notes . . .

28 **Mr. Frank.** Burn them. All of them.

29 **Miep.** Burn *this?*

30 (*She hands him a paperbound notebook.*)

31 **Mr. Frank** (*quietly*). Anne's diary. (*He opens the diary and begins to read.*) "Monday, the sixth of July, nineteen forty-two." (*to* Miep) Nineteen forty-two. Is it possible, Miep? . . . Only three years ago. (*As he continues his reading, he sits down on the couch.*) "Dear Diary, since you and I are going to be great friends, I will start by telling you about myself. My name is Anne Frank. I am thirteen years old. I was born in Germany the twelfth of June, nineteen twenty-nine. As my family is Jewish, we emigrated to Holland when Hitler came to power."

CONTRASTS AND CONTRADICTIONS

Notice & Note: Mark what Mr. Frank tells Miep to do with the papers she brings to him.

Compare: Recall what Mr. Frank did with the glove he found. How do his actions contrast with his words about the papers? What might explain his behavior?

NOTICE & NOTE

32 (*As* Mr. Frank *reads on, another voice joins his, as if coming from the air. It is* Anne's Voice.)

33 **Mr. Frank and Anne.** "My father started a business, importing spice and herbs. Things went well for us until nineteen forty. Then the war came, and the Dutch capitulation, followed by the arrival of the Germans. Then things got very bad for the Jews."

34 (Mr. Frank's Voice *dies out.* Anne's Voice *continues alone. The lights dim slowly to darkness. The curtain falls on the scene.*)

35 **Anne's Voice.** You could not do this and you could not do that. They forced Father out of his business. We had to wear yellow stars.[1] I had to turn in my bike. I couldn't go to a Dutch school any more. I couldn't go to the movies, or ride in an automobile, or even on a streetcar, and a million other things. But somehow we children still managed to have fun. Yesterday Father told me we were going into hiding. Where, he wouldn't say. At five o'clock this morning Mother woke me and told me to hurry and get dressed. I was to put on as many clothes as I could. It would look too suspicious if we walked along carrying suitcases. It wasn't until we were on our way that I learned where we were going. Our hiding place was to be upstairs in the building where

[1] **yellow stars**: the six-pointed Stars of David that the Nazis ordered all Jews to wear for identification.

MEMORY MOMENT

Notice & Note: In paragraphs 31–35, mark time words that indicate this is a Memory Moment.

Infer: What information do these memories provide? Why might the playwrights have chosen to include them?

ANALYZE DRAMA

Annotate: Mark details in paragraphs 32–34 that describe how the speech shifts from Mr. Frank's voice to Anne's voice.

Interpret: Why might the playwrights have written the stage directions in this way? How might this affect the mood?

NOTICE & NOTE

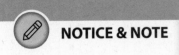

Father used to have his business. Three other people were coming in with us . . . the Van Daans and their son Peter . . . Father knew the Van Daans but we had never met them . . .

36 (*During the last lines the curtain rises on the scene. The lights dim on.* Anne's Voice *fades out.*)

Scene 2

ANALYZE PLOT DEVELOPMENT

Annotate: Mark the new date indicated in Scene 2. Then look back at paragraph 6.

Analyze: What indicates that this is a flashback? How does this flashback affect the mood of what is happening on the stage? What questions does this change raise for the audience?

37 *It is early morning, July, 1942. The rooms are bare, as before, but they are now clean and orderly.*

38 Mr. Van Daan, *a tall, portly man in his late forties, is in the main room, pacing up and down, nervously smoking a cigarette. His clothes and overcoat are expensive and well cut.*

39 Mrs. Van Daan *sits on the couch, clutching her possessions, a hatbox, bags, etc. She is a pretty woman in her early forties. She wears a fur coat over her other clothes.*

40 Peter Van Daan *is standing at the window of the room on the right, looking down at the street below. He is a shy, awkward boy of sixteen. He wears a cap, a raincoat, and long Dutch trousers, like "plus fours." At his feet is a black case, a carrier for his cat.*

conspicuous
(kən-spĭk´yo͞o-əs) *adj.*
Something *conspicuous* is obvious or very easy to see.

41 *The yellow Star of David is* **conspicuous** *on all of their clothes.*

ANALYZE PLOT DEVELOPMENT

Annotate: Mark details in paragraphs 42–47 that indicate that Mrs. Van Daan is worried about something.

Draw Conclusions: What is she worried about?

42 **Mrs. Van Daan** (*rising, nervous, excited*). Something's happened to them! I know it!

43 **Mr. Van Daan.** Now, Kerli!

44 **Mrs. Van Daan.** Mr. Frank said they'd be here at seven o'clock. He said . . .

45 **Mr. Van Daan.** They have two miles to walk. You can't expect . . .

46 **Mrs. Van Daan.** They've been picked up. That's what's happened. They've been taken . . .

47 (Mr. Van Daan *indicates that he hears someone coming.*)

48 **Mr. Van Daan.** You see?

49 (Peter *takes up his carrier and his schoolbag, etc., and goes into the main room as* Mr. Frank *comes up the stairwell from below.* Mr. Frank *looks much younger now. His movements are brisk, his manner confident. He wears an overcoat and carries his hat and a small cardboard box. He crosses to the* Van Daans, *shaking hands with each of them.*)

50 **Mr. Frank.** Mrs. Van Daan, Mr. Van Daan, Peter. (*then, in explanation of their lateness*) There were too many of the Green Police[2] on the streets . . . we had to take the long way around.

51 (*Up the steps come* Margot Frank, Mrs. Frank, Miep *[not pregnant now] and* Mr. Kraler. *All of them carry bags, packages, and so forth. The Star of David is conspicuous on all of the* Franks' *clothing.* Margot *is eighteen, beautiful, quiet, shy.* Mrs. Frank *is a young mother, gently bred, reserved. She, like* Mr. Frank, *has a slight German accent.* Mr. Kraler *is a Dutchman, dependable, kindly.*

52 *As* Mr. Kraler *and* Miep *go upstage to put down their parcels,* Mrs. Frank *turns back to call* Anne.)

53 **Mrs. Frank.** Anne?

54 (Anne *comes running up the stairs. She is thirteen, quick in her movements, interested in everything, mercurial in her emotions. She wears a cape, long wool socks and carries a schoolbag.*)

55 **Mr. Frank** (*introducing them*). My wife, Edith. Mr. and Mrs. Van Daan (Mrs. Frank *hurries over, shaking hands with them.*) . . . their son, Peter . . . my daughters, Margot and Anne.

56 (Anne *gives a polite little curtsy as she shakes* Mr. Van Daan's *hand. Then she immediately starts off on a tour of investigation of her new home, going upstairs to the attic room.* Miep *and* Mr. Kraler *are putting the various things they have brought on the shelves.*)

57 **Mr. Kraler.** I'm sorry there is still so much confusion.

58 **Mr. Frank.** Please. Don't think of it. After all, we'll have plenty of leisure to arrange everything ourselves.

59 **Miep** (*to* Mrs. Frank). We put the stores of food you sent in here. Your drugs are here . . . soap, linen here.

60 **Mrs. Frank.** Thank you, Miep.

61 **Miep.** I made up the beds . . . the way Mr. Frank and Mr. Kraler said. (*She starts out.*) Forgive me. I have to hurry. I've got to go to the other side of town to get some ration books[3] for you.

62 **Mrs. Van Daan.** Ration books? If they see our names on ration books, they'll know we're here.

[2] **Green Police:** the Nazi police, who wore green uniforms.

[3] **ration books:** books of stamps or coupons issued by the government in wartime. With these coupons, people could purchase scarce items, such as food, clothing, and gasoline.

NOTICE & NOTE

LANGUAGE CONVENTIONS

Annotate: The first word in a sentence always begins with a capital letter, as do people's names (such as Margot or Mr. Frank). Mark other words that are capitalized in paragraphs 50–51.

Analyze: What other words are capitalized? Why?

NOTICE & NOTE

ANALYZE DRAMA

Annotate: Mark the stage directions that reveal how Mr. Kraler and Miep respond to Mrs. Van Daan's comment about the ration books.

Interpret: What does that stage direction mean? Why might the playwrights have used it?

63 **Mr. Kraler.** There isn't anything . . .

64 **Miep**. Don't worry. Your names won't be on them. (*as she hurries out*) I'll be up later.

Together

65 **Mr. Frank.** Thank you, Miep.

66 **Mrs. Frank** (*to* Mr. Kraler). It's illegal, then, the ration books? We've never done anything illegal.

67 **Mr. Frank.** We won't be living here exactly according to regulations. (*As* Mr. Kraler *reassures* Mrs. Frank, *he takes various small things, such as matches, soap, etc., from his pockets, handing them to her.*)

68 **Mr. Kraler.** This isn't the black market,[4] Mrs. Frank. This is what we call the white market . . . helping all of the hundreds and hundreds who are hiding out in Amsterdam.

69 (*The carillon is heard playing the quarter-hour before eight.* Mr. Kraler *looks at his watch.* Anne *stops at the window as she comes down the stairs.*)

70 **Anne.** It's the Westertoren!

71 **Mr. Kraler.** I must go. I must be out of here and downstairs in the office before the workmen get here. (*He starts for the stairs leading out.*) Miep or I, or both of us, will be up each day to bring you food and news and find out what your needs are. Tomorrow I'll get you a better bolt for the door at the foot of the stairs. It needs a bolt that you can throw yourself and open only at our signal. (*to* Mr. Frank) Oh . . .You'll tell them about the noise?

72 **Mr. Frank.** I'll tell them.

73 **Mr. Kraler.** Good-bye then for the moment. I'll come up again, after the workmen leave.

74 **Mr. Frank.** Good-bye, Mr. Kraler.

75 **Mrs. Frank** (*shaking his hand*). How can we thank you? (*The others murmur their good-byes.*)

76 **Mr. Kraler.** I never thought I'd live to see the day when a man like Mr. Frank would have to go into hiding. When you think— (*He breaks off, going out.* Mr. Frank *follows him down the steps, bolting the door after him. In the interval before he returns,* Peter *goes over to* Margot, *shaking hands with her. As* Mr. Frank *comes back up the steps,* Mrs. Frank *questions him anxiously.*)

77 **Mrs. Frank.** What did he mean, about the noise?

---

[4] **black market:** a system for selling goods illegally, in violation of rationing and other restrictions.

NOTICE & NOTE

78 **Mr. Frank.** First let us take off some of these clothes. (*They all start to take off garment after garment. On each of their coats, sweaters, blouses, suits, dresses, is another yellow Star of David.* Mr. *and* Mrs. Frank *are underdressed quite simply. The others wear several things, sweaters, extra dresses, bathrobes, aprons, nightgowns, etc.*)

79 **Mr. Van Daan.** It's a wonder we weren't arrested, walking along the streets . . . Petronella with a fur coat in July . . . and that cat of Peter's crying all the way.

80 **Anne** (*as she is removing a pair of panties*). A cat?

81 **Mrs. Frank.** (*shocked*). Anne, please!

82 **Anne.** It's all right. I've got on three more. (*She pulls off two more. Finally, as they have all removed their surplus clothes, they look to* Mr. Frank, *waiting for him to speak.*)

83 **Mr. Frank.** Now. About the noise. While the men are in the building below, we must have complete quiet. Every sound can be heard down there, not only in the workrooms, but in the offices too. The men come at about eight-thirty, and leave at about five-thirty. So, to be perfectly safe, from eight in the morning until six in the evening we must move only when it is necessary, and then in stockinged feet. We must not speak above a whisper. We must not run any water. We cannot use the sink, or even, forgive me, the w.c.[5] The pipes go down through the workrooms. It would be heard. No trash . . . (Mr. Frank *stops abruptly as he hears the sound of marching feet from the street below. Everyone is motionless, paralyzed with fear.* Mr. Frank *goes quietly into the room on the right to look down out of the window.* Anne *runs after him, peering out with him. The tramping feet pass without stopping. The tension is relieved.* Mr. Frank, *followed by* Anne, *returns to the main room and resumes his instructions to the group.*) . . . No trash must ever be thrown out which might reveal that someone is living up here . . . not even a potato paring. We must burn everything in the stove at night. This is the way we must live until it is over, if we are to survive.

84 (*There is silence for a second.*)

85 **Mrs. Frank.** Until it is over.

86 **Mr. Frank** (*reassuringly*). After six we can move about . . . we can talk and laugh and have our supper and read and play games . . . just as we would at home. (*He looks at his watch.*) And now I think it would be wise if we all went to our rooms,

ANALYZE PLOT DEVELOPMENT

Annotate: Mark details in paragraphs 83–84 about how the residents of the Secret Annex must behave in order to survive.

Interpret: What is the main conflict, or problem, in the plot? How do Mr. Frank's words add tension, or suspense, to the plot?

[5] **w.c.:** water closet; toilet.

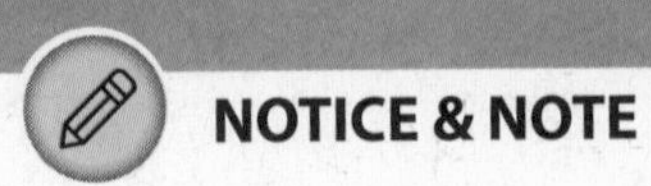

and were settled before eight o'clock. Mrs. Van Daan, you and your husband will be upstairs. I regret that there's no place up there for Peter. But he will be here, near us. This will be our common room, where we'll meet to talk and eat and read, like one family.

87 **Mr. Van Daan.** And where do you and Mrs. Frank sleep?

88 **Mr. Frank.** This room is also our bedroom.

89 **Mrs. Van Daan.** That isn't right. We'll sleep here and you take the room upstairs } *Together*

90 **Mrs. Van Daan.** It's your place.

91 **Mr. Frank.** Please. I've thought this out for weeks. It's the best arrangement. The only arrangement.

MEMORY MOMENT

Notice & Note: Review paragraphs 92–93. Mark what Mr. Frank recalls when Mrs. Van Daan tries to thank him for taking her family into the Annex.

Analyze: What does this Memory Moment reveal about the characters?

92 **Mrs. Van Daan** (*to* Mr. Frank). Never, never can we thank you. (*then to* Mrs. Frank) I don't know what would have happened to us, if it hadn't been for Mr. Frank.

93 **Mr. Frank.** You don't know how your husband helped me when I came to this country . . . knowing no one . . . not able to speak the language. I can never repay him for that. (*going to* Van Daan) May I help you with your things?

94 **Mr. Van Daan.** No. No. (*to* Mrs. Van Daan) Come along, *liefje*.[6]

95 **Mrs. Van Daan.** You'll be all right, Peter? You're not afraid?

96 **Peter** (*embarrassed*). Please, Mother.

97 (*They start up the stairs to the attic room above.* Mr. Frank *turns to* Mrs. Frank.)

98 **Mr. Frank.** You too must have some rest, Edith. You didn't close your eyes last night. Nor you, Margot.

99 **Anne.** I slept, Father. Wasn't that funny? I knew it was the last night in my own bed, and yet I slept soundly.

100 **Mr. Frank.** I'm glad, Anne. Now you'll be able to help me straighten things in here. (*to* Mrs. Frank *and* Margot) Come with me . . . You and Margot rest in this room for the time being. (*He picks up their clothes, starting for the room on the right.*)

101 **Mrs. Frank.** You're sure . . . ? I could help . . . And Anne hasn't had her milk . . .

102 **Mr. Frank.** I'll give it to her. (*to* Anne *and* Peter) Anne, Peter . . . it's best that you take off your shoes now, before you forget. (*He leads the way to the room, followed by* Margot.)

103 **Mrs. Frank.** You're sure you're not tired, Anne?

[6] ***liefje*** (lēf′yə) *Dutch:* little darling.

104 **Anne.** I feel fine. I'm going to help Father.

105 **Mrs. Frank.** Peter, I'm glad you are to be with us.

106 **Peter.** Yes, Mrs. Frank.

107 (Mrs. Frank *goes to join* Mr. Frank *and* Margot.

108 *During the following scene* Mr. Frank *helps* Margot *and* Mrs. Frank *to hang up their clothes. Then he persuades them both to lie down and rest. The* Van Daans *in their room above settle themselves. In the main room* Anne *and* Peter *remove their shoes.* Peter *takes his cat out of the carrier.*)

109 **Anne.** What's your cat's name?

110 **Peter.** Mouschi.[7]

111 **Anne.** Mouschi! Mouschi! Mouschi! (*She picks up the cat, walking away with it. To* Peter.) I love cats. I have one . . . a darling little cat. But they made me leave her behind. I left some food and a note for the neighbors to take care of her . . . I'm going to miss her terribly. What is yours? A him or a her?

112 **Peter.** He's a tom. He doesn't like strangers.

113 (*He takes the cat from her, putting it back in its carrier.*)

114 **Anne** (*unabashed*). Then I'll have to stop being a stranger, won't I? Is he fixed?

115 **Peter** (*startled*). Huh?

116 **Anne.** Did you have him fixed?

117 **Peter.** No.

118 **Anne.** Oh, you ought to have him fixed—to keep him from—you know, fighting. Where did you go to school?

[7] **Mouschi** (mo͞o′shē)

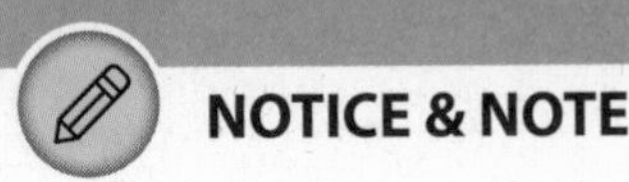

ANALYZE PLOT DEVELOPMENT

Annotate: In paragraphs 121–125, underline details that describe Anne. Circle details that describe Peter.

Compare: What does Peter mean when he says he is "a lone wolf"? What contrast do the playwrights reveal between the two characters?

119 **Peter.** Jewish Secondary.

120 **Anne.** But that's where Margot and I go! I never saw you around.

121 **Peter.** I used to see you . . . sometimes . . .

122 **Anne.** You did?

123 **Peter.** . . . in the school yard. You were always in the middle of a bunch of kids. (*He takes a penknife from his pocket.*)

124 **Anne.** Why didn't you ever come over?

125 **Peter.** I'm sort of a lone wolf. (*He starts to rip off his Star of David.*)

126 **Anne.** What are you doing?

127 **Peter.** Taking it off.

128 **Anne.** But you can't do that. They'll arrest you if you go out without your star.

129 (*He tosses his knife on the table.*)

130 **Peter.** Who's going out?

131 **Anne.** Why, of course! You're right! Of course we don't need them any more. (*She picks up his knife and starts to take her star off.*) I wonder what our friends will think when we don't show up today?

132 **Peter.** I didn't have any dates with anyone.

133 **Anne.** Oh, I did. I had a date with Jopie to go and play ping-pong at her house. Do you know Jopie de Waal?[8]

134 **Peter.** No.

135 **Anne.** Jopie's my best friend. I wonder what she'll think when she telephones and there's no answer? . . . Probably she'll go over to the house . . . I wonder what she'll think . . . we left everything as if we'd suddenly been called away . . . breakfast dishes in the sink . . . beds not made . . . (*As she pulls off her star, the cloth underneath shows clearly the color and form of the star.*) Look! It's still there! (Peter *goes over to the stove with his star.*) What're you going to do with yours?

136 **Peter.** Burn it.

137 **Anne** (*She starts to throw hers in, and cannot.*) It's funny, I can't throw mine away. I don't know why.

138 **Peter.** You can't throw . . . ? Something they branded you with . . . ? That they made you wear so they could spit on you?

[8] **Jopie de Waal** (yō´pē də väl´)

139 **Anne.** I know. I know. But after all, it is the Star of David, isn't it?

140 (*In the bedroom, right,* Margot *and* Mrs. Frank *are lying down.* Mr. Frank *starts quietly out.*)

141 **Peter.** Maybe it's different for a girl.

142 (Mr. Frank *comes into the main room.*)

143 **Mr. Frank.** Forgive me, Peter. Now let me see. We must find a bed for your cat. (*He goes to a cupboard.*) I'm glad you brought your cat. Anne was feeling so badly about hers. (*getting a used small washtub*) Here we are. Will it be comfortable in that?

144 **Peter** (*gathering up his things*). Thanks.

145 **Mr. Frank** (*opening the door of the room on the left*). And here is your room. But I warn you, Peter, you can't grow any more. Not an inch, or you'll have to sleep with your feet out of the skylight. Are you hungry?

146 **Peter.** No.

147 **Mr. Frank.** We have some bread and butter.

148 **Peter.** No, thank you.

149 **Mr. Frank.** You can have it for luncheon then. And tonight we will have a real supper . . . our first supper together.

150 **Peter.** Thanks. Thanks.

151 (*He goes into his room. During the following scene he arranges his possessions in his new room.*)

152 **Mr. Frank.** That's a nice boy, Peter.

153 **Anne.** He's awfully shy, isn't he?

154 **Mr. Frank.** You'll like him, I know.

155 **Anne.** I certainly hope so, since he's the only boy I'm likely to see for months and months.

156 (Mr. Frank *sits down, taking off his shoes.*)

157 **Mr. Frank.** Annele,[9] there's a box there. Will you open it? (*He indicates a carton on the couch.* Anne *brings it to the center table. In the street below there is the sound of children playing.*)

158 **Anne** (*as she opens the carton*). You know the way I'm going to think of it here? I'm going to think of it as a boarding house. A very peculiar summer boarding house, like the one that we—(*She breaks off as she pulls out some photographs.*) Father! My movie stars! I was wondering where they were! I

[9] **Annele/Anneke:** a nickname for Anne.

NOTICE & NOTE

ANALYZE PLOT DEVELOPMENT

Annotate: In paragraphs 158–160, mark the gifts that Mr. Frank gives Anne.

Interpret: What do these gifts reveal about Mr. Frank? How does the diary tie to the events in Scene 1?

WORDS OF THE WISER

Notice & Note: Review paragraphs 168–169. Mark the advantages to living in the Secret Annex that Mr. Frank points out to Anne.

Interpret: How does Mr. Frank probably think Anne is feeling in paragraphs 164–167? How does Mr. Frank use what he knows about his daughter to comfort her?

was looking for them this morning . . . and Queen Wilhelmina! How wonderful!

159 **Mr. Frank.** There's something more. Go on. Look further. (*He goes over to the sink, pouring a glass of milk from a thermos bottle.*)

160 **Anne** (*pulling out a pasteboard-bound book*). A diary! (*She throws her arms around her father.*) I've never had a diary. And I've always longed for one. (*She looks around the room.*) Pencil, pencil, pencil, pencil. (*She starts down the stairs.*) I'm going down to the office to get a pencil.

161 **Mr. Frank.** Anne! No! (*He goes after her, catching her by the arm and pulling her back.*)

162 **Anne** (*startled*). But there's no one in the building now.

163 **Mr. Frank.** It doesn't matter. I don't want you ever to go beyond that door.

164 **Anne** (*sobered*). Never . . . ? Not even at nighttime, when everyone is gone? Or on Sundays? Can't I go down to listen to the radio?

165 **Mr. Frank.** Never. I am sorry, Anneke. It isn't safe. No, you must never go beyond that door.

166 (*For the first time* Anne *realizes what "going into hiding" means.*)

167 **Anne.** I see.

168 **Mr. Frank.** It'll be hard, I know. But always remember this, Anneke. There are no walls, there are no bolts, no locks that anyone can put on your mind. Miep will bring us books. We will read history, poetry, mythology. (*He gives her the glass of milk.*) Here's your milk. (*With his arm about her, they go over to the couch, sitting down side by side.*) As a matter of fact, between us, Anne, being here has certain advantages for you. For instance, you remember the battle you had with your mother the other day on the subject of overshoes? You said you'd rather die than wear overshoes. But in the end you had to wear them? Well now, you see, for as long as we are here you will never have to wear overshoes! Isn't that good? And the coat that you inherited from Margot, you won't have to wear that any more. And the piano! You won't have to practice on the piano. I tell you, this is going to be a fine life for you!

169 (Anne's *panic is gone.* Peter *appears in the doorway of his room, with a saucer in his hand. He is carrying his cat.*)

170 **Peter.** I . . . I . . . I thought I'd better get some water for Mouschi before . . .

171 **Mr. Frank.** Of course.

172 (*As he starts toward the sink the carillon begins to chime the hour of eight. He tiptoes to the window at the back and looks down at the street below. He turns to* Peter, *indicating in pantomime that it is too late.* Peter *starts back for his room. He steps on a creaking board. The three of them are frozen for a minute in fear. As* Peter *starts away again,* Anne *tiptoes over to him and pours some of the milk from her glass into the saucer for the cat.* Peter *squats on the floor, putting the milk before the cat.* Mr. Frank *gives* Anne *his fountain pen, and then goes into the room at the right. For a second* Anne *watches the cat, then she goes over to the center table, and opens her diary.*

173 *In the room at the right,* Mrs. Frank *has sat up quickly at the sound of the carillon.* Mr. Frank *comes in and sits down beside her on the settee, his arm comfortingly around her.*

174 *Upstairs, in the attic room,* Mr. *and* Mrs. Van Daan *have hung their clothes in the closet and are now seated on the iron bed.* Mrs. Van Daan *leans back exhausted.* Mr. Van Daan *fans her with a newspaper.*

175 Anne *starts to write in her diary. The lights dim out, the curtain falls.*

176 *In the darkness* Anne's Voice *comes to us again, faintly at first, and then with growing strength.*)

177 **Anne's Voice.** I expect I should be describing what it feels like to go into hiding. But I really don't know yet myself. I only know it's funny never to be able to go outdoors . . . never to breathe fresh air . . . never to run and shout and jump. It's the silence in the nights that frightens me most. Every time I hear a creak in the house, or a step on the street outside, I'm sure they're coming for us. The days aren't so bad. At least we know that Miep and Mr. Kraler are down there below us in the office. Our protectors, we call them. I asked Father what would happen to them if the Nazis found out they were hiding us. Pim said that they would suffer the same fate that we would . . . Imagine! They know this, and yet when they come up here, they're always cheerful and gay as if there were nothing in the world to bother them . . . Friday, the twenty-first of August, nineteen forty-two. Today I'm going to tell you our general news. Mother is unbearable. She insists on treating me like a baby, which I **loathe.** Otherwise things are going better. The weather is . . .

178 (*As* Anne's Voice *is fading out, the curtain rises on the scene.*)

loathe
(lōth) *v.* To *loathe* something is to dislike it very much.

ANALYZE PLOT DEVELOPMENT

Annotate: Mark the stage direction that tells you how much time has passed since the end of Scene 2.

Predict: During that time, what kinds of tensions do you think have grown among the residents of the Secret Annex, and why? How might those tensions create subplots in this drama?

Scene 3

179 *It is a little after six o'clock in the evening, two months later.*

180 Margot *is in the bedroom at the right, studying.* Mr. Van Daan *is lying down in the attic room above.*

181 *The rest of the "family" is in the main room.* Anne *and* Peter *sit opposite each other at the center table, where they have been doing their lessons.* Mrs. Frank *is on the couch.* Mrs. Van Daan *is seated with her fur coat, on which she has been sewing, in her lap. None of them are wearing their shoes.*

182 *Their eyes are on* Mr. Frank, *waiting for him to give them the signal which will release them from their day-long quiet.* Mr. Frank, *his shoes in his hand, stands looking down out of the window at the back, watching to be sure that all of the workmen have left the building below.*

183 *After a few seconds of motionless silence,* Mr. Frank *turns from the window.*

184 **Mr. Frank** (*quietly, to the group*). It's safe now. The last workman has left. (*There is an immediate stir of relief.*)

185 **Anne** (*Her pent-up energy explodes*). WHEE!

186 **Mrs. Frank** (*startled, amused*). Anne!

187 **Mrs. Van Daan.** I'm first for the w.c. (*She hurries off to the bathroom.* Mrs. Frank *puts on her shoes and starts up to the sink to prepare supper.* Anne *sneaks* Peter's *shoes from under the table and hides them behind her back.* Mr. Frank *goes in to* Margot's *room.*)

188 **Mr. Frank** (*to* Margot). Six o'clock. School's over.

189 (Margot *gets up, stretching.* Mr. Frank *sits down to put on his shoes. In the main room* Peter *tries to find his.*)

190 **Peter** (*to* Anne). Have you seen my shoes?

191 **Anne** (*innocently*). Your shoes?

192 **Peter.** You've taken them, haven't you?

193 **Anne.** I don't know what you're talking about.

194 **Peter.** You're going to be sorry!

195 **Anne.** Am I? (Peter *goes after her.* Anne, *with his shoes in her hand, runs from him, dodging behind her mother.*)

196 **Mrs. Frank** (*protesting*). Anne, dear!

197 **Peter.** Wait till I get you!

198 **Anne.** I'm waiting! (Peter *makes a lunge for her. They both fall to the floor.* Peter *pins her down, wrestling with her to get the shoes.*) Don't! Don't! Peter, stop it. Ouch!

199 **Mrs. Frank.** Anne! . . . Peter! (*Suddenly* Peter *becomes self-conscious. He grabs his shoes roughly and starts for his room.*)

200 **Anne** (*following him*). Peter, where are you going? Come dance with me.

201 **Peter.** I tell you I don't know how.

202 **Anne.** I'll teach you.

203 **Peter.** I'm going to give Mouschi his dinner.

204 **Anne.** Can I watch?

205 **Peter.** He doesn't like people around while he eats.

206 **Anne.** Peter, please.

207 **Peter.** No! (*He goes into his room.* Anne *slams his door after him.*)

208 **Mrs. Frank.** Anne, dear, I think you shouldn't play like that with Peter. It's not dignified.

209 **Anne.** Who cares if it's dignified? I don't want to be dignified.

210 (Mr. Frank *and* Margot *come from the room on the right.* Margot *goes to help her mother.* Mr. Frank *starts for the center table to correct* Margot's *school papers.*)

211 **Mrs. Frank** (*to* Anne). You complain that I don't treat you like a grownup. But when I do, you resent it.

212 **Anne.** I only want some fun . . . someone to laugh and clown with . . . After you've sat still all day and hardly moved, you've got to have some fun. I don't know what's the matter with that boy.

213 **Mr. Frank.** He isn't used to girls. Give him a little time.

214 **Anne.** Time? Isn't two months time? I could cry. (*catching hold of* Margot) Come on, Margot . . . dance with me. Come on, please.

215 **Margot.** I have to help with supper.

216 **Anne.** You know we're going to forget how to dance . . . When we get out we won't remember a thing.

217 (*She starts to sing and dance by herself.* Mr. Frank *takes her in his arms, waltzing with her.* Mrs. Van Daan *comes in from the bathroom.*)

218 **Mrs. Van Daan.** Next? (*She looks around as she starts putting on her shoes.*) Where's Peter?

NOTICE & NOTE

CONTRASTS AND CONTRADICTIONS

Notice & Note: In paragraphs 208–212, underline how Anne feels when her mother doesn't treat her like a grownup. Circle how she feels when her mother *does* treat her like a grownup.

Infer: What does this contradiction reveal about Anne? What does it reveal about her relationship with her mother?

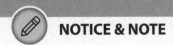

219 **Anne** (*as they are dancing*). Where would he be!

220 **Mrs. Van Daan.** He hasn't finished his lessons, has he? His father'll kill him if he catches him in there with that cat and his work not done.

221 (Mr. Frank *and* Anne *finish their dance. They bow to each other with extravagant formality.*) Anne, get him out of there, will you?

222 **Anne** (*at* Peter's *door*). Peter? Peter?

223 **Peter** (*opening the door a crack*). What is it?

224 **Anne.** Your mother says to come out.

225 **Peter.** I'm giving Mouschi his dinner.

226 **Mrs. Van Daan.** You know what your father says. (*She sits on the couch, sewing on the lining of her fur coat.*)

227 **Peter.** For heaven's sake, I haven't even looked at him since lunch.

228 **Mrs. Van Daan.** I'm just telling you, that's all.

229 **Anne.** I'll feed him.

230 **Peter.** I don't want you in there.

231 **Mrs. Van Daan.** Peter!

232 **Peter** (*to* Anne). Then give him his dinner and come right out, you hear? (*He comes back to the table.* Anne *shuts the door of* Peter's *room after her and disappears behind the curtain covering his closet.*)

233 **Mrs. Van Daan** (*to* Peter). Now is that any way to talk to your little girl friend?

234 **Peter.** Mother . . . for heaven's sake . . . will you please stop saying that?

235 **Mrs. Van Daan.** Look at him blush! Look at him!

236 **Peter.** Please! I'm not . . . anyway . . . let me alone, will you?

237 **Mrs. Van Daan.** He acts like it was something to be ashamed of. It's nothing to be ashamed of, to have a little girl friend.

238 **Peter.** You're crazy. She's only thirteen.

239 **Mrs. Van Daan.** So what? And you're sixteen. Just perfect. Your father's ten years older than I am. (*to* Mr. Frank) I warn you, Mr. Frank, if this war lasts much longer, we're going to be related and then . . .

240 **Mr. Frank.** *Mazeltov!*[10]

[10]***Mazeltov!*** (mä´zəl-tôf´) *Hebrew:* Congratulations!

241 **Mrs. Frank** (*deliberately changing the conversation*). I wonder where Miep is. She's usually so prompt. (*Suddenly everything else is forgotten as they hear the sound of an automobile coming to a screeching stop in the street below. They are tense, motionless in their terror. The car starts away. A wave of relief sweeps over them. They pick up their occupations again.* Anne *flings open the door of* Peter's *room, making a dramatic entrance. She is dressed in* Peter's *clothes.* Peter *looks at her in fury. The others are amused.*)

242 **Anne.** Good evening, everyone. Forgive me if I don't stay. (*She jumps up on a chair.*) I have a friend waiting for me in there. My friend Tom. Tom Cat. Some people say that we look alike. But Tom has the most beautiful whiskers, and I have only a little fuzz. I am hoping . . . in time . . .

243 **Peter.** All right, Mrs. Quack Quack!

244 **Anne** (*outraged—jumping down*). Peter!

245 **Peter.** I heard about you . . . How you talked so much in class they called you Mrs. Quack Quack. How Mr. Smitter made you write a composition . . . "'Quack, quack,' said Mrs. Quack Quack."

246 **Anne.** Well, go on. Tell them the rest. How it was so good he read it out loud to the class and then read it to all his other classes!

247 **Peter.** Quack! Quack! Quack . . . Quack . . . Quack . . .

248 (Anne *pulls off the coat and trousers.*)

249 **Anne.** You are the most intolerable, insufferable boy I've ever met!

250 (*She throws the clothes down the stairwell.* Peter *goes down after them.*)

251 **Peter.** Quack, quack, quack!

252 **Mrs. Van Daan** (*to* Anne). That's right, Anneke! Give it to him!

253 **Anne.** With all the boys in the world . . . Why I had to get locked up with one like you! . . .

254 **Peter.** Quack, quack, quack, and from now on stay out of my room!

255 (*As* Peter *passes her,* Anne *puts out her foot, tripping him. He picks himself up, and goes on into his room.*)

256 **Mrs. Frank** (*quietly*). Anne, dear . . . your hair. (*She feels* Anne's *forehead.*) You're warm. Are you feeling all right?

NOTICE & NOTE 

ANALYZE PLOT DEVELOPMENT

Annotate: In paragraphs 241–249, underline details that show how Anne teases Peter. Circle what Peter says about Anne.

Draw Conclusions: What do Anne and Peter tease each other about? What conclusions can you draw about Anne and Peter based on their actions, their speech, and the descriptions provided by the playwrights?

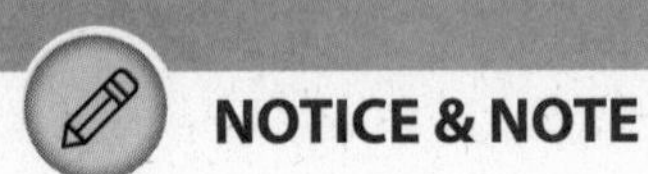

257 **Anne.** Please, Mother. (*She goes over to the center table, slipping into her shoes.*)

258 **Mrs. Frank** (*following her*). You haven't a fever, have you?

259 **Anne** (*pulling away*). No. No.

260 **Mrs. Frank.** You know we can't call a doctor here, ever. There's only one thing to do . . . watch carefully. Prevent an illness before it comes. Let me see your tongue.

261 **Anne.** Mother, this is perfectly absurd.

262 **Mrs. Frank.** Anne, dear, don't be such a baby. Let me see your tongue. (*As* Anne *refuses,* Mrs. Frank *appeals to* Mr. Frank.) Otto . . . ?

263 **Mr. Frank.** You hear your mother, Anne. (Anne *flicks out her tongue for a second, then turns away.*)

264 **Mrs. Frank.** Come on—open up! (*as* Anne *opens her mouth very wide*) You seem all right . . . but perhaps an aspirin . . .

265 **Mrs. Van Daan.** For heaven's sake, don't give that child any pills. I waited for fifteen minutes this morning for her to come out of the w.c.

266 **Anne.** I was washing my hair!

267 **Mr. Frank.** I think there's nothing the matter with our Anne that a ride on her bike, or a visit with her friend Jopie de Waal wouldn't cure. Isn't that so, Anne?

268 (Mr. Van Daan *comes down into the room. From outside we hear faint sounds of bombers going over and a burst of ack-ack.*)

269 **Mr. Van Daan.** Miep not come yet?

270 **Mrs. Van Daan.** The workmen just left, a little while ago.

271 **Mr. Van Daan.** What's for dinner tonight?

272 **Mrs. Van Daan.** Beans.

273 **Mr. Van Daan.** Not again!

274 **Mrs. Van Daan.** Poor Putti! I know. But what can we do? That's all that Miep brought us.

275 (Mr. Van Daan *starts to pace, his hands behind his back.* Anne *follows behind him, imitating him.*)

276 **Anne.** We are now in what is known as the "bean cycle." Beans boiled, beans en casserole, beans with strings, beans without strings . . .

277 (Peter *has come out of his room. He slides into his place at the table, becoming immediately absorbed in his studies.*)

278 **Mr. Van Daan** (*to* Peter). I saw you . . . in there, playing with your cat.

279 **Mrs. Van Daan.** He just went in for a second, putting his coat away. He's been out here all the time, doing his lessons.

280 **Mr. Frank** (*looking up from the papers*). Anne, you got an excellent in your history paper today . . . and very good in Latin.

281 **Anne** (*sitting beside him*). How about algebra?

282 **Mr. Frank.** I'll have to make a confession. Up until now I've managed to stay ahead of you in algebra. Today you caught up with me. We'll leave it to Margot to correct.

283 **Anne.** Isn't algebra *vile,* Pim!

284 **Mr. Frank.** Vile!

285 **Margot** (*to* Mr. Frank). How did I do?

286 **Anne** (*getting up*). Excellent, excellent, excellent, excellent!

287 **Mr. Frank** (*to* Margot). You should have used the subjunctive here . . .

288 **Margot.** Should I? . . . I thought . . . look here . . . I didn't use it here . . . (*The two become absorbed in the papers.*)

289 **Anne.** Mrs. Van Daan, may I try on your coat?

290 **Mrs. Frank.** No, Anne.

291 **Mrs. Van Daan** (*giving it to* Anne). It's all right . . . but careful with it. (Anne *puts it on and struts with it.*) My father gave me that the year before he died. He always bought the best that money could buy.

292 **Anne.** Mrs. Van Daan, did you have a lot of boy friends before you were married?

293 **Mrs. Frank.** Anne, that's a personal question. It's not courteous to ask personal questions.

294 **Mrs. Van Daan.** Oh I don't mind. (*to* Anne) Our house was always swarming with boys. When I was a girl we had . . .

295 **Mr. Van Daan.** Oh, God. Not again!

296 **Mrs. Van Daan** (*good-humored*). Shut up! (*Without a pause,* to Anne. Mr. Van Daan *mimics* Mrs. Van Daan, *speaking the first few words in unison with her.*) One summer we had a big house in Hilversum. The boys came buzzing round like bees around a jam pot. And when I was sixteen! . . . We were wearing our skirts very short those days and I had good-looking legs. (*She pulls up her skirt, going to* Mr. Frank.) I still have 'em. I may not be as pretty as I used to be, but I still have my legs. How about it, Mr. Frank?

MEMORY MOMENT

Notice & Note: In paragraphs 294–296, mark the words that signal that Mrs. Van Daan is about to share a memory with Anne.

Interpret: How does Mr. Van Daan react when his wife begins to share her memory? Why does he react that way?

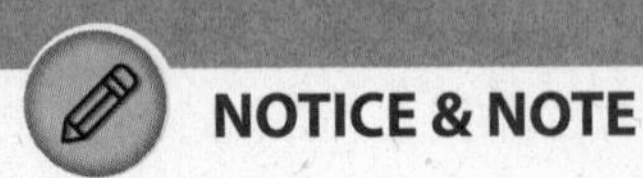

NOTICE & NOTE

297 **Mr. Van Daan.** All right. All right. We see them.

298 **Mrs. Van Daan.** I'm not asking you. I'm asking Mr. Frank.

299 **Peter.** Mother, for heaven's sake.

AGAIN AND AGAIN

Notice & Note: In paragraphs 300–302, mark the words that Mrs. Van Daan's father told her to tell boys who got "fresh." Then mark the same words where Anne repeats them.

Interpret: Why might the playwrights have made Anne repeat those lines?

300 **Mrs. Van Daan.** Oh, I embarrass you, do I? Well, I just hope the girl you marry has as good. (*then to* Anne) My father used to worry about me, with so many boys hanging round. He told me, if any of them gets fresh, you say to him . . . "Remember, Mr. So-and-So, remember I'm a lady."

301 **Anne.** "Remember, Mr. So-and-So, remember I'm a lady." (*She gives* Mrs. Van Daan *her coat.*)

302 **Mr. Van Daan.** Look at you, talking that way in front of her! Don't you know she puts it all down in that diary?

303 **Mrs. Van Daan.** So, if she does? I'm only telling the truth!

304 (Anne *stretches out, putting her ear to the floor, listening to what is going on below. The sound of the bombers fades away.*)

305 **Mrs. Frank** (*setting the table*). Would you mind, Peter, if I moved you over to the couch?

306 **Anne** (*listening*). Miep must have the radio on.

307 (Peter *picks up his papers, going over to the couch beside* Mrs. Van Daan.)

308 **Mr. Van Daan** (*accusingly, to* Peter). Haven't you finished yet?

309 **Peter.** No.

310 **Mr. Van Daan.** You ought to be ashamed of yourself.

311 **Peter.** All right. All right. I'm a dunce. I'm a hopeless case. Why do I go on?

312 **Mrs. Van Daan.** You're not hopeless. Don't talk that way. It's just that you haven't anyone to help you, like the girls have. (*to* Mr. Frank) Maybe you could help him, Mr. Frank?

313 **Mr. Frank.** I'm sure that his father . . . ?

314 **Mr. Van Daan.** Not me. I can't do anything with him. He won't listen to me. You go ahead . . . if you want.

315 **Mr. Frank** (*going to* Peter). What about it, Peter? Shall we make our school coeducational?

316 **Mrs. Van Daan** (*kissing* Mr. Frank). You're an angel, Mr. Frank. An angel. I don't know why I didn't meet you before I met that one there.

317 Here, sit down, Mr. Frank . . . (*She forces him down on the couch beside* Peter.) Now, Peter, you listen to Mr. Frank.

318 **Mr. Frank.** It might be better for us to go into Peter's room. (Peter *jumps up eagerly, leading the way.*)

319 **Mrs. Van Daan.** That's right. You go in there, Peter. You listen to Mr. Frank. Mr. Frank is a highly educated man. (*As* Mr. Frank *is about to follow* Peter *into his room,* Mrs. Frank *stops him and wipes the lipstick from his lips. Then she closes the door after them.*)

320 **Anne** (*on the floor, listening*). Shh! I can hear a man's voice talking.

321 **Mr. Van Daan** (*to* Anne). Isn't it bad enough here without your sprawling all over the place? (Anne *sits up.*)

322 **Mrs. Van Daan** (*to* Mr. Van Daan). If you didn't smoke so much, you wouldn't be so bad-tempered.

323 **Mr. Van Daan.** Am I smoking? Do you see me smoking?

324 **Mrs. Van Daan.** Don't tell me you've used up all those cigarettes.

325 **Mr. Van Daan.** One package. Miep only brought me one package.

326 **Mrs. Van Daan.** It's a filthy habit anyway. It's a good time to break yourself.

327 **Mr. Van Daan.** Oh, stop it, please.

328 **Mrs. Van Daan.** You're smoking up all our money. You know that, don't you?

329 **Mr. Van Daan.** Will you shut up? (*During this,* Mrs. Frank *and* Margot *have studiously kept their eyes down. But* Anne, *seated on the floor, has been following the discussion interestedly.* Mr. Van Daan *turns to see her staring up at him.*) And what are you staring at?

330 **Anne.** I never heard grownups quarrel before. I thought only children quarreled.

331 **Mr. Van Daan.** This isn't a quarrel! It's a discussion. And I never heard children so rude before.

332 **Anne** (*rising,* ***indignantly***). *I,* rude!

333 **Mr. Van Daan.** Yes!

334 **Mrs. Frank** (*quickly*). Anne, will you get me my knitting? (Anne *goes to get it.*) I must remember, when Miep comes, to ask her to bring me some more wool.

335 **Margot** (*going to her room*). I need some hairpins and some soap. I made a list. (*She goes into her bedroom to get the list.*)

indignantly
(ĭn-dĭg´nənt-lē) *adv.* Someone who does something *indignantly* acts in a way that shows anger or shock over something that is unjust or unfair.

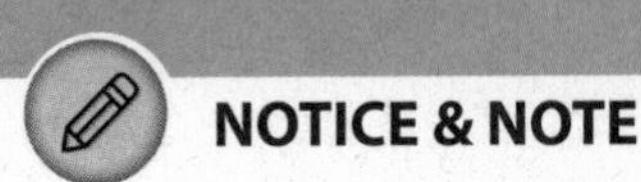

NOTICE & NOTE

336 **Mrs. Frank** (*to* Anne). Have you some library books for Miep when she comes?

337 **Anne.** It's a wonder that Miep has a life of her own, the way we make her run errands for us. Please, Miep, get me some starch. Please take my hair out and have it cut. Tell me all the latest news, Miep.

338 (*She goes over, kneeling on the couch beside* Mrs. Van Daan.) Did you know she was engaged? His name is Dirk, and Miep's afraid the Nazis will ship him off to Germany to work in one of their war plants. That's what they're doing with some of the young Dutchmen . . . they pick them up off the streets—

339 **Mr. Van Daan** (*interrupting*). Don't you ever get tired of talking? Suppose you try keeping still for five minutes. Just five minutes. (*He starts to pace again. Again* Anne *follows him, mimicking him.* Mrs. Frank *jumps up and takes her by the arm up to the sink, and gives her a glass of milk.*)

340 **Mrs. Frank.** Come here, Anne. It's time for your glass of milk.

341 **Mr. Van Daan.** Talk, talk, talk. I never heard such a child. Where is my . . . ? Every evening it's the same, talk, talk, talk. (*He looks around.*) Where is my . . . ?

342 **Mrs. Van Daan.** What're you looking for?

343 **Mr. Van Daan.** My pipe. Have you seen my pipe?

344 **Mrs. Van Daan.** What good's a pipe? You haven't got any tobacco.

345 **Mr. Van Daan.** At least I'll have something to hold in my mouth! (*opening Margot's bedroom door*) Margot, have you seen my pipe?

346 **Margot.** It was on the table last night.

347 *(Anne puts her glass of milk on the table and picks up his pipe, hiding it behind her back.)*

348 **Mr. Van Daan.** I know. I know. Anne, did you see my pipe? . . . Anne!

349 **Mrs. Frank.** Anne, Mr. Van Daan is speaking to you.

350 **Anne.** Am I allowed to talk now?

351 **Mr. Van Daan.** You're the most aggravating . . . The trouble with you is, you've been spoiled. What you need is a good old-fashioned spanking.

352 **Anne** (*mimicking* Mrs. Van Daan). "Remember, Mr. So-and-So, remember I'm a lady." (*She thrusts the pipe into his mouth, then picks up her glass of milk.*)

ANALYZE PLOT DEVELOPMENT

Annotate: In paragraphs 348–358, underline details that show how Mr. Van Daan expects girls and women to behave. Circle what Anne wants for herself.

Compare: How do these differences highlight the conflict in values between Mr. Van Daan and Anne?

353 **Mr. Van Daan** (*restraining himself with difficulty*). Why aren't you nice and quiet like your sister Margot? Why do you have to show off all the time? Let me give you a little advice, young lady. Men don't like that kind of thing in a girl. You know that? A man likes a girl who'll listen to him once in a while . . . a domestic girl, who'll keep her house shining for her husband . . . who loves to cook and sew and . . .

354 **Anne.** I'd cut my throat first! I'd open my veins! I'm going to be remarkable! I'm going to Paris . . .

355 **Mr. Van Daan** (*scoffingly*). Paris!

356 **Anne.** . . . to study music and art.

357 **Mr. Van Daan.** Yeah! Yeah!

358 **Anne.** I'm going to be a famous dancer or singer . . . or something wonderful. (*She makes a wide gesture, spilling the glass of milk on the fur coat in* Mrs. Van Daan's *lap.* Margot *rushes quickly over with a towel.* Anne *tries to brush the milk off with her skirt.*)

359 **Mrs. Van Daan.** Now look what you've done . . . you clumsy little fool! My beautiful fur coat my father gave me . . .

360 **Anne.** I'm so sorry.

361 **Mrs. Van Daan.** What do you care? It isn't yours . . . So go on, ruin it! Do you know what that coat cost? Do you? And now look at it! Look at it!

362 **Anne.** I'm very, very sorry.

363 **Mrs. Van Daan.** I could kill you for this. I could just kill you! (Mrs. Van Daan *goes up the stairs, clutching the coat.* Mr. Van Daan *starts after her.*)

364 **Mr. Van Daan.** Petronella . . . *liefje! Liefje!* . . . Come back . . . the supper . . . come back!

365 **Mrs. Frank.** Anne, you must not behave in that way.

366 **Anne.** It was an accident. Anyone can have an accident.

367 **Mrs. Frank.** I don't mean that. I mean the answering back. You must not answer back. They are our guests. We must always show the greatest courtesy to them. We're all living under terrible tension. (*She stops as* Margot *indicates that* Van Daan *can hear. When he is gone, she continues.*) That's why we must control ourselves . . . You don't hear Margot getting into arguments with them, do you? Watch Margot. She's always courteous with them. Never familiar. She keeps her distance. And they respect her for it. Try to be like Margot.

WORDS OF THE WISER

Notice & Note: Mark the reason that Mrs. Frank gives for why Anne must not answer back or behave rudely to the Van Daans.

Infer: What does Mrs. Frank understand about people that Anne has yet to learn?

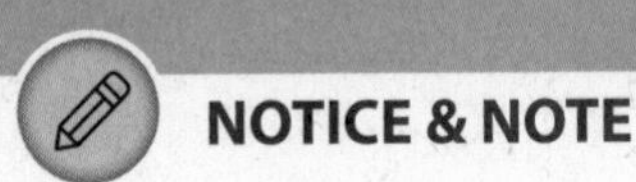

368 **Anne.** And have them walk all over me, the way they do her? No, thanks!

369 **Mrs. Frank.** I'm not afraid that anyone is going to walk all over you, Anne. I'm afraid for other people, that you'll walk on them. I don't know what happens to you, Anne. You are wild, self-willed. If I had ever talked to my mother as you talk to me . . .

370 **Anne.** Things have changed. People aren't like that any more. "Yes, Mother." "No, Mother." "Anything you say, Mother." I've got to fight things out for myself! Make something of myself!

371 **Mrs. Frank.** It isn't necessary to fight to do it. Margot doesn't fight, and isn't she . . . ?

372 **Anne** (*violently rebellious*). Margot! Margot! Margot! That's all I hear from everyone . . . how wonderful Margot is . . . "Why aren't you like Margot?"

373 **Margot** (*protesting*). Oh, come on, Anne, don't be so . . .

374 **Anne** (*paying no attention*). Everything she does is right, and everything I do is wrong! I'm the goat around here! . . . You're all against me! . . . And you worst of all!

375 (*She rushes off into her room and throws herself down on the settee, stifling her sobs.* Mrs. Frank *sighs and starts toward the stove.*)

376 **Mrs. Frank** (*to* Margot). Let's put the soup on the stove . . . if there's anyone who cares to eat. Margot, will you take the bread out? (Margot *gets the bread from the cupboard.*) I don't know how we can go on living this way . . . I can't say a word to Anne . . . she flies at me . . .

377 **Margot.** You know Anne. In half an hour she'll be out here, laughing and joking.

378 **Mrs. Frank.** And . . . (*She makes a motion upwards, indicating the* Van Daans.) . . . I told your father it wouldn't work . . . but no . . . no . . . he had to ask them, he said . . . he owed it to him, he said. Well, he knows now that I was right! These quarrels! . . . This bickering!

379 **Margot** (*with a warning look*). Shush. Shush.

380 (*The buzzer for the door sounds.* Mrs. Frank *gasps, startled.*)

381 **Mrs. Frank.** Every time I hear that sound, my heart stops!

382 **Margot** (*starting for* Peter's *door*). It's Miep. (*She knocks at the door.*) Father?

383 (Mr. Frank *comes quickly from* Peter's *room.*)

384 **Mr. Frank.** Thank you, Margot. (*as he goes down the steps to open the outer door*) Has everyone his list?

385 **Margot.** I'll get my books. (*giving her mother a list*) Here's your list.

386 (Margot *goes into her and* Anne's *bedroom on the right.* Anne *sits up, hiding her tears, as* Margot *comes in.*) Miep's here.

387 (Margot *picks up her books and goes back.* Anne *hurries over to the mirror, smoothing her hair.*)

388 **Mr. Van Daan** (*coming down the stairs*). Is it Miep?

389 **Margot.** Yes. Father's gone down to let her in.

390 **Mr. Van Daan.** At last I'll have some cigarettes!

391 **Mrs. Frank** (*to* Mr. Van Daan). I can't tell you how unhappy I am about Mrs. Van Daan's coat. Anne should never have touched it.

392 **Mr. Van Daan.** She'll be all right.

393 **Mrs. Frank.** Is there anything I can do?

394 **Mr. Van Daan.** Don't worry.

395 (*He turns to meet* Miep. *But it is not* Miep *who comes up the steps. It is* Mr. Kraler, *followed by* Mr. Frank. *Their faces are grave.* Anne *comes from the bedroom.* Peter *comes from his room.*)

396 **Mrs. Frank.** Mr. Kraler!

397 **Mr. Van Daan.** How are you, Mr. Kraler?

398 **Margot.** This is a surprise.

399 **Mrs. Frank.** When Mr. Kraler comes, the sun begins to shine.

400 **Mr. Van Daan.** Miep is coming?

401 **Mr. Kraler.** Not tonight.

402 (Kraler *goes to* Margot *and* Mrs. Frank *and* Anne, *shaking hands with them.*)

403 **Mrs. Frank.** Wouldn't you like a cup of coffee? . . . Or, better still, will you have supper with us?

404 **Mr. Frank.** Mr. Kraler has something to talk over with us. Something has happened, he says, which demands an immediate decision.

405 **Mrs. Frank** (*fearful*). What is it?

406 (Mr. Kraler *sits down on the couch. As he talks he takes bread, cabbages, milk, etc., from his briefcase, giving them to* Margot *and* Anne *to put away.*)

NOTICE & NOTE

ANALYZE PLOT DEVELOPMENT

Annotate: In paragraphs 407–419, mark the request that Mr. Kraler makes of Mr. Frank and the others.

Interpret: Remember that a subplot can add a new conflict to a main plot. How does Mr. Kraler's request create a new problem for the residents of the Secret Annex?

407 **Mr. Kraler.** Usually, when I come up here, I try to bring you some bit of good news. What's the use of telling you the bad news when there's nothing that you can do about it? But today something has happened . . . Dirk . . . Miep's Dirk, you know, came to me just now. He tells me that he has a Jewish friend living near him. A dentist. He says he's in trouble. He begged me, could I do anything for this man? Could I find him a hiding place? . . . So I've come to you . . . I know it's a terrible thing to ask of you, living as you are, but would you take him in with you?

408 **Mr. Frank.** Of course we will.

409 **Mr. Kraler** (*rising*). It'll be just for a night or two . . . until I find some other place. This happened so suddenly that I didn't know where to turn.

410 **Mr. Frank.** Where is he?

411 **Mr. Kraler.** Downstairs in the office.

412 **Mr. Frank.** Good. Bring him up.

413 **Mr. Kraler.** His name is Dussel . . . Jan Dussel.

414 **Mr. Frank.** Dussel . . . I think I know him.

415 **Mr. Kraler.** I'll get him. (*He goes quickly down the steps and out.* Mr. Frank *suddenly becomes conscious of the others.*)

416 **Mr. Frank.** Forgive me. I spoke without consulting you. But I knew you'd feel as I do.

417 **Mr. Van Daan.** There's no reason for you to consult anyone. This is your place. You have a right to do exactly as you please. The only thing I feel . . . there's so little food as it is . . . and to take in another person . . .

418 (Peter *turns away, ashamed of his father.*)

419 **Mr. Frank.** We can stretch the food a little. It's only for a few days.

420 **Mr. Van Daan.** You want to make a bet?

421 **Mrs. Frank.** I think it's fine to have him. But, Otto, where are you going to put him? Where?

422 **Peter.** He can have my bed. I can sleep on the floor. I wouldn't mind.

423 **Mr. Frank.** That's good of you, Peter. But your room's too small . . . even for *you*.

424 **Anne.** I have a much better idea. I'll come in here with you and Mother, and Margot can take Peter's room and Peter can go in our room with Mr. Dussel.

425 **Margot.** That's right. We could do that.

426 **Mr. Frank.** No, Margot. You mustn't sleep in that room . . . neither you nor Anne. Mouschi has caught some rats in there. Peter's brave. He doesn't mind.

427 **Anne.** Then how about *this?* I'll come in here with you and Mother, and Mr. Dussel can have my bed.

428 **Mrs. Frank.** No. No. *No!* Margot will come in here with us and he can have her bed. It's the only way. Margot, bring your things in here. Help her, Anne.

429 (Margot *hurries into her room to get her things.*)

430 **Anne** (*to her mother*). Why Margot? Why can't I come in here?

431 **Mrs. Frank.** Because it wouldn't be proper for Margot to sleep with a . . . Please, Anne. Don't argue. Please. (Anne *starts slowly away.*)

432 **Mr. Frank.** (*to* Anne). You don't mind sharing your room with Mr. Dussel, do you, Anne?

433 **Anne.** No. No, of course not.

434 **Mr. Frank.** Good. (Anne *goes off into her bedroom, helping* Margot. Mr. Frank *starts to search in the cupboards.*) Where's the cognac?

435 **Mrs. Frank.** It's there. But, Otto, I was saving it in case of illness.

436 **Mr. Frank.** I think we couldn't find a better time to use it. Peter, will you get five glasses for me?

437 (Peter *goes for the glasses.* Margot *comes out of her bedroom, carrying her possessions, which she hangs behind a curtain in the main room.* Mr. Frank *finds the cognac and pours it into the five glasses that* Peter *brings him.* Mr. Van Daan *stands looking on sourly.* Mrs. Van Daan *comes downstairs and looks around at all the bustle.*)

438 **Mrs. Van Daan.** What's happening? What's going on?

439 **Mr. Van Daan.** Someone's moving in with us.

440 **Mrs. Van Daan.** In here? You're joking.

441 **Margot.** It's only for a night or two . . . until Mr. Kraler finds him another place.

442 **Mr. Van Daan.** Yeah! Yeah!

443 (Mr. Frank *hurries over as* Mr. Kraler *and* Dussel *come up.* Dussel *is a man in his late fifties, meticulous, finicky . . . bewildered now. He wears a raincoat. He carries a briefcase, stuffed full, and a small medicine case.*)

444 **Mr. Frank.** Come in, Mr. Dussel.

445 **Mr. Kraler.** This is Mr. Frank.

446 **Dussel.** Mr. Otto Frank?

447 **Mr. Frank.** Yes. Let me take your things. (*He takes the hat and briefcase, but* Dussel *clings to his medicine case.*) This is my wife Edith . . . Mr. and Mrs. Van Daan . . . their son, Peter . . . and my daughters, Margot and Anne.

448 (Dussel *shakes hands with everyone.*)

449 **Mr. Kraler.** Thank you, Mr. Frank. Thank you all. Mr. Dussel, I leave you in good hands. Oh . . . Dirk's coat.

450 (Dussel *hurriedly takes off the raincoat, giving it to* Mr. Kraler. *Underneath is his white dentist's jacket, with a yellow Star of David on it.*)

451 **Dussel** (*to* Mr. Kraler). What can I say to thank you . . .?

452 **Mrs. Frank** (*to* Dussel). Mr. Kraler and Miep . . . They're our life line. Without them we couldn't live.

453 **Mr. Kraler.** Please. Please. You make us seem very heroic. It isn't that at all. We simply don't like the Nazis. (*to* Mr. Frank, *who offers him a drink*) No, thanks. (*then going on*) We don't like their methods. We don't like . . .

454 **Mr. Frank** (*smiling*). I know. I know. "No one's going to tell us Dutchmen what to do with our damn Jews!"

455 **Mr. Kraler** (*to* Dussel). Pay no attention to Mr. Frank. I'll be up tomorrow to see that they're treating you right. (*to* Mr. Frank) Don't trouble to come down again. Peter will bolt the door after me, won't you, Peter?

456 **Peter.** Yes, sir.

457 **Mr. Frank.** Thank you, Peter. I'll do it.

458 **Mr. Kraler.** Good night. Good night.

459 **Group.** Good night, Mr. Kraler. We'll see you tomorrow, (*etc., etc.*)

460 (Mr. Kraler *goes out with* Mr. Frank. Mrs. Frank *gives each one of the "grownups" a glass of cognac.*)

461 **Mrs. Frank.** Please, Mr. Dussel, sit down.

462 (Mr. Dussel *sinks into a chair.* Mrs. Frank *gives him a glass of cognac.*)

463 **Dussel.** I'm dreaming. I know it. I can't believe my eyes. Mr. Otto Frank here! (*to* Mrs. Frank) You're not in Switzerland

then? A woman told me . . . She said she'd gone to your house . . . the door was open, everything was in disorder, dishes in the sink. She said she found a piece of paper in the wastebasket with an address scribbled on it . . . an address in Zurich. She said you must have escaped to Zurich.

464 **Anne.** Father put that there purposely . . . just so people would think that very thing!

465 **Dussel.** And you've been here all the time?

466 **Mrs. Frank.** All the time . . . ever since July.

467 (Anne *speaks to her father as he comes back.*)

468 **Anne.** It worked, Pim . . . the address you left! Mr. Dussel says that people believe we escaped to Switzerland.

469 **Mr. Frank.** I'm glad . . . And now let's have a little drink to welcome Mr. Dussel. (*Before they can drink,* Mr. Dussel *bolts his drink.* Mr. Frank *smiles and raises his glass.*) To Mr. Dussel. Welcome. We're very honored to have you with us.

470 **Mrs. Frank.** To Mr. Dussel, welcome.

471 (*The* Van Daans *murmur a welcome. The "grown-ups" drink.*)

472 **Mrs. Van Daan.** Um. That was good.

473 **Mr. Van Daan.** Did Mr. Kraler warn you that you won't get much to eat here? You can imagine . . . three ration books among the seven of us . . . and now you make eight.

474 (Peter *walks away, humiliated. Outside a street organ is heard dimly.*)

475 **Dussel** (*rising*). Mr. Van Daan, you don't realize what is happening outside that you should warn me of a thing like that. You don't realize what's going on . . . (*As* Mr. Van Daan *starts his characteristic pacing, Dussel turns to speak to the others.*) Right here in Amsterdam every day hundreds of Jews disappear . . . They surround a block and search house by house. Children come home from school to find their parents gone. Hundreds are being deported . . . people that you and I know . . . the Hallensteins . . . the Wessels . . .

476 **Mrs. Frank** (*in tears*). Oh, no. No!

477 **Dussel.** They get their call-up notice . . . come to the Jewish theatre on such and such a day and hour . . . bring only what you can carry in a rucksack. And if you refuse the call-up notice, then they come and drag you from your home and ship you off to Mauthausen.[11] The death camp!

[11] **Mauthausen** (mout´hou´zən): a Nazi concentration camp in Austria.

NOTICE & NOTE

CONTRASTS AND CONTRADICTIONS

Notice & Note: In paragraphs 473–474, mark how Peter reacts to his father's words to Mr. Dussel.

Compare: What causes Peter's embarrassment? How does Mr. Van Daan's behavior contrast with how we would expect a person to behave?

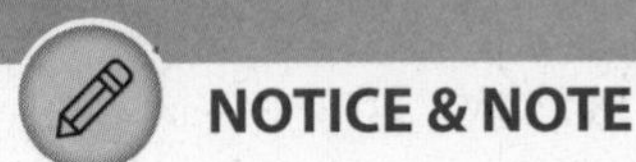

478 **Mrs. Frank.** We didn't know that things had got so much worse.

479 **Dussel.** Forgive me for speaking so.

480 **Anne** (*coming to* Dussel). Do you know the de Waals? . . . What's become of them? Their daughter Jopie and I are in the same class. Jopie's my best friend.

481 **Dussel.** They are gone.

482 **Anne.** Gone?

483 **Dussel.** With all the others.

484 **Anne.** Oh, no. Not Jopie!

485 (*She turns away, in tears.* Mrs. Frank *motions to* Margot *to comfort her.* Margot *goes to* Anne, *putting her arms comfortingly around her.*)

486 **Mrs. Van Daan.** There were some people called Wagner. They lived near us . . . ?

487 **Mr. Frank** (*interrupting, with a glance at* Anne). I think we should put this off until later. We all have many questions we want to ask . . . But I'm sure that Mr. Dussel would like to get settled before supper.

488 **Dussel.** Thank you. I would. I brought very little with me.

489 **Mr. Frank** (*giving him his hat and briefcase*). I'm sorry we can't give you a room alone. But I hope you won't be too uncomfortable. We've had to make strict rules here . . . a schedule of hours . . . We'll tell you after supper. Anne, would you like to take Mr. Dussel to his room?

490 **Anne** (*controlling her tears*). If you'll come with me, Mr. Dussel? (*She starts for her room.*)

491 **Dussel** (*shaking hands with each in turn*). Forgive me if I haven't really expressed my gratitude to all of you. This has been such a shock to me. I'd always thought of myself as Dutch. I was born in Holland. My father was born in Holland, and my grandfather. And now . . . after all these years . . . (*He breaks off.*) If you'll excuse me.

492 (Dussel *gives a little bow and hurries off after* Anne. Mr. Frank *and the others are subdued.*)

493 **Anne** (*turning on the light*). Well, here we are.

494 (Dussel *looks around the room. In the main room* Margot *speaks to her mother.*)

495 **Margot.** The news sounds pretty bad, doesn't it? It's so different from what Mr. Kraler tells us. Mr. Kraler says things are improving.

496 **Mr. Van Daan.** I like it better the way Kraler tells it.

497 (*They resume their occupations, quietly.* Peter *goes off into his room. In* Anne's *room,* Anne *turns to* Dussel.)

498 **Anne.** You're going to share the room with me.

499 **Dussel.** I'm a man who's always lived alone. I haven't had to adjust myself to others. I hope you'll bear with me until I learn.

500 **Anne.** Let me help you. (*She takes his briefcase.*) Do you always live all alone? Have you no family at all?

501 **Dussel.** No one. (*He opens his medicine case and spreads his bottles on the dressing table.*)

502 **Anne.** How dreadful. You must be terribly lonely.

503 **Dussel.** I'm used to it.

504 **Anne.** I don't think I could ever get used to it. Didn't you even have a pet? A cat, or a dog?

505 **Dussel.** I have an allergy for fur-bearing animals. They give me asthma.

506 **Anne.** Oh, dear. Peter has a cat.

507 **Dussel.** Here? He has it here?

508 **Anne.** Yes. But we hardly ever see it. He keeps it in his room all the time. I'm sure it will be all right.

509 **Dussel.** Let us hope so.

510 (*He takes some pills to fortify himself.*)

511 **Anne.** That's Margot's bed, where you're going to sleep. I sleep on the sofa there. (*indicating the clothes hooks on the wall*) We cleared these off for your things. (*She goes over to the window.*) The best part about this room . . . you can look down and see a bit of the street and the canal. There's a houseboat . . . you can see the end of it . . . a bargeman lives there with his family . . . They have a baby and he's just beginning to walk and I'm so afraid he's going to fall into the canal some day. I watch him . . .

512 **Dussel** (*interrupting*). Your father spoke of a schedule.

513 **Anne** (*coming away from the window*). Oh, yes. It's mostly about the times we have to be quiet. And times for the w.c. You can use it now if you like.

514 **Dussel** (*stiffly*). No, thank you.

515 **Anne.** I suppose you think it's awful, my talking about a thing like that. But you don't know how important it can get to be, especially when you're frightened . . . About this room, the

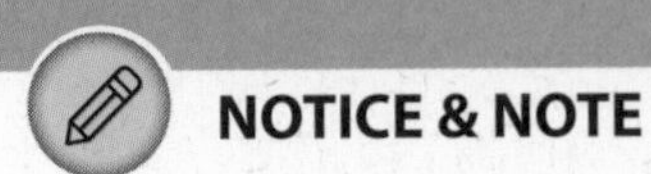

way Margot and I did . . . she had it to herself in the afternoons for studying, reading . . . lessons, you know . . . and I took the mornings. Would that be all right with you?

516 **Dussel.** I'm not at my best in the morning.

517 **Anne.** You stay here in the mornings then. I'll take the room in the afternoons.

518 **Dussel.** Tell me, when you're in here, what happens to me? Where am I spending my time? In there, with all the people?

519 **Anne.** Yes.

520 **Dussel.** I see. I see.

521 **Anne.** We have supper at half past six.

522 **Dussel** (*going over to the sofa*). Then, if you don't mind . . . I like to lie down quietly for ten minutes before eating. I find it helps the digestion.

523 **Anne.** Of course. I hope I'm not going to be too much of a bother to you. I seem to be able to get everyone's back up.

524 (Dussel *lies down on the sofa, curled up, his back to her.*)

CONTRASTS AND CONTRADICTIONS

Notice & Note: In paragraphs 525–529, mark lines that show a surprising contrast between how Mr. Dussel and Anne expect to get along and how they actually get along.

Interpret: What might explain this contradiction?

525 **Dussel.** I always get along very well with children. My patients all bring their children to me, because they know I get on well with them. So don't you worry about that.

526 (Anne *leans over him, taking his hand and shaking it gratefully.*)

527 **Anne.** Thank you. Thank you, Mr. Dussel.

528 (*The lights dim to darkness. The curtain falls on the scene.* Anne's Voice *comes to us faintly at first, and then with increasing power.*)

529 **Anne's Voice.** . . . And yesterday I finished Cissy Van Marxvelt's latest book. I think she is a first-class writer. I shall definitely let my children read her. Monday the twenty-first of September, nineteen forty-two. Mr. Dussel and I had another battle yesterday. Yes, Mr. Dussel! According to him, nothing, I repeat . . . nothing, is right about me . . . my appearance, my character, my manners. While he was going on at me I thought . . . sometime I'll give you such a smack that you'll fly right up to the ceiling! Why is it that every grownup thinks he knows the way to bring up children? Particularly the grownups that never had any. I keep wishing that Peter was a girl instead of a boy. Then I would have someone to talk to. Margot's a darling, but she takes everything too seriously. To

pause for a moment on the subject of Mrs. Van Daan. I must tell you that her attempts to flirt with Father are getting her nowhere. Pim, thank goodness, won't play.

530 (*As she is saying the last lines, the curtain rises on the darkened scene.* Anne's Voice *fades out.*)

Scene 4

531 *It is the middle of the night, several months later. The stage is dark except for a little light which comes through the skylight in* Peter's *room.*

532 *Everyone is in bed.* Mr. *and* Mrs. Frank *lie on the couch in the main room, which has been pulled out to serve as a makeshift double bed.*

533 Margot *is sleeping on a mattress on the floor in the main room, behind a curtain stretched across for privacy. The others are all in their accustomed rooms.*

534 *From outside we hear two drunken soldiers singing "Lili Marlene." A girl's high giggle is heard. The sound of running feet is heard coming closer and then fading in the distance. Throughout the scene there is the distant sound of airplanes passing overhead.*

535 *A match suddenly flares up in the attic. We dimly see* Mr. Van Daan. *He is getting his bearings. He comes quickly down the stairs, and goes to the cupboard where the food is stored. Again the match flares up, and is as quickly blown out. The dim figure is seen to steal back up the stairs.*

536 *There is quiet for a second or two, broken only by the sound of airplanes, and running feet on the street below.*

537 *Suddenly, out of the silence and the dark, we hear* Anne *scream.*

538 **Anne** (*screaming*). No! No! Don't . . . don't take me!

539 (*She moans, tossing and crying in her sleep. The other people wake, terrified.* Dussel *sits up in bed, furious.*)

540 **Dussel.** Shush! Anne! Anne, for God's sake, shush!

541 **Anne** (*still in her nightmare*). Save me! Save me!

542 (*She screams and screams.* Dussel *gets out of bed, going over to her, trying to wake her.*)

543 **Dussel.** For God's sake! Quiet! Quiet! You want someone to hear?

ANALYZE PLOT DEVELOPMENT

Annotate: In paragraphs 531–535, mark where Mr. Van Daan goes in the dark.

Predict: What do you think Mr. Van Daan is doing? How might his action cause trouble in the future?

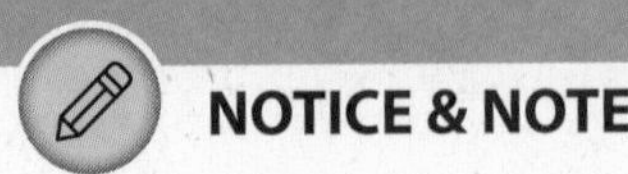

544 (*In the main room* Mrs. Frank *grabs a shawl and pulls it around her. She rushes in to* Anne, *taking her in her arms.* Mr. Frank *hurriedly gets up, putting on his overcoat.* Margot *sits up, terrified.* Peter's *light goes on in his room.*)

545 **Mrs. Frank** (*to* Anne, *in her room*). Hush, darling, hush. It's all right. It's all right. (*over her shoulder to* Dussel) Will you be kind enough to turn on the light, Mr. Dussel? (*back to* Anne) It's nothing, my darling. It was just a dream.

546 (Dussel *turns on the light in the bedroom.* Mrs. Frank *holds* Anne *in her arms. Gradually* Anne *comes out of her nightmare, still trembling with horror.* Mr. Frank *comes into the room, and goes quickly to the window, looking out to be sure that no one outside had heard* Anne's *screams.* Mrs. Frank *holds* Anne, *talking softly to her. In the main room* Margot *stands on a chair, turning on the center hanging lamp. A light goes on in the* Van Daans' *room overhead.* Peter *puts his robe on, coming out of his room.*)

547 **Dussel** (*to Mrs. Frank, blowing his nose*). Something must be done about that child, Mrs. Frank. Yelling like that! Who knows but there's somebody on the streets? She's endangering all our lives.

548 **Mrs. Frank.** Anne, darling.

549 **Dussel.** Every night she twists and turns. I don't sleep. I spend half my night shushing her. And now it's nightmares!

550 (Margot *comes to the door of* Anne's *room, followed by* Peter. Mr. Frank *goes to them, indicating that everything is all right.* Peter *takes* Margot *back.*)

551 **Mrs. Frank** (*to* Anne). You're here, safe, you see? Nothing has happened. (*to* Dussel) Please, Mr. Dussel, go back to bed. She'll be herself in a minute or two. Won't you, Anne?

552 **Dussel** (*picking up a book and a pillow*). Thank you, but I'm going to the w.c. The one place where there's peace! (*He stalks out.* Mr. Van Daan, *in underwear and trousers, comes down the stairs.*)

553 **Mr. Van Daan** (*to* Dussel). What is it? What happened?

554 **Dussel.** A nightmare. She was having a nightmare!

555 **Mr. Van Daan.** I thought someone was murdering her.

556 **Dussel.** Unfortunately, no.

557 (*He goes into the bathroom.* Mr. Van Daan *goes back up the stairs.* Mr. Frank, *in the main room, sends* Peter *back to his own bedroom.*)

558 **Mr. Frank.** Thank you, Peter. Go back to bed.

559 (Peter *goes back to his room.* Mr. Frank *follows him, turning out the light and looking out the window. Then he goes back to the main room, and gets up on a chair, turning out the center hanging lamp.*)

560 **Mrs. Frank** (*to* Anne). Would you like some water? (Anne *shakes her head.*) Was it a very bad dream? Perhaps if you told me . . . ?

561 **Anne.** I'd rather not talk about it.

562 **Mrs. Frank.** Poor darling. Try to sleep then. I'll sit right here beside you until you fall asleep.

563 (*She brings a stool over, sitting* there.)

564 **Anne.** You don't have to.

565 **Mrs. Frank.** But I'd like to stay with you . . . very much. Really.

566 **Anne.** I'd rather you didn't.

567 **Mrs. Frank.** Good night, then. (*She leans down to kiss* Anne. Anne *throws her arm up over her face, turning away.* Mrs. Frank, *hiding her hurt, kisses* Anne's *arm.*) You'll be all right? There's nothing that you want?

568 **Anne.** Will you please ask Father to come.

569 **Mrs. Frank** (*after a second*). Of course, Anne dear. (*She hurries out into the other room.* Mr. Frank *comes to her as she comes in.*) *Sie verlangt nach Dir!*[12]

570 **Mr. Frank** (*sensing her hurt*). Edith, *Liebe, schau . . .*[13]

571 **Mrs. Frank.** *Es macht nichts! Ich danke dem lieben Herrgott, dass sie sich wenigstens an Dich wendet, wenn sie Trost braucht! Geh hinein, Otto, sie ist ganz hysterisch vor Angst.*[14] (*as* Mr. Frank *hesitates*) *Geh zu ihr.*[15] (*He looks at her for a second and then goes to get a cup of water for* Anne. Mrs. Frank *sinks down on the bed, her face in her hands, trying to keep from sobbing aloud.* Margot *comes over to her, putting her arms around her.*) She wants nothing of me. She pulled away when I leaned down to kiss her.

572 **Margot.** It's a phase . . . You heard Father . . . Most girls go through it . . . they turn to their fathers at this age . . . they give all their love to their fathers.

ANALYZE DRAMA

Annotate: In paragraphs 569–571, notice the lines that Mr. and Mrs. Frank speak in German. Mark the English translations in the footnotes.

Infer: Why might the playwrights have chosen to have the characters speak German in this part of the script?

---

[12] ***Sie verlangt nach Dir*** (zē fer-längt´näKH dîr) *German:* She is asking for you.

[13] ***Liebe, schau*** (lē´bə shou´) *German:* Dear, look.

[14] ***Es macht . . . vor Angst*** (ĕs mäKHt´ nĭKHts´! ĭKH dängk´ə dām lē´bən hĕr´gôt´, däs zē zĭKH´ vāN´ĭKHshtənz än dĭKH´ vĕn´dət, vĕn zē trôst´ brouKHt´! gā hĭn-īn´, ôt´tô; zē ĭst gänts hüstĕr´ĭsh fôr ängst´) *German:* It's all right. I thank dear God that at least she turns to you when she needs comfort. Go in, Otto; she is hysterical with fear.

[15] ***Geh zu ihr*** (gā´ tso͞o îr´) *German:* Go to her.

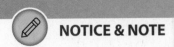

573 **Mrs. Frank.** You weren't like this. You didn't shut me out.

574 **Margot.** She'll get over it . . . (*She smooths the bed for* Mrs. Frank *and sits beside her a moment as* Mrs. Frank *lies down. In* Anne's *room* Mr. Frank *comes in, sitting down by* Anne. Anne *flings her arms around him, clinging to him. In the distance we hear the sound of ack-ack.*)

575 **Anne.** Oh, Pim. I dreamed that they came to get us! The Green Police! They broke down the door and grabbed me and started to drag me out the way they did Jopie.

576 **Mr. Frank.** I want you to take this pill.

577 **Anne.** What is it?

578 **Mr. Frank.** Something to quiet you.

579 (*She takes it and drinks the water. In the main room* Margot *turns out the light and goes back to her bed.*)

580 **Mr. Frank** (*to* Anne). Do you want me to read to you for a while?

581 **Anne.** No. Just sit with me for a minute. Was I awful? Did I yell terribly loud? Do you think anyone outside could have heard?

582 **Mr. Frank.** No. No. Lie quietly now. Try to sleep.

583 **Anne.** I'm a terrible coward. I'm so disappointed in myself. I think I've conquered my fear . . . I think I'm really grown-up . . . and then something happens . . . and I run to you like a baby . . . I love you, Father. I don't love anyone but you.

584 **Mr. Frank** (*reproachfully*). Annele!

585 **Anne.** It's true. I've been thinking about it for a long time. You're the only one I love.

586 **Mr. Frank.** It's fine to hear you tell me that you love me. But I'd be happier if you said you loved your mother as well . . . She needs your help so much . . . your love . . .

587 **Anne.** We have nothing in common. She doesn't understand me. Whenever I try to explain my views on life to her she asks me if I'm constipated.

588 **Mr. Frank.** You hurt her very much just now. She's crying. She's in there crying.

589 **Anne.** I can't help it. I only told the truth. I didn't want her here . . . (*then, with sudden change*) Oh, Pim, I was horrible, wasn't I? And the worst of it is, I can stand off and look at myself doing it and know it's cruel and yet I can't stop doing it. What's the matter with me? Tell me. Don't say it's just a phase! Help me.

TOUGH QUESTIONS

Notice & Note: Mark how Anne describes her behavior toward her mother.

Interpret: What question does Anne ask her father? What internal conflict does this question reveal?

590 **Mr. Frank.** There is so little that we parents can do to help our children. We can only try to set a good example . . . point the way. The rest you must do yourself. You must build your own character.

591 **Anne.** I'm trying. Really I am. Every night I think back over all of the things I did that day that were wrong . . . like putting the wet mop in Mr. Dussel's bed . . . and this thing now with Mother. I say to myself, that was wrong. I make up my mind, I'm never going to do *that* again. Never! Of course I may do something worse . . . but at least I'll never do that again! . . . I have a nicer side, Father . . . a sweeter, nicer side. But I'm scared to show it. I'm afraid that people are going to laugh at me if I'm serious. So the mean Anne comes to the outside and the good Anne stays on the inside, and I keep on trying to switch them around and have the good Anne outside and the bad Anne inside and be what I'd like to be . . . and might be . . . if only . . . only . . . (*She is asleep.* Mr. Frank *watches her for a moment and then turns off the light, and starts out. The lights dim out. The curtain falls on the scene.* Anne's Voice *is heard dimly at first, and then with growing strength.*)

592 **Anne's Voice.** . . . The air raids are getting worse. They come over day and night. The noise is terrifying. Pim says it should be music to our ears. The more planes, the sooner will come the end of the war. Mrs. Van Daan pretends to be a fatalist. What will be, will be. But when the planes come over, who is the most frightened? No one else but Petronella! . . . Monday, the ninth of November, nineteen forty-two. Wonderful news! The Allies have landed in Africa. Pim says that we can look for an early finish to the war. Just for fun he asked each of us what was the first thing we wanted to do when we got out of here. Mrs. Van Daan longs to be home with her own things, her needle-point chairs, the Beckstein piano her father gave her . . . the best that money could buy. Peter would like to go to a movie. Mr. Dussel wants to get back to his dentist's drill. He's afraid he is losing his touch. For myself, there are so many things . . . to ride a bike again . . . to laugh till my belly aches . . . to have new clothes from the skin out . . . to have a hot tub filled to overflowing and wallow in it for hours . . . to be back in school with my friends . . .

593 (*As the last lines are being said, the curtain rises on the scene. The lights dim on as* Anne's Voice *fades away.*)

LANGUAGE CONVENTIONS

Annotate: To use correct capitalization, you need to capitalize the names of religions, religious texts, and important symbols or artifacts. Review paragraph 594 and mark three words that are capitalized.

Identify: Into which category, or group, does each word fall? Note that many religions also capitalize words to show respect for their deity. What other words are capitalized in paragraph 595?

Scene 5

594 *It is the first night of the Hanukkah*[16] *celebration.* Mr. Frank *is standing at the head of the table on which is the Menorah.*[17] *He lights the Shamos, or servant candle, and holds it as he says the blessing. Seated listening is all of the "family," dressed in their best. The men wear hats,* Peter *wears his cap.*

595 **Mr. Frank** (*reading from a prayer book*). "Praised be Thou, oh Lord our God, Ruler of the universe, who has sanctified us with Thy commandments and bidden us kindle the Hanukkah lights. Praised be Thou, oh Lord our God, Ruler of the universe, who has wrought wondrous deliverances for our fathers in days of old. Praised be Thou, oh Lord our God, Ruler of the universe, that Thou has given us life and sustenance and brought us to this happy season." (Mr. Frank *lights the one candle of the Menorah as he continues.*) "We kindle this Hanukkah light to celebrate the great and wonderful deeds wrought through the zeal with which God filled the hearts of the heroic Maccabees, two thousand years ago. They fought against indifference, against tyranny and oppression, and they restored our Temple to us. May these lights remind us that we should ever look to God, whence cometh our help." Amen. [Pronounced O-mayn.]

596 **All.** Amen.

597 (Mr. Frank *hands* Mrs. Frank *the prayer book.*)

598 **Mrs. Frank** (*reading*). "I lift up mine eyes unto the mountains, from whence cometh my help. My help cometh from the Lord who made heaven and earth. He will not suffer thy foot to be moved. He that keepeth thee will not slumber. He that keepeth Israel doth neither slumber nor sleep. The Lord is thy keeper. The Lord is thy shade upon thy right hand. The sun shall not smite thee by day, nor the moon by night. The Lord shall keep thee from all evil. He shall keep thy soul. The Lord shall guard thy going out and thy coming in, from this time forth and forevermore." Amen.

599 **All.** Amen.

600 (Mrs. Frank *puts down the prayer book and goes to get the food and wine.* Margot *helps her.* Mr. Frank *takes the men's hats and puts them aside.*)

---

[16] **Hanukkah** (hä´nə-kə): a Jewish holiday, celebrated in December and lasting eight days.

[17] **Menorah** (mə-nôr´ə): a candleholder with nine branches, used in the celebration of Hanukkah.

NOTICE & NOTE

601 **Dussel** (*rising*). That was very moving.

602 **Anne** (*pulling him back*). It isn't over yet!

603 **Mrs. Van Daan.** Sit down! Sit down!

604 **Anne.** There's a lot more, songs and presents.

605 **Dussel.** Presents?

606 **Mrs. Frank.** Not this year, unfortunately.

607 **Mrs. Van Daan.** But always on Hanukkah everyone gives presents . . . everyone!

608 **Dussel.** Like our St. Nicholas's Day.[18] (*There is a chorus of "no's" from the group.*)

609 **Mrs. Van Daan.** No! Not like St. Nicholas! What kind of a Jew are you that you don't know Hanukkah?

610 **Mrs. Frank** (*as she brings the food*). I remember particularly the candles . . . First one, as we have tonight. Then the second night you light two candles, the next night three . . . and so on until you have eight candles burning. When there are eight candles it is truly beautiful.

611 **Mrs. Van Daan.** And the potato pancakes.

612 **Mr. Van Daan.** Don't talk about them!

613 **Mrs. Van Daan.** I make the best *latkes*[19] you ever tasted!

614 **Mrs. Frank.** Invite us all next year . . . in your own home.

615 **Mr. Frank.** God willing!

---

[18] **St. Nicholas's Day:** December 6, the day that Christian children in the Netherlands receive gifts.

[19] ***latkes*** (lät´kəz): potato pancakes.

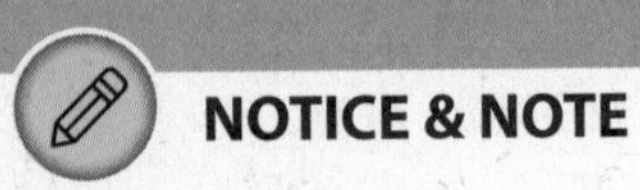

NOTICE & NOTE

MEMORY MOMENT

Notice & Note: Review paragraphs 610–622. Mark the Memory Moment that Margo has.

Connect: How does Margot's memory relate to what Anne does next in the play?

---

616 **Mrs. Van Daan.** God willing.

617 **Margot.** What I remember best is the presents we used to get when we were little . . . eight days of presents . . . and each day they got better and better.

618 **Mrs. Frank** (*sitting down*). We are all here, alive. That is present enough.

619 **Anne.** No, it isn't. I've got something . . .

620 (*She rushes into her room, hurriedly puts on a little hat improvised from the lamp shade, grabs a satchel bulging with parcels and comes running back.*)

621 **Mrs. Frank.** What is it?

622 **Anne.** Presents!

623 **Mrs. Van Daan.** Presents!

624 **Dussel.** Look!

625 **Mr. Van Daan.** What's she got on her head?

626 **Peter.** A lamp shade!

627 **Anne** (*She picks out one at random*). This is for Margot. (*She hands it to* Margot, *pulling her to her feet.*) Read it out loud.

628 **Margot** (*reading*).
"You have never lost your temper.
You never will, I fear,
You are so good.
But if you should,
Put all your cross words here."
(*She tears open the package.*)
A new crossword puzzle book!
Where did you get it?

629 **Anne.** It isn't new. It's one that you've done. But I rubbed it all out, and if you wait a little and forget, you can do it all over again.

630 **Margot** (*sitting*). It's wonderful, Anne. Thank you. You'd never know it wasn't new.

631 (*From outside we hear the sound of a streetcar passing.*)

632 **Anne** (*with another gift*). Mrs. Van Daan.

633 **Mrs. Van Daan** (*taking it*). This is awful . . . I haven't anything for anyone . . . I never thought . . .

634 **Mr. Frank.** This is all Anne's idea.

635 **Mrs. Van Daan** (*holding up a bottle*). What is it?

NOTICE & NOTE

636 **Anne.** It's hair shampoo. I took all the odds and ends of soap and mixed them with the last of my toilet water.

637 **Mrs. Van Daan.** Oh, Anneke!

638 **Anne.** I wanted to write a poem for all of them, but I didn't have time. (*offering a large box to* Mr. Van Daan) Yours, Mr. Van Daan, is really something . . . something you want more than anything. (*as she waits for him to open it*) Look! Cigarettes!

639 **Mr. Van Daan.** Cigarettes!

640 **Anne.** Two of them! Pim found some old pipe tobacco in the pocket lining of his coat . . . and we made them . . . or rather, Pim did.

641 **Mrs. Van Daan.** Let me see . . . Well, look at that! Light it, Putti! Light it.

642 (Mr. Van Daan *hesitates.*)

643 **Anne.** It's tobacco, really it is! There's a little fluff in it, but not much.

644 (*Everyone watches intently as* Mr. Van Daan *cautiously lights it. The cigarette flares up. Everyone laughs.*)

645 **Peter.** It works!

646 **Mrs. Van Daan.** Look at him.

647 **Mr. Van Daan** (*spluttering*). Thank you, Anne. Thank you.

648 (Anne *rushes back to her satchel for another present.*)

649 **Anne** (*handing her mother a piece of paper*). For Mother, Hanukkah greeting. (*She pulls her mother to her feet.*)

650 **Mrs. Frank** (*She reads.*) "Here's an I.O.U. that I promise to pay. Ten hours of doing whatever you say. Signed, Anne Frank." (Mrs. Frank, *touched, takes* Anne *in her arms, holding her close.*)

651 **Dussel** (*to* Anne). Ten hours of doing what you're told? *Anything* you're told?

652 **Anne.** That's right.

653 **Dussel.** You wouldn't want to sell that, Mrs. Frank?

654 **Mrs. Frank.** Never! This is the most precious gift I've ever had!

655 (*She sits, showing her present to the others.* Anne *hurries back to the satchel and pulls out a scarf, the scarf that* Mr. Frank *found in the first scene.*)

656 **Anne** (*offering it to her father*). For Pim.

657 **Mr. Frank.** Anneke . . . I wasn't supposed to have a present! (*He takes it, unfolding it and showing it to the others.*)

ANALYZE DRAMA

Annotate: In the stage directions, mark the gift that Anne gives her father.

Connect: How is the scarf connected to Act One, Scene 1? Why is it important for the audience to make this connection?

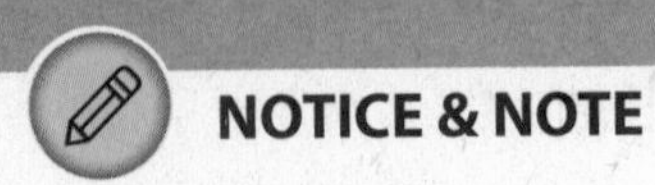

658 **Anne.** It's a muffler . . . to put round your neck . . . like an ascot, you know. I made it myself out of odds and ends . . . I knitted it in the dark each night, after I'd gone to bed. I'm afraid it looks better in the dark!

659 **Mr. Frank** (*putting it on*). It's fine. It fits me perfectly. Thank you, Annele.

660 (Anne *hands* Peter *a ball of paper, with a string attached to it.*)

661 **Anne.** That's for Mouschi.

662 **Peter** (*rising to bow*). On behalf of Mouschi, I thank you.

663 **Anne** (*hesitant, handing him a gift*). And . . . this is yours . . . from Mrs. Quack Quack. (*as he holds it gingerly in his hands*) Well . . . open it . . . Aren't you going to open it?

664 **Peter.** I'm scared to. I know something's going to jump out and hit me.

665 **Anne.** No. It's nothing like that, really.

666 **Mrs. Van Daan** (*as he is opening it*). What is it, Peter? Go on. Show it.

667 **Anne** (*excitedly*). It's a safety razor!

668 **Dussel.** A what?

669 **Anne.** A razor!

670 **Mrs. Van Daan** (*looking at it*). You didn't make that out of odds and ends.

671 **Anne** (*to* Peter). Miep got it for me. It's not new. It's second-hand. But you really do need a razor now.

672 **Dussel.** For what?

673 **Anne.** Look on his upper lip . . . you can see the beginning of a mustache.

674 **Dussel.** He wants to get rid of that? Put a little milk on it and let the cat lick it off.

675 **Peter** (*starting for his room*). Think you're funny, don't you.

676 **Dussel.** Look! He can't wait! He's going in to try it!

677 **Peter.** I'm going to give Mouschi his present! (*He goes into his room, slamming the door behind him.*)

678 **Mr. Van Daan** (*disgustedly*). Mouschi, Mouschi, Mouschi.

679 (*In the distance we hear a dog persistently barking.* Anne *brings a gift to* Dussel.)

680 **Anne.** And last but never least, my roommate, Mr. Dussel.

NOTICE & NOTE

681 **Dussel.** For me? You have something for me? (*He opens the small box she gives him.*)

682 **Anne.** I made them myself.

683 **Dussel** (*puzzled*). Capsules! Two capsules!

684 **Anne.** They're ear-plugs!

685 **Dussel.** Ear-plugs?

686 **Anne.** To put in your ears so you won't hear me when I thrash around at night. I saw them advertised in a magazine. They're not real ones . . . I made them out of cotton and candle wax. Try them . . . See if they don't work . . . see if you can hear me talk . . .

687 **Dussel** (*putting them in his ears*). Wait now until I get them in . . . so.

688 **Anne.** Are you ready?

689 **Dussel.** Huh?

690 **Anne.** Are you ready?

691 **Dussel.** Good God! They've gone inside! I can't get them out! (*They laugh as* Mr. Dussel *jumps about, trying to shake the plugs out of his ears. Finally he gets them out. Putting them away.*) Thank you, Anne! Thank you!

692 **Mr. Van Daan.** A real Hanukkah!
693 **Mrs. Van Daan.** Wasn't it cute of her?
694 **Mrs. Frank.** I don't know when she did it.
695 **Margot.** I love my present.
} *Together*

696 **Anne** (*sitting at the table*). And now let's have the song, Father . . . please . . . (*to* Dussel) Have you heard the Hanukkah song, Mr. Dussel? The song is the whole thing! (*She sings.*) "Oh, Hanukkah! Oh Hanukkah! The sweet celebration . . ."

697 **Mr. Frank** (*quieting her*). I'm afraid, Anne, we shouldn't sing that song tonight. (*to* Dussel) It's a song of jubilation, of rejoicing. One is apt to become too enthusiastic.

698 **Anne.** Oh, please, please. Let's sing the song. I promise not to shout!

699 **Mr. Frank.** Very well. But quietly now . . . I'll keep an eye on you and when . . .

700 (*As* Anne *starts to sing, she is interrupted by* Dussel, *who is snorting and wheezing.*)

701 **Dussel** (*pointing to* Peter). You . . . You! (Peter *is coming from his bedroom,* ***ostentatiously*** *holding a bulge in his coat as if he*

ostentatiously
(ŏs´tĕn-tā´shəs-lē) *adv.*
Someone who does something *ostentatiously* acts in an exaggerated way in order to attract attention.

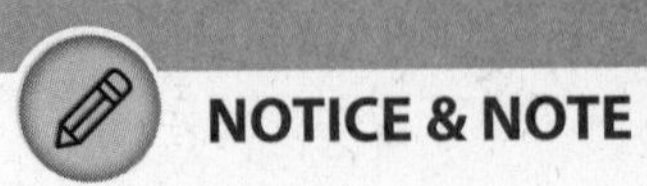

were holding his cat, and dangling Anne's *present before it.*) How many times . . . I told you . . . Out! Out!

702 **Mr. Van Daan** (*going to* Peter). What's the matter with you? Haven't you any sense? Get that cat out of here.

703 **Peter** (*innocently*). Cat?

704 **Mr. Van Daan.** You heard me. Get it out of here!

705 **Peter.** I have no cat. (*Delighted with his joke, he opens his coat and pulls out a bath towel. The group at the table laugh, enjoying the joke.*)

706 **Dussel** (*still wheezing*). It doesn't need to be the cat . . . his clothes are enough . . . when he comes out of that room . . .

707 **Mr. Van Daan.** Don't worry. You won't be bothered any more. We're getting rid of it.

708 **Dussel.** At last you listen to me. (*He goes off into his bedroom.*)

709 **Mr. Van Daan** (*calling after him*). I'm not doing it for you. That's all in your mind . . . all of it! (*He starts back to his place at the table.*) I'm doing it because I'm sick of seeing that cat eat all our food.

710 **Peter.** That's not true! I only give him bones . . . scraps . . .

711 **Mr. Van Daan.** Don't tell me! He gets fatter every day! Damn cat looks better than any of us. Out he goes tonight!

712 **Peter.** No! No!

713 **Anne.** Mr. Van Daan, you can't do that! That's Peter's cat.

714 **Mrs. Frank** (*quietly*). Anne.

715 **Peter** (*to* Mr. Van Daan). If he goes, I go.

716 **Mr. Van Daan.** Go! Go!

717 **Mrs. Van Daan.** You're not going and the cat's not going! Now please . . . this is Hanukkah . . . Hanukkah . . . this is the time to celebrate . . . What's the matter with all of you? Come on, Anne. Let's have the song.

718 **Anne** (*singing*). "Oh, Hanukkah! Oh, Hanukkah! The sweet celebration."

719 **Mr. Frank** (*rising*). I think we should first blow out the candle . . . then we'll have something for tomorrow night.

720 **Margot.** But, Father, you're supposed to let it burn itself out.

721 **Mr. Frank.** I'm sure that God understands shortages. (*before*

blowing it out) "Praised be Thou, oh Lord our God, who hast sustained us and permitted us to celebrate this joyous festival."

722 (*He is about to blow out the candle when suddenly there is a crash of something falling below. They all freeze in horror, motionless. For a few seconds there is complete silence.* Mr. Frank *slips off his shoes. The others noiselessly follow his example.* Mr. Frank *turns out a light near him. He motions to* Peter *to turn off the center lamp.* Peter *tries to reach it, realizes he cannot and gets up on a chair. Just as he is touching the lamp he loses his balance. The chair goes out from under him. He falls. The iron lamp shade crashes to the floor. There is a sound of feet below, running down the stairs.*)

723 **Mr. Van Daan** (*under his breath*). God Almighty! (*The only light left comes from the Hanukkah candle.* Dussel *comes from his room.* Mr. Frank *creeps over to the stairwell and stands listening. The dog is heard barking excitedly.*) Do you hear anything?

724 **Mr. Frank** (*in a whisper*). No. I think they've gone.

725 **Mrs. Van Daan.** It's the Green Police. They've found us.

726 **Mr. Frank.** If they had, they wouldn't have left. They'd be up here by now.

727 **Mrs. Van Daan.** I know it's the Green Police. They've gone to get help. That's all. They'll be back!

728 **Mr. Van Daan.** Or it may have been the Gestapo,[20] looking for papers . . .

729 **Mr. Frank** (*interrupting*). Or a thief, looking for money.

730 **Mrs. Van Daan.** We've got to do something . . . Quick! Quick! Before they come back.

731 **Mr. Van Daan.** There isn't anything to do. Just wait.

732 (Mr. Frank *holds up his hand for them to be quiet. He is listening intently. There is complete silence as they all strain to hear any sound from below. Suddenly* Anne *begins to sway. With a low cry she falls to the floor in a faint.* Mrs. Frank *goes to her quickly, sitting beside her on the floor and taking her in her arms.*)

733 **Mrs. Frank.** Get some water, please! Get some water!

734 (*Margot starts for the sink.*)

735 **Mr. Van Daan** (*grabbing* Margot). No! No! No one's going to run water!

736 **Mr. Frank.** If they've found us, they've found us. Get the water.

[20]**Gestapo** (gə-stä´pō): the Nazi secret police force, known for its terrorism and brutality.

NOTICE & NOTE

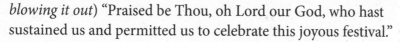

ANALYZE PLOT DEVELOPMENT

Annotate: Reread the stage directions in paragraph 722 and identify two key events—one downstairs and one in the Annex. Underline details describing the sounds downstairs and circle details about what causes noise in the Annex.

Cause and Effect: What has just happened? What effects could these events have on future events in the plot?

(Margot *starts again for the sink.* Mr. Frank, *getting a flashlight*) I'm going down.

737 (Margot *rushes to him, clinging to him.* Anne *struggles to consciousness.*)

738 **Margot.** No, Father, no! There may be someone there, waiting . . . It may be a trap!

739 **Mr. Frank.** This is Saturday. There is no way for us to know what has happened until Miep or Mr. Kraler comes on Monday morning. We cannot live with this uncertainty.

740 **Margot.** Don't go, Father!

741 **Mrs. Frank.** Hush, darling, hush. (Mr. Frank *slips quietly out, down the steps and out through the door below.*) Margot! Stay close to me.

742 (Margot *goes to her mother.*)

743 **Mr. Van Daan.** Shush! Shush!

744 (Mrs. Frank *whispers to* Margot *to get the water.* Margot *goes for it.*)

745 **Mrs. Van Daan.** Putti, where's our money? Get our money. I hear you can buy the Green Police off, so much a head. Go upstairs quick! Get the money!

746 **Mr. Van Daan.** Keep still!

747 **Mrs. Van Daan** (*kneeling before him, pleading*). Do you want to be dragged off to a concentration camp? Are you going to stand there and wait for them to come up and get you? Do something, I tell you!

748 **Mr. Van Daan** (*pushing her aside*). Will you keep still! (*He goes over to the stairwell to listen.* Peter *goes to his mother, helping her up onto the sofa. There is a second of silence, then* Anne *can stand it no longer.*)

749 **Anne.** Someone go after Father! Make Father come back!

750 **Peter** (*starting for the door*). I'll go.

751 **Mr. Van Daan.** Haven't you done enough?

752 (*He pushes* Peter *roughly away. In his anger against his father* Peter *grabs a chair as if to hit him with it, then puts it down, burying his face in his hands.* Mrs. Frank *begins to pray softly.*)

753 **Anne.** Please, please, Mr. Van Daan. Get Father.

754 **Mr. Van Daan.** Quiet! Quiet!

755 (Anne *is shocked into silence.* Mrs. Frank *pulls her closer, holding her protectively in her arms.*)

NOTICE & NOTE 

756 **Mrs. Frank** (*softly, praying*). "I lift up mine eyes unto the mountains, from whence cometh my help. My help cometh from the Lord who made heaven and earth. He will not suffer thy foot to be moved . . . He that keepeth thee will not slumber . . ." (*She stops as she hears someone coming. They all watch the door tensely.* Mr. Frank *comes quietly in.* Anne *rushes to him, holding him tight.*)

757 **Mr. Frank.** It was a thief. That noise must have scared him away.

758 **Mrs. Van Daan.** Thank God.

759 **Mr. Frank.** He took the cash box. And the radio. He ran away in such a hurry that he didn't stop to shut the street door. It was swinging wide open. (*A breath of relief sweeps over them.*) I think it would be good to have some light.

760 **Margot.** Are you sure it's all right?

761 **Mr. Frank.** The danger has passed. (Margot *goes to light the small lamp.*) Don't be so terrified, Anne. We're safe.

762 **Dussel.** Who says the danger has passed? Don't you realize we are in greater danger than ever?

763 **Mr. Frank.** Mr. Dussel, will you be still!

764 (Mr. Frank *takes* Anne *back to the table, making her sit down with him, trying to calm her.*)

765 **Dussel** (*pointing to* Peter). Thanks to this clumsy fool, there's someone now who knows we're up here! Someone now knows we're up here, hiding!

766 **Mrs. Van Daan** (*going to* Dussel). Someone knows we're here, yes. But who is the someone? A thief! A thief! You think a thief is going to go to the Green Police and say . . . I was robbing a place the other night and I heard a noise up over my head? You think a thief is going to do that?

767 **Dussel.** Yes. I think he will.

768 **Mrs. Van Daan** (*hysterically*). You're crazy! (*She stumbles back* to *her seat at the table.* Peter *follows protectively, pushing* Dussel *aside.*)

769 **Dussel.** I think some day he'll be caught and then he'll make a bargain with the Green Police . . . if they'll let him off, he'll tell them where some Jews are hiding!

770 (*He goes off into the bedroom. There is a second of* ***appalled*** *silence.*)

771 **Mr. Van Daan.** He's right.

ANALYZE PLOT DEVELOPMENT

Annotate: In paragraphs 758–768, underline Mr. Frank's explanation for what caused the noise downstairs. Circle Mr. Dussel's fears about what will happen as a result of this.

Predict: Remember that when a writer hints at future events, it is called foreshadowing. Do you think the playwrights are foreshadowing what will actually happen in the future—that the Annex residents will be caught because of the thief? Explain your prediction.

appalled
(ə-pôld´) *adj.* To be *appalled* is to feel horror and shock about something.

NOTICE & NOTE

772 **Anne.** Father, let's get out of here! We can't stay here now . . . Let's go . . .

773 **Mr. Van Daan.** Go! Where?

774 **Mrs. Frank** (*sinking into her chair at the table*). Yes. Where?

775 **Mr. Frank** (*rising, to them all*). Have we lost all faith? All courage? A moment ago we thought that they'd come for us. We were sure it was the end. But it wasn't the end. We're alive, safe. (Mr. Van Daan *goes to the table and sits.* Mr. Frank *prays.*) "We thank Thee, oh Lord our God, that in Thy infinite mercy Thou hast again seen fit to spare us." (*He blows out the candle, then turns to* Anne.) Come on, Anne. The song! Let's have the song! (*He starts to sing.* Anne *finally starts falteringly to sing, as* Mr. Frank *urges her on. Her voice is hardly audible at first.*)

ANALYZE DRAMA

Annotate: Review paragraphs 775–784. Mark details in the stage directions that reveal how the characters sing the Hanukkah song.

Interpret: How does the gradual change in the way the characters are singing reveal their feelings? How does this change affect the mood, or emotional atmosphere, at the end of Act One?

776 **Anne** (*singing*). "Oh, Hanukkah! Oh, Hanukkah! The sweet . . . celebration . . . " (*As she goes on singing, the others gradually join in, their voices still shaking with fear.* Mrs. Van Daan *sobs as she sings.*)

777 **Group.** "Around the feast . . . we . . . gather
In complete . . . jubilation . . .
Happiest of sea . . . sons
Now is here. Many are the reasons for good cheer."

778 (Dussel *comes from the bedroom. He comes over to the table, standing beside* Margot, *listening to them as they sing.*)

779 "Together
We'll weather
Whatever tomorrow may bring."

780 *(As they sing on with growing courage, the lights start to dim.)*

781 "So hear us rejoicing
And merrily voicing
The Hanukkah song that we sing.
Hoy!"

782 *(The lights are out. The curtain starts slowly to fall.)*

783 "Hear us rejoicing
And merrily voicing
The Hanukkah song that we sing."

784 *(They are still singing, as the curtain falls.)*

785 *The Curtain Falls.*

CHECK YOUR UNDERSTANDING

Answer these questions before moving on to the **Analyze the Text** section on the following page.

1 A major difference in Mr. Frank between Scene 1 and Scene 2 is that in Scene 1, —

A he feels gratitude for the help provided by Miep Gies

B he is overwhelmed by a mix of grief and bitterness

C he wishes that he had taken his family out of Amsterdam

D he is haunted by memories of life in a concentration camp

2 In Act One, the dialogue between Anne and Peter reveals that —

F they have a number of things in common

G they did not have many friends when they were at school

H Anne looks up to Peter because he is a few years older

J Anne is lively and sociable, but Peter is shy and awkward

3 The arrival of Mr. Dussel increases tension because —

A the Annex residents do not trust strangers

B Dussel insists on having his own room

C Dussel is not used to being around children

D there is barely enough food for everyone

ANALYZE THE TEXT

Support your responses with evidence from the text. NOTEBOOK

1. **Identify Patterns** How many scenes are there in Act One of this play? Why might the playwrights have begun a new scene after paragraph 178?
2. **Draw Conclusions** Examine paragraphs 351–363. What do the stage directions and dialogue reveal about the characters?
3. **Analyze** What subplot or subplots have the playwrights introduced in Act One? For each subplot you identify, what is the conflict?
4. **Cause/Effect** Plot events are often related by cause and effect; that is, one event causes something else to happen. How does the arrival of Mr. Dussel affect life in the Annex?
5. **Notice & Note** Review paragraph 589. What might explain the contradictions in Anne's feelings and behavior toward her mother?

MAKE PREDICTIONS

Predicting is a reading strategy that involves using text clues to make a reasonable guess about what will happen next in a story. To make predictions, think about what events have already taken place. Also consider how the plot is developing. What events, if any, have been foreshadowed? Is there rising tension between characters? Are there certain actions or events—either in the main plot or in a subplot—that you predict will have certain effects, or consequences?

Based on what you have read, make predictions about what will happen in Act Two. Record your predictions in the chart. Then, as you read Act Two, note which predictions are confirmed by the text, and correct those predictions that did not come true.

MY PREDICTION	WHAT HAPPENS

ACT TWO
Scene 1

1 *In the darkness we hear* Anne's Voice, *again reading from the diary.*

2 **Anne's Voice.** Saturday, the first of January, nineteen forty-four. Another new year has begun and we find ourselves still in our hiding place. We have been here now for one year, five months and twenty-five days. It seems that our life is at a standstill.

3 *The curtain rises on the scene. It is late afternoon. Everyone is bundled up against the cold. In the main room* Mrs. Frank *is taking down the laundry which is hung across the back.* Mr. Frank *sits in the chair down left, reading.* Margot *is lying on the couch with a blanket over her and the many-colored knitted scarf around her throat.* Anne *is seated at the center table, writing in her diary.* Peter, Mr. *and* Mrs. Van Daan, *and* Dussel *are all in their own rooms, reading or lying down.*

4 *As the lights dim on,* Anne's Voice *continues, without a break.*

5 **Anne's Voice.** We are all a little thinner. The Van Daans' "discussions" are as violent as ever. Mother still does not understand me. But then I don't understand her either. There is one great change, however. A change in myself. I read somewhere that girls of my age don't feel quite certain of themselves. That they become quiet within and begin to think of the miracle that is taking place in their bodies. I think that what is happening to me is so wonderful . . . not only what can be seen, but what is taking place inside. Each time it has happened I have a feeling that I have a sweet secret. (*We hear the chimes and then a hymn being played on the carillon outside.*) And in spite of any pain, I long for the time when I shall feel that secret within me again.

6 (*The buzzer of the door below suddenly sounds. Everyone is startled,* Mr. Frank *tiptoes cautiously to the top of the steps and listens. Again the buzzer sounds, in* Miep's *V-for-Victory signal.*)

7 **Mr. Frank.** It's Miep! (*He goes quickly down the steps to unbolt the door.* Mrs. Frank *calls upstairs to the* Van Daans *and then to* Peter.)

8 **Mrs. Frank.** Wake up, everyone! Miep is here! (Anne *quickly puts her diary away.* Margot *sits up, pulling the blanket around her shoulders.* Mr. Dussel *sits on the edge of his bed, listening, disgruntled.* Miep *comes up the steps, followed by* Mr. Kraler.

ANALYZE DRAMA

Annotate: Mark the date of Anne's diary entry at the beginning of Act Two, Scene 1.

Draw Conclusions: How much time has passed between the end of Act One and the beginning of Act Two? What does this suggest about the suspected thief who may have heard noise from the Annex?

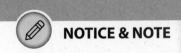

They bring flowers, books, newspapers, etc. Anne *rushes to* Miep, *throwing her arms affectionately around her.*) Miep . . . *and* Mr. Kraler . . . What a delightful surprise!

9 **Mr. Kraler.** We came to bring you New Year's greetings.

10 **Mrs. Frank.** You shouldn't . . . you should have at least one day to yourselves. (*She goes quickly to the stove and brings down teacups and tea for all of them.*)

11 **Anne.** Don't say that, it's so wonderful to see them! (*sniffing at* Miep's *coat*) I can smell the wind and the cold on your clothes.

12 **Miep** (*giving her the flowers*). There you are. (*then to* Margot, *feeling her forehead*) How are you, Margot? . . . Feeling any better?

13 **Margot.** I'm all right.

14 **Anne.** We filled her full of every kind of pill so she won't cough and make a noise. (*She runs into her room to put the flowers in water.* Mr. *and* Mrs. Van Daan *come from upstairs. Outside there is the sound of a band playing.*)

15 **Mrs. Van Daan.** Well, hello, Miep. Mr. Kraler.

16 **Mr. Kraler** (*giving a bouquet of flowers to* Mrs. Van Daan). With my hope for peace in the New Year.

17 **Peter** (*anxiously*). Miep, have you seen Mouschi? Have you seen him anywhere around?

18 **Miep.** I'm sorry, Peter. I asked everyone in the neighborhood had they seen a gray cat. But they said no.

19 (Mrs. Frank *gives* Miep *a cup of tea.* Mr. Frank *comes up the steps, carrying a small cake on a plate.*)

20 **Mr. Frank.** Look what Miep's brought for us!

21 **Mrs. Frank** (*taking it*). A cake!

22 **Mr. Van Daan.** A cake! (*He pinches* Miep's *cheeks gaily and hurries up to the cupboard.*) I'll get some plates.

23 (Dussel, *in his room, hastily puts a coat on and starts out to join the others.*)

24 **Mrs. Frank.** Thank you, Miepia. You shouldn't have done it. You must have used all of your sugar ration for weeks. (*giving it to* Mrs. Van Daan) It's beautiful, isn't it?

25 **Mrs. Van Daan.** It's been ages since I even saw a cake. Not since you brought us one last year. (*without looking at the cake, to* Miep) Remember? Don't you remember, you gave us one on New Year's Day? Just this time last year? I'll never forget it

because you had "Peace in nineteen forty-three" on it. (*She looks at the cake and reads.*) "Peace in nineteen forty-four!"

26 **Miep.** Well, it has to come sometime, you know. (*as* Dussel *comes from his room*) Hello, Mr. Dussel.

27 **Mr. Kraler.** How are you?

28 **Mr. Van Daan** (*bringing plates and a knife*). Here's the knife, *liefje*. Now, how many of us are there?

29 **Miep.** None for me, thank you.

30 **Mr. Frank.** Oh, please. You must.

31 **Miep.** I couldn't.

32 **Mr. Van Daan.** Good! That leaves one . . . two . . . three . . . seven of us.

33 **Dussel.** Eight! Eight! It's the same number as it always is!

34 **Mr. Van Daan.** I left Margot out. I take it for granted Margot won't eat any.

35 **Anne.** Why wouldn't she!

36 **Mrs. Frank.** I think it won't harm her.

37 **Mr. Van Daan.** All right! All right! I just didn't want her to start coughing again, that's all.

38 **Dussel.** And please, Mrs. Frank should cut the cake.

39 **Mr. Van Daan.** What's the difference?

40 **Mrs. Van Daan.** It's not Mrs. Frank's cake, is it, Miep? It's for all of us.

} *Together*

41 **Dussel.** Mrs. Frank divides things better.

42 **Mrs. Van Daan** (*going to* Dussel). What are you trying to say?

43 **Mr. Van Daan.** Oh, come on! Stop wasting time!

} *Together*

44 **Mrs. Van Daan** (*to* Dussel). Don't I always give everybody exactly the same? Don't I?

45 **Mr. Van Daan.** Forget it, Kerli.

46 **Mrs. Van Daan.** No. I want an answer! Don't I?

47 **Dussel.** Yes. Yes. Everybody gets exactly the same . . . except Mr. Van Daan always gets a little bit more.

48 (Mr. Van Daan *advances on* Dussel, *the knife still in his hand.*)

49 **Mr. Van Daan.** That's a lie!

50 (Dussel *retreats before the onslaught of the* Van Daans.)

ANALYZE DRAMA

Annotate: Review paragraphs 38–51. Mark the lines that reveal who Mr. Dussel thinks should cut the cake and why.

Interpret: Think about Mr. and Mrs. Van Daan's reaction to Dussel's comments, and what Mr. Frank says. What does the characters' dialogue reveal about them?

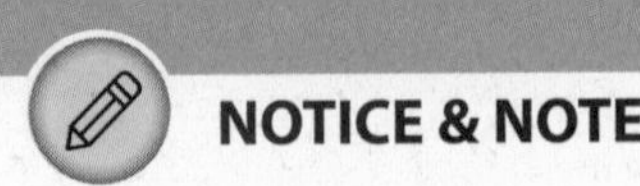

51 **Mr. Frank.** Please, please! (*then to* Miep) You see what a little sugar cake does to us? It goes right to our heads!

52 **Mr. Van Daan** (*handing* Mrs. Frank *the knife*). Here you are, Mrs. Frank.

53 **Mrs. Frank.** Thank you. (*then to* Miep *as she goes to the table to cut the cake*) Are you sure you won't have some?

54 **Miep** (*drinking her tea*). No, really, I have to go in a minute.

55 (*The sound of the band fades out in the distance.*)

56 **Peter** (*to* Miep). Maybe Mouschi went back to our house . . . they say that cats . . . Do you ever get over there . . . ? I mean . . . do you suppose you could . . . ?

57 **Miep.** I'll try, Peter. The first minute I get I'll try. But I'm afraid, with him gone a week . . .

58 **Dussel.** Make up your mind, already someone has had a nice big dinner from that cat!

inarticulate
(ĭn´är-tĭk´yə-lĭt) *adj.* Someone who is *inarticulate* is unable to speak in a clear way.

59 (Peter *is furious,* ***inarticulate****. He starts toward* Dussel *as if to hit him.* Mr. Frank *stops him.* Mrs. Frank *speaks quickly to ease the situation.*)

60 **Mrs. Frank** (*to* Miep). This is delicious, Miep!

61 **Mrs. Van Daan** (*eating hers*). Delicious!

62 **Mr. Van Daan** (*finishing it in one gulp*). Dirk's in luck to get a girl who can bake like this!

63 **Miep** (*putting down her empty teacup*). I have to run. Dirk's taking me to a party tonight.

64 **Anne.** How heavenly! Remember now what everyone is wearing, and what you have to eat and everything, so you can tell us tomorrow.

65 **Miep.** I'll give you a full report! Good-bye, everyone!

66 **Mr. Van Daan** (*to* Miep). Just a minute. There's something I'd like you to do for me. (*He hurries off up the stairs to his room.*)

67 **Mrs. Van Daan** (*sharply*). Putti, where are you going? (*She rushes up the stairs after him, calling hysterically.*) What do you want? Putti, what are you going to do?

68 **Miep** (*to* Peter). What's wrong?

69 **Peter** (*his sympathy is with his mother*). Father says he's going to sell her fur coat. She's crazy about that old fur coat.

70 **Dussel.** Is it possible? Is it possible that anyone is so silly as to worry about a fur coat in times like this?

71 **Peter.** It's none of your darn business . . . and if you say one more thing . . . I'll, I'll take you and I'll . . . I mean it . . . I'll . . .

72 (*There is a piercing scream from* Mrs. Van Daan *above. She grabs at the fur coat as* Mr. Van Daan *is starting downstairs with it.*)

73 **Mrs. Van Daan.** No! No! No! Don't you dare take that! You hear? It's mine! (*Downstairs* Peter *turns away, embarrassed, miserable.*) My father gave me that! You didn't give it to me. You have no right. Let go of it . . . you hear?

74 (Mr. Van Daan *pulls the coat from her hands and hurries downstairs.* Mrs. Van Daan *sinks to the floor, sobbing. As* Mr. Van Daan *comes into the main room the others look away, embarrassed for him.*)

75 **Mr. Van Daan** (*to* Mr. Kraler). Just a little—discussion over the advisability of selling this coat. As I have often reminded Mrs. Van Daan, it's very selfish of her to keep it when people outside are in such desperate need of clothing . . . (*He gives the coat to* Miep.) So if you will please to sell it for us? It should fetch a good price. And by the way, will you get me cigarettes. I don't care what kind they are . . . get all you can.

76 **Miep.** It's terribly difficult to get them, Mr. Van Daan. But I'll try. Good-bye.

77 (*She goes.* Mr. Frank *follows her down the steps to bolt the door after her.* Mrs. Frank *gives* Mr. Kraler *a cup of tea.*)

78 **Mrs. Frank.** Are you sure you won't have some cake, Mr. Kraler?

79 **Mr. Kraler.** I'd better not.

80 **Mr. Van Daan.** You're still feeling badly? What does your doctor say?

81 **Mr. Kraler.** I haven't been to him.

82 **Mrs. Frank.** Now, Mr. Kraler! . . .

83 **Mr. Kraler** (*sitting at the table*). Oh, I tried. But you can't get near a doctor these days . . . they're so busy. After weeks I finally managed to get one on the telephone. I told him I'd like an appointment . . . I wasn't feeling very well. You know what he answers . . . over the telephone . . . Stick out your tongue! (*They laugh. He turns to* Mr. Frank *as* Mr. Frank *comes back.*) I have some contracts here . . . I wonder if you'd look over them with me . . .

84 **Mr. Frank** (*putting out his hand*). Of course.

85 **Mr. Kraler** (*He rises*). If we could go downstairs . . . (Mr. Frank *starts ahead,* Mr. Kraler *speaks to the others.*) Will you forgive

AGAIN AND AGAIN

Notice & Note: In paragraph 75, mark the word that Mr. Van Daan uses to refer to the quarrel he and his family have been having. Then look back at paragraph 331 from Act One.

Interpret: What have the Van Daans been arguing about? What is the impact of Mr. Van Daan's using the word *discussion* again rather than *quarrel*?

us? I won't keep him but a minute. (*He starts to follow* Mr. Frank *down the steps.*)

86 **Margot** (*with sudden foreboding*). What's happened? Something's happened! Hasn't it, Mr. Kraler?

87 (Mr. Kraler *stops and comes back, trying to reassure* Margot *with a pretense of casualness.*)

88 **Mr. Kraler.** No, really. I want your father's advice . . .

89 **Margot.** Something's gone wrong! I know it!

90 **Mr. Frank** (*coming back, to* Mr. Kraler). If it's something that concerns us here, it's better that we all hear it.

91 **Mr. Kraler** (*turning to him, quietly*). But . . . the children . . . ?

92 **Mr. Frank.** What they'd imagine would be worse than any reality.

93 (*As* Mr. Kraler *speaks, they all listen with intense apprehension.* Mrs. Van Daan *comes down the stairs and sits on the bottom step.*)

ANALYZE PLOT DEVELOPMENT

Annotate: Mark the problem that Mr. Kraler tells the group about in paragraphs 94–96.

Analyze: How does this problem affect the plot?

94 **Mr. Kraler.** It's a man in the storeroom . . . I don't know whether or not you remember him . . . Carl, about fifty, heavy-set, near-sighted . . . He came with us just before you left.

95 **Mr. Frank.** He was from Utrecht?

96 **Mr. Kraler.** That's the man. A couple of weeks ago, when I was in the storeroom, he closed the door and asked me . . . how's Mr. Frank? What do you hear from Mr. Frank? I told him I only knew there was a rumor that you were in Switzerland. He said he'd heard that rumor too, but he thought I might know something more. I didn't pay any attention to it . . . but then a thing happened yesterday . . . He'd brought some invoices to the office for me to sign. As I was going through them, I looked up. He was standing staring at the bookcase . . . your bookcase. He said he thought he remembered a door there . . . Wasn't there a door there that used to go up to the loft? Then he told me he wanted more money. Twenty guilders[1] more a week.

97 **Mr. Van Daan.** Blackmail!

98 **Mr. Frank.** Twenty guilders? Very modest blackmail.

99 **Mr. Van Daan.** That's just the beginning.

100 **Dussel** (*coming to* Mr. Frank). You know what I think? He was the thief who was down there that night. That's how he knows we're here.

---

[1] **guilders** (gĭl´dərz): the basic monetary unit of the Netherlands at the time.

101 **Mr. Frank** (*to* Mr. Kraler). How was it left? What did you tell him?

102 **Mr. Kraler.** I said I had to think about it. What shall I do? Pay him the money? . . Take a chance on firing him . . . or what? I don't know.

103 **Dussel** (*frantic*). For God's sake don't fire him! Pay him what he asks . . . keep him here where you can have your eye on him.

104 **Mr. Frank.** Is it so much that he's asking? What are they paying nowadays?

105 **Mr. Kraler.** He could get it in a war plant. But this isn't a war plant. Mind you, I don't know if he really knows . . . or if he doesn't know.

106 **Mr. Frank.** Offer him half. Then we'll soon find out if it's blackmail or not.

107 **Dussel.** And if it is? We've got to pay it, haven't we? Anything he asks we've got to pay!

108 **Mr. Frank.** Let's decide that when the time comes.

109 **Mr. Kraler.** This may be all my imagination. You get to a point, these days, where you suspect everyone and everything. Again and again . . . on some simple look or word, I've found myself . . . (*The telephone rings in the office below.*)

110 **Mrs. Van Daan** (*hurrying to* Mr. Kraler). There's the telephone! What does that mean, the telephone ringing on a holiday?

111 **Mr. Kraler.** That's my wife. I told her I had to go over some papers in my office . . . to call me there when she got out of church. (*He starts out.*) I'll offer him half then. Good-bye . . . we'll hope for the best!

112 (*The group call their good-byes half-heartedly.* Mr. Frank *follows* Mr. Kraler, *to bolt the door below. During the following scene,* Mr. Frank *comes back up and stands listening, disturbed.*)

113 **Dussel** (*to* Mr. Van Daan). You can thank your son for this . . . smashing the light! I tell you, it's just a question of time now. (*He goes to the window at the back and stands looking out.*)

114 **Margot.** Sometimes I wish the end would come . . . whatever it is.

115 **Mrs. Frank** (*shocked*). Margot!

116 (Anne *goes to* Margot, *sitting beside her on the couch with her arms around her.*)

117 **Margot.** Then at least we'd know where we were.

118 **Mrs. Frank.** You should be ashamed of yourself! Talking that way! Think how lucky we are! Think of the thousands dying in the war, every day. Think of the people in concentration camps.

119 **Anne** (*interrupting*). What's the good of that? What's the good of thinking of misery when you're already miserable? That's stupid!

120 **Mrs. Frank.** Anne!

121 (*As* Anne *goes on raging at her mother,* Mrs. Frank *tries to break in, in an effort to quiet her.*)

122 **Anne.** We're young, Margot and Peter and I! You grownups have had your chance! But look at us . . . If we begin thinking of all the horror in the world, we're lost! We're trying to hold onto some kind of ideals . . . when everything . . . ideals, hopes . . . everything, are being destroyed! It isn't our fault that the world is in such a mess! We weren't around when all this started! So don't try to take it out on us!

123 (*She rushes off to her room, slamming the door after her. She picks up a brush from the chest and hurls it to the floor. Then she sits on the settee, trying to control her anger.*)

124 **Mr. Van Daan.** She talks as if we started the war! Did we start the war? (*He spots* Anne's *cake. As he starts to take it,* Peter *anticipates him.*)

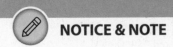

ANALYZE DRAMA

Annotate: In paragraphs 125–128, mark details in the stage directions and dialogue that reveal Peter's changing feelings toward Anne.

Infer: What do you infer from Peter's actions and words?

125 **Peter.** She left her cake. (*He starts for* Anne's *room with the cake. There is silence in the main room.* Mrs. Van Daan *goes up to her room, followed by* Van Daan. Dussel *stays looking out the window.* Mr. Frank *brings* Mrs. Frank *her cake. She eats it slowly, without relish.* Mr. Frank *takes his cake to* Margot *and sits quietly on the sofa beside her.* Peter *stands in the doorway of* Anne's *darkened room, looking at her, then makes a little movement to let her know he is there.* Anne *sits up, quickly, trying to hide the signs of her tears.* Peter *holds out the cake to her.*) You left this.

126 **Anne** (*dully*). Thanks.

127 (Peter *starts to go out, then comes back.*)

128 **Peter.** I thought you were fine just now. You know just how to talk to them. You know just how to say it. I'm no good . . . I never can think . . . especially when I'm mad . . . That Dussel . . . when he said that about Mouschi . . . someone eating him . . . all I could think is . . . I wanted to hit him. I wanted to give him such a . . . a . . . that he'd . . . That's what I used to do when there was an argument at school . . . That's the way I . . . but here . . . And an old man like that . . . it wouldn't be so good.

129 **Anne.** You're making a big mistake about me. I do it all wrong. I say too much. I go too far. I hurt people's feelings . . .

130 (Dussel *leaves the window, going to his room.*)

131 **Peter.** I think you're just fine . . . What I want to say . . . if it wasn't for you around here, I don't know. What I mean . . .

132 (Peter *is interrupted by* Dussel's *turning on the light.* Dussel *stands in the doorway, startled to see* Peter. Peter *advances toward him forbiddingly.* Dussel *backs out of the room.* Peter *closes the door on him.*)

133 **Anne.** Do you mean it, Peter? Do you really mean it?

134 **Peter.** I said it, didn't I?

135 **Anne.** Thank you, Peter!

136 (*In the main room* Mr. *and* Mrs. Frank *collect the dishes and take them to the sink, washing them.* Margot *lies down again on*

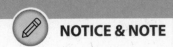

the couch. Dussel, *lost, wanders into* Peter's *room and takes up a book, starting to read.)*

137 **Peter** (*looking at the photographs on the wall*). You've got quite a collection.

138 **Anne.** Wouldn't you like some in your room? I could give you some. Heaven knows you spend enough time in there . . . doing heaven knows what . . .

139 **Peter.** It's easier. A fight starts, or an argument . . . I duck in there.

140 **Anne.** You're lucky, having a room to go to. His lordship is always here . . . I hardly ever get a minute alone. When they start in on me, I can't duck away. I have to stand there and take it.

141 **Peter.** You gave some of it back just now.

142 **Anne.** I get so mad. They've formed their opinions . . . about everything . . . but we . . . we're still trying to find out . . . We have problems here that no other people our age have ever had. And just as you think you've solved them, something comes along and bang! You have to start all over again.

ANALYZE DRAMA

Annotate: In paragraphs 143–146, underline details in the dialogue that reveal Anne's relationship with her mother. Circle details that reveal her relationship with her father.

Compare: Contrast these two relationships. Why do you think Anne has such different relationships with her father and mother?

143 **Peter.** At least you've got someone you can talk to.

144 **Anne.** Not really. Mother . . . I never discuss anything serious with her. She doesn't understand. Father's all right. We can talk about everything . . . everything but one thing. Mother. He simply won't talk about her. I don't think you can be really intimate with anyone if he holds something back, do you?

145 **Peter.** I think your father's fine.

146 **Anne.** Oh, he is, Peter! He is! He's the only one who's ever given me the feeling that I have any sense. But anyway, nothing can take the place of school and play and friends of your own age . . . or near your age . . . can it?

147 **Peter.** I suppose you miss your friends and all.

148 **Anne.** It isn't just . . . (*She breaks off, staring up at him for a second.*) Isn't it funny, you and I? Here we've been seeing each other every minute for almost a year and a half, and this is the first time we've ever really talked. It helps a lot to have someone to talk to, don't you think? It helps you to let off steam.

149 **Peter** (*going to the door*). Well, any time you want to let off steam, you can come into my room.

150 **Anne** (*following him*). I can get up an awful lot of steam. You'll have to be careful how you say that.

151 **Peter.** It's all right with me.

152 **Anne.** Do you mean it?

153 **Peter.** I said it, didn't I?

154 (*He goes out.* Anne *stands in her doorway looking after him. As* Peter *gets to his door he stands for a minute looking back at her. Then he goes into his room.* Dussel *rises as he comes in, and quickly passes him, going out. He starts across for his room.* Anne *sees him coming, and pulls her door shut.* Dussel *turns back toward* Peter's *room.* Peter *pulls his door shut.* Dussel *stands there, bewildered, forlorn.*

155 *The scene slowly dims out. The curtain falls on the scene.* Anne's Voice *comes over in the darkness . . . faintly at first, and then with growing strength.*)

156 **Anne's Voice.** We've had bad news. The people from whom Miep got our ration books have been arrested. So we have had to cut down on our food. Our stomachs are so empty that they rumble and make strange noises, all in different keys. Mr. Van Daan's is deep and low, like a bass fiddle. Mine is high, whistling like a flute. As we all sit around waiting for supper, it's like an orchestra tuning up. It only needs Toscanini[2] to raise his baton and we'd be off in the Ride of the Valkyries.[3] Monday, the sixth of March, nineteen forty-four. Mr. Kraler is in the hospital. It seems he has ulcers. Pim says we are his ulcers. Miep has to run the business and us too. The Americans have landed on the southern tip of Italy. Father looks for a quick finish to the war. Mr. Dussel is waiting every day for the warehouse man to demand more money. Have I been skipping too much from one subject to another? I can't help it. I feel that spring is coming. I feel it in my whole body and soul. I feel utterly confused. I am longing . . . so longing . . . for everything . . . for friends . . . for someone to talk to . . . someone who understands . . . someone young, who feels as I do . . .

157 (*As these last lines are being said, the curtain rises on the scene. The lights dim on.* Anne's Voice *fades out.*)

---

[2] **Toscanini** (tŏs´kə-nē´nē): Arturo Toscanini, a famous Italian orchestral conductor.

[3] **Ride of the Valkyries** (văl-kîr´əz): an exciting passage from an opera by Richard Wagner, a German composer.

Scene 2

158 *It is evening, after supper. From outside we hear the sound of children playing. The "grownups," with the exception of* Mr. Van Daan, *are all in the main room.* Mrs. Frank *is doing some mending,* Mrs. Van Daan *is reading a fashion magazine.* Mr. Frank *is going over business accounts.* Dussel, *in his dentist's jacket, is pacing up and down, impatient to get into his bedroom.* Mr. Van Daan *is upstairs working on a piece of embroidery in an embroidery frame.*

ANALYZE DRAMA

Annotate: Mark details in paragraphs 159–161 that reveal what Peter and Anne are doing at the beginning of Scene 2.

Predict: What do these stage directions suggest will happen next? Why did the playwrights choose to include those details about Peter and Anne?

159 *In his room* Peter *is sitting before the mirror, smoothing his hair. As the scene goes on, he puts on his tie, brushes his coat and puts it on, preparing himself meticulously for a visit from* Anne. *On his wall are now hung some of* Anne's *motion picture stars.*

160 *In her room* Anne *too is getting dressed. She stands before the mirror in her slip, trying various ways of dressing her hair.* Margot *is seated on the sofa, hemming a skirt for* Anne *to wear.*

161 *In the main room* Dussel *can stand it no longer. He comes over, rapping sharply on the door of his and* Anne's *bedroom.*

162 **Anne** (*calling to him*). No, no, Mr. Dussel! I am not dressed yet. (Dussel *walks away, furious, sitting down and burying his head in his hands.* Anne *turns to* Margot.) How is that? How does that look?

163 **Margot** (*glancing at her briefly*). Fine.

164 **Anne.** You didn't even look.

165 **Margot.** Of course I did. It's fine.

166 **Anne.** Margot, tell me, am I terribly ugly?

167 **Margot.** Oh, stop fishing.

168 **Anne.** No. No. Tell me.

169 **Margot.** Of course you're not. You've got nice eyes . . . and a lot of animation, and . . .

170 **Anne.** A little vague, aren't you?

171 (*She reaches over and takes a brassière out of* Margot's *sewing basket. She holds it up to herself, studying the effect in the mirror. Outside,* Mrs. Frank, *feeling sorry for* Dussel, *comes over, knocking at the girls' door.*)

172 **Mrs. Frank** (*outside*). May I come in?

173 **Margot.** Come in, Mother.

174 **Mrs. Frank** (*shutting the door behind her*). Mr. Dussel's impatient to get in here.

175 **Anne** (*still with the brassière*). Heavens, he takes the room for himself the entire day.

176 **Mrs. Frank** (*gently*). Anne, dear, you're not going in again tonight to see Peter?

177 **Anne** (*dignified*). That is my intention.

178 **Mrs. Frank.** But you've already spent a great deal of time in there today.

179 **Anne.** I was in there exactly twice. Once to get the dictionary, and then three-quarters of an hour before supper.

180 **Mrs. Frank.** Aren't you afraid you're disturbing him?

181 **Anne.** Mother, I have some intuition.

182 **Mrs. Frank.** Then may I ask you this much, Anne. Please don't shut the door when you go in.

183 **Anne.** You sound like Mrs. Van Daan! (*She throws the brassière back in* Margot's *sewing basket and picks up her blouse, putting it on.*)

184 **Mrs. Frank.** No. No. I don't mean to suggest anything wrong. I only wish that you wouldn't expose yourself to criticism . . . that you wouldn't give Mrs. Van Daan the opportunity to be unpleasant.

185 **Anne.** Mrs. Van Daan doesn't need an opportunity to be unpleasant!

186 **Mrs. Frank.** Everyone's on edge, worried about Mr. Kraler. This is one more thing . . .

187 **Anne.** I'm sorry, Mother. I'm going to Peter's room. I'm not going to let Petronella Van Daan spoil our friendship.

188 (Mrs. Frank *hesitates for a second, then goes out, closing the door after her. She gets a pack of playing cards and sits at the center table, playing solitaire. In* Anne's *room* Margot *hands the finished skirt to* Anne. *As* Anne *is putting it on,* Margot *takes off her high-heeled shoes and stuffs paper in the toes so that* Anne *can wear them.*)

189 **Margot** (*to* Anne). Why don't you two talk in the main room? It'd save a lot of trouble. It's hard on Mother, having to listen to those remarks from Mrs. Van Daan and not say a word.

190 **Anne.** Why doesn't she say a word? I think it's ridiculous to take it and take it.

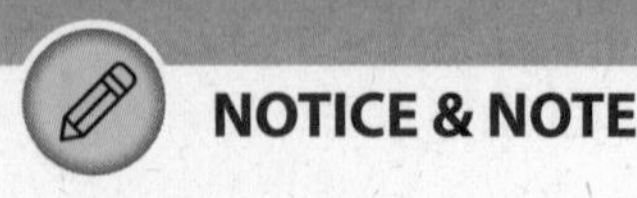

NOTICE & NOTE

WORDS OF THE WISER

Notice & Note: In paragraphs 189–191, mark the explanation Margot gives Anne for why Mrs. Frank doesn't react to Mrs. Van Daan's remarks.

Infer: What wisdom do Margot's words reveal?

191 **Margot.** You don't understand Mother at all, do you? She can't talk back. She's not like you. It's just not in her nature to fight back.

192 **Anne.** Anyway . . . the only one I worry about is you. I feel awfully guilty about you.

193 (*She sits on the stool near* Margot, *putting on* Margot's *high-heeled shoes.*)

194 **Margot.** What about?

195 **Anne.** I mean, every time I go into Peter's room, I have a feeling I may be hurting you. (Margot *shakes her head.*) I know if it were me, I'd be wild. I'd be desperately jealous, if it were me.

196 **Margot.** Well, I'm not.

197 **Anne.** You don't feel badly? Really? Truly? You're not jealous?

198 **Margot.** Of course I'm jealous . . . jealous that you've got something to get up in the morning for . . . But jealous of you and Peter? No.

199 (Anne *goes back to the mirror.*)

200 **Anne.** Maybe there's nothing to be jealous of. Maybe he doesn't really like me. Maybe I'm just taking the place of his cat . . . (*She picks up a pair of short white gloves, putting them on.*) Wouldn't you like to come in with us?

201 **Margot.** I have a book.

202 (*The sound of the children playing outside fades out. In the main room* Dussel *can stand it no longer. He jumps up, going to the bedroom door and knocking sharply.*)

203 **Dussel.** Will you please let me in my room!

204 **Anne.** Just a minute, dear, dear Mr. Dussel. (*She picks up her Mother's pink stole and adjusts it elegantly over her shoulders, then gives a last look in the mirror.*) Well, here I go . . . to run the gauntlet.[4] (*She starts out, followed by* Margot.)

205 **Dussel** (*as she appears—sarcastic*). Thank you so much.

206 (Dussel *goes into his room.* Anne *goes toward* Peter's *room, passing* Mrs. Van Daan *and her parents at the center table.*)

207 **Mrs. Van Daan.** My God, look at her! (Anne *pays no attention. She knocks at* Peter's *door.*) I don't know what good it is to have a son. I never see him. He wouldn't care if I killed myself. (Peter *opens the door and stands aside for* Anne *to come in.*) Just

[4] **to run the gauntlet:** to endure a series of troubles or difficulties.

a minute, Anne. (*She goes to them at the door.*) I'd like to say a few words to my son. Do you mind? (Peter *and* Anne *stand waiting.*) Peter, I don't want you staying up till all hours tonight. You've got to have your sleep. You're a growing boy. You hear?

208 **Mrs. Frank.** Anne won't stay late. She's going to bed promptly at nine. Aren't you, Anne?

209 **Anne.** Yes, Mother . . . (*to* Mrs. Van Daan) May we go now?

210 **Mrs. Van Daan.** Are you asking me? I didn't know I had anything to say about it.

211 **Mrs. Frank.** Listen for the chimes, Anne dear.

212 (*The two young people go off into* Peter's *room, shutting the door after them.*)

213 **Mrs. Van Daan** (*to* Mrs. Frank). In my day it was the boys who called on the girls. Not the girls on the boys.

214 **Mrs. Frank.** You know how young people like to feel that they have secrets. Peter's room is the only place where they can talk.

215 **Mrs. Van Daan.** Talk! That's not what they called it when I was young.

216 (Mrs. Van Daan *goes off to the bathroom.* Margot *settles down to read her book.* Mr. Frank *puts his papers away and brings a chess game to the center table. He and* Mrs. Frank *start to play. In* Peter's *room,* Anne *speaks to* Peter, *indignant, humiliated.*)

217 **Anne.** Aren't they awful? Aren't they impossible? Treating us as if we were still in the nursery.

218 (*She sits on the cot.* Peter *gets a bottle of pop and two glasses.*)

219 **Peter.** Don't let it bother you. It doesn't bother me.

220 **Anne.** I suppose you can't really blame them . . . they think back to what *they* were like at our age. They don't realize how much more advanced we are . . . When you think what wonderful discussions we've had! . . . Oh, I forgot. I was going to bring you some more pictures.

221 **Peter.** Oh, these are fine, thanks.

222 **Anne.** Don't you want some more? Miep just brought me some new ones.

223 **Peter.** Maybe later. (*He gives her a glass of pop and, taking some for himself, sits down facing her.*)

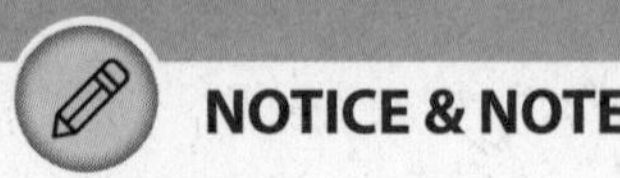

NOTICE & NOTE

MEMORY MOMENT

Notice & Note: Mark the memories that Anne has as she looks at the photos that Miep brought her.

Interpret: How does Anne feel that she's changed since the days when she played ping-pong with her friends?

224 **Anne** (*looking up at one of the photographs*). I remember when I got that . . . I won it. I bet Jopie that I could eat five ice-cream cones. We'd all been playing ping-pong . . . We used to have heavenly times . . . we'd finish up with ice cream at the Delphi, or the Oasis, where Jews were allowed . . . there'd always be a lot of boys . . . we'd laugh and joke . . . I'd like to go back to it for a few days or a week. But after that I know I'd be bored to death. I think more seriously about life now. I want to be a journalist . . . or something. I love to write. What do you want to do?

225 **Peter.** I thought I might go off some place . . . work on a farm or something . . . some job that doesn't take much brains.

226 **Anne.** You shouldn't talk that way. You've got the most awful inferiority complex.

227 **Peter.** I know I'm not smart.

228 **Anne.** That isn't true. You're much better than I am in dozens of things . . . arithmetic and algebra and . . . well, you're a million times better than I am in algebra. (*with sudden directness*) You like Margot, don't you? Right from the start you liked her, liked her much better than me.

229 **Peter** (*uncomfortably*). Oh, I don't know.

230 (*In the main room* Mrs. Van Daan *comes from the bathroom and goes over to the sink, polishing a coffee pot.*)

231 **Anne.** It's all right. Everyone feels that way. Margot's so good. She's sweet and bright and beautiful and I'm not.

232 **Peter.** I wouldn't say that.

233 **Anne.** Oh, no, I'm not. I know that. I know quite well that I'm not a beauty. I never have been and never shall be.

234 **Peter.** I don't agree at all. I think you're pretty.

235 **Anne.** That's not true!

236 **Peter.** And another thing. You've changed . . . from at first, I mean.

237 **Anne.** I have?

238 **Peter.** I used to think you were awful noisy.

239 **Anne.** And what do you think now, Peter? How have I changed?

240 **Peter.** Well . . . er . . . you're . . . quieter.

241 (*In his room* Dussel *takes his pajamas and toilet articles and goes into the bathroom to change.*)

242 **Anne.** I'm glad you don't just hate me.

243 **Peter.** I never said that.

244 **Anne.** I bet when you get out of here you'll never think of me again.

245 **Peter.** That's crazy.

246 **Anne.** When you get back with all of your friends, you're going to say . . . now what did I ever see in that Mrs. Quack Quack.

247 **Peter.** I haven't got any friends.

248 **Anne.** Oh, Peter, of course you have. Everyone has friends.

249 **Peter.** Not me. I don't want any. I get along all right without them.

250 **Anne.** Does that mean you can get along without me? I think of myself as your friend.

251 **Peter.** No. If they were all like you, it'd be different.

252 (*He takes the glasses and the bottle and puts them away. There is a second's silence and then* Anne *speaks, hesitantly, shyly.*)

253 **Anne.** Peter, did you ever kiss a girl?

254 **Peter.** Yes. Once.

255 **Anne** (*to cover her feelings*). That picture's crooked. (Peter *goes over, straightening the photograph.*) Was she pretty?

256 **Peter.** Huh?

257 **Anne.** The girl that you kissed.

258 **Peter.** I don't know. I was blindfolded. (*He comes back and sits down again.*) It was at a party. One of those kissing games.

259 **Anne** (*relieved*). Oh. I don't suppose that really counts, does it?

260 **Peter.** It didn't with me.

261 **Anne.** I've been kissed twice. Once a man I'd never seen before kissed me on the cheek when he picked me up off the ice and I was crying. And the other was Mr. Koophuis, a friend of Father's who kissed my hand. You wouldn't say those counted, would you?

262 **Peter.** I wouldn't say so.

263 **Anne.** I know almost for certain that Margot would never kiss anyone unless she was engaged to them. And I'm sure too that Mother never touched a man before Pim. But I don't know . . . things are so different now . . . What do you think? Do you think a girl shouldn't kiss anyone except if she's engaged or

something? It's so hard to try to think what to do, when here we are with the whole world falling around our ears and you think . . . well . . . you don't know what's going to happen tomorrow and . . . What do you think?

264 **Peter.** I suppose it'd depend on the girl. Some girls, anything they do's wrong. But others . . . well . . . it wouldn't necessarily be wrong with them. (*The carillon starts to strike nine o'clock.*) I've always thought that when two people . . .

265 **Anne.** Nine o'clock. I have to go.

266 **Peter.** That's right.

267 **Anne** (*without moving*). Good night.

268 (*There is a second's pause, then* Peter *gets up and moves toward the door.*)

269 **Peter.** You won't let them stop you coming?

270 **Anne.** No. (*She rises and starts for the door.*) Sometime I might bring my diary. There are so many things in it that I want to talk over with you. There's a lot about you.

271 **Peter.** What kind of things?

272 **Anne.** I wouldn't want you to see some of it. I thought you were a nothing, just the way you thought about me.

273 **Peter.** Did you change your mind, the way I changed my mind about you?

274 **Anne.** Well . . . You'll see . . .

275 (*For a second* Anne *stands looking up at* Peter, *longing for him to kiss her. As he makes no move she turns away. Then suddenly* Peter *grabs her awkwardly in his arms, kissing her on the cheek.* Anne *walks out dazed. She stands for a minute, her back to the people in the main room. As she regains her poise she goes to her mother and father and* Margot, *silently kissing them. They murmur their good nights to her. As she is about to open her bedroom door, she catches sight of* Mrs. Van Daan. *She goes quickly to her, taking her face in her hands and kissing her first on one cheek and then on the other. Then she hurries off into her room.* Mrs. Van Daan *looks after her, and then looks over at* Peter's *room. Her suspicions are confirmed.*)

276 **Mrs. Van Daan** (*She knows*). Ah hah!

277 (*The lights dim out. The curtain falls on the scene. In the darkness* Anne's Voice *comes faintly at first and then with growing strength.*)

NOTICE & NOTE

278 **Anne's Voice.** By this time we all know each other so well that if anyone starts to tell a story, the rest can finish it for him. We're having to cut down still further on our meals. What makes it worse, the rats have been at work again. They've carried off some of our precious food. Even Mr. Dussel wishes now that Mouschi was here. Thursday, the twentieth of April, nineteen forty-four. Invasion fever is mounting every day. Miep tells us that people outside talk of nothing else. For myself, life has become much more pleasant. I often go to Peter's room after supper. Oh, don't think I'm in love, because I'm not. But it does make life more bearable to have someone with whom you can exchange views. No more tonight. P.S. . . . I must be honest. I must confess that I actually live for the next meeting. Is there anything lovelier than to sit under the skylight and feel the sun on your cheeks and have a darling boy in your arms? I admit now that I'm glad the Van Daans had a son and not a daughter. I've outgrown another dress. That's the third. I'm having to wear Margot's clothes after all. I'm working hard on my French and am now reading *La Belle Nivernaise.*

279 (*As she is saying the last lines—the curtain rises on the scene. The lights dim on, as* Anne's Voice *fades out.*)

Scene 3

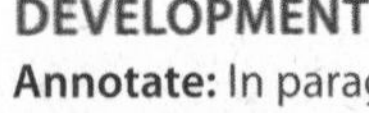

ANALYZE PLOT DEVELOPMENT

Annotate: In paragraphs 280–299, mark details in the stage directions and dialogue that introduce a new conflict to the drama.

Connect: What conflict arises in this scene? What event earlier in the play foreshadowed this conflict?

280 *It is night, a few weeks later. Everyone is in bed. There is complete quiet. In the* Van Daans' *room a match flares up for a moment and then is quickly put out.* Mr. Van Daan, *in bare feet, dressed in underwear and trousers, is dimly seen coming stealthily down the stairs and into the main room, where* Mr. *and* Mrs. Frank *and* Margot *are sleeping. He goes to the food safe and again lights a match. Then he cautiously opens the safe, taking out a half-loaf of bread. As he closes the safe, it creaks. He stands rigid.* Mrs. Frank *sits up in bed. She sees him.*

281 **Mrs. Frank** (*screaming*). Otto! Otto! *Komme schnell!*[5]

282 (*The rest of the people wake, hurriedly getting up.*)

283 **Mr. Frank.** *Was ist los? Was ist passiert?*[6]

284 (Dussel, *followed by* Anne, *comes from his room.*)

285 **Mrs. Frank** (*as she rushes over to* Mr. Van Daan). *Er stiehlt das Essen!*[7]

[5] ***Komme schnell!*** (kôm´e shnĕl´) *German:* Come quickly!

[6] ***Was ist los? Was ist passiert?*** (väs ĭst lôs´? väs ĭst pä-sērt´?) *German:* What's the matter? What has happened?

[7] ***Er stiehlt das Essen!*** (ĕr shtēlt´ däs ĕs´ən) *German:* He is stealing food!

286 **Dussel** (*grabbing* Mr. Van Daan). You! You! Give me that.

287 **Mrs. Van Daan** (*coming down the stairs*). Putti . . . Putti . . . what is it?

288 **Dussel** (*his hands on* Van Daan's *neck*). You dirty thief . . . stealing food . . . you good-for-nothing . . .

289 **Mr. Frank.** Mr. Dussel! For God's sake! Help me, Peter!

290 (Peter *comes over, trying, with* Mr. Frank, *to separate the two struggling men.*)

291 **Peter.** Let him go! Let go!

292 (Dussel *drops* Mr. Van Daan, *pushing him away. He shows them the end of a loaf of bread that he has taken from* Van Daan.)

293 **Dussel.** You greedy, selfish . . . !

294 (Margot *turns on the lights.*)

295 **Mrs. Van Daan.** Putti . . . what is it?

296 (*All of* Mrs. Frank's *gentleness, her self-control, is gone. She is outraged, in a frenzy of indignation.*)

297 **Mrs. Frank.** The bread! He was stealing the bread!

298 **Dussel.** It was you, and all the time we thought it was the rats!

299 **Mr. Frank.** Mr. Van Daan, how could you!

300 **Mr. Van Daan.** I'm hungry.

301 **Mrs. Frank.** We're all of us hungry! I see the children getting thinner and thinner. Your own son Peter . . . I've heard him moan in his sleep, he's so hungry. And you come in the night and steal food that should go to them . . . to the children!

302 **Mrs. Van Daan** (*going to* Mr. Van Daan *protectively*). He needs more food than the rest of us. He's used to more. He's a big man.

303 (Mr. Van Daan *breaks away, going over and sitting on the couch.*)

304 **Mrs. Frank** (*turning on* Mrs. Van Daan). And you . . . you're worse than he is! You're a mother, and yet you sacrifice your child to this man . . . this . . . this . . .

305 **Mr. Frank.** Edith! Edith!

306 (Margot *picks up the pink woolen stole, putting it over her mother's shoulders.*)

307 **Mrs. Frank** (*paying no attention, going on to* Mrs. Van Daan). Don't think I haven't seen you! Always saving the choicest bits

CONTRASTS AND CONTRADICTIONS

Notice & Note: Mark details in paragraphs 301–313 that reveal how Mrs. Frank feels about the theft and what she wants to happen as a result of it.

Analyze: How does Mrs. Frank's behavior contradict what you would expect of her? Do you think she would have reacted the same way at the beginning of the play? Explain.

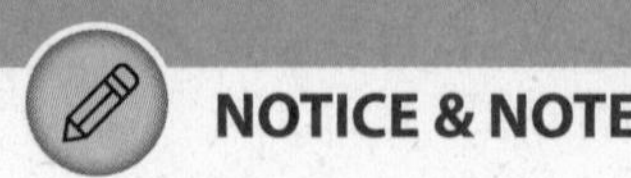

for him! I've watched you day after day and I've held my tongue. But not any longer! Not after this! Now I want him to go! I want him to get out of here!

308 **Mr. Frank.** Edith!

309 **Mr. Van Daan.** Get out of here?

310 **Mrs. Van Daan.** What do you mean?

Together

MAKE PREDICTIONS

Annotate: As you read this scene, mark details that match predictions you made at the end of Act One. In the chart on page 462, describe what actually happens.

Predict: Make a new prediction about what will happen as a result of Mr. Van Daan's being caught stealing food. Use details from the play to support your prediction.

311 **Mrs. Frank.** Just that! Take your things and get out!

312 **Mr. Frank** (*to* Mrs. Frank). You're speaking in anger. You cannot mean what you are saying.

313 **Mrs. Frank.** I mean exactly that!

314 (Mrs. Van Daan *takes a cover from the* Franks' *bed, pulling it about her.*)

315 **Mr. Frank.** For two long years we have lived here, side by side. We have respected each other's rights . . . we have managed to live in peace. Are we now going to throw it all away? I know this will never happen again, will it, Mr. Van Daan?

316 **Mr. Van Daan.** No. No.

317 **Mrs. Frank.** He steals once! He'll steal again!

318 (Mr. Van Daan, *holding his stomach, starts for the bathroom.* Anne *puts her arms around him, helping him up the step.*)

319 **Mr. Frank.** Edith, please. Let us be calm. We'll all go to our rooms . . . and afterwards we'll sit down quietly and talk this out . . . we'll find some way . . .

320 **Mrs. Frank.** No! No! No more talk! I want them to leave!

321 **Mrs. Van Daan.** You'd put us out, on the streets?

322 **Mrs. Frank.** There are other hiding places.

323 **Mrs. Van Daan.** A cellar . . . a closet. I know. And we have no money left even to pay for that.

324 **Mrs. Frank.** I'll give you money. Out of my own pocket I'll give it gladly. (*She gets her purse from a shelf and comes back with it.*)

325 **Mrs. Van Daan.** Mr. Frank, you told Putti you'd never forget what he'd done for you when you came to Amsterdam. You said you could never repay him, that you . . .

326 **Mrs. Frank** (*counting out money*). If my husband had any obligation to you, he's paid it, over and over.

327 **Mr. Frank.** Edith, I've never seen you like this before. I don't know you.

328 **Mrs. Frank.** I should have spoken out long ago.

329 **Dussel.** You can't be nice to some people.

330 **Mrs. Van Daan** (*turning on* Dussel). There would have been plenty for all of us, if you hadn't come in here!

331 **Mr. Frank.** We don't need the Nazis to destroy us. We're destroying ourselves.

332 (*He sits down, with his head in his hands.* Mrs. Frank *goes to* Mrs. Van Daan.)

333 **Mrs. Frank** (*giving* Mrs. Van Daan *some money*). Give this to Miep. She'll find you a place.

334 **Anne.** Mother, you're not putting *Peter* out. Peter hasn't done anything.

335 **Mrs. Frank.** He'll stay, of course. When I say I must protect the children, I mean Peter too.

336 (Peter *rises from the steps where he has been sitting.*)

337 **Peter.** I'd have to go if Father goes.

338 (Mr. Van Daan *comes from the bathroom.* Mrs. Van Daan *hurries to him and takes him to the couch. Then she gets water from the sink to bathe his face.*)

339 **Mrs. Frank** (*while this is going on*). He's no father to you . . . that man! He doesn't know what it is to be a father!

340 **Peter** (*starting for his room*). I wouldn't feel right. I couldn't stay.

341 **Mrs. Frank.** Very well, then. I'm sorry.

342 **Anne** (*rushing over to* Peter). No, Peter! No! (Peter *goes into his room, closing the door after him.* Anne *turns back to her mother, crying.*) I don't care about the food. They can have mine! I don't want it! Only don't send them away. It'll be daylight soon. They'll be caught . . .

343 **Margot** (*putting her arms comfortingly around* Anne). Please, Mother!

344 **Mrs. Frank.** They're not going now. They'll stay here until Miep finds them a place. (*to* Mrs. Van Daan) But one thing I insist on! He must never come down here again! He must never come to this room where the food is stored! We'll divide what we

NOTICE & NOTE

WORDS OF THE WISER

Notice & Note: Mark the lines of dialogue that reveal what Mr. Frank believes is destroying the group in the Annex.

Infer: What does Mr. Frank mean?

have . . . an equal share for each! (Dussel *hurries over to get a sack of potatoes from the food safe.* Mrs. Frank *goes on, to* Mrs. Van Daan.) You can cook it here and take it up to him.

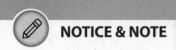

345 (Dussel *brings the sack of potatoes back to the center table.*)

346 **Margot.** Oh, no. No. We haven't sunk so far that we're going to fight over a handful of rotten potatoes.

347 **Dussel** (*dividing the potatoes into piles*). Mrs. Frank, Mr. Frank, Margot, Anne, Peter, Mrs. Van Daan, Mr. Van Daan, myself . . . Mrs. Frank . . .

348 (*The buzzer sounds in Miep's signal.*)

349 **Mr. Frank.** It's Miep! (*He hurries over, getting his overcoat and putting it on.*)

350 **Margot.** At this hour?

351 **Mrs. Frank.** It is trouble.

352 **Mr. Frank** (*as he starts down to unbolt the door*). I beg you, don't let her see a thing like this!

353 **Mr. Dussel** (*counting without stopping*). . . . Anne, Peter, Mrs. Van Daan, Mr. Van Daan, myself . . .

354 **Margot** (*to Dussel*). Stop it! Stop it!

355 **Dussel.** . . . . Mr. Frank, Margot, Anne, Peter, Mrs. Van Daan, Mr. Van Daan, myself, Mrs. Frank . . .

356 **Mrs. Van Daan.** You're keeping the big ones for yourself! All the big ones . . . Look at the size of that! . . . And that! . . .

357 (Dussel *continues on with his dividing.* Peter, *with his shirt and trousers on, comes from his room.*)

358 **Margot.** Stop it! Stop it!

359 (*We hear* Miep's *excited voice speaking to* Mr. Frank *below.*)

ANALYZE PLOT DEVELOPMENT

Annotate: In paragraphs 360–373, mark details that reveal what Miep has come to tell everyone about.

Summarize: Why do the residents of the Annex go "crazy" and have a "wild demonstration"?

360 **Miep.** Mr. Frank . . . the most wonderful news! . . . The invasion has begun!

361 **Mr. Frank.** Go on, tell them! Tell them!

362 (Miep *comes running up the steps, ahead of* Mr. Frank. *She has a man's raincoat on over her nightclothes and a bunch of orange-colored flowers in her hand.*)

363 **Miep.** Did you hear that, everybody? Did you hear what I said? The invasion has begun! The invasion!

364 (*They all stare at* Miep, *unable to grasp what she is telling them.* Peter *is the first to recover his wits.*)

365 **Peter.** Where?

366 **Mrs. Van Daan.** When? When, Miep?

367 **Miep.** It began early this morning . . .

368 (*As she talks on, the realization of what she has said begins to dawn on them. Everyone goes crazy. A wild demonstration takes place.* Mrs. Frank *hugs* Mr. Van Daan.)

369 **Mrs. Frank.** Oh, Mr. Van Daan, did you hear that? (Dussel *embraces* Mrs. Van Daan. Peter *grabs a frying pan and parades around the room, beating on it, singing the Dutch National Anthem.* Anne *and* Margot *follow him, singing, weaving in and out among the excited grownups.* Margot *breaks away to take the flowers from* Miep *and distribute them to everyone. While this pandemonium is going on* Mrs. Frank *tries to make herself heard above the excitement.*)

370 **Mrs. Frank** (*to* Miep). How do you know?

371 **Miep.** The radio . . . The B.B.C.! They said they landed on the coast of Normandy!

372 **Peter.** The British?

373 **Miep.** British, Americans, French, Dutch, Poles, Norwegians . . . all of them! More than four thousand ships! Churchill spoke, and General Eisenhower! D-Day they call it!

374 **Mr. Frank.** Thank God, it's come!

375 **Mrs. Van Daan.** At last!

376 **Miep** (*starting out*). I'm going to tell Mr. Kraler. This'll be better than any blood transfusion.

377 **Mr. Frank** (*stopping her*). What part of Normandy did they land, did they say?

378 **Miep.** Normandy . . . that's all I know now . . . I'll be up the minute I hear some more! (*She goes hurriedly out.*)

379 **Mr. Frank** (*to* Mrs. Frank). What did I tell you? What did I tell you?

380 (Mrs. Frank *indicates that he has forgotten to bolt the door after* Miep. *He hurries down the steps.* Mr. Van Daan, *sitting on the couch, suddenly breaks into a convulsive sob. Everybody looks at him, bewildered.*)

381 **Mrs. Van Daan** (*hurrying to him*). Putti! Putti! What is it? What happened?

382 **Mr. Van Daan.** Please. I'm so ashamed.

383 (Mr. Frank *comes back up the steps.*)

384 **Dussel.** Oh, for God's sake!

385 **Mrs. Van Daan.** Don't, Putti.

386 **Margot.** It doesn't matter now!

387 **Mr. Frank** (*going to* Mr. Van Daan). Didn't you hear what Miep said? The invasion has come! We're going to be liberated! This is a time to celebrate!

388 (*He embraces* Mrs. Frank *and then hurries to the cupboard and gets the cognac and a glass.*)

389 **Mr. Van Daan.** To steal bread from children!

390 **Mrs. Frank.** We've all done things that we're ashamed of.

391 **Anne.** Look at me, the way I've treated Mother . . . so mean and horrid to her.

392 **Mrs. Frank.** No, Anneke, no.

393 (Anne *runs to her mother, putting her arms around her.*)

394 **Anne.** Oh, Mother, I was. I was awful.

395 **Mr. Van Daan.** Not like me. No one is as bad as me!

396 **Dussel** (*to* Mr. Van Daan). Stop it now! Let's be happy!

397 **Mr. Frank** (*giving* Mr. Van Daan *a glass of cognac*). Here! Here! *Schnapps! L'chaim!*[8] (Van Daan *takes the cognac. They all watch him. He gives them a feeble smile.* Anne *puts up her fingers in a V-for-Victory sign. As* Van Daan *gives an answering V-sign, they are startled to hear a loud sob from behind them. It is* Mrs. Frank, *stricken with remorse. She is sitting on the other side of the room.*)

398 **Mrs. Frank** (*through her sobs*). When I think of the terrible things I said . . .

399 (Mr. Frank, Anne, *and* Margot *hurry to her, trying to comfort her.* Mr. Van Daan *brings her his glass of cognac.*)

400 **Mr. Van Daan.** No! No! You were right!

401 **Mrs. Frank.** That I should speak that way to you! . . . Our friends! . . . Our guests! (*She starts to cry again.*)

402 **Dussel.** Stop it, you're spoiling the whole invasion!

403 (*As they are comforting her, the lights dim out. The curtain falls.*)

---

[8] ***Schnapps!*** (shnäps) *German:* Brandy!
L'chaim! (lə khä´yĭm) *Hebrew:* To life!

NOTICE & NOTE

ANALYZE DRAMA

Annotate: In paragraph 404, mark details that show how the mood in the Annex changes immediately after the residents learn about D-Day (the Allied invasion on June 6, 1944) and a month later.

Interpret: What has happened in the month since D-Day? How has this affected people's spirits?

404 **Anne's Voice** (*faintly at first and then with growing strength*). We're all in much better spirits these days. There's still excellent news of the invasion. The best part about it is that I have a feeling that friends are coming. Who knows? Maybe I'll be back in school by fall. Ha, ha! The joke is on us! The warehouse man doesn't know a thing and we are paying him all that money! . . . Wednesday, the second of July, nineteen forty-four. The invasion seems temporarily to be bogged down. Mr. Kraler has to have an operation, which looks bad. The Gestapo have found the radio that was stolen. Mr. Dussel says they'll trace it back and back to the thief, and then, it's just a matter of time till they get to us. Everyone is low. Even poor Pim can't raise their spirits. I have often been downcast myself . . . but never in despair. I can shake off everything if I write. But . . . and that is the great question . . . will I ever be able to write well? I want to so much. I want to go on living even after my death. Another birthday has gone by, so now I am fifteen. Already I know what I want. I have a goal, an opinion.

405 (*As this is being said—the curtain rises on the scene, the lights dim on, and* Anne's Voice *fades out.*)

Scene 4

406 *It is an afternoon a few weeks later . . . Everyone but* Margot *is in the main room. There is a sense of great tension.*

407 *Both* Mrs. Frank *and* Mr. Van Daan *are nervously pacing back and forth,* Dussel *is standing at the window, looking down fixedly at the street below.* Peter *is at the center table, trying to do his lessons.* Anne *sits opposite him, writing in her diary.* Mrs. Van Daan *is seated on the couch, her eyes on* Mr. Frank *as he sits reading.*

408 *The sound of a telephone ringing comes from the office below. They all are rigid, listening tensely.* Mr. Dussel *rushes down to* Mr. Frank.

409 **Dussel.** There it goes again, the telephone! Mr. Frank, do you hear?

410 **Mr. Frank** (*quietly*). Yes. I hear.

411 **Dussel** (*pleading, insistent*). But this is the third time, Mr. Frank! The third time in quick succession! It's a signal! I tell you it's Miep, trying to get us! For some reason she can't come to us and she's trying to warn us of something!

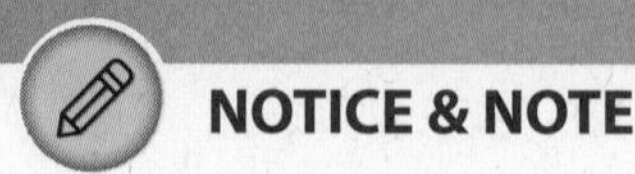

412 **Mr. Frank.** Please. Please.

413 **Mr. Van Daan** (*to* Dussel). You're wasting your breath.

414 **Dussel.** Something has happened, Mr. Frank. For three days now Miep hasn't been to see us! And today not a man has come to work. There hasn't been a sound in the building!

415 **Mrs. Frank.** Perhaps it's Sunday. We may have lost track of the days.

416 **Mr. Van Daan** (*to* Anne). You with the diary there. What day is it?

417 **Dussel** (*going to* Mrs. Frank). I don't lose track of the days! I know exactly what day it is! It's Friday, the fourth of August. Friday, and not a man at work. (*He rushes back to* Mr. Frank, *pleading with him, almost in tears.*) I tell you Mr. Kraler's dead. That's the only explanation. He's dead and they've closed down the building, and Miep's trying to tell us!

418 **Mr. Frank.** She'd never telephone us.

419 **Dussel** (*frantic*). Mr. Frank, answer that! I beg you, answer it!

420 **Mr. Frank.** No.

421 **Mr. Van Daan.** Just pick it up and listen. You don't have to speak. Just listen and see if it's Miep.

422 **Dussel** (*speaking at the same time*). For God's sake . . . I ask you.

423 **Mr. Frank.** No. I've told you, no. I'll do nothing that might let anyone know we're in the building.

424 **Peter.** Mr. Frank's right.

425 **Mr. Van Daan.** There's no need to tell us what side you're on.

426 **Mr. Frank.** If we wait patiently, quietly, I believe that help will come.

427 (*There is silence for a minute as they all listen to the telephone ringing.*)

428 **Dussel.** I'm going down. (*He rushes down the steps.* Mr. Frank *tries ineffectually to hold him.* Dussel *runs to the lower door, unbolting it. The telephone stops ringing.* Dussel *bolts the door and comes slowly back up the steps.*) Too late. (Mr. Frank *goes to* Margot *in* Anne's *bedroom.*)

429 **Mr. Van Daan.** So we just wait here until we die.

430 **Mrs. Van Daan** (*hysterically*). I can't stand it! I'll kill myself! I'll kill myself!

431 **Mr. Van Daan.** For God's sake, stop it!

432 (*In the distance, a German military band is heard playing a Viennese waltz.*)

433 **Mrs. Van Daan.** I think you'd be glad if I did! I think you want me to die!

434 **Mr. Van Daan.** Whose fault is it we're here? (Mrs. Van Daan *starts for her room. He follows, talking at her.*) We could've been safe somewhere . . . in America or Switzerland. But no! No! You wouldn't leave when I wanted to. You couldn't leave your things. You couldn't leave your precious furniture.

435 **Mrs. Van Daan.** Don't touch me!

436 (*She hurries up the stairs, followed by* Mr. Van Daan. Peter, *unable to bear it, goes to his room.* Anne *looks after him, deeply concerned.* Dussel *returns to his post at the window.* Mr. Frank *comes back into the main room and takes a book, trying to read.* Mrs. Frank *sits near the sink, starting to peel some potatoes.* Anne *quietly goes to* Peter*'s room, closing the door after her.* Peter *is lying face down on the cot.* Anne *leans over him, holding him in her arms, trying to bring him out of his despair.*)

437 **Anne.** Look, Peter, the sky. (*She looks up through the skylight.*) What a lovely, lovely day! Aren't the clouds beautiful? You know what I do when it seems as if I couldn't stand being cooped up for one more minute? I *think* myself out. I think myself on a walk in the park where I used to go with Pim. Where the jonquils and the crocus and the violets grow down the slopes. You know the most wonderful part about *thinking* yourself out? You can have it any way you like. You can have roses and violets and chrysanthemums all blooming at the same time . . . It's funny . . . I used to take it all for granted . . . and now I've gone crazy about everything to do with nature. Haven't you?

438 **Peter.** I've just gone crazy. I think if something doesn't happen soon . . . if we don't get out of here . . . I can't stand much more of it!

439 **Anne** (*softly*). I wish you had a religion, Peter.

440 **Peter.** No, thanks! Not me!

441 **Anne.** Oh, I don't mean you have to be Orthodox[9] . . . or believe in heaven and hell and purgatory and things . . . I just mean some religion . . . it doesn't matter what. Just to believe in something! When I think of all that's out there . . . the

[9] **Orthodox:** Orthodox Jews who strictly observe Jewish laws and traditions.

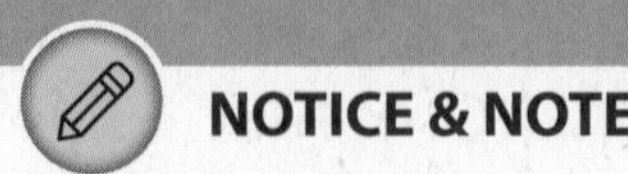

trees . . . and flowers . . . and seagulls . . . when I think of the dearness of you, Peter . . . and the goodness of the people we know . . . Mr. Kraler, Miep, Dirk, the vegetable man, all risking their lives for us every day . . . When I think of these good things, I'm not afraid any more . . . I find myself, and God, and I . . . (Peter *interrupts, getting up and walking away.*)

442 **Peter.** That's fine! But when I begin to think, I get mad! Look at us, hiding out for two years. Not able to move! Caught here like . . . waiting for them to come and get us . . . and all for what?

CONTRASTS AND CONTRADICTIONS

Notice & Note: Mark what Anne says to Peter in paragraph 443. Then look back at the dialogue between Anne and her mother in paragraphs 118–119 of Act Two.

Interpret: What contrast do these lines reveal? What does this contrast reveal about Anne?

443 **Anne.** We're not the only people that've had to suffer. There've always been people that've had to . . . sometimes one race . . . sometimes another . . . and yet . . .

444 **Peter.** That doesn't make me feel any better!

445 **Anne** (*going to him*). I know it's terrible, trying to have any faith . . . when people are doing such horrible . . . But you know what I sometimes think? I think the world may be going through a phase, the way I was with Mother. It'll pass, maybe not for hundreds of years, but some day . . . I still believe, in spite of everything, that people are really good at heart.

446 **Peter.** I want to see something now . . . Not a thousand years from now! (*He goes over, sitting down again on the cot.*)

447 **Anne.** But, Peter, if you'd only look at it as part of a great pattern . . . that we're just a little minute in the life . . . (*She breaks off.*) Listen to us, going at each other like a couple of stupid grownups! Look at the sky now. Isn't it lovely? (*She holds out her hand to him.* Peter *takes it and rises, standing with her at the window looking out, his arms around her.*) Some day, when we're outside again, I'm going to . . .

448 (*She breaks off as she hears the sound of a car, its brakes squealing as it comes to a sudden stop. The people in the other rooms also become aware of the sound. They listen tensely. Another car roars up to a screeching stop.* Anne *and* Peter *come from* Peter's *room.* Mr. *and* Mrs. Van Daan *creep down the stairs.* Dussel *comes out from his room. Everyone is listening, hardly breathing. A doorbell clangs again and again in the building below.* Mr. Frank *starts quietly down the steps to the door.* Dussel *and* Peter *follow him. The others stand rigid, waiting, terrified.*

449 *In a few seconds* Dussel *comes stumbling back up the steps. He shakes off* Peter's *help and goes to his room.* Mr. Frank *bolts the door below, and comes slowly back up the steps. Their eyes are all*

NOTICE & NOTE

on him as he stands there for a minute. They realize that what they feared has happened. Mrs. Van Daan *starts to whimper.* Mr. Van Daan *puts her gently in a chair, and then hurries off up the stairs to their room to collect their things.* Peter *goes to comfort his mother. There is a sound of violent pounding on a door below.*)

450 **Mr. Frank** (*quietly*). For the past two years we have lived in fear. Now we can live in hope.

451 (*The pounding below becomes more insistent. There are muffled sounds of voices, shouting commands.*)

452 **Men's Voices.** *Auf machen! Da drinnen! Auf machen! Schnell! Schnell! Schnell! etc., etc.*[10]

453 (*The street door below is forced open. We hear the heavy tread of footsteps coming up.* Mr. Frank *gets two school bags from the shelves, and gives one to* Anne *and the other to* Margot. *He goes to get a bag for* Mrs. Frank. *The sound of feet coming up grows louder.* Peter *comes to* Anne, *kissing her good-bye, then he goes to his room to collect his things. The buzzer of their door starts to ring.* Mr. Frank *brings* Mrs. Frank *a bag. They stand together, waiting. We hear the thud of gun butts on the door, trying to break it down.*

454 Anne *stands, holding her school satchel, looking over at her father and mother with a soft, reassuring smile. She is no longer a child, but a woman with courage to meet whatever lies ahead.*

455 *The lights dim out. The curtain falls on the scene. We hear a mighty crash as the door is shattered. After a second* Anne's Voice *is heard.*)

456 **Anne's Voice.** And so it seems our stay here is over. They are waiting for us now. They've allowed us five minutes to get our things. We can each take a bag and whatever it will hold of clothing. Nothing else. So, dear Diary, that means I must leave you behind. Good-bye for a while. P.S. Please, please, Miep, or Mr. Kraler, or anyone else. If you should find this diary, will you please keep it safe for me, because some day I hope . . .

457 (*Her voice stops abruptly. There is silence. After a second the curtain rises.*)

WORDS OF THE WISER

Notice & Note: Mark what Mr. Frank tells the group after they hear pounding on the door downstairs.

Interpret: What does Mr. Frank mean?

[10] ***Auf machen! . . . Schnell!*** (ouf´ mäKH´ən! dä drĭn´ən! ouf´ mäKH´ən! shnĕl! shnĕl! shnĕl!) *German:* Open up! Inside there! Open up! Quick! Quick! Quick!

Scene 5

ANALYZE PLOT DEVELOPMENT

Annotate: Mark details in the stage directions at the opening of Scene 5 that reveal the time and place of that scene.

Interpret: How does the setting of Scene 5 complete the structure of the play?

458 *It is again the afternoon in November, 1945. The rooms are as we saw them in the first scene.* Mr. Kraler *has joined* Miep *and* Mr. Frank. *There are coffee cups on the table. We see a great change in* Mr. Frank. *He is calm now. His bitterness is gone. He slowly turns a few pages of the diary. They are blank.*

459 **Mr. Frank.** No more. (*He closes the diary and puts it down on the couch beside him.*)

460 **Miep.** I'd gone to the country to find food. When I got back the block was surrounded by police . . .

461 **Mr. Kraler.** We made it our business to learn how they knew. It was the thief . . . the thief who told them.

462 (Miep *goes up to the gas burner, bringing back a pot of coffee.*)

463 **Mr. Frank** (*after a pause*). It seems strange to say this, that anyone could be happy in a concentration camp. But Anne was happy in the camp in Holland where they first took us. After two years of being shut up in these rooms, she could be out . . . out in the sunshine and the fresh air that she loved.

464 **Miep** (*offering the coffee to* Mr. Frank). A little more?

465 **Mr. Frank** (*holding out his cup to her*). The news of the war was good. The British and Americans were sweeping through France. We felt sure that they would get to us in time. In September we were told that we were to be shipped to Poland . . . The men to one camp. The women to another. I was sent to Auschwitz. They went to Belsen. In January we were freed, the few of us who were left. The war wasn't yet over, so it took us a long time to get home. We'd be sent here and there behind the lines where we'd be safe. Each time our train would stop . . . at a siding, or a crossing . . . we'd all get out and go from group to group . . . Where were you? Were you at Belsen? At Buchenwald? At Mauthausen? Is it possible that you knew my wife? Did you ever see my husband? My son? My daughter? That's how I found out about my wife's death . . . of Margot, the Van Daans . . . Dussel. But Anne . . . I still hoped . . . Yesterday I went to Rotterdam. I'd heard of a woman there . . . She'd been in Belsen with Anne . . . I know now.

466 (*He picks up the diary again, and turns the pages back to find a certain passage. As he finds it we hear* Anne's Voice.)

467 **Anne's Voice.** In spite of everything, I still believe that people are really good at heart.

468 (Mr. Frank *slowly closes the diary.*)

469 **Mr. Frank.** She puts me to shame. (*They are silent.*)

470 *The Curtain Falls.*

NOTICE & NOTE 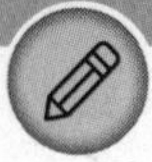

ANALYZE PLOT DEVELOPMENT

Annotate: Mark the lines that cause Mr. Frank to say that Anne "puts [him] to shame."

Analyze: What does Mr. Frank mean? Why might the playwrights have chosen to end the play with this line?

CHECK YOUR UNDERSTANDING

Answer these questions before moving on to the **Analyze the Text** section on the following page.

1 Which of the following scenes take place after WWII has ended?

A Act One, Scenes 1 and 2

B Act One, Scenes 2–5 and Act Two, Scenes 1–4

C Act One, Scenes 1–5

D Act One, Scene 1 and Act Two, Scene 5

2 Reread paragraph 86 of Act Two.

> **Margot** (*with sudden foreboding*). What's happened? Something's happened! Hasn't it, Mr. Kraler?

The playwrights include these lines to suggest that —

F Margot doesn't trust Mr. Kraler any longer

G Margot is afraid that Mr. Kraler has informed on them

H Margot fears that a thief has broken into the office

J Margot senses that Mr. Kraler has bad news

3 In Act Two, what results in a temporary easing of the tensions in the Annex?

A Mr. Kraler's release from his hospitalization

B News that the Allies have landed in Normandy

C The sharing of Miep's cake on New Year's Day

D The Franks' promise that they will take care of Peter

ANALYZE THE TEXT

Support your responses with evidence from the text. NOTEBOOK

1. **Analyze** Briefly summarize Act One and then Act Two, identifying the main focus of each. How do the two acts work together to develop the action in this drama?
2. **Predict** In Scene 5, Mr. Kraler reveals who told the police about the Franks' hiding place. Did this outcome confirm or contradict a prediction you had made? Explain.
3. **Cause/Effect** Examine the dialogue in paragraphs 281–307 that describes the aftermath of Mr. Van Daan's theft. Explain the effect of this event and how it propels the action of the story.
4. **Evaluate** How do the playwrights use a flashback to tell the story of life in the Annex? Does the use of a nonlinear plot add to or detract from the impact of this play? Note how the play would be different if it had a linear plot as you explain your opinion.
5. **Notice & Note** How do Anne's wise words in paragraph 437 relate to what her father told her in Act One, Scene 2? Why might the playwrights have had Anne speak these words to Peter in Act Two?

RESEARCH TIP

You will be able to find many World War II timelines online. However, each may have a different focus, and much of the information may not be relevant. To find events that focus on the Nazi regime and its effects on Jews in Europe, you might try search terms such as "Nazi rise to power timeline," "the rise of the Nazi party," or "Holocaust timeline."

RESEARCH

Most of the events in *The Diary of Anne Frank* focus on a two-year period toward the end of the Second World War. World War II began in 1939, but the Nazis' rise to power had begun 20 years earlier. Using several sources, research key events in the rise of the Nazi regime and the effects those events had on Jewish people. Present your findings in a timeline. Each date or year entry should include a detailed caption to make its significance clear. As you research, record your notes in this chart, continuing on a separate sheet of paper as necessary.

DATE	EVENT

Extend With a partner or group, create a parallel timeline of key events in Anne Frank's life. Then discuss how the events taking place in Europe impacted her and her family.

CREATE AND DRAMATIZE

Make a Poster Setting influences character development in literature just as people's surroundings affect their values, beliefs, and actions in real life. Create a poster to convey how the characters in the drama were affected by their time in the Secret Annex during World War II.

- ❑ As a group, choose three Annex residents to depict.
- ❑ Analyze how the conditions in the Annex affected each character. Explain each character's motivations, actions, and reactions in relation to others and to the historical context. Cite details from the text to support your analysis.
- ❑ Create a poster to show the effects of setting on each character, and how these effects change or remain the same over time. As a group, present your poster to the class.

Dramatize a Relationship Act out (or do a dramatic reading of) two sections of the drama to demonstrate how a relationship between two characters changes over time.

- ❑ As a group, discuss how the subplot of Anne's relationship with Peter develops throughout the play. How does each character's personality affect the way the relationship develops?
- ❑ Choose two short sections of the play that show how Anne and Peter's relationship changes over time. Rehearse the lines. Then act them out for the class.

RESPOND TO THE ESSENTIAL QUESTION

What can we learn from Anne Frank?

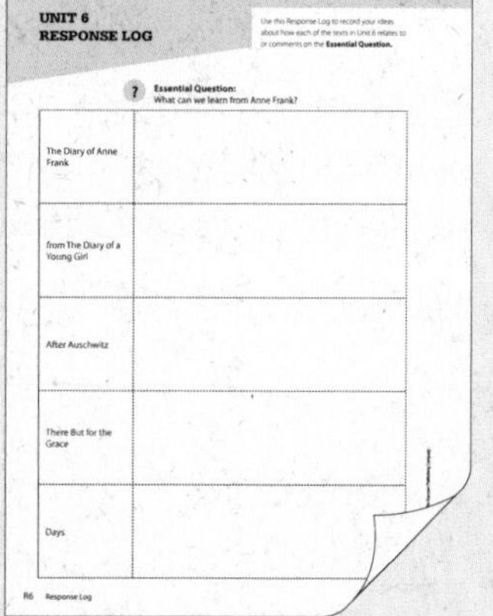

Gather Information Review your annotations and notes on *The Diary of Anne Frank*. Then, add relevant details to your Response Log. As you determine which information to include, think about:

- the types of conflicts Anne had with others
- the ways in which her relationships changed over time
- the wisdom Anne gained through her interactions and experiences

At the end of the unit, you may use your notes to help you write a personal narrative.

ACADEMIC VOCABULARY

As you write and discuss what you learned from the drama, be sure to use the Academic Vocabulary words. Check off each of the words that you use.

- ❑ **communicate**
- ❑ **draft**
- ❑ **liberation**
- ❑ **philosophy**
- ❑ **publish**

RESPOND

WORD BANK
conspicuous
loathe
indignantly
ostentatiously
appalled
inarticulate

CRITICAL VOCABULARY

Practice and Apply Complete each sentence in a way that shows the meaning of the Critical Vocabulary word.

1. If you wanted to be **conspicuous** in a crowd, you might . . .
2. My friends **loathe** that TV show because . . .
3. The player spoke **indignantly** to the coach when . . .
4. The pop star dressed **ostentatiously** because . . .
5. The hostess of the party was **appalled** when . . .
6. The politician suddenly became **inarticulate** because . . .

VOCABULARY STRATEGY: Use Prefixes

Go to **Common Roots, Prefixes, and Suffixes** in the **Vocabulary Studio** for more on using prefixes.

A **prefix** is a word part that has been added to the beginning of a base word to form a new word. You can sometimes use prefixes to figure out the meanings of unfamiliar words. Imagine, for example, that aren't sure what *inarticulate* means but you know that someone who is articulate speaks clearly and you know that the prefix *in-* means "not." Then you can figure out that someone who is inarticulate does not speak clearly. Here are some common prefixes and their meanings:

PREFIX	MEANING
dis-, in-, im-, non-, un-	not
pre-	before
re-	back or again

Practice and Apply Choose a prefix to add to each of these base words. (In each case, more than one prefix is possible.) Then, use each new word in an original sentence.

1. view

2. arrange

3. committed

4. pulse

LANGUAGE CONVENTIONS: Correct Capitalization

You already know a lot about correct capitalization. For example, you know that the first word in a sentence is always capitalized. You also know that certain proper nouns, such as a person's name and the city in which you live, are always capitalized. But there are other types of words—many having to do with government and culture—that also need to be capitalized. The chart lists types of words to capitalize, along with examples.

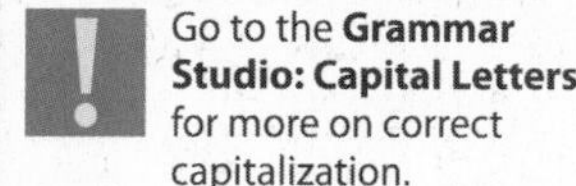

Go to the **Grammar Studio: Capital Letters** for more on correct capitalization.

TYPES OF WORDS TO CAPITALIZE	EXAMPLES
Languages	English, Spanish, German, Japanese
Countries and continents	Holland (the Netherlands), Mexico; Europe, North America
Nationalities and regional affiliations	American, Dutch, Chinese; European, Asian
Ethnicities	Hispanic, Native American, Jewish, Asian
Political parties	Democrats, Republicans, Nazis, Socialists
Religions	Judaism, Islam, Christianity, Buddhism
Religious words (texts, symbols, and words referring to a deity)	Bible, Koran; Menorah, Star of David; Thou, God, Ruler

Practice and Apply Rewrite the following sentences, correcting any errors in capitalization. A sentence may contain more than one error.

1. Not all germans wanted the nazis to be in control.
2. For many europeans, it was dangerous to practice judaism.
3. Because they were jewish, the Franks fled to holland to escape persecution.
4. Anne Frank's diary was translated into many languages, including english.
5. The first Country that Hitler's army invaded was Poland.

When you have finished, share your sentences with a partner and compare your use of capitalization.

ANALYZE & APPLY

from THE DIARY OF A YOUNG GIRL

Diary by **Anne Frank**

? ESSENTIAL QUESTION:

What can we learn from Anne Frank?

QUICK START

Asking questions before you read a selection can help you realize what you'd like to learn from it and what you think you already know. What questions do you have about Anne's diary? Jot them down.

ANALYZE A PRIMARY SOURCE

A source is anything that supplies information. **Secondary sources,** such as encyclopedia articles, are those produced by people who have learned about an event through research. **Primary sources** are those created by people who witnessed or took part in the event. Diaries are primary sources.

A **diary** is a record of its author's thoughts and feelings during a particular time. They often contain headings and salutations, as shown below. As you read Anne Frank's diary, notice what you learn about life during World War II.

MONDAY EVENING, NOVEMBER 8, 1943

Dearest Kitty,

If you were to read all my letters in one sitting, you'd be struck by the fact that they were written in a variety of moods.

The **heading** contains the date on which the entry was made.

The **salutation** reveals to whom the entry has been addressed.

GENRE ELEMENTS: DIARY

- is a type of autobiographical writing
- uses first-person point of view
- includes a daily record of a writer's thoughts, experiences, and feelings
- uses date headings—text features that help to structure and organize the writing

MAKE INFERENCES

Since Anne does not explain everything she writes about, readers must fill in gaps in their understanding by making **inferences,** or logical guesses, from clues in the text and their prior knowledge. For example, in this passage, readers must infer why the doorbell frightens Anne:

> **This evening, when Bep was still here, the doorbell rang long and loud. I instantly turned white, my stomach churned, and my heart beat wildly—and all because I was afraid.**

What the text says:	+	What I know:	=	Inference:
The doorbell rang.	+	The Franks are hiding from the Nazis.	=	Anne is afraid they have been discovered.

As you read and analyze *The Diary of a Young Girl,* use clues in the text and your knowledge of the Franks' situation as well as what it's like to be a teenager to make inferences about events and experiences that Anne does not fully explain.

CRITICAL VOCABULARY

implore **splendid** **conjecture**

To see how many Critical Vocabulary words you already know, use them to complete the sentences.

1. The event was __________, thanks to everyone's hard work and preparation.
2. Once the results became clear, we learned that his __________ was correct.
3. I __________ you to stay longer because I will struggle without your help.

LANGUAGE CONVENTIONS

Parentheses In this lesson, you will learn how to use parentheses to enclose less important details or comments without interrupting the flow of a sentence, as in the example below.

My bike had a flat tire (second time this month), so I walked to school.

As you read *The Diary of a Young Girl*, note Anne Frank's use of parentheses.

ANNOTATION MODEL

NOTICE & NOTE

As you read, notice primary source elements that help you learn about Anne Frank. In the model, you can see one reader's notes about *The Diary of a Young Girl*.

MONDAY EVENING, NOVEMBER 8, 1943

Dearest Kitty,

1 If you were to read all my letters in one sitting, you'd be struck by the fact that they were written in a variety of moods. It annoys me to be so dependent on the moods here in the Annex, but I'm not the only one: we're all subject to them.

Anne addresses her diary as "Kitty" and uses the pronoun "you" to suggest how Kitty would respond.

Anne understands that everyone is struggling to cope with life in the Annex.

BACKGROUND

Anne Frank *(1929–1945) was 13 years old when she and her family went into hiding to avoid being sent to concentration camps by the Nazis. During the two years she spent living in an attic, she kept a diary. After the war, Anne's father, the only family member to survive the concentration camps to which the family was eventually sent, chose to publish the diary. The selection you are about to read consists of entries taken from throughout the work.*

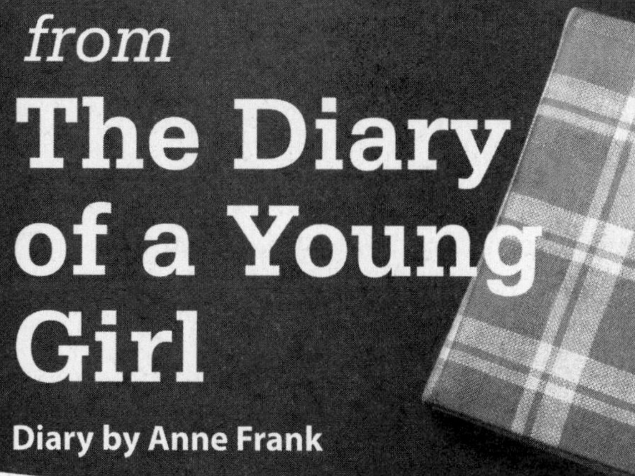

from The Diary of a Young Girl

Diary by Anne Frank

SETTING A PURPOSE

As you read, think about which of Anne's thoughts and feelings are similar to those of any teenager and which are unique to her family's particularly dire, or urgent, situation.

Notice & Note

Use the side margins to notice and note signposts in the text.

MONDAY EVENING, NOVEMBER 8, 1943

Dearest Kitty,

1 If you were to read all my letters in one sitting, you'd be struck by the fact that they were written in a variety of moods. It annoys me to be so dependent on the moods here in the Annex, but I'm not the only one: we're all subject to them. If I'm engrossed in a book, I have to rearrange my thoughts before I can mingle with other people, because otherwise they might think I was strange. As you can see, I'm currently in the middle of a depression. I couldn't really tell you what set it off, but I think it stems from my cowardice, which confronts me at every turn. This evening, when Bep was still here, the doorbell rang long and loud. I instantly turned white, my stomach churned, and my heart beat wildly—and all because I was afraid.

NOTICE & NOTE

2 At night in bed I see myself alone in a dungeon, without Father and Mother. Or I'm roaming the streets, or the Annex is on fire, or they come in the middle of the night to take us away and I crawl under my bed in desperation. I see everything as if it were actually taking place. And to think it might all happen soon!

3 Miep often says she envies us because we have such peace and quiet here. That may be true, but she's obviously not thinking about our fear.

MAKE INFERENCES

Annotate: In paragraph 4, mark what Anne compares to "a castle in the air."

Infer: What reasons might Anne have for making this comparison?

4 I simply can't imagine the world will ever be normal again for us. I do talk about "after the war," but it's as if I were talking about a castle in the air, something that can never come true.

5 I see the eight of us in the Annex as if we were a patch of blue sky surrounded by menacing black clouds. The perfectly round spot on which we're standing is still safe, but the clouds are moving in on us, and the ring between us and the approaching danger is being pulled tighter and tighter. We're surrounded by darkness and danger, and in our desperate search for a way out we keep bumping into each other. We look at the fighting down below and the peace and beauty up above. In the meantime, we've been cut off by the dark mass of clouds, so that we can go neither up nor down. It looms before us like an impenetrable wall, trying to crush us, but not yet able to. I can only cry out and **implore**, "Oh, ring, ring, open wide and let us out!"

implore
(ĭm-plôr´) *v.* To *implore* is to beg for something urgently.

Yours, Anne

THURSDAY, NOVEMBER 11, 1943

Dearest Kitty,

6 I have a good title for this chapter:

Ode to My Fountain Pen
In Memoriam

7 My fountain pen was always one of my most prized possessions; I valued it highly, especially because it had a thick nib, and I can only write neatly with thick nibs. It has led a long and interesting fountain-pen life, which I will summarize below.

LANGUAGE CONVENTIONS

Annotate: Parentheses can be used to enclose information that is helpful but not essential to the meaning of a sentence. In paragraph 8, mark the text in parentheses.

Analyze: Explain how the details in parentheses relate to the rest of the sentence.

8 When I was nine, my fountain pen (packed in cotton) arrived as a "sample of no commercial value" all the way from Aachen,[1] where my grandmother (the kindly donor) used to live. I lay in bed with the flu, while the February winds howled

[1] **Aachen** (ä´kən): a city in Germany.

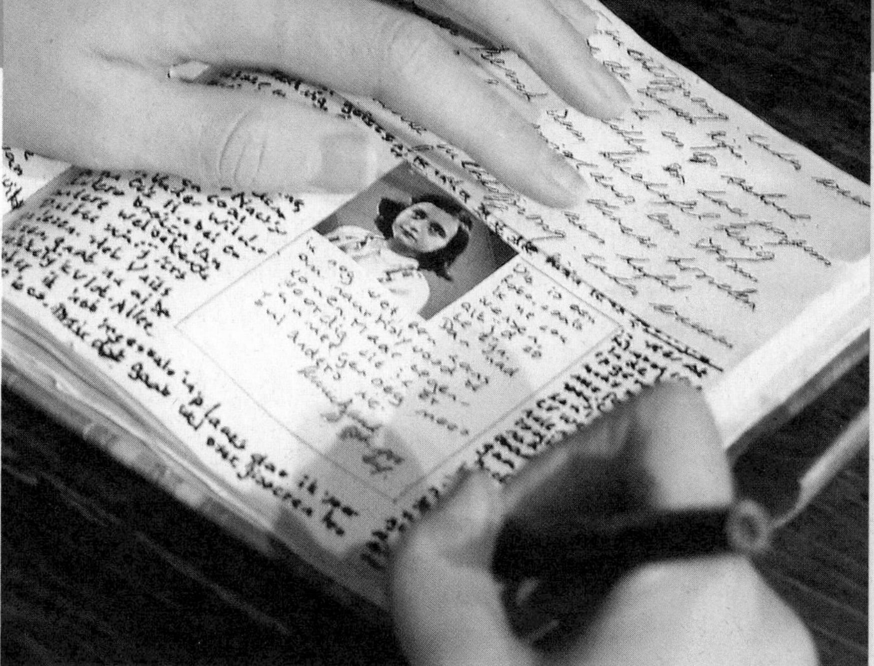

NOTICE & NOTE

around the apartment house. This **splendid** fountain pen came in a red leather case, and I showed it to my girlfriends the first chance I got. Me, Anne Frank, the proud owner of a fountain pen.

splendid
(splĕn´dĭd) *adj.* If something is *splendid*, it is magnificent or very good.

9 When I was ten, I was allowed to take the pen to school, and to my surprise, the teacher even let me write with it. When I was eleven, however, my treasure had to be tucked away again, because my sixth-grade teacher allowed us to use only school pens and inkpots. When I was twelve, I started at the Jewish Lyceum and my fountain pen was given a new case in honor of the occasion. Not only did it have room for a pencil, it also had a zipper, which was much more impressive. When I was thirteen, the fountain pen went with me to the Annex, and together we've raced through countless diaries and compositions. I'd turned fourteen and my fountain pen was enjoying the last year of its life with me when . . .

10 It was just after five on Friday afternoon. I came out of my room and was about to sit down at the table to write when I was roughly pushed to one side to make room for Margot and Father, who wanted to practice their Latin. The fountain pen remained unused on the table, while its owner, sighing, was forced to make do with a very tiny corner of the table, where she began rubbing beans. That's how we remove mold from the beans and restore them to their original state. At a quarter to six I swept the floor, dumped the dirt into a newspaper, along with the rotten beans, and tossed it into the stove. A giant flame shot up, and I thought it was wonderful that the stove, which had been gasping its last breath, had made such a miraculous recovery.

MAKE INFERENCES

Annotate: Mark details in paragraph 10 that describe Anne's actions.

Infer: What can you infer about Anne's relationship with her family based on these details?

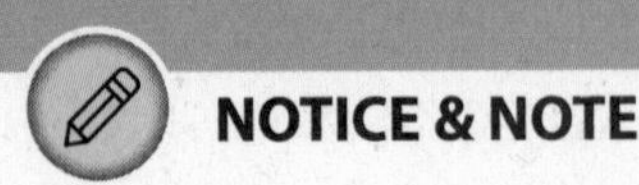

NOTICE & NOTE

11 All was quiet again. The Latin students had left, and I sat down at the table to pick up where I'd left off. But no matter where I looked, my fountain pen was nowhere in sight. I took another look. Margot looked, Mother looked, Father looked, Dussel looked. But it had vanished.

12 "Maybe it fell into the stove, along with the beans!" Margot suggested.

13 "No, it couldn't have!" I replied.

14 But that evening, when my fountain pen still hadn't turned up, we all assumed it had been burned, especially because celluloid is highly inflammable. Our darkest fears were confirmed the next day when Father went to empty the stove and discovered the clip, used to fasten it to a pocket, among the ashes. Not a trace of the gold nib was left. "It must have melted into stone," Father **conjectured.**

conjecture
(kən-jĕk´chər) *v.* If you *conjecture*, you guess or suppose.

15 I'm left with one consolation, small though it may be: my fountain pen was cremated,[2] just as I would like to be someday!

SATURDAY, JANUARY 15, 1944

My dearest Kitty,

16 There's no reason for me to go on describing all our quarrels and arguments down to the last detail. It's enough to tell you that we've divided many things like meat and fats and oils and are frying our own potatoes. Recently we've been eating a little extra rye bread because by four o'clock we're so hungry for dinner we can barely control our rumbling stomachs.

17 Mother's birthday is rapidly approaching. She received some extra sugar from Mr. Kugler, which sparked off jealousy on the part of the van Daans, because Mrs. van D. didn't receive any on her birthday. But what's the point of boring you with harsh words, spiteful conversations and tears when you know they bore us even more?

ANALYZE A PRIMARY SOURCE

Annotate: Mark names and third-person pronouns in paragraphs 17–19.

Draw Conclusions: Although diaries are written from the first-person point of view, clues in the text may provide insight into the character traits and feelings of others. What conclusions can you draw about the people Anne mentions based on the details she includes?

18 Mother has expressed a wish, which isn't likely to come true any time soon: not to have to see Mr. van Daan's face for two whole weeks. I wonder if everyone who shares a house sooner or later ends up at odds with their fellow residents. Or have we just had a stroke of bad luck? At mealtime, when Dussel helps himself to a quarter of the half-filled gravy boat and leaves the rest of us to do without, I lose my appetite and feel like jumping to my feet, knocking him off his chair and throwing him out the door.

[2] **cremated** (krē´māt´əd): burned to ashes.

19 Are most people so stingy and selfish? I've gained some insight into human nature since I came here, which is good, but I've had enough for the present. Peter says the same.

20 The war is going to go on despite our quarrels and our longing for freedom and fresh air, so we should try to make the best of our stay here.

21 I'm preaching, but I also believe that if I live here much longer, I'll turn into a dried-up old beanstalk. And all I really want is to be an honest-to-goodness teenager!

Yours, Anne

NOTICE & NOTE

ANALYZE A PRIMARY SOURCE

Annotate: Mark words and phrases that suggest Anne's feelings and outlook on life in paragraphs 20–21.

Analyze: In what ways does Anne's outlook relate to her current situation? Which emotions are shared by many teenagers?

CHECK YOUR UNDERSTANDING

Answer these questions before moving on to the **Analyze the Text** section on the following page.

1 Which word from paragraph 1 helps the reader understand the meaning of cowardice?

A *depression*

B *confront*

C *churned*

D *afraid*

2 The story of Anne's fountain pen allows her to recall —

F events that led her to stop writing

G pleasant memories from her past

H her fondness for her sister

J her fear of the future

3 In paragraphs 16–17, Anne explains that she will not describe many details about the arguments among her family members and the van Daans because —

A she wants to avoid dwelling on the conflicts

B she disagrees with the way her parents interpret events

C the information was included in earlier entries

D writing about the quarrels will make her hungry

RESPOND

ANALYZE THE TEXT

Support your responses with evidence from the text. NOTEBOOK

1. **Infer** What is Anne Frank's view of the tension among all eight people living in the Annex? Cite evidence to support your response.
2. **Interpret** A **simile** makes a comparison between two unlike things using the word *like* or *as*. Reread paragraph 5. What does Anne reveal about her perspective with her use of the simile "I see the eight of us in the Annex as if we were a patch of blue sky surrounded by menacing black clouds"?
3. **Draw Conclusions** Review the introduction to the entry for Thursday, November 11, 1943. Notice that the elements of this entry differ from the others. Why might Anne have used a slightly different form here?
4. **Compare** How does Anne's emotional state in paragraphs 1–2 compare with her feelings in paragraphs 18–21? Does your comparison support Anne's statement that her reader would be "struck by the fact" that her entries are "written in a variety of moods"? Explain.
5. **Draw Conclusions** Over what span of time are the entries in this excerpt from the diary written? What does Anne reveal has been happening during this period?

RESEARCH TIP
Online encyclopedias provide reliable information about prominent historical figures and works of literature. When researching a particular work, official websites of authors, publishers, museums, or historical organizations may provide helpful information.

RESEARCH

Using at least two sources, research how Anne Frank's diary was found and became published. Record what you learn in the chart.

QUESTION	ANSWER
How did Otto Frank receive his daughter's diary?	
How was the published format of the diary decided?	
What was the response to the published book?	

Connect Consider what you have learned about how the published format of *The Diary of a Young Girl* was chosen. In a small group, discuss ways in which different decisions in creating the published form of the diary may have affected responses to the book.

CREATE AND DISCUSS

Create a Comic Create an illustrated comic retelling of the fountain pen story that Anne shares in *The Diary of a Young Girl.*

- ❑ Review Anne's November 11, 1943, entry for details of the fountain pen story. Decide which elements you will include in your comic.
- ❑ Plan what words and images each panel will show, and create a layout of the number and size of your panels.
- ❑ Sketch your comic. Then create a final version by adding elements such as ink, color, captions, and word balloons.

Discuss with a Partner How do Anne's ideas and reactions compare with yours and those of your friends? Discuss this question with a partner.

- ❑ Review The *Diary of a Young Girl* to identify ideas and reactions with which you agree or disagree. Connect each idea or reaction with a particular value or trait to which you can relate.
- ❑ Discuss your ideas with a partner. Share any questions you generated in your discussion with the rest of the class.

Go to the **Speaking and Listening Studio: Participating in Collaborative Discussions** for help with having a discussion.

RESPOND TO THE ESSENTIAL QUESTION

? What can we learn from Anne Frank?

Gather Information Review your annotations and notes on *The Diary of a Young Girl.* Then, add relevant details to your Response Log. As you determine which details to include, think about:

- what you learn about Anne and what life was like in the Annex
- reasons Anne includes certain details and descriptions
- ways in which Anne is similar to other teenagers

At the end of the unit, you can use your notes to help you write a personal narrative.

ACADEMIC VOCABULARY

As you write and discuss what you learned from the diary, be sure to use the Academic Vocabulary words. Check off each of the words that you use.

- ❑ **communicate**
- ❑ **draft**
- ❑ **liberation**
- ❑ **philosophy**
- ❑ **publish**

WORD BANK
implore
splendid
conjecture

CRITICAL VOCABULARY

Practice and Apply To demonstrate that you understand the Critical Vocabulary words, choose an appropriate response to each question below and explain why you chose it.

1. Which of the following would you describe as conjecturing? Why?
   explaining a problem — guessing an answer
2. Which of the following would you describe as imploring? Why?
   correcting a mistake — begging for help
3. Which of the following would you describe as splendid? Why?
   a lovely view — a draft of a story

VOCABULARY STRATEGY: Connotation and Denotation

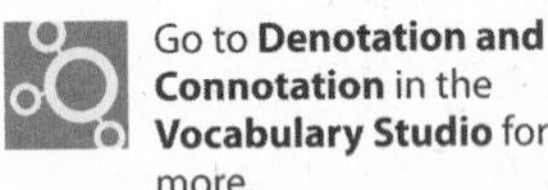

Go to **Denotation and Connotation** in the **Vocabulary Studio** for more.

Many words have both a denotation and a connotation. A word's **denotation** is its dictionary definition. A word's **connotations** are the ideas and feelings associated with the word. You can use your knowledge of a word's connotation as a context clue to help you determine the meaning of other words. Study this example from *The Diary of a Young Girl.*

> **Are most people so stingy and selfish?**

While the denotation of *stingy* is "giving or spending reluctantly," the negative connotation of *selfish* can help you realize that stingy also has a negative connotation. *Stingy* suggests unkindness, in contrast to its synonyms *sparing* or *frugal*, which have more positive connotations and suggest carefulness and a desire to avoid waste.

Practice and Apply Tell how the meaning of each sentence would change if the underlined word were replaced by the word in parentheses.

1. Anne dreams of being in a <u>prison</u> without her parents. (dungeon)
2. The view from a certain window in the Annex was <u>splendid</u>. (fine)
3. Anne was bothered by the <u>conflicts</u> between the families. (battles)

LANGUAGE CONVENTIONS: Parentheses

Parentheses are punctuation marks that are used to set off useful but less-important information that does not fit neatly into the sentence. The chart shows some reasons writers use parentheses.

REASON	EXAMPLE
to enclose information that is related but not of primary importance	The play (we all loved it) runs about ninety minutes.
to add directions or other information that explains or clarifies something	Lizzi's (the bakery) is giving out free samples today.
to repeat numbers or figures to ensure accuracy	The fee for the service is thirty dollars ($30).

Use parentheses so that information that you want to include but that is not of great importance doesn't interrupt the flow of a sentence.

Practice and Apply For each sentence, put parentheses around the word or words that should be enclosed by them.

1. Antonio introduced us to Deshawn I think his last name is Jackson at the party last weekend.

2. Paris often called the City of Lights is one of the world's most popular tourist destinations.

3. The banquet will be held at Nicholson Hall on Harris Street on Tuesday evening.

4. Our team won by 6 points 48–42.

ANALYZE & APPLY

AFTER AUSCHWITZ

Speech by **Elie Wiesel**

? ESSENTIAL QUESTION:

What can we learn from Anne Frank?

QUICK START

The speech you are about to read was given at a ceremony to mark the 50th anniversary of the liberation of Auschwitz, a Nazi concentration camp. With the class, discuss why people take the time to hold such ceremonies. Why might it be important to remember horrible crimes committed in the past?

ANALYZE APPEALS

In "After Auschwitz," Elie Wiesel's goal is to persuade, or convince, his audience to adopt a particular viewpoint and support his claim. To do so, he appeals to his audience's feelings and values. Appeals are one kind of rhetorical device used to make an argument more persuasive.

- An **emotional appeal** is a message that creates strong feelings in order to make an impact. These appeals can tap into people's feelings such as fear, pity, or vanity. In the passage from his speech provided on the chart, Elie Wiesel appeals to feelings of sympathy and compassion for others.
- In an **ethical appeal**, a speaker or writer links a claim to a widely accepted value in order to gain moral support for the claim and to establish a bond with the audience as someone who shares their values. In his speech, Wiesel appeals to the established belief that human beings should neither murder one another nor be indifferent to suffering.

View the chart below for examples of each kind of appeal. As you read the speech, notice other places Wiesel appeals to his audience's emotions and their ethics.

GENRE ELEMENTS: SPEECH

- is a talk or public address presented to an audience
- may have one or more purposes, such as to entertain, to explain, or to persuade
- is often delivered on a special occasion
- may be recorded or transcribed for later reading and analysis

TYPE OF APPEAL	EXAMPLES FROM THE SPEECH
Emotional appeal	Close your eyes and listen. Listen to the silent screams of terrified mothers, the prayers of anguished old men and women. Listen to the tears of children, Jewish children . . .
Ethical appeal	And it worked. The killers killed, the victims died and the world was the world and everything else was going on, life as usual.

GET READY

ANALYZE RHETORICAL DEVICES

Appeals to emotion and ethics are just two of many **rhetorical devices,** or techniques writers use to enhance their arguments and communications. Here are two other rhetorical devices that writers often use to enhance the effectiveness of speeches in particular.

- **Repetition** is a rhetorical device in which a sound, word, phrase, clause, or line is repeated for emphasis or to give a text or speech a sense of unity. Repetition also helps reinforce meaning and can create an appealing rhythm, as in this example.

  After Auschwitz, the human condition is no longer the same. After Auschwitz, nothing will ever be the same.

- **Parallelism** is the use of words, phrases, clauses, or lines that have a similar structure or grammatical form. Like repetition, parallelism can emphasize meaning and also produce an engaging rhythm.

  In this place of darkness and malediction we can but stand in awe and remember its stateless, faceless and nameless victims.

As you read and analyze the speech, pay attention to the rhetorical devices Elie Wiesel uses.

ANNOTATION MODEL

NOTICE & NOTE

As you read, note examples of the speaker's appeals to both emotions and ethics, and examine other rhetorical devices. This model shows one reader's notes about the beginning of "After Auschwitz."

1 *"After Auschwitz, the human condition is not the same, nothing will be the same."*

2 Here heaven and earth are on fire.

3 I speak to you as a man, who 50 years and nine days ago had no name, no hope, no future and was known only by his number, A7713.

"human condition" suggests ethical concerns

parallel phrases with "no" create a rhythm that produces a tone of hopelessness

Elie Wiesel *(1928–2016) was born in Romania. After the Germans invaded his town, he and his family were sent to Auschwitz, a concentration camp. Only Wiesel and two of his sisters survived. Wiesel wrote about his experiences in the book* Night, *which has sold millions of copies in many different languages. After its publication, Wiesel devoted himself to ensuring that the deaths of millions of Jews would never be forgotten, and that other human beings would never be subjected to such crimes. In 1986, Wiesel was awarded the Nobel Peace Prize for his life's work.*

AFTER AUSCHWITZ

Speech by Elie Wiesel

BACKGROUND

The Auschwitz concentration camp complex opened in 1940 in southern Poland. Concentration camps were used to incarcerate Jews and other supposed enemies of the state. Auschwitz played a major role in the Nazi plan to exterminate all the Jews in Europe. Inside, Nazis forced prisoners into hard labor. Anyone unable to work was executed upon arrival. Between 1940 and 1945, more than one million Jews and others including Poles, Roma, and Soviet prisioners of war were sent to Auschwitz. Few survived. Auschwitz was finally abandoned by German soldiers as the Soviet army advanced upon it in 1945.

SETTING A PURPOSE

The horrible crimes committed in Nazi concentration camps occurred long ago. As you read, think about why the author continues to reflect on these events. Why does he believe people need to be reminded of them? Write down any questions you have.

Notice & Note

Use the side margins to notice and note signposts in the text.

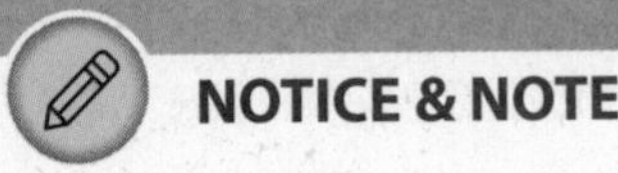

NOTICE & NOTE

EXTREME OR ABSOLUTE LANGUAGE

Notice & Note: In paragraphs 1–3, mark words and phrases that suggest certainty or completeness.

Infer: What can you infer from these statements about Wiesel's perspective on Auschwitz?

ANALYZE APPEALS

Annotate: Mark the words in paragraph 6 in which Wiesel asks the audience to do something.

Analyze: Does this paragraph appeal to the audience's emotions or ethics? Explain the effect it would most likely have on an audience.

1 *"After Auschwitz, the human condition is not the same, nothing will be the same."*

2 Here heaven and earth are on fire.

3 I speak to you as a man, who 50 years and nine days ago had no name, no hope, no future and was known only by his number, A7713.[1]

4 I speak as a Jew who has seen what humanity has done to itself by trying to exterminate an entire people and inflict suffering and humiliation and death on so many others.

5 In this place of darkness and malediction[2] we can but stand in awe and remember its stateless, faceless and nameless victims. Close your eyes and look: endless nocturnal processions are converging here, and here it is always night. Here heaven and earth are on fire.

6 Close your eyes and listen. Listen to the silent screams of terrified mothers, the prayers of anguished old men and women. Listen to the tears of children, Jewish children, a beautiful little girl among them, with golden hair, whose vulnerable tenderness has never left me. Look and listen as they quietly walk towards dark flames so gigantic that the planet itself seemed in danger.

[1] **A7713:** the identification number tattooed on Wiesel at Auschwitz.

[2] **malediction** (măl ĭ-dĭk´shən): curse.

NOTICE & NOTE 

7 All these men and women and children came from everywhere, a gathering of exiles drawn by death.

8 **Yitgadal veyitkadash, Shmay Rabba.**[3]

9 In this kingdom of darkness there were many people. People who came from all the occupied lands of Europe. And then there were the Gypsies and the Poles and the Czechs … It is true that not all the victims were Jews. But all the Jews were victims.

10 Now, as then, we ask the question of all questions: what was the meaning of what was so routinely going on in this kingdom of eternal night. What kind of demented mind could have invented this system?

11 And it worked. The killers killed, the victims died and the world was the world and everything else was going on, life as usual. In the towns nearby, what happened? In the lands nearby, what happened? Life was going on where God's creation was condemned to blasphemy[4] by their killers and their accomplices.

12 **Yitgadal veyitkadash, Shmay Rabba.**

[3] **Yitgadal veyitkadash, Shmay Rabba:** the words that begin a Jewish prayer for the dead.

[4] **blasphemy** (blăs´fə-mē): a disrepect for religion.

NOTICE & NOTE

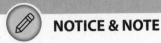

ANALYZE RHETORICAL DEVICES

Annotate: Mark the phrase that is repeated in paragraph 13.

Connect: What effect does the repetition of this phrase help to create and what is the resulting impact of that effect?

ANALYZE APPEALS

Annotate: Mark words and phrases in paragraphs 17–18 that Wiesel uses to appeal to the audience's emotions and ethics.

Compare: Paragraph 17 uses a **rhetorical question**—that is, a question that Wiesel does not expect the audience to answer—to be persuasive. Compare this question to the statement in the next paragraph. What impact does each have on the audience?

13 Turning point or watershed,[5] Birkenau[6] produced a mutation[7] on a cosmic scale, affecting man's dreams and endeavours. After Auschwitz, the human condition is no longer the same. After Auschwitz, nothing will ever be the same.

14 **Yitgadal veyitkadash, Shmay Rabba.**

15 As we remember the solitude and the pain of its victims, let us declare this day marks our commitment to commemorate their death, not to celebrate our own victory over death.

16 As we reflect upon the past, we must address ourselves to the present and the future. In the name of all that is sacred in memory, let us stop the bloodshed in Bosnia, Rwanda and Chechnia; the vicious and ruthless terror attacks against Jews in the Holy Land.[8] Let us reject and oppose more effectively religious fanaticism and racial hate.

17 Where else can we say to the world "*Remember the morality of the human condition,*" if not here?

18 For the sake of our children, we must remember Birkenau, so that it does not become their future.

[5] **watershed:** a place that marks a change of course or direction.
[6] **Birkenau:** the sub-camp at Auschwitz where prisoners were killed.
[7] **mutation** (myo͞o-tā´shən): change.
[8] **Holy Land:** the ancient kingdom of Israel.

19 **Yitgadal veyitkadash, Shmay Rabba:** Weep for Thy children whose death was not mourned then: weep for them, our Father in heaven, for they were deprived of their right to be buried, for heaven itself became their cemetery.

CHECK YOUR UNDERSTANDING

Answer these questions before moving on to the **Analyze the Text** section on the following page.

1 Why does Wiesel use the present tense in paragraph 2, "Here heaven and earth are on fire"?

A He is telling a story about the concentration camp.

B He wants Auschwitz to be burned down and forgotten.

C He believes Auschwitz still affects us today.

D He is still angry about what happened to him.

2 What is the main idea of paragraph 16?

F Nothing in today's world is as bad as the Holocaust.

G We must forget what happened at Auschwitz and move on.

H People who are being persecuted should fight back against their oppressors.

J The example of the Holocaust should make us oppose similar persecutions today.

3 The speech's title means that after Auschwitz —

A Wiesel not only survived but became a successful man

B the world is a dark place haunted by the ghosts of the dead

C former enemies can be friends if they acknowledge the evil that was done

D people can no longer be indifferent to the suffering of others

RESPOND

ANALYZE THE TEXT

Support your responses with evidence from the text. NOTEBOOK

1. **Analyze** Wiesel's speech begins: "After Auschwitz, the human condition is not the same, nothing will be the same." Identify where similar language is repeated later in his speech. What is the effect of this repetition?
2. **Analyze** Reread paragraphs 3–4 and identify the examples of parallelism. What impact does the parallelism create? How does it contribute to the writer's **tone,** or the attitude he expresses?
3. **Interpret** Imagery consists of descriptive words and phrases that create sensory experiences for the reader. Wiesel writes: "Here heaven and earth are on fire." What image is he communicating? What effect might it have on his audience?
4. **Evaluate** The sentence *Yitgadal veyitkadash, Shmay Rabba* is stated four times in the speech. Is Wiesel's repetition of this prayer as a rhetorical device effective? Why or why not?
5. **Notice & Note** Review Wiesel's ethical appeal in paragraphs 16–18. What values is he asking his audience to consider? What impact does his use of absolute language have on this appeal?

RESEARCH TIP
You just read the transcription of a speech. You can use the Internet to find video or audio recordings of many speeches. Hearing and seeing the speaker can enhance the impact of a speech that you have read.

RESEARCH

The Nobel Peace Prize is one of the highest honors in the world. With a partner, research more about Elie Wiesel's work as a humanitarian and activist. Use what you learn to answer these questions, as well as one additional question you have about him after reading the speech.

QUESTION	ANSWER
What genre is Wiesel's most famous book, *Night*?	
Aside from writing and activism, what was Wiesel's primary vocation?	
Finish this quote: "The opposite of love is not hate, but ________."	
Question:	

Extend Share your questions and answers with the class and discuss any similarities and differences you find among them.

CREATE AND PRESENT

Make a Poster Choose a quotation from "After Auschwitz" that moved you. You might find it by reading the notes you took on the selection or by rereading the speech. Then create a poster that amplifies the message of this quotation.

- ❑ Write the quotation prominently on your poster.
- ❑ Research the Holocaust and/or current events to find facts, dates, and other details that support the message expressed by the quotation you chose.
- ❑ Add to your poster the most powerful pieces of relevant information and visual details you found during your research.
- ❑ Explain your completed work to the class in an oral presentation.

Discuss with a Group In a small group, discuss how you might follow Wiesel's direction to "reject and oppose more effectively religious fanaticism and racial hate." What successful efforts do you know of? What problems exist today, and how might you help solve them?

- ❑ Choose a persecuted group that you know of from reading the news or doing research.
- ❑ Discuss these questions: Why is the group being persecuted? What global or national groups are helping the persecuted?
- ❑ Using your knowledge of how conflicts between groups of people have been resolved before, discuss how you think the current conflict can come to a just resolution.

Go to the **Speaking and Listening Studio** for help with giving a presentation and participating in a discussion.

RESPOND TO THE ESSENTIAL QUESTION

? What can we learn from Anne Frank?

Gather Information Review your annotations and notes on "After Auschwitz." Then, add relevant details to your Response Log. As you determine which information to include, think about:

- why it is important to know what happened in World War II concentration camps
- the best way to respond to that knowledge

At the end of the unit, you can use your notes to help you write a personal narrative.

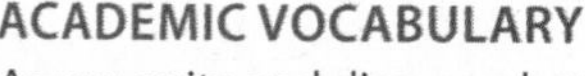

ACADEMIC VOCABULARY

As you write and discuss what you learned from the speech, be sure to use the Academic Vocabulary words. Check off each of the words that you use.

- ❑ **communicate**
- ❑ **draft**
- ❑ **liberation**
- ❑ **philosophy**
- ❑ **publish**

POEM

THERE BUT FOR THE GRACE

by **Wisława Szymborska**

pages 525–527

COMPARE POEMS

The poems you are about to read have similar messages and moods. As you read, compare the ways in which each poet uses techniques such as sound devices or figurative language to convey the theme. After reading, you will collaborate with a small group on a final project.

? *ESSENTIAL QUESTION:*

What can we learn from Anne Frank?

POEM

DAYS

by **Billy Collins**

pages 528–529

QUICK START

Think of a "close call" you had. It could be a time when you narrowly avoided an accident or almost made a mistake. Write down how you felt during and after the close call.

WHAT HAPPENED	HOW I FELT

ANALYZE SOUND DEVICES

Like songs, poems are meant to be heard. When poets choose certain words for their connection to the sense of hearing, they're using **sound devices.** The use of sound devices not only affects how a poem sounds. It can also create **mood** (the feeling or atmosphere that a writer creates for the reader), reveal **tone** (the writer's attitude toward the subject), and contribute to a poet's **voice** (the unique use of language that suggests a personality behind the words).

As you read each poem, look for these sound devices. Consider why the poet chose that device. How does it affect you as a reader?

GENRE ELEMENTS: POETRY

- uses imagery and figurative language to convey meaning and mood
- uses sound devices such as alliteration and assonance to unify the poem
- expresses a theme, or a message about life
- includes a speaker who "talks" to the reader, like a narrator in fiction; the speaker is not necessarily the poet

SOUND DEVICE	DEFINITION	EXAMPLE FROM THE POEMS
alliteration	repetition of consonant sounds at the beginnings of words	What would have happened had not a hand . . .
assonance	repetition of vowel sounds within non-rhyming words	or set upon your forehead moments before you open your eyes.
consonance	repetition of consonant sounds within and at the ends of words	It happened sooner. Later. Nearer. Farther.
onomatopoeia	the use of words whose sounds echo their meanings	you whisper, then holding your breath, place this cup on yesterday's saucer without the slightest clink.
repetition	a technique in which a sound, word, phrase, or line is repeated for emphasis or unity	It could have happened. It had to happen. It happened sooner. Later.

GET READY

ANALYZE FIGURATIVE LANGUAGE

Writers—especially poets—use **figurative language** to help readers see things in new ways. Figurative language is language used imaginatively in ways that go beyond literal definitions.

A **simile** is one type of figurative language that compares two unlike things using the words *like* or *as*. For instance, you might say, "My little sister's face is *like* a storm cloud." A **metaphor** is also a comparison between things that are basically unlike. However, unlike a simile, a metaphor does not contain the words *like* or *as*. In the example below from "Days," the poet compares a window to a "calm eye."

EXAMPLE FROM "DAYS"	EFFECT
Through the calm eye of the window	emphasizes the peacefulness of the scene

While reading "There But for the Grace" and "Days," consider the impact of the poets' use of figurative language. In what ways does the figurative language add interest and support meaning?

ANNOTATION MODEL

NOTICE & NOTE

As you read, mark striking examples of sound devices and figurative language, and jot down notes about their impact and meaning. In the model below, you can see one reader's notes about the first two stanzas of "Days."

Each one is a gift, no doubt,
mysteriously placed in your waking hand
or set upon your forehead
moments before you open your eyes.

Today begins cold and bright,
the ground heavy with snow
and the thick masonry of ice,
the sun glinting off the turrets of clouds.

The title "Days," and the word "Today" at the beginning of the second stanza help me infer that "each one" refers to "each day." The metaphor comparing each day to a gift highlights the idea that we never know what each day will bring.

BACKGROUND

On September 1, 1939, Germany invaded Poland, triggering the start of World War II. Many Polish soldiers and citizens were slaughtered by the German army. Surviving Polish political leaders, Jews, and others were later gathered and sent to concentration camps. By the end of the war, more than five million Poles had died. Poet ***Wisława Szymborska*** *(1923–2012) was born in a small town in western Poland. She was in high school when Germany invaded her country, and she was fortunate to avoid imprisonment and death. She published more than a dozen poetry collections and won the Nobel Prize for Literature in 1996.*

There But for the Grace

Poem by Wisława Szymborska

PREPARE TO COMPARE

As you read the poem, note how the author uses sound devices and figurative language to emphasize ideas and convey mood.

It could have happened.
It had to happen.
It happened sooner. Later.
Nearer. Farther.
It happened not to you.

You survived because you were the first.
You survived because you were the last.
Because you were alone. Because of people.
Because you turned left. Because you turned right.
Because rain fell. Because a shadow fell.
Because sunny weather prevailed.[1]

[1] **prevailed:** was common or frequent.

Notice & Note

Use the side margins to notice and note signposts in the text.

ANALYZE SOUND DEVICES

Annotate: Mark the repetition in lines 6–11.

Analyze: How does the repetition in these lines impact the mood and meaning of the poem?

Luckily there was a wood.
Luckily there were no trees.
Luckily there was a rail, a hook, a beam, a brake,
a frame, a bend, a millimeter, a second.
Luckily a straw was floating on the surface.

Thanks to, because, and yet, in spite of.
What would have happened had not a hand, a foot,
by a step, a hairsbreadth[2]
by sheer coincidence.

---

[2] **hairsbreadth:** a tiny space.

So you're here? Straight from a moment still ajar?
The net had one eyehole, and you got through it?
There's no end to my wonder, my silence.
Listen
how fast your heart beats in me.

ANALYZE FIGURATIVE LANGUAGE

Annotate: Mark the metaphor that relates to survival in lines 21–25.

Analyze: What does this metaphor mean? What ideas does this use of figurative language emphasize?

CHECK YOUR UNDERSTANDING

Answer these questions about "There But for the Grace" before moving on to the next selection.

1 In lines 10–11, the words rain, shadow, and sunny weather most likely —

A relate to good times and hard times

B describe the hopes of the speaker

C convey an upbeat, jaunty tone

D add to the positive, optimistic mood

2 In lines 12–16, the speaker most likely repeats the word luckily to —

F express gratitude that the world is such a lucky place

G emphasize that survival often depends on luck

H encourage people to focus on the positive

J explain steps people can take to survive a tragedy

3 What is an important idea in "There But for the Grace"?

A Being prepared can help people avoid tragedy.

B Nature and hope are comforts in times of trouble.

C Nothing is impossible with a positive attitude.

D Good or bad fortune can suddenly change a life.

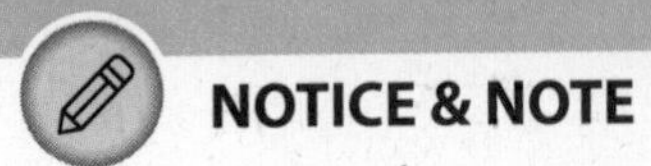

BACKGROUND

Billy Collins *(b. 1941) is perhaps the most popular poet in North America. When he served as the U.S. Poet Laureate from 2001 to 2003, he created the 180 Project, which provided high schools across the country with poems to be read along with daily announcements. His goal was to make poetry part of everyday life for young people.*

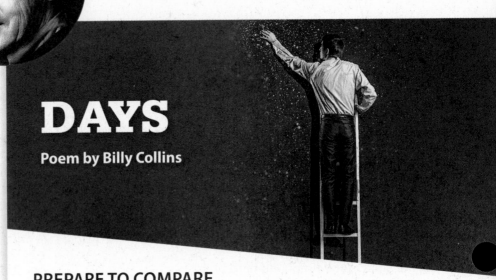

DAYS

Poem by Billy Collins

PREPARE TO COMPARE

As you read, think about how the poet uses figurative language to create vivid images and help convey a message, or theme. As you read the poem, note how the author uses sound devices and figurative language to emphasize ideas and convey mood.

Notice & Note

Use the side margins to notice and note signposts in the text.

Each one is a gift, no doubt,
mysteriously placed in your waking hand
or set upon your forehead
moments before you open your eyes.

Today begins cold and bright,
the ground heavy with snow
and the thick masonry of ice,
the sun glinting off the turrets of clouds.

Through the calm eye of the window
everything is in its place
but so precariously
this day might be resting somehow

ANALYZE SOUND DEVICES: ASSONANCE

Annotate: Mark examples of assonance in lines 5–8.

Analyze: How does the assonance affect the mood of the poem?

on the one before it,
all the days of the past stacked high
like the impossible tower of dishes
entertainers used to build on stage.

No wonder you find yourself
perched on the top of a tall ladder
hoping to add one more.
Just another Wednesday

you whisper,
then holding your breath,
place this cup on yesterday's saucer
without the slightest clink.

NOTICE & NOTE 

ANALYZE FIGURATIVE LANGUAGE

Annotate: Mark the simile in lines 12–16.

Analyze: What two unlike things does the speaker compare? How does this comparison impact the meaning of the poem?

ANALYZE SOUND DEVICES: ONOMATOPOEIA

Annotate: Mark the words in line 21–24 that sound like their meaning.

Analyze: Describe how these words help you hear Billy Collins's voice.

CHECK YOUR UNDERSTANDING

Answer these questions about "Days" before moving on to the **Analyze the Text** section on the following page.

1 The figurative language in the poem suggests that the days in a life are —

A beautiful and limitless

B cold yet calm

C precious but fragile

D boring and repetitive

2 Which of the following lines in the poem contains alliteration?

F *Today begins cold and bright*

G *perched on the top of a tall ladder*

H *Just another Wednesday*

J *then holding your breath*

3 Line 14 emphasizes that —

A a person's life can come crashing down without warning

B there is beauty even in bitterly cold winter weather

C it's important to keep track of events and tasks before they pile up

D entertaining others is the key to a happy life

ANALYZE THE TEXT

Support your responses with evidence from the texts. NOTEBOOK

1. **Identify Patterns** Choose an example of repetition in "There But for the Grace," and explain how the repetition helps emphasize the message of the poem.

2. **Infer** Reread lines 21–25 of "There But for the Grace." In your opinion, what does the metaphor about the heart mean? How does this metaphor impact the meaning of the poem?

3. **Analyze** Examine line 16. Identify the sound device used, and explain how it affects the ending of the stanza.

4. **Compare** How does the mood of lines 1–4 of "Days" compare with the mood of lines 21–24?

5. **Evaluate** What other words and phrases in "Days" relate to the simile in lines 14–16? What impact does this extended comparison have on the poem's overall meaning? Cite text evidence in your response.

RESEARCH TIP

Because you will be presenting your research results to the class, you may want to display photographs of statues, memorials, museums, or other sites. Keep track of where you find each image, and include a credit line that lists source information. For print sources, include the title, author, publisher, publication date, and page number. For online sources, include the website, URL, article title, author, and access date.

RESEARCH

Both the poems you read in this lesson have to do with the fragility and temporary nature of life. Wislawa Szymborska lived through the Nazi invasion of Poland. Like other poets of her generation, she grappled with the Holocaust in her work. In what other ways do people remember victims of the Holocaust? With a partner, research Holocaust memorials or other sites dedicated to promoting remembrance and tolerance. What do these memorials have in common? What effect do they have on visitors?

MEMORIAL	DESCRIPTION

Extend With your group, share your research findings with the class. Identify a museum or memorial focused on tolerance that is near you, or present a suggestion for a new memorial. Come up with one or two questions that you would like to continue to explore.

CREATE AND RECITE

Illustrate Figurative Language Make a drawing or other artwork to represent one of the examples of figurative language in "There But for the Grace" or "Days."

- ❑ Review the poems to select an example of figurative language. Think about which example appeals most to you.
- ❑ Decide how you will represent the figurative language visually.
- ❑ Create your artwork. Your illustration could be a drawing, collage, or painting.
- ❑ Present your artwork to the class. Explain what the illustration shows and how it represents the example of figurative language.

Recite a Poem With a small group, present a recitation of "There But for the Grace" or "Days" for the class.

- ❑ Work with your group to select which poem you will present.
- ❑ Plan how you will present the poem. Will you take turns reciting different stanzas, or recite stanzas in unison?
- ❑ Memorize your lines and rehearse with your group.
- ❑ Present the poem with appropriate rate, volume, and expression.

RESPOND TO THE ESSENTIAL QUESTION

What can we learn from Anne Frank?

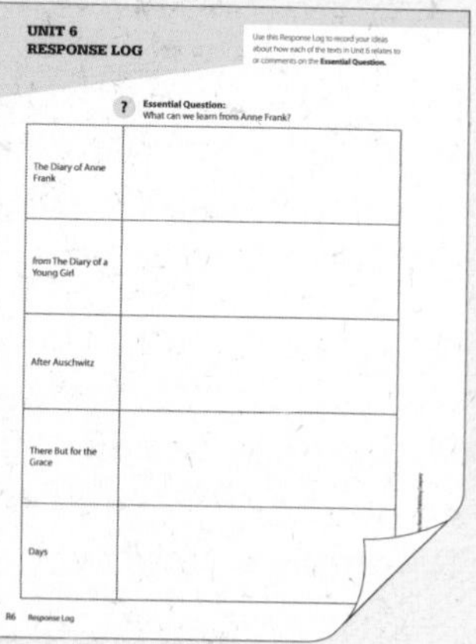

UNIT 6
RESPONSE LOG

Use this Response Log to record your ideas about how each of the texts in Unit 6 relates to or comments on the **Essential Question.**

? **Essential Question:** What can we learn from Anne Frank?

The Diary of Anne Frank	
from The Diary of a Young Girl	
After Auschwitz	
There But for the Grace	
Days	

R6 Response Log

Gather Information Review your annotations and notes on both poems. Then, add relevant details to your Response Log. As you determine which information to include, think about:

- literary devices each poet uses to convey meaning
- ways in which the messages in both poems relate to other selections in the unit
- connections you make between the poems, your own life, and society

At the end of the unit, you will use your notes to help you write a personal narrative.

ACADEMIC VOCABULARY

As you write and discuss what you learned from the poems, be sure to use the Academic Vocabulary words. Check off each of the words that you use.

- ❑ **communicate**
- ❑ **draft**
- ❑ **liberation**
- ❑ **philosophy**
- ❑ **publish**

Collaborate & Compare

THERE BUT FOR THE GRACE
Poem by Wisława Szymborska

DAYS
Poem by Billy Collins

COMPARE POEMS

Both "There But for the Grace" and "Days" have similar themes—in other words, similar messages about life. To analyze a poem's theme, ask yourself these questions:

- ❏ What is your first reaction after reading the poem? What message do you believe the poet wants to share?
- ❏ What evidence do you have to support your reaction? How does the poet use word choice and figurative language to get his or her message across?
- ❏ What is the on-the-surface (explicit) meaning of the poem, and what is the beneath-the-surface (implicit) meaning?
- ❏ What is the writer's tone, or attitude toward the subject?

Now that you have had time to read and think about both poems, compare and contrast their themes. In a small group, use this chart to record your thoughts. Summarize each poem's theme, and list words or phrases from the poem that support your interpretation of the theme.

POEM	THEME	EVIDENCE FROM POEM
"There But for the Grace"		
"Days"		

ANALYZE THE TEXTS

Discuss these questions in your group.

1. **Compare** With your group, review the details in your chart. In what ways are the themes of both poems similar? In what ways are they different? Explain.
2. **Critique** Which poem do you believe has a stronger or a more compelling theme? Cite evidence to support your ideas.
3. **Compare** Does the tone of each poem remain the same, or change? Explain.
4. **Interpret** How does the figurative language in each poem emphasize its theme? Include evidence from the poems to support your answer.

ANALYZE AND SHARE

Continue exploring the ideas in these poems by analyzing their connections to the other selections in this unit. Follow these steps:

1. **Identify Connections** Think about similarities between these poems and the other Unit 6 selections. Ask yourself:
   - ❑ How are the themes (messages about life) related?
   - ❑ What ideas do they share?
   - ❑ How are their explicit and implicit meanings similar?
   - ❑ Which poem connects more closely to the other selections in the unit? Why?

Use this chart to record your thoughts.

OTHER UNIT SELECTIONS	CONNECTIONS TO "THERE BUT FOR THE GRACE"	CONNECTIONS TO "DAYS"
The Diary of Anne Frank		
The Diary of a Young Girl		
"After Auschwitz"		

2. **Discuss Ideas** Join a group and compare the connections you have made. Discuss your interpretations of the themes. Listen carefully, and make sure to speak respectfully even if you disagree with others' interpretations. Be willing to adjust your responses to the poems based on what others say.
3. **Select Information** Working independently, use the information you generated on your own and in the group to decide which poem is a better fit for the unit.
4. **Draft and Share** Write an analysis that explains which poem best captures the spirit of the unit and why. Cite text evidence to support your ideas. Share your analysis with a partner, and use your partner's feedback to revise your analysis.
5. **Publish Your Analysis** Include your analysis in a collection you can share with the whole class.

Go to the **Speaking and Listening Studio** for a lesson on having a collaborative discussion.

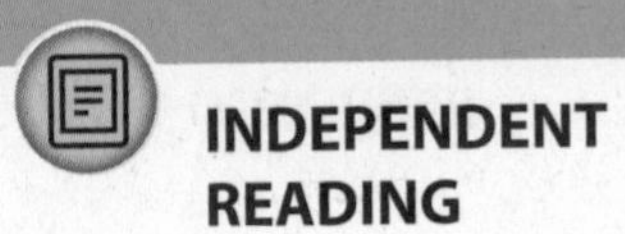

INDEPENDENT READING

? ESSENTIAL QUESTION:

What can we learn from Anne Frank?

Reader's Choice

Setting a Purpose Select one or more of these options from your eBook to continue your exploration of the Essential Question.

- Read the descriptions to see which text grabs your interest.
- Think about which genres you enjoy reading.

Notice & Note

In this unit, you practiced noticing and noting three signposts: **Words of the Wiser, Memory Moment,** and **Contrasts and Contradictions.** As you read independently, these signposts and others will aid your understanding. Below are the anchor questions to ask when you read literature and nonfiction.

Reading Literature: Stories, Poems, and Plays		
Signpost	**Anchor Question**	**Lesson**
Contrasts and Contradictions	Why did the character act that way?	p. 3
Aha Moment	How might this change things?	p. 3
Tough Questions	What does this make me wonder about?	p. 152
Words of the Wiser	What's the lesson for the character?	p. 406
Again and Again	Why might the author keep bringing this up?	p. 2
Memory Moment	Why is this memory important?	p. 153

Reading Nonfiction: Essays, Articles, and Arguments		
Signpost	**Anchor Question(s)**	**Lesson**
Big Questions	What surprised me? What did the author think I already knew? What challenged, changed, or confirmed what I already knew?	p. 77
Contrasts and Contradictions	What is the difference, and why does it matter?	p. 241
Extreme or Absolute Language	Why did the author use this language?	p. 76
Numbers and Stats	Why did the author use these numbers or amounts?	p. 325
Quoted Words	Why was this person quoted or cited, and what did this add?	p. 77
Word Gaps	Do I know this word from someplace else? Does it seem like technical talk for this topic? Do clues in the sentence help me understand the word?	p. 240

You can preview these texts in Unit 6 of your eBook.

Then, check off the text or texts that you select to read on your own.

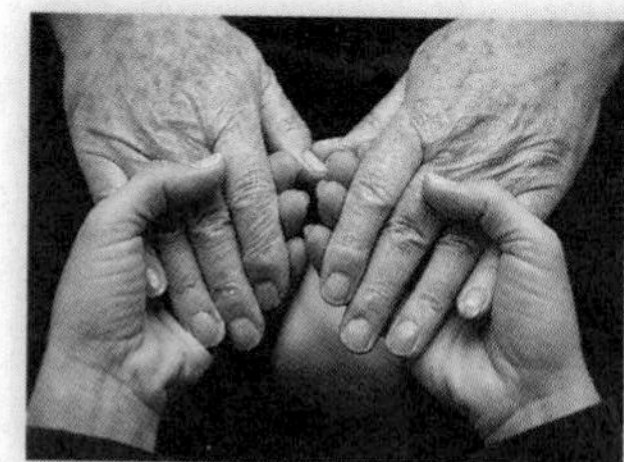

ESSAY

Peace Can Happen
Christine Kingery

Forgiveness and compassion can heal all wounds—one person at a time.

POEMS

The Butterfly
Pavel Friedmann
On a Sunny Evening
Anonymous

Young prisoners in a concentration camp hunger for the natural world.

SHORT STORY

The Singing Women
Rebecca Makkai

An attempt to preserve a fragile culture puts it in harm's way.

ARTICLE

***from* A Tragedy Revealed: A Heroine's Last Days**
Ernst Schnabel

This historical account details the fate of Anne and the other residents of the Secret Annex.

SPEECH

Nobel Prize Acceptance Speech
Elie Wiesel

A survivor of the Holocaust argues for our common humanity and against injustice.

Collaborate and Share With a partner, discuss what you learned from at least one of your independent readings.

- Give a brief synopsis or summary of the text.
- Describe any signposts that you noticed in the text and explain what they revealed to you.
- Describe what you most enjoyed or found most challenging about the text. Give specific examples.
- Decide if you would recommend the text to others. Why or why not?

Go to the **Reading Studio** for more resources on **Notice & Note.**

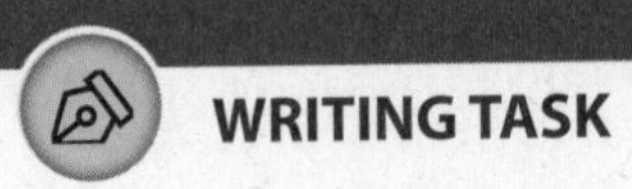

Write a Personal Narrative

Go to the **Writing Studio** for help writing a personal narrative.

This unit focuses on Anne Frank, a Jewish girl in the Netherlands whose family hid from the Nazis during World War II. In her diary, she wrote about a pen she valued. For this writing task, create a short personal narrative about an emotional experience involving an object you value. For a narrative you can use as a mentor text, review the entry for November 11, 1943, in *The Diary of a Young Girl.*

As you write your personal narrative, you can use the notes from your Response Log, which you filled out after reading the texts in this unit.

Writing Prompt

Read the information in the box below.

This is the context or inspiration for your personal narrative.

> **One of Anne Frank's most treasured possessions was a fountain pen, which was inadvertently destroyed while she was in hiding in the Secret Annex with her family.**

This is the Essential Question for this unit. How would you answer this question, based on the texts in the unit?

Think carefully about the following question.

> **What can we learn from Anne Frank?**

Now mark the words that identify exactly what you are being asked to produce.

Write a personal narrative about an experience involving an object that you value.

Be sure to —

Review these points as you write and again when you finish. Make any needed changes or edits.

- ☐ provide an attention-getting opening
- ☐ focus on a single incident
- ☐ include vivid, specific, and sensory details
- ☐ describe events in an order that makes sense
- ☐ use transitions to make the sequence of events clear and to connect ideas within and across paragraphs
- ☐ include your thoughts and feelings
- ☐ conclude by explaining why the experience was meaningful to you

1 Plan

Before you start writing your first draft, you need to plan your personal narrative. Think about the prompt. What object has been meaningful to you? What event demonstrates its importance? To help you gather ideas, jot down a list of some of your most treasured objects, going all the way back to early childhood. Discuss ideas with a classmate, and also review Anne Frank's diary or other personal narratives.

Next, consider your purpose and audience. Who might most enjoy hearing about your experience? Keep in mind that your word choice and tone for a group of classmates or friends may differ from what it would be for a group of adults.

Use the table below for help in planning your draft.

Personal Narrative Planning Table	
Genre	Personal narrative
Topic	An experience with a valued object
Some of my most valued objects	
Ideas from discussion with classmates	
Ideas from reading other narratives	
Purpose	
Audience	

Background Reading Review the notes you took in your Response Log after reading *The Diary of a Young Girl*. Your responses to Anne's diary might give you ideas for your own personal narrative.

Go to **Writing as a Process: Task, Purpose, and Audience** for help planning your personal narrative.

Notice & Note

From Reading to Writing

As you plan your personal narrative, apply what you've learned about signposts to your own writing. Remember that writers use common features, called signposts, to help convey their message to readers. Think about how you can incorporate a **Memory Moment** into your narrative.

Go to the **Reading Studio** for more resources on Notice & Note.

Use the notes from your Response Log as you plan your personal narrative.

UNIT 6 RESPONSE LOG

Essential Question: What can we learn from Anne Frank?

The Diary of Anne Frank	
from The Diary of a Young Girl	
After Auschwitz	
There But for the Grace	
Days	

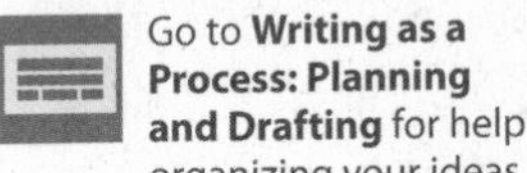

Go to **Writing as a Process: Planning and Drafting** for help organizing your ideas.

Organize Your Ideas After you have planned your narrative, you need to organize your ideas in a way that will help you write your first draft. You can use the chart below to record each part of the experience in chronological order.

Main Topic: Experience with a Valued Possession		
How the valued object entered your life	Experience that caused you to appreciate its importance to you	Reflection on the event and the significance of the object
Key Details	Key Details	Key Details

2 Develop a Draft

When you're ready to begin drafting, refer to the chart above, as well as any notes you took as you studied *The Diary of a Young Girl*. These will provide a kind of map for you to follow as you write.

You may prefer to draft your personal narrative online.

Your personal narrative should include the following elements:

- a well-structured, effectively paced sequence of events
- vivid, specific details about the incident
- your thoughts and feelings about the experience
- reflection on why the experience was meaningful to you

Use the Mentor Text

Author's Craft

Your introduction is the first place to get your reader's attention as you present your topic in an engaging way. Note how Anne Frank opens the following passage from *The Diary of a Young Girl.*

Dearest Kitty,

I have a good title for this chapter:
Ode to My Fountain Pen
In Memoriam

The author (Anne) begins with a humorous title. Odes are poems that express strong feelings of love or respect. Here, the author suggests that she has such feelings about a simple object—a pen—that is unimportant to most people.

Apply What You've Learned To capture your reader's attention, you might open your narrative with a surprising, unexpected comparison or an unusual expression.

Genre Characteristics

To develop an important idea and draw readers into a narrative, writers sometimes include dialogue. Notice how Anne Frank uses dialogue to convey her feelings about the lost fountain pen.

. . . Margot looked, Mother looked, Father looked, Dussel looked. But it had vanished.

"Maybe it fell into the stove, along with the beans!" Margot suggested.

"No, it couldn't have!" I replied.

The author's frantic denial of her sister's suggestion indicates that she greatly valued the pen.

Apply What You've Learned To help your readers better understand the events in your narrative, consider adding dialogue. Think about other people who were part of the experience that you have chosen. What did you say to them—or what did they say to you—that might help show why you valued the object or why the experience was an emotional one?

3 Revise

Go to **Writing as a Process: Revising and Editing** for help revising your personal narrative.

On Your Own Once you have written your draft, you'll want to go back and look for ways to improve it. As you reread and revise, think about whether you have achieved your purpose. The Revision Guide will help you focus on specific elements to make your writing stronger.

Revision Guide		
Ask Yourself	**Tips**	**Revision Techniques**
1. Does my opening grab readers' attention?	**Underline** interesting or surprising statements.	**Add** an attention-getting statement.
2. Are events in an order that makes sense? Do transitions connect paragraphs and make the sequence of events clear?	**Number** the events in the narrative. **Check** that they are in the correct order. **Underline** transitional words and phrases.	**Rearrange** events in the order in which they occurred, if necessary. **Add** transitions to link events and make connections between paragraphs.
3. Is dialogue relevant to the purpose?	**Note** any dialogue that seems unnecessary.	**Add** dialogue that reveals character and advances the action.
4. Do vivid sensory details make the experience seem real?	**Highlight** vivid, specific, and sensory details.	**Add** more sensory details. **Delete** irrelevant details.
5. Have I included my thoughts and feelings?	**Put a check mark** next to statements of feelings or thoughts.	**Add** specific details about feelings and thoughts, if necessary.
6. Does my conclusion reveal why the experience was meaningful to me?	**Underline** the statement about why the experience was meaningful.	**Add** a statement that explains why the experience was important.

ACADEMIC VOCABULARY

As you conduct your **peer review,** be sure to use these words.

- ❑ **communicate**
- ❑ **draft**
- ❑ **liberation**
- ❑ **philosophy**
- ❑ **publish**

With a Partner Once you and your partner have worked through the Revision Guide on your own, exchange papers and evaluate each other's draft in a **peer review.** Focus on providing revision suggestions for at least three of the items mentioned in the chart. Explain why you think your partner's draft should be revised and what your specific suggestions are.

When receiving feedback from your partner, listen attentively and ask questions to make sure you fully understand the revision suggestions.

4 Edit

Improve your personal narrative. Edit it for the proper use of standard English conventions and correct any misspellings or grammatical errors.

Language Conventions

Correct Capitalization When editing your draft, check for correct capitalization. Keep these categories in mind:

Go to the **Grammar Studio** to learn more about using correct capitalization.

CATEGORY	EXAMPLES
Capitalize the first word in a sentence.	"Burn them. All of them."
Capitalize the pronoun *I*.	I'm seething with rage, yet I can't show it.
Capitalize proper nouns.	
Names of people and animals	Anne Frank, Father, Mrs. Van Daan, Mouschi, Tom Cat
Nationalities, races, peoples	Jewish, German, Dutch, Europeans, Maccabees
Languages	Dutch, Latin, German, English
Organizations, government bodies	Jewish Lyceum, Nazis, Green Police, Allies
Historical periods and events	World War II, the Holocaust
Days, months, and holidays	Friday, February, Hanukkah, St. Nicholas's Day
Titles of literary works	*The Diary of a Young Girl*, "Ode to My Fountain Pen"
Capitalize geographical names.	
Cities, states, countries, continents	Chicago, Texas, Switzerland, Europe
Regions, bodies of water, mountains	the West, Atlantic Ocean, Alps
Buildings, bridges, monuments	Westertoren, London Bridge, the Annex

Example of correct capitalization from *The Diary of a Young Girl*
It was just after five on **Friday** afternoon. **I** came out of my room and was about to sit down at the table to write when **I** was roughly pushed to one side to make room for **Margot** and **Father**, who wanted to practice their **Latin**.

5 Publish

Choose one of these options for sharing your personal narrative:

- Post your personal narrative on a classroom or school website.
- Submit your personal narrative to a literary magazine.

WRITING TASK

Use the scoring guide to evaluate your personal narrative.

Writing Task Scoring Guide: Personal Narrative			
	Organization/Progression	**Development of Ideas**	**Use of Language and Conventions**
4	• The narrative has a coherent sequence that builds to a logical conclusion. • Well-chosen events result in effective pacing. • Transitions clearly show the sequence of events.	• The opening catches the reader's attention and sets the scene. • The focus is on a single incident. • The conclusion of the narrative makes clear the significance of the experience to the writer.	• Precise words and vivid, sensory language are used throughout to bring people, places, and events to life. • Spelling is correct. • Grammar, usage, and mechanics are correct.
3	• Some events are presented in a sensible order, but others are not. • Pacing is, for the most part, effective. • A few more transitions are needed to clarify the sequence of events and other details.	• The opening could be more engaging. The scene is set adequately. • The narrative focuses primarily on a single incident but includes some extraneous events. • The conclusion of the narrative suggests but doesn't make clear the significance of the event to the writer.	• Precise words and vivid, sensory details are often used to describe people, places, and events. • There are only a few spelling errors. • Grammar, usage, and mechanics are mostly correct with only a few errors.
2	• The sequence of events is confusing. • Pacing is uneven. • More transitions are needed to show the sequence of events.	• The opening is not very engaging. • The narrative may relate more than one incident but still focuses on the most important one. • The conclusion of the narrative offers conflicting interpretations of the significance of the event to the writer.	• Precise words and vivid details are used only occasionally; descriptions are often vague and general. • Spelling is often incorrect but does not make reading difficult. • Some grammatical and usage errors exist but do not obscure the writer's meaning.
1	• Events are presented in random order, with no logical connections. • Pacing is dull. • No transitions are used, making the narrative difficult to follow.	• The opening is uninteresting or is missing altogether. • The narrative wanders from incident to incident, with little or no focus. • The conclusion of the narrative fails to convey the significance of the event to the writer.	• Language is vague and confusing. • Many spelling errors are present. • Many grammatical and usage errors confuse the writer's ideas.

Reflect on the Unit

By completing your personal narrative, you have created a writing product that takes inspiration from Anne Frank's writing and explores how everyday objects and moments can be meaningful. Now reflect on what you have learned throughout this unit.

UNIT 6 SELECTIONS
- *The Diary of Anne Frank*
- *The Diary of a Young Girl*
- "After Auschwitz"
- "There But for the Grace"
- "Days"

Reflect on the Essential Question

- What can we learn from Anne Frank? How did your answer to this question change as you read the selections in this unit?

- What are some examples from the texts you've read that show the kinds of lessons people can learn from Anne Frank's experiences?

Reflect on Your Reading

- Which selections were the most interesting or surprising to you?

- Did you prefer reading Anne Frank's diary or the play based on her diary? Why?

- From which selection did you learn the most about the lessons we can learn from Anne Frank?

Reflect on the Writing Task

- What was the most exciting or vivid detail in your narrative? Why do you think so?

- How did writing a personal narrative help you better understand how you felt about your experience or what its significance might be?

- What improvements did you make to your personal narrative as you were revising?

RESOURCES

HMH *INTO LITERATURE* STUDIOS

For more instruction and practice, visit the HMH *Into Literature* Studios.

Reading Studio

Writing Studio

Speaking & Listening Studio

Grammar Studio

Vocabulary Studio

UNIT 1 RESPONSE LOG

Use this Response Log to record your ideas about how each of the texts in Unit 1 relates to or comments on the **Essential Question.**

Essential Question:
Does technology improve or control our lives?

The Brave Little Toaster	
Are Bionic Superhumans on the Horizon?	
Interflora	
The Automation Paradox	
Heads Up, Humans	

UNIT 2 RESPONSE LOG

Use this Response Log to record your ideas about how each of the texts in Unit 2 relates to or comments on the **Essential Question.**

? **Essential Question:**
Why do we sometimes like to feel frightened?

What Is the Horror Genre?	
The Tell-Tale Heart	
The Hollow	
The Monkey's Paw (short story)	
from The Monkey's Paw (film clip)	

UNIT 3
RESPONSE LOG

Use this Response Log to record your ideas about how each of the texts in Unit 3 relates to or comments on the **Essential Question.**

? **Essential Question:**
What are the places that shape who you are?

My Favorite Chaperone	
from The Book of Unknown Americans	
Spirit Walking in the Tundra	
New Immigrants Share Their Stories	
A Common Bond: Teens Forge Friendships Despite Differences	

UNIT 4 RESPONSE LOG

Use this Response Log to record your ideas about how each of the texts in Unit 4 relates to or comments on the **Essential Question.**

? **Essential Question:**
What will people risk to be free?

from Narrative of the Life of Frederick Douglass, an American Slave	
from Harriet Tubman: Conductor on the Underground Railroad	
The Drummer Boy of Shiloh	
O Captain! My Captain!	
Not My Bones	
from Fortune's Bones	

UNIT 5 RESPONSE LOG

Use this Response Log to record your ideas about how each of the texts in Unit 5 relates to or comments on the **Essential Question.**

? **Essential Question:**
How do your teenage years prepare you for adulthood?

The Debt We Owe to the Adolescent Brain	
from Bronx Masquerade	
Hanging Fire	
Summer of His Fourteenth Year	
from It's Complicated: The Social Lives of Networked Teens	
Outsmart Your Smartphone	

UNIT 6 RESPONSE LOG

Use this Response Log to record your ideas about how each of the texts in Unit 6 relates to or comments on the **Essential Question.**

Essential Question:
What can we learn from Anne Frank?

The Diary of Anne Frank	
from The Diary of a Young Girl	
After Auschwitz	
There But for the Grace	
Days	

Using a Glossary

A glossary is an alphabetical list of vocabulary words. Use a glossary just as you would a dictionary—to determine the meanings, parts of speech, pronunciation, and syllabification of words. (Some technical, foreign, and more obscure words in this book are defined for you in the footnotes that accompany many of the selections.)

Many words in the English language have more than one meaning. This glossary gives the meanings that apply to the words as they are used in the selections in this book.

The following abbreviations are used to identify parts of speech of words:

adj. adjective ***adv.*** adverb ***n.*** noun ***v.*** verb

Each word's pronunciation is given in parentheses. A guide to the pronunciation symbols appears in the Pronunciation Key below. The stress marks in the Pronunciation Key are used to indicate the force given to each syllable in a word. They can also help you determine where words are divided into syllables.

For more information about the words in this glossary or for information about words not listed here, consult a dictionary.

Pronunciation Key

Symbol	Examples
ă	**pat**
ā	**pay**
ä	**father**
âr	**care**
b	**bib**
ch	**church**
d	**deed, milled**
ĕ	**pet**
ē	**bee**
f	**fife, phase, rough**
g	**gag**
h	**hat**
hw	**which**
ĭ	**pit**
ī	**pie, by**
îr	**pier**
j	**judge**
k	**kick, cat, pique**
l	**lid, needle*** (nēd´l)

Symbol	Examples
m	**mum**
n	**no, sudden*** (sud´n)
ng	**thing**
ŏ	**pot**
ō	**toe**
ô	**caught, paw**
oi	**noise**
o͝o	**took**
o͞o	**boot**
o͝or	**lure**
ôr	**core**
ou	**out**
p	**pop**
r	**roar**
s	**sauce**
sh	**ship, dish**
t	**tight, stopped**
th	**thin**
th	**this**
ŭ	**cut**

Symbol	Examples
ûr	**urge, term, firm, word, heard**
v	**valve**
w	**with**
y	**yes**
z	**zebra, xylem**
zh	**vision, pleasure, garage**
ə	**about, item, edible, gallop, circus**
ər	**butter**

Sounds in Foreign Words

Symbol	Examples
KH	*German* **ich, ach;** *Scottish* **loch**
N	*French,* **bon** (bôN)
œ	*French* **feu, œuf;** *German* **schön**
ü	*French* **tu;** *German* **über**

*In English the consonants *l* and *n* often constitute complete syllables by themselves.

Stress Marks

The relative emphasis with which the syllables of a word or phrase are spoken, called stress, is indicated in three different ways. The strongest, or primary, stress is marked with a bold mark (´). An intermediate, or secondary, level of stress is marked with a similar but lighter mark (´). The weakest stress is unmarked. Words of one syllable show no stress mark.

GLOSSARY OF ACADEMIC VOCABULARY

access (ăk´sĕs) *n.* a way of approaching or making use of

civil (sĭv´əl) *adj.* of, or related to, citizens and their relations with each other and the state

commentary (kŏm´ən-tĕr´ē) *n.* explanation or interpretation in the form of comments or observations

communicate (kə-myo͞o´nĭ-kāt´) *v.* to convey information or exchange ideas

contribute (kən-trĭb´yo͞ot) *v.* to give or supply for a common purpose

convention (kən-vĕn´shən) *n.* a practice or procedure widely used by a group; a custom

debate (dĭ-bāt´) *v.* to engage in arguments by discussing opposing points

deduce (dĭ-do͞os´) *v.* to reach a conclusion or decision through reasoning

demonstrate (dĕm´ən-strāt´) *v.* to show clearly and deliberately

document (dŏc´yə-mənt) *n.* written or printed paper that provides evidence or information

draft (drăft) *n.*; *v.* an early version or stage of a written document or plan; to write such a version

immigrate (ĭm´ĭ-grāt´) *v.* to enter and settle in a new country

liberation (lĭb´ə-rā´shən) *n.* the act of freeing or the state of being free

license (lī´səns) *n.* a document that is issued as proof of legal permission to do something

occupation (ŏk´yə-pā´shən) *n.* an activity that serves as one's source of income

option (ŏp´shən) *n.* something chosen or available as a choice

philosophy (fĭ-lŏs´ə-fē) *n.* an underlying theory or set of ideas relating to life as a whole

predict (prĭ-dĭkt´) *v.* to tell about in advance, especially on the basis of special knowledge

psychology (sī-kŏl´ə-jē) *n.* the study of mental processes and behaviors

publish (pŭb´lĭsh) *v.* to prepare and issue a book or other material to the public

reaction (rē-ăk´shən) *n.* a response to something

relocate (rē-lō´kāt) *v.* to move to a new place

shifting (shĭft´ĭng) *adj.* changing attitudes, judgments, or emphases

speculate (spĕk´yə-lāt´) *v.* to reason or form a theory about something based on available evidence

sufficient (sə-fĭsh´ənt) *adj.* being enough, or as much as needed

summary (sŭm´ə-rē) *n.* a condensed, or shorter, report that includes the main points of a text or event

symbolize (sĭm´bə-līz´) *v.* to serve as a symbol of, or represent, something else

technique (tĕk-nēk´) *n.* the systematic or orderly procedure by which a task is accomplished

technology (tĕk-nŏl´ə-jē) *n.* the application of science to make products; electronic or digital products and systems

trend (trĕnd) *n.* the general direction of something; a current style

GLOSSARY OF CRITICAL VOCABULARY

abode (ə-bōd´) *n.* An *abode* is a home.

adaptable (ə-dăp´tə-bəl) *adj.* *Adaptable* means able to survive under certain conditions.

ample (ăm´pəl) *adj.* To be *ample* is to be plentiful or enough.

anonymous (ə-nŏn´ə-məs) *adj.* To be *anonymous* means to be unknown or unidentified by name.

appalled (ə-pôld´) *adj.* To be *appalled* is to feel horror and shock about something.

appease (ə-pēz´) *v.* To *appease* means to pacify or lessen the anger of, usually by making concessions.

apprehension (ăp´rĭ-hĕn´shən) *n.* *Apprehension* is the fear or dread of the future.

askew (ə-skyōō´) *adj.* When something is *askew,* it is off center.

assimilate (ə-sĭm´ə-lāt´) *v.* To *assimilate* means to blend into or become similar to the prevailing culture.

assure (ə-shŏŏr´) *v.* To *assure* is to state something positively, so as to remove doubt about it.

audacity (ô-dăs´ĭ-tē) *n.* *Audacity* is shameless daring or boldness.

cajole (kə-jōl´) *v.* When you *cajole,* you coax or urge gently.

capitalize (kăp´ĭ-tl-īz´) *v.* To *capitalize* on something means to use it to one's advantage.

chafe (chāf) *v.* To *chafe* is to annoy or bother someone.

collaborate (kə-lăb´ə-rāt´) *v.* To *collaborate* means to work together.

commence (kə-mĕns´) *v.* When things *commence,* they begin or start.

compensation (kŏm´pən-sā´shən) *n.* *Compensation* is something, such as money, that is received as payment.

conceive (kən-sēv´) *v.* When you *conceive* an idea, you think of it.

condole (kən-dōl´) *v.* If you *condole* with someone, you express sympathy or sorrow.

confer (kən-fûr´) *v.* To *confer* is to share ideas or make a decision with one or more other people.

confide (kən-fīd´) *v.* To *confide* means to share private or secret information.

conjecture (kən-jĕk´chər) *v.* If you *conjecture,* you guess or suppose.

conspicuous (kən-spĭk´yōō-əs) *adj.* Something *conspicuous* is obvious or very easy to see.

consternation (kŏn´stər-nā´shən) *n.* *Consternation* is a feeling of alarm or fear.

convene (kən-vēn´) *v.* To *convene* is to come together for a purpose.

credulity (krĭ-dōō´lĭ-tē) *n.* *Credulity* is a tendency to believe too readily.

crevice (krĕv´ĭs) *n.* A *crevice* is a narrow crack.

deliberate (dĭ-lĭb´ər-ĭt) *adj.* *Deliberate* decision-making activity is the process of making a choice only after carefully considering its likely effects.

denunciation (dĭ-nŭn´sē-ā´shən) *n.* A *denunciation* is the public condemnation of something as wrong or evil.

dependent (dĭ-pĕn´dənt) *adj.* *Dependent* means relying on or requiring the aid or support of another.

deplete (dĭ-plēt´) *v.* To *deplete* means to use up or to reduce to a very small amount.

derision (dĭ-rĭzh´ən) *n.* *Derision* is jeering laughter or ridicule.

diagnostics (dī´əg-nŏs´tĭks) *n.* *Diagnostics* are tools a computer uses to identify problems.

disheveled (dĭ-shĕv´əld) *adj.* When something is *disheveled,* it is messy or untidy.

dispatcher (dĭs-păch´ər) *n.* A *dispatcher* is a person who sends out vehicles according to a schedule.

dispel (dĭ-spĕl´) *v.* When you ***dispel*** something, you drive it away.

dynamic (dī-năm´ĭk) *n.* A ***dynamic*** is a system in which conflicting or competing forces are at work.

eligible (ĕl´ĭ-jə-bəl) *adj.* ***Eligible*** means qualified to be selected.

eloquence (ĕl´ə-kwəns) *n.* ***Eloquence*** is the ability to speak powerfully and persuasively.

embrace (ĕm-brās´) *v.* To ***embrace*** an idea means to accept and support it.

enhancement (ĕn-hăns´mənt) *n.* An ***enhancement*** improves or adds to the quality or function of something.

evoke (ĭ-vōk´) *v.* When you ***evoke*** something, you bring it to mind.

exotic (ĕg-zŏt´ĭk) *adj.* Something that is ***exotic*** is unusual or different.

expansive (ĕk-spăns´sĭv) *adj.* ***Expansive*** means broad in size, range, or degree of openness.

fate (fāt) *n.* ***Fate*** is a power that is thought to determine the course of events.

froth (frôth) *n.* A ***froth*** is a fit of frustration or excitement.

grimace (grĭm´ĭs) *n.* A ***grimace*** is a facial expression of pain or disgust.

hunker (hŭng´kər) *v.* To ***hunker*** down means to stay in a place and focus on a task for a period of time.

hypocritical (hĭp´ə-krĭt´ĭ-kəl) *adj.* If someone is ***hypocritical,*** the person is false or deceptive.

implant (ĭm-plănt´) *v.* To ***implant*** a device means to place it inside the body through surgery.

implore (ĭm-plôr´) *v.* To ***implore*** is to beg for something urgently.

impulsive (ĭm-pŭl´sĭv) *adj.* To be ***impulsive*** means to act quickly, before thinking about the consequences.

inarticulate (ĭn´är-tĭk´yə-lĭt) *adj.* Someone who is ***inarticulate*** is unable to speak in a clear way.

indignantly (ĭn-dĭg´nənt-lē) *adv.* Someone who does something ***indignantly*** acts in a way that shows anger or shock over something that is unjust or unfair.

inert (ĭn-ûrt´) *adj.* ***Inert*** means unable to move or act.

inhibited (ĭn-hĭb´ĭt-əd) *adj.* If you feel ***inhibited*** you feel restrained, held back, or self-conscious.

instill (ĭn-stĭl´) *v.* When you ***instill*** something, you establish or implant it gradually.

insulate (ĭn´sə-lāt´) *v.* To ***insulate*** means to surround or cover to prevent the passage of heat, electricity, or sound.

integrity (ĭn-tĕg´rĭ-tē) *n.* ***Integrity*** is following a strict code of ethical conduct.

intensify (ĭn-tĕn´sə-fī´) *v.* If you ***intensify*** something, you make it grow in strength.

intimacy (ĭn´tə-mə-sē) *n.* ***Intimacy*** refers to a state of personal closeness that is usually experienced in privacy.

justify (jŭs´tə-fī´) *v.* If you ***justify*** something, you prove it is right or valid.

legitimately (lə-jĭt´ə-mĭt-lē) *adv.* When you do something ***legitimately,*** you do it lawfully.

lethal (lē´thəl) *adj.* ***Lethal*** means causing or capable of causing death.

linger (lĭng´gər) *v.* To ***linger*** is to remain or stay longer.

loathe (lō*th*) *v.* To ***loathe*** something is to dislike it very much.

melodrama (mĕl´ə-drä´mə) *n.* ***Melodrama*** is behavior characterized by exaggerated emotions.

muted (myōō´tĭd) *adj.* When something is ***muted,*** it is softened or muffled.

ostentatiously (ŏs´tĕn-tā´shəs-lē) *adv.* Someone who does something ***ostentatiously*** acts in an exaggerated way in order to attract attention.

paradox (păr´ə-dŏks´) *n.* A ***paradox*** is a person, thing, or situation that is contradictory.

parallel (păr´ə-lĕl´) *adj.* If things are ***parallel,*** they have comparable or similar parts.

peril (pĕr´əl) *n.* A *peril* is something that is dangerous.

perspective (pər-spĕk´tĭv) *n.* A *perspective* is a viewpoint on or understanding of something.

predominantly (prĭ-dŏm´ə-nənt-lē) *adv.* *Predominantly* refers to the most important, obvious, or typical aspect(s) of something.

prosaic (prō-zā´ĭk) *adj.* If something is *prosaic,* it is dull or ordinary.

prudence (pro͞od´ns) *n.* *Prudence* is the wise handling of practical matters.

quest (kwĕst) *n.* A *quest* is a search.

ravage (răv´ĭj) *v.* To *ravage* is to cause serious damage or destruction.

redistribute (rē´dĭ-strĭb´yo͞ot) *v.* To *redistribute* means to distribute again but differently.

reintegrate (rē-ĭn´tĭ-grāt´) *v.* To *reintegrate* is to come together, as when similar materials are collected for recycling.

relevant (rĕl´ə-vənt) *adj.* Something is *relevant* to a topic when it is related or important to that topic.

relish (rĕl´ĭsh) *v.* To *relish* is to take great joy or pleasure in something.

reminisce (rĕm´ə-nĭs´) *v.* When you *reminisce*, you think or talk about past experiences.

renowned (rĭ-nound´) *adj.* Someone or something that is *renowned* is famous.

resignation (rĕz´ĭg-nā´shən) *n.* *Resignation* is the acceptance of something that is inescapable.

resolute (rĕz´ə-lo͞ot´) *adj.* If you are *resolute,* you are firm or determined.

retract (rĭ-trăkt´) *v.* To *retract* is to pull in.

robustly (rō-bŭst´lē) *adv.* *Robustly* means in a strong, healthy way.

scrutinize (skro͞ot´n-īz´) *v.* To *scrutinize* is to examine or inspect with great care.

scuffle (skŭf´əl) *n.* A *scuffle* is a disorderly fight.

sector (sĕk´tər) *n.* A *sector* is a part or division, as of a city or a national economy.

snicker (snĭk´ər) *n.* A *snicker* is a superior, partially suppressed laugh.

solemn (sŏl´əm) *adj.* If an event is *solemn,* it is deeply serious.

splendid (splĕn´dĭd) *adj.* If something is *splendid,* it is magnificent or very good.

sponsor (spŏn´sər) *v.* If you *sponsor* someone, you support his or her admission into a group.

stifle (stī´fəl) *v.* If you *stifle* something, you smother it.

stimulant (stĭm´yə-lənt) *n.* A *stimulant* is an agent that excites or temporarily speeds up mental and/or physical functions.

strew (stro͞o) *v.* If you *strew* something, you spread it here and there, or scatter it.

stun (stŭn) *v.* To *stun* someone is to make him or her feel shocked or dazed.

sullen (sŭl´ən) *adj.* *Sullen* people show silent resentment.

tirade (tī´rād) *n.* A *tirade* is a long, angry speech.

unabated (ŭn´ə-bā´tĭd) *adj.* If something is *unabated,* it keeps its full force without decreasing.

unrest (ŭn-rĕst´) *n.* *Unrest* refers to an unstable or turbulent condition that is often marked by protests or riots.

vehemently (vē´ə-mənt-lē) *adv.* If you do something *vehemently,* you do it with intense emotion.

vex (vĕks) *v.* If you *vex* someone, you annoy that person.

vindication (vĭn´dĭ-kā´shən) *n.* *Vindication* is the evidence or proof that someone's claim is correct.

vindictive (vĭn-dĭk´tĭv) *adj.* Something is *vindictive* if it is intended to hurt or punish someone.

whimper (hwĭm´pər) *v.* To *whimper* is to sob or let out a soft cry.

INDEX OF SKILLS

INDEX OF TITLES AND AUTHORS

ACKNOWLEDGMENTS

"After Auschwitz" by Elie Wiesel. Text copyright © 1995 by Elie Wiesel. Reprinted by permission of Georges Borchardt, Inc.

Excerpts from *The American Heritage Dictionary of The English Language, Fifth Edition.* Text copyright © 2016 by Houghton Mifflin Harcourt Publishing Company. Reprinted by permission of Houghton Mifflin Harcourt Publishing Company.

"Are Bionic Superhumans on the Horizon" by Ramez Naam from CNN.com April 25, 2013. Text copyright © 2013 by Turner Broadcast Systems. Reprinted by permission of PARS International on behalf of Turner Broadcast Systems. All rights reserved. Protected by the Copyright Laws of the United States. The printing, copying, redistribution, or retransmission of this Content without express written permission is prohibited. http://www.cnn.com

"The Automation Paradox" by James Bessen, from *The Atlantic Monthly*, January 19, 2016. Text copyright © 2016 by The Atlantic Monthly. Reprinted by permission of Tribune Content Agency.

Excerpt from *The Book of Unknown Americans* by Cristina Henríquez. Text copyright © 2014 by Cristina Henríquez. Reprinted by permission of Alfred A. Knopf, an imprint of the Knopf Doubleday Publishing Group, a division of Penguin Random House LLC and Canongate Books. All rights reserved. Any third party use of this material, outside this publication, is prohibited. Interested parties must apply directly to Penguin Random House LLC for permission.

"The Brave Little Toaster" from *TRSF* by Cory Doctorow. Text copyright © 2014 by Cory Doctorow. Reprinted by permission of Cory Doctorow.

"Days" from *The Art of Drowning* by Billy Collins. Text copyright © 1995 by Billy Collins. Reprinted by permission of University of Pittsburgh Press.

"The Debt We Owe to the Adolescent Brain" by Jeanne Miller from *Odyssey* March 2015. Text copyright © 2015 by Carus Publishing Company. Reprinted by permission of Carus Publishing Company. All Cricket Media material is copyrighted by Carus Publishing Company d/b/a Cricket Media, and/or various authors and illustrators. Any commercial use or distribution of material without permission is strictly prohibited. Please visit http://cricketmedia.com/licensing for licensing and http://www.cricketmedia.com for subscriptions.

"Devon Hope" by Nikki Grimes; "Open Mike: Bronx Masquerade" by Devon Hope; "Open Mike: If" by Diondra Jordan; "Diondra Jordan," and "Tyrone" from *Bronx Masquerade* by Nikki Grimes. Text copyright © 2002 by Nikki Grimes. Reprinted by permission of Dial Books for Young Readers, an imprint of Penguin Young Readers Group, a division of Penguin Random House LLC, Curtis Brown Limited and Recorded Books. All rights reserved. Any third party use of this material, outside this publication, is prohibited. Interested parties must apply directly to Penguin Random House LLC for permission.

Excerpt(s) from *The Diary of a Young Girl: The Definitive Editions* by Anne Frank, edited by Otto H. Frank and Mirjam Pressler, translated by Susan Massotty. Text copyright © 1991 by The Anne Frank-Fonds, Basle, Switzerland. Translation copyright © 1995 by Penguin Random House LLC. Any third party use of this material, outside of this publication, is prohibited. Interested parties must apply directly to Penguin Random House LLC for permission. Reprinted by permission of Doubleday, an imprint of the Knopf Doubleday Publishing Group, a division of Penguin Random House LLC and Penguin Books Ltd. All rights reserved.

The Diary of Anne Frank by Frances Goodrich and Albert Hackett. Text copyright © 1956 by Albert Hackett, Frances Goodrich Hackett and Otto Frank. Copyright renewed 1984 by Albert Hackett. Reprinted by permission of Random House, an imprint and division of Penguin Random House LLC and Flora Roberts, Inc. All rights reserved. Any third-party use of this material, outside of this publication, is prohibited. Interested parties must apply directly to Penguin Random House LLC for permission.

"The Drummer Boy of Shiloh" from *The Saturday Evening Post,* April 30, 1960 by Ray Bradbury. Text copyright © 1960 by the Curtis Publishing Company, renewed 1988 by Ray Bradbury. Reprinted by permission of Don Congdon Associates, Inc.

"Fortune's Bones" from *Fortune's Bones: The Manumission Requiem* by Marilyn Nelson. Text copyright © 2004 by Pamela Espeland. Reprinted by permission of Highlights for Children, Inc.

"Hanging Fire" from *The Collected Poems of Audre Lorde* by Audre Lorde. Text copyright © 1978 by The Audre Lorde Estate. Reprinted by permission of W.W. Norton and Company and Charlotte Sheedy Literary Agency.

Harriet Tubman: Conductor on the Underground Railroad by Ann Petry. Text copyright © 1955, © 1983 by Ann Petry. Reprinted by permission of Hannigan Salky Getzler Agency as agents for the author.

"The Hollow" by Kelly Deschler. Text copyright by Kelly Deschler. Reprinted by permission of Kelly Deschler.

"Interflora" by Susan Hamlyn. Text copyright and permission by Susan Hamyln.

Excerpt from *It's Complicated: The Social Lives of Networked Teens* by Danah Boyd. Text copyrighted © 2014 by Danah Boyd. Reprinted by permission of Yale University Press.

"My Favorite Chaperone" by Jean Davies Okimoto. Text copyright © 2004 by Jean Davies Okimoto. Reprinted with permission of Jean Davies Okimoto.

"Not My Bones" from *Fortune's Bones: The Manumission Requiem* by Marilyn Nelson. Text copyright © 2004 by Marilyn Nelson. Reprinted by permission of Highlights for Children, Inc.

Quote by Henning Mankell from "All along the watchtower" by Nick Hasted from *The Guardian*, January 11, 2002. Text copyright © 2002 by Guardian News & Media Limited. Reprinted courtesy of Guardian News & Media Limited.

ACKNOWLEDGMENTS

"Spirit Walking in the Tundra" from *Conflict Resolution for Holy Beings: Poems* by Joy Harjo. Text copyright © 2015 by Joy Harjo. This selection may not be reproduced, stored in a retrieval system, or transmitted in any form or by any means without the prior written permission of the publisher. Reprinted by permission of W.W. Norton & Company, Inc.

"Summer of His Fourteenth Year" from *Wind Chimes* by Gloria Amescua. Text copyright © 2004 by Altura Press. Reprinted by permission of Gloria Amescua.

"There But for the Grace" from *Sounds, Feelings, Thoughts: Seventy Poems by Wislawa Szymborska* by Wislawa Szymborska translated by Magnus J. Krynski and Robert A. Maguire. Text copyright © 1981 by Princeton University Press. Reprinted by permission Copyright Clearance Center on behalf of Princeton University Press.

Excerpt from "What is the Horror Genre?" by Stephen King from *Stephen King: a Critical Companion* by Sharon A. Russell. Text copyright © 1996 by Sharon A. Russell. Reprinted by permission of Copyright Clearance Center.